The Accusation Model Before the International Criminal Court

AF794112

Hanna Kuczyńska

The Accusation Model Before the International Criminal Court

Study of Convergence of Criminal Justice Systems

Springer

Hanna Kuczyńska
Institute of Law Studies
Polish Academy of Sciences
Warsaw
Poland

Updated and extended text based on the translation from the Polish language edition: Model oskarzenia przed Miedzynarodowym Trybunalem Karnym by Hanna Kuczyńska, © C.H. Beck 2014. All rights reserved.

ISBN 978-3-319-36738-5 ISBN 978-3-319-17626-0 (eBook)
DOI 10.1007/978-3-319-17626-0

Springer Cham Heidelberg New York Dordrecht London
© Springer International Publishing Switzerland 2015
Softcover reprint of the hardcover 1st edition 2015
This work is subject to copyright. All rights are reserved by the Publisher, whether the whole or part of the material is concerned, specifically the rights of translation, reprinting, reuse of illustrations, recitation, broadcasting, reproduction on microfilms or in any other physical way, and transmission or information storage and retrieval, electronic adaptation, computer software, or by similar or dissimilar methodology now known or hereafter developed.
The use of general descriptive names, registered names, trademarks, service marks, etc. in this publication does not imply, even in the absence of a specific statement, that such names are exempt from the relevant protective laws and regulations and therefore free for general use.
The publisher, the authors and the editors are safe to assume that the advice and information in this book are believed to be true and accurate at the date of publication. Neither the publisher nor the authors or the editors give a warranty, express or implied, with respect to the material contained herein or for any errors or omissions that may have been made.

Printed on acid-free paper

Springer International Publishing AG Switzerland is part of Springer Science+Business Media (www.springer.com)

Preface

This monograph examines the accusation model used before the International Criminal Court (hereinafter: ICC) from a comparative point of view.[1] It highlights elements of the accusation model used in four different countries and before the *ad hoc* tribunals and the ICC and explains why a certain structure of prosecution has been used before the ICC. The study addresses questions on the main differences between the continental law and common law judicial traditions and on how changing one of the institutions of criminal procedure influences the remaining institutions. It examines how the functioning of the International Criminal Court has become a forum of convergence of procedural solutions known in these legal traditions. Four countries were selected as primary examples of these two legal traditions: the United States, England and Wales, Germany and Poland.

The first layer of analysis focuses on selected elements of the model of accusation that are crucial to the model adopted by the ICC. These are development of the notion of the ICC Prosecutor's independence in view of their ties to the States Parties and the Security Council, the nature and limits of the Prosecutor's discretional powers to initiate proceedings before the ICC, the reasons behind the prosecutor's choice of both defendants and charges, the role he plays in the procedure of disclosure of evidence and consensual termination of proceedings and the determinants of the model of accusation used during trial and appeal proceedings.

The second layer of the book consists in an analysis of the motives behind applying particular solutions to create the model of accusation before the ICC. It also shows how the model of accusation gradually evolved in proceedings before the military and *ad hoc* tribunals: ICTY and ICTR. Moreover, the question of compatibility of procedural institutions is addressed: in what ways does adopting a certain element of criminal procedure, e.g. discretional powers of the prosecutor

[1] The research project was financed from the funds of the National Centre of Science (Narodowe Centrum Nauki) on the basis of a decision No. DEC-2012/05/B/HS5/00653.

to initiate criminal proceedings, influence the remaining procedural elements, e.g. the existence of the *dossier* of a case or the powers of a judge to modify the legal characterisation of facts appearing in the indictment? Moreover, it should be borne in mind that both the specific powers and the practical role of prosecutors in any legal order depend not only on the legal and the criminal law systems in place but also on historical circumstances and historical development of the law, the cultural and legal impact of other countries, as well as the existing culture of which the legal culture is only a small part.

Warsaw, Poland Hanna Kuczyńska

List of Abbreviations

§	Paragraph
CC	The polish Criminal Code
CCP	The Polish Code of Criminal Proceedings
CPIA	Criminal Procedure and Investigation Act 1996.
CPS	Crown Prosecution Service
DPP	Director of Public Prosecutions
Dz.U.	Dziennik Ustaw (the Polish Journal of Laws)
ECHR	Convention for the Protection of Human Rights and Fundamental Freedoms (European Convention on Human Rights)
ECtHR	European Court of Human Rights
ICC	International Criminal Court
ICTR	International Criminal Tribunal for Rwanda
ICTY	International Criminal Tribunal for the former Yugoslavia
IMT	International Military Tribunal
IMTFE	International Military Tribunal for the Far East
NGO	Non-governmental organisation
OTP	Office of the Prosecutor
OTP ICC	Office of the Prosecutor of the International Criminal Court
OTP ICTY	Office of the Prosecutor of the International Criminal Tribunal for the former Yugoslavia
RPE	Rules of Procedure and Evidence
RPE ICC	Rules of Procedure and Evidence of the International Criminal Court
RPE ICTR	Rules of Procedure and Evidence of the International Criminal Tribunal for Rwanda
RPE ICTY	Rules of Procedure and Evidence of the International Criminal Tribunal for the former Yugoslavia
SC	Security Council
SN	Sąd Najwyższy (the Polish Supreme Court)
StGB	Strafgesetzbuch
StPO	Strafprocessordnung

TK	Trybunał Konstytucyjny (the Polish Constitutional Tribunal)
UN	United Nations
UN SC	United Nations Security Council
US	United States

Contents

Chapter 1
The Procedure Before International Criminal Tribunals

Abstract This chapter shows an outline of the process in which the accusation model before the ICC was created as the result of a discussion between representatives of the continental and the common law systems. This discussion was aimed at finding how to build a criminal procedure model that would meet the major objectives set by the ICC, taking advantage of the experiences of various legal systems in order to prevent the impunity of perpetrators of the most severe crimes of international significance, simultaneously ensuring compensation for victims of crimes and a fair trial for the accused. This discussion started with the creation of the first international criminal tribunals and the adoption of the first set of procedural rules for the operation of international criminal (military) tribunals: in Nuremberg and Tokyo, and continued during the operation of the ad hoc tribunals. The finally adopted accusation model before the ICC is presented by using a set of basic components that were selected on the basis of the fact that they cover the framework of the entire course of proceedings before the ICC, and they are regulated in both the common law and the continental law systems in a manner that is both distinct and different. They were also selected in a way that demonstrates to the fullest extent why certain solutions are consistent with the common law approach while others are based on the continental tradition.

1.1 Preliminary Issues of Convergence of Criminal Justice Systems

The international procedural criminal law governs the role and powers of a prosecutor who is an accuser before international criminal tribunals in a manner that is a *sui generis* solution when compared to national legal orders. Through the adoption of criminal procedure components derived from various legal systems and traditions, a distinct model of accusation was established that was unrelated to the legal system of any one specific state. It is often presented as the result of a conflict between common law and civil law traditions, which is a paradigm used to explain

© Springer International Publishing Switzerland 2015

H. Kuczyńska, *The Accusation Model Before the International Criminal Court*,
DOI 10.1007/978-3-319-17626-0_1

the dynamics of international procedure.[1] Procedural institutions were selected in such a way as to facilitate the optimum administration of international justice. In consequence, criminal procedure before international criminal tribunals has become an amalgam of procedural institutions functioning in various states. It has become a forum for bringing closer and converging legal traditions introducing a new quality to the area of legal proceedings.

The literature on international criminal procedure often focuses on the analysis of procedural institutions in terms of their continental and common law background. Traditionally, the continental law systems (which in the Anglo-Saxon doctrine are known as civil law or inquisitorial (non-adversarial) systems and are considered to have been derived from Roman law and the impact of Napoleon's codes on Continental Europe) are juxtaposed with the common law systems (the law of the Anglo-Saxon states, also referred to as the adversarial system) based on the assumption that these are two distinct traditions. Such a dichotomy is purely a matter of convention. We could as well talk about Anglo-American and Roman-German legal orders,[2] confessional states (e.g., Islamic) and secular states,[3] North and South states[4] or common law and statutory law states. A division based on a larger number of systems may also be adopted, in which case we could discuss, for example, the states of the common law area, the civil law and *sui generis* states[5] or the systems of Christian, Islamic, Confucian and Buddhist states.[6] We could also rely on the approach that analyses the types of authority and justice and, in consequence, distinguishes between two models of justice systems: hierarchical and coordinated officialdom or policy-implementing and conflict-solving justice types of procedure. The main difference between these types is characterised by the presence (or absence) of a hierarchical structure of authority, a strict hierarchical ordering and technical standards for decision-making.[7] While all these features are characteristic for hierarchical officialdom, coordinated officialdom's distinctive features comprise the absence of specialised officials, as justice is performed by lay people, who belong to a "single echelon of authority". While the first type is associated with non-adversarial systems and the mode of procedure structures as an official inquiry, the second one responds to the adversarial mode of proceeding and takes its shape from a contest or a dispute.[8]

---

[1] See: Mégret (2009), p. 41.

[2] Which would explain the differentiation applied herein—Ambos (2009), p. 605. This dichotomy presented also by many more authors, e.g., Ambos (2007) p 429; Bohlander (2011) p 393; Knoops (2005) p 6-7; Kuczyńska (2014) p 3; Ohlin (2009) p 81; Orie (2002) p 1450; Safferling (2001) p 55; Schuon (2010) p 25; Tochilovsky (2001) p 627; Wiliński (2008) p 640; Wilhelmi (2004) p 7.

[3] Elewa Badar (2011), pp. 411–433.

[4] Van Sliedregt (2011).

[5] That may be exemplified by the Democratic Republic of China as in: Ambos (2000), p. 89; Damaška (1986), p. 3.

[6] Bassiouni (1993), p. 248.

[7] So-called *logical legalism*—Damaška (1986), p. 23.

[8] This approach was also adopted by A. Heinze. Using these two models of justice systems, this author analysed procedural solutions used before the ICC on the example of disclosure of evidence. Heinze (2014), p. 145.

Even the above-mentioned divisions are sometimes considered to be too simple to capture systemic solutions. The notions of common law (adversarial) tradition and continental (inquisitorial) tradition seem to be more like labels than strict divisions as they cover certain features in shifting combinations.[9] Much confusion is due to the fact that certain criteria remain uncertain for the inclusion of specific traits into a specific type of procedure.[10] It is not possible to use them in order to describe legal traditions in a dichotomous way, as the main features of these two model procedures are present in legal systems with both common law and continental traditions. The most characteristic features of these models are often equally well known as ill-defined, as it is "not at all clear which sets of features are determinative of the 'adversary' as opposed to the 'non-adversary' system".[11] In both continental and Anglo-Saxon scholarship, the expressions "adversary" and "inquisitorial" are used in a variety of senses and certain features of these types of proceeding are polarised to excess for better comparativist effect.

However, because differentiation between the common law and continental law traditions is a common point of reference in the majority of research studies on international criminal law, in both the areas of national and international criminal procedures, these concepts will be used here in a comparative analysis of international criminal procedure. The dichotomy was already in use in the twelfth century, and nowadays it came to be used by comparativists on a broader scale.[12] Although the dichotomy between these two legal traditions is actually disappearing, it is still the best point of reference and still constitutes a useful analytical device. This method will be adopted here, as the diversity of legal systems has to be somehow reduced to a "manageable set of patterns".[13] It will be assumed that the systems of criminal procedure in England, Wales and the United States of America belong to the common law tradition, whereas Poland and Germany represent continental legal systems. Comparative analysis on the basis of the defined legal systems is practical, as comparing "examples" of adversarial and inquisitorial systems enables to articulate concrete differences and concrete similarities between these systems and the ICC model of accusation and prevents analysing mere "patterns".[14]

It is noteworthy that there is no consistency in calling a given method of resolving legal and criminal issues a "system" (by using the phrase "the continental law system"). The following phrases are alternatively used: type of proceeding,[15] model,[16] method[17] and tradition[18] or legal families.[19] In the literature, the term

[9] Damaška (1972–1973), p. 552.

[10] Damaška (1986), p. 4.

[11] *Ibidem*.

[12] *Ibidem*, p. 3.

[13] *Ibidem*, p. 3.

[14] As analysed by Damaška (1986), pp. 5 et seq.

[15] See: Damaška (1986), p. 23; Damaška (1974–1975), p. 481.

[16] Langbein and Wienreb (1978), p. 1551.

[17] Hauck (2008).

[18] Van Sliedregt (2011), p. 390; Heinze (2014), p. 105.

[19] As in: Bohlander (2014), p. 493; Campbell (2013), p. 156.

"common law system" occurs most frequently, although the use of the notion "legal traditions", rather than "legal systems", to describe legal orders seems to be more accurate. The notion "tradition" is defined as "a set of deeply rooted, historically conditioned attitudes about the nature of law, about the role of law in society and the politics, about the proper organization and operation of a legal system, and about the way the law is or should be made, applied, studied, perfected and taught".[20] This notion seems to be the most appropriate in analysing procedural aspects of international criminal procedure. In turn, the concept of a "model" may be understood primarily as a "specimen" structure or procedure. The best definition of the term "model" in the theory of the criminal proceedings seems to be that of a "set of basic components of a system that allows differentiating it from other systems".[21] In this sense, this word will be used in the analysis of the accusation model presented in this monograph. The notion "model" is usually considered to be signifying a structure that is coherent and complete. Therefore, one could argue that the whole system of criminal procedure should be described to constitute a "model", as "accusation" is just one of the functions of this procedure and cannot be treated as a whole. However, we cannot save this notion solely for the needs of describing a whole system of criminal procedure. It is often observed that models can serve as "convenient shorthand to indicate generalities rather than specifics, and they must therefore be seen only as an aid to, and as a substitute for, understanding".[22] While analysing a certain component of criminal trial (or a function performed by one of the actors in trial), "modelling" becomes useful in order to explain and show why certain elements tend to have certain features. Notwithstanding the shortcomings of the "modelling", using a model description cannot be abandoned. Therefore, when speaking of the common law and continental "legal tradition", it will be assumed that a "system" of law can operate in one state only and a "model" of procedure (that is, a set of basic components) is not the same as system and tradition.

International criminal procedure is often referred to as "cultural and legal hybrid".[23] It was created as the result of a discussion between representatives of the continental and the common law systems. This discussion was aimed at finding how to build—from scratch—a criminal procedure that would meet the major objectives set by the ICC, taking advantage of the experiences of various legal systems in order to prevent the impunity of perpetrators of the most severe crimes of international significance, simultaneously ensuring compensation for the victims and a fair trial for the accused. This discussion started with the creation of the first international military tribunals and the adoption of the first set of procedural rules

[20] Cit. after: Merryman and Pérez-Perdomo (2007), p. 2.

[21] As defined by Waltoś (1968), p. 9.

[22] Cit. after: Heinze (2014), p. 114.

[23] This notion is used quite commonly, e.g.: Cryer et al. (2010), p. 427; Van Sliedregt (2011), p. 389; Boas et al. (2011), pp. 15–16.

for their operation: in Nuremberg and Tokyo. Usually, therefore, analysis of procedural models before the ICC starts with these.

1.2 Evolution of Procedure Before International Criminal Tribunals

1.2.1 International Military Tribunals: Establishing a Precedent

Regulation of the procedure before the International Military Tribunal (IMT) in Nuremberg was the first historical instance of establishing criminal procedure rules from scratch, independently of any national legal orders.[24] The proceedings were conducted pursuant to the IMT Charter, which constituted an attachment to the London Agreement of August 8th 1945 for the Prosecution and Punishment of the Major War Criminals of the European Axis. Its provisions were complemented by Rules of Procedure.[25] The provisions of the Charter and the Rules contain only an outline of solutions, leaving the resolution of ongoing procedural problems to judges and prosecutors. This model of procedure came to life, shaped by a variety of legal orders from the victorious countries, representing both the common law and the continental law systems. The states managed to achieve a compromise that resulted in, as we would call it today, convergence of legal traditions. Based on the continental tradition, it was decided that the trial would be led by a judge who would also issue a verdict, as the jury had not been introduced. *In absentia* trials were also allowed, and the accused had the right to provide explanations (they were not acting in the capacity of witnesses). In turn, a strictly adversarial trial framework was borrowed from the Anglo-Saxon system, in which the parties were to present the evidence and interrogate witnesses pursuant to the principles of cross-examination, composing the dialectic method of presentation of evidence.[26]

When a project of procedural rules for the Tribunal was presented by the American delegation, the representatives of France and the Soviet Union "shuddered".[27] Differences between common law systems and continental law systems led to misunderstandings and long negotiations. The earliest disagreements that occurred between the representatives of the two legal traditions concerned the

[24] International Military Tribunal for the Far East Charter (IMTFE Charter) of 19 January 1946: http://web.archive.org/web/19990222030537/http://www.yale.edu/lawweb/avalon/imtfech.htm. Accessed 8 Jan 2015.

[25] Adopted on 29 October 1945, at http://avalon.law.yale.edu/imt/imtrules.asp. Accessed 9 Sept 2014.

[26] But Cassese (2008), p. 384; Fairlie (2004), p. 245 otherwise.

[27] See: Ginsburg and Kudriavtsev (1990), pp. 67–31; Cyprian and Sawicki (1948), pp. 5–38; Gardocki (1985), pp. 22–33.

adoption of particular procedural institutions. There was a particular backlash against the use of a purely adversarial model before an international criminal tribunal, as it was considered to turn a criminal trial into a "mere contest of skills". Another problem occurred in relation to the limited content of the indictment and the related "classification" of incriminating evidence until the time of trial, which, according to representatives of continental systems, impaired the fairness of the trial. Even at that time, precedent-based procedure caused a lot of controversy—mainly due to the possibility of abuse of their broad prerogatives by judges and the unpredictability of the proceedings. Also, the suitability of adopting solutions characteristic of the purely adversarial model was generally challenged, as it was argued that neither the accused nor their defence counsels knew the system, which put them in an unfavourable position relative to the prosecutors, who came from a background of common law orders (two out of the four members of the Committee of Prosecutors).[28] Finally, however, it was decided that the use of an adversarial framework for the Nuremberg trials was "pragmatic".[29]

There is no doubt that the model employed in Nuremberg served as guidance for the further development of international criminal procedure. It was both "novel and experimental".[30] The model of criminal procedure that was finally adopted turned out to be unexpectedly effective, and the trials were completed within 10 months. They became a proof that it was possible to establish a *sui generis* criminal procedure model that would not duplicate the legal procedure of any of the states and that justice could be efficiently administered on an international forum, in this "most delicate kind of trial".[31] However, the political situation under which military tribunals operated was entirely different from the situation in which international criminal tribunals function today. Moreover, military tribunals were to adopt and apply "to the greatest possible extent expeditious and nontechnical procedure" (as in Article 19 of the Charter). As a result, the course of their operation was based mainly on decisions taken by judges in specific cases, as the charters of the tribunals were formulated in exceptionally general terms. It seems that the fact of establishing a precedent in the form of a tribunal issuing verdicts on the most serious international law crimes was, in itself, considered by the founders to be more important than establishing coherent and durable rules of procedure.[32]

---

[28] Kremens (2010), p. 34.

[29] As observes: Cassese (2008), pp. 377–378. It was also due to the United States' involvement, which became the "driving force" behind the Nuremberg trials—not least in economic terms—as in: Ambos and Beck (2012), p. 491.

[30] The opening speech by Justice Robert H. Jackson as reported in: Roche (2011), p. 139.

[31] Cit. after: May and Wierda (2002), p. 20.

[32] It also seems that the underlying criticism towards strictly adversarial solutions used on an international forum continues to be valid in relation to today's development of the procedure before international criminal tribunals.

1.2.2 *ICTY and ICTR: "Living Laboratories"*

The International Criminal Tribunal for the former Yugoslavia (ICTY)[33] and the International Criminal Tribunal for Rwanda (ICTR), established on the basis of Security Council Resolution,[34] are known as *ad hoc* tribunals—as their jurisdiction was restricted to a specific time and territorial framework. They were appointed by the Security Council as a means of restoring international peace and security pursuant to Chapter VII of the UN Charter.[35] They were the first two modern international criminal tribunals administering international justice pursuant to a dedicated, independent set of procedural rules. Until the moment of establishing the ICC, they were the basic forum for the development of international criminal procedure. The procedural framework of the *ad hoc* tribunals is set out in their Statutes: the ICTY and ICTR Statutes, which comprise, respectively, 32 and 34 articles. These documents are, however, general and schematic, and as such they had to be complemented with the Rules of Procedure and Evidence (RPE).[36] They constitute a specific source of procedural law. They were adopted by the judges of the Tribunal, who may also amend them at any time. The benefit of this solution is in achieving high flexibility of the rules. As a result of such development, the specific shape of procedural rules depends mainly on the resolutions of judges. This method of legislation raises two concerns. First, it allows the judges to play a dual role as a drafting organ and as an organ applying the rules—they act as *quasi*-legislators. In consequence, judges act both as entities establishing and interpreting the law. Second, it leaves the judges with almost unlimited discretion in framing the rules and principles of procedure—considering that the content of the Statue is the only limitation of their discretion and that this document is very laconic. On the other hand, flexibility of the Rules is an important asset in dealing with the many unprecedented situations and unpredicted legal issues confronting the tribunals; it makes it possible to adjust them to the ongoing tasks and demands of the tribunals.[37]

Before the *ad hoc* tribunals, international criminal procedure has been developed as a separate branch of law. In the frequently cited decision in the case of *Prosecutor v. Tadić*, the ICTY made a statement on the unique nature of the criminal procedure model adopted by this Tribunal:[38] "As a body unique in

[33] UN Doc. SC Rep. 808, of 22.2.1993.

[34] UN Doc. SC Rep. 955, of 8.11.1994.

[35] As it reads in Article 39: "The Security Council shall determine the existence of any threat to the peace, breach of peace or act of aggression, and shall make recommendations, or decide what measures shall be taken in accordance with Articles 41 and 42, to maintain or restore international peace and security".

[36] Rules of Procedure and Evidence ICTY, version of 22.05.2013; Rules of Procedure and Evidence ICTR, version of 9.02.2010.

[37] In general, see: May and Wierda (2002), pp. 22–23; Bassiouni and Manikas (1996), pp. 199–225, 819–820.

[38] *Prosecutor v. Tadić*, IT-94-1, Decision on the Prosecutor's Motion Requesting Protective Measures for Victims and Witnesses, 10 August 1995, § 20–23.

international law, the International Tribunal has little precedent to guide it. The international criminal tribunals at Nuremberg and Tokyo both had only rudimentary rules of procedure. The rules of procedure at Nuremberg barely covered three and a half pages, with a total of 11 rules, and all procedural problems were resolved by individual decisions of the Tribunal. At Tokyo there were nine rules of procedure contained in its Charter and, again, all other matters were left to the case-by-case ruling of the Tribunal. (…) Another unique characteristic of the International Tribunal is its utilization of both common law and civil law aspects. Although the Statute adopts a largely common law approach to its proceedings, it deviates in several respects from the purely adversarial model (…) As such, the International Tribunal constitutes an innovative amalgam of these two systems" and "was able to mold its Rules and procedures to fit the task at hand". Thus, the model does not follow the principles of only one of these systems. It has been assumed that despite the fact that the procedural institutions known from specific legal systems were used, the interpretation of a given provision should not be automatically applied: "A Rule may have a common law or civilian origin but the final product may be an amalgam of both common law and civilian elements, so as to render it sui generis".[39] Despite such systemic assumptions, it cannot be denied that in the initial period of operation of the ICTY and ICTR, the vision for the criminal procedure was derived from the common law tradition. This observation does not arise from the Statutes of these tribunals but from analysis of procedural solutions contained in the Rules of Procedure and Evidence, whose draft version was presented by the US delegation. It is claimed that judges received proposals regarding the model of procedure from a number of states and organisations, but the proposal that came from the United States was "by far most comprehensive and the one that proved to be particularly influential".[40] Moreover, the judges (unsurprisingly) were inclined to draw upon models of procedure that were the most readily available—the precedent of Nuremberg and Tokyo. The judges adjudicating in the initial period of the tribunals' functioning also came from these legal systems. It was admitted that "it was not a secondary factor that a slight majority of the judges who drafted the Rules came from common law countries".[41] The approach of both the creators of the procedure, as well as those who applied it, had a direct impact on the main characteristics of the procedure before the *ad hoc* tribunals and led to the conclusion that it was a model of mainly "adversarial inclination".[42]

---

[39] *Prosecutor v. Delalić*, IT-96-21, Decision on the Motion on Presentation of Evidence by the Accused, Esad Landzo, 1 May 1997, § 15.

[40] In similar words: Morris and Scharf (1995), p. 177. Also in: Bassiouni and Manikas (1996), p. 863; Schuon (2010), p. 196; Jackson and M'Boge (2013), p. 949.

[41] Cit. after: Langer (2005), p. 859.

[42] The majority of authors agree on that: Ambos (2003), p. 18; Bassiouni and Manikas (1996), p. 863; May and Wierda (2002), pp. 328–329; Mégret (2009), p. 43.

The experience of the *ad hoc* tribunals shows the pursuit of an accusation model that would be most compatible with the profile of international criminal tribunals. The proceedings before the ICTY and ICTR became a forum for testing the effectiveness of procedural institutions derived from various legal systems. These tribunals became a "living laboratory", examining the effectiveness of specific legal solutions in the environment of an international tribunal. Due to the flexibility of procedural rules, it was possible to seek solutions tailored to the specific tasks of the international criminal tribunal.

"The competition between the adversarial and inquisitorial systems in the early years of ICTY was a competition about which of these two techniques would better enable ICTY to achieve its goals. But it also was a competition between cultures".[43] Each of the components comprising the accusation model—the role of the prosecutor in a trial, his discretion in initiating an investigation, subjecting his right to bring the indictment before a court to judicial review, the prosecutor's obligation to disclose evidence to the accused, the possibility of a consensual termination of criminal proceedings and the prosecutor's tasks during the trial and the appeal proceedings—has become a field of conflict between two legal traditions during proceedings before the *ad hoc* tribunals. Each of these components has been altered and adapted in order to administer international justice, not always in a manner predicted—or even approved—by the tribunals' founders. These alterations were often made in the course of a specific case, which provided a background for the adoption of a new solution. When confronted with a specific procedural problem, the solutions applied by the tribunals' creators needed to be adapted, through proper judicial interpretation, to the requirements and rules of the international tribunal. Even the most basic principles of criminal procedure have been reviewed, as in the case of gradual departure from perceiving a prosecutor solely as an accuser in the criminal procedure and recognising him to be a "guardian of law" or as in the case of acknowledging the need for proactive participation by a judge in a trial and imposing on him an obligation to establish the material truth.

As their name suggests, the *ad hoc* tribunals are not universal authorities. They may be treated as experiments that, having succeeded, have made it possible to undertake work on a universal model of criminal procedure, adjusted to the needs of the tribunals prosecuting the most severe crimes under international law. The functioning of the ICTY and ICTR had the greatest impact on the accusation model adopted before the ICC.[44] The proceedings held before the ICC are based on the principles developed by the *ad hoc* tribunals, while taking into account their experiences, as well as amendments introduced in their jurisdiction. Some of the legal institutions used before the ICTY were transferred unchanged to the ICC, some were modified to a certain extent and the remaining ones were regulated in a completely different way.

---

[43] Cit. after: Langer (2005), p. 848.

[44] *Inter alia*: Roberts (2001), p. 561; Kirsch (2005), p. 293.

As far as the model of accusation before the ICTR is concerned, it differs in some aspects from that adopted by the ICTY. Due to numerous similarities, the proceedings before this Tribunal will be presented only in cases when it has adopted solutions different from those of the ICTY, or such, that are particularly important for illustrating a specific trend or functioning of a specific procedural institution. The same approach—due to the growing volume of the manuscript—had to be adopted towards the rules of functioning of the IMTFE in Tokyo.

1.2.3 *International Criminal Court: Normative Balance Between Two Traditions*

The final stage in the development of international criminal procedure involves the establishment of a permanent tribunal, a universal authority of justice adjudicating in cases pertaining to the most serious crimes of international law. The Rome Statute of the International Criminal Court is an international agreement, adopted at a diplomatic conference in Rome on 7 July 1998. It became effective on 1 July 2002, having achieved the agreed threshold of 60 ratifications. As opposed to the *ad hoc* tribunals established by the Security Council pursuant to the UN mandate, the State Parties to the Rome Statute themselves agreed to execute and ratify the Statute. Establishing a permanent and—presumably—neutral court marked the next stage in the development of international justice, considering that international military tribunals had been established by the winners of the World War and the *ad hoc* tribunals—by forces that were external to the domestic conflicts taking place at a specific time and in a specific territory.

The criminal procedure before the ICC is based on the Rome Statute, which provides very detailed solutions for the majority of procedural issues (with 128 articles). Despite this level of detail, its provisions are also complemented by the Rules of Procedure and Evidence (RPE)[45] and Regulations of the Court.[46] Amendments to the Rules of Procedure and Evidence can enter into force only upon adoption by a two-thirds majority of the members of the Assembly of States Parties. The amendments can be proposed by each State Party, the ICC Prosecutor and the judges acting by an absolute majority. This amendment procedure makes them less flexible than the procedural rules before the *ad hoc* tribunals and prevents them from being modified in response to a specific demand.[47] Such a demand will definitely occur, as

[45] Rules of Procedure and Evidence, Preparatory Commission for the International Criminal Court, New York 2000, U.N. Doc PCNICC/2000/1/Add.1.

[46] Regulations of the Court, ICC-BD/01-03-11, Adopted by the judges of the Court on 26 May 2004, http://www.icc-cpi.int/NR/rdonlyres/50A6CD53-3E8A-4034-B5A9-8903CD9CDC79/0/RegulationsOfTheCourtEng.pdf. Accessed 11 Feb 2015. Altogether almost 700 provisions: Lee (2001), p. 548; Fernandez de Gurmendi and Friman (2009), pp. 797–824.

[47] Successfully, so far.

there is no way of foreseeing each procedural problem that may be faced by the ICC. The fact that their content is controlled by the states is intended to discourage potential amendments. The Regulations of the Court can, however, be amended by the judges acting by an absolute majority, which proves that there is always a tendency to use flexible rules established by judges as a basis for international criminal proceedings and to seek the efficiency of actions by ensuring flexibility of the applied regulations.[48]

A number of years were spent on developing detailed procedural solutions in the course of drafting the ICC Statute. Each time, they were a result of long-term negotiations and the outcome of the compromise between the representatives of states with various legal traditions. The ICC Statute was the first document that was not developed in a haphazard manner, with an intention to create procedural rules in the process of their application by means of transforming them by judges; the latter approach prevailed in the international military tribunals and *ad hoc* tribunals that were set up—as their name indicates—in response to a specific demand and only for a specific period of time. It was of paramount importance that the need to reach a consensus between the states signing the Rome Statute—between the delegations of about 120 states—played a major role in developing the accusation model before the ICC.[49] The establishment of the Court by means of the execution of an international agreement forced a compromise in the area of procedural solutions between its creators. In order to ensure adoption of the Statute, some of the most controversial issues were dropped and replaced by more neutral solutions: as in the case of "indictment", which was finally replaced by "charges".[50] Such method sometimes led to prejudicial effects on coherence and effectiveness of the procedural system of the ICC.

Finally, the criminal procedure before the ICC was developed in such a way as to respond optimally to the needs of the international criminal court. This manner, however, did not resemble any of the legal systems from which the specific institutional solutions were borrowed. Although a majority of institutions and mechanisms may be described as institutions and mechanisms derived from a specific legal system, they have become *sui generis* solutions due to their application and functioning before the international criminal tribunal. They are not dominated by one legal culture. Some stages of proceedings are conducted according to the Anglo-Saxon model. At the same time, the impact of the continental system on the development of the procedure is also evident, and it is not difficult to observe that some stages of the proceedings were derived from this procedure. According to repeated rumour, when the American delegation (in a manner known from the ICTY and ICTR creation process) presented a proposal of procedure completely based on the American legal tradition, the French delegation produced a new alternative concept overnight, this one based completely on the principles of the

---

48 The Regulations have been amended three times, so far: on 14 June, on 14 November 2007 and on 2 November 2011.

49 See: Guariglia (2002), p. 1119; Roberts (2001), p. 572; Swart and Sluiter (1999), p. 127.

50 See: Sluiter et al. (2013), p. 50.

French procedure. It was only such a confrontation that led to finding the balance between the two legal traditions.[51] On the other hand, as a result, none of the legal systems prevails in this procedural model. Thus, two legal traditions, which had previously been considered irreconcilable, were reconciled in the proceedings before the ICC. As a result, however, the procedural framework of the ICC is also extremely complex and lacks transparency; its normative structure can be described as “byzantine”.

1.2.4 *Quasi-International Courts and Tribunals: Embedded in Domestic Law*

In addition to international criminal tribunals, there are numerous courts whose jurisdiction is limited, both in terms of time and geography, to the territory of one state and a specific armed conflict. They are appointed by the UN authorities in consultation with governments of certain states or independently by the states with the participation of international community. These are known as internationalised criminal courts,[52] because they form a part of the national justice authorities. They constitute a unique combination of the systems of national and international justice. Among such tribunals the following are known: Extraordinary Chambers in the Courts of Cambodia for the Prosecution of Crimes Committed during the Period of Democratic Kampuchea,[53] Panels with Jurisdiction over Serious Criminal Offences,[54] Special Court for Sierra Leone,[55] Special Tribunal for Lebanon,[56] and finally there is the Supreme Iraqi Criminal Tribunal.[57]

Each of these tribunals operates differently, depending on the internal situation and international arrangements that have determined their establishment. As they are an element of the national legal system, it was necessary to combine procedure before the tribunals with domestic procedural law. The work of *quasi*-international tribunals is most often governed by internal law of the state in which the proceedings are pending; it is sometimes modified by adding the elements of international procedure. The fact that the procedural law does not differ much from the procedure known to national courts enhances its recognition and legitimisation in a given state; implementation of an entirely new procedure could impair legal

[51] See: De Hert (2003), p. 79.

[52] Or *quasi*-international tribunals, mixed or hybrid tribunals, as, *inter alia*, defined by: Bassiouni (2003), Cryer et al. (2010), and Ambos and Bock (2012).

[53] Law of 10.8.2001, http://www.eccc.gov.kh. Accessed 3 Nov 2014.

[54] On the basis of S/RES/1272 (1999) 25 October 1999.

[55] S/RES/1315 (2000) 14 August 2000. Althought the Special Court for Sierra Leone is often considered to constitute an ad hoc tribunal, just as the two above described ad hoc tribunals. E.g., Ambos and Bock (2012) p 488; Knoops (2005) p 119; Sluiter et al. (2013) p 15.

[56] S/RES/1757 (2007) 30 May 2007, Annex and Statute of the Tribunal included.

[57] Official Gazette of the Republic of Iraq, 18.10.2005.

certainty due to the fact that the tribunal is not anchored to a given legal system.[58] Therefore, the *sui generis* criminal procedure has not been developed in their case. The powers of prosecutors acting on behalf of tribunals are to a large extent based on the procedure of each of these states. The model of accusation adopted by this group of tribunals is not as uniform as the solutions adopted before the *ad hoc* tribunals and the ICC.

1.3 The Accusation Model Before International Criminal Tribunals

Each time we tend to present a model of a certain constituent, it needs to be decided what "set of basic components" is of key importance in the description of a given model. Therefore, because of the necessity to present a (relatively) concise analysis, the method of comparing the models of accusation had to be limited to the basic elements of the accusation only. While analysing the accusation model before the ICC, major components that determine its unique form have been identified.

There are seven issues that have turned out to be of principal importance in the development of the accusation model before the ICC. Analysis of the function of the accusation and the role of the ICC Prosecutor in the system of international criminal justice is of key significance here: the prosecutor may be seen as a guardian of the law or solely as an accusing authority. Also, the adopted scope of discretion (and its limits) in the selection of specific suspects under a specifically developed principle of opportunism is highly important. The scope of judicial review of the Prosecutor's actions in an investigation, which, in practice, turned out to be much broader than was originally planned by the creators of the Rome Statute, is another issue that has a significant impact on the model of accusation; gradual broadening of the scope of this review in the judicial practice has become a characteristic feature of the ICC procedure. According to the ICC judges, this solution was intended to replace the system of hierarchical and political review, non-existent in the case of the ICC Prosecutor. The information obligations arising from the disclosure of evidence institution turned out to be surprisingly similar to those developed in the legal system of one of the countries, i.e., the United States of America, although, in this case, the continental model of access to a case file would seem to be better adjusted to the needs of the international criminal tribunal. On the other hand, the impact of the Prosecutor on the consensual termination of criminal proceedings before the ICC turned out, contrary to the solutions existing in common law systems, to be limited. Issues subsequently analysed include seeking the proper balance between the proactive approach of the Prosecutor and the judge during trial, as well as the possibility of lodging an appeal against a judgement of the Trial Chamber under the appeal procedure. The aforementioned issues are not

[58] More information in: Romano et al. (2004) p 3 et seq. and: Tochilovsky (2004), pp. 319–344.

exhaustive as far as the powers and tasks of the ICC Prosecutor are concerned. These features were selected on the basis of the fact that they cover the framework of the entire course of proceedings before the ICC, and they are regulated in both the common law and the continental law traditions in a manner that is both distinct and different. They were also selected in a way that demonstrates to the fullest extent why certain solutions are consistent with the common law approach while others are based on the continental systems.

The development of the presented procedural institutions shows that it is possible to establish a distinct model of accusation that can be adjusted to the needs of international criminal tribunals. On the basis of specific procedural solutions and institutions of criminal proceedings, it will be presented, first, how the institutions related to the development of the accusation model were derived from specific legal systems and, second, what the course of the process of amending them in the ICTY and ICTR forum was and thus how they have been adopted to the tasks of international justice and the specific forum in which they were to operate from the moment of establishment of the ICC. Therefore, the analysis of the model of accusation before the ICC was combined with legal comparative research.[59] Comparative law is therefore used not as a single legal body but only as a method of analysing the law before the ICC, as understanding the accusation model and analysis of the procedural institutions depend on the understanding and analysis of the origin and content of a given institution in the state from which it derives, as well as by taking the context of its application into account.[60] The presented analysis is to achieve a double aim: it presents technical rules of procedure, while at the same time it also analyses the reasons why a certain solution was chosen. Moreover, it is not limited to a static description of an instant image of international criminal procedure at a given moment but presents a wider view of evolution of norms over time, showing how rapidly and significantly they have changed over a relatively short period.[61] Therefore, this analysis also aims to present "the transformations the idea may undergo when initially transferred from the source to the target legal system".[62]

The different systemic positioning and powers of public prosecutors were analysed during the works on the Rome Statute. Negotiations on the final model of accusation before the International Criminal Court served as a workshop during which experiences of various legal traditions and cultures were studied. During these negotiations, several legal orders were examined. From among these orders,

---

[59] The use of comparative law to describe the issues of international criminal law is a common tool of legal analysis, as M. Delmas-Marty states: "by postulating a relationship between comparative law and international criminal law, as an extension of the interaction between international and national legal systems, it suggests a pluralist conception of international criminal law": Delmas-Marty (2003), p. 13.

[60] As in Heinze (2014), p. 187.

[61] Trying to avoid errors committed in analysis of the international criminal procedure topics as mentioned by Mégret (2009), p. 41.

[62] In the words of Langer (2004), p. 33.

three were selected for the needs of this study. This selection was necessitated by the need to limit the scope of the comparative study to those selected legal systems that would be most representative of the ICC accusation model. It was assumed, for this study, that the German and Polish systems would be used as representative of the continental tradition, while the English and American systems would serve as representative of the Anglo-Saxon tradition. The systems of England and the United States were considered to be both most influencial and best known by the authors of the Rome Statute. The system of German law was selected as a representative for the national systems of continental law because it has attributes that are characteristic for all systems of Germanic states, as well as due to the fact that it has also had the highest impact on the development of the law in this part of our continent. The Polish model of accusation is, in turn, the most familiar to the author of this monograph; it should also not be ignored that this system is rooted in the legacy of Germanic law and largely influenced by French law. It is also interesting to notice that the Polish model of criminal procedure is presently undergoing serious changes that shift it towards the Anglo-Saxon model and away from the German tradition. Therefore, it will become a poor example for the needs of this comparative research. This text is being prepared in the time of a monumental re-codification, during an extended *vacatio legis* of the Act of 27 of September 2013 amending the Code of Criminal Proceedings (on the 1st of July 2015) which makes it difficult to apply rigid schemes to the Polish criminal procedure system at the moment. At the same time, these changes prove how the main features of a given legal tradition can shift and change not during centuries but while preparing one book.

This study will analyse the procedural institutions derived from the four legal systems that have determined the accusation model before the ICC. Naturally, it is not the objective of this work to present a detailed description of the development of the aforementioned institutions but rather to present some basic assumptions and to demonstrate how they have been implemented into the model of accusation before the ICC. Neither does this study aim at comparing the different criminal proceeding systems, but it constitutes an attempt at building a theoretical model based on the main determinants that have been captured generally.

References

Ambos K (2000) Status, role, accountability of the Prosecutor of the International Criminal Court: a comparative overview on the basis of 33 national reports. Eur J Crime Crim Law Crim Justice 8:89

Ambos K (2003) International criminal procedure: "adversarial", "inquisitorial" or mixed? Int Crim Law Rev 3:1

Ambos K (2007) The structure of international procedure: "adversarial", "inquisitorial" or mixed. In: Bohlander M (ed) International criminal justice: a critical analysis of institutions and procedures. Cameron May, London

Ambos K (2009) 'Witness Proofing' before the ICC: neither legally admissible nor necessary. In: Stahn C, Sluiter G (eds) The emerging practice of the International Criminal Court. Martinus Nijhoff, Leiden/Boston

Ambos K, Bock S (2012) Procedural regimes. In: Reydams L, Wouters J, Ryngaert C (eds) International prosecutors. Oxford University Press, Oxford

Bassiouni MC (1993) Human rights in the context of criminal justice: identifying international procedural protections and equivalent protections in national constitutions. Duke J Comp Int Law 3:235

Bassiouni MC (2003) Introduction to international criminal law. Transnational Publishers, New York

Bassiouni MC, Manikas P (1996) The law of the International Criminal Tribunal for the former Yugoslavia. Transnational Publishers, New York

Boas G, Bischoff J, Reid N, Taylor BD (2011) International criminal procedure. Cambridge University Press, Cambridge

Bohlander M (2011) Radbruch Redux: the need for revisiting the conversation between common and civil law at root level at the example of international criminal justice. Leiden J Int Law 2:393

Bohlander M (2014) Language, culture, legal traditions, and international criminal justice. J Int Crim Justice 12:491

Campbell K (2013) The making of global legal culture and international criminal law. Leiden J Int Law 26:155

Cassese A (2008) International criminal law. Oxford University Press, Oxford

Cryer R, Friman H, Robinson D, Wilmshurst E (2010) An introduction to international criminal law and procedure, 2nd edn. Cambridge University Press, Cambridge

Cyprian T, Sawicki J (1948) Prawo Norymberskie. Bilans i perspektywy. Eugeniusz Kuthan, Warszawa-Kraków

Damaška M (1972–1973) Evidentiary barriers to conviction and two models of criminal procedure: a comparative study. Univ Pa Law Rev 121:508

Damaška M (1974–1975) Structures of authority and comparative criminal procedure. Yale Law J 84:481

Damaška M (1986) The faces of justice and state authority. Yale University Press, New Haven/London

De Hert P (2003) Legal procedures at the International Criminal Court. A comparative law analysis of procedural basic rights. In: Haveman R, Kavran O, Nicholls J (eds) Supranational criminal law: a system sui generis. Intersentia, Antwerp/Oxford/New York

Delmas-Marty M (2003) Comparative law to a pluralist conception of international criminal law. J Int Crim Justice 1:13

Elewa Badar M (2011) Islamic law (Sharii'a) and the jurisdiction of the International Criminal Court. Leiden J Int Law 24:411

Fairlie M (2004) The marriage of common and continental law at the ICTY and its progeny, due process deficit. Int Crim Law Rev 4:243

Fernandez de Gurmendi P, Friman H (2009) The Rules of Procedure and Evidence and the Regulations of the Court. In: Daria J, Gasser H-P, Bassiouni MC (eds) The legal regime of the International Criminal Court. Essays in honour of Professor Igor Blishchenko. Martinus Nijhoff, Leiden/Boston

Gardocki L (1985) Zarys prawa karnego międzynarodowego. PWN, Warszawa

Ginsburg G, Kudriavtsev VN (eds) (1990) The Nuremberg trial and international law. Martinus Nijhoff, Leiden/Boston

Guariglia F (2002) The Rules of Procedure and Evidence for the International Criminal Court: a new development in international adjudication of individual criminal responsibility. In: Cassese A, Gaeta P, Jones WD (eds) The Rome Statute of the International Criminal Court: a commentary. Oxford University Press, Oxford

Hauck P (2008) Judicial decisions in the pre-trial phase of criminal proceedings in France, Germany, and England: a comparative analysis responding to the law of the International Criminal Court. Nomos Verlagsgesellschaft, Baden-Baden

Heinze A (2014) International criminal procedure and disclosure. An attempt to better understand and regulate disclosure and communication at the ICC on the basis of a comprehensive and comparative theory of criminal procedure. Duncker & Humblot, Berlin

Jackson J, M'Boge Y (2013) The effect of legal culture on the development of international evidentiary practice: from the 'Robing Room' to the 'Melting Pot'. Leiden J Int Law 26:947

Kirsch P (2005) The International Criminal Court: a new and necessary institution meriting continued international support. Fordham Int Law Rev 28:292

Knoops G-J (2005) Theory and practice of international and internationalized criminal proceedings. Kluwer Law International, The Hague/London/Boston

Kremens K (2010) Dowody osobowe w międzynarodowym postępowaniu karnym. TNOiK, Toruń

Kuczyńska H (2014) Model oskarżenia przed Międzynarodowym Trybunałem Karnym. C.H. Beck, Warszawa

Langbein JH, Wienreb LL (1978) Continental criminal procedure: myth and reality. Yale Law J 87:1549

Langer M (2004) From legal transplants to legal translations: the globalization of plea bargaining and the Americanization thesis in criminal procedure. Harv Int Law J 45:1

Langer M (2005) The rise of managerial judging in international criminal law. Am J Comp Law 53:835

Lee RP (ed) (2001) The International Criminal Court. Elements of Crimes and Rules of Procedure and Evidence. Transnational Publishers, New York

May R, Wierda M (2002) International criminal evidence. Transnational Publishers, Ardsley, NY

Mégret F (2009) Beyond "Fairness": understanding the determinants of international criminal procedure. UCLA J Int Law Foreign Aff 14:37

Merryman JH, Pérez-Perdomo R (2007) The civil law tradition, an introduction to the legal systems in Europe and Latin America, 3rd edn. Stanford University Press, Stanford, CA

Morris V, Scharf M (1995) An insider's guide to the International Criminal Tribunal for the former Yugoslavia: a documentary history and analysis. Martinus Nijhoff, Leiden/Boston

Ohlin J (2009) A meta-theory of international criminal procedure: vindicating the rule of law. UCLA J Int Law Foreign Aff 14:81

Orie A (2002) Accusatorial v. Inquisitorial approach in international criminal proceedings prior to the establishment of the ICC and in the proceedings before the ICC. In: Cassese A, Gaeta P, Jones WD (eds) The Rome Statute of the International Criminal Court: a commentary. Oxford University Press, Oxford

Roberts K (2001) Aspects of the ICTY contribution to the criminal procedure of the ICC. In: May R, Tolbert D, Hocking J (eds) Essays on ICTY procedure and evidence in honour of Gabrielle Kirk McDonald. Kluwer Law International, The Hague/London/Boston

Roche A (2011) Does international criminal justice work? In: Meron T (ed) The making of international criminal justice. A view from the Bench. Selected speeches. Oxford University Press, Oxford

Romano C, Nollkaemper A, Kleffner J (2004) Internationalized criminal courts. Oxford University Press, Oxford

Safferling C (2001) Towards an international criminal procedure, Oxford monographs in international law. Oxford University Press, Oxford

Schuon C (2010) International criminal procedure. A clash of legal cultures. T. M. C. Asser Press, The Hague

Sluiter G, Friman H, Linton S, Vasiliev S, Zappala S (2013) International criminal procedure. Principles and rules. Oxford University Press, Oxford

Swart B, Sluiter G (1999) The International Criminal Court and International Criminal Cooperation. In: von Hebel H, Bos A, Lammers JG, Schukking J (eds) Reflections on the International Criminal Court, essays in honour of Adriaan Bos. T.M.C. Asser Press, The Hague

Tochilovsky V (2001) Legal systems and cultures in the International Criminal Court: the experience from the international criminal tribunal for the former Yugoslavia. In: Fischer H, Kreß C, Lüder P (eds) International and national prosecution of crimes under international law. Current developments. Arno Spitz, Berlin

Tochilovsky V (2004) International criminal justice: "Strangers In The Foreign System". Crim Law Forum 15:319

Van Sliedregt E (2011) Introduction: common civility – international criminal law as cultural hybrid. Leiden J Int Law 24:389

Waltoś S (1968) Model postępowania przygotowawczego na tle prawnoporównawczym. PWN, Warszawa

Wilhelmi T (2004) Die Verfahrensordnung des Internationalen Strafgerichtshofs – Modell eines universalen Strafverfahrensrecht? Rechtspolitisches Forum. Legal Policy Forum 24:7

Wiliński P (2008) Wpływ systemów common law i civil law na kształtowanie się międzynarodowego postępowania karnego. In: Jakubowska-Hara J, Skupiński J (eds), Reforma prawa karnego: propozycje i komentarze. Księga pamiątkowa Prof. Barbary Kunickiej-Michalskiej, Scholar, Warszawa

Chapter 2
Prosecutor as an Organ of International Criminal Tribunals

Abstract To begin with an analysis of the accusation model, we have to "clear the terminological foreground". Therefore, first we need to establish what will be understood by the notion "accusation", which is close to other concepts: "prosecution" and "investigative steps". Second, we have to "embed" the meaning of this notion in an international environment, taking into consideration the role that the ICC Prosecutor plays in the area of international politics as a member of the international community. Third, as the model of accusation is shaped both by the systemic location of the prosecutor as an accuser in criminal cases as well as by the powers vested in him in specific stages of criminal proceedings, the location and organisation of the OTP must be presented. As to the powers of the Prosecutor, the most important on the first stage of their analysis is determining whether the ICC Prosecutor is an independent judiciary organ (a so-called guardian of the law or a minister of justice) or a strictly accusing organ—a "partisan advocate", who is driven by the goal to win the trial "combat". Finally, in this introductory chapter, two different models of accusation that are driven by different assumptions and that grant various competences to the prosecutor, the Anglo-Saxon model and the Continental model, will be described in general terms, and their main assumption will be explained.

2.1 The Role of the Prosecutor of International Criminal Tribunals

2.1.1 In an Internal Aspect: As an Accusatory Organ

The role of the prosecutor at an international criminal tribunal may be considered in two aspects. First, it is a role arising from his powers within the operation of every tribunal that may be defined as an internal role. Second, there is the external role of "the most political office in international criminal justice".[1]

---

[1] Cit. after: Coté (2012), p. 321.

© Springer International Publishing Switzerland 2015

H. Kuczyńska, *The Accusation Model Before the International Criminal Court*,
DOI 10.1007/978-3-319-17626-0_2

In the internal aspect, the main task of the prosecutor is similar to the role envisaged in national proceedings: "it is the implementation of the procedural function of criminal prosecution, leading to fair penalisation of the person guilty of committing a crime".[2] While the national prosecutor is usually responsible for supervising investigation and supporting the accusation before the court, the prosecutor at the international criminal tribunal is obliged not only to carry out investigation on his own but also to exercise investigative steps usually reserved for the police in national orders, as well as to prepare an indictment and support it before the Trial Chamber. There are two basic principles upon which the accusation model is built. First, the ICC Prosecutor acts according to the officiality maxim—he is the exclusively competent public authority to initiate and conduct criminal proceedings and bring the accusation before the Court. Private rights of criminal action do not exist—private individuals may also not challenge the decision of the Prosecutor not to initiate an investigation based on information provided by private individuals.[3] He retains the exclusive right to shape the course of criminal proceedings, deciding on their instigation, conduct, discontinuation, depending on whether—in his opinion—there exist legal and factual grounds to accuse a given person. Second, the ICC also operates according to the principle of accusation, which is manifested by the rule that the scope of charges as confirmed by the Pre-Trial Chamber at the confirmation hearing is binding for the Trial Chamber. The Trial Chamber may not expand the trial to other persons than the accused, and it may not expand it to other crimes (understood as certain facts not legal characterisation thereof) of the accused.

In the literature, the term "accusation" is understood in many different ways. It may mean lodging of an indictment (complaint) before a court—bringing charges for the commission of a specific crime, the demand to penalise a perpetrator for committing a specific crime—and also all actions taken by the prosecutor before the court, being a synonym of the procedural function of accusing.[4] Certain ambiguities may also arise from the use of the notions of "accusation" (*oskarżenie*) and "prosecution" (*ściganie*); they are not always deemed to be distinctly different concepts.[5] For the purpose of this monograph, it will be assumed that accusation is a broader notion, covering not only decision to direct criminal prosecution against a certain person—whether to prosecute that person or not, bringing an indictment, selecting a defendant and formulating appropriate charges (these actions are understood by the notion "prosecution")—but also, later at the trial stage, accusation and

[2] Cit. after: Grzegorczyk and Tylman (2007), p. 288.

[3] As it is observed by: Röben (2003), p. 520.

[4] See: Daszkiewicz (1960), pp. 6–9; Daszkiewicz (1961), p. 46; Razowski (2005), p. 24; Stachowiak (1975), pp. 63–64, 84; and Stachowiak (1989), p. 299 also rely on the differing interpretation of the term.

[5] Where investigative steps imply the implementation of investigative functions, "the procedural operations aimed mainly at detecting and penalising the person guilty of committing a crime, demonstrated mainly in the preparation of the indictment in the investigation"—Razowski (2005), p. 24, and, similarly, Płachta (2007), p. 479.

all the actions undertaken by the prosecutor during evidentiary proceedings and later during appeal proceedings.[6]

In this study, these terms will be treated as denoting two separate groups of actions.[7] It will be assumed that the "accusation" function manifests itself both in prosecution—selecting a defendant, preparation of an indictment, lodging it before a court—and in acting as an accusatory authority during the proceedings before the court. The study will not cover "investigative steps" understood as actions related to the collection and recording of evidence under investigation (pursuant to Part IX of the Rome Statue). Thus, "accusation" covers both the steps related to lodging of the indictment and the accusation before the court, namely the powers and obligations of the prosecutor in the court and appeal proceedings.[8]

Another concept that requires explanation in relation to internal aspects of the role of a prosecutor is the meaning of the term prosecutor itself. According to some views expressed in the Polish legal science, the term "prosecutor" may be understood as "the party lodging a motion to penalise the accused and supporting this motion in the course of the proceedings"[9] or "as an entity that, pursuant to its own procedural powers or acting as a state authority, demands that a court penalises an accused"[10] or as "a state authority that on its own behalf brings and/or supports the indictment where the law orders or permits to prosecute a crime through a public complaint".[11] Naturally, in the case of international criminal tribunals, the prosecutor does not "act as a state authority", as he is not a state authority but rather an organ of an autonomous tribunal appointed for prosecuting offences of a specific type. In this case, he plays the role of an accuser before a specific international criminal tribunal. Based on the concepts used in the literature, we may conclude that he is a prosecutor only in relation to defined types of crimes and only before a specific authority appointed to prosecute these crimes. He is entitled to act pursuant to an international agreement or a resolution of the Security Council that established the tribunal. It could be said that it is the international community (or such a part of it that is interested in establishing a tribunal) that delegates the task of prosecuting the most severe crimes of international law to the prosecutor.

[6] The scope and meaning of all the functions of a prosecutor, including "prosecution", "accusation" and "investigative steps", are explained in: Kremens (2014), p. 26.

[7] In the same way as it was done in: Kremens (2014), p. 26.

[8] It is worth noting that even the ICC observed that "a note of caution" is necessary in relation to the understanding of the terms "investigation" and "prosecution". The terms used in the various official language versions of the Statute appear to differ in their meaning—as the Court noticed—given that the terminology is based on the criminal law traditions of specific countries. See: The Prosecutor v. William Samoei Ruto, Henry Kiprono Kosgey And Joshua Arap Sang, ICC-01/09-01/11, Judgment on the appeal of the Republic of Kenya against the decision of Pre-Trial, Chamber II of 30 May 2011 entitled "Decision on the Application by the Government of Kenya Challenging the Admissibility of the Case Pursuant to Article 19(2)(b) of the Statute, § 23".

[9] Cit. after: Cieślak (1984), pp. 37–38.

[10] Cit. after: Daszkiewicz (1960), p. 9.

[11] Cit. after: Grzegorczyk and Tylman (2007), p. 285, and similarly: Waltoś (2008), p. 181.

The prosecutor acquires the power to prosecute by will of the international community.

2.1.2 *In an External Aspect: As a Political Player*

In the external aspect, the prosecutor's role in proceedings before international criminal tribunals depends to a large extent on the position that the tribunal itself has in the light of international law and the role it plays in international politics. In many cases, on the other hand, the effectiveness of international justice depends on the prosecutor's actions. For this reason, he should always take into account the political context of his actions. In fact, the prosecutor outlines the actual scope of interest of each international criminal court and, in consequence, the limits of impact of international criminal law. As it is the case with national systems, the prosecutor's role is a key to understanding how the systems of international justice operate. There are two major characteristics that allow us to acknowledge the prosecutor's paramount role: first, he must "stand at the entrance gate to the criminal justice system and control the transition from the investigative phase to adjudication in court, essentially determining the fate of each suspect". Second, "through his case-processing decisions, the prosecutor also makes or implements general criminal policy".[12]

The external aspect of activities of the international criminal tribunal prosecutor, that is, criminal proceedings as an element of international politics, sets it apart from prosecutorial tasks taken in the national context.[13] The mandate that the prosecutor receives from the international community is not limited solely to bringing to justice perpetrators of the most serious crimes of international law. The scope of the ICC Prosecutor's interest is limited only by the factual and financial capabilities of the Office of the Prosecutor. The prosecutors of the *ad hoc* tribunals have not enjoyed such liberty and have not held such responsibility (mainly political) for taking a decision to prosecute, as they had to act within the limits of factual circumstances determined by the scope of the Tribunal's jurisdiction. The ICC Prosecutor, on the other hand, is free to perform a preliminary examination of a case and to bring charges every time he concludes that international law crimes falling under the Tribunal's jurisdiction have been committed. As a result, he is the only agent deciding whether a case is brought before the ICC. Of course, such situations occur not only in Africa, although all pending investigations that are carried out by the Prosecutor at the moment focus on this continent.

[12] Both citations after: Weigend (2012), p. 377.

[13] "To ignore the political realities would subject the Court to a form of suicide in so far as it would become marginalised in its relations with states and, ultimately, in its ability to enforce international justice". Cit. after: Brubacher (2004), p. 94. See also: Kuczyńska (2010) p. 53.

The prosecutor at an international criminal tribunal may play the political role in many different ways. The fact that the ICC Prosecutor is a narrator of the conflict[14] is often indicated as the first of the most important tasks he shoulders. He takes part in seeking and developing a historical record of events. He presents the events that form the background of a crime and identifies the parties to a conflict. He becomes a historian, demographer and forensic scientist. Assembled documentation and testimonies do not only serve as evidence in criminal proceedings but also become the archives of fragments of a national history. The volume of evidence the Prosecutor collects is so overwhelming that it presents a unique chance to create a historical record of events.[15] The evidentiary material collected by the Prosecutor enables the judges to prepare historical parts of reasoned statements of the Trial Chamber's findings, describing in detail events, the roles of perpetrators and the harm done.

The next aspect of the prosecutor's activity is related to the role of international criminal tribunals as instruments for uniting societies divided by conflicts and mechanisms for reaching peace and justice (in the process of establishing post-conflict justice). It is noteworthy that the differing organisation and functioning of tribunals and the role of the prosecutor within international justice result mainly from the different ways of resolving post-conflict situations in specific cases.[16] Every international criminal tribunal should become a "tool for promoting reconciliation and restoring true peace".[17] In order to bring conflicted parties to an agreement, it is necessary to satisfy their sense of justice, acting reasonably and impartially—as there can be "no healing without peace; there can be no peace without justice".[18] The actions of the international criminal tribunal prosecutor have added value to the ongoing debate on the peace processes. The question, whether peace and justice may be achieved at the same time, has to be posed every time again. This role of the prosecutor was also important when the *ad hoc* tribunals were established and when they were operating. Both *ad hoc* tribunals were established by the Security Council acting in accordance with the UN Charter, as a measure necessary in order to restore international peace and security. This task found confirmation in the jurisprudence of these tribunals, which stated that: "This Tribunal (ICTY) has been created not only to administer justice in respect of the accused that stands before you, but there is an expectation that in so doing you will contribute to a lasting peace in the country that was once Yugoslavia".[19] Every tribunal needs to find the balance between preventing the impunity of perpetrators and achieving tasks of retributive and restorative justice. Most often, however, its task involves seeking a balance between international politics and the

---

[14] "He writes history": Turković (2008), p. 30.

[15] As in: Sluiter et al. (2013), p. 60.

[16] In general see: Bassiouni (2003), p. 543; Bassiouni (2002), p. 8; Morris (2002), p. 135.

[17] As in the SC Resolution Doc. S/1994/1007 of 29.8.1994, § 16.

[18] Cit. after: Greenawalt (2007), p. 604.

[19] ICTY in *Prosecutor v. Tadić*, IT-94-1-T, trial transcript, 7 May 1996, § 1113. In general see: see also: Greenawalt (2007), pp. 604 and 646; Rodman (2009), pp. 125–126; Sluiter et al. (2013), pp. 56–60.

administration of justice. We should also not forget about the tribunals' role as catalysts of and the driving force behind social and political changes.

Moreover, the effect that a prosecution may have on the legal status of the conflict is one of the elements that should be taken into consideration in determining whether to proceed with an indictment. It is considered to constitute an element of the wider concept evaluated whether the investigation is in the interest of justice.[20] The ICC Prosecutor has, undoubtedly, became one of the political players whose intervention in the form of an indictment was a bargaining chip in the pending peace processes. The Prosecutor is responsible for a "delicate challenges of pursuing justice in the midst of international efforts to resolve some of the world's most complex and deadliest conflicts".[21] While initiation of proceedings shows only that the Court is interested in a situation, presentation of an indictment becomes a clear signal of the ICC's condemnation of specific acts committed by identified persons. First of all, in some situations the initiation of proceedings before the Court may directly impact the actions of a state's government. In this aspect, the factor of the proper timing of an intervention should also be taken into consideration. Issuing an indictment too early may jeopardise political efforts to conclude a peace agreement by disrupting a fragile political situation.[22] But having lodged an indictment, the Prosecutor loses his only bargaining chip and he always risks that, when presenting an indictment in one case, he will be accused of a lack of impartiality. Second, it may have an impact on the de-legitimisation of a criminal government in the eyes of the international community. The Prosecutor's involvement in a case always stirs a lot of emotions, defining a specific group, be it political, social or national, as the "bad ones" who committed crimes of international law leading to their political marginalisation and their victims as the "good ones", who require protection by the international community. The role it plays has had a particular importance in the process of political transformations, especially recently in North Africa. Presentation of charges to the regime leaders sent a message to the entire world: the Court does not support the old regime and thinks that it should be replaced. This aspect of the Prosecutor's activity leads to further reflection on the role of tribunals as a tool of governance and management of the international situation.[23] It also inevitably leads to perceiving them as "politicians' toys".[24] Accusations of bias are, however, directed not only towards the prosecutor representing international justice—they are also quite commonly thrown at national enforcement authorities.

---

[20] See: Brubacher (2004), p. 81; Ohlin (2009), p. 192.

[21] Cit. after: Geis and Mundt (2009), p. 2.

[22] As in the case of Uganda, see: Fish (2010), p. 1708; Locke (2012), pp. 620–624.

[23] Extensive literature on this topic, among others: Findlay (2008), pp. 132–135; Yañez-Barnuevo and Escobar Hernández (2003), p. 52; Donat-Cattin (2003), p. 70; Arbour (1999b), p. 24; Greenawalt (2007), p. 585; Findlay (2008), pp. 112–116; Safferling (2001), pp. 83–84, 483.

[24] Cit. after: Scharf (2000), p. 934.

2.2 Systemic Location of the Prosecutor's Office

The model of accusation is shaped both by the systemic location of the prosecutor as an accuser in criminal cases as well as by the powers vested in him in specific stages of criminal proceedings. Both the systemic location of the prosecutor's office and the powers and organisation of prosecutors' activities in a given state have been determined by the historical development of its legal system.[25] Both of these aspects of the accusation model vary from country to country. Based on the classification presented in literature, there are two prevailing models of accusation: continental (in civil law states) and Anglo-Saxon (in common law states). The first group is further categorised into countries with the institution of the investigating magistrate[26] and countries with the prosecutorial system.[27]

2.2.1 *Continental Law Model*

In the analysed continental states, no single systemic location of the prosecutor's office and of the prosecutor has been developed. It is often unclear what the systemic location of the prosecutor's office is: whether it is an organ of the executive or of the judiciary. What is more, where the prosecutor is, as in Germany, located in the court (§ 141 GVG),[28] it is even difficult to unambiguously determine if it is a judicial or an executive authority. Some assume that a prosecutor in Germany is a judicial authority, similar to a court.[29] However, it remains separate from the court and independent from the judiciary. J. H. Langbein argues that this conception of the prosecutorial office, which gave it a curious "double character" as both an executive and a judicial office, can be traced back as far as Savigny, the Prussian minister of justice, who participated in constructing and defining the prosecutorial office.[30] Therefore, a common opinion is also that it neither belongs fully to the executive nor forms part of the judiciary.[31] However, unlike the court, it is not an independent authority as it is subject to administrative review by the Minister of Justice, which would support the view that it is a politically specific legal protection authority.[32] There is no centralised state prosecution authority, and

[25] See: Rogacka-Rzewnicka (2007), pp. 47–48.

[26] Such as France, Belgium, Spain.

[27] Including, *inter alia*, Germany, Poland, Russia—see divisions presented in: Ambos (2000), p. 90 and also: Kijowski (2013), p. 132.

[28] Gerichtsverfassungsgesetz, In der Fassung der Bekanntmachung vom 09.05.1975 (BGBl. I S. 1077), zuletzt geändert durch Gesetz vom 26.06.2013 (BGBl. I S. 1738).

[29] See: Safferling (2001), p. 66.

[30] A detailed history of the German prosecution service presented in: Langbein (1973–1974), p. 448.

[31] Such a conclusion in: Huber (2008), p. 326.

[32] In that respect agree: Morré (2000), p. 341; Volk (2006), p. 24; Beulke (2005), pp. 50, 53, 54.

the Federal Minister of Justice has no power to direct the heads of prosecution authorities of particular lands. The federal state prosecution service is parallel to the prosecution service in lands, not subordinate. It is hierarchically structured and responsible to the ministers of justice of particular lands who are entitled to give directions. Adopting a hierarchical structure of the prosecution entails that prosecutors are bound by the directives and instructions of their supervisors. The competent federal or state ministers of justice, who are executive organs, exercise general control over the manner in which the prosecutor performs his functions. These instructions may be turned hierarchically to all the prosecutors below. However, the scope of interference in a criminal case is rather limited. The factual and legal assessment of a case—that is, how to evaluate the evidence and what conclusions to draw or whether to ask for an acquittal or a conviction—is the responsibility of the prosecutor in charge, not of his supervisors or the minister of justice. Therefore, the prosecutor cannot be obliged by a superior to initiate an investigation or to refrain from instigating one against his legal judgment.

In the Polish system, similar to the German model, there is no agreement as to what location of the prosecutor's office ensues from the provisions governing its functioning. It is most often assumed that the prosecutor's office is a control and law enforcement authority. This theory stems from the framework that has the legal protection authorities divided into three groups: the authorities in charge of resolving conflicts, control of legality organs and legal aid authorities. There are also authors who qualify the prosecution as an "advocate of the public interest" and include it in the last group.[33]

Characteristically for these systems, prosecutors are appointed for life. Generally, they can be removed from office before their age of retirement for disciplinary reasons only or as a consequence of committing a crime, in a formal way. In both legal systems, unlike in the case of the Crown Prosecution Service in England and Wales, the prosecution is not merely "the final clearing-house for the decision to prosecute"[34] but is also the master of the investigation from the very beginning—*Herr der Ermittlungverfahrens*. Similarly in both systems, although the prosecution must be present in court during the whole trial, it does not have to be represented by the same prosecutor in person—according to the doctrine of "uniformity" of the prosecution, it does not matter which prosecutor took an action. It is attributed to the prosecution as a whole.

The Constitution does not resolve uniformly the systemic location of the prosecutor's office. In some states (as France), the prosecutor's office is a constitutional authority.[35] Such a location is not only evidence of the legal and political significance of this organ but is also an outcome of certain regulatory techniques and culture as well as of the historical legacy. Neither in Germany nor in Poland does the Constitution contain any provisions pertaining to the prosecutor's office.

---

[33] Goławski and Żmigrodzki (2005), p. 375, see also: Olszewski (2014) p. 50.

[34] Cit. after: Bohlander (2012), p. 56. For more information on different types of public prosecutor see: Perrodet (2004) pp. 415–483.

[35] Article 64 of the Constitution of the V Republic of 5 October 1958.

However, in Poland, it has for many years been indicated the need for providing systemic foundations for the existence of the prosecutor's office in the constitution, and the lack of constitutional foundations for the prosecutor's office's activities has often come under criticism.[36] Including provisions regulating the functioning of this office in a chapter of the Constitution would resolve the dilemma of its systemic nature; their inclusion in Chapter 8: "Courts and Tribunals" would indicate that this authority is constitutionally linked to the judiciary. On the other hand, their incorporation in Chapter 9: "State Control and Legal Protection Organs" would support the assumption concerning the independence and separation of the prosecutor's office and the judiciary.[37] It has also been shown that such an inclusion is directly related to the adopted model of accusation. The assumption that the prosecutor's office forms part of the judiciary emphasises its role as an accusing authority. Its location as part of control authorities would, in turn, put the focus on its controlling function with respect to the rule of law.

As far as the second aspect of the accusation model—the prosecutor's powers—is concerned, there are specific components that constitute the "continental model of accusation". The German variant of the model, which has also operated in Poland, has certain very distinct features.[38] First, it treats the prosecutor as an impartial authority in pursuit of the material truth and having a statutory obligation to act in favour of the accused. Another characteristic feature is the existence of a comprehensive stage of investigation during which the prosecutor exhaustively examines a case. In this model, the court proceedings are mainly intended to verify his findings. The third characteristic feature is the fact that there is only one "case"—the accusation case (according to the terminology used in common law states)—that is handled from the beginning by a professional enforcement authority. This model also assumes that case files, which are an official record of an investigation submitted to a court with an indictment, are handled by the prosecutor (or the police). Finally, at the stage of court proceedings, two characteristic features of the accusation model may be distinguished, both of which result in the loss of control over the line of prosecution (the prosecution case) by the prosecutor: first, presentation of the evidence collected by the prosecutor is done solely upon the court's permission, and second, the legal characterisation of facts presented by a prosecutor is of a non-binding character for the court. Therefore, the judge becomes the central figure of the court proceedings.

---

[36] Judgment of the Constitutional Tribunal of 6 March 2007, SK 54/06, OTK-A 2007, No 3, pos. 23.

[37] See: Kardas (2012), pp. 15, 27–34; Stankowski (2009), pp. 5–15.

[38] See also: Trüg (2003), pp. 7–25.

2.2.2 Common Law Model

The central prosecutor's office has been established in common law states only recently, following a positive assessment of its effectiveness in continental law systems. Prior to 1985, a centralised and public prosecution service did not exist in England and Wales. Prosecution was handled by the local police and lawyers hired by the police, who formed the accusation system lacking a central structure. It was only in 1985 that the Prosecution of Offences Act brought into force the Crown Prosecution Service (CPS), headed by the Director of Public Prosecutions (DPP).[39] The chief prosecutor is the Attorney General, who is a Government Minister and is the head of the department known as the Attorney General's Office. The Attorney General also plays an important role in criminal proceedings—his consent is necessary to prosecute certain offences and may terminate criminal proceedings on indictment before a judge and jury by the entry of a *nolle prosequi*. His discretion in this regard is very wide and cannot be questioned by the court. The Crown Prosecution Service undertakes most prosecutions and is politically independent, although the Attorney General is responsible to Parliament for its functioning and its penal policy (including the budget). The CPS does not conduct an investigation, as the latter is the responsibility of the police. It brings an indictment before the court and takes over criminal proceedings instituted by the police, who handled the investigation. It is also responsible for making a decision on whether an indictment will be brought before the court. The CPS functions according to the rules provided for by the Code for Crown Prosecutors. It is issued by the Director of Public Prosecutions.[40] The Code, updated from time to time, contains a set of rules that should be followed by a prosecutor in performing his statutory tasks, for example, in making a decision on whether to prosecute or not. The Code is not a source of law, but it forms basic guidelines to procedure, and its breach may have legal consequences in a subsequent case. This is a public document, drawn up by the DPP and laid before Parliament for scrutiny—which can be seen as a form of accountability to the legislature. It is based on the policy drawn up by the government.[41]

In the United States, the authority of the public prosecutor has been known from the very beginning of this country's existence. Both state and federal prosecutors are always part of the executive branch of the government. Some derive their powers from the Constitution of the United States—Article 2, section 3, states that the executive branch of the federal government "shall take care that the laws are faithfully executed". As a result, this constitutional duty was mandated to

---

[39] This tendency is considered to constitute a part of "a global trend toward an enlarged role for government – so dramatically evident in Britain"—Damaška (1986), p. 231.

[40] Code for Crown Prosecutors, http://www.cps.gov.uk/publications/docs/code_2013_accessible_english.pdf. Accessed 13 Feb 2015.

[41] See in general: Darbyshire (2008), p. 128; Padfield (2008), p. 162; Sprack (2012), p. 66; Sanders (2000), p. 300; Gandy (1988).

prosecutors.[42] In the US, prosecutors are divided into federal prosecutors and state prosecutors. They have to be licensed attorneys, but they are not judicial officers. Federal prosecutors (US Attorneys) represent the federal government before district and appeal courts. They operate under the federal prosecutors' regulations (The United States Attorneys' Manual)[43] that contain a set of guidelines related both to the organisational structure of the prosecutor's office as well as to the manner of prosecuting federal law offences. It is an internal document in the Department of Justice. Such guidelines are adopted both at a federal level and internally, as policies of individual states or counties—in most cases, they are modelled on the federal system. However, when it comes to state prosecutors, in the case of the United States it is rather difficult to present coherent rules of operation for the prosecutor's office where even its name differs from state to state.[44] Both their systemic location and the scope of powers are so different that it is impossible to present a uniform analysis. In most cases, they are local government officials: in 45 states, prosecutors are elected officials (which makes them directly accountable to the public), who run for office as political party nominees; in five states, they are nominated by the Governor (or Attorney General). Where prosecutors are appointed, they may be required to explain their decisions to a higher political authority. Since they are appointed government officials, they can be removed for cause at the pleasure of the appointing official. If they are elected, they respond directly to the voters. As some observe in either case, the prosecutor should be careful to perform his duties in conformity with the expression of the popular will of the people.[45] However, in either case, the prosecutor is solely responsible for the manner in which a case is handled, and no higher official may exercise supervision or control over the performance of his duties. They may not be forced to initiate a prosecution or to refrain from prosecuting a particular case. On the other hand, US Attorneys are supervised by the Attorney General who establishes policy for the US Department of Justice and exercises general control over the manner in which all federal prosecutors perform their duties.[46] As a consequence, it is not easy to conduct a coherent analysis of the systemic location of the US prosecutor's office.

Characteristic components of the "Anglo-Saxon model of accusation" manifest themselves in two basic systemic features. First, a strict understanding of the adversarial nature of criminal proceedings results in perceiving the criminal proceedings as a dispute, a contest between prosecution and defence, both of which have equal rights. The trial before common law courts is a procedure managed by the parties. Each of the parties establishes its own version of a case, which gives rise

---

[42] This conclusion presented in: Worrall (2007), p. 293.

[43] http://www.justice.gov/usao/eousa/foia_reading_room/usam/. Accessed 10 Feb 2015.

[44] They are called, for example, city attorney, county prosecutor, district attorney, district attorney general, prosecuting attorney, state prosecutor, state attorney, chief law enforcement officer—as noticed by LaFave et al. (2009).

[45] E.g., Michelich (2000), p. 483.

[46] *Ibidem.*

to the two case approach, with two versions of a case being consequently presented by parties. Thus, the prosecutor is one of the parties involved in a dispute held before an impartial court. His powers are clearly defined: he should achieve conviction of the accused. The prosecutor independently decides on the scope of the evidence presented in order to support the indictment. This limits the scope of an investigation to the steps that allow the accuser to prepare a case to be brought before a court. The court's role is only that of an arbiter. Its task is to ensure that the parties, while presenting their version of events, comply with the rules of procedure. The court may not even evaluate the evidence presented by the parties, as that is the task of the jury. The prosecutor remains the master of the prosecution case.

The other fundamental feature of this model is the assumption that the legal and criminal reaction to a crime (the scope and manner of response) is left to the discretion of the prosecutor's office. This principle stems from the application of the principle of prosecutorial opportunism. Particularly noteworthy are the consequences of this principle, i.e., wide discretion in pursuing prosecution and in deciding on the intensity of criminal reaction. The prosecutor decides whether there will be a confrontation of parties in a trial or whether a legal and criminal conflict will be resolved in a non-confrontational (consensual) manner, e.g., by way of an agreement with the accused regarding the essence of the accusation. Another consequence of leaving the manner and scope of the legal and criminal response to the prosecutor's discretion is the binding nature of the legal characterisation of facts contained in the indictment for the court.

2.2.3 Prosecutors of International Military Tribunals

The prosecutors of the international military tribunals created after World War II acted on behalf of the states setting up the tribunal. The Charter of the International Military Tribunal (IMT) in Nuremberg regulated both the rules of appointing the prosecutors and their powers. It did not envisage the establishment of the prosecutor's office, and the function of a single chief prosecutor did not exist. It was concluded that the existence of "mutual trust" between the allied forces eliminated the need to establish a centralised prosecutor's office.[47] Each of the signatories to the London Agreement appointed a Chief Prosecutor for the investigation of the charges against and the prosecution of major war criminals accused before the IMT (Article 14 of the Charter). Each Prosecutor was to act using the means and specialists assigned to assist him by the government of each state. The Chief Prosecutors acted as a committee for the purposes of agreeing upon a plan of the individual work of each of the Chief Prosecutors and his staff, settling the final designation of major war criminals to be tried by the Tribunal, approving the indictment and the documents to be submitted therewith and finally lodging the

[47] In general see: Townsend (2012), pp. 173–208; Ginsburg and Kudriavtsev (1990), p. 31.

indictment and the accompanying documents with the Tribunal. In all the above matters, the Committee was supposed to act by a majority vote. It was to appoint a Chairman as might be convenient and in accordance with the principle of rotation. In the case of an equal division of vote concerning the designation of a defendant to be tried by the Tribunal, or the crimes with which he should be charged, that proposal was to be adopted that had been made by the party that had proposed that the particular defendant be tried or the particular charges be preferred against him.

The Chief Prosecutors, acting individually, or in collaboration with one another, had the following duties: investigation, collection and production before or at the trial of all necessary evidence; the preparation of the indictment for approval by the Committee of Prosecutors; the preliminary examination of all necessary witnesses and of all defendants. Moreover, they were obliged to act as prosecutor at the trial, to appoint representatives to carry out such duties as may be assigned them and to undertake such other matters as may appear necessary to them for the purposes of the preparation for and conduct of the trial. As far as the distribution of work between them was concerned, each of the Prosecutors could undertake any investigative steps and, having lodged an indictment, could act as accuser (Article 15 of the Charter). The Prosecutors' task was also "to draw up and recommend to the Tribunal for its approval draft rules of procedure". The Tribunal had the power to accept, with or without amendments, or to reject the rules so recommended (Article 14(e) of the Charter). It was a unique solution: the drafting of procedural regulations was delegated to an enforcement authority that was to follow them in proceedings it was just about to conduct.

The function of the Chief of Counsel was provided for by the International Military Tribunal for the Far East Charter. The Chief of Counsel was to be designated by the Supreme Commander for the Allied Powers. He was responsible for the investigation and prosecution of charges against war criminals within the jurisdiction of this Tribunal. He did not enjoy any independence from the government of the United States. Also, any state with which Japan had been at war could appoint an Associate Counsel to assist the Chief of Counsel (Articles 8a and 8 of the IMTFE Charter).[48]

The proceedings before the international military tribunals were carried out pursuant to distinct procedures. None of them, however, guaranteed independence of prosecutors. The sole objective of the tribunals was to punish the crimes committed by only one of the parties to the international conflict, and both were set up by occupying forces, during an ongoing occupation. They also operated on the occupied territory of the defeated side, whose representatives were to be prosecuted. We also should not forget about their military character, which had an obvious impact on the lack of decision-making independence by prosecutors.

[48] The International Military Tribunal for the Far East Charter (IMTFE Charter), 19 January 1946: http://web.archive.org/web/19990222030537/http://www.yale.edu/lawweb/avalon/imtfech.htm. Accessed 17 Nov 2014.

The prosecutors of these tribunals were officials of the state, investigating and prosecuting on behalf and under the control of certain states. Even indictments were formulated with the name of each state against all of the accused. The prosecutors were given instructions regarding the accused persons, charges that should be formulated, as well as the specific manner for handling a case. In such a situation, there was no doubt that the prosecutors of the International Military Tribunals were not independent and that their decisions were entirely dependent on the will of the victorious states.

2.2.4 The ICTY Office of the Prosecutor

In proceedings before the *ad hoc* tribunals, the International Criminal Tribunal for the former Yugoslavia and the International Criminal Tribunal for Rwanda, it was assumed that the prosecutor would be a permanent organ of the tribunal. The Statutes of both of these tribunals provide for identical organisational solutions for the prosecutor's office location (also, the Rules of Procedure and Evidence are similar, and major differences appeared only after several amendments introduced by the ICTY judges during the course of functioning). The Prosecutor is one of the three independent organs of the ICTY, along with the Chambers and the Registry (Article 16 ICTY Statute). The Prosecutor is appointed by the Security Council at the nomination of the UN Secretary General (the candidates are presented by the states). The Statute requires him to be of high moral character and possess the highest level of competence and experience in the conduct of investigations and prosecutions of criminal cases. He serves for a 4-year term and is eligible for reappointment.

Similar requirements are set for the staff members of the Office of the Prosecutor. They are to perform the functions of the Prosecutor on his behalf, under his supervision and pursuant to his instructions. The Rules provide that the ICTY Prosecutor's powers and duties under the Rules may be exercised by staff members of the Office of the Prosecutor authorised by the Prosecutor or by any person acting under the Prosecutor's direction (Rules 37 and 38 ICTY RPE). Their professionalism is of key importance for the reliability of operations of the Office of the Prosecutor. The staff of the Office of the Prosecutor is appointed by the Secretary General on the recommendation of the Prosecutor. They are selected pursuant to the rules applicable in the UN HR system. A Deputy Prosecutor is appointed by the Secretary General of the United Nations, on the recommendation of the Prosecutor. He exercises the functions of the Prosecutor in the event of the latter's absence from duty or inability to act or upon the Prosecutor's express instructions.[49]

The Office of the Prosecutor consists of the investigation unit, conducting activities in the field and the prosecution unit, constituted by experienced court

[49] In general see: Bassiouni and Manikas (1996), pp. 828–836.

lawyers, as well as the Office of the Prosecutor and Special Advisory Unit. The powers of the international criminal tribunal prosecutor remained unchanged from the times of the IMT in Nuremberg: he is expected not only to conduct investigations and perform all investigative steps, usually reserved for the police in national orders, but also to prepare an indictment and support it before the court. According to the ICTY and ICTR Statutes, the Prosecutor can make proposals for amendment of the Rules of Procedure and Evidence, and therefore he can exert impact on the procedure employed before the tribunals (Rule 6(A) RPE ICTY).

Also, as far as organisational structure and the systemic location of the prosecutor are concerned, the *ad hoc* tribunals have served as "laboratories" for the establishment of the model adopted by the ICC.[50] The practice of the *ad hoc* tribunals showed that it was usually the first prosecutor of a given tribunal who had to find the proper model of operation and develop methods of acting.

2.2.5 The ICC Office of the Prosecutor

According to Article 42(1) of the Rome Statute, the Office of the Prosecutor (OTP) shall act independently as a separate organ of the Court. When creating the Statute, there was no doubt that the Office of the Prosecutor was to be an independent organ of the Court. The Office is headed by the Prosecutor. He has full authority over the management and administration of the Office, including the staff, the facilities and its other resources. The Prosecutor is assisted by one or more Deputy Prosecutors, who shall be entitled to carry out any of the acts required of the Prosecutor under this Statute. Provisions of both the Statute and Rules of Procedure and Evidence are intended to ensure the highest possible professional standards for the Office's members. In agreement with the Presidency and the Prosecutor, the Secretary submits Regulations for the Office of the Prosecutor,[51] which define the term of office and the terms and conditions for appointing, compensating and dismissing the staff. All decisions on behalf of the Prosecutor are issued by himself or one of his two Deputies. Rules of Procedure and Evidence provide that the Prosecutor or a Deputy Prosecutor may authorise staff members of the Office of the Prosecutor to represent him in the exercise of his functions. This prevents the establishment of a complex hierarchical system of organisation with each prosecutor issuing decisions on his own behalf but remaining obliged to report to numerous higher ranks of prosecutors. Each decision is issued on behalf of the Prosecutor, which may lead to the conclusion on the uniformity of the ICC Office of Prosecutor.[52]

The Office of the Prosecutor is divided into three functional divisions: the Jurisdiction, Complementarity and Cooperation Division, the Investigation

[50] See: Boed (2002), p. 496.

[51] Regulations of the Office of the Prosecutor, ICC-BD/05-01-09, 23 April 2009.

[52] In general see: Bergsmo and Harhoff (2008), p. 974; Schabas (2010), p. 578.

Division and the Prosecution Division—which correspond to the three major areas of activity of the OTP. Within these divisions, there are the-so called joint teams assigned to a specific case. A joint team is formed upon a decision to proceed with an investigation in a situation, for the purpose of conducting the investigation. The composition and size of each joint team depends on the needs and stage of the investigation. Each joint team is composed of staff from the three Divisions in order to ensure a coordinated approach throughout the investigation. Each team is headed by the Special Prosecutor. He leads the investigation and is assigned to a specific case, leading a team of the Tribunal's officials. He manages the investigation under the supervision and in agreement with the Senior Prosecutor, who is then responsible for presenting an indictment at the trial. Upon confirmation of the charges, an inter-divisional trial team is formed to carry out prosecutions.[53]

All the members of the Office act in accordance with the Code of Conduct for the Office of the Prosecutor, which entered into force on the 5th of September 2013.[54] The Code establishes a set of minimum standards of conduct, among which as general standards it provides for independence of the Office; professional ethics and integrity; fair, impartial, effective and expeditious investigation and prosecution; respect for confidentiality of investigations and prosecutions; respect for human rights and fundamental freedoms recognised by international law in conformity with the Statute and non-discrimination against any individual or groups of individuals; and a shared culture rooted in the principles and purposes of the Statute, without bias for the rules and methods of any national system.

The tasks of the Prosecutor include receiving referrals and any substantiated information on crimes within the jurisdiction of the Court, examining them and conducting investigations and prosecutions before the Court. Upon completion of the investigation, he turns to the Pre-Trial Chamber with a request to authorise initiation of an investigation. During trial, he acts as an accusatory before the Trial Chamber, presenting the prosecution case. Also, the ICC Prosecutor enjoys the power to propose amendments to the Rules of Procedure and Evidence—which can enter into force upon adoption by a two-thirds majority of the members of the Assembly of States Parties (Article 51(2) of the Statute).

2.3 Independence of the ICC Prosecutor

2.3.1 Organisational Guarantees of Independence

The basic systemic aspect of the international criminal tribunal prosecutor is his independence. Similar to judicial independence, it is protected by means of legal regulations, as the status of both of these offices and the need to ensure their

[53] Regulations of the Office of the Prosecutor, ICC-BD/05-01-09, 23 April 2009.

[54] Code of Conduct for the Office of the Prosecutor: Date of entry into force: 5 September 2013.

autonomy in the international arena are very similar and equally important. The challenges arising from prosecution of international law crimes make the prosecutor's independence a key guarantee of the reliability of both the prosecutor's office and of the tribunal. It would not be an overstatement to claim that the reliability of each tribunal depends on whether the prosecutor is capable of acting in an independent manner.[55]

The prosecutor's independence has two aspects: internal and external. In the internal aspect, the prosecutor's independence is mostly affected by the systemic location of his office. Article 16(2) of the ICTY Statute (15(2) of the ICTR Statute) provides that the Prosecutor shall act independently as a separate organ of the International Tribunal. He shall not seek or receive instructions from any government or from any other source. The independence of the Prosecutor should be also seen in the light of the rules of appointment—he is appointed by the Security Council at the nomination of the UN Secretary General. The Statute ensures his professional and personal qualifications by requiring him to be a person of high moral character and possess the highest level of competence and experience in the conduct of investigations and prosecutions of criminal cases (Article 16(4) ICTY Statute). However, the Statute contains no information on the possibility of removing the Prosecutor from office.

Numerous organisational guarantees of internal independence of the Prosecutor were implemented in the ICC Statute and Rules of Procedure and Evidence.

Firstly, in order to ensure independence as well as geographical equality, it was decided that the Prosecutor and the Deputy Prosecutors shall be of different nationalities. Secondly, similar to the case of the *ad hoc* tribunals, neither the Prosecutor nor a Deputy Prosecutor shall engage in any activity that is likely to interfere with his prosecutorial functions or to affect confidence in his independence. Moreover, they should not engage in any other occupation of a professional nature.

Thirdly, the Statute ensures the independence of the members of the Office, constituting that they shall not seek or act on instructions from any external source. Very detailed instructions as to how to ensure full staff independence are presented in the Code of Conduct for the Office of the Prosecutor.[56] Firstly, the Prosecutor is entrusted with the task of insuring this independence. Secondly, the members themselves are obliged to follow the subsequent rules: remain unaffected by any individual or sectional interests and, in particular, by any pressure from any State or any international, intergovernmental or non-governmental organisation or the media; refrain from any activity that is likely to negatively affect the confidence of others in the independence or integrity of the Office; refrain from any activity that may lead to any reasonable inference that their independence has been compromised; refrain from the exercise of other occupations of a professional

[55] See: Rwalamira (1999), p. 167.

[56] Date of entry into force September 5, 2013, http://www.icc-cpi.int/iccdocs/oj/otp-COC-Eng.PDF. Accessed 11 Feb 2015.

nature without the prior approval of the Prosecutor; and refrain from any activity that is likely to interfere with the performance of duties and the exercise of their functions as Members of the Office. Moreover, staff members who are confronted with an attempt by any source to induce them to violate their obligation of loyalty and independence shall promptly report this to a Head of Division or Section, the Prosecutor or the Deputy Prosecutor(s), who then should provide guidance on how to proceed.

The fourth guarantee of impartiality is the institution of disqualification of the Prosecutor or a Deputy Prosecutor. There are three modes of disqualification: *ex officio*, at the request of the Prosecutor (or a Deputy Prosecutor) or at the request of the person being investigated or prosecuted (similarly to the approach adopted in the Polish Code of Criminal Proceedings). According to the general rule, they cannot participate in any matter in which their impartiality might reasonably be doubted on any ground. This provision mentions explicitly two examples when their impartiality will always be impaired. They shall be disqualified from a case, first, if they have previously been involved in any capacity in that case before the Court and, second, if they have participated in a related criminal case at the national level involving the person being investigated or prosecuted (Article 42(7) ICC Statute). Moreover, a detailed list of possible grounds for disqualification is included in Rule 34 of RPE. The list explains which situations (*inter alia*) will be regarded as giving rise to a suspicion of impartiality: personal interest in the case, including a spousal, parental or other close family, personal or professional relationship, or a subordinate relationship, with any of the parties; involvement, in his or her private capacity, in any legal proceedings initiated prior to his or her involvement in the case, or initiated by him or her subsequently, in which the person being investigated or prosecuted was or is an opposing party; performance of functions, prior to taking office, during which he or she could be expected to have formed an opinion on the case in question, on the parties or on their legal representatives that, objectively, could adversely affect the required impartiality of the person concerned; expression of opinions, through the communications media, in writing or in public actions, that, objectively, could adversely affect the required impartiality of the person concerned.

If such a situation appears, the Prosecutor cannot refrain from investigating a particular case on his own. When the person being investigated or prosecuted requests *disqualification*, indicating existence of grounds leading to impartiality, or a request as to the disqualification was presented by the Prosecutor or a Deputy Prosecutor, it shall be decided by the Appeals Chamber (Article 42(8) Statute).[57]

The institution of "disqualification" should not be mistaken with the institution known as "excusal". Article 42(6) provides that the Presidency of the Court has a discretionary power to excuse the Prosecutor or a Deputy Prosecutor from acting in a particular case at his request. There may be variety of reasons, personal or other,

---

[57] In general see: Bergsmo and Harhoff (2008), pp. 978–979; and Schabas (2010), p. 582.

behind the request to be excused. This request is then treated as confidential as well as the reasons given to support it.

The Prosecutor may also be temporally suspended from duty by the Bureau of the Assembly of States Parties in the case that the Presidency transmits to the Bureau a complaint of a "sufficiently serious nature" filed against the ICC Prosecutor (Rule 28 RPE).

The guarantee of independence is also ensured by the highest level of professionalism expected of the Prosecutor. The Prosecutor and the Deputy Prosecutors "shall be persons of high moral character, be highly competent in and have extensive practical experience in the prosecution or trial of criminal cases" (Article 42(3)). Moreover, they should have an excellent knowledge of and be fluent in at least one of the working languages of the Court. However, in the earliest days of the ICC, there was a tendency to avoid engaging prosecutors who had previously worked before the *ad hoc* tribunals. Therefore, it was hardly possible to expect the appointed Prosecutor to be a person with any experience in handling international cases.

Another measure planned as a guarantee of the Prosecutor's independence is the manner of his appointment. As a rule, this is more democratic than in the case of the *ad hoc* tribunals. The Prosecutor is elected by secret ballot by an absolute majority of the members of the Assembly of States Parties (Article 42(3) of the Statute). This method of election was intended as one of the guarantees of the Prosecutor's independence. Its goal was to prevent his selection *via* diplomatic routes that are in principle considered to be confidential and lack transparency.[58] This rule has not disrupted the election of the first candidate by way of "informal consultations", in which process only one candidate emerged (who, to nobody's surprise, was elected single-votedly with no abstentions). As W. Schabas observes, there were no indications as to by which states he was nominated.[59] The election seems to be always a matter of reaching a consensus.[60] The Deputy Prosecutors are elected in the same way from a list of candidates provided by the Prosecutor. The Prosecutor nominates three candidates for each position of Deputy Prosecutor. Unless a shorter term is decided upon at the time of their election, the Prosecutor and the Deputy Prosecutors shall hold office for a term of 9 years and shall not be eligible for re-election. Despite the fact that such a democratic method was adopted, there is still some criticism related to the fact that the ICC suffers from a "democratic deficit", which is manifested by the way of selection of the Prosecutor on a "one-state-one-vote basis".[61] Moreover, neither the Statute nor the RPE indicate who may nominate the candidates. This matter was decided only in the resolution adopted at the first session of the Assembly of the States Parties. It constitutes that the candidates are

[58] See: Coté (2012), p. 345.

[59] Schabas (2010), p. 581.

[60] Wei (2007), p. 27.

[61] Cit. after: Greenawalt (2007), p. 657.

nominated by the States Parties during the nomination period.[62] This resolution highlights that such nominations should (preferably) be made by a group of states and supported by more than just one state.

Finally, independence is also ensured by the rule that both the Prosecutor and his Deputy Prosecutors cannot be re-elected. In consequence, there is no incentive for them to try to gather further support from States to secure their subsequent election. At a personal level, this independence allows everybody to believe that the Prosecutor will not see any reason to favour one situation over another, or to specifically target one situation over another, in order to gather support from the States.[63]

For the first time, the Rome Statute provides for a procedure of removal from office of the Prosecutor (Article 46). Such a decision is made by the Assembly of States Parties, by secret ballot by an absolute majority of the States Parties. It can be taken only in two situations, provided for by the Statute: in cases where that person

(a) is found to have committed serious misconduct or a serious breach of his or her duties under this Statute, as provided for in the Rules of Procedure and Evidence; or
(b) is unable to exercise the functions required by this Statute.

It seems that the provision sets an obligation on the decisive organ in every case when such a conduct takes place. Moreover, in order to secure a strict and coherent interpretation of these grounds of removal, Rule 24 RPE provides a detailed definition of "serious misconduct" and "serious breach of duty".

As far as the external independence of the prosecutor of an international criminal tribunal is concerned, this always raises the greatest concerns. It was most clearly visible in the practice of the *ad hoc* tribunals. The external independence of the prosecutor is related to the necessity of remaining independent from external sources—states and international organisations, such as the Security Council.[64] As an example, it may be observed that since the Security Council established the *ad hoc* tribunals pursuant to a resolution, it may easily pass another resolution to terminate their operations or amend their operating principles by amending the Statute. It can already be observed that the Council does use resolutions to affect the ongoing operations of the *ad hoc* tribunals. However, analysis of this issue shows that whereas there is no independence of the *ad hoc* tribunals' prosecutors from external political factors, the ICC operates in a relatively independent way.

Independence from a higher executive power may also be perceived as a component of external independence. In many states, the prosecutor acts as a government official reporting to a complex structure of "official supervisors" and cannot be considered to be an independent authority. He is subject to the official supervision of the Minister of Justice or that of a General Prosecutor. M. Damaška

---

[62] Procedure for the nomination and election of judges, the Prosecutor and Deputy Prosecutors of the International Criminal Court, ICC-ASP/1/Res.2, § 3 and 24.

[63] See: Wouters et al. (2008), p. 273.

[64] See: Brubacher (2004), p. 85; and Coté (2012), p. 337.

leaves no doubt that the hierarchical structure may lead to "less visible but extremely important internal constraints on the exercise of prosecutorial freedom". In consequence, prosecutors often presse charges *contre coeur* or against their personal wishes, led to their decisions by normative directives or—more probably—by the wishes of their superiors.[65] In Poland, the principle of hierarchical subordination prevents the prosecutor from remaining independent in his actions—Articles 8a and 8b of the Act on the Public Prosecutor's Office (ustawa o Prokuraturze) are quite clear about it.[66] Although Article 8 claims that "while performing the activities set forth in legal acts, the prosecutor is independent", subsequent provisions undermine this claim. Namely, the prosecutor is obliged to perform the orders and implement the guidelines and instructions of a superior prosecutor. Moreover, a directly superior prosecutor is authorised to amend or repeal the subordinate prosecutor's decisions. He can also take over the cases handled by subordinate prosecutors and conduct it further. Citing the words of S. Waltoś, it may not be assumed that the regulatory requirement of prosecutor's "independence" will mean that a prosecutor will be, at the same time "as objective as a judge, and as obedient as a reliable link in the chain of hierarchical subordination".[67]

In the case of the ICC, there are two views on the issue of hierarchical independence of the Prosecutor. According to one of them, organisationally, the Prosecutor should not be seen in separation from the OTP. Therefore, the structure of the OTP should be evaluated as a whole. Then it could also be concluded that it is a hierarchical organ: "a pyramid-shaped organ", headed by the Prosecutor and his Deputies.[68] In consequence, the Prosecutor has full authority over the management and administration of the office. However, in the light of the assumption on the uniformity of the ICC Office of Prosecutor, as each decision is issued on behalf of the Prosecutor, it seems that the Office should be evaluated as a whole. Therefore, the organisational independence of the OTP should be seen in the light of the position as an organ of the Court. Although the internal structure is hierarchical, the whole organ is still independent from other organs of the ICC and from external bodies.[69] The Prosecutor himself is not dependent on any "institutional superior" as it is the case in the hierarchical structure of continental states' prosecution services.

The third aspect of independence is functional independence. It signifies the scope of powers and autonomy of the prosecutor in criminal proceedings. The basic manifestation of functional independence is discretion in deciding on initiating an investigation and in lodging an indictment before the court.[70]

---

[65] Cit. after: Damaška (1974–1975), p. 480.

[66] Act of 20.6.1985 of the Prosecution, Dz. U. of 2011, No. 270, pos. 1599.

[67] Cit. after: Waltoś (2002), p. 6.

[68] Cit. after Heinze (2014), p. 250.

[69] Which is highlighted in most of the cases, as in: Coté (2012), p. 337, see also: Olásolo (2003) p. 89.

[70] See: Turone (2002), p. 1138.

2.3.2 Limits of Independence

Despite the numerous guarantees of the ICC Prosecutor's independence, there is also criticism pertaining to the actual possibilities of maintaining it. It pertains both to the various internal and external aspects of systemic location of the Prosecutor's Office and to procedural aspects.

2.3.2.1 Internal Limits of Independence

Organisational Context

As far as the internal independence in the organisational context is concerned, the organisational aspect has to be analysed. It has been indicated that the OTP is a division of an international organ that has a jurisdiction over crimes of international law. On the one hand, it may be concluded that a prosecutor forms part of the judiciary's power, being an authority established at the court (following the example of such legal systems as France or Belgium). However, we may also conclude that the Court as a whole is an inquisitorial authority as it combines two functions of the criminal process that are usually exercised by two independent authorities on behalf of the state.

In this context, there arise concerns as to the actual possibility of maintaining the prosecutor's independence from the judges. In the case of the ICC, the Prosecutor is in many ways dependent on the judicial authority, both in the organisational and the procedural aspects. As far as the former is concerned, first, there is no doubt that there is close co-operation between the tribunals' judges and prosecutors. Second, both divisions of this system of justice are physically located in the same building.[71] Third, personal influence and the impact of the authority of some judges may not be ignored. In practice, especially when hearing the earliest cases before the *ad hoc* tribunals, prosecutors searched for a "golden measure" that would enable them to maintain their practical independence in the decision-making process.

Procedural Context

Particularly conspicuous is the procedural dependence of the Prosecutor's actions on the judicial authority. There are numerous procedural institutions subjecting his actions to the control of the judges or conditioning them on their approval.

The first such institution involves the judges' impact on the selection of the accused by the prosecutor. This impact can easily be observed on the example of the ICTY. The Security Council 1534 Resolution instructs that the ICTY ensures that

[71] See: Schabas (2010), p. 578, who mentions the dangers of sharing a common cafeteria on the same floor and Tochilovsky (2001), p. 594.

indictments "concentrate on one or more of the most senior leaders suspected of being most responsible for crimes within the jurisdiction of the Tribunal".[72] Pursuant to Rule 28 RPE ICTY, which was amended in 2004, the ICTY judges have the power to control whether the ICTY Prosecutor in fact brings the indictment against such officials. The ICTY Prosecutor strongly opposed implementation of this principle, concluding that it violates his independence. This opinion was shared by judges—however, of the second *ad hoc* tribunal, ICTR—who refused to accept such a solution. The implementation of this rule is the more surprising since, prior to this amendment, the ICTY Appeals Chamber found that "The Statute leaves it entirely to the Prosecutor to investigate serious violations of international humanitarian law in the territory of the former Yugoslavia, and to determine against whom an indictment is to be brought. No government or other institution or person, including the judges of the Tribunal, can direct the Prosecutor as to whom he or she is to investigate or to charge".[73]

The necessity of having an indictment approved by the judicial authority accounts for another institution limiting the procedural independence of the prosecutor, common for all international criminal tribunals. Without its approval, it is not possible to move from the stage of investigation to the stage of trial. In the case of the ICC Prosecutor, the necessity of authorisation by the judicial authority also pertains to the decision on the initiation of an investigation.

Third, the institution of Pre-Trial Conference was introduced before the *ad hoc* tribunals. Prior to the commencement of the trial, on the basis of Rule 73bis (D) RPE, the judges may control the scope of the evidence that the Prosecutor intends to present during the trial and, as a result, have an impact on its limitation. Namely, they may direct (rather than only invite) the Prosecutor to select the counts in the indictment on which to proceed. Judges may "instruct" the Prosecutor, in a binding manner, to drop charges in order to limit the indictment by, e.g., one-thirds. Also, the ICC Trial Chamber may exercise certain control over the evidence that is to be presented at trial. Regulation 54 of the ICC Regulation of the Court formulates only a general rule, which allows the judges to during a Status Conference issue any order in the interests of justice for the purposes of the proceedings on, *inter alia*, issues of the length and content of legal arguments and the opening and closing statements, a summary of the evidence the participants intend to rely on, the length of the evidence to be relied on, the length of questioning of the witnesses and to limit the checklist of issues to be raised in a trial and to guarantee that the manner of their presentation will not lead to a lengthy trial. From the wording of this rule, many powers can be drawn.

From the perspective of the common law states' representatives, the possibility of modifying the legal characterisation presented by the prosecutor in an indictment

---

[72] SC Resolution 1534, UN Doc. S/RES/1534 (2004), § 5, http://www.icty.org/x/file/Legal%20Library/Statute/statute_1534_2004_en.pdf. Accessed 12 Feb 2015.

[73] *Prosecutor v. Milošević*, IT-02-54, Reasons for Refusal of Leave to Appeal from Decision to Impose Time Limit, 16 May 2002, § 12.

is also a factor limiting the prosecutor's independence; in the case of the ICC, this can be done both by the Pre-Trial Chamber during the confirmation hearing as well as by the Trial Chamber during the trial. Similarly, representatives of this system may consider as limiting the assumption that the procedural deals executed between the prosecutor and the accused are not binding for the court.

The above examples may lead us to the conclusion that currently the power of the prosecutor at an international criminal tribunal may be limited in favour of the judicial authority, both in terms of who the accused is and of what offence. In proceedings before the ICTY, both the selection of the defendant by the Prosecutor was limited, as his decision as to the charges he chose to press could be controlled by the Presidency of the Court. In proceedings held before the ICC, however, control over the object of prosecution was introduced in a specific shape only since the Pre-Trial Chamber took the power to modify the legal characterisation adopted by the Prosecutor in an indictment.

2.3.2.2 External Limits of Independence

Independence of Political Organs

As far as external independence is concerned, what causes major concern is the dependence of the *ad hoc* tribunals on the UN authorities. They were in fact appointed as the tribunals of this organisation. In light of the statement that the ICTY and ICTR prosecutors "shall not seek or receive instructions from any Government or from any other source" (in Article 16(2) ICTY Statute), their relationship with the Security Council seems to be rather problematic. The dependence of the *ad hoc* tribunal prosecutors' decisions on the will of the Security Council is a distinct feature of the model of prosecution before these tribunals.[74]

First, not only did the Security Council establish both of these *ad hoc* tribunals, but it also outlined the scope of their powers in terms of territory, subject matter and time, drawing the mandate for such operations from the UN Charter.[75] Second, the prosecutors' dependence on the Council's decisions is demonstrated by the fact that they operate pursuant to the regulations set forth by this entity to govern their powers. There is no doubt that the Security Council appears here as the entity providing a legal framework for the international criminal procedure. The competence of the tribunals' judges to set forth binding procedural rules as part of the Rules of Procedure and Evidence is derived from the powers granted by the Council. The Security Council, however, does not have any impact on the content of the Rules themselves—it is decided exclusively by the judges. The third manifestation of dependence is the selection of the prosecutors by the Council.

[74] See: Bassiouni and Manikas (1996), p. 210.

[75] Irrespective of the fact whether it had legitimate powers to conduct such action in the light of international law or not. See: Buisman (2003), p. 190.

In consequence, when the Security Council is not satisfied with the performance of the prosecutor, it could decide to appoint a different prosecutor—this time a more co-operating one.[76] Moreover, appointment of the staff of the OTP by the UN Secretary General affects their independence and submits them to the bureaucracy and politics of the UN system.[77] On the other hand, in practice this relationship is a formal one and the Secretary General does not induce any influence on the selection process of the new staff.[78]

The fourth manifestation of this dependence is the management of ongoing operations of the tribunals by means of resolutions. The greatest impact is of resolutions setting time frames for completion of work by these tribunals. This puts a particular pressure on the operations of the ICTY and its Prosecutor, which in many cases has led to amendments in the penal procedure aimed at expediting proceedings. Such amendments, primarily intended only to expedite and improve the course of proceedings, in consequence simultaneously limited significantly the powers of the Prosecutor. First of all, the point was to enable the judges to control whether the Prosecutor prosecutes "sufficiently high-ranking government officials" pursuant to Rule 28 RPE ICTY. Second, the option to "order" that a number of charges brought in an indictment and the number of sites or events presented by the Prosecutor to support charges should be limited (Rule 73bis(D)) resulted in the court's power to exercise impact on the content of the indictment during a pre-trial hearing.

Analysing the subject from the point of view of organisational structure, the supervision of the Security Council over the operations of the *ad hoc* tribunals may be compared to administrative supervision performed by the Minister of Justice (or a Chief Prosecutor) by means of issuing the guidelines in national legal systems. The ICTY President stated that "it is entirely appropriate for the Security Council to define (...) broad goals and directives. (...) it would not be appropriate for the Council to go into great detail in such directives, because such directives should not encroach on the prosecutorial independence of the Prosecutor".[79] Finally, pressure of a non-formal character should not be ignored either: when the ICTY trials did not start as expected, the first ICTY Prosecutor was informed that if he did not indict someone within the next month, the Tribunal would not be given money for operation for the following year.[80]

In the light of all the above-described limitations to independence, it seems debatable whether the Prosecutor of the ICTY is sufficiently independent.[81]

In the case of the ICC Prosecutor, the aspect of external independence manifests itself in a different way. As a rule, he is independent of political bodies such as the

[76] Buisman (2003), p. 197.

[77] See: Bassiouni and Manikas (1996), p. 833.

[78] See: Safferling (2001), p. 79.

[79] Cit. after: Coté (2012), p. 339.

[80] Goldstone (2002), p. 281.

[81] Buisman (2003), p. 198.

UN and its organs. Compared to the situation of the ICTY, in proceedings before the ICC the competence of the Security Council is relatively limited.[82] M. Płachta even talks about "liberation from the paralysing dependence on a strictly political body".[83] There are only three aspects in which the Council may influence the operations of the ICC Prosecutor. First, it may make a referral that a crime has been committed within the Court's jurisdiction. Second, it may prompt the Pre-Trial Chamber to review the Prosecutor's decision on refusal to handle an investigation or refusal to lodge an indictment. Third, pursuant to Article 16 of the ICC Statute, it may postpone the commencement or handling of investigation or prosecution by the ICC Prosecutor for a period of 12 months by issuing a resolution pursuant to Chapter 7 of the UN Charter. The binding nature of the Security Council's crime referral remains a controversial issue.[84] Acknowledgement of its binding nature for the Prosecutor could lead to the question on whether the Security Council is going to use the ICC in the same way as the *ad hoc* tribunals it has established. Obligatory following of the Council's requests would turn the Court into a "court of the Security Council". Generally, it should be considered that the ICC operates as a tribunal independent of the Security Council. However, adopting this provision in the Statute leaves many questions unanswered. And these are questions crucial for the actual balance between these two organs and for the evaluation of the Prosecutor's independence.

Financial Independence

The manner of financing the operations of the tribunal should also be considered as an indication of its external dependence.[85] In fact, the practical scope of prosecutorial actions and the number of the accused and, in consequence, their selection will depend on the manner and efficiency of financing. In the case of the *ad hoc* tribunals, their operations were mostly financed by the United Nations (as well as with voluntary contributions of states), which gave the Council the mandate to consider itself responsible for influencing the number of cases handled by the *ad hoc* tribunals and the allocated time framework.[86] In the first place, if the funding is inadequate, the tribunal is forced to limit new investigations. In the second place, as the budget for the ICTY is approved on a semi-annual basis, its actual amount may

---

[82] As observed also by numerous authors: Greenawalt (2007), p. 665; Gallant (2003), p. 30; Yañez-Barnuevo and Escobar Hernández (2003), p. 51; Wei (2007), p. 15.

[83] Cit. after: Płachta (2007), p. 481.

[84] See: Ohlin (2009), p. 189.

[85] A fact noticed by: Wouters et al. (2008), p. 288: "Financial predictability is indeed key to the Office of the Prosecutor's being able to plan ahead and to move forward on certain issues".

[86] In general see: Bassiouni and Manikas (1996), pp. 212 and 217; Gallant (2003), p. 22; Bibas and Burke-White (2009–2010), p. 677.

be understood as “a clear message to the Tribunal to produce results”.[87] The budget anyway indicates the number of cases that can be dealt with by the tribunal.

In the case of the ICC, the budget is planned and approved by the Assembly of States Parties. Expenses are covered from the following sources: agreed contributions paid by the States Parties; the funds allocated by the United Nations upon approval of the General Assembly, which are, in particular, to cover the costs incurred in relation to the presentation of cases by the Security Council. This may suggest that in matters referred by the Security Council, the Prosecutor’s decision depends to a certain extent on the amount of funds allocated by the Council for case handling. However, after the first case had been referred by the Council pursuant to Resolution 1593[88] (pertaining to the situation in Sudan), the Resolution included a statement that “none of the expenses incurred in connection with the referral including expenses related to investigations or prosecutions in connection with that referral, shall be borne by the United Nations and that such costs shall be borne by the parties to the Rome Statute and those States that wish to contribute voluntarily”.[89] This assumption is obviously not in compliance with Article 115(b) of the Rome Statute. It leaves us with the question, which act should prevail, the Security Council Resolution or the Rome Statute?

The question of the ICC Prosecutor’s independence leads inevitably to a debate on how to achieve a proper balance between independence and accountability. The method of adopting a complicated set of multiple checks and balances was supposed to eliminate the argument of “a renegade Prosecutor that is accountable to no one”;[90] however, it leaves open a discussion as to whether the Prosecutor is still independent. The second discussion may begin with a question as to whether this model of strongly limited independence leaves any room for taking up successful actions, whether it does not “render the bulldog potentially toothless”[91] and whether it is true that “there is more to fear from an impotent than from an overreaching Prosecutor”.[92] It seems that the search for the right balance is still continuing.

Despite the numerous guarantees of independence that were provided in the Rome Statute, the Prosecutor has not been, and most likely never will be, able to avoid accusations of a lack of impartiality and being driven by political goals—in both the internal and external aspects. On the other hand, his independence has become the reason for the US’s refusal to ratify the Statute. The United States claimed that the prosecutor left without any “supervision” and acting “arbitrarily” could conduct overtly anti-American proceedings causing major moral, financial

[87] Cit. after Buisman (2003), p. 203.

[88] UN Doc. S/Res/1593 of 2005.

[89] The meaning of this provisions discussed by: Krzan (2009), p. 159. Similarly: Bergsmo and Harhoff (2008), p. 975, and Ohlin (2009), p. 193.

[90] Cit. after: Wouters et al. (2008), p. 288.

[91] *Ibidem*, p. 316.

[92] As in: Arbour (1999a) p. 217.

and political losses for this country by the mere fact of accusing American citizens. According to the representatives of the United States, the Prosecutor should act exclusively under the supervision and control of the Security Council, similar to the *ad hoc* tribunals.[93]

2.4 Prosecutor: Minister of Justice or an Accusator?

2.4.1 *Two Conceptions of the Prosecutor's Role*

It is also of key importance for the model of accusation to determine whether a prosecutor is an independent judiciary organ (a so-called guardian of the law, in German—*Wächter des Gesetzes*), referred to as "minister of justice" in Anglo-Saxon states, or a strictly accusing organ—a "partisan advocate", who is driven by the goal to win the trial "combat", "which might mean obtaining the full-extent conviction and maximum sentence for the accused".[94]

Again, there are two conceptions of a prosecutor's role. In the common law states, the function of accusation is understood literally—it is the prosecutor's task to have a person convicted. In England and in the United States, the prosecutor is an authority specialised in criminal prosecution and trial before a court. This means that the prosecutor only looks for evidence to prove the guilt of the accused and presents to court only such evidentiary material as supports the formulated charges. In Anglo-Saxon states, the prosecutor is never considered a "seeker of the objective truth". This assumption would be contrary to, for example, the broad practice of negotiating procedural agreements between the prosecutor and the accused. In common law jurisdictions, the prosecutor's obligation to act also in favour of the accused is in principle limited to the disclosure of exculpatory material in his or her possession without the additional requirement to search actively for it. The active search is left to the accused through counsel who, at least in theory, is provided with adequate resources to conduct defence investigations.[95]

Prosecutors from the continental tradition should, in turn, act as "guardians of the law". Civil law jurisdictions generally conceive the prosecutor not as a party but rather as another public official whose role also is to investigate the truth. This is why the prosecutor, like the judge, has a duty to gather both incriminating and exculpatory evidence.[96] In the context of criminal proceedings, this means that the prosecutor is obliged to act as "an impartial organ of justice". The notion of the prosecutor as the "guardian of the law" is derived from the German legal tradition[97]

---

93 See: Schabas (2010), pp. 294–297.

94 Cit. after: Vasiliev (2012), p. 704.

95 In general see: Buisman (2014), p. 206; Mathias (2004), p. 479; Sprack (2012), p. 68; LaFave et al. (2009), pp. 29–30 and 714.

96 See: Langer (2005), p. 840.

97 It was used for the first time in 1846—Waltoś (2002), p. 17; Cieślak (1984), p. 42.

where the prosecutor is obliged to remain objective and to establish not only incriminating but also exonerating circumstances (§ 160(II) *Strafprozeßordnung* (StPO)). According to representatives of the German doctrine, such an approach is consistent with the assumption that not only courts but also law enforcement services should look for the material truth and comply with presumption of innocence.[98] This allows the defence to adopt a passive role during an investigation (and sometimes during trial as well) and concentrate simply on checking the correctness of the prosecution's and the courts' activities. However, there are certain consequences of such assumption: as the prosecutor seeks to act for the sake of broader concerns, first, he may forsake the interests of the victim, and second, the proceedings no longer involve the clash of two partisan interests but rather involve "a clash between the aggregate interests of the state and the partisan interests of an individual".[99]

The Polish CCP also imposes the obligation to act according to the principle of material truth on all authorities involved in criminal proceedings; therefore, the prosecutor is expected to base his opinions on all gathered evidence, evaluating it freely by using his reasonable judgement, expertise and life experience. This task draws him closer, especially in an investigation, to a judge. For this reason, his role is sometimes referred to as "*quasi*-judicial".[100] The prosecutor also controls all procedural steps of an investigation taken by other authorities (such as the police), issuing binding opinions regarding their requests—also in this aspect, his role is *quasi*-judicial. There is no doubt that it is the duty of the prosecutor in Poland to remain objective (Article 4 CCP) and to seek truth, as well as to "look critically at the outcomes of the 'work' performed by himself and by the adjudicating court".[101] This principle of objectivity requires him to take into account circumstances that act both in favour of and against the accused. Even lodging an indictment and the obligation to support it before a court do not exempt the prosecutor from the necessity to evaluate evidence collected and presented at trial. Neither at the stage of judicial proceedings may he seek, at any cost, to demonstrate the guilt of the accused if, in his opinion, the evidence proves the accused innocent. Pursuant to Article 32(2) of the Act on the Public Prosecutor's Office, he should discontinue prosecution if the outcomes of judicial proceedings failed to confirm charges articulated in an indictment. On the other hand, the prosecutor's withdrawal from supporting a lodged indictment is not binding on the court (Article 14(2) CCP). Prosecutorial impartiality also manifests itself in the power to submit an appeal in favour of the accused.

Moreover, in the continental model of prosecution, the prosecutor also fulfils objective functions as guarantors of the observance of the law by all involved in the proceedings, including the court.[102] In the Polish system, the prosecutor's function

---

[98] See: Safferling (2001), p. 74; Beulke (2005), pp. 57 and 234; Volk (2006), p. 24.

[99] Damaška (1986), p. 103.

[100] Waltoś (2002), p. 6.

[101] Cit. after: Sowiński (2005), p. 116.

[102] Bohlander (2012).

as a "guardian of the law" is also demonstrated by the broad range of his competences: not only is he obliged to prosecute crimes; he is also responsible, and equally so, for ensuring the observance of law. This task is construed in view of Article 2 of the Constitution of the Republic of Poland as "guarding that the Polish state is in fact a democratic state of law" and that "law is respected by all its addressees".[103] As a result, the provision of Article 3 of the Act on the Public Prosecutor's Office contains a long list of tasks to be handled by prosecutors and the Prosecutor General, *inter alia,* in their capacity as public interest commissioners in civil and administrative proceedings. The accusation model established in this way is not limited to penal prosecution, and it is consistently maintained, despite the numerous changes in the structure of the prosecution and even more numerous amendments to the Act on the Public Prosecutor's Office.

On a side note, the above represents a model approach, and there are plenty of exceptions to these ideal assumptions.[104] It is true that in the continental tradition the prosecutor evaluates the evidence in an objective way during an investigation because he has to assess whether there are grounds to draft an indictment that he will need to support in court. Thus, this objective evaluation can be also seen as driven by practicality: the prosecutor should not lodge an indictment where the guilt of an accused cannot be proven. Moreover, once before the court he ceases to be an objective authority and becomes the accuser, as he presents only such evidence that proves the guilt of the accused rather than all of the evidence discovered in a case in an objective manner and in separation from the role of the accuser. The prosecutor in continental tradition might be perceived as having "two faces" in one procedural figure and as fulfilling a "dichotomous" task.[105]

In Anglo-Saxon states, there is also a gradual departure from seeing a prosecutor as a strictly accusing authority. In the English legal system, more and more often the neutral role of the prosecutor is highlighted. Moreover—it is considered to be a beneficial trophy from the continental tradition. After establishing the Crown Prosecution Service in England and Wales, new tasks and objectives were set for the prosecution service. There is no doubt that the prosecutor has special prerogatives when compared to the defence; he has the institution of state coercion and the police at his disposal, which allows him to obtain evidence much more easily than the defence. It is hard to ignore the fact that the prosecutor does not enter proceedings on the same terms as the defence. Currently, it is believed that "to win the case at all costs" is not his only objective. Naturally, the prosecutor should indict "with all proper vigour and guile".[106] However, he "ought not to struggle for the verdict against the prisoner, but they ought to bear themselves rather in the character of ministers of justice assisting in the administration of justice".[107]

---

[103] Cit. after: Waltoś (2002), p. 6.

[104] See: Weigend (2012), p. 382.

[105] Cit. after: Vasiliev (2012), p. 704.

[106] Sprack (2012), p. 314.

[107] *Ibidem*, p. 314, and the case law there analysed.

Because of this approach, the prosecutor is expected to seek to disclose actual circumstances of a case rather than confine himself to indicting. Therefore, if the defence suggests execution of a deal, the prosecutor should not take his decision solely on the basis of holding sufficient evidence to convict the accused, but he should, first of all, take into account whether the proposed way of dealing with a case is fair.[108] The CPS's duty has become to ensure that the court is furnished with all the relevant evidence that might be probative in proving innocence or guilt. To this extent, the English prosecutor's role is becoming more akin to the neutral one performed by their continental colleagues in inquisitorial systems. Moreover, according to some opinions, we can deduce the existence of an ethical obligation of diligence. This obligation may require common law prosecutors to seek exonerating information not yet within their knowledge and possession. Therefore, prosecutors cannot ignore the obvious evidence of the accused's innocence, even if "it will damage the prosecution's case or aid the accused".[109] However, the extent to which this neutral role fits into the adversarial nature of the English adversarial trail is debatable and not really clear.[110]

2.4.2 Conception of the Prosecutor's Role Before International Criminal Tribunals

According to R. Jackson, the prosecutor of the International Military Tribunal in Nuremberg, his role was to be interpreted narrowly. He claimed that he could not play the role of accuser and seeker of the material truth at the same time: "our duty is to present the case for the Prosecution. I do not, in any instance, serve two masters".[111] However, there were severe factual problems in the proceedings before this Tribunal, arising from the adoption of such a conception of the prosecutor's role. It turned out from the very beginning that the collection of evidence at the site was a major obstacle for the accused to prepare properly for the defence. It was necessary to seek the assistance of states. Taking these difficulties into account, an ultimate solution was adopted, offering the accused some assistance from the Tribunal in preparation of the evidence for his defence, by, for example, enabling him to request that the Tribunal summons witnesses for the defence.

Comprehensive examination of a case by the prosecutor was neither provided for in the Statutes of the ICTY and ICTR. The only type of action undertaken in favour of the accused related to fulfilling the duties under the institution of disclosure of evidence. The prosecutor was expected to disclose to the defence any material that in his actual knowledge might suggest the innocence or mitigate the guilt of the

[108] *Ibidem*, p. 315.

[109] The conception and citation after: Buisman (2014), p. 206.

[110] Fionda (1995), p. 58.

[111] Citation found in: May and Wierda (2002), p. 33.

accused or affect the credibility of prosecution evidence (Rule 68 RPE ICTY). However, there was no obligation to seek such evidence intentionally.

The ICTY's attitude to the prosecutor's role seems to be somewhat unclear. On the one hand, as early as in 1998, the judges were claiming that despite the lack of his statutory duty to act as a seeker of the objective truth, the prosecutor's role should be perceived otherwise than it had initially been conceived by the creators of this Tribunal. They pointed out that the prosecutor's role was no longer limited to the tasks provided for in the Statute: "the Prosecutor of the Tribunal is not, or not only, a Party to adversarial proceedings, but is an organ of the Tribunal and an organ of international criminal justice whose objective is not simply to secure a conviction, but to present the case for the Prosecution, which includes not only incriminating, but also exculpatory evidence, in order to assist the Chamber to discover the truth in a judicial setting".[112] Despite the above statement, the ICTY Prosecutor has neither the powers, nor the tools, to act in the interest of the accused. He is not obliged nor entitled to collect evidence exonerating the accused. The judges therefore seem to require from the Prosecutor more than he actually can and may do in the context of adversarial trial proceedings.[113] However, on the other hand, it must be admitted that the Statute does not prohibit taking of actions to help the accused, for example, bringing an appeal in his case.

On the other hand, however, in 2002 the judges of this Tribunal found that the primary responsibility for investigating the charges against the accused, including seeking and gathering information related to those charges, "lies with his or her defence counsel".[114] In *Prosecutor v. Blagojević,* due to the lack of the defence counsel's awareness of the strictly adversarial nature of the proceedings, no defence witness was interrogated in relation to the specific circumstances. The defence counsel of the accused observed: "It was the first time (in my career as an attorney) that I come across the problem of "my witness and your witness", because in the area in which we worked, we usually had witnesses of the Court". In response, the defence counsel was instructed by the presiding judge that the trial was conducted according to rules of the adversarial system, which is totally different from the inquisitorial system with which lawyers from Continental Europe are familiar and pursuant to which neither the prosecutor nor the judges are obliged to proactively search for the evidence in favour of the accused.[115] The judges seemed to ignore the argument that for the defence equality of arms means not only procedural equality but also substantive (material) equality, which signifies assuring the means and resources necessary for conducting an effective defence. They have recently confirmed their opinion on this subject quite clearly on another occasion—"the rights

[112] *Prosecutor v. Kupreskić*, IT-95-16, Trial Chamber Decision on Communication between the Parties and Their Witnesses, 21 October 1998.

[113] See: Vasiliev (2012), p. 708.

[114] *Prosecutor v. Blagojević*, IT-02-60, Joint Decision on Motions Related to Production of Evidence, 12 December 2002, § 26.

[115] *Prosecutor v. Kupreškić*, IT-95-16, Trial Chamber II, trial transcript of 27 August 1998.

of the accused and equality between the parties should however not be confused with the equality of means and resources".[116]

The prosecutor's role was clearly defined only in the proceedings before the ICC. During the negotiations on the Rome Statute, there was a dispute on the essence of the role played by the ICC Prosecutor—whether he is to be an impartial authority or a strictly accusing authority. Finally, it was adopted that the ICC Prosecutor has a duty to establish the truth (Article 54 of the Statute). In order to do that, he should extend the investigation to cover all facts and evidence relevant to an assessment of whether there is criminal responsibility under this Statute and, in doing so, investigate incriminating and exonerating circumstances equally. The goal of his action should be to establish the legal truth and not only "to present the facts and evidence as seen by him or her in order to accuse and to secure the indictee's conviction".[117] The ICC Statute mandates the Prosecutor not to be solely a party to the trial but to be equally "an objective and impartial body of justice", a truth-seeking organ, comparable to prosecutors in civil law countries. His functions are closer to a continental "quasi-judicial" position.[118] As a matter of fact, this assumption finds its origin in a German proposal.[119] However, even though the obligation described in Article 54(1)(a) finds its origin in civil law, we have seen that presently some sources of common law principles of ethics also require prosecutors to be on the lookout for exonerating evidence.[120]

For the purposes of ensuring full compliance of the OTP with this obligation, the Code of Conduct defines in detail what will be considered to constitute fulfilling the obligation to "investigate incriminating and exonerating circumstances". Foremost, this duty should be related equally to all steps involved in the planning and conduct of investigative and prosecutorial activities. In particular, members of the Office are under an obligation to conduct investigations with the goal of establishing the truth and in the interests of justice. In doing so, they should consider all relevant circumstances when assessing evidence, irrespective of whether they are to the advantage or the disadvantage of the prosecution. During these activities, they must ensure that all necessary and reasonable enquiries are made. Moreover, they should report to the Prosecutor concerns that, if substantiated, would tend to render a previous conviction made by the Court unsafe, bring the administration of justice into disrepute or constitute a miscarriage of justice. Every decision of the Office should be impartial. The OTP should refrain from prosecuting any person whom they believe to be innocent of the charges.

---

[116] *Prosecutor v. Prisić*, IT-04-81, Decision on Motion to Appoint *Amicus Curiae* to Investigate Equality of Arms, 18 June 2007, § 8. In general, see Tochilovsky (2001), p. 9.

[117] Cit. after: Cassese (1999).

[118] As to that fact the majority of authors agree, e.g.: Wouters et al. (2008) and also: Turone (2002), p. 1164; Coté (2012), pp. 359–360; Bergsmo and Kruger (2008), p. 1080; Izydorczyk and Wiliński (2005), p. 36; Schabas (2010), p. 675; Jackson (2009), p. 26.

[119] See: Buisman (2014), p. 206.

[120] At least to some extent—Buisman (2014), p. 206.

As a result, the ICC Prosecutor became another authority, next to the judge, expected to assess impartially a suspect's guilt, and only after such an analysis may he proceed with the prosecution. Assisting the judge in establishing the truth and achieving true "justice" became the "ideological pillars and ultimate goals of international prosecution".[121] Imposing the duty of truth seeking on the Prosecutor did not only arise from the necessity of ensuring equality between the parties to the proceedings, but it was also necessary in view of the nature of cases handled by the Tribunal. It resulted from the huge discrepancies between the actual means of obtaining evidence by the prosecution and by the defence. There is an obvious imbalance in power and resources between the defence and prosecution. The prosecution also significantly benefits from the assistance of the UN and NGOs, which are also often more reluctant to co-operate with the defence. Governments are often reluctant to offer the same services to the defence as to the prosecution. Only the organs of the Court have at their disposal the mechanisms for ensuring co-operation of states. In consequence, the accused (or the suspect) is not always capable of collecting evidence at the site. Another question is whether the Prosecutor fulfils adequately in practice the obligation he is burdened with when conducting an investigation. We can find examples demonstrating that the prosecution has so far largely ignored its obligation under Article 54(1)(a) to investigate incriminating and exonerating circumstances equally in any of the pending or completed cases.[122]

Another provision of the ICC Statute has the Prosecutor act in the name of broadly interpreted "interests of justice" by granting him the right to appeal on behalf of the accused. The Prosecutor may take advantage of this power in a situation where he considers it is necessary to lodge an appeal; he may also use this right when, in absence of adequate representation, the accused did not have a fair trial. This power to appeal in favour of the accused neutralises the Prosecutor's role as the accusing authority, and, again, it emphasises his role as a seeker and defender of the material truth.[123] It provides another example of departure from the accusation model typical for strictly adversarial proceedings, known from the operations of international military tribunals and the *ad hoc* tribunals.

In the context of the statutory obligation to act to the advantage of the accused, a question arises whether this obligation entails that the accused may demand that the Prosecutor undertakes specific actions to search for or record evidence favourable for him.[124] The Statute, however, does not impose any obligation on the Prosecutor to undertake such actions. It seems that in the lack of a basis for the Prosecutor's actions in this respect, other than the Statute and the RPE, the Prosecutor will undertake such steps only when he considers it necessary—and not on request. It does not mean, however, that the accused is left to his own devices, as he may count

[121] Cit. after: Vasiliev (2012), p. 711.

[122] See on that topic comprehensively: Buisman (2014), p. 223.

[123] See: Roth and Henzelin (2002), p. 1543; Safferling (2001), p. 86.

[124] Such a question poses: Kirsch (2008), p. 58.

on the supplementary role of the Pre-Trial Chamber, which may undertake actions requested by the accused. For example, at the request of a detained person or a person who has appeared upon the summons of the Tribunal, the Chamber may (and shall) issue orders or seek co-operation from a State Party under Part IX of the Statute that is necessary to assist such a person in preparation for defence. Rule 116 (1) RPE states in more detail that the Pre-Trial Chamber may undertake such actions only where it is satisfied that such an order would facilitate the collection of evidence that may be material to the proper determination of the issues being adjudicated or to the proper preparation of the person's defence. This competence of the Tribunal was designed to enable the defence to take actions in accordance with the principle of equality of parties to an investigation. In this way, the Statute allows the judicial authority to play a proactive role in the collection of evidence already at this stage of proceedings.

Interestingly, in *The Prosecutor v. Mbarushimana*, the question appeared whether the Pre-Trial Chamber has powers to examine the scope of fulfilment of the Prosecutor's obligation under Article 54 of the Statute: whether the prosecution had not sought enough to obtain exonerating information. In that case, the prosecution argued that in doing so the Pre-Trial Chamber exceeded its role as a confirmation chamber. However, the Appeals Chamber found no error on the part of the Pre-Trial Chamber.[125] On the other hand, in other cases (as in *The Prosecutor v. Abu Garda*) the Pre-Trial Chamber did not examine the arguments of the defence concerning the alleged investigative failures. It concluded that by doing so it would exceed its role during a confirmation hearing. The alleged failures can be viewed only in the context of the purpose of the confirmation hearing and should thus be regarded as a means of seeking a decision declining to confirm the charges. Such a conclusion only may have an impact on the Chamber's assessment of whether the Prosecutor's evidence as a whole has met the threshold of "substantial grounds to believe that a crime within the jurisdiction of the Court has been or is being committed".[126] Therefore, the Chamber cannot decline to confirm the charges on the basis of a finding that the Prosecutor has not complied with his duty stemming from Article 54. Thus, in two cases the ICC expressed opinions that contradict each other. In between these two positions, in the next case (*The Prosecutor v. Kenyatta*) the Pre-Trial Chamber found that "the Prosecutor should not seek to have the charges against a suspect confirmed before having conducted a full and thorough investigation in order to have a sufficient overview of the evidence available and the theory of the case", emphasising that the Prosecutor "is not responsible for establishing the truth only at the trial stage by presenting a complete evidentiary

---

[125] *The Prosecutor v. Callixte Mbarushimana*, ICC-01/04-01/10, Prosecution's Document in Support of Appeal against the "Decision on the Confirmation of Charges", 12 March 2012 and Judgment on the appeal of the Prosecutor against the decision of Pre-Trial Chamber I of 16 December 2011 entitled "Decision on the confirmation of charges", 30 May 2012. Cases analysed in: Buisman (2014), p. 220.

[126] *The Prosecutor v. Bahar Idriss Abu Garda*, ICC-02/05-02/09-243-Red, Pre-Trial Chamber I, Decision on the Confirmation of Charges, 8 February 2010, § 48.

record, but is also expected to present a reliable version of events at the confirmation hearing". In consequence, the Prosecutor's investigative failures were seemingly important factors in finding that the Prosecutor had failed to prove to the requisite confirmation standard of "sufficient grounds to believe".[127] Fulfilment of Article 54 duties is another of the Prosecutor's powers that fell into the scope of judicial control. And again it seems that the Prosecutor's powers tend to be seriously limited by judicial interpretation of this provision. Thus, the balance between the autonomy of the Prosecutor and the powers of the judges may seem to be distorted.

2.5 Conclusion

The first issues that required explanation were clearing out the terminology used and the scope of analysis that was to be undertaken. The term "accusation" covers the prosecutor's actions from the moment of directing prosecution against a certain person by making a decision on whether this person should be brought before the Tribunal, through drafting of the indictment, as well as the actions of prosecutors in court and appeal proceedings. As a result of the broad understanding of this term, the analysis of the accusation model used before international criminal tribunals pertains to both drafting charges and the accusation before the Trial Chamber.

The second step required in order to clear out the terminology was presenting the two major prosecution traditions and choosing their most important components. There are two major factors affecting the model of accusation.

The first of these is the systemic location of the prosecutor's office. The adoption of a specific organisational structure determines the degree of independence of the prosecutor. Tracing back in time different models of accusation adopted by international criminal tribunals, we have seen that the characteristic feature of the model of accusation before the IMT in Nuremberg and Tokyo was that prosecutors acted on behalf of the victorious states and their decisions were entirely dependent on the will of the states establishing the tribunals. The prosecutor of international criminal tribunals became an autonomous and independent authority only with the establishment of the Office of the Prosecutor before the ICTY and ICTR. The systemic location of the *ad hoc* tribunals' prosecutors was, on the other hand, significantly affected by the fact that they had been established under the resolutions of the Security Council, which, in addition to establishing these tribunals, may also impact the functioning of the tribunals and of the prosecutor himself using a number of non-procedural instruments. Not only does the Council determine their temporal framework and territorial jurisdiction but also, *via* financing their operations, affects the necessity and the manner of selection of the accused appearing before

[127] *The Prosecutor v. Uhuru Muigai Kenyatta*, ICC-01/09-02/11-728, Trial Chamber, Decision on Defense Application Pursuant to Article 64(4) and Related Requests, 26 April 2013, § 119.

these tribunals. The ICC Prosecutor was the first autonomous prosecutorial organ of international justice, acting independently of the states' will (winning states, as in the case of the International Military Tribunals in Nuremberg and Tokyo) or the Security Council (as the establishing authority, controlling the course and tempo of its work, as well as its financing, as in the case of the ICTY and ICTR). The independence of the ICC Prosecutor is protected under a number of guarantees, both organisational and procedural. In the case of the ICC, the impact of the Security Council is scarce, and definitely highly limited in comparison to the original plans of the creators of the ICC, although there are some competences envisaged for this authority in relation to the Court. The aforementioned considerations show that the Prosecutor's independence is significantly limited in the internal aspect, by means of a judicial authority's control.

The second factor affecting the accusation model is the procedural aspect that defines the role of a prosecutor during criminal proceedings.

It became a characteristic feature of the model of accusation before international criminal tribunals that its components are selected from two differing legal traditions. There is no doubt that there are two different models of accusation that are driven by different assumptions and that grant various competences to the prosecutor: the Anglo-Saxon model and the continental model. Whereas in the Anglo-Saxon model of accusation the prosecutor plays a strictly accusatory role, acting as one of the parties to a dispute held before an impartial arbiter, in the continental procedure, he is perceived as an impartial guardian of the law, seeking, just as the court does, also evidence in favour of the accused and the material truth. Also, the availability of consensual termination of proceedings for the prosecutor and the possibility of affecting the intensity of the criminal law response are governed in a different way. In Anglo-Saxon states, not only does he have the power to decide whether there are grounds to commence proceedings, but, once commenced, he may conclude a deal with the accused pertaining to legal responsibility that is binding on the court; he may decide on the scope of the evidentiary proceedings that are carried out to support the case for prosecution; also, his criminal and legal evaluation of the conduct of the accused expressed in a form of characterisation presented in an indictment is binding on the court. In the continental procedure, the prosecutor, at the moment of bringing the indictment before a court, loses control over his case, both in terms of the possibility of controlling evidence to support the line of prosecution and in terms of the legal characterisation charged in the indictment. Also, the option to conclude a procedural agreement is significantly limited compared to the Anglo-Saxon model.

In view of the differences between the solutions adopted in these two models of accusation, there is no doubt that the model of prosecution before international criminal tribunals is a *sui generis* solution. The procedural conception of the accusation model before the ICC has the attributes of both the Anglo-Saxon and the continental models. The concept of the criminal trial as a procedure managed by the parties was borrowed from the Anglo-Saxon tradition. The "two-cases-approach" model, that is, the model of two versions of a case presented to the court by the parties, was applied. The ICC Prosecutor independently decides on the scope of the evidence presented to support the charges during trial. This does not, however, mean that proceedings before the ICC share with the Anglo-Saxon model the latter's fundamental characteristic, involving the limitation of the scope of the proceedings to activities undertaken to prepare the case and to accuse during the trial. This is prevented by the fact that the accusation model borrows also from the continental model, which manifests itself in three main aspects. First, the role of the Prosecutor as solely being an accuser in criminal cases has been re-evaluated. Currently, he is to act as a guardian of the law, seeking also exonerating evidence and the material truth. Second, he is not a "master" of the proceedings: he may not determine the intensity of criminal prosecution by concluding procedural agreements. Third, his criminal and legal evaluation of the conduct of the accused expressed in a form of characterisation of facts presented in the indictment is not binding on the court. Because of the above aspects, the model of accusation before the ICC reconciles two legal traditions that, until recently, were considered to be completely distinct.

Another important component of this model is the external aspect of the activities taken by the prosecutor at international criminal tribunals, who may not ignore the political context of his case. His role is not limited to seeking conviction of perpetrators of the most severe international law crimes. He also performs an important task searching for and determining the truth pertaining to the committed crimes, applying international justice as one of the mechanisms of achieving peace and justice. When initiating proceedings, he may affect the political situation in a given state; many times, he also performs a diplomatic function. The prosecutor at the international criminal tribunal has become an organ responsible for bringing peace and ending wars. His function is a distant departure from the function of the national prosecutor.

References

Ambos K (2000) Status, role, accountability of the prosecutor of the International Criminal Court: a comparative overview on the basis of 33 National Reports. Eur J Crime Crim Law Crim Justice 8:89

Arbour L (1999a) The need for an independent and effective prosecutor in the permanent International Criminal Court. Windsor Yearbook of Access to Justice 17:217

Arbour L (1999b) Access to justice: the prosecution of international crimes: prospects and pitfalls. Wash Univ J Law Policy 1:24

Bassiouni MC (2003) Introduction to international criminal law. Transnational Publishers, New York

Bassiouni MC (2002) Accountability for violations of international humanitarian law and other serious violations of human rights. In: Bassiouni MC (ed) Post-conflict justice. Transnational Publishers, New York

Bassiouni MC, Manikas P (1996) The law of the international criminal tribunal for the former Yugoslavia. Transnational Publishers, New York

Bergsmo M, Harhoff F (2008) In: Triffterer O (ed) Commentary on the Rome Statute of the International Criminal Court – observers' notes, article by article, 2nd edn. Hart/Nomos Verlagsgesellschaft/C.H. Beck, München/Oxford
Bergsmo M, Kruger P (2008) In: Triffterer O (ed.), Commentary on the Rome Statute of the International Criminal Court – Observers' Notes, Article by Article, 2nd edn, Hart Publishing, Nomos Verlagsgesellschaft, C. H. Beck, München/Oxford
Beulke W (2005) Strafprozessrecht, 12th edn. C.F. Müller, Heidelberg
Bibas S, Burke-White W (2009-2010) International idealism meets domestic-criminal-procedure realism. Duke Law J 59:637
Boed R (2002) The International Criminal Tribunal for Rwanda. In: Bassiouni MC (ed) Post-conflict justice. Transnational Publishers, New York
Bohlander M (2012) Principles of German criminal procedure. Hart, Oxford and Portland/Oregon
Brubacher M (2004) Prosecutorial discretion within the ICC. J Int Crim Justice 2:85
Buisman C (2014) The prosecutor's obligation to investigate incriminating and exonerating circumstances equally: illusion or reality? Leiden J Int Law 27:205
Buisman C (2003) Defence and fair trial. In: Haveman R, Kavran O, Nicholls J (eds) Supranational criminal law: a system sui generis. Intersentia, Antwerp/Oxford/New York
Cassese A (1999) The Statute of the International Criminal Court: some preliminary reflections. Eur J Int Law 10:168
Cieślak M (1984) Polska procedura karna. PWN, Warszawa
Coté L (2012) Independence and impartiality. In: Reydams L, Wouters J, Ryngaert C (eds) International prosecutors. Oxford University Press, Oxford
Damaška M (1974–1975) Structures of authority and comparative criminal procedure. Yale Law J 84:480
Damaška M (1986) The faces of justice and state authority. Yale University Press, New Haven/London
Darbyshire P (2008) England and Wales. In: Vogler R, Huber B (eds) Criminal procedures in Europe. Duncker & Humblot, Berlin
Daszkiewicz W (1960) Oskarżyciel w polskim procesie karnym. Warszawa
Daszkiewicz W (1961) Odstąpienie oskarżyciela publicznego od oskarżenia a zasada legalizmu. Palestra 8:46
Donat-Cattin D (2003) Decision-making in the International Criminal Court: functions of the assembly of state parties and independence of the judicial organs. In: Lattanzi F, Schabas W (eds) Essays on the Rome Statute of the International Criminal Court, vol 2. Il Sirente, Ripa di Fagnano Alto
Findlay M (2008) Governing through globalised crime. Futures for international criminal justice. Willian Publishing, Portland
Fionda J (1995) Public prosecutors and discretion. A comparative study. Clarendon, Oxford
Fish E (2010) Peace through complementarity: solving the ex post problem in International Criminal Court prosecutions. Yale Law J 119:1708
Gallant K (2003) The ICC in the system of states and international organizations. In: Lattanzi F, Schabas W (eds) Essays on the Rome Statute of the International Criminal Court, vol 2. Il Sirente, Ripa di Fagnano Alto
Gandy D (1988) The Crown Prosecution Service: its organization and philosophy. In: Hall Williams JE (ed) The role of the prosecutor. Report of the International Criminal Justice seminar held at the London School of Economics and Political Science, January 1987. Gower Publishing Company Limited, Avebury
Geis J, Mundt A (2009) When to indict? The impact of timing of international criminal indictments on peace processes and humanitarian action. The Brookings Institution-University of Bern Project on Internal Displacement. http://www.brookings.edu/~/media/research/files/papers/2009/4/peace%20and%20justice%20geis/04_peace_and_justice_geis.pdf
Goldstone R (2002) Prosecuting rape as a war crime. Case Western Reserve J Int Law 34:277

Ginsburg G, Kudriavtsev VN (eds) (1990) The Nuremberg trial and international law. Martinus Nijhoff, Leiden/Boston
Goławski A, Żmigrodzki M (2005) In: Szmulik B, Żmigrodzki M (eds) Ustrój organów ochrony prawnej. Wydawnictwo UMCS, Lublin
Greenawalt A (2007) Justice without politics? Prosecutorial discretion and the International Criminal Court. NYU J Int Law Polit 39:583
Grzegorczyk T, Tylman J (2007) Polskie postępowanie karne. LexisNexis, Warszawa
Heinze A (2014) International criminal procedure and disclosure. An attempt to better understand and regulate disclosure and communication at the ICC on the basis of a comprehensive and comparative theory of criminal procedure. Duncker & Humblot, Berlin
Huber B (2008) Germany. In: Vogler R, Huber B (eds) Criminal procedures in Europe. Duncker & Humblot, Berlin
Izydorczyk J, Wiliński P (2005) Pozycja i zakres uprawnień Prokuratora Międzynarodowego Trybunału Karnego. Prokuratura i Prawo 6:35
Jackson J (2009) Finding the best epistemic fit for international criminal tribunals. Beyond the adversarial-inquisitorial dichotomy. J Int Crim Justice 7:17
Kardas P (2012) Rola i miejsce prokuratury w systemie organów demokratycznego państwa prawnego. Prokuratura i Prawo 9:15
Kijowski K (2013) Pozycja prawno-ustrojowa prokuratury w wybranych państwach Europy Środkowej i Wschodniej. Prokuratura i Prawo 4:132
Kirsch S (2008) Finding the truth at international criminal tribunals. In: Kruessmann T (ed) ICTY: towards a fair trial? Neuer Wissenschaftlicher Verlag, Wien/Graz
Kremens K (2014) Prokuratura wobec reformy postępowania karnego. Rozważania o rozdziale funkcji śledczych i oskarżycielskich na tle angielskiego procesu karnego. Przegląd Sądowy 5:7
Krzan B (2009) Kompetencje Rady Bezpieczeństwa ONZ w międzynarodowym sądownictwie karnym. TNOiK, Toruń
Kuczyńska H (2010) Rola prokuratora w postępowaniu przed międzynarodowymi trybunałami karnymi. Studia Prawnicze 4:53
LaFave W, Israel J, King N, Kerr O (2009) Criminal procedure, 5th edn. West Academic Publishing, St. Paul
Langbein JH (1973–1974) Controlling prosecutorial discretion in Germany. Univ Chic Law Rev 41:439
Langer M (2005) The rise of managerial judging in international criminal law. Am J Comp Law 53:835
Locke J (2012) Indictments. In: Reydams L, Wouters J, Ryngaert C (eds) International prosecutors. Oxford University Press, Oxford
Mathias E (2004) The police and public prosecutor. In: Delmas-Marty M, Spencer J (eds) European criminal procedures. Cambridge University Press, Cambridge
May R, Wierda M (2002) International criminal evidence. Transnational Publishers, Ardsley, NY
Michelich J (2000) United States of America. In: Arbour L, Eser A, Ambos K, Sanders A (eds) The prosecutor of a permanent International Criminal Court. International workshop in co-operation with the Office of the Prosecutor of the International Criminal Tribunals (ICTY and ICTR). Edition Iuscrim, Freiburg im Breisgau
Morré P (2000) Germany. In: Arbour L, Eser A, Ambos K, Sanders A (eds) The Prosecutor of a Permanent International Criminal Court. International workshop in co-operation with the Office of the Prosecutor of the International Criminal Tribunals (ICTY and ICTR). Edition Iuscrim, Freiburg im Breisgau
Morris M (2002) Lacking a Leviathan: the quandaries of peace and accountability. In: Bassiouni MC (ed) Post-conflict justice. Transnational Publishers, New York
Ohlin JD (2009) Peace, security, and prosecutorial discretion. In: Stahn C, Sluiter G (eds) The emerging practice of the International Criminal Court. Martinus Nijhoff, Leiden/Boston
Olásolo H (2003) The Prosecutor of the ICC before the initiation of investigations: a quasi-judicial or a political body? Int Crim Law Rev 3:87

Olszewski R (2014) Rola prokuratora w postępowaniu karnym. Prokuratura i Prawo 1:50
Padfield N (2008) Text and materials on the criminal justice process. Oxford University Press, Oxford
Perrodet A (2004) The public prosecutor. In: Delmas-Marty M, Spencer J (eds) European criminal procedures. Cambridge University Press, Cambridge
Płachta M (2007) Prokurator Międzynarodowego Trybunału Karnego: między legalizmem a oportunizmem ścigania. In: Menkes J (ed) Prawo międzynarodowego. Księga pamiątkowa Profesor Renaty Szafarz. Warszawa
Razowski T (2005) Formalna i merytoryczna kontrola oskarżenia w polskim procesie karnym. Zakamycze, Kraków
Röben V (2003) The procedure of the ICC: status and function of the Prosecutor. Max Planck Yearbook United Nations Law 7:520
Rodman K (2009) Is peace in the interests of justice? The case for broad prosecutorial discretion at the International Criminal Court. Leiden J Int Law 1:99
Rogacka-Rzewnicka M (2007) Oportunizm i legalizm ścigania przestępstw w świetle współczesnych przeobrażeń procesu karnego. Zakamycze, Warszawa
Roth R, Henzelin M (2002) The appeal procedure of the ICC. In: Cassese A, Gaeta P, Jones WD (ed) The Rome Statute of the International Criminal Court: a commentary. Oxford University Press, Oxford
Rwalamira M (1999) Composition and administration of the Court. In: Lee RP (ed) The International Criminal Court: the making of the Rome Statute: issues, negotiations and results. Kluwer Law International, The Hague
Safferling C (2001) Towards an international criminal procedure, Oxford monographs in international law. Oxford University Press, Oxford
Sanders A (2000) England and Wales. In: Arbour L, Eser A, Ambos K, Sanders A (eds) The prosecutor of a permanent International Criminal Court. International workshop in co-operation with the Office of the Prosecutor of the International Criminal Tribunals (ICTY and ICTR). Edition Iuscrim, Freiburg im Breisgau
Schabas W (2010) The International Criminal Court. A commentary on the Rome Statute. Oxford University Press, Oxford
Scharf MP (2000) The tools for enforcing international criminal justice in the new millennium: lessons from the Yugoslavia tribunal. Int Crim Justice 49:925
Sluiter G, Friman H, Linton S, Vasiliev S, Zappala S (2013) International criminal procedure. Principles and rules. Oxford University Press, Oxford
Sowiński P (2005) W kwestii bezstronności prokuratora. Uwagi na tle przepisów art. 47 oraz art. 48 k.p.k. In: Zięba-Załucka H, Kijowski M (eds) Godność obywatela, urzędu i instytucji. Zmiany prawnoustrojowe prokuratury RP, Rzeszów
Sprack J (2012) A practical approach to criminal procedure. Oxford University Press, Oxford
Stachowiak S (1975) Funkcje zasady skargowości w polskim procesie karnym. Zakłady Graficzne UAM, Poznań
Stachowiak S (1989) Zawisłość sprawy w sądzie a odstąpienia oskarżyciela publicznego od oskarżenia w polskim procesie karnym. Wojskowy Przegląd Prawniczy 3:299
Stankowski A (2009) Propozycja unormowań Prokuratury w Konstytucji RP. Prokuratura i Praw 10:5
Tochilovsky V (2001) Special commentary International Criminal Justice: some flaws and misperceptions. Crim Law Forum 22:593
Townsend G (2012) Structure and management. In: Reydams L, Wouters J, Ryngaert C (eds) International prosecutors. Oxford University Press, Oxford
Trüg G (2003) Lösungskonvergenzen trotz Systemdivergenzen im deutschen und US-amerikanischen Strafverfahren. Ein strukturanalytischer Vergleich am Beispiel der Wahrheitserforschung. Mohr Siebeck, Tübingen
Turković K (2008) The value of the ICTY as a historiographical tool. In: Kruessmann T (ed) ICTY: towards a fair trial? Neuer Wissenschaftlicher Verlag, Wien

Turone G (2002) Powers and duties of the Prosecutor. In: Cassese A, Gaeta P, Jones WD (eds) The Rome Statute of the International Criminal Court: a commentary. Oxford University Press, Oxford

Vasiliev S (2012) Trial. In: Reydams L, Wouters J, Ryngaert C (eds) International prosecutors. Oxford University Press, Oxford

Volk K (2006) Grundkurs. StPO, 5th edn. C.H. Beck, München

Waltoś (2008) Proces karny. Zarys systemu, 9th edn. LexisNexis, Warszawa

Waltoś S (2002) Prokuratura – jej miejsce wśród organów władzy, struktura i funkcje. Państwo i Prawo 4:6

Weigend T (2012) A judge by another name? Comparative perspectives on the role of the public prosecutor. In: Luna E, Wade M (eds) The prosecutor in transnational perspective. Oxford University Press, Oxford

Worrall J (2007) Criminal procedure: from first contact to appeal, 2nd edn. Pearson Allyn & Bacon, Boston

Wouters J, Verhoeven S, Demeyere B (2008) The International Criminal Court's Office of the Prosecutor: navigating between independence and accountability? Int Crim Law Rev 8:273

Wei W (2007) Die Rolle des Anklägers eines internationalen Strafgerichtshofs. Peter Lang, Frankfurt am Main

Yañez-Barnuevo JA, Escobar Hernández C (2003) The ICC and the UN – a complex and vital relationship. In: Lattanzi F, Schabas W (eds) Essays on the Rome Statute of the International Criminal Court. vol 2. Il Sirente, Ripa di Fagnano Alto

Chapter 3
Initiation of an Investigation

Abstract One of the most significant components of the model of accusation before the ICC is the existence of the ICC Prosecutor's power to independently initiate an investigation. However, although the ICC Prosecutor is entitled to initiate proceedings at his discretion, his decision must be always authorised by the Pre-Trial Chamber, which brings up questions about the extended scope of judicial control over his actions. Moreover, while deciding whether to initiate an investigation, the Prosecutor must consider the conditions set up in the Rome Statute: whether the information available to the Prosecutor provides a "reasonable basis to believe that a crime within the jurisdiction of the Court has been or is being committed", whether the case is admissible and whether taking into account "the gravity of the crime" and the interests of victims, there are nonetheless substantial reasons to believe that an investigation "would not serve the interests of justice". The wording of this provisions leads to a question whether these factors constitute a basis for the principle of opportunism or the principle of legalism. It will be presented how the attitude towards this issue depends on the model of accusation the interpreting author belongs to: these coming from the Anglo-Saxon tradition have a tendency to search for elements of the principle of opportunism; those from the civil law states assume that the model of accusation operates according to the principle of legalism.

3.1 Functions of an Investigation

In proceedings before the international criminal tribunals, the functions and the form of an investigation have been dominated by the idiosyncratic principles governing the tribunals' operation. There are four issues that have turned out to be fundamental for the model of accusation:

- Firstly, the objective of an investigation had to be established.
- Secondly, the decision whether the prosecutor may independently initiate criminal proceedings has garnered much attention.
- Thirdly, the conditions of initiating an investigation had to be defined.

© Springer International Publishing Switzerland 2015

H. Kuczyńska, *The Accusation Model Before the International Criminal Court*,
DOI 10.1007/978-3-319-17626-0_3

– Finally, international criminal tribunals had to decide whether the prosecutor should act pursuant to the principle of legalism (mandatory prosecution) or that of opportunism (prosecutorial discretion).

The international criminal tribunals had to make a choice between the various methods of conducting an investigation that were differently regulated under two legal systems. Although in every national legal system the purpose of an investigation is to gather and organise relevant material for the court, the implications and extent of the notion of "preparation" are fundamentally different. In continental systems, the investigative process fulfils multiple functions: in Polish criminal proceedings, Article 297(1)(5) of CCP orders an investigation to be conducted in such a manner as to not only establish whether a prohibited act has been committed, whether it constitutes an offence and detect the perpetrator, but also collect data concerning all the personal and official circumstances of the accused, including a community enquiry, to elucidate the circumstances of the case, including the extent of the damage, and to collect, secure and record evidence to the extent required or even "to elucidate circumstances favourable to the commission of the act". This model of investigation requires concentration of the prosecutor's activities at the preliminary stage of the proceedings rather than at the trial stage. It also prolongs the investigation and diminishes the importance of the main trial, depreciating the court proceeding stage, which—in extreme cases—is reduced to the presentation of findings of the investigation. S. Waltoś highlights that "an ideal criminal proceedings system would be one in which the investigation stage could be entirely dispensed with. It would be a system in which the immediacy principle would almost always triumph".[1]

It is worth to mention, however, that this model is undergoing serious changes at the moment. An amendment of the Code of Criminal Proceedings by way of the Act of 27 September 2013 (which comes into force as late as 1st of July 2015)[2] enhances the adversarial nature of Polish criminal proceedings. Among other various elements of this new model of criminal procedure, the scope of investigation (so called preparatory proceedings) is supposed to be narrowed down. Beginning from 1st of July, the prosecutor should follow the directive of gathering and recording evidence only to such an extent as deems necessary in order to support the indictment and to fulfil his role at the trial stage.

In the Anglo-Saxon investigation model, on the other hand, it needs to be established whether the prosecution serves public interest and whether the evidence is sufficient for the conviction. In these systems, preparation of a case for the court boils down to collection of evidence sufficient to convince the jury that the accused is guilty. The prosecutor is not obliged to conduct a "comprehensive clarification of

[1] See: Waltoś (1968), p. 98. Similarly: Kulesza (2011), pp. 271–301.

[2] Act of 27 September 2013 amending the Act—Code of Criminal Proceedings, Dz.U. of 2013, pos. 1282.

a case" or even a "clarification of a case" in a situation where he only collects evidence incriminating the person charged and where the latter's guilt is to be proven at a trial. As prosecutorial functions remained for a long time in private hands, the preparatory stages of process were never as tightly integrated into the subsequent stages as was the case with continental preliminary stages.[3]

In the proceedings before international criminal tribunals the influence of both legal tradition can be seen. First, the assumptions of an investigation were basically adopted from the investigative model applied in common law states. An investigation aims neither at a "comprehensive clarification of a case" nor at a "clarification of a case" as such but at establishing if there are "substantial grounds to believe that the person committed the crime charged" (Article 19 ICTY Statute, Article 61 ICC Statute) and in consequence whether it is reasonable to file an indictment.

The second problem relating to conditions of initiating an investigation, however, has been regulated differently before the *ad hoc* tribunals and the ICC. While the first ones use a flexible and an enigmatic threshold of a "prima facie case", the ICC introduces a set of parameters, whose existence has to be established by the Prosecutor before initiating an investigation and accepted by the Pre-Trial Chamber.

Also, the third issue has been regulated differently before the *ad hoc* tribunals and the ICC. The existence of the prosecutor's power to independently initiate an investigation is one of those elements of the accusation model that makes it impossible to speak of a common prosecution model before international criminal tribunals. While in the proceedings before the *ad hoc* tribunals the prosecutors may exercise this right, the distinctive way in which the competence to initiate an investigation is regulated has become a characteristic feature of the proceedings before the ICC. In practice, the ICC Prosecutor is entitled to initiate proceedings at his discretion, but his decision must be always authorised by the Pre-Trial Chamber. Implementation of the judicial review of the decision to initiate proceedings has specific procedural consequences. The requirement to have a case confirmed as early as at the pre-investigation stage has inevitably strengthened the formality of the Prosecutor's actions, which led to the emergence of the verifying stage in a form of a preliminary examination of the case.

Finally, the fourth issue has been resolved similarly in the proceedings before all tribunals. Despite some divergences in the literature on this subject, it may be assumed that they follow the principle of opportunism, albeit in a specific form, adjusted to the tasks of international tribunals.

---

[3] Damaška (1986), p. 57.

3.2 Initiation of an Investigation Before the ICC

3.2.1 The Prosecutor's Powers to Initiate Investigation proprio motu

The power of the prosecutor to initiate an investigation on his own initiative is one of the main elements of the accusation model. The existence of this right is a staple of every national system, but its granting to the ICC Prosecutor has taken long negotiation.

The ICTY and ICTR Prosecutors initiate proceedings "ex-officio or on the basis of information obtained from any source, particularly from Governments, United Nations organs, intergovernmental and nongovernmental organisations" (Article 18 (1)). They enjoy the competence to assess the information received and decide whether there is sufficient basis to proceed. The ICTY and ICTR Statutes instruct the Prosecutor in such a situation as to initiate an investigation, collect information and prepare an indictment based on evidentiary material. It results from the phrasing of Article 18 that the Prosecutor need not obtain any authorisation to initiate and proceed with investigation.[4]

While designating the powers of the ICC Prosecutor during the negotiation stage, his independent power to start an investigation became one of the most disputed and controversial problems.[5]

Many states supported a solution where the Prosecutor could start an investigation only by demand of one of the States Parties to the Statute or the Security Council. Prosecutorial discretion has been seen as a danger in the ICC system. During negotiations, many states strongly opposed granting the Prosecutor the power to initiate investigations *proprio motu*. Most prominently, the United States was strongly opposed to giving these powers to the Prosecutor, indicating that his discretion to start an investigation would not allow him to proceed in an unbiased way, drawing his attention to political questions and problems and making him a political player. They expressed anxiety about "frivolous" or even "malicious" accusations made by an "unpredictable" prosecutor.[6] Anyway, such a solution was adopted in the Draft Statute of the ICC.[7] The final adoption of the *proprio motu* Prosecutor's powers to initiate an investigation became (supposedly) the main reason for the US's refusal to ratify the Statute. However, both supporters and opponents of this solution agreed as to one thing: this power was to have a key

---

[4] See: Bassiouni and Manikas (1996), pp. 867–875.

[5] Which is often mentioned in the literature: Schabas (2010), p. 317; Bergsmo and Pejić (2008), p. 582; Goldstone and Fritz (2000), p. 657; Brubacher (2004), p. 73; Greenawalt (2007), p. 585; Coté (2012), p. 404.

[6] Cit after: Płachta (2007), p. 480; Turone (2002), p. 1146.

[7] 1994 ILC Draft Statute, Article 25(1), http://legal.un.org/ilc/texts/instruments/english/draft%20articles/7_4_1994.pdf. Accessed 13 Feb 2015.

significance for the ICC's competences. It was to become a test of its independence.[8]

Finally, the version promoted by the European states prevailed, and on the basis of Article 15(1) "The Prosecutor may initiate investigations proprio motu on the basis of information on crimes within the jurisdiction of the Court". The power to make this decision was given to the Prosecutor of the ICC rather than to the States Parties or the Security Council. He is the sole organ of the Court that decides who will be prosecuted and who will be not. It empowers the Prosecutor to decide about the factual scope of the ICC's jurisdiction. This power was, however, surrendered to the control of the Pre-Trial Chamber, which must authorise initiation of an investigation before a case can enter the stage of investigation. Upon examination of the request of the Prosecutor to start an investigation and of the supporting material, the Pre-Trial Chamber considers whether there is a reasonable basis to proceed with an investigation. When the case appears to fall within the jurisdiction of the Court, it confirms the commencement of the investigation. The wording of the Statute stresses that the Prosecutor has only the power to "initiate" investigations and not to "start" it. It is only the decision of the Pre-Trial Chamber that may become a basis for the "commencement" of the investigation.[9]

No limitations were imposed in respect of the sources of information from which the Prosecutor may obtain communications on the commission of crimes within the jurisdiction of the Court. It is the Prosecutor himself who decides whether a given source is reliable. The OTP adopted the term "communication" to describe this type of information coming from independent sources. The enigmatic wording of Article 15(1) does not clarify whether the Rome Statute does confer discretion upon the Prosecutor to completely disregard the *notitia criminis* without having taken further action. On the one hand, Article 15(2) uses the term "may", which should be interpreted as leaving the decision, whether to react to such a communication, to the Prosecutor. On the other hand, some authors believe that the Prosecutor is under an obligation to react to such a communication. Accordingly, by communication of the *notitia criminis* the informants would acquire the right to demand performance of certain actions by the Prosecutor, e.g. to properly assess the *notitia criminis* and to inform the informant of her decision not to proceed with an investigation, or not to request the Pre-Trial Chamber the authorisation to initiate an investigation.[10] However, the latter theory is not convincing—especially taking into consideration the number of communications received by the Office of the Prosecutor.

Acting *proprio motu*, the ICC Prosecutor "initiated" two investigations. In both cases, his decision was authorised by the Pre-Trial Chamber. The first investigation pertained to the civil war in Kenya. On 31 March 2010, the Pre-Trial Chamber issued a decision permitting the Prosecutor to proceed with the investigation. It emphasised therein that Kenya demonstrated a lack of will to prosecute perpetrators

---

[8] See: Coté (2012), p. 353; Bergsmo and Harhoff (2008), p. 972. Izydorczyk, Wiliński (2005) p. 38

[9] See: Bergsmo and Pejić (2008), pp. 585 and 590.

[10] See: Olásolo (2005), pp. 65 et seq.; Olásolo (2005), p. 119.

of crimes and therefore it was necessary to refer to international justice. On the other hand, however, the state (primarily) agreed to co-operate with the ICC Prosecutor and to submit all required information pertaining to crimes, including classified information. The political context of the Prosecutor's decision has also been highlighted. The Prosecutor himself declared that addressing the issue of Kenya is aimed at discouraging other African states from exercising violence during elections.[11] The second case in which the Prosecutor initiated proceedings *proprio motu* pertained to the situation in Côte d'Ivoire. This state is not a party to the Rome Statute, but it accepted the ICC jurisdiction in respect of the specific period and specific actions on 18 April 2003, pursuant to Article 12(3) of the Statute. On 3 October 2011, the Pre-Trial Chamber approved the Prosecutor's decision on the initiation of investigation of the crimes that could have been committed there between 28 November 2008 and the moment of filing the indictment.

3.2.2 *Initiation of an Investigation on the Basis of* notitia criminis

The Statute provides for three different "triggering mechanisms". While it is only the Prosecutor who may initiate the investigation, he may do so not only acting *proprio motu*, on the basis of communications from independent sources. The other two 'triggering mechanisms" are referrals made by a) State Parties and b) the Security Council. According to Article 13 of the Statute, the Court may exercise its jurisdiction if

a) a situation in which one or more of such crimes appears to have been committed is referred to the Prosecutor by a State Party and
b) in a situation in which one or more of such crimes appears to have been committed is referred to the Prosecutor by the Security Council acting under Chapter VII of the Charter of the United Nations.

The information on the commission of international law crimes (*notitia criminis*) that is referred by the Security Council (Article 13(b)) has the strongest position. The Security Council may collect information using the measures as foreseen in the UN Charter in every case where it deems it necessary in order to maintain or restore international peace and security. This "peculiar" hierarchy highlights the strong position of the Security Council and the national sovereignty.[12]

[11] *The Situation in the Republic of Kenya*, ICC-01/09, Decision Pursuant to Article 15 of the Rome Statute on the Authorization of an Investigation into the Situation in the Republic of Kenya, 31 March 2010; ICC—ICC Prosecutor: Kenya Can Be an Example to the World, press release of 18 September 2009, ICC-OTP-20090918-PR452. See also: Aresi (2013) p. 615.

[12] This notion used by: Turone (2002), p. 1144.

The second group is information provided by States Parties. According to Article 14 of the Statute, "A State Party may refer to the Prosecutor a situation in which one or more crimes within the jurisdiction of the Court appear to have been committed, requesting the Prosecutor to investigate the situation for the purpose of determining whether one or more specific persons should be charged with the commission of such crimes. As far as possible, a referral shall specify the relevant circumstances and be accompanied by such supporting documentation as is available to the State referring the situation".

When "a situation" has been "referred" by one of the two privileged organs, the starting of an investigation by the Prosecutor does not require authorisation by the Pre-Trial Chamber. The absence of this requirement has led to calling this manner of proceedings initiation "fast track" proceedings.[13] When an investigation has been initiated by the Prosecutor acting *proprio motu*, on the basis of *notitia criminis* referred to the Prosecutor by other sources, it cannot be proceeded with without a specific authorisation by the Pre-Trial Chamber.

There is a major difference between "referral of a situation" by one of the privileged entities and initiating an investigation. Particularly problematic is the issue of binding effect of a "referral". The wording used in the Statute, stating that the privileged authority "refers a situation", is sufficiently ambiguous to multiply doubts as to whether it is a request, a demand for the Prosecutor to proceed with the investigation in a given situation or merely a suggestion.

Pursuant to the first theory, the fact that a given situation was referred by one of the privileged entities does not impose on the Prosecutor a duty to proceed with the investigation. In such a situation, his only duty is to carry out a preliminary examination of the case in order to determine whether there are grounds for the initiation of the investigation. The Prosecutor cannot be released from this obligation as he may not refrain from acting having received a *notitia criminis*. This is the difference between the specific nature of information coming from the privileged entity and information provided by other sources.[14]

Proponents of the second theory claim that the nature of the UN Security Council's actions conducted pursuant to the UN Charter Chapter VII should be considered binding and that offering the Prosecutor discretion as to whether to initiate an investigation in a case referred by the Security Council would be inconsistent with the basic principles of international law and the properly understood role of the Security Council.[15] Article 103 of the Charter requires that "in the event of a conflict between the obligations of the Members of the United Nations under the present Charter and their obligations under any other international agreement, their obligations under the present Charter shall prevail". The hierarchy of sources of international law should lead to a conclusion that the provisions of the Charter have priority over the provisions of the Rome Statute. It should be

[13] See: Turone (2002), p. 1144.

[14] See: Bergsmo and Harhoff (2008), pp. 974–977; Schabas (2010), p. 299.

[15] See: Ohlin (2009), pp. 189–190.

impossible to enact a law that would cancel the powers of the UN authorities. Therefore, the Court should not have the right to deny the powers articulated in the UN Charter. However, this hierarchy is not recognised by the Rome Statute, which explicitly governs the powers of the Security Council in an entirely different way from what would follow from the UN Charter. Pursuant to this theory, it leads to violation of the Charter by the Rome Statute.

This assumption gives rise two fundamental issues. First, in this situation referral of a situation by the Security Council prevents the Prosecutor from evaluating whether the conditions of initiation of an investigation as set up in Article 53 have been fulfilled, thus limiting prosecutorial discretion in assessing whether there is "a reasonable basis to proceed under this Statute". Neither would he be capable of performing an independent assessment as to whether an investigation "would not serve the interests of justice" and whether it is in the "interests of victims". The second problem that may appear is that by assuming that the Prosecutor is obliged to proceed with a case referred by the Security Council, the ICC becomes the "the Security Council court", hearing cases *de facto* charged by this authority, and not as a result of the Prosecutor's free decision.[16] This would lead to a situation where the ICC takes over the function that is currently fulfilled by *ad hoc* tribunals. Although the ICC Prosecutor's powers should not be considered separately from the role of the Court itself as a body restoring peace and security, or from the international political situation, it certainly was not the Court founders' intention to condition his actions on the decisions of a political authority such as the Security Council. There is no doubt that decisions made by the Council are, in principle, political rather than taken solely to serve the interests of international justice.[17] It should also be said that the text of the Charter should not lead to amendments of the provisions of the Rome Statute. It is the Statute, and not the Charter, that governs the procedural issues before the ICC. As it is highlighted, the Court operates pursuant to the Statute, not to the UN Charter.[18]

Therefore, the first view should be considered correct, especially that Article 103 of the Charter seems not to relate to the powers of the ICC Prosecutor. It may be noticed, however, that despite the fact that the Prosecutor himself has emphasised the non-binding nature of the referral made by privileged entities, every time one of them referred a situation to the ICC, the Prosecutor initiated an investigation.

Moreover, in the context of the nature of referrals provided by privileged entities, the difference between a "situation" and a "case" is of a particular importance. In accordance with the principles governing his actions, the ICC Prosecutor investigates specific "cases" within a certain "situation". Privileged entities make a "referral of a situation" on the basis of which the ICC Prosecutor defines specific "cases". A situation is defined in general terms of geography, of time and, on occasion, of the (many) persons involved. Therefore, while the "situation" referred to in Article 13, which justifies the initiation of the proceedings

---

16 Such risk has been perceived by: Ohlin (2009), pp. 192–195.

17 This danger is presented in: Gallant (2003), p. 21; deGuzman and Schabas (2013), p. 132.

18 E.g. by: Gallant (2003), p. 30; Friman (2003), p. 202.

before the Court, includes a whole range of behaviours restricted to time, venue and potential perpetrators, the "case" refers to the specific event constituting one of the crimes falling within the Court's jurisdiction: "is used herein to denote one or more defendants and one or more charges stemming from one or more related incidents".[19] The Registrar even keeps a separate record for each "situation" and each "case". When a "case" is commenced, its record is completed with copies of the relevant documents from the "situation" record.[20] Therefore, the decision to prosecute a case consists of these two decisions: first, whether to investigate a situation and, second, whether to prosecute a particular case. It should then be borne in mind that even if privileged entities entrust the Prosecutor with the conduct of proceedings in a specific conflict situation, the Prosecutor is still entitled to select specific perpetrators and to focus his investigation on specific fragments of this situation.[21]

There is an interesting concept of "dormant jurisdiction" of the ICC arising in this context.[22] When a situation is referred by an authorised entity, the Prosecutor's power to initiate any number of cases under the reported situation (most frequently, a specific conflict) is activated. Results of the referral could be compared to the Security Council's definition of *ad hoc* tribunals' jurisdiction (pursuant to the resolution establishing the basis of their operations), which, from the moment of their establishment, was limited by these two aspects: geography and time. These two parameters are defined by the entity referring a given situation before the ICC, setting the limits for the Prosecutor's freèdom of selecting specific cases and pressing charges against specific suspects. The Prosecutor's power extends over the whole territory of the conflict and all its participants. In the limits of a single situation, the Prosecutor may initiate a number of proceedings.

However, it may not be ruled out that the "situation" referred by an entity will be narrow enough so as to restrict the Prosecutor's choice. Both the Security Council and the State Party have the powers to conduct an initial examination of a conflict and may refer the situation to the ICC only when they identify the perpetrators and formulate a list of charges.[23] In fact, in the first referred situation in Sudan, the Security Council emphasised in its resolution that the Prosecutor should focus on the crimes committed only by one of the parties to the conflict.[24]

Adopting the concept of a "dormant jurisdiction" gives rise to further questions. Firstly, we need to ask for how long the ICC jurisdiction is activated in respect of a specific situation. Can we assume that once a referral triggers the Court's

[19] Cit. after: deGuzman and Schabas (2013), p. 132.

[20] See: Olásolo (2012), p. 26.

[21] In general see: Turone (2002), p. 1147; Olásolo (2005), pp. 37–38 and 48 et seq. In more detail about the criteria that govern the Prosecutor's choice of defendants in: Selection of defendants before the ICC: between the principle of opportunism and legalism, published in the Polish Yearbook of International Law 2015.

[22] This concept was presented and analysed by: Olásolo (2005), pp. 39 et seq.

[23] A different view: Olásolo (2003), p. 99.

[24] Resolution of 31 March 2005, S/RES/1593 (2005): http://www.icc-cpi.int/NR/rdonlyres/85FEBD1A-29 F8-4EC4-9566-48EDF55CC587/283244/N0529273.pdf. Accessed 11 Feb 2015. It was the *Lord's Resistance Army*. The whole situation analysed in: Schabas (2010), p. 299.

jurisdiction, there is no temporal limitation to the Prosecutor's powers to initiate an investigation? It seems that this is precisely the case, and the Prosecutor can suspend such an investigation or discontinue it and later reopen it at any time without having to go through the triggering procedure again.[25]

Secondly, considering the above discussion of the binding nature of the Security Council's referral, does the Prosecutor also have powers not to activate "dormant jurisdiction" and not to proceed with a case?[26] As it was said earlier, it should be concluded that he has such powers.

The earliest communications regarding committed crimes were made by the Security Council and the interested States Parties.

The first two investigations conducted by the Prosecutor in the Democratic Republic of Congo (DRC) and in Uganda were initiated pursuant to the procedure set forth in Article 13(a), in conjunction with Article 14 of the Statute. These two states provided the Prosecutor with information suggesting the commission of crimes falling within the Court's jurisdiction. This came as a surprise even to the authors of the Statute, as they had not expected that this mechanism of "self-denunciation" would have so much practical importance for the operation of the Court.[27] In the case of the Democratic Republic of Congo, it was the president himself who provided incriminating information on July 2003.[28] Upon a preliminary examination of the case, the Prosecutor concluded that there were grounds for initiation of an investigation.

In the case of Uganda, the state was divided between two hostile parties, and the referral pertained exclusively to crimes committed by only one of them.[29] The international community exerted some pressure on the ICC Prosecutor to address the situation in Uganda as his first case. Some Ugandan sources even claim that the Prosecutor himself suggested that the president of Uganda referred the case to the ICC as he did not want to initiate his first case *proprio motu*. The fact that the Prosecutor proceeded with the case was very comfortable for the President of Uganda: first of all, it presented the rebels as "criminals" whose acts deserved condemnation; second, it presented all parties (including foreign states) that provided assistance to the rebels as co-perpetrators of these acts. Moreover, the costs of the prosecution and of criminal proceedings against all criminals were covered by

[25] See: Olásolo (2005), p. 53. A different view: Krzan (2009), p. 155.

[26] Such a question was asked by: Olásolo (2005), p. 53.

[27] In general see: Ambos (2007), p. 434, and Burke-White (2005), pp. 557–590; Wierczyńska (2013) pp. 127-129.

[28] Press release: Prosecutor receives referral of the situation in the Democratic Republic of Congo, ICC-OTP-20040419-50: http://icc-cpi.int/en_menus/icc/press%20and%20media/press%20releases/2004/Pages/prosecutor%20receives%20referral%20of%20the%20situation%20in%20the%20democratic%20republic%20of%20congo.aspx. Accessed 11 Feb 2015.

[29] Press release: President of Uganda refers situation concerning the Lord's Resistance Army (LRA) to the ICC, ICC-20040129-44, http://icc-cpi.int/en_menus/icc/press%20and%20media/press%20releases/2004/Pages/president%20of%20uganda%20refers%20situation%20concerning%20the%20lord_s%20resistance%20army%20_lra_%20to%20the%20icc.aspx. Accessed 11 Feb 2015.

the international body. As far as the ICC Prosecutor was concerned, these proceedings validated the grounds for his existence within 1 year of his appointment.[30]

The case of the Central African Republic was also referred to the ICC by the government of this state, notifying the Court about violations of law committed during the pending armed conflict between the government and rebel forces.[31] On 13 July 2012, the Court received a referral from the government of Mali.[32] As the Government of Ukraine on 17 April 2014 lodged a declaration accepting the jurisdiction of the International Criminal Court under Article 12(3) of the Rome Statute over alleged crimes committed on its territory from 21 November 2013 to 22 February 2014, this situation became the next one to be referred to by a State Party. Upon receipt of such a declaration, the Office of the Prosecutor, as a matter of policy, opened a preliminary examination of the situation at hand.

Following the referral of the Uganda case, some observers started asking whether it was the Prosecutor's duty to indict perpetrators representing both sides of the conflict. It was argued that law enforcement by international courts should not be transformed into victor's justice.[33] It could not be overlooked that, so far, in the case of three self-referrals, the referring state asked the Prosecutor to investigate crimes allegedly committed by "rebels" fighting against the central authorities.[34] It was asked whether—to prevent accusations of arbitrariness in selection of the accused—the Prosecutor's aim should be to strive for equilibrium between both sides of the conflict is concerned. And if so - should the equilibrium express itself e.g. in the number of indicted perpetrators on both sides. After receiving the referral, the Prosecutor notified the authorities referring the situation that he would address all cases of crimes within this situation, regardless of who committed them. He argued that it was his competence to address the whole situation first and that he would outline the limits of the case—by selecting the perpetrators and formulating charges—only after completing a preliminary examination. By this decision, he asserted his right to prosecute also those criminals who had not been included in the referral. He decided that the complaint of a state should be treated as a call to investigate the entire situation.[35]

The Prosecutor's decision sent a message to other states referring situations to the ICC: that in subsequent cases, the investigating Prosecutor will not restrain himself to the personal limits determined by a given referral but will rather take into account the entire territorial and temporal scope of a given conflict reported in the referral. On the one hand, this is a reflection of the desired equality of parties

[30] In general see: Geis and Mundt (2009), pp. 7–8; Schabas (2009), p. 238; Locke (2012), p. 622.

[31] Press release: Prosecutor receives referral concerning Central African Republic, ICC-OTP-20050107-86.

[32] See: http://icc-cpi.int/NO./rdonlyres/A245A47F-BFD1-45B6-891C-3BCB5B173F57/0/ReferralLetterMali130712.pdf. Accessed 18 June 2013.

[33] As in: Coté (2012), pp. 366–370; Olásolo (2003), p. 95; Schabas (2010), pp. 750–753; de Vlaming (2012), p. 567.

[34] See: Cassese (2006), p. 436.

[35] This is emphasised by: Cryer (2005), p. 225. Detailed analysis in: Ambos (2007), p. 441; Schabas (2008), pp. 752–753.

involved in a conflict: the referring party does not enjoy special protection by the international administration of justice. In practice, however, the situation developed contrary to the Prosecutor's claims. Although he emphasised that despite the fact that the conflict had been referred by one of the involved parties he was obliged to address all crimes committed during the conflict, from the very beginning he focused on the crimes committed by the forces opposing the government. Responding to the criticism that ensued, the Prosecutor argued that the crimes allegedly committed by the "rebels" were of a higher gravity than alleged crimes committed by any other group.[36]

The Security Council has made two referrals. In 2005, it addressed international law crimes committed in Sudan, referring the case to the Court.[37] Naturally, in a situation where the Prosecutor considers it necessary to accuse the presiding head of a state, he may not expect to have the situation referred by that state. As the Security Council referred the case for the ICC's investigation, the President of Sudan became the first governing president accused before the ICC. On the one hand, the Prosecutor's decision was criticised for ruining the chances for peace, but on the other it was praised for having demonstrated that even the head of a state is not immune from prosecution.[38] For obvious reasons, the ICC may not force the government of Sudan to co-operate with it in order to surrender the accused. Therefore, a practical problem arises: if the Prosecutor fails to bring the perpetrator before the Court, he might lose his credibility. Should he give up then the prosecution to protect the credibility of his office[39] or should he rather keep formulating indictments without any hope of bringing the accused to justice, only to convey the condemnation expressed by the international community or in order to achieve current political goals?

The Security Council also referred the situation in Libya.[40] It passed a resolution to impose on the authorities of Libya (which is not, however, a State Party to the Statute) an obligation to co-operate with the Court and its Prosecutor.

3.2.3 Preliminary Examination of a Case

The preliminary examination of a case is the stage of proceedings when information on committed crimes is analysed in order to determine whether the initiation of an investigation is justified. It may be noticed that the more formalised an investigation

[36] Office of the Prosecutor, Report on the Activities Performed During the First Three Years (June 2003–June 2006), 12 September 2006, The Hague, p. 14.

[37] Resolution of 31 March 2005, S/RES/1593 (2005).

[38] See: Geis and Mundt (2009), pp. 10–13; Locke (2012), p. 622; Milik (2012), pp. 133–141.

[39] Stating that prosecution without the likelihood of any effective investigation being possible would not serve the interest of justice. Some say he should—Wouters et al. (2008), p. 291.

[40] Resolution No. 1970(2011), 26.2.2011, S/RES/1970 (2011).

is, the greater the need to precede it with non-formalised actions aimed at checking whether its instigation is necessary (admissible). In continental systems, the degree of formalisation of investigation resulted in the development of a statutory practice of preliminary examination whose objective is to check whether "there is a justified suspicion of commission of a crime". Only when this suspicion is confirmed may a formal investigation be started. In Polish criminal trials, a verification of the facts in the matter may be carried out on the basis of Article 307 CCP, or the necessary inquiries, as foreseen by Article 308 CPP; in the German procedure, it is the *Vorermittlungen* performed pursuant to Article 152(2) StPO that is undertaken to establish whether there are "sufficient factual preconditions" (*zureichende tatsächliche Anhaltspunkte*).[41] During this procedure, information contained in the notice of the offence committed can be completed and verified. All these actions are conducted informally. If needed, such actions are recorded in the form of "official notes" that cannot, however, be presented during the trial. In the verifying proceedings, no evidence from an expert opinion or actions requiring records are undertaken. These actions cannot be considered the initial form of an investigation because they precede its initiation. Only upon their completion is the investigation formally initiated—or abandoned, in which case "discontinuation prior to initiation" takes place, which is an unusual mechanism, not only from the semantic point of view. The existence of this institution is justified by the argument that the more preliminary examinations are performed to verify the suitability (admissibility) of an investigation, the less investigations end in discontinuation.[42] However, it can be very difficult to draw a clear line between preliminary checks and the "formal" initiation of proceedings.[43]

In proceedings before the *ad hoc* tribunals, the stage of an investigation has been de-formalised in a manner that follows the common law model. No distinction was made between the verification activities and an investigation (Rule 2 RPE ICTY). The ICTY procedure defines "investigation" as all activities undertaken by the Prosecutor in order to confirm the fact of commission of crimes within the Tribunal's jurisdiction. All of these activities are finalised with the preparation of an indictment and its filing in the Trial Chamber.

Before the ICC, numerous elements formalising an investigation were introduced. Of key importance is the requirement that the Prosecutor's decision on the initiation of proceedings must be confirmed by the Pre-Trial Chamber. This requirement was the reason why, following the example of continental states, it was considered necessary to implement a particular stage, which is not yet an investigation but is considered as a sort of "pre-investigation". Its aim is to determine whether there are reasonable and sufficient grounds to initiate a proper "investigation". It should be carried out before requesting the authorisation to

[41] Beulke (2005), p. 179.

[42] See: Grzegorczyk (2008), p. 640; Waltoś (1968), p. 106.

[43] Damaška (1986), p. 155.

investigate a case and precisely with this aim—to gather information and evaluate if it constitutes sufficient basis for authorisation.

In proceedings before the ICC, the sole suspicion that an international law crime has been committed or a notification about this fact should never be considered sufficient to start (and also to "initiate" by the Prosecutor acting *proprio motu*) an investigation, and they always require implementation of verifying procedure. Article 15(2) of the Rome Statute provides that the Prosecutor, after receiving information on crimes within the jurisdiction of the Court, and before initiation of an investigation, "shall analyse the seriousness of the information received. For this purpose, he or she may seek additional information". This stage is referred to as "preliminary examination" in paragraph 6 of this provision. Thus, two stages have been distinguished: there is a distinction between a preliminary examination of information regulated in Article 15 of the Statute, carried out in order to establish whether there is a reasonable basis to proceed with an investigation, and investigation under Article 53, whose goal is to prepare charges and submit it to the Trial Chamber.

It is obvious that on the basis of preliminary information available to the Prosecutor, it is often still not possible to define specific events and perpetrators. The preliminary analysis of a case is designed to determine these factors: it serves to single out the "case" limited to specific events and persons referred by one of the information sources from a whole range of events included in a "situation". The initiated investigation must pertain to a specific event and a specific perpetrator, i.e., to a "case" rather than to a "situation".

Preliminary examination of a case has only one goal: collecting information, which would enable taking the decision as to whether it is reasonable to initiate an investigation. Primary analysis of a case provides a tool to verify and confirm potential doubts about the credibility of communications received. The Statute provides the Prosecutor with measures to analyse the seriousness of the information received. For this purpose, he may seek additional information from States, organs of the United Nations, intergovernmental or non-governmental organisations or other reliable sources that he or she deems appropriate and may receive written or oral testimony at the seat of the Court—but only from those who chose to appear at the seat of the Court willingly. In practice, the Prosecutor can also take part in field missions, as he did, for instance, in 2008 in Columbia or in November 2014 in Kiev. Having obtained information in this way, the Prosecutor must decide whether, within the investigated situation, specific events and perpetrators of crimes falling within the jurisdiction of the Court may be indicated with sufficient precision.

Already at the stage of preliminary examination of a case and prior to taking the decision on initiation of prosecution, the Prosecutor must also assess the issues of admissibility listed in Article 17 of the Statute. It is at this stage that the Prosecutor investigates whether the criterion of complementarity is satisfied, justifying the Court's jurisdiction.

The relation between Article 15(3) and Article 53 of the ICC Statute, both introducing parameters for initiation of an investigation, is not clear. It is not easy to reconcile these two provisions. It has been indicated that the discrepancies between Article 53 and Article 15(3) arise from the fact that these provisions have not been consolidated by the authors of the Rome Statute. The origins of these two provisions can be found in two different proposals presented by two different states and were dealt with not only by different working groups but by different delegates. Consequently, there was no stage where these two provisions could be reconciled.[44]

In the case law, it is now recognised that the criteria used to assess the suitability of an indictment are, simultaneously, the criteria used by the Prosecutor during the preliminary examination of a case to verify whether it is reasonable to initiate an investigation.[45] According to the opinion of the Pre-Trial Chamber, the drafting history of Articles 15 and 53 of the Statute reveals that the intention was to use exactly the same standard for these provisions. According to Article 15(2) and (3) of the Statute, the Prosecutor, after having analysed the seriousness of the information received from different sources, may conclude that there is "a reasonable basis to proceed with an investigation". In reaching this conclusion, Rule 48 RPE dictates that the Prosecutor shall consider the factors set out in Article 53, paragraph 1(a) to (c). It signifies the need to analyse the criteria justifying a decision on the confirmation of charges at the stage of the initiation of an investigation, even when the investigation is not yet in progress.[46]

In addition to the concept expressed by the Pre-Trial Chamber, there are two further theories regarding the mutual relation of these two provisions. First, it may be assumed that Article 15(3) provides guidelines for the Prosecutor as to when to initiate an investigation *proprio motu*. Article 53 governs situations that are referred to the Prosecutor by the Security Council or States Parties.[47] One may also encounter the theory that Article 15 refers to preliminary examinations, that is, to preliminary gathering of information in order to determine whether to proceed to request the Pre-Trial Chamber to authorise a full investigation, whereas Article 53 refers to "the commencement or start of a full investigation with a view to determining whether to prepare an indictment and prosecute".[48]

In regard to the issues of preliminary examination of a case, a question arises as to how far a preliminary examination of a case may go without the Pre-Trial Chamber's authorisation. There are no rules regulating the duration of this stage of proceedings. This issue was considered by the Pre-Trial Chamber in relation to the preliminary examination of the situation in Kenya. The organ concluded that the answer might be found in Article 53(1) of the Rome Statute. According to this conception, the Prosecutor is entitled to continue gathering additional information until he feels sufficiently confident about the actual existence of a "reasonable basis

---

44 See: Olásolo (2003), p. 70.

45 In: *Situation in the Republic of Kenya*, ICC-01/09, Decision Pursuant to Article 15 of the Rome Statute on the Authorization of an Investigation into the Situation in the Republic of Kenya, 31 March 2010.

46 The same conclusions also in: Stegmiller (2011), p. 322; Olásolo (2003), pp. 63 et seq.; Turone (2002), p. 1147.

47 This opinion presented by: Schabas (2010), p. 659.

48 This conclusion expressed by: Bergsmo and Pejić (2008), p. 1067.

to proceed with the investigation" or lack thereof. So far, none of the preliminary examinations conducted by the Prosecutor have lasted more than 2 years. However, when the Prosecutor was investigating the case of the Central African Republic (CAR), he was asked by the Pre-Trial Chamber (which referred to the right of the State Party that reported the situation to be informed about the course of the case) to provide information on the current state of the preliminary examination of the case, as well as on the expected term of its completion and the decision on the initiation of an investigation.[49] The Prosecutor submitted a description of the current status of the preliminary examination of the CAR situation; he even applied for authorisation of the investigation within the next 6 months. At the same time, though, he observed that the prosecutorial discretion to examine a case on a preliminary stage and time thereof are not susceptible to judicial review by the Pre-Trial Chamber.[50] He indicated that the role of the Pre-Trial Chamber is limited solely to controlling a decision on the initiation of, or refusal to initiate, an investigation and is not extended to the preliminary examination of a case. On the one hand, the Prosecutor emphasised that it was not his duty to reply to a question asked in this form, but on the other it can be seen that a new type of judicial review was exerted in the form of an official enquiry about the current status of the case. The development of the situation demonstrates that the role the Pre-Trial Chamber plays in an investigation is very similar to that of official supervision in hierarchically structured prosecution offices, especially in the light of seizing even more controlling powers than provided expressly by the Statute. This tendency shows how, even when lacking a hierarchical structure, the ICC Prosecutor's actions do not remain unsupervised. Similarly, even in the absence of time limits for the completion of the preliminary examination of a case, it cannot go on without end.

In light of the considerations pertaining to the binding character of the referrals received by the Security Council, there is also the question of whether, having received information from this source, the Prosecutor has the power (or even the obligation) to carry out a preliminary examination to analyse the reliability of the information received. Such a requirement seems to arise from the Rules of Procedure and Evidence, which provide that in each case, whether it is the initiation of proceedings *proprio motu* or following the referral made by the privileged authority, "in acting pursuant to Article 53, paragraph 1, the Prosecutor shall, in evaluating the information made available to him or her, analyse the seriousness of the information received" (Rule 104 RPE). Therefore, there should be no doubt that the preliminary examination should be conducted regarding all kinds of information—from both privileged and other sources.[51] The practice shows that, even in the case

[49] *Situation in the Central African Republic*, ICC-01/05-6, Decision requesting Information on the Status of the Preliminary examination of the Situation in CAR, 30 November 2006, p. 5.

[50] *Situation in the Central African Republic*, ICC-01/05, Prosecution's Report Pursuant to Pre-Trial Chamber III's 30 November 2006 Decision Requesting Information on the Status of the Preliminary Examination of the Situation in the Central African Republic, ICC 01/05, 15 December 2006, § 1.

[51] See: Turone (2002), p. 1147.

of receiving information from the Security Council, regarding the situation in Sudan, the Prosecutor, independently from this authority's opinion, had conducted a preliminary analysis of the available information and concluded that there was a "reasonable basis to proceed with an investigation". There are opinions that he had done so in order to emphasise his liberty to take decisions as to the validity of grounds for initiation of an investigation independently from the assessment of the Security Council.[52] It was highlighted that the Prosecutor already acted this way in relation to the first case referred by the Security Council, thus defining the relations between the ICC and this organ at the first opportunity. It is also noted in the doctrine that the preliminary examination should be conducted regarding all kinds of information—from both privileged and other sources.[53]

After evaluating the information received during the preliminary analysis of the case, the Prosecutor shall "initiate an investigation unless he or she determines that there is no reasonable basis to proceed under this Statute" (Article 53(1) of the ICC Statute). If the Prosecutor concludes that there is a reasonable basis to proceed with an investigation, he shall submit to the Pre-Trial Chamber a request for authorisation of an investigation, together with any supporting material collected—if the analysis was initiated *proprio motu*. Authorisation of an investigation is the borderline between preliminary examination of a case by the Prosecutor and the investigation proper. If, however, a case is referred by one of the privileged entities, the borderline is constituted by the Prosecutor's decision itself to proceed with (rather than to initiate) an examination, in accordance with Article 53(1) of the Rome Statute. Therefore, when the informant is the Security Council or a Sate Party, an investigation is automatically opened if the Prosecutor decides that there is a "reasonable basis to proceed".[54] No judicial review is provided for in the "fast-track procedure". In such a situation, the procedure described below does not need to be conducted.

3.3 Conditions of Initiation of an Investigation Before the ICC

3.3.1 Powers of the Pre-Trial Chamber

The Prosecutor may initiate an investigation that, however, can commence only after this decision has been authorised by the Pre-Trial Chamber—if it has been initiated *proprio motu*. This decision is taken after an examination of the supporting material submitted by the Prosecutor, including witnesses' and victims'

[52] In general see: Ohlin (2009), p. 187; Schabas (2010), p. 301; Williams and Schabas (2008), p. 570.

[53] See: Turone (2002), p. 1147; Wouters et al. (2008), p. 294.

[54] So: Olásolo (2003), p. 104.

statements (which, however, do not have the status of testimony). The Pre-Trial Chamber assesses whether there is a reasonable basis to proceed with an investigation and whether the case appears to fall within the jurisdiction of the Court. The judicial authority's intervention constitutes a borderline between the preliminary examination of a case and the proper investigation. As representatives of some states claimed that the Prosecutor had been given too much political power, the authorisation procedure was considered necessary in order to control prosecutorial discretion in the selection of cases that are to be brought to the Court's attention.

The institution of confirmation of the Prosecutor's decisions to initiate criminal proceedings is not known to any of the analysed legal systems. This stage is also absent from the proceedings before the *ad hoc* tribunals. The ICTY Prosecutor's decision to initiate an investigation has not been formalised and is not subject to review by a judicial authority.

Article 53(1) of the Rome Statute provides that the Prosecutor may initiate an investigation "unless he or she determines that there is no reasonable basis to proceed under this Statute". This provision defines the conditions for the preliminary assessment of suitability and admissibility of a case to be brought before the Court. They serve a twofold purpose: first, they provide guidelines for the Prosecutor as to when he should initiate an investigation and, second, they are a basis for the Pre-Trial Chamber's assessment as to whether his decision should be authorised. The general principle remains that judicial organs themselves have the competence to decide whether they have jurisdiction over a given case and whether this case is admissible.[55] Namely, while deciding whether to initiate an investigation, the Prosecutor shall consider the following conditions:

(a) the information available to the Prosecutor provides a reasonable basis to believe that a crime within the jurisdiction of the Court has been or is being committed;
(b) the case is or would be admissible under Article 17; and
(c) taking into account the gravity of the crime and the interests of victims, there are nonetheless substantial reasons to believe that an investigation would not serve the interests of justice.

Sometimes an additional fourth condition is added. Bearing in mind that Article 1 of the Rome Statute defines the scope of the Court's jurisdiction, which should pertain solely to "the most serious crimes of concern to the international community as a whole", the Prosecutor may initiate an investigation only in the situation where the reported situation concerns the commission of such crimes.[56]

When submitting his decision to initiate proceedings for the Pre-Trial Chamber's confirmation, the Prosecutor must properly justify his point of view, making references to the materials collected during a preliminary examination of the

[55] See: Oosthuizen (1999), p. 321.
[56] Bergsmo and Pejić (2008), p. 586.

case. He must also prove that the crimes that have been committed are not common crimes but are rather crimes of concern to the international community. He needs to establish the existence of every element of crime: if he suspects that crimes against humanity have been committed, he must prove that the acts when committed were not a single case constituted but a part of a "widespread or systematic attack directed against any civilian population, with knowledge of the attack" (Article 7 (1) of the Statute). Therefore, it is necessary for the Prosecutor to present information that would show the *nexus* between specific offences and their proliferation. As an example, the preliminary examination of the situation in Venezuela can be mentioned, as a result of which the Prosecutor decided that despite the suspicion that crimes against humanity had been committed there, the acquired materials did not support the conviction that the alleged crimes constituted "a part of a widespread or systematic attack".[57]

3.3.2 Reasonable Basis to Proceed with an Investigation

When submitting his decision to proceed with an investigation for the Pre-Trial Chamber's confirmation, the Prosecutor must demonstrate that "the information available to the Prosecutor provides a reasonable basis to believe that a crime within the jurisdiction of the Court has been or is being committed" (Article 53(1)(a) of the Statute). Despite the consistent use of the term "reasonable basis" in the English text of Article 53, both in paragraph 1 and paragraph 1(a), the Polish legislator decided to differentiate between these two provisions. As a result, in the Polish version of the Statute, Article 53(1) provides that "The Prosecutor shall, having evaluated the information made available to him or her, initiate an investigation unless he or she determines that there is no justified basis (Pol. uzasadniona podstawa) to proceed under this Statute", whereas Article 53(1)(a) provides that when submitting his decision to proceed with the investigation for the Pre-Trial Chamber's confirmation, the Prosecutor must demonstrate that "the information available to the Prosecutor provides a reasonable basis (Pol. rozsądna podstawa) to believe that a crime within the jurisdiction of the Court has been or is being committed".[58]

This phrasing entails that the Prosecutor does not have to prove a suspect's guilt "beyond reasonable doubt", which is a condition for charging the latter with alleged crimes. For an investigation to be initiated, it is sufficient to initially determine that there are grounds to suspect that a person has committed an offence falling within the Court's jurisdiction. In order for the Prosecution to meet its evidentiary burden, it must offer concrete and tangible proof demonstrating a clear line of reasoning

[57] *Update on Communications Received by the Prosecutor*, statement of 10 February 2006, Annex: Venezuela response, p. 4.

[58] See: Milik (2012), p. 107.

underpinning its specific allegations.[59] In *The Prosecutor v. Bahar Idriss Abu Garda*, the Prosecutor charged the suspect with commission of war crimes during the domestic conflict in Darfur, treating him as co-perpetrator within the meaning of Article 25(3)(a) of the Rome Statute. The Pre-Trial Chamber decided, however, that the evidence presented by the Prosecutor during the hearing to confirm the charges is "scant and unreliable" and, as a consequence, refused to confirm charges.

The Pre-Trial Chamber emphasised that it is "the lowest evidentiary standard provided for in the Statute". As the confirmation hearing should not be turned into a mini-trial, its purpose should be limited to confirming that sufficiently compelling charges going beyond mere theory or suspicion have been brought. Thus, the information available to the Prosecutor is neither expected to be "comprehensive" nor "conclusive"—if compared to evidence gathered during the investigation. The above is a distinctive feature of all legal systems: the existance of a justified suspicion that a crime has been committed is sufficient to proceed with an investigation (e.g., Article 303 CCP, § 203 StPO).

A detailed interpretation of the significance of the conditions set forth in Article 53 of the Statute was presented in the case of the situation in the Republic of Kenya, pertaining to the commission of crimes against humanity during the conflict that took place during parliamentary elections, which was the first of the two cases so far in which the Prosecutor has proceeded *proprio motu*.[60] In this case, the Appeals Chamber found that the standard of proof justifying the investigation proceedings did not require the evidence to lead to the only reasonable conclusion on the suspect's guilt. It is sufficient that the commission of crimes by the suspect is "possible and reasonable to confirm", along with other potential versions of events. The Prosecutor does not need to prove beyond any doubt that no other solution is possible. Determination as to whether there are reasonable grounds to proceed with an investigation should be analysed, taking into account specific facts, and, therefore, the Prosecutor's presentation of general facts pertaining to a specific case is not sufficient. He must at least indicate groups of persons suspected of having committed specific crimes, even if he is not yet able to prove the names of suspects or present specific charges. Even the Prosecutor's selection of charges and suspects is, by its nature, preliminary and non-binding for the purposes of preparing a further indictment brought to the Court.

Also, when adjudicating on the confirmation of an investigation into the situation in Côte d'Ivoire pertaining to alleged crimes against humanity during the civil unrests that broke out after the presidential election in the period of 16 December

---

[59] *The Prosecutor v. Bahar Idriss Abu Garda*, ICC-02/05-02/09, Decision on the Confirmation of Charges, 8.2.2010, § 37.

[60] *Situation in the Republic of Kenya*, ICC-01/09, Decision Pursuant to Article 15 of the Rome Statute on the Authorization of an Investigation into the Situation in the Republic of Kenya, 31 March 2010, § 21 et seq.; The same opinion is expressed in: The Prosecutor v. *Omar Hassan Ahmad Al Bashir*, ICC-02/05-01/09, Judgment on the appeal of the Prosecutor against the "Decision on the Prosecution's Application for a Warrant of Arrest against Omar Hassan Ahmad Al Bashir", 3 February 2010, § 30.

2010–12 April 2011, the Pre-Trial Chamber confirmed that at such an early stage of proceedings, the Chamber may review only potential "cases" chosen from a broader "situation" as part of which a crime under international law could have been committed. We may speak of a "potential case" when the following two conditions are met: there is a specific group of persons that is likely to become the subject of the Prosecutor's interest, and there is a suspicion that crimes have been committed that fall within the Court's jurisdiction (and are serious enough for their scale, nature, manner of performance and impact on the victims to be brought before the Court).[61] The Prosecutor does not indicate potential suspects but must only prove that specific crimes have been committed, providing information to support that specific acts were not isolated but together constitute a single crime of concern to the international community as a whole. At this stage of proceedings, the Chamber refers not to the "evidence" but rather to the "information provided by the Prosecutor", and it takes its decision not on the basis of specific evidence but rather on the basis of "available information".

As part of the decision to proceed with an investigation, the Prosecutor has to determine the time framework for proceedings to be held before the Court. However, similarly as with the final formulation of charges, the time when crimes were committed does not have to be specified in detail. In the case pertaining to the commission of war crimes and crimes against humanity in Congo, the Pre-Trial Chamber decided that "such a situation can include not only crimes that had already been or were being committed at the time of the referral, but also crimes committed after that time, in so far as they are sufficiently linked to the situation of crisis referred to the Court as ongoing at the time of the referral".[62] The above entails that the Chamber confirms proceedings related to acts that have not been committed yet but will have been committed by the time the Prosecutor formulates charges and presents them for the Pre-Trial Chamber's authorisation (as was the case with Côte d'Ivoire).

3.3.3 The Parameter of Admissibility

The Pre-Trial Chamber acknowledges that there are reasonable grounds to conduct the proceedings if the Prosecutor demonstrates that the case is, or would be, considered admissible pursuant to Article 17 of the Statute. The Prosecutor needs to prove that a given act constitutes a crime as defined in Article 5 of the ICC Statute (that it meets the *ratione materiae* conditions), was committed in a period

---

[61] *Situation in the Republic of Côte d'Ivoire*, ICC-02/11, Decision Pursuant to Article 15 of the Rome Statute on the Authorisation of an Investigation into the Situation in the Republic of Côte d'Ivoire, 3 October 2011, § 23–25.

[62] *The Prosecutor v. Callixte Mbarushimana*, ICC-01/04-01/07, Decision on the Prosecutor's Application for a Warrant of Arrest against Callixte Mbarushimana, 28 September 2010, § 6.

enabling the ICC to exercise its jurisdiction (Article 11—jurisdiction *ratione temporis*) and complies with the conditions of Article 12—the suspect is a national of a state that ratified the Statute or committed the act on the territory of such a state (jurisdiction *ratione loci* or *ratione personae*).

The admissibility of a case handled by the Prosecutor also depends on the compliance with a fourth precondition of the ICC jurisdiction—the requirement of Article 17(1)(d) relating to the "gravity of the case"—which should "justify further action by the Court". As the last criterion is of a fully discretionary character, the parameter of admissibility of a case, evaluated as a whole, can be called "a fluctuating parameter"[63]: being both non-discretionary (as the first criteria of jurisdiction) and discretionary—depending on the specific issues of admissibility that come into consideration.

3.3.4 Principle of Complementary Jurisdiction

When examining whether there are reasonable grounds to proceed with an investigation, the Prosecutor needs to demonstrate each time that the Court has the jurisdiction in a given case pursuant to the principle of complementarity. The Preamble to the Rome Statute emphasises that the "International Criminal Court established under this Statute shall be complementary to national criminal jurisdictions". Also in Article 1 of the Statute, we find confirmation of the principle that "the Court shall be complementary to national criminal jurisdictions". According to this principle—unlike the *ad hoc* Tribunals for the former Yugoslavia and for Rwanda—the ICC does not have primacy over national systems.

In Article 17, the Rome Statute defines what should be understood by the notion of "shall be complementary to national criminal jurisdictions". In order to come to such a conclusion, the Court should determine whether:

(1) the case is being investigated or prosecuted by a State that has jurisdiction over it, unless the State is unwilling or unable genuinely to carry out the investigation or prosecution;
(2) the case has been investigated by a State that has jurisdiction over it and the State has decided not to prosecute the person concerned, unless the decision resulted from the unwillingness or inability of the State genuinely to prosecute[64];

---

[63] The notion used by: Turone (2002), p. 1152.

[64] Or also entrusting the ICC with a case: as in *The Prosecutor v. Katanga*, ICC-01/04-01/07-T-67-1213, Reasons for the Oral Decision on the Motion Challenging the Admissibility of the Case, 12 June 2009. These notions analysed in: Batros (2010), pp. 343–362, and Sacouto and Cleary (2010), pp. 363–374.

(3) the person concerned has already been tried for conduct that is the subject of the complaint, and a trial by the Court is not permitted under Article 20(3) of the Statute.

In consequence, only if in a given state having jurisdiction are there ongoing investigations or prosecutions (*lis pendens* premise)—or there have been investigations in the past (*ne bis in idem* premise)—and as their result it has been decided not to prosecute the person concerned, can the Prosecutor examine the question of unwillingness and inability to act. Examining unwillingness and inability before establishing facts as to former and ongoing investigations would amount to, quoting the Court's judges, "putting the cart before the horse".[65] Both notions are defined in the ICC Statute in order to avoid any prospective ambiguities. It provides that in order to determine unwillingness within the meaning of the Statute in a particular case, the Court considers, having regard to the principles of due process recognised by international law, whether one or more of the following exist, as applicable:

(a) The proceedings were or are being undertaken, or the national decision was made for the purpose of shielding the person concerned from criminal responsibility for crimes within the jurisdiction of the Court referred to in Article 5.
(b) There has been an unjustified delay in the proceedings that in the circumstances is inconsistent with an intent to bring the person concerned to justice.
(c) The proceedings were not or are not being conducted independently or impartially, and they were or are being conducted in a manner that, in the circumstances, is inconsistent with an intent to bring the person concerned to justice.

In order to determine inability in a particular case, the Court considers whether, due to a total or substantial collapse or unavailability of its national judicial system, the State is unable to obtain the accused or the necessary evidence and testimony or otherwise unable to carry out criminal proceedings.

The Paper on some policy issues adopted on September 2003 by the OTP presents the official analysis of what will be meant under the principle of complementarity of jurisdiction by the Office.[66] The OTP expressed an opinion that the ICC is not intended to replace national courts. The reason behind adopting the principle of complementarity was to create an institution that is global in scope while recognising the primary responsibility of States themselves to exercise their *ius puniendi*. The system of international accountability before the ICC is based on the assumption that states do not only have a right but that they also have an

[65] *The Prosecutor v. Katanga*, ICC-01/04-01/07-1497, Judgment on the Appeal of Mr. Germain Katanga against the Oral Decision of Trial Chamber II of 12 June 2009 on the Admissibility of the Case, 25 September 2009, § 78, also in: *Situation in the Republic of Côte d'Ivoire*, ICC-02/11, Decision Pursuant to Article 15 of the Rome Statute on the Authorisation of an Investigation into the Situation in the Republic of Côte d'Ivoire, 3 October 2011, § 193.

[66] Paper on some policy issues before the Office of the Prosecutor, September 2003, on the following websites: http://www.icc-cpi.int/NO./rdonlyres/1FA7C4C6-DE5F-42B7-8B25-60AA962ED8B6/143594/030905_Policy_Paper.pdf. Accessed 18 Mar 2013, pp. 4–5.

obligation to prosecute crimes falling within the Court's jurisdiction. The Office also indicated that States will generally be more effective in conducting investigations as they have the best access to evidence and witnesses. In line with the official opinion of the Office, the provision of the Statute that defines the notions of "inability" and "unwillingness" of a state to prosecute these crimes was established in order to allow the Prosecutor to conduct an investigation in a situation where there was a lack of central government or a state of chaos due to the conflict or crisis or public disorder leading to collapse of national systems that prevents the State from discharging its duties to investigate and prosecute crimes within the jurisdiction of the Court. We may also envisage a situation in which a state concludes that the Court is more capable of handling the proceedings. This may happen when, as a result of collapse of the state's normal functioning, the national justice system also becomes disorganised and also when there are two interest groups that seek an impartial forum to decide on the criminal liability of perpetrators.

During the examination of the complementarity principle in respect of the situation in Kenya, discrepancies in understanding of this concept occurred. The meaning of the phrase "the case is being investigated or prosecuted by a State" was analysed when Kenya challenged the correctness of the Pre-Trial Chamber's findings about the admissibility of the case.[67] The state claimed that the Court had wrongly decided, based on the information provided by the Prosecutor, that the case being heard by the Court was not subject to national criminal proceedings in Kenya as there were ongoing investigations into this situation. Kenya argued that it had been prosecuting the same conduct as was examined by the Prosecutor during investigation. It further submitted that, although the national proceedings were not conducted in respect of the same persons as suspected by the Court of committing certain acts, they were conducted in respect of "persons at the same level in the hierarchy as those being investigated by the ICC". In consequence, it should be acknowledged that they constituted an obstacle preventing the proceedings from being initiated before the Court. Kenya submitted that the Court had not yet authoritatively established the meaning of the word "case" in Article 17(1) of the Statute. In the view of Kenya, it was sufficient to conclude that there is an investigation "in the case" and not necessarily "against a certain person". The theory according to which a case can be inadmissible before the Court only when a national jurisdiction is investigating the same person and for the same conduct as in the case already before the Court ("same person/same conduct" test) should be therefore rejected.

The Pre-Trial Chamber, however, did not agree with this reasoning. It found that the condition that "the case is being investigated or prosecuted by a State which has jurisdiction over it" is only fulfilled when the "same person/same conduct" test is

---

[67] *The Prosecutor v. William Samoei Ruto, Henry Kiprono Kosgey And Joshua Arap Sang*, ICC-01/09-01/11, Judgment on the appeal of the Republic of Kenya against the decision of Pre-Trial, Chamber II of 30 May 2011 entitled "Decision on the Application by the Government of Kenya Challenging the Admissibility of the Case Pursuant to Article 19(2)(b) of the Statute", 30 August 2011, § 27–28.

applied. At this stage of proceedings, the conclusion that the case "is being investigated" (although at other, earlier stages the contours of the likely cases will often be relatively vague) cannot be considered sufficient. The statement that the proceedings are held in relation to the same conduct that falls within the Court's interest but against different persons is also insufficient. The State must be carrying out steps directed at ascertaining whether these suspects are responsible for substantially the same conduct as is the subject of the proceedings before the Court. The objective of this provision of the Statute was primarily to ensure that specific persons would not be able to avoid criminal responsibility for committed acts.[68] Moreover, in such a situation, there is no risk that a person will be tried twice for the same offence and the question of a conflict of jurisdictions does not exist.

In turn, when examining the complementarity principle with respect to the situation in Côte d'Ivoire, the Prosecutor informed that although no proceedings regarding acts falling within the Court's jurisdiction were in progress in this state (in relation to the persons most involved in the conflict), lawyers of the state's president had notified a French court about the commission of crimes against humanity. The Prosecutor had to analyse the cases pending in France but finally concluded that none of them pertained to the events or persons that were within his interest.[69] He also found that the national proceedings did not concern the persons who were to the greatest extent responsible for the events undergoing examination.

Introducing of the complementarity principle aims at encouraging states to exercise their own jurisdiction over crimes that fall within the Court's jurisdiction.[70] The Statute provided for certain mechanisms of co-operation with states to share information that should ensure that, at any time, a state can choose to exercise its jurisdiction over a given case. Within 1 month of receipt of that notification, a state may inform the Court that it is investigating or has investigated its nationals or others within its jurisdiction with respect to criminal acts that may constitute crimes referred to in Article 5 and that relate to the information provided in the notification to states. At the request of that state, the Prosecutor shall defer to the State's investigation of those persons unless the Pre-Trial Chamber, on the application of

---

[68] *The Prosecutor v. William Samoei Ruto, Henry Kiprono Kosgey And Joshua Arap Sang*, ICC-01/09-01/11, Judgment on the appeal of the Republic of Kenya against the decision of Pre-Trial, Chamber II of 30 May 2011 entitled "Decision on the Application by the Government of Kenya Challenging the Admissibility of the Case Pursuant to Article 19(2)(b) of the Statute", decision of 30 August 2011, § 45–47.

[69] *Situation in the Republic of Côte d'Ivoire*, Prosecution's provision of additional information in relation to its request for authorisation of an investigation pursuant to Article 15, ICC-02/11-7-Red, 16 August 2011, § 9.

[70] Paper on some policy issues before the Office of the Prosecutor, September 2003, on the following websites: http://www.icc-cpi.int/nr/rdonlyres/1fa7c4c6-de5f-42b7-8b25-60aa962ed8b6/143594/030905_policy_paper.pdf. Accessed 18 Mar 2013, pp. 4–5. The same problems analysed extensively in: Hall (2009), pp. 219–220; Milik (2012), p. 190; Cryer (2005), pp. 145–149.

the Prosecutor, decides to authorise the investigation (Article 18(2) of the Statute).[71]

On the other hand, the solution provided for in the Statute was also intended to prevent the impunity of perpetrators. There are two mechanisms that enable the Prosecutor to control the actions of a state in the deferred case. The first institution is the state's obligation to provide information: "When the Prosecutor has deferred an investigation in accordance with paragraph 2, the Prosecutor may request that the State concerned periodically inform the Prosecutor of the progress of its investigations and any subsequent prosecutions. The State's Parties shall respond to such requests without undue delay". The second mechanism involves a review conducted to verify whether the state fulfilled its obligation to prosecute: "The Prosecutor's deferral to a State's investigation shall be open to review by the Prosecutor six months after the date of deferral or at any time when there has been a significant change of circumstances based on the State's unwillingness or inability genuinely to carry out the investigation" (Article 18(3) of the Rome Statute). If the review demonstrates that the state is still "unwilling or genuinely unable to carry out the investigation or prosecution", the precondition of complementarity of the ICC's jurisdiction is activated again. In consequence, the adopted regulation of the complementarity principle is "complicated and baroque". As G. Turone observes "this regulation is liable to give rise to an inextricable entanglement of notifications, counter-notifications, challenges, complaints, judicial reviews entrusted to the Pre-trial Chamber and appeals, such as to substantially hamper any serious investigation".[72] Writing 12 years later it is hard to disagree, although no such problems have yet occurred.

3.3.5 *Interests of Justice*

Despite taking the gravity of crimes and interests of the victims into account, there may still appear significant reasons to believe that an investigation would not serve the interests of justice. The Prosecutor may refuse to initiate an investigation if he demonstrates "that an investigation would not serve the interests of justice" (Article 53(1)(c) of the Statute). This decision must be taken on the basis of all the circumstances of the case, in particular the gravity of the crime and the interests of victims. It does not mean, though, that the Prosecutor must prove a positive thesis (as was in the case of the former paragraphs of Article 53(1)): that an investigation "would serve the interests of justice". In fact, the Prosecutor needs to notify the Chamber only when he concludes that there are no interests of justice in the

[71] It is obvious that without authorisation, there can be no investigation in the case when the Prosecutor initiates an investigation *proprio motu*. If the case is not pending, then it cannot be transferred.

[72] Cit. after: Turone (2002), p. 1142.

prosecution. It has not been specified, however, what the Prosecutor should consider as serving (or not) the interests of justice; "the Prosecutor is invited to balance all relevant circumstances".[73] The assessment of this parameter is entirely arbitrary and depends on the Prosecutor's discretion. The standard of "not serving the interests of justice" may be defined more precisely by the Pre-Trial Chamber when the Prosecutor refuses for the first time to initiate an investigation on the basis of the above precondition. So far, the Prosecutor has never relied on this parameter to support his decision not to initiate an investigation.

In order to shed more light on this precondition, the Office of the Prosecutor published the Policy Paper on the Interests of Justice in September 2007.[74] These guidelines encourage the Prosecutor to take into account the following circumstances when analysing whether or not proceeding with a case would serve the interest of justice:

- the gravity of the crime;
- the interests of the victims;
- the particular circumstances of the accused—for example, international justice may not be served by the prosecution of a terminally ill defendant or a suspect who has been the subject of abuse amounting to serious human rights violations;
- the alleged status or hierarchical level of the accused or implication in particularly serious or notorious crimes, that is, the significance of the role of the accused in the overall commission of crimes and the degree of the accused's involvement (actual commission, ordering, indirect participation).

The guidelines indicate that, first of all, the Prosecutor needs to bear in mind that his task is to ensure to put an end to impunity and to ensure that the most serious crimes do not go unpunished. Therefore, he should assess whether prosecution by the ICC is the only way to punish perpetrators and whether the concerned states themselves would be able to perform the obligation to prosecute. The Prosecutor should consider the state of a conflict under which the crimes were committed and any potential adverse impact on security and crime prevention that the Court's intervention may have. Pursuant to these guidelines, only in exceptional circumstances will the Prosecutor of the ICC conclude that an investigation or a prosecution may not serve the interests of justice: there is a presumption in favour of an investigation or prosecution. The document also emphasises that it would be hard to imagine criminal proceedings on international law crimes that would not serve the interests of justice.[75]

---

[73] Cit. after: deGuzman and Schabas (2013), p. 146.

[74] Policy Paper on the Interest of Justice, September 2007, p. 7, http://icc-cpi.int/NO./rdonlyres/772C95C9-F54D-4321-BF09-73422BB23528/143640/ICCOTPInterestsOfJustice.pdf. Accessed 19 Sept 2014.

[75] More on the guidelines: Ohlin (2009), p. 188; Guariglia (2009), p. 210; Schabas (2008), p. 749; Brubacher (2004), pp. 80–84.

By enumerating factors that may stand behind the decision, the OTP admitted that when taking a decision to initiate proceedings, the Prosecutor needs to take into account not only the interests of justice but also those of peace and international security. It stressed that the two concepts should not be identified with one another. It further conceded that there might be a conflict between these two. First of all, it should not be forgotten that "the broader matter of international peace and security is not the responsibility of the Prosecutor; it falls within the mandate of other institutions". Moreover, political factors should never hamper punishment of the guilty. Differentiation between the interests of justice and interests of peace gives rise to some interpretative concerns with regard to the powers of the Security Council. Namely, it may lead to the assumption that there are no grounds for the Security Council to make a "referral of a situation" to the ICC as it has powers to make it by the UN Charter, i.e., when it aims at protecting the "interests of peace" but not the interests of justice.[76]

When considering the meaning of the term "interests of justice" as presented by the Office of the Prosecutor, it should be borne in mind that these guidelines are a document prepared solely for the Office's internal needs. They are not binding for other participants in the proceedings. They do not necessarily have to overlap with the definition adopted by the Court's judges. The assumptions presented in the guidelines are also not binding for the Court. The participants in the proceedings may not rely on them as a valid interpretation of this provision before the Court. Moreover, they should not be treated as a precedent. They are the words of the Prosecutor that held the office at that time, and the current Prosecutor may even express a different opinion.[77]

3.3.6 Gravity of the Case

The parameter that is absent from Article 53 but that is also decisive for the admissibility of the Court's jurisdiction pursuant to Article 17(1)(d) of the Statute is the gravity of the case. The concept lacks definition; it must be, however, "sufficient to justify further actions by the Court". It must be also distinguished from the concept used in Article 53, which provides that the Prosecutor, evaluating whether an investigation "would not serve the interests of justice", has to take into consideration "the gravity of the crime". In this context, "gravity of the crime" occurs as an element of evaluation of the "reasonable basis to proceed". These two concepts should be assessed separately. On the other hand, it is difficult not to

[76] The difference between these two concepts is also emphasised by: Schabas (2010), p. 749; Ohlin (2009), p. 200; Stahn (2009), p. 269. At the same time it has been stated that "the Prosecutor has been given the necessary political discretion to evaluate the convenience of starting a criminal prosecution in order to achieve a certain political goal identified as the 'interests of justice'", cit. after: Olásolo (2003), p. 110.

[77] See: Ohlin (2009), p. 200; Stahn (2009), p. 263.

notice that all cases of international law crimes fall into the category of "grave" cases.[78] As a result, it became necessary to establish certain preconditions to assist the Prosecutor in deciding whether the gravity of a case provides the grounds to initiate proceedings.

The first group of preconditions includes criteria adopted through case law. In *The Prosecutor v. Lubanga*, the Court concluded that "the gravity threshold is in addition to the drafters' careful selection of crimes included in articles 6 to 8 of the Statute [. . .]. Hence, the fact that a case addresses one of the most serious crimes for the international community as a whole is not sufficient for it to be admissible before the Court".[79]

The Pre-Trial Chamber indicated that when examining whether this threshold has been met, it takes the following factors into account:

(1) whether the committed acts were widespread and systematic;
(2) the seriousness of the impact of the acts on the international peace;
(3) whether the person who has been accused of committing the acts may be included in the category of "top leaders" in the case in question.

The judges of the Pre-Trial Chamber had no doubts about the relationship between the gravity of the case and the position held in a state hierarchy by the accused. The obligation to focus on cases that are sufficiently grave should entail that only the "top officials" are charged. Their role should be assessed on the basis of the following three elements: their position in the hierarchy of authority, the role played by them in this hierarchy at the time when their government was involved in the commission of crimes and the role played by them in the commission of crimes. The same preconditions are used for the selection of cases to be prosecuted.[80] The Chamber reasoned that focusing on individuals that satisfy these requirements would maximise the ICC's deterrent effects since persons in such positions are the ones who would be most likely to be able to prevent or stop the commission of large-scale or systematic crimes.

Furthermore, the Pre-Trial Chamber found that "the social alarm in the international community caused by the extent of the crimes"[81] was a significant component in the evaluation of a case's gravity. The existence of a "social alarm" can be proven, *inter alia*, through UN reports presenting circumstances of the committed crimes.

In the same decision, however, the judges failed to acknowledge that the invasion in Iraq and the acts committed by the British soldiers that constituted war crimes, including torturing of prisoners, caused any "social alarm".

---

[78] This conclusion is repeated by many authors, e.g.: Schabas (2008), p. 232; Murphy (2006), pp. 282 et seq.

[79] *The Prosecutor v. Lubanga*, Decision on the Prosecutor's Application for a warrant of arrest. Article 58, ICC-01/04-01/06-8-Corr, § 41.

[80] See: Schabas (2008), pp. 740–741; Smith (2008), pp. 337–338.

[81] See: Schabas (2008), pp. 740–741.

Moreover, in its decision authorising the Prosecutor's decision to initiate the investigation in the situation in Côte d'Ivoire, the Pre-Trial Chamber argued that the gravity of a case should be assessed following a quantitative as well as a qualitative approach. The Pre-Trial Chamber admitted that certainly all crimes that fall within the jurisdiction of the Court are serious, and thus the reference to the lack of gravity is an "additional safeguard" that prevents the Court from investigating, prosecuting and trying "peripheral" cases.[82] Also in the case of Bahar Idriss Abu Garda, who was charged with committing war crimes in Sudan, the Pre-Trial Chamber stated that the gravity of a given case should not be assessed only from a quantitative perspective, i.e. by considering the number of victims, but also their significance—the "qualitative dimension" of the crime—should be taken into consideration.[83]

Second, the Pre-Trial Chamber found that certain factors that may be of relevance to the assessment of gravity are listed in Rule 145(1)(c) RPE. This Rule relates to the determination of sentence. The rule makes reference to "the extent of damage caused, in particular, the harm caused to victims and their families, the nature of the unlawful behaviour and the means employed to execute the crime". Those factors could serve as useful guidelines for the Prosecutor in the process of evaluation of the gravity threshold required by Article 17(l)(d) of the Statute.[84]

It may be noticed that the adoption of such preconditions in the judicial decision significantly limits the discretion of the Prosecutor in making an independent assessment of the gravity of the case.

Documents presented by the Office of the Prosecutor have become the third source of information as to what preconditions are decisive in establishing whether a case can be considered "grave".

First, there are decisions refusing initiation of proceedings due to the lack of sufficient gravity. Of key importance here is the widely criticised decision by which the Prosecutor refused to initiate proceedings following notifications of war crimes committed by British soldiers in Iraq. In 2005, when considering the possibility of initiation of proceedings pertaining to the situation in Iraq, the Prosecutor took into account mainly the number of people killed and victimised as a result of particularly serious crimes that had been committed there and the number of potential victims. He claimed that—having analysed all available information—he was able to establish a reasonable ground to suspect the commission of crimes falling within the jurisdiction of the Court. The Prosecutor highlighted that many various factors should be considered in assessing gravity of this case. However, he came to a conclusion that "a key consideration is the number of victims of particularly serious crimes, such as wilful killing or rape. The number of potential victims of crimes

[82] *Situation in the Republic of Côte d'Ivoire*, ICC-02/11, Decision Pursuant to Article 15 of the Rome Statute on the Authorisation of an Investigation into the Situation in the Republic of Côte d'Ivoire, 3 October 2011, § 201–204.

[83] *The Prosecutor v. Bahar Idriss Abu Garda*, ICC-02/05-02/09, Decision on the Confirmation of Charges, 8 February 2010, § 31–34.

[84] Ibidem.

within the jurisdiction of the Court in this situation – 4 to 12 victims of wilful killing and a limited number of victims of inhuman treatment – was of a different order than the number of victims found in other situations under investigation or analysis by the Office. It is worth bearing in mind that the OTP is currently investigating three situations involving long-running conflicts in Northern Uganda, the Democratic Republic of Congo and Darfur. Each of the three situations under investigation involves thousands of wilful killings as well as intentional and large-scale sexual violence and abductions. Collectively, they have resulted in the displacement of more than 5 million people".[85] The Prosecutor concluded that compared to other cases, the numbers quoted in the case at hand did not justify initiation of an investigation. Its gravity could not be compared with that of other cases in which the Prosecutor examined crimes involving thousands of victims (e.g. 8,000 victims in the Democratic Republic of Congo). The rationale behind other cases indicated that their gravity was considered in quantitative terms. What is the most interesting part of this case, is that on the 13th of May 2014 the Prosecutor decided to "re-open" (using the words of the OTP) the preliminary examination of the situation in Iraq after it had received new communications alleging the responsibility of officials of the United Kingdom for war crimes involving systematic detainee abuse in Iraq from 2003 until 2008. According to the OTP, these communications provided further information that was not available to the Office in 2006. In particular, the communication alleged a higher number of cases of ill-treatment of detainees and provides further details on the factual circumstances and the geographical and temporal scope of the alleged crimes. During the "re-opened" preliminary examination the Prosecutor will again analyse the seriousness of the information received and ultimately determine whether there is a reasonable basis to proceed with an investigation. There are two conclusions that can be drawn from the wording used in this decision – first, it seems that it is still the same "situation" – concerning the same events that were subject to analysis in 2006. Second, what results from the first observation, the Prosecutor recognised his right to analyse every situation without any limits, even if the informal proceedings has been earlier discontinued (as refusal to initiate an investigation should be treated in the same terms as a discontinuation of a case, as it is the case in continental systems). It is noteworthy, however, that while the Prosecutor refused to initiate the proceedings to investigate the situation in Iraq due to the low number of victims, in the case of *The Prosecutor v. Lubanga* that he initiated due to a large number of victims, he did not formulate any charges of genocide but restricted himself to charging the suspect with the crime of child recruitment.[86] This decision shows that, in practice, the gravity precondition was used by the Prosecutor as an excuse for not addressing the situation referred to him. This way, it had become an instrument for justifying decisions that he took in his sole discretion.[87] It has also become an instrument of

[85] Update on Communications Received by the Prosecutor, representation of 10 February 2006, Annex: Iraq response, p. 8.

[86] These issues are discussed comprehensively by: Schabas (2008), p. 735.

[87] See: deGuzman and Schabas (2013), p. 144.

justifying non-prosecution of non-senior leaders, which leads to inability to exercise their jurisdiction over an accused standing lower in the hierarchy, however "'repugnant', 'bestial', 'sadistic', and 'cold-blooded'" he had been. "Such a situation will undoubtedly cause a crisis of confidence in the Court and its ability to effectively cope with the challenges it was designed to confront".[88]

It can also be noted, however, how the "scope of harm" in situations under examination is becoming more limited as compared to the first situations referred to the ICC. The situation in South Korea, where there is an ongoing preliminary examination, concerns the shelling of an island that resulted in the death of four people and the sinking of a warship that killed 46. Another situation pertains to a *coup d'etat* in Honduras that caused six deaths and two instances of sexual violence.[89]

The second group of documents explaining the meaning of the term "gravity" are Papers published by the OTP that were presented after the Prosecutor had familiarised himself with the first case law of the Pre-Trial Chamber pertaining to the gravity parameter. The OTP explained that, when examining the gravity of a case, the Prosecutor would take into account such criteria as scale of the crimes (where the key factor is the quantity of victims), the nature of the crimes, the manner of their commission and their impact.[90]

3.3.7 Sufficient Basis for a Prosecution

The parameters of initiation of an investigation are reassessed by the Prosecutor against the evidence collected during the investigation, when presenting the charges for authorisation by the Pre-Trial Chamber. At this stage of the proceedings, in addition to the aforementioned parameters (that have already been assessed once), the Statute requires that the Prosecutor examines the so-called factual parameter. According to Article 53(2) of the Statute:

> if, upon investigation, the Prosecutor concludes that there is not a sufficient basis for a prosecution because:
> (a) There is not a sufficient legal or factual basis to seek a warrant or summons under Article 58;
> (b) The case is inadmissible under Article 17; or
> (c) A prosecution is not in the interests of justice, taking into account all the circumstances, including the gravity of the crime, the interests of victims and the age or infirmity of the

[88] Cit. after: Smith (2008), p. 350.

[89] Which leads in consequence to an expansion of jurisdiction of the ICC; see: deGuzman (2012–2013), p. 43.

[90] Policy Paper on the Interest of Justice, September 2007. On the sideline, it is worth mentioning that, in the situation where the Security Council refers a case to the Prosecutor, the latter's refusal to proceed with it due to the "insufficient gravity of a case" would be believed to undermine the Court's credibility. As noticed by: Ohlin (2009), p. 200; and Schabas (2008), p. 233.

> alleged perpetrator, and his or her role in the alleged crime – he should inform the Pre-Trial Chamber and the State making a referral or the Security Council, of his or her conclusion and the reasons for the conclusion.

This parameter is assessed by the Prosecutor upon completion of the investigation. The Prosecutor refuses to proceed with a case if he decides that there is no sufficient basis for prosecution due to the lack of sufficient—legal or factual—basis for formulating charges. This will happen, for example, in a situation where the Prosecutor has failed to find the perpetrators of crimes. On the basis of the evidence collected during the investigation, the Prosecutor also examines whether he is going to be able to prove that the accused has committed the alleged crime and that all criteria of the crime have been met and that the accused assumed a particular role. Using this provision as a basis, the Prosecutor may, therefore, refuse to proceed in the event of lack of evidence.[91] This can happen before or after selecting a defendant - both in a situation where the Prosecutor has failed to find the perpetrators of crimes or proof of the perpetrator's guilt.

When examining the reasons for the refusal to proceed with an investigation, at this stage of the case the Prosecutor needs to reconsider whether the case is admissible pursuant to Article 17 and whether a prosecution is not in the interests of justice—taking into account all the circumstances, including the gravity of the crime, the interests of victims and the age or infirmity of the alleged perpetrator and his or her role in the alleged crime. Thus, these factors are assessed twice by the Prosecutor (earlier pursuant to Article 53(1) of the Statute). In paragraph 2 of Article 53, however, they appear in a different context. Actually, only at this stage of the proceedings that the Prosecutor is able to conclude whether the case is admissible pursuant to Article 17 of the Statute, as he was only then capable of indicating the perpetrator. As long as he was unable to do so, he was also unable to determine beyond any doubt whether the condition of nationality was met or whether the proceedings are consistent with the principle of complementarity. The assessment of whether interests of justice exist or not must, in this context, be made from another perspective. Only when the perpetrator is determined can his age and health be assessed, together with his role in the commission of a crime.

The refusal of the Pre-Trial Chamber to authorise the investigation does not mean that the *ne bis in idem* principle can be applied. The Prosecutor may collect new facts and evidence proving that the crime has been committed and present to the Pre-Trial Chamber a new request to authorise this decision to initiate an investigation (Article 15(5) of the ICC Statute).

---

[91] See: Schabas (2010), p. 666, and Bergsmo and Kruger (2008), p. 1073.

3.4 Model of Mandatory Prosecution Versus Prosecutorial Discretion

The decision to initiate an investigation by the international criminal tribunal prosecutor has been an element of a broader discussion concerning the operation of the principle of opportunism vs. principle of legalism. Application of either of these two principles is one of the defining components of the accusation model adopted in a given legal system.[92] In national legal systems, the principle of opportunism (opportunité des poursuites) is usually identified with the principle of prosecutorial discretion associated with common law states (mostly Anglo-Saxon). Both principles are based on a presumption that it is only for the prosecutor to decide which offences and offenders should be prosecuted and on which counts. The prosecutorial discretion principle gives investigative authorities liberty to decide on how to proceed in cases of punishable acts that have come to their attention—whether to initiate criminal proceedings, to choose another, non-penal, way of reacting to law infringement or whether to take no action at all. The authority is not so much obliged as it is entitled to act. It is said that, historically, the informality of proceedings and the absence of lawyers and of regular channels of review "provided an ample room for 'discretionary' departure from instructions contained in manuals"; decision-making by local justices of the peace was "strongly influenced by prevailing community norms, rather than by technical legal rules detached from their social matrix".[93]

As opposed to that principle, *Legalitätsprinzip* or principle of *legalité de poursuites* prevails in continental legal systems, where all those who infringe the law must be prosecuted (the so-called *principle of mandatory prosecution*). In such a model, there is no prosecutorial discretion—the mandatory prosecution principle "establishes the obligation to initiate and to conduct the proceedings" because "no person should be exempted from liability for the committed crime"[94]; it is a "directive pursuant to which the sheer probability that a crime has been committed obliges the competent authorities to initiate and conduct criminal proceedings".[95] The model of accusation based on this principle requires prosecution of all offences where sufficient evidence exists of the guilt of the defendant. Discretion is minimised and limited by the frames of the law, and the prosecutor is precluded from taking a proactive diversionary role. However, at the same time, it cannot be denied that discretion can also function as well within the system of mandatory prosecution—although in certain limits provided by the law and in smaller quantities. "Claims that prosecutorial discretion has been eliminated, or is supervised

[92] Damaška (1986), p. 22.

[93] Damaška (1986), p. 41.

[94] Cit. after: Waltoś (2005), pp. 289 and 291.

[95] Cit. after: Cieślak (1984), p. 291, and more information about these two principles in numerous positions, e.g.: Cassese (2009), p. 471; Langbein (1973–1974), p. 443; Herrmannt (1973–1974), p. 468; Tylman (1965), pp. 42 and 112; Rogacka-Rzewnicka (2007), p. 46; Weigend (1976), pp. 17 et seq.

closely, are exaggerated", as discretion is exercised in each of the systems for reasons similar to those supporting it in the United States, although by the use of different means: e.g., by manipulating legal characterisation of facts or extending the notion of minor guilt or lack of social interest or definition of a socially dangerous act—which leads to excluding such an act from the category of crimes.[96]

Nowadays, it can hardly be said that a certain system of criminal procedure is strictly opportunist or legalist. The proliferation of exemptions that favour the principle of opportunism in continental systems is a result of the gradually growing emphasis on the pragmatism of prosecution and the desired cost-effectiveness of the administration of justice.[97] However, even in the situation where all the systems of criminal procedure are more and more subjected to convergence, nobody dares to deny the central role of opportunism and legalism for the certain legal tradition.[98] Still two models can be isolated: states where the principle of opportunism is the legal rule and in which the principle of legalism is the main rule, states that traditionally adopt one legal principle.

3.4.1 *Model of Opportunism in the United States*

In common law states, the sole fact that investigative organs have information about a crime does not mean that they will start an investigation. The prosecutor's discretion in deciding whether to start an investigation, or whether to discontinue it or file an indictment, is almost unlimited. This decision is taken on the basis of assessment of profitability of the case: both in financial and legal terms. This power is often referred to as "prosecutorial discretion". This notion means that it is up to the prosecutor to decide whether a specific case and a certain defendant (defendants) will be brought to criminal trial.[99]

Discretion is seen as a positive achievement of the systems of common law states: as it "can individualize the implementation of the law, softening the harshness or injustices that sometimes arise from rules dispassionately applied".[100]

---

[96] E.g. Goldstein and Marcus (1977), p. 280. The same problem discussed in: Kuczyńska (2015) in print.

[97] See opinions expressed in: Rogacka-Rzewnicka (2007), pp. 96 and 127; Volk (2006), p. 113; Safferling (2001), p. 174.

[98] Extensively on this topic: Rogacka-Rzewnicka (2007), pp. 19 and 129; Tylman (1965), pp. 112 and 42; Ambos (2000b), pp. 98–101. Discussing the principles of opportunity and legality, M. Andrzejewska rightly indicates that "the most important dogma of criminal proceedings at the turn of the 19th and 20th centuries is the principal role of directive models governing the most important procedural issues. It is symptomatic that the procedural principles developed in the past have been consistently functioning, i.e. despite the numerous divergences, nobody dares to eliminate them from the procedure": Andrzejewska (2013), p. 141.

[99] See this notion defined in e.g.: Cane and Conaghan (2008), p. 330; Cassese (2009), p. 471; Fionda (1995), p. 9.

[100] Cit. after: Cane and Conaghan (2008), p. 330.

In such a model of accusation, the mere commission of an offence and probable guilt of a given offender do not necessarily trigger the formal legal procedure of prosecution and trial. In consequence, the prosecutor is not obliged to prosecute any case simply because it can be prosecuted. Therefore, we can see that prosecutors have powers to set the boundaries of a coherent criminal justice policy. This power allows them to decide about intensification of criminal reaction they choose to apply in a given case. In the literature, it is concluded that discretionary non-prosecution arises out of practical policies—"if the rule of compulsory prosecution were strictly applied, the growth of new categories of minor crime in the statutes and the increase of reported crimes of all types would submerge the prosecution of serious crime in a sea of less important cases".[101] In the Anglo-Saxon doctrine, it is believed that it is simply not possible to prosecute all the criminal acts: "as the volume of crime increases and offense categories proliferate, even serious crimes are not fully prosecuted because it might be unduly time consuming to conduct a full investigation".

The prosecutor's discretion may include many factors. Foremost, he has to decide if there was a crime: if a certain human act or omission fulfils all the elements of a crime. It relates also to a decision as to whom to prosecute: the prosecutor has the power to select defendants from all the persons possibly involved in a criminal conduct. Moreover, he also chooses what criminal behaviour to accuse the defendant (both referring to factual and legal borders of a certain behaviour expressed in the form of the legal charaterisation of facts). He also decides about the timing of an indictment—when to initiate an investigation. Last but not least, he decides whether to engage in the *plea bargaining* process: whether to apply his discretion in order to stop criminal reaction in exchange for a guilty plea and quick termination of the proceedings. This leads to the problem of prosecutor's powers to intensify criminal prosecution in general, whether to initiate criminal reaction to a certain behaviour or to restrain from bringing the social conflict to the court and limit the judicial influence on a situation to making a bargain in a process of negotiations between the suspect and the prosecutor. Therefore, the result of using discretionary powers by the prosecutor is selectivity of prosecution: meaning not only selective choice of persons that are brought to justice but also the law to be enforced.[102] It leads also to obvious disadvantageous results: the same crimes are not treated alike. As it allows an individual to act as that individual chooses, the choice of that method must accept the consequences: the individual may act on the basis of improper considerations, substituting personal standards for public, legal standards.

The United States have become the state, where this principle occurs in its most pure form. The U.S. Supreme Court—in the most cited case on that subject—emphasised that "so long as the prosecutor has probable cause to believe that the accused committed an offense defined by statute, the decision whether or not to

[101] Cit after: Langbein (1973–1974), p. 459.

[102] in similar words in: Kuczyńska (2015), in print. .

prosecute, and what charge to file or bring before a grand jury, generally rests entirely in his discretion".[103] Within the limits set by the legislature, the conscious exercise of some selectivity in enforcement is not, in itself, a federal constitutional violation so long as the selection is not deliberately based upon an unjustifiable standard such as race, religion or other arbitrary classification. It is not even considered inappropriate to make this assessment based on the prospects for "winning" the case—that is, assessing whether the jury would find the accused guilty. In consequence, the American prosecutor will not file an indictment in a case that he would consider to be doomed to fail.[104]

The US legal practice shows that the freedom to decide whether to seek an indictment proves indispensable where some factors prevent prosecution of all perpetrators of prohibited acts. Among these factors, several of the most common are named: "overcriminalisation"—as the criminal laws are drafted without regard to possible enforceability or changing social concepts; limitations in available enforcement resources: both in personal as in financial terms; a need to apply criminal laws in an individualised way, adapted to the individual position and interests of the defendant, also in order to relieve him from unnecessary harm; finally, the opinion expressed by the victim, who may not be willing to prosecute the offender, especially when the harm done by the offender can be corrected without prosecution.[105]

Moreover, "the discretion of investigative organs in deciding how to react to a crime is a consequence of the adopted structure of investigation, which lacks formal requirements and rigid procedures and is characterized by pragmatism typical for the whole common law tradition".[106] An obvious consequence of this liberty is the right to conclude procedural agreements with the accused (in a process of plea bargaining). Due to the broad applicability of the principle of opportunism in the United States and investigators' right to restrain from prosecuting certain acts, and to alter the legal characterisation of facts to one that is more favourable for the accused in exchange for them pleading guilty, the conclusion of a plea agreement is the main way to wind up a criminal case.

Prosecutorial discretion is, however, not unlimited. There are numerous restrictions on the decision to prosecute. Some stem from statutes or similar sources, such as internal policies, while others are of a non-legal nature.

Most commonly, statutes decide that the prosecutor's decision is taken on the basis of two factors:

(a) sufficiency of evidence test, and
(b) if the evidence is sufficient, whether there are reasons not to prosecute.

---

[103] *Bordenkircher v. Hayes*, 434 U.P. 357 (1978), Supreme Court, 18 January 1978.

[104] See: Ambos (2000b), p. 98; Trüg (2003), p. 95.

[105] In more detail: LaFave et al. (2009), pp. 710–711 and 733–736.

[106] Cit. after: Rogacka-Rzewnicka (2007), p. 21.

The most obvious reason for non-prosecution is insufficiency of evidence. We may encounter two situations here: first, the prosecutor, after analysing the evidence presented to him by the police, may decide that the suspect is clearly innocent. Second, he may come to the conclusion that, despite his personal belief in the guilt of the accused, the evidentiary material does not satisfy the standard that would be sufficient to prove the guilt of the accused beyond reasonable doubt.[107]

Another source of restrictions on prosecutorial discretion is the manuals and sets of standards prepared by prosecutor's offices. They present the general policies that are to guide the exercise of prosecutorial discretion, describing the factors that should be taken into consideration by the prosecutors. They are also supposed to ensure consistent charging and prosecuting policy.[108] One such set of guidelines (which will be used here as an example of this general practice) is found in the United States Attorneys' Manual.[109] It includes extensive instructions as to when the attorney for the government should commence prosecution: if he believes that the person's conduct constitutes a Federal offence and that the admissible evidence will probably be sufficient to obtain and sustain a conviction, unless, in his judgment, prosecution should be declined because

- no substantial Federal interest would be served by prosecution (and defines the meaning of this criterion),
- the person is subject to effective prosecution in another jurisdiction,
- there exists an adequate non-criminal alternative to prosecution.

Non-legal restrictions may vary and are subject to the prosecutor's own assessment. Thus, the prosecutor may resign from pursuing an indictment at the victim's request or upon deciding that it would be not fair or reasonable to prosecute a given person for a crime he has committed.[110] The prosecutor's ability to assess whether his personal sense of justice is not at odds with the indictment may have more significance in systems that have more restrictive criminal law. In many jurisdictions, such as Texas, California, Washington, Arkansas and Arizona, there operates (in differing versions) the doctrine of the "three strikes law".[111] According to this doctrine, a three-time offender is required to serve life imprisonment if two of his previous offences were included in a list of serious crimes. However, the third violation can be of any type. In such a situation, the prosecutor's sensibility may lead him to a decision not to prosecute the third concurrent offence. Another factual factor behind non-prosecution may result from economic concerns—where the costs of the prosecution would be excessive, considering the nature of the violation,

---

[107] As regards the American system stated in: Worrall (2007), p. 310.

[108] In general see: LaFave et al. (2009), p. 714.

[109] The United States Attorneys' Criminal Resource Manual, 9-27.220: http://www.justice.gov/usao/eousa/foia_reading_room/usam/title9/27mcrm.htm#9-27.200. Accessed 9 Sept 2014.

[110] See: Worrall (2007), pp. 310 and 312.

[111] Texas Penal Code Section 1242(d); California Penal Code Sections 667(e)(2)(A)(ii) and 1170.12(c)(2)(A)(ii).

the prosecutor may take a decision not to proceed with prosecution as it would be not cost-effective and would lead to a waste of the taxpayers' money.

The law may also define situations in which the prosecutor cannot bring charges. There are three important reasons why the prosecutor may not prosecute a particular case: first, if such a prosecution would be unfair and selective, when a prosecution would be pursued for vindictive reasons and when it could be assessed as being in disregard of statutory intent.[112] Prosecution is selective when an individual is prosecuted merely because he belongs to a certain group and was selected on arbitrary grounds. Here, the Manual lists by which factors the prosecutor should not be influenced: the person's race, religion, sex, national origin or political association, activities or beliefs; the attorney's own personal feelings concerning the person, the person's associates or the victim; or the possible effect of the decision on the attorney's own professional or personal circumstances. As an example of such a decision, a case decided by the Wisconsin Court of Appeals is commonly mentioned. In this case, a female dancer was prosecuted, while her male patrons were not, although the Wisconsin law penalised both behaviours.[113] When the prosecutor brings charges against an individual because he is motivated by revenge, prosecution is vindictive.[114] The US Supreme Court had no doubts that if a prosecutor changes an indictment by lodging more serious charges against a defendant in retaliation for filing an appeal by this defendant, he does it for vindictive reasons.

The third reason for non-prosecution is applicable only when there are two different statutes that are duplicative or overlapping and they provide for different sanctions for the same behaviour. In such a situation, the prosecutor should conclude that the intent of the legislature was to limit criminal responsibility to the statute providing for lower penalty.[115] If he neglects the existence of duplicative statutes, the defendant may challenge the prosecutor's selection of a statutory scheme under which the prosecutor acted.[116]

Prosecutorial discretion is also applied to the decision to proceed on particular charges: lesser charges or a smaller number of charges than it would be possible to lodge against the defendant. This attitude stays in compliance with the general belief according to which full enforcement of the criminal statutes is neither possible nor desired.[117]

---

[112] See: *The United States Attorneys' Manual*, Section 9-27.260: http://www.justice.gov/usao/eousa/foia_reading_room/usam/title9/27mcrm.htm#9-27.200. Accessed 9 Sept 2014.

[113] *State v. McCollum*, 159 Wip.2d 184 (1990), Court of Appeals of Wisconsin, 14.11.1990.

[114] *Blackledge v. Perry*, 417 U.P. 21 (1974), Supreme Court, 20 May 1974; *United States v. Goodwin*, 457 U.P. 368 (1982), Supreme Court, 18 June 1982.

[115] *United States v. Batchelder*, 442 U.P. 114 (1979), Supreme Court, 4 June 1979.

[116] See: LaFave et al. (2009), p. 737.

[117] See: LaFave et al. (2009), p. 710.

3.4.2 Model of Opportunism in England and Wales

There are two distinctive features of the English model of opportunism. First of all, this model provides for a broad range of alternatives to prosecution, depending on the nature of the suspected offence. These are e.g. administering a formal caution (including also conditional caution) and issuing a fixed penalty notice.[118] These measures can be administered by the police, in co-operation with the prosecutor, as it is the prosecutor who decides whether a suspect should be charged and whether administering a caution would better serve the interests of justice.[119] The second characteristic feature of this model is introducing detailed criteria that have to be taken into consideration by the prosecutor when deciding to initiate a prosecution.

These detailed criteria pursuant to which the prosecutor is to decide whether to initiate the proceedings and what charges should be presented are provided for in the Code for Crown Prosecutors.[120] Pursuant to the Code, the prosecutor must, foremost, decide whether a particular case meets the following two conditions (the so-called *Full Code Test*): the *sufficiency of evidence test* and the *public interest test* (section 4.1 of the Code). The first condition signifies that prosecutors must be satisfied that there is sufficient evidence to provide a "realistic prospect of conviction against each suspect on each charge". They must consider what the defence case may be and how it is likely to affect the prospects of conviction. In the process, they should take into consideration whether an objective, impartial and reasonable jury or bench of magistrates or judge hearing a case alone, properly directed and acting in accordance with the law, is more likely than not to convict the defendant of the charge alleged. In order to answer that question, the prosecutor should consider certain circumstances, as provided in the Code (section 4.6):

(1) Can the evidence be used in court—if there is any question over the admissibility of certain evidence

    (a) The likelihood of that evidence being held as inadmissible by the court; and
    (b) The importance of that evidence in relation to the evidence as a whole.

(2) Is the evidence reliable?—whether there are any reasons to question the reliability of the evidence, including its accuracy or integrity;
(3) Is the evidence credible?—whether there are any reasons to doubt the credibility of the evidence.

A case that does not pass the evidential stage must not proceed, no matter how serious or sensitive it may be. On the other hand, the availability of sufficient

[118] See: Sprack (2012), pp. 75–79; Padfield (2008), p. 164.

[119] Criminal Justice Act 2003, section 22(2), http://www.legislation.gov.uk/ukpga/2003/44/section/22. Accessed 9 Sept 2014.

[120] Code for Crown Prosecutors, http://www.cpp.gov.uk/publications/docs/code_2013_accessible_english.pdf. Accessed 9 Sept 2014.

evidence itself should not automatically result in a prosecution. In every case, where there is sufficient evidence to justify prosecution, prosecutors must go on to consider whether a prosecution is required in the public interest. This test is also made on the basis of factors as provided by the Code for Crown Prosecutors (section 4.12). Examining the possible existence of the public interest in prosecution, prosecutors should consider each of the questions set out in the Code so as to identify and determine the relevant public interest factors tending for and against prosecution:

(a) How serious is the committed offence? Usually, the more serious the offence is, the more likely it is that a prosecution is required. They should include among the factors for consideration the suspect's culpability and the harm to the victim.
(b) What is the level of culpability of the suspect? The greater the suspect's level of culpability is, the more likely it is that prosecution is required. According to the Code, this level is determined by such factors as the suspect's level of involvement; the extent to which the offending was premeditated and/or planned; whether he has previous criminal convictions and/or out-of-court disposals and any offending while on bail or while subject to a court order; whether the offending was or is likely to be continued, repeated or escalated; and the suspect's age or maturity.
(c) What are the circumstances of and the harm caused to the victim? As a general rule, the greater is the vulnerability of the victim (because of his age or a position of trust or authority that exists between the suspect and the victim), the greater public interest there is in prosecution. In deciding whether a prosecution is required in the public interest, prosecutors should take into account the views expressed by the victim (or victim's family) about the impact that the offence has had.
(d) Was the suspect under the age of 18 at the time of the offence?
(e) What is the impact on the community?
(f) Is prosecution a proportionate response? The relevant factors are the cost to the CPS and possibility of effective case management. The prosecutor is advised to consider whether, in a case involving multiple suspects, prosecution might be reserved for the main participants in order to avoid excessively long and complex proceedings.
(g) Do sources of information require protecting?

The list of the factors is not, of course, exhaustive.[121] They should also not be assessed separately. The prosecutor should decide how important each factor is in this particular case and make an overall assessment. Another important aspect of these factors is their specificity that significantly limits the prosecutorial discretion in deciding whether to file an indictment and leaves one asking whether in the case

[121] For more information on the Code and the Full Code Test, see: Ward and Wragg (2005), p. 535; Padfield (2008), p. 166 and 184–191; Sprack (2012), pp. 79–80.

of the English model one can still speak of the opportunism of prosecution. Some scholars argue that putting in writing the rules to be followed by prosecutors while making decisions whether to proceed with prosecution imposes certain limitations on the principle of opportunism that, as a result, is never unconditional.[122]

In addition to the decision whether to prosecute or not, there is also the question of adopting the appropriate legal characterisation of the facts of the case. The Code requires that charges should be formulated according to certain rules. Prosecutors should select charges that

- reflect the seriousness and extent of the offending supported by the evidence;
- give the court adequate powers to sentence and impose appropriate post-conviction orders; and
- enable the case to be presented in a clear and simple way (section 6.1 of the Code).

Prosecutors should never go ahead with more charges than are necessary simply to encourage a defendant to plead guilty to a few. In the same way, they should never go ahead with a more serious charge just to encourage a defendant to plead guilty to a less serious one.

In the criminal procedure of England and Wales, the decision to adopt a given legal characterisation of facts is of principal importance for two reasons:

(1) Firstly, the characterisation of an act adopted by the prosecutor determines the mode of trial. There are three types of crimes tried subject to separate procedures. These are a trial involving a jury in the Crown Court (trial on indictment) or summary trial before Magistrates' Courts. The third group includes crimes that may be tried in two ways, and it is up to the prosecutor to decide which approach should be adopted (*offences triable either way*). The prosecutor must choose between these modes when making submissions to the Magistrates' Court about where the defendant should be tried. Speed must never be the only reason for asking for a case to stay in the Magistrates' Court. But prosecutors should consider the effect of any likely delay if a case is sent to the Crown Court and the possible effect on any victim or witness if the case is delayed (section 8.2).
(2) Secondly, the characterisation adopted by the prosecutor is binding for the court. The latter may only adjudicate as to whether the defendant has committed an act as described by the elements of a crime in a form of a certain legal characterisation but may not adopt its own. Once an indictment has been lodged before a court, modification of the legal characterisation of facts, leading to changes in the procedure, may be allowed in exceptional cases only. However, this is offset by the operation of the unique principle of judicial review of the prosecutor's decisions. The legal characterisation of facts presented by the prosecutor may be challenged by the accused who may claim that a different

[122] Conclusion presented by: Rogacka-Rzewnicka (2007), pp. 218–219.

characterisation, more accurately reflecting the true facts of the case, would enable a trial involving a jury.[123]

3.4.3 *Principle of Legalism in Poland and Germany*

Unlike in common law systems, according to the continental tradition, the prosecutor is obliged to issue a decision on the initiation of an investigation every time there is a justified suspicion that a crime has been committed. In its essence, the principle of legalism[124] deprives the prosecution of the option to assess whether evidence is convincing for the court or even whether there are reasonable grounds for prosecution. It imposes on the competent authorities "the obligation to initiate and proceed with criminal proceedings".[125] There is not much room left for discretion to prosecute: whenever the evidence collected in a case makes commission of a crime probable, investigation must be initiated.

The principle of legalism has become a staple in states that remain under the influence of German legal culture. It is demonstrated in §152(2) of the German StPO, according to which: "except as otherwise provided by law, the public prosecution office shall be obliged to take action in relation to all prosecutable criminal offences, provided there are sufficient factual indications" (so-called *Legalitätsprinzip*). Also, Article 10 of the Polish Code of Criminal Proceedings provides that "the agency responsible for prosecuting offences shall have the duty to institute and conduct the preparatory proceedings, and the public prosecutor shall have also the obligation to bring and support charges, with respect to an offence prosecuted". In the continental tradition, the "legality maxim" is often considered to be the expression of the rule of law, which is understood as enforcing the law whenever it is violated; this doctrine accepts that equal treatment of the perpetrators of crimes necessitates their equal prosecution, as only such a model of accusation provides for equality before the law.[126] The prosecutor issues an order instituting investigation always when "there is good reason to suspect that an offence has been committed" (Article 303 CCP; § 160 StPO). Thus, whereas common law states provide prosecutors with long lists of criteria that must be followed when deciding whether to file an indictment before the court, in continental systems the existence of a "suspicion" that a crime has been committed (*der Verdacht* in German) has become a determinant of the decision to initiate an investigation. Therefore, the

[123] *R v. Redbridge Justices, ex parte Whitehouse*, (1992) 94 Cr App R 332; *R v. Sheffield Justices, ex parte Director of Public Prosecutions*, [1993] Crim LR 136. In general see: Sprack (2012), p. 127; Fionda (1995), pp. 51–52.

[124] Known also as "the rule of compulsory prosecution"; see: Langbein (1973–1974), p. 443; Herrmannt (1973–1974), p. 468.

[125] The limits and scope of this obligation discussed, e.g., in: Cieślak (1984), p. 291; Rogacka-Rzewnicka (2007), p. 46; Weigend (1976), pp. 17 et seq.

[126] See: Herrmannt (1973–1974), p. 470; Trüg (2003), pp. 72–75; Röben (2003), p. 523.

definition of a "reasonable (grounded) suspicion" is a central issue for the prosecutor's decision to initiate proceedings. Only when such a suspicion is acknowledged is the principle of procedural legalism actualised.[127]

In the continental tradition, legal conditions of a trial (prerequisites) provide a basis for the refusal to institute or discontinue investigation. They play a major role in the assessment as to whether there is "a justified/reasonable suspicion" of the commission of a crime. The prerequisites defined in Article 17(1)(1) CCP provide for a "sufficiency of evidence test" of sorts, similar to that applied in the Anglo-Saxon systems. If it is not fulfilled, criminal proceedings shall not be instituted, or, if previously instituted, shall be discontinued. The acknowledgement that an act has not been committed or that there is insufficient information to support the suspicion of its commission or that an act does not fulfil the elements of a crime is, in practice, based on the fact that there is no evidence to prove the facts of a case. This means that the obligation to prosecute is not absolute, and often on the ground that there "has not been sufficient information to suspect that an offence has been committed", the prosecutor will discontinue investigation, whereas in England he would consider that there is insufficient evidence to convince a reasonable jury or bench of magistrates or judge of the guilt of the defendant. The difference is that in Poland and Germany "the prosecutor's liberty to decide pertains to the examination of facts of the case and assessment as to whether factual circumstances justify initiation of procedural actions, whereas in systems based on the opportunist model, prosecutorial liberty also extends to the stage when it is decided whether accusation is desirable in a situation when the facts of the case provide grounds to acknowledge the commission of a crime".[128] Another difference can be seen in the fact that "unlike the American situation, the discretion of the prosecutor in this system is strictly limited by the Code of Criminal Procedure; it is guided by statutory standards and, to a certain extent, is controlled by the courts".[129]

In the systems favouring the principle of legalism, there have been an increasing number of exceptions to the obligation to prosecute: "Legalitätsprinzip has been steadily eroded in the twentieth century".[130] They sometimes become so far-reaching that we are no longer in a position to speak of the principle of legalism in its "pure form" but rather of the existence of a "mixed system". In fact, the exceptions lead to the application of the principle of opportunism (the so-called *improper*[131] or *tempered opportunism*) in respect of certain types of crimes or trial situations. For example, it is possible to resign from prosecution due to the minor nature of an offence. One way to do it would be through the use of institution of an "absorptive discontinuation" or "insignificant secondary penalties". This institution allows for dispensing with prosecuting an offence if the penalty or the measure of

[127] Beulke (2005), pp. 178–179; Grzegorczyk (2008), p. 78.

[128] Cit. after: Rogacka-Rzewnicka (2007), p. 86.

[129] Cit. Herrmannt (1973–1974), p. 468.

[130] Cit. after: Langbein (1973–1974), p. 451.

[131] This term used by Rogacka-Rzewnicka (2007), p. 86.

reform and prevention in which the prosecution might result is not particularly significant in addition to a penalty or measure of reform and prevention that has been imposed with binding effect upon the accused for another offence. Another example would be, in Germany, when the public prosecution office may dispense with prosecution with the approval of the court competent to open the main proceedings if the perpetrator's guilt is considered to be of a minor nature and there is no public interest in the prosecution (§ 153 StPO). Another possibility is provisional dispensing with court action, which may lead to termination of the proceedings—this institution allows the prosecutor, with the consent of the accused and of the court competent to order the opening of the main proceedings, to dispense with preferment of public charges and concurrently impose conditions and instructions upon the accused if these are of such a nature as to eliminate the public interest in criminal prosecution and if the degree of guilt does not present an obstacle (§ 153a StPO and similarily the new provision of the Polish criminal law - Article 59a CC).[132]

Moreover, while analysing prosecutorial discretion, we cannot forget that in some cases the prosecutor who has decided that the evidence in a case is sufficient to obtain a conviction cannot always prosecute. First, some criminal offences, involving primarily violations of personal interests (such as stealing from a next of kin), can be prosecuted only after the victim has filed a motion for prosecution. The victim in these cases is given an option to file a motion and have the offender prosecuted or not file and thereby protect his personal affairs from the intrusion of a police investigation and the publicity of a trial. Second, in cases of certain criminal behaviours (such as slander or insulting), the victim has a right to file a private indictment, and the prosecutor may prosecute such a behaviour only when he decides—and he rarely does—that there is a public interest in prosecuting such a case by a state authority.

Finally, the principle of legalism should be also analysed in the light of implications arising from the material definition of a crime and its procedural consequences set forth in the Criminal Code (e.g., Article 17 § 1(3) CCP)—the requirement not to institute proceedings or to discontinue initiated ones, in a situation when the act constitutes an insignificant social danger.[133] As a matter of fact, such an act does not constitute a crime at all—therefore, no prosecution is even allowed. Moreover, it should be seen in relation to the theory of separating "offences" (where in this group we include misdemeanors and crimes) from "petty infractions" (lesser misdemeanors, *Ubertretungen*), according to which the latter offences remain prohibited (they are still included in the group of "prohibited acts", which include both "offences" and "petty infractions"), but they are conceptualised differently and subjected to different procedures.[134] Conducting

[132] In general see: Beulke (2005), pp. 183 and 193–201; Fionda (1995), pp. 135–136; Weigend (1976), p. 13.

[133] Such a view is expressed by: Hofmański et al. (2011), p. 120; Cieślak (1984), p. 292. A different view is presented in: Grzegorczyk (2008), p. 78.

[134] Langbein (1973–1974), p. 451; Herrmannt (1973–1974), p. 481.

such a separation leads to so-called contraventionalisation—"decriminalisation" of certain behaviours, meaning interpreting certain behaviour as petty infractions and not an offence.[135]

3.4.4 The Model Chosen by the International Criminal Court

The founders of international criminal tribunals have always had to choose between the application of the principles of opportunism and legalism. In line with the goals imposed on the prosecutor, they had to answer the question whether the prosecutor should be "a servant to an act of law" (as is the case of legalism) or "the first judge" (who assesses the reasonability of prosecution under the principle of opportunism, as in the case of common law systems.[136] In the practice of international criminal tribunals, we have always seen a tendency to indict only the most responsible perpetrators.

There were two characteristic features of the model of initiating an investigation procedure before the international military tribunals. First, they did not offer prosecutors any guarantees of independence. Prosecutors of these tribunals were state officials, acting on behalf of certain states and under their control.[137] In practice, although according to the Charter of the Tribunal the Chief Prosecutors were responsible for "designation of the defendants", they were chosen by the governments of the victorious states. The second feature was that the procedural system of initiating criminal proceedings in Nuremberg and Tokyo reflected the strong influence of common law systems. It was designed on the basis of the model of opportunism—and in this model discretionary selection of defendants was possible. However, prosecutors did not enjoy any discretion: the final choice of defendants was made by governmental institutions. Therefore, we can make an assumption that in this case there was a separation between the principle of opportunism and prosecutorial discretion. While the international military tribunals operated according to the principle of opportunism, their prosecutors did not take decisions on the choice of defendants discretionally.

It was only with the establishment of the *ad hoc* international criminal tribunals that the discussion of the scope of prosecutorial discretion in the international justice system has begun. There was no doubt that they would not be able to try all persons suspected of having committed crimes in their jurisdiction, especially in light of the primacy of jurisdiction over national courts criterion applicable. As in

---

[135] Such as in the case of, e.g., theft penalised under Article 278 of the Polish Criminal Code; this provision can be used only if the stolen property is worth more than 400 PLN—approximately 100 euro. Stealing property of lower value is not considered to be an offence.

[136] According to the terminology used by: Rogacka-Rzewnicka (2007), p. 46.

[137] As to this fact agree: Coté (2012), pp. 372–373; Schabas (2008), p. 731; Brubacher (2004), p. 71; Ambos and Bock (2012), p. 492; Ohlin (2009), p. 185; Boister and Cryer (2008), pp. 51–52; deGuzman and Schabas (2013), p. 133; and Stahn (2009), p. 185.

the case of other procedural solutions, the standardisation of the reaction to information concerning committed crimes falling within the jurisdiction of a tribunal was based on the common law model.[138] This model assumed the applicability of procedural opportunism.

Article 18(1) of the ICTY Statute constitutes that "The Prosecutor shall initiate investigations ex-officio or on the basis of information obtained from any source, particularly from Governments, United Nations organs, intergovernmental and nongovernmental organisations. The Prosecutor shall assess the information received or obtained and decide whether there is sufficient basis to proceed". Accordingly, it is assumed the assessment as to whether there is a "sufficient basis to proceed" belongs solely to the Prosecutor. It was a widely accepted conclusion that discretion was essential to the operation of the ICTY, which would be paralysed without the ability to choose defendants.[139] As a consequence of the practice adopted by the Prosecutor and approved by the Chambers, there can be no doubt that the Prosecutor acts according to the principle of opportunism and uses his wide discretionary powers to select cases for investigation; he indicts only some of the alleged perpetrators.

Naturally, it is worth mentioning that the prosecutorial discretion is not unlimited, and several factors influence the final decision of the ICTY Prosecutor. Firstly, this discretion is submitted to the control of a judge, who can analyse the Prosecutor's decision to indict a particular perpetrator. What differs this model from the one adopted by the ICC is that the judges of the ICTY have powers only to assess the decision to prosecute. The decision not to prosecute does not fall within the scope of the judicial review. Secondly, the discretionary powers of the Prosecutor are limited by the Security Council Resolution no. 1534, which "calls on each Tribunal, in reviewing and confirming any new indictments, to ensure that any such indictments concentrate on the most senior leaders suspected of being most responsible for crimes within the jurisdiction of the relevant Tribunal".[140] This appeal was combined with a demand from the Security Council to complete all cases, first by the end of 2008 and then by the end of 2014.[141] Thirdly, on the basis of this Resolution, in 2004, Rule 28(A) RPE ICTY was adopted, which allows the Bureau of the Tribunal to control whether the indictment, *prima facie*, concentrates on the persons as indicated in the Resolution. If the Bureau determines that the indictment does not meet this standard, the President shall return the indictment to the Registrar to communicate this finding to the Prosecutor. This provision constitutes an indication

---

[138] This theory is represented, *inter alia*, by: Ambos (2003), p. 18; May and Wierda (2002), pp. 328–329; Greenawalt (2007), p. 636; Cryer (2005), pp. 214–216; Coté (2012), pp. 376–379; Jallow (2005), p. 150; Schabas (2008), p. 733; de Vlaming (2012), pp. 548–571; Schuon (2010), p. 196.

[139] See: Jallow (2005), p. 145, and Coté (2005), p. 165.

[140] Resolution of the Security Council No. S/RES/1503 (2003), § 5–6, No. 1534 S/RES/1534 (2004), § 5, and then No. 1966, S/RES/1966(2010), § 3.

[141] See: Schabas (2008), p. 733; Ambos and Bock (2012), p. 503; de Vlaming (2012), pp. 548–571; Heller (2012), pp. 901–902; Smith (2008), p. 338.

for the Prosecutor on how to proceed with the selection of the defendants. At the same time, it becomes the next tool for exercising judicial control over the actions of the Prosecutor. Finally, the Chambers of the ICTY have on numerous occasions determined the limits of prosecutorial discretion in their jurisprudence, setting the standards as to the choice of cases and defendants (and charges).[142]

Article 15(3) of the Rome Statute was drafted in a similar way as the ICTY Statute. It provides that "If the Prosecutor concludes that there is a reasonable basis to proceed with an investigation, he or she shall submit to the Pre-Trial Chamber a request for authorization of an investigation, together with any supporting material collected". The conditions on which the Prosecutor may initiate an investigation are set in Article 53(1) of the Statute.

However, based on the wording of these two provisions, both arguments supporting the principle of opportunism and the principle of legalism have been presented. It is interesting to observe that in most cases the attitude towards this issue depends on the model of accusation the interpreting author belongs to: these coming from the Anglo-Saxon tradition have a tendency to search for elements of the principle of opportunism; those from the continental law states assume that the model of accusation operates according to the principle of legalism. It seems that the main difference in interpretation depends on the decision whether the parameter "reasonable basis to proceed" is of a mandatory or discretionary character.

The most common opinion is that the elements mentioned in Article 53(1) are of an opportunist nature.[143] The term "interests of justice" signifies that the Prosecutor independently assesses whether the conditions justifying initiation of an investigation have been fulfilled: that is, the parameters of "reasonable basis to proceed", "gravity of the crime" and the lack of "interests of justice". Admissibility of the case being a non-discretionary parameter does not change the general outcome of the interpretation of this provision.[144] This power is referred to as "prosecutorial discretion" or even "absolute discretion". With this notion, all decisions during the investigation are described: the decision to initiate an investigation, the decision whom to prosecute and the decision for what crimes. He enjoys the full independence to select situations and cases to investigate.

However, even if we accept applications of the principle of opportunism, it should be remembered that the discretion of the Prosecutor is limited by the controlling powers of the Pre-Trial Chamber. The Chamber enjoys two powers: to authorise the initiation of an investigation (Article 15) and to confirm charges before trial (Article 61). Therefore, sometimes the notion of a "controlled opportunity" is being used.[145] The discretion of the Prosecutor may therefore be

---

[142] As, e.g., in the case: *Prosecutor v. Delalić*, IT-96-21, Appeal Chamber, 20 February 2001, § 601.

[143] E.g.: Schabas (2010), p. 663, and Greenawalt (2007), p. 599.

[144] In: Vasiliev (2012), p. 702; Ohlin (2009), p. 187; Olásolo (2003), p. 136.

[145] This notion is used by: Płachta (2007), p. 494. Similar observations in: Kuczyńska (2015), in print.

understood only as the power to examine a case and not as the power to start an investigation.

According to the second theory, the model of accusation operates in line with the principle of legalism. The representatives of this theory claim that the notion "shall initiate" in connection with the exception of "the interests of justice" is typically used when it induces the operation of the principle of legality, and therefore the wording used by the Statute "sounds very close to the principle of legality in the Continental tradition".[146] Thus, when the three criteria introduced by Article 53 (1) of the Statute occur, there is sufficient evidence that a grave crime within the jurisdiction of the Court occurred, the case would be admissible and when it is not against the interest of justice the Prosecutor is obliged to initiate proceedings.[147]

The second argument supporting this theory is connected to the seriousness of crimes the ICC deals with. The Preamble states that "Affirming that the most serious crimes of concern to the international community as a whole must not go unpunished and that their effective prosecution must be ensured by taking measures at the national level and by enhancing international cooperation, determined to put an end to impunity for the perpetrators of these crimes and thus to contribute to the prevention of such crimes (. . .)". Accordingly, the Preamble seems to assume that investigation of all the crimes it mentions is obligatory. The principle of legalism would be in compliance with the obligation to treat all the crimes in the same way and, therefore, with the principle of equality before the law. Moreover, it would send a clear signal to all the states that all situations and cases within the jurisdiction of the ICC will be treated on equal terms—independently of the personal opinions of the present Prosecutor of the ICC.

However, even representatives of this theory agree that it is not practically possible to investigate all the cases of crimes of international law, and in some cases it is necessary to use "an exemplary prosecution".[148] They agree that the ICC does not possess the factual means to ensure the legal standards consistent with the principle of legalism. Therefore, this principle has to undergo a certain adaptation to the goals of the ICC. This adaptation relates to the operations of the complementarity principle. It means that the principle of legalism will find application only in cases where the jurisdiction of the ICC would come into force in cases of states' unwillingness or being unable to investigate the crimes in the Court's jurisdiction. This attitude highlights the primary responsibility of the states to prosecute the perpetrators of international law crimes.

In addition to the two above-mentioned theories, there are also a number of mixed theories. Their representatives usually agree that neither a strict principle of legalism nor opportunism was adopted.[149] In result, the solution adopted in Article 53(1) of the Rome Statute is mixed system, a "hybridization between various

[146] E.g.: Safferling (2001), p. 176; Ntanda Nsereko (1994), pp. 518–519.

[147] See: Bergsmo and Pejić (2008), p. 589; Stegmiller (2008), p. 330.

[148] E.g. Orentlicher (1991), p. 2598. This conception is also mentioned by: Turone (2002), p. 1154.

[149] See: Stegmiller (2011), p. 262.

national traditions".[150] The most frequently supported attitude divides conditions in Article 53 (1) between non-discretionary parameters and discretionary parameters. The non-discretionary parameters, such as the scope of jurisdiction, cannot be freely evaluated by the Prosecutor.[151] However, both "gravity" of the crime and "lack of interests of justice" are of a discretionary character. They allow using the prosecutorial discretion in order to determine whether to proceed with an investigation following authorisation by the Pre-Trial Chamber. In consequence, these parameters can be assessed as "opportunist elements", exception to the generally applicable principle of legalism. Although there is a general obligation to initiate an investigation, as the Statute uses the "shall" expression, the provision introduces also an exemption (or "the backdoor"[152]).

It seems that the main difference between opportunism and legalism depends on a decision whether the assessment of the parameter "reasonable basis to proceed" and its elements, existence of interests of justice and gravity of the crime, leads to a mandatory reaction or the reaction is of a discretionary character. Using other words it can be also said that it depends on whether existence of a reasonable basis to proceed (or lack thereof) should be assessed subjectively (by the Prosecutor) or according to an objective test. While the first interpretation is characteristic of the common law tradition, the second is used by continental states. The latter interpretation assumes that taking a decision to start an investigation the prosecutor must take into consideration an objective evaluation of a situation, and act according to this idealistic assessment, rejecting at the same time the possibility to apply his personal judgment. It means that initiation of an investigation is mandatory if the prosecutor comes to a conclusion that objectively there is a reasonable basis to proceed. At the same time, the common law tradition leaves the evaluation of existence of a reasonable basis to the discretion of the prosecutor, not subjecting him to objective tests (as a rule)—other than the limitations provided for by the legal act. Basing on such a view, we can observe that the same wording of a legal provision leads to completely different interpretations in two legal traditions. The whole cultural and legal heritage of a given state seems to weight upon this interpretation and the meaning given to a certain phrase.

At this point, again, making a clear distinction between a situation and a case is especially relevant. The differentiation between a situation and a case seems to resemble continental structure of an investigation, which is divided into two phases: *in rem* and *in personam*. Whereas during the first stage the prosecutor (also the ICC Prosecutor) analyses the whole factual situation and allegation as to committing of a crime, the second stage refers to a specific person and specific charges, which are presented in the charging document. The decision to prosecute a case consists of

---

[150] Cit. after: Delmas-Marty (2006), p. 9. As a matter of fact, most systems are mixed nowadays, with the characteristic combinations of various elements of these two principles being determined by practical necessity, constitutional rules, historical and sociological background or political demands. See comprehensive consideration in: Fionda (1995), p. 10.

[151] See: Turone (2002), p. 1152. Bergsmo (2008), pp. 589 and 1068.

[152] Cit. after: Stegmiller (2011), p. 262.

these two decisions: first, whether to investigate a situation and, second, whether to prosecute a particular case. A case is separated from a situation when the situation is already under investigation and the Prosecutor issues an arrest warrant against a certain person to be confirmed by the Pre-Trial Chamber. It is the first moment in which the defendant is mentioned. In the moment of issuing an arrest warrant (or summoning the person to appear) the Prosecutor manifests his decision to prosecute a certain person. It means that there is no need for a formal decision to consider a person to become a suspect: it is enough to direct against this person factual actions. From the point of view of prosecutorial discretion, we can say that it comes into play on two stages of initiating an investigation: the first stage being selecting a situation for investigation, the second—selecting a case and a defendant for prosecution.

3.5 Discretion of the ICC Prosecutor and the Strategy Behind

The prosecutorial discretion cannot be analysed in separation from the objectives and the reality of the international criminal tribunal, which are in their substance different from those of the state systems and do not allow easy comparisons. Taking into consideration two conditions influencing actions of the ICC Prosecutor: almost unlimited scope of jurisdiction and limited (both personally and financially) means to execute it, it seems obvious that it is not possible to prosecute all the perpetrators of the crimes in jurisdiction of the ICC, even in a situation when the Prosecutor could consider the leading of an investigation to be reasonable. The scope of jurisdiction itself constitutes a strong argument for opportunism: it is too wide to assume that it is possible to apply the principle of legalism. The number of communications coming to the OTP causes that the Prosecutor is not practically capable of bringing to justice every person suspected of having committed a crime within the jurisdiction of the ICC. The scale of the problem is best shown by the numbers: between 1 November 2013 and 31 October 2014, the Office received 579 communications relating to Article 15 of the Rome Statute (of which 462 were manifestly outside the Court's jurisdiction, 44 warranted further analysis, 49 were linked to a situation already under analysis and 24 were linked to an investigation or prosecution). The Office has received a total of 10,797 communications since July 2002.[153] Even in a situation when the Prosecutor acquires evidence in support of the information about committing a crime within the jurisdiction of the ICC, he will always face the necessity to select the alleged perpetrators he indicts—on the basis of the criteria named in Article 53(1): gravity of crimes, interests of justice, reasonability of initiating an investigation. In consequence, the general relations

[153] Report on Preliminary Examination Activities 2014, § 17–18: http://www.icc-cpi.int/iccdocs/otp/OTP-Pre-Exam-2014.pdf. Accessed 19 Jan 2015.

of crimes investigated (9 situations under investigation—Democratic Republic of the Congo, Uganda, Central African Republic, Darfur, Sudan, Kenya, Libya, Cote d'Ivoire, Mali, Central African Republic II—which include 21 cases and 8 preliminary examinations) to crimes communicated must diverge to the detriment in comparison to state systems. Crimes investigated by the Prosecutor of the ICC entail large numbers of perpetrators, sometimes even thousands of them, and it is virtually impossible to bring them all to face the ICC. The workload would lead to a total paralysis of the Court. It is necessary to limit the number of persons accused by the Prosecutor—and as a result those judged by the Court—to an absolute minimum.[154] It cannot be done without the selection of defendants.

Only the principle of opportunism allows the Prosecutor to investigate only the most serious cases in which circumstances suggest—such a high position in hierarchy of the alleged perpetrator or the significance of the legal issues—that an international judicial organ should deal with them. Legalism rejects discretionary selection of defendants, as all perpetrators should be treated alike. This assumption clearly contradicts the reality of every international criminal tribunal. It seems that also tempered legalism does not allow introducing any new criteria for selecting defendants, accepting that the parameters from Article 53(1) should be applied equally in every case, basing on an objective test. So even legalism adapted by the use of complementarity principle does not solve the problem of multiplicity of perpetrators. Only within the principle of opportunism that it is possible to accept that the Prosecutor may select defendants among the large number of alleged perpetrators.

The most commonly adopted concept on the selection of defendants assumes that only the most responsible persons should be prosecuted.[155] This strategy was also presented by the OTP, which developed a prosecutorial strategy in its strategy papers and policy papers published in 2003 and in 2007. Pursuant to the Policy Paper of 2003, the concept of prosecuting the highest ranking officials responsible for the commission of a crime was adopted as a basic rule: "the Office of the Prosecutor should focus its investigative and prosecutorial efforts and resources on those who bear the greatest responsibility, such as the leaders of the State or organisation allegedly responsible for those crimes". The Office is aware that such selection of cases leaves an "impunity gap". According to the Office, however, such a gap should be "patched" if national authorities co-operate with the Court to ensure that all appropriate means for bringing other perpetrators to justice are used. In the Office's opinion, other offenders, who will not be prosecuted by the OTP, can wait for the strengthening or rebuilding of national justice systems, whereas the most guilty ones should not wait.[156] The Policy Paper explains that prosecuting the

[154] The so-called *screening* and *gatekeeping competence* as in: Bibas and Burke-White (2009–2010), p. 681. The same opinions expressed by numerous authors: Stegmiller (2011), p. 257; earlier the same opinion was expressed by: Ntanda Nsereko (1994), p. 125; Wei (2007), p. 173; Greenawalt (2007), p. 620; Ambos and Beck (2012), p. 541; Cassese (2009), p. 472.

[155] See: Greenawalt (2007), p. 627; Schabas (2010), pp. 745–746; Płachta (2004), p. 487.

[156] Paper on some policy issues before the Office of the Prosecutor, September 2003, pp. 6–7: http://www.icc-cpi.int/NO./rdonlyres/1FA7C4C6-DE5F-42B7-8B25-60AA962ED8B6/143594/030905_Policy_Paper.pdf. Accessed 9 Sept 2014.

most responsible perpetrators might encourage national authorities to deal with other cases. Also in the Policy Paper on the Interests of Justice of 2007, the OTP concluded that the Prosecutor's actions inevitably lead to the occurrence of the "impunity gap".[157] Again in this Paper, it was stressed that such a gap may be eliminated by designing comprehensive strategies to combat impunity, fully endorsing the complementary role that can be played by domestic prosecutions, truth seeking, reparations programs, institutional reform and traditional justice mechanisms in the pursuit of a broader justice.

It is only in the Prosecutorial strategy 2009–2012 that we can find straightforward information that the OTP prosecutes in a selective way. Namely, it adopted "a policy of focused investigations and prosecutions", meaning "it will investigate and prosecute those who bear the greatest responsibility for the most serious crimes, based on the evidence that emerges in the course of an investigation. Thus, the Office will select for prosecution those situated at the highest echelons of responsibility, including those who ordered, financed, or otherwise organized the alleged crimes".[158] According to the OTP "a policy of focused investigations" also means that "cases inside a situation are selected according to gravity, taking into account factors such as the scale, nature, manner of commission, and impact of the alleged crimes". A limited number of incidents are selected. This allows the Office to "carry out short investigations; to limit the number of persons put at risk by reason of their interaction with the Office; and to propose expeditious trials while aiming to represent the entire range of victimization". While the Office's mandate does not include production of comprehensive historical records for a given conflict, incidents are selected to provide a sample that is reflective of the gravest incidents and the main types of victimisation.163 Moreover, against those chosen on this basis, the Office brings representative charges only. However, which person and what charges the Prosecutor will choose to make an example of remain to his own personal discretion.

In fact, the ICC Prosecutor's actions are illustrative of the application of the policy of focusing on the prosecution of "those who bear the greatest responsibility". In this context it is important to highlight that there is no equation between the concepts of "senior leaders" and "those most responsible".[159] Prosecuting senior leaders means prosecuting only the senior state officials, whereas prosecuting the most responsible leads to a conclusion that also mid-level perpetrators can be held responsible if an investigation of a certain type of crimes or those officers lower down the chain of command is necessary for the whole case. Also, the OTP realises that there is a distinction between these two groups as the group of "those who bear the greatest responsibility" may include "the leaders of the State or organisation

[157] Policy Paper on the Interest of Justice, September 2007, p. 7: http://icc-cpi.int/NO./rdonlyres/772C95C9-F54D-4321-BF09-73422BB23528/143640/ICCOTPInterestsOfJustice.pdf. Accessed 9 Sept 2014.

[158] Prosecutorial strategy 2009–2012, 1 February 2010, The Hague, § 19–20: http://www.icc-cpi.int/NR/rdonlyres/66A8DCDC-3650-4514-AA62-D229D1128F65/281506/OTPProsecutorialStrategy20092013.pdf. Accessed 28 Jan 2015.

[159] Stegmiller (2011), p. 260.

allegedly responsible for those crimes" and also other perpetrators. Both Article 1 of the Rome Statute and the OTP Papers refer to prosecuting "persons for the most serious crimes of international concern" and do not allow to restrict prosecution only to the senior leaders. In *The Prosecutor v. Lubanga*, the Pre-Trial Chamber considered that the intent of the aggravated gravity threshold in Article 17(1)(d) was to ensure that the ICC "initiates cases only against the most senior leaders suspected of being the most responsible" for the commission of the ICC crimes committed in any situation under investigation. Adopting this approach in jurisdiction "solidified the impunity gap" and "needlessly destroyed the ability of the OTP to temporarily or permanently alter its prosecutorial focus in response to external political pressures".[160] This approach, however, when used in another case by the Pre-Trial Chamber, *The Prosecutor v. Ntaganda*, was rejected by the Appeals Chamber. It concluded that even if Ntaganda was not the most senior leader in the given conflict, also lower and mid-level operatives sometimes are (and should be) arrested to help build a case against the most senior leaders.[161] In consequence, his case is pending before the ICC.

The approach adopted by the Appeals Chamber gives to the Prosecutor possibility to use a flexible approach. A strict inadmissibility of cases concerning lower level perpetrators would lead to even greater impunity gap.[162]

As a result, the Prosecutor can prosecute persons, whose prosecution would lead to indicating to the guilty ones and demonstrating the condemnation for given behaviours on behalf of the international community and satisfy the sense of justice for the victims. This method of choosing the defendants is commonly referred to as "exemplary prosecution".

However, in the doctrine, it is widely agreed that selectivity of the Prosecutor's actions may cnstitute a threat to the ICC's legitimacy. The ICC Prosecutor is often criticised for applying a non-coherent policy of prosecuting, which depends on the specific state where he intervenes and the position of the suspect. Therefore, it is highlighted that there exists a need to introduce additional guidelines for prosecution that would provide a framework within which decision-making takes place. Several propositions have been presented.[163]

First, it is proposed that certain basic principles should govern the selection process: independence, impartiality and non-discrimination.[164] Second, it is suggested that when selecting perpetrators, the Prosecutor should bear in mind criteria of a more political character, as the concerns that certain crimes may have

---

[160] Cit. after: Smith (2008), p. 342.

[161] ICC-01/04-169, Situation in the Democratic Republic of the Congo, Judgment on the Prosecutor's Appeal against the Decision of Pre-Trial Chamber I entitled "Decision on the Prosecutor's Application for Warrants of Arrest, Article 58", § 77.

[162] See: Stegmiller (2011), p. 75; Smith (2008), p. 343.

[163] See: Greenawalt (2007), p. 651; Brubacher (2004), p. 72; Stegmiller (2011), pp. 240–260; Muller-Rappard (2002), p. 918; Locke (2012), pp. 610–612; Danner (2003), p. 511; Goldstone and Fritz (2000), p. 664; Schabas (2009), p. 242; deGuzman (2011-2012) p. 271.

[164] Such possible criteria proposed by: Guariglia (2009), pp. 212–213.

caused in the international community and the political ramifications of an investigation on the political environment of the state over which he is exercising jurisdiction where he would have to weigh the risk that an investigation or prosecution may have on a political situation.[165] However, even these criteria would depend on personal evaluation and subjective decision-making of the Prosecutor (his Office). They would constitute rather a "guidance" than a binding order.[166]

Moreover, there are different ideas that tend to take away the decision-making from the Prosecutor and offer it to another organ. The first one is to shift the decision-making from the ICC Prosecutor to the judges.[167] There are also proposals to "outsource" the decision-making process to the Security Council.[168] This time, it seems that all of the above-mentioned propositions would not only endanger the subtle balance that exists presently between the Prosecutor and the judicial organ (described in the next chapter) but also call in question the existence of independence of the organ.

Before the ICC, we observe the importance of setting the correct extent to prosecutorial discretion, resulting from the universal scope of the ICC jurisdiction. Because of this scope, selection of defendants stands at the basis of its effective and correct functioning. Although there are opinions that the Rome Statute obliges the Prosecutor to act according to the principle of legalism—adapted to the role of the ICC by the way of complementarity of jurisdiction—the OTP assumed that the "impunity gap" is an indispensible—and therefore necessary—element of the selection strategy. This assumption equals to foundation of the principle of opportunism. Even if we assumed that the ICC Statute operates on the basis of the principle of legalism, we could come to a conclusion that the legality maxim remains solely an assumption made in the written law of the Rome Statue—it was never the aim of the ICC Prosecutor to follow the maxim. In this situation, we can conclude that the obligation to act, which is mentioned in Article 53 (1) of the ICC Statute by the use of the words "shall act", was supposed to relate only to a situation when the Prosecutor (subjectively) considers that the conditions from this Article have been fulfilled. The Prosecutor concentrates not on the "shall" notion but rather on the discretionary possibilities that are given by the coming afterwards criteria.

---

[165] See: Brubacher (2004), pp. 81–82; Schabas (2008), p. 742.

[166] In general see: Greenawalt (2007), p. 630; Locke (2012), p. 612.

[167] See: Greenawalt (2007), p. 660. Or create an investigative chamber by, for instance, equipping the Pre-Trial Chamber with investigative powers. See: De Hemptinne (2007), p. 416 and later described also in: Stegmiller (2011), p. 265.

[168] As it stated: Greenawalt (2007), p. 672.

3.6 Conclusion

The principle of procedural opportunism applied by international criminal tribunals underlies the model of the initiation of an investigation. In view of the almost unlimited range of jurisdiction and limited (in terms of personnel and finances) resources to exercise it, selective prosecution turned out to be unavoidable. This principle, in its variant adopted by international criminal tribunals, has numerous implications that define specific components of the accusation model.

First, every prosecutor of the international criminal tribunal enjoys a broad discretion in the selection of cases. Before the international criminal tribunals, we can witness a practical need to be selective. No legal system is currently capable of prosecuting all cases of criminal law infringement. In national systems, selectivity is introduced either through provisions of the substantive law (using the criteria of a socially dangerous act) or by implementation of the prosecutorial opportunism principle.[169] In the case of the ICC, substantive law does not solve the problem, as it leaves us with an indefinite number of possible perpetrators—and one court only. The ICC Prosecutor's power to select suspects is limited only by the factual (and financial) capabilities of the Court. There is still the principle of complementarity, in accordance to which it is mainly the state's responsibility to prosecute perpetrators of international law crimes. However, it seems that national jurisdictions are not able, prepared or willing to fill the "impunity gap". Therefore, the Prosecutor's discretion to initiate and to proceed with an investigation leads to "selective prosecution". A component of this approach is also the option to press only some of the numerous charges that could be brought against suspects. Simultaneously, the necessity to implement transparent and coherent principles for the selection of suspects is emphasised. We have experienced what importance for the practical operations of the Court, its credibility and efficiency has a coherent and clear method of selection of defendants. One problem cannot be overlooked—selectivity of prosecution leads to selective legal responsibility and selectivity of enforcement of the ICC's jurisdiction. Moreover, selectivity of the Prosecutor's actions has so far led to instituting prosecutions mainly against citizens of states that are weak actors in the international arena or that fail to enjoy the support of powerful nations.[170]

The second characteristic feature of the model of accusation before the international criminal tribunals is adopting the objective of an investigation in accordance with the Anglo-Saxon model of accusation: it aims at determining whether "there is sufficient evidence to justify the suspicion that the suspect has committed the alleged crime" and whether prosecution is "reasonable". Determining whether there is a suspicion that the offence was committed as is the case in continental systems is not sufficient. Due to the application of the principle of procedural opportunism, even when there is a suspicion that a crime has been committed

---

[169] This tendency highlighted by: Cryer (2005), p. 192; Ambos (2000a), pp. 495 and 505–509.

[170] See: Damaška (2008), p. 361.

falling within the Court's jurisdiction, the ICC Prosecutor is not obligated to prosecute.

The manner of operation of the *ad hoc* tribunals established the principle of broad prosecutorial discretion in initiating cases *proprio motu* that was used also by the ICC. However, significant changes were introduced in the proceedings before the ICC compared to the proceedings before *ad hoc* tribunals as to other components of the model of investigation.

The first characteristic element of the model of investigation before the ICC is the judicial authority's review of the Prosecutor's decision to initiate an investigation. Although the broad discretion of the Prosecutor in the selection of cases remains a distinctive feature of the process, the Prosecutor's decision has been subjected to judicial control. It is characteristic that this type of control is used only in those cases where the Prosecutor initiates proceedings *propio motu*. In the situation where proceedings are instigated as a result of a referral made by one of the privileged entities—the Security Council or the State Party to the Statute—the Prosecutor's decision is not subject to review. In this aspect, the binding nature of such a "referral of a situation" by one of the entities has led to much controversy. The solution adopted before the ICC is a reflection of the need to ensure balance between prosecutorial discretion to initiate proceedings *proprio motu* and the necessity to subject the Prosecutor's choices of cases to some type of review. In the situation where states and political authorities do not have any (statutory) impact on the Prosecutor's actions, the Pre-Trial Chamber has decided to exercise stronger control. This pursuit of equilibrium between the functions of the Prosecutor and the Pre-Trial Chamber has become one of the characteristic features of the accusation model before the ICC.

Moreover, the Statute provides the Prosecutor with a list of parameters that he should assess when making a decision to initiate an investigation. These include the same criteria as are taken into account by the Pre-Trial Chamber when confirming the Prosecutor's decision. They are also similar to the catalogues of preconditions known to common law systems that, in practice, put restrictions on the principle of prosecutorial discretion. It was assumed before the ICC that the Prosecutor should initiate proceedings when the available information provides a reasonable basis to believe that a crime has been or is being committed and that it falls within the jurisdiction of the Court; the Court's jurisdiction is or would be considered admissible; despite taking the gravity of a crime and interest of victims into account, there are significant reasons to believe that an investigation would not serve the interests of justice; and it pertains to the gravest crimes of international relevance.

These parameters are gradually defined in the case law of the Court. Also by developing documents by the Office of the Prosecutor itself, some efforts have been made to render the statutory conditions as specific as possible. This indicates an intention to reduce prosecutorial discretion and subject it to restrictions by providing specific points of reference. Especially worth noting is the manner in which these parameters are defined, which, in addition to being interpreted for internal purposes, are simultaneously published on the Internet. This is symptomatic of the ICC entering the era of digital society. It also supports the public review of the

Prosecutor's actions and gives entities interested in referring a situation an opportunity to check whether their communication may be successful. Due to their publication, a specific interpretation of a given concept by the Office of the Prosecutor becomes binding before the public.

The introduction of a preliminary examination phase, during which the "reasonableness" of initiation of an investigation is assessed, as well as the selection of a specific "case" limited to specific events and persons out of a wider "situation" referred to a Prosecutor is conducted, has become the third novelty compared to the model of accusation applied before the *ad hoc* tribunals.

The prosecutor's powers and his role in an investigation have changed since the establishment of the first international criminal tribunals. The investigation before these tribunals was first modelled on the basis of common law systems. Later on, the main assumptions of investigation changed, evolving in the practice of these tribunals. When the Rome Statute was drafted, it largely took into account the role of the prosecutor as it was understood in continental systems; the Statute formalised the investigation phase, subjected the ICC Prosecutor's actions in an investigation to judicial review and introduced a preliminary examination of a case. In the end, the ICC Prosecutor's powers were shaped differently not only from those observed in specific states, but even from those adopted before the *ad hoc* tribunals, drawing in equal measure on both the continental and the common law states' models.

References

Ambos K (2000a) Comparative summary of the national reports. In: Arbour L, Eser A, Ambos K, Sanders A (eds) The prosecutor of a permanent International Criminal Court. International workshop in co-operation with the Office of the Prosecutor of the International Criminal Tribunals (ICTY and ICTR). Edition Iuscrim, Freiburg im Breisgau

Ambos K (2000b) Status, role, accountability of the Prosecutor of the International Criminal Court: a comparative overview on the basis of 33 national reports. Eur J Crime Crim Law Crim Justice 8:89

Ambos K (2003) International criminal procedure: "adversarial", "inquisitorial" or mixed? Int Crim Law Rev 3:18

Ambos K (2007) The structure of international procedure: "adversarial", "inquisitorial" or mixed. In: Bohlander M (ed) International criminal justice: a critical analysis of institutions and procedures. Cameron May, London

Ambos K, Bock S (2012) Procedural regimes. In: Reydams L, Wouters J, Ryngaert C (eds) International prosecutors. Oxford University Press, Oxford

Andrzejewska M (2013) Adaptacja koncepcji Thomasa Kuhna dla postępowania karnego. Prokuratura i Prawo 3:136

Aresi B (2013) L'autonomie du Procureur et la supervision du Juge dans l'activation de la competence de la Cour Penale internationale: l'affaire du Kenya. In: Boschiero N, Scovazzi T, Pitea C, Ragni C (eds) International courts and the development of international law. Essays in honour of Tullio Treves. Asser Press, The Hague

Bassiouni MC, Manikas P (1996) The law of the international criminal tribunal for the former Yugoslavia. Transnational Publishers, New York

Batros B (2010) The judgment on the Katanga admissibility appeal: judicial restraint at the ICC. Leiden J Int Law 23:343

Bergsmo M, Harhoff F (2008) In: Triffterer O (ed) Commentary on the Rome Statute of the International Criminal Court – observers' notes, article by article, 2nd edn. Hart/Nomos Verlagsgesellschaft/C.H. Beck, München/Oxford
Bergsmo M, Kruger P (2008) In: Triffterer O (ed) Commentary on the Rome Statute of the International Criminal Court – observers' notes, article by article, 2nd edn. Hart/Nomos Verlagsgesellschaft/C.H. Beck, München/Oxford
Bergsmo M, Pejić J (2008) In: Triffterer O (ed) Commentary on the Rome Statute of the International Criminal Court – observers' notes, article by article, 2nd edn. Hart/Nomos Verlagsgesellschaft/C.H. Beck, München/Oxford
Beulke W (2005) Strafprozessrecht, 12th edn. C.F. Müller, Heidelberg
Bibas P, Burke-White WW (2009–2010) International idealism meets domestic-criminal-procedure realism. Duke Law J 59:637
Boister N, Cryer R (2008) The Tokyo International Military Tribunal: a reappraisal. Oxford University Press, Oxford
Brubacher M (2004) Prosecutorial discretion within the ICC. J Int Crim Justice 2:71
Burke-White WW (2005) Complementarity in practice: the International Criminal Court as part of a system of multi-level global governance in the democratic Republic of Congo. Leiden J Int Law 18:557
Cane P, Conaghan J (ed) (2008) The new Oxford companion to law. Oxford University Press, Oxford
Cassese A (2006) Is the ICC still having teething problems? J Int Crim Justice 4:434
Cassese A (ed) (2009) The Oxford companion to international criminal law. Oxford University Press, Oxford
Cieślak M (1984) Polska procedura karna. Podstawowe założenia teoretyczne, 3rd edn. PWN, Warszawa
Coté L (2005) Reflections on the exercise of prosecutorial discretion in international criminal law. J Int Crim Justice 3:162
Coté L (2012) Independence and impartiality. In: Reydams L, Wouters J, Ryngaert C (eds) International prosecutors. Oxford University Press, Oxford
Cryer R (2005) Prosecuting international crimes: selectivity and the international criminal law regime. Cambridge University Press, Cambridge
Damaška M (1986) The faces of justice and state authority. Yale University Press, New Haven/London
Damaška M (2008) What is the point of international criminal justice? Chic Kent Law Rev 83:329
Danner AM (2003) Enhancing the legitimacy and accountability of prosecutorial discretion at the International Criminal Court. Am J Int Law 97:510
deGuzman MM (2011–2012) Choosing to prosecute: expressive selection at the International Criminal Court. Mich J Int Law 33:265
deGuzman MM (2012–2013) How serious are international crimes? The gravity problem in international criminal law. Columbia J Transnatl Law 51:18
deGuzman MM, Schabas W (2013) Initiation of investigation and selection of cases. In: Sluiter G, Friman H, Linton S, Vasiliev S, Zappala S (eds) International criminal procedure. Principles and rules. Oxford University Press, Oxford
De Hemptinne J (2007) The creation of investigating chamber at the ICC: an option worth pursuing? J Int Crim Justice 5:402
de Vlaming F (2012) Selection of defendants. In: Reydams L, Wouters J, Ryngaert C (eds) International prosecutors. Oxford University Press, Oxford
Delmas-Marty M (2006) Criminal law in the preliminary phase of trial at the ICC. J Int Crim Justice 4:2
Fionda J (1995) Public prosecutors and discretion. A comparative study. Clarendon, Oxford
Friman H (2003) An introduction. In: Lattanzi F, Schabas W (eds) Essays on the Rome Statute of the International Criminal Court, vol 2. Il Sirente, Ripa di Fagnano Alto

Gallant K (2003) The ICC in the system of states and international organizations. In: Lattanzi F, Schabas W (eds) Essays on the Rome Statute of the International Criminal Court, vol 2. Il Sirente, Ripa di Fagnano Alto

Geis J, Mundt A (2009) When to indict? The impact of timing of international criminal indictments on peace processes and humanitarian action. The Brookings Institution-University of Bern Project on Internal Displacement: http://www.brookings.edu/~/media/research/files/papers/2009/4/peace%20and%20justice%20geis/04_peace_and_justice_geis.pdf. Accessed 13 Feb 2015

Goldstein A, Marcus A (1977) The myth of judicial supervision in three "Inquisitorial" systems: France, Italy and Germany. Yale Law J 87:240

Goldstone R, Fritz N (2000) In the interest of justice and the independent referral: the ICC prosecutor unprecedented power. Leiden J Int Law 13:655

Greenawalt A (2007) Justice without politics? Prosecutorial discretion and the International Criminal Court. NYU J Int Law Polit 39:583

Grzegorczyk T (2008) Kodeks postępowania karnego oraz Ustawa o świadku koronnym. Komentarz, 5th edn. Wolter Kluwer, Warszawa

Guariglia F (2009) The selection of cases by the Office of the Prosecutor of the International Criminal Court. In: Stahn C, Sluiter G (eds) The emerging practice of the International Criminal Court. Martinus Nijhoff, Leiden/Boston

Hall CK (2009) Developing and implementing an effective positive complementarity prosecution strategy. In: Stahn C, Sluiter G (eds) The emerging practice of the International Criminal Court. Martinus Nijhoff, Leiden/Boston

Heller KJ (2012) Completion. In: Reydams L, Wouters J, Ryngaert C (eds) International prosecutors. Oxford University Press, Oxford

Herrmannt J (1973–1974) The rule of compulsory prosecution and the scope of prosecutorial discretion in Germany. Univ Chic Law Rev 41:468

Hofmański P, Sadzik E, Zgryzek K (2011) Kodeks postępowania karnego. Komentarz, vol 2, 4th edn. C.H. Beck, Warszawa

Izydorczyk J, Wiliński P (2005) Pozycja i zakres uprawnień Prokuratora Międzynarodowego Trybunału Karnego. Prouratura i Prawo 6:35

Jallow HB (2005) Prosecutorial discretion and international criminal justice. J Int Crim Justice 3:145

Krzan B (2009) Kompetencje Rady Bezpieczeństwa ONZ w międzynarodowym sądownictwie karnym. TNOiK, Toruń

Kuczyńska H (2015) Selection of defendants before the ICC: between the principle of opportunism and legalism. Polish Yearb Int Law 34 (in print)

Kulesza C (2011) Deprecjacja rozprawy głównej w procesie karnym z perspektywy obrońcy – uwagi na tle prawno-porównawczym. In: Przyborowska-Klimczak A, Tarach A (eds) Iudicium et Scientia. Księga Jubileuszowa Profesora Romulada Kmiecika, Warszawa

LaFave W, Israel J, King N, Kerr O (2009) Criminal procedure, 5th edn. West Academic Publishing, St. Paul

Langbein JH (1973–1974) Controlling prosecutorial discretion in Germany. Univ Chic Law Rev 41:439

Locke J (2012) Indictments. In: Reydams L, Wouters J, Ryngaert C (eds) International prosecutors. Oxford University Press, Oxford

May R, Wierda M (2002) International criminal evidence. Transnational Publishers, Ardsley, NY

Milik P (2012) Komplementarność jurysdykcji Międzynarodowego Trybunału Karnego i trybunałów hybrydowych. Dom Wydawniczy Elipsa, Warszawa

Muller-Rappard E (2002) International cooperation in prosecution and punishment. In: Bassiouni MC (ed) Post-conflict justice. Transnational Publishers, New York

Murphy R (2006) Gravity issues and the International Criminal Court. Crim Law Forum 17:281

Ntanda Nsereko DD (1994) Rules of Procedure and Evidence of the International Tribunal for the former Yugoslavia. Crim Law Forum 5:507

Ohlin JD (2009) Peace, security, and prosecutorial discretion. In: Stahn C, Sluiter G (eds) The emerging practice of the International Criminal Court. Martinus Nijhoff, Leiden/Boston

Olásolo H (2003) The Prosecutor of the ICC before the initiation of investigations: a quasi-judicial or a political body? Int Crim Law Rev 3:87

Olásolo H (2005) The triggering procedure of the International Criminal Court. Martinus Nijhoff, Leiden/Boston

Olásolo H (2012) Essays on international criminal justice. Hart, Oxford and Portland/Oregon

Oosthuizen GH (1999) Some preliminary remarks on the relationship between the envisaged International Criminal Court and the UN Security Council. Netherlands Int Law Rev 46:313

Orentlicher D (1991) Settling accounts: the duty to prosecute human rights violations of a prior regime. Yale Law J 100:2537

Padfield N (2008) Text and materials on the criminal justice process, 4th edn. Oxford University Press, Oxford

Płachta M (2004) Międzynarodowy Trybunał Karny. Zakamycze, Kraków

Płachta M (2007) Prokurator Międzynarodowego Trybunału Karnego: między legalizmem a oportunizmem ścigania. In: Menkes J (ed) Prawo międzynarodowego. Księga pamiątkowa Profesor Renaty Szafarz. WSHiP, Warszawa

Röben V (2003) The procedure of the ICC: status and function of the Prosecutor. Max Planck Yearbook United Nations Law 7:520

Rogacka-Rzewnicka M (2007) Oportunizm i legalizm ścigania przestępstw w świetle współczesnych przeobrażeń procesu karnego. Zakamycze, Warszawa

Sacouto P, Cleary K (2010) The *Katanga* complementarity decisions: sound law but flawed policy. Leiden J Int Law 23:363

Safferling C (2001) Towards an international criminal procedure, Oxford monographs in international law. Oxford University Press, Oxford

Schabas W (2008) Prosecutorial Discretion v. Judicial Activism at the International Criminal Court. J Int Crim Justice 6:731

Schabas W (2009) Prosecutorial discretion and gravity. In: Stahn C, Sluiter G (eds) The emerging practice of the International Criminal Court. Martinus Nijhoff, Leiden/Boston

Schabas W (2010) The International Criminal Court. A commentary on the Rome Statute. Oxford University Press, Oxford

Schuon C (2010) International criminal procedure. A clash of legal cultures. T.M.C. Asser Press, The Hague

Smith SE (2008) Inventing the laws of gravity: the ICC's initial *Lubanga* decision and its regressive consequences. Int Crim Law Rev 8:331

Sprack J (2012) A practical approach to criminal procedure. Oxford University Press, Oxford

Stahn C (2009) Judicial review of prosecutorial discretion: five years on. In: Stahn C, Sluiter G (eds) The emerging practice of the International Criminal Court. Martinus Nijhoff, Leiden/Boston

Stegmiller I (2008) The pre-investigation stage of the ICTY and ICC compared. In: Kruessmann T (ed.), ICTY: towards a fair trial? Neuer Wissenschaftlicher Verlag, Wien.

Stegmiller I (2011) The pre-investigation stage of the ICC. Criteria for situation selection. Duncker & Humblot, Berlin

Trüg G (2003) Lösungskonvergenzen trotz Systemdivergenzen im deutschen und US-amerikanischen Strafverfahren. Ein strukturanalytischer Vergleich am Beispiel der Wahrheitserforschung. Mohr Siebeck, Tübingen

Turone G (2002) Powers and duties of the Prosecutor. In: Cassese A, Gaeta P, Jones WD (eds) The Rome Statute of the International Criminal Court: a commentary. Oxford University Press, Oxford

Tylman J (1965) Zasada legalizmu w procesie karnym (The principle of legality in the legal procedure). Warszawa

Vasiliev P (2012) Trial. In: Reydams L, Wouters J, Ryngaert C (eds) International prosecutors. Oxford University Press, Oxford

Volk K (2006) Grundkurs. StPO, 5th edn. C.H. Beck, München
Waltoś S (1968) Model postępowania przygotowawczego na tle porównawczym. PWN, Warszawa
Waltoś S (2005) Proces karny. Zarys systemu, 8th edn. LexisNexis, Warszawa
Ward R, Wragg A (2005) Walker and Walker's English legal system, 9th edn. Oxford University Press, Oxford
Wei W (2007) Die Rolle des Anklägers eines Internationalen Strafgerichtshofs. Peter Lang, Frankfurt am Main
Weigend T (1976) Anklagepflicht und Ermessen. Die Stellung des Staatsanwalts zwischen Legalität- und Opportunitätprinzip nach deutschem und amerikanischen Recht. Nomos Verlagsgesellschaft, Baden-Baden
Wierczyńska K (2013) Dekada działalności Międzynarodowego Trybunału Karnego – sukcesy i porażki międzynarodowego wymiaru sprawiedliwości. Studia Prawnicze 2:127
Williams P, Schabas W (2008) In: Triffterer O (ed) Commentary on the Rome Statute of the International Criminal Court – observers' notes, article by article, 2nd edn. Hart/Nomos Verlagsgesellschaft/C.H. Beck, München/Oxford
Worrall J (2007) Criminal procedure: from first contact to appeal, 2nd edn. Pearson Allyn & Bacon, Boston
Wouters J, Verhoeven S, Demeyere B (2008) The International Criminal Court's Office of the Prosecutor: navigating between independence and accountability? Int Crim Law Rev 8:273

Chapter 4
Judicial Control of an Accusation

Abstract The method and scope of the judicial control over the indictment has a significant impact on the model of accusation. The broad extent of judicial control over the Prosecutor's actions has become a characteristic feature of the ICC proceedings. Not only the Pre-Trial Chamber has powers to approve the decision to initiate an investigation, but later it also authorises the charges filed by the Prosecutor, at a contradictory hearing. Moreover, the judicial review performed by the Pre-Trial Chamber covers the grounds for non-prosecution. Both the Pre-Trial Chamber and the Trial Chamber have the authority to modify the legal characterisation of facts presented in an indictment—which deprives the Prosecutor of control over the formulated charges. In this chapter, the "interplay" between the Prosecutor and the ICC Chambers will be shown and the ways in which the role of the judicial authority matches the role of the Prosecutor in bringing an indictment. Moreover, reflections on this aspect of the Prosecutor's role should be related to a broader discussion of the objectives of international criminal law as analysis of the accusation model would not be complete without considering the political aspect of indictments presented by the ICC Prosecutor.

4.1 The Role of Judicial Control of an Accusation

Following the filing of an indictment and prior to the setting of a trial, the second stage of proceedings takes place, which is referred to as "proceedings between instances" (the so-called "inter-instance" procedure, in German: *das Zwischenverfahren*) when the indictment is reviewed. The purpose of this stage of proceedings is similar in all legal systems: the objective of the preliminary judicial scrutiny of the indictment is to prevent situations in which cases insufficiently prepared in terms of completeness and legal correctness of procedural steps are sent to trial or a hearing in which the court adjudicates on the subject of the trial.[1] The first area of judicial review in this respect is releted to assesment whether it is

[1] The so-called *filtering of cases* or *negative controlling function*—see: Hauck (2008), pp. 54 and 48 respectively; Ambos and Miller (2007), p. 355.

© Springer International Publishing Switzerland 2015

H. Kuczyńska, *The Accusation Model Before the International Criminal Court*,
DOI 10.1007/978-3-319-17626-0_4

reasonable to set forth a trial based on the sufficiency of evidence. Only such persons should be committed to trial against whom sufficiently compelling charges going beyond mere theory or suspicion have been brought. Its role is also to protect the defendant against abusive and unfounded accusations.[2] Such review is conducted by a professional judge who becomes a barrier between the prosecutor and the court. It is the court itself that decides whether a trial will be held.

In various states' legislation, we encounter various models of this review. The specific type and method of judicial review is closely related to the model for the pre-trial stage of criminal proceedings and the adopted accusation model. This area of judicial control constitutes a part of a wider topic of judicial review over the prosecutor's action in an investigation and at the pre-trial stage that is characteristic of a certain state's system of checks and balances. Most importantly, the mechanism of review is different: in continental systems, it is the judge who evaluates whether an indictment is correct in formal terms and whether it is justified (most frequently, parties do not take part in the hearing), whereas in the systems of common law states, an indictment's review involves a mandatory confirmation of the indictment by a judicial authority in an adversary hearing. However, the main difference is the practical dimension of functioning of this mechanism. In continental systems, the indictment review aims at finding "a manifest absence of any factual basis for charge" rather than merely demonstrating that there are reasons for finding the accused guilty of the alleged act. As a consequence, only a small percentage of cases are discontinued at this stage of proceedings as a result of a judicial review. In Anglo-Saxon systems, however, judges evaluate evidence presented by the prosecutor in support of his case as part of the review and already at this stage examine the alleged offence and take a decision whether there is a *prima facie* case, i.e., whether the evidence collected by the prosecution is sufficient to prove the commission of a crime by the accused.

The second area of judicial review, apart from reviewing whether the triggering of a criminal process by the prosecutor is reasonable, is the power of a judicial authority to control prosecutorial inaction. It is in this area of judicial review that the most material differences between legal systems occur. In common law systems, the judicial review of the prosecutor's decision not to start proceedings is considered to be "an interference with the prosecutor's authority". Meanwhile, in continental systems, it is one of the most common methods of a judicial control over the prosecutor's actions in investigation. It is also in this aspect that we encounter the most evident differences between the accusation model before the *ad hoc* tribunals and before the International Criminal Court: whereas the former comply with common law principles and are reluctant to review this area of prosecutorial discretion, in proceedings before the International Criminal Court the Prosecutor's decision on the refusal to initiate proceedings was subjected to review of the

[2] E.g., "selective or vindictive" prosecutions—see: Stahn (2009), p. 247. See also the case law, e.g.: *The Prosecutor v. Lubanga*, Confirmation of charges decision, 29 January 2007, § 37.

Pre-Trial Chamber (albeit to a very limited extent)—thus introducing elements of continental origin.

The third area of judicial review is control of the form and contents of an indictment. There are a number of issues related to this subject:

(1) When drafting an indictment, the prosecutor constitutes the scope of the case being tried.
(2) Another issue related to the drafting of an indictment is the possibility of presenting alternative charges. In common law systems, this solution is widely used due to the fact that the court may not modify the legal characterisation presented by the prosecutor in an indictment.
(3) The issue of filing an indictment is related to the consequences of its defective drafting. Whereas in common law criminal proceedings this may lead to finding the accused not guilty as the court has no impact on the adopted legal characterisation and scope of evidence presented by the Prosecutor, in continental systems it is not only the court but also the Prosecutor himself that has a broad spectrum of options to remedy defects in an indictment—including after the trial has begun.
(4) Finally, it should be assessed to what extent the prosecutor's findings made in an indictment are binding for the court: whether upon issuing of this document a judicial authority may influence its contents. There are two ways of affecting the indictment: first, the court may change the contents of charges; second, it may change the legal evaluation of an offence made by the prosecutor and presented in the form of a legal characterisation of facts. In proceedings before the *ad hoc* tribunals, the first type of review could be applied in the preparatory hearing where the judicial authority enjoys the power to reduce the number of counts charged in the indictment. However, while the contents of charges cannot be affected in proceedings before the International Criminal Court, the Trial Chamber has the authority to modify the legal characterisation of facts presented in an indictment, that is to say, to present a different assessment of elements of the alleged offence and form of criminal liability. Thus, there is a relationship between the form and contents of the indictment and any subsequent judgment. Moreover, these powers were also awarded to the Pre-Trial Chamber at the confirmation hearing stage.

Each of these issues is not only regulated differently in the two legal systems in question, but there are also differences between the models adopted by the *ad hoc* tribunals and the International Criminal Court. It is clear that in resolving such issues, the *ad hoc* tribunals are inspired by common law systems. Before the International Criminal Court, however, the question of the scope and methods of judicial control has been resolved in accordance with the model adopted in continental criminal trial: the model of greater judicial control over prosecutors' activities.

4.2 Problems of Drafting an Indictment

4.2.1 Form and Contents of an Indictment

The Charter of the International Military Tribunal in Nuremberg contained only concise provisions pertaining to the technical requirements (the form, which by Anglo-Saxon lawyers could be known as "lay-out") and contents of an indictment. Article 16(a) provided that "in order to ensure fair trial for the Defendants (...) the Indictment shall include full particulars specifying in detail the charges against the Defendants". Each of the four Chief Prosecutors was responsible for preparation of their thematic section of the indictment; as a result, each section demonstrated an approach unique for a given legal system. The French and Soviet Union sections (pertaining to War crimes and Crimes against humanity—for the western and eastern front, respectively) were very detailed. The section prepared by the representatives of the United Kingdom (dealing with Crimes against peace) had one page only; the United States drafted 13 pages on a count dealing with a common plan or conspiracy to wage an aggressive war (as it is mentioned, it had the narrative style of an antitrust indictment). As eventually drafted, the indictment was only 65 pages long.[3]

The statutory requirements concerning the form and contents of an indictment in the proceedings before the *ad hoc* tribunals are equally general in nature. Article 18 (4) of the ICTY Statute provides only that "upon a determination that a prima facie case exists, the Prosecutor shall prepare an indictment containing a concise statement of the facts and the crime or crimes with which the accused is charged under the Statute". Rule 47(C) adds: "the indictment shall set forth the name and particulars of the suspect and a concise statement of the facts of the case and of the crime with which the suspect is charged". Due to the concise nature of these provisions, the requirements as to the form and contents of an indictment were developed in the course of judicial practice. It is in the jurisprudence of the *ad hoc* tribunals that the foundations for the theory of drafting indictments in international criminal proceedings have been laid.[4]

Initially, two trends could be observed in the practice of the ICTY. First, it was decided that indictments would be prepared on the basis of the common law model. At the beginning of its functioning, there were evident differences in the way specific indictments were drafted. What was missing was a uniform model. It was uncertain which legal system should be followed by the ICTY. The Prosecutor himself had to decide about the form of a particular indictment. The defence attorneys expected the indictments brought before the ICTY to be as detailed as in the former Yugoslavian states, where references had to be made to specific evidence while describing specific charges.[5] However, in consequence of the

[3] See: Cryer et al. (2010), p. 114; May and Wierda (2002), p. 40; Townsend (2012), p. 200.

[4] *The Prosecutor v. Lubanga*, ICC-01/04-01/06, Decision on the confirmation of charges, 29 January 2007, § 153.

[5] See: Tochilovsky (2004), pp. 319–344; Keegan and Mundis (2001), pp. 124–125.

adoption of the common law model, each indictment was challenged by the defence counsels for being too general and had to be corrected by the Prosecutor at least once. The Trial Chamber was unwilling—although it possessed the relevant powers—to check the technical form of the indictment *ex officio*: "It is not the function of a Trial Chamber to check for itself whether the form of an indictment complies with the pleading principles which have been laid down. The Trial Chamber is, of course, entitled proprio motu to raise issues as to the form of an indictment but, unless it does so, it waits until a specific complaint is made by the accused before ruling upon the compliance of the indictment with those pleading principles. This is fundamental to the primarily adversarial system adopted for the Tribunal by its Statute".[6]

The second trend concerned the contents of indictments. In the rulings of the *ad hoc* tribunals, it was adopted, similarly as in common law,[7] that the essence of an indictment was the presentation of "material facts".[8] The court would decide that an indictment includes "a concise statement of facts" if it described material facts in a sufficiently accurate manner so as to provide clear information to an accused necessary for the preparation of a defence.[9] The accused had to be informed in detail of the nature and cause of charges and the evidence on the basis of which his responsibility for these acts was to be determined. In the jurisprudence, we can find indicated what elements must appear in an indictment for it to be considered as containing material facts:

(1) A description of the specific conduct of the accused constituting the offence he is alleged to have committed: the particulars of facts of the offence, though concise, must contain all the essential elements of the offence that the accused has been charged with and be accompanied by a case summary that sets out the allegations that the Prosecutor intends to prove. It is also vital for the indictment to specify at least on what legal basis of the Statute an individual is being charged.
(2) Circumstances rendering a specific infringement of law a crime under international law, prosecuted under international jurisdiction, e.g., the circumstances pertaining to the massive scale of a crime.[10]
(3) The elements relative to the circumstances of the committed act: the identity of the victim or victims, the places and the approximate date of those acts and the

[6] *Prosecutor v. Brđanin*, IT-99-36, Decision on Objections by Momir Talic to the Form of the amended Indictment, 20 February 2001, § 23.

[7] As, e.g., *Federal Rules of Criminal Procedure*, Rule 7.1., of 1.12.2012, http://www.law.cornell.edu/rules/frcrmp/rule_5.1. Accessed 1 Sept 2014.

[8] This concept was also interpreted in: Tochilovsky (2008), p. 2; Tochilovsky (2004), pp. 319–344; Tochilovsky (2009), pp. 829–832; Keegan and Mundis (2001), pp. 154–159.

[9] See, e.g., *Prosecutor v. Blaškić*, IT-95-14, Appeals Chamber, 29 July 2004, § 207.

[10] *Prosecutor v. Kvočka*, IT-98-30/1, Decision on the Defence Preliminary Motion on the Form of the Indictment, 12 April 1999.

means by which the offence was committed (but where the precise date cannot be specified, a reasonable range of dates may be sufficient).[11]

(4) It should also specify the elements of *mens rea*, describing a special form of intent (or lack of it).

(5) In the event of cases based upon individual responsibility where it is not alleged that the accused personally did the acts for which he is to be held responsible—where the accused is being placed in greater proximity to the acts of other persons—the most material is the conduct of the accused by which he may be found to have planned, instigated, ordered, committed or otherwise aided and abetted in the planning, preparation or execution of those acts. In the case of acting as part of a common purpose or design, or as part of a common criminal enterprise, the indictment must inform the accused of the nature or purpose of the joint criminal enterprise (or its "essence"), the time at which or the period over which the enterprise is said to have existed, the identity of those engaged in the enterprise—so far as their identity is known, but at least by reference to their category as a group—and the nature of the participation by the accused in that enterprise.[12] If an indictment does not specify the precise form of perpetration of the alleged crimes, the evidence produced at trial will not be able to remedy such defects.[13]

(6) The legal characterisation of the alleged act, and, if required, presented in a form of cumulative or alternative charges.

The ICTY judges did not, however, indicate a comprehensive list of circumstances that need to be included in an indictment: "material facts" are defined on a case-to-case basis; what is understood under this notion depends on the nature of a specific case, mainly the nature of the alleged criminal conduct. They found that the requirements relating to the precise drafting of an indictment in cases concerning mass criminality might not be interpreted in the same manner as in the case of crimes heard by national courts. While deciding how precise an indictment should be, the Prosecutor needs to take numerous factors into account: the type of crimes, their extent, the circumstances of commission, the period in which they were committed, the relation between other circumstances and the main act the defendant is charged with. If possible, the Prosecutor should include the victims' personal data. The Tribunal may not, however, require him to perform an impossible task, e.g., to present the identity of 800,000 victims.[14] The mass scale of the offences

[11] See, e.g., *Prosecutor v. Blaškić*, IT-95-14, judgment of the Appeal Chamber, 29 July 2004, § 207–210; *Prosecutor v. Krnojelac*, IT-97-25, Decision on the Defence Preliminary Motion on the Form of the Indictment, 24 February 1999.

[12] *Prosecutor v. Brđanin*, IT-99-36, Decision on Objections by Momir Talić to the Form of the Indictment, 20 February 2001, § 19–20.

[13] *Prosecutor v. Krnojelac*, IT-97-25, Decision on the Defence Preliminary Motion on the Form of the Indictment, 24 February 1999.

[14] *Prosecutor v. Todorović*, IT-95-9/1, Decision on Todorović Defence Motion on the Form of the Joint Amended Indictment, 21 March 2006, § 17.

"would make [it] impracticable"[15] to require a high degree of specificity regarding the identity of victims, time of alleged offences and place of events. Therefore, according to the jurisprudence, where a precise identification of the victim or victims cannot be specified, a reference to their category or position as a group may be sufficient. Where the prosecution is unable to specify matters such as these, it must make it clear in the indictment that it is unable to do so and that it has provided the best information it can. On the other hand, it may turn out to be necessary to expand the contents of an indictment compared to national systems by presenting additional facts defining the nature of the crime: e.g., the demographic, geographical or historical facts, demonstrating the (massive) scale of the committed crimes.

In proceedings before the International Criminal Court, the statutory requirements for indictments are more detailed. However, the ICC Prosecutor does not prepare an indictment. A special phrase is used in the Rome Statute declaring that "within a reasonable time before the hearing, the person shall be provided with a copy of the document containing the charges on which the Prosecutor intends to bring the person to trial" (Article 61(3)(a)). Thus, it is not a classical indictment but a "document containing the charges". Interestingly, the form and contents of this document were specified neither in the Statute nor in the Rules but in the Regulations of the Court (Regulation 52).[16] These Regulations state that

the document containing the charges referred to in article 61 shall include:
a) The full name of the person and any other relevant identifying information;
b) A statement of the facts, including the time and place of the alleged crimes, which provides a sufficient legal and factual basis to bring the person or persons to trial, including relevant facts for the exercise of jurisdiction by the Court;
c) A legal characterisation of the facts to accord both with the crimes under articles 6, 7 or 8 and the precise form of participation under articles 25 and 28.

There is no obligation to refer to evidence in an indictment.[17] However, in order to support all material facts that are provided in the document containing the charges, the Prosecutor should present the evidence at the confirmation hearing that has been disclosed prior to this hearing in the *disclosure of evidence* procedure. We have to keep in mind the interrelation between drafting the charges and the necessity of complying with the disclosure of evidence obligation. The Prosecutor should avoid including charges—or even describing the circumstances in which an act was committed—if supporting evidence has not been (or cannot be) disclosed.[18]

---

[15] Cit. after: Knoops (2005), p. 156.

[16] Regulations of the Court, ICC-BD/01-03-11, Adopted by the judges of the Court on 26 May 2004, http://www.icc-cpi.int/NR/rdonlyres/50A6CD53-3E8A-4034-B5A9-8903CD9CDC79/0/RegulationsOfTheCourtEng.pdf. Accessed 11 Feb 2015.

[17] *Prosecutor v. Krnojelac*, IT-97-25, Decision on the Defence Preliminary Motion on the Form of the Indictment, 24 February 1999.

[18] See: Keegan and Mundis (2001), pp. 134 and 127–129.

Taking into consideration the existing legal framework and doctrinal considerations, we can observe that a threefold test has been established. The legal requirements of an indictment before the ICC relate to the standard of proof (which will be discussed later), legal sufficiency (compliance with Regulation 52 requirements) and specificity.[19] The last parameter examines whether the indictment sets out the material facts of the prosecution case.

In the first confirmation hearing before the International Criminal Court, the accused claimed that ambiguity, the general nature of charges and lack of specificity of the document containing charges made it impossible to prepare for defence. Also, the Pre-Trial Chamber acknowledged that it was imprecise both in relation to the facts of the case and the effective legislation; in its opinion, the Prosecutor failed to demonstrate that the crimes had been committed within the scope of a conflict of an international character. Ultimately, however, the Chamber concluded that the form and contents of charges should be read together with a list of pieces of evidence presented at the confirmation hearing. In consequence, in spite of the indicated deficiencies, the formulation of charges still enabled preparation for defence and was not prejudicial to their rights, and therefore the indictment could have been approved.[20]

There is no doubt that the preparation of an indictment in cases pertaining to international law crimes is a difficult task. An indictment needs to have a reporting function: to present charges in the context of specific facts and within a specific conflict. Thus, preparation of a broader background for incriminating events has always been very significant. In consequence, indictments submitted before the international criminal courts will always be much longer than those in national legal orders. On the other hand, as M. Damaška observes, "when judges aspire to paint a broader historical tableau, the issues involved in trial may become staggeringly complicated".[21] An example of such an attitude could be seen when while trying *Prosecutor v. Milosević* case judges intended to produce a record of events accompanying the disintegration of Yugoslavia. The indictment related to crimes committed within a period of 8 years and contained 66 counts. Therefore, it should be seen as doubtful to attempt to use criminal proceedings to provide a comprehensive portrayal of events surrounding massive human rights violations. Prosecutors should not go beyond what's regarded as common sense. It is the Prosecutor's task in every international criminal court to seek balance between the required precision of drafting an indictment and a rational approach that requires this document to be clear and coherent.

[19] See: Locke (2012), p. 624.

[20] *The Prosecutor v. Lubanga*, ICC-01/04-01/06, Decision on the confirmation decision, 29 January 2007, § 153. See in general also: Schabas (2010), p. 738.

[21] Cit. after: Damaška (2008), p. 340.

4.2.2 *Alternative and Cumulative Charging*

A key element of an indictment is a proper formulation of the legal characterisation of the suspect's alleged act. Each legal system allows for using more than one legal characterisation to describe the conduct of the defendant, which may simultaneously infringe several criminal law provisions and can consequently be classified as a concourse of legal provisions. In the Polish and German continental law systems, cumulative legal charging may be used under the concurrence of legal provisions (in German: either in a form of *Realkonkurrenz* or *Idealkonkurrenz*). English law differentiates between two regimes: charges founded on the same facts (cumulative charges) and alternative charges. The former approach is designed to describe a situation in which a single act by the defendant gives rise to several offences—leads to the violation of several provisions and results in several charges. As to alternative counts, they may be included in an indictment when the accused's conduct, depending on his state of mind at the relevant time and/or consequences of his act, might make him guilty of one of a number of offences of differing degrees of gravity, and therefore a prosecutor is not sure what charge he will be able to prove with the evidence collected and presented in the trial.[22] In such a case, he will include in the indictment all possible legal characterisations of facts acceptable on the basis of the evidence at their disposal.

In proceedings before the *ad hoc* tribunals, it was agreed that the prosecutor may present more than one legal characterisation of facts to define a single act; some provisions of the ICTY Statute have such a broad scope that they may overlap. The ICTY addressed this issue for the first time in *Prosecutor v. Kupreškić*.[23] The Trial Chamber indicated that although the matter was fundamental for the adjudication before international criminal tribunals, it had neither been regulated by the legislation nor dealt with in depth by an international criminal court.

Judges decided to fill the gaps in the doctrine of international criminal law by relying on the general principles of international criminal law and, if no such principle is found, on the principles common to the various legal systems of the world, in particular those shared by most civil law and common law criminal systems. In consequence, they presented what they considered to be "the correct legal standards" based on the model adopted in the common law tradition.[24]

First, they decided that the ICTY Prosecutor may present cumulative charges whenever he contends that the facts charged violate simultaneously two or more provisions of the Statute under each relevant provision; in such a case, we may differentiate between partial concurrence (referred to as "reciprocal speciality") and

[22] In English criminal trial: Sprack (2012), pp. 244–248.

[23] *Prosecutor v. Kupreškić*, IT-95-16, Trial Chamber, 14 January 2000, § 637–748.

[24] See: *Prosecutor v. Kunarac*, IT-96-23, Appeals Chamber, 12 June 2002, § 167–174; *Prosecutor v. Delalić*, IT-96-21, Appeals Chamber, 20 February 2001, § 389–425, and the same case analysed in: Tochilovsky (2008), p. 33; Tochilovsky (2009), pp. 833–834; Eser (2008), p. 215; Locke (2012), pp. 635–638.

total concurrence (adopting the "lesser included offence" doctrine existing in common law).

Partial concurrence means that the Prosecutor must demonstrate that each of the crimes meets an additional criterion in relation to another. In so far as each crime contains a materially distinct legal element, cumulative convictions are permitted. Cumulative legal charging may then refer solely to the situation in which the conduct of the accused itself violates two legal standards and each of them requires evidence that an additional criterion is met in relation to the other standard. In the Tribunal's opinion, cumulative legal charging allows the entirety of the criminal content of the offender's act to be presented. It also offers some advantages to the Prosecutor—if it turns out that he is not able to present satisfactory evidence for some of the charges, the Tribunal may still convict the offender for another act cited in the legal characterisation of facts. If this test, however, is not passed, one legal characterisation of facts is applied in accordance with the doctrine of *lex specialis derogat generali*. In such a situation, the Prosecutor must rely on the law that relates to the crime more specifically, or it is assumed that there is an inclusion relation (total concurrence, *lesser included offence*). There is no need for cumulative conviction then.

Cumulative legal charging was also applied in proceedings before the ICTR. In the procedure before this Tribunal, however, the French *concours ideal d'infractions* regime was adopted as the basis "which permits multiple convictions for the same act under certain circumstances". In *Prosecutor v. Akayesu*, the Tribunal found that "It may, depending on the case, be necessary to record a conviction for more than one of these offences in order to reflect what crimes an accused committed".[25] The Chamber concluded that it is acceptable to convict the accused of two offences in relation to the same set of facts in the following circumstances:

(1) where the offences have different elements; or
(2) where the provisions creating the offences protect different interests; or
(3) where it is necessary to record a conviction for both offences in order fully to describe what the accused did.[26]

Second, as the ICTY judges indicated, the possibility of using cumulative charging should be differentiated from alternative description of facts.

At the initial stage of the functioning of the ICTY, there was no consensus as to the possibility of alternative charging. The ICTY judges coming from continental systems argued that it was not possible to plead in the alternative, especially not to the extent that the counts contradicted each other.[27] Ultimately, however, the ICTY stated that this practice was acceptable. Currently, it is recognised that presenting charges alternatively supports the effectiveness of an indictment; even if the

---

[25] *Prosecutor v. Akayesu*, ICTR-96-4, Trial Chamber, 2 September 1998, § 469.

[26] *Ibidem*, § 468.

[27] *Prosecutor v. Stakić*, IT-97-24, Status conference, 18 February 2002.

Tribunal finds one of the charges to be unclear or insufficiently proven, it may convict the accused on the basis of an alternative legal characterisation of facts. If an indictment lacks such an alternative, this may not be remedied at the stage of court proceedings. Inadequately formulated charges or charges based on an inappropriate legal characterisation of facts lead to a futile presentation of evidence that could be used in support of these charges if they had been phrased otherwise. In such a situation, the Prosecutor should charge in the alternative rather than cumulatively whenever an offence appears to be in breach of more than one provision, depending on the elements of the crime the prosecution is able to prove. The Prosecutor may legitimately fear that, if he fails to prove the required legal and factual elements necessary to substantiate a charge, the count may be dismissed even if in the course of the trial it has turned out that other elements were present supporting a different and perhaps even a lesser charge. Thanks to this solution, the Prosecutor does not need to select one form of complicity for a given act but may formulate alternative charges, e.g., of aiding and abetting, liability of superiors and being part of a joint criminal enterprise. As a result, the Trial Chamber may, having rejected the main charge (e.g., acting as a main perpetrator or in complicity), still convict the accused for aiding and abetting.[28] Presentation of alternative charges allows the Trial Chamber to decide which legal characterisation of facts is more suitable for the presented evidence or which form of complicity should be adopted in relation to the accused.[29] As the judges concluded: "The Trial Chamber is better poised, after the parties' presentation of the evidence, to evaluate which of the charges may be retained, based upon the sufficiency of the evidence".[30]

The judges went even further and provided the Prosecutor with a set of "guidelines" that specified the violation of which provisions should be presented so as to, in the event there is no possibility of proving the violation of the Statute of a more material nature, prevent acquittal and to lead to conviction for another, alternatively specified, crime: "The efficient fulfilment of the Prosecution's mission favours a system that is not hidebound by formal requirements of pleading in the indictment". The judges indicated that the Prosecutor should present an alternative rather than a cumulative characterisation of facts whenever he concludes that the acts with which the accused is charged simultaneously violate two or more provisions of the Statute, and in his opinion he may prove that only some of the criteria of the crime have been met, depending on the elements of the crime the Prosecutor is able to prove. For instance, the prosecution may characterise the same act as a crime against humanity and, in the alternative, as a war crime. Indeed, in case of doubt, it is appropriate from a prosecutorial point of view to suggest that a certain act falls under a stricter and more serious provision of the Statute, adding, however, that if

---

[28] *Prosecutor v. Brđanin*, IT-99-36, Decision on Form of Third Amended Indictment, 21 September 2001, § 22.

[29] See: *Prosecutor v. Naletilić*, IT-98-34, Appeals Chamber, 3 May 2006, § 103; *Prosecutor v. Delalić*, IT-96-21, Appeals Chamber, 20 February 2001, § 400.

[30] See: *Prosecutor v. Naletilić*, IT-98-34, Appeals Chamber, 3 May 2006, § 103.

proof to this effect is not convincing, the act falls under a less serious provision: "it may also prove appropriate to charge the indictee with a crime envisaged in a provision that is – at least in some respects – special vis-à-vis another and, in the alternative, with a violation of a broader provision, so that if the evidence turns out to be insufficient with regard to the special provision (the lex specialis), it may still be found compelling with respect to a violation of the broader provision (the lex generalis). The prosecution should make clear that these are alternative formulations by use of the word 'or' between the crimes against humanity and war crimes charges, for example, and refrain in these circumstances from using the word 'and', to make clear the disjunctive and alternative nature of the charges being brought".[31]

It seems, however, that the differentiation between cumulative and alternative charges is not entirely consistent.[32] The Tribunal found that "Cumulative charging on the basis of the same acts is generally allowed on the basis that prior to the presentation of all of the evidence, it is not possible to determine to a certainty which of the charges brought against an accused will be proven". In the same case, the Tribunal admitted that "The same reasoning allows for alternative charging".[33] Moreover, it can be stated that cumulative charges and cumulative convictions leave little space for alternative charges. However, using alternative charges is considered to constitue a method specifically used for securing conviction as to different forms of criminal responsibility; superior responsibility is subsidiary to other modes of liability, and commission excludes a conviction for also planning and aiding and abetting.[34]

Application of cumulative charging is possible in proceedings before the International Criminal Court—although subject to certain conditions. The ICC judges have not, however, differentiated between alternative and cumulative charging. They defined both of these approaches as "cumulative charging", which they understood as a situation in which "the same criminal conduct can be prosecuted under two different counts"[35]—regardless of whether legal provisions are cumulated or excluded. In *The Prosecutor v. Bemba*, the Prosecutor decided to charge both rape and, using the same conduct, torture (the act of rape being the instrument of torture) as crimes against humanity, in addition to charging rape and outrages against personal dignity as war crimes, again using the same acts. However, the Pre-Trial Chamber made it clear that "the Prosecutorial practice of cumulative charging is detrimental to the rights of the Defence since it places an undue burden on the Defence. The Chamber considers that, as a matter of fairness and

[31] *Prosecutor v. Kupreškić*, IT-95-16, Trial Chamber, 14 January 2000, § 727.

[32] On many occasions, these two separate systems of evaluation of charges are considered to be identical, as, e.g., in Friman et al. (2013), p. 389.

[33] See: *Prosecutor v. Naletilić*, IT-98-34, Appeals Chamber, 3 May 2006, § 103.

[34] See: Cryer et al. (2010), p. 459.

[35] *The Prosecutor v. Bemba*, ICC-01/05-01/08, Decision Pursuant to Article 61(7)(9a) and (b) of the Rome Statute on the Charges of the Prosecutor Against J-P Bemba Gombo, 15 June 2009, § 199.

expeditiousness of the proceedings, only distinct crimes may justify a cumulative charging approach and, ultimately, be confirmed as charges. This is only possible if each statutory provision allegedly breached in relation to one and the same conduct requires at least one additional material element not contained in the other".[36] It also instructed the Prosecutor on the theory of application of the concurrence of legal regulations: its application should be restricted to instances where the same conduct gives rise to an "additional material element". The Chamber did not agree with the Prosecutor's argument, who claimed that it was not his intention to present alternative charges for the purpose of "unfairly securing conviction on multiple counts" and that he only wanted to "capture the full extent of the criminal conduct of the accused". The Prosecutor also indicated that as long as all charges are supported by the evidence, the choice of counts to prosecute at trial is a right guaranteed only the prosecutor. However, the Pre-Trial Chamber emphasised that "it is not its role to accept every charge presented to it". In its opinion, the Prosecutor should choose the most appropriate characterisation (*choisir la qualification la plus pertinente*). It indicated that the Prosecutor should ensure that the same criminal conduct should not be prosecuted under two different counts, as this might create an impression that the accused was twice held responsible for the same criminal act. When charging for violation of too many provisions of the Statute in the indictment, the Prosecutor is risking subjecting the defence to the burden of responding to multiple charges for the same facts and at the same time delaying the proceedings. The Chamber considered that, as a matter of fairness and expeditiousness of the proceedings, only distinct crimes might justify a cumulative charging approach and, ultimately, be confirmed. This is only possible if each statutory provision allegedly breached in relation to one and the same conduct requires at least one "additional material element" not contained in the other. Thus, the International Criminal Court has not rejected the practice of cumulative charging but has introduced limitations to its application. In the subsequent decision issued in this case, the Pre-Trial Chamber rejected two out of three charges presented by the Prosecutor on the basis of the same facts. It decided that in this particular case the count of outrage upon personal dignity is fully subsumed by the count of rape, which is the most appropriate legal characterisation of the conduct presented.[37] Moreover, the Chamber selected between the forms of complicity presented in (cumulative) charges by the Prosecutor and decided that although it could not accept the charge of complicity, it would accept the charge of directing the commission of acts of a crime (based on superior responsibility).[38] At the same time, the Chamber stressed that "it did not purport to impinge upon the Prosecutor's functions as regards the formulation of the appropriate charges or to advise the Prosecutor on how best to prepare the document containing the charges".

---

[36] *The Prosecutor v. Bemba*, Decision of 15 June 2009, § 202.

[37] *Ibidem*, § 312.

[38] *The Prosecutor v. Bemba*, Decision of 15 June 2009, § 403.

However, we could observe an example of inconsistency in this approach. In *The Prosecutor v. Al Bashir*, the Pre-Trial Chamber accepted cumulative charges from the Prosecutor when it issued an arrest warrant concerning the counts of both acts of extermination and murder as crimes against humanity that were based on the same underlying conduct.[39] Also in *The Prosecutor v. Ruto*, the Pre-Trial Chamber accepted the later view, adopting the jurisprudence of the ICTY, known from the *Kupreskić* judgment.[40] It stated namely, rejecting the claims of the defence based on an earlier finding of this Chamber in *The Prosecutor v. Bemba* confirmation of charges decision, that cumulative charging of multiple crimes for the same behaviour is permissible—provided that each of the charges involved a materially distinct element. We could also claim that this changing approach is not a sign of inconsistency but a sign of an evolution of the approach.[41] Nonetheless, this inconsistency results in the lack of clarity, which, in turn, leads to insecurity as to what interpretation will be adopted in the next case.

Two observations appear when interpreting this jurisprudence. First, we could note a re-evaluation of the international criminal law (characteristic of common law tradition) doctrine according to which, where the charges are supported by evidence, the choice of counts to prosecute at trial is a right granted only to the Prosecutor. This power was used willingly by the prosecutors of the *ad hoc* tribunals. It seems that the ICC Prosecutor "walked into the shoes" of these prosecutors, assuming that the ICC will adopt the same attitude towards cumulative and alternative charging as it was the case before these tribunals. Meanwhile, the ICC judges decided to narrow the scope of the prosecutorial discretion as to the choice of counts. This re-evaluation constitutes an example of tension between the ICC Prosecutor and the Chambers "in assessing which organ of the Court has the authority to decide which charges should be tried".[42]

It should be also noted that the issue of application of alternative charging should be contemplated in combination with the competence of a court to change the legal characterisation of facts presented by a prosecutor in an indictment. If the court has the right to modify it, then the prosecutor's decision as to legal characterisation of facts does not have to be final: it does not determine the legal basis of the conviction. In this aspect, the ICC legal framework differs from that of the *ad hoc* tribunals. Under Regulation 55 of the Regulations of the Court, the Trial Chamber may re-characterise a crime to give it the most appropriate legal characterisation. Therefore, before the ICC, there is no need for the Prosecutor to adopt an alternative charging approach and present all possible characterisations in order to ensure that at least one could be retained by the Chamber. It is for the Chamber to

[39] *The Prosecutor v. Al Bashir*, Decision on the Prosecution's Application for a Warrant of Arrest against Omar Hassan Ahmad Al Bashir, 14 March 2009, § 95–96.

[40] *The Prosecutor v. Ruto*, Decision on the Confirmation of Charges Pursuant to Article 61(7) (a) and (b) of the Rome Statute, 23 January 2012, § 279–281.

[41] Friman et al. (2013), p. 393.

[42] Cit. after: Locke (2012), p. 637.

characterise the facts put forward by the Prosecutor. It appears that the application of alternative charging is a remnant of relying on the common law tradition by the *ad hoc* tribunals, in which the characterisation of facts presented by the Prosecutor was binding for the judges. In this model, alternative charging constitutes a safeguard against a situation in which the court decides that the presented evidence proves that the elements of crime have not been fulfilled. In proceedings before the International Criminal Court, this practice is no longer justified. It may, then, seem somewhat surprising that in such a situation, the judges of the ICC did not rely on the advanced doctrine of concurrence of legal provisions (real and formal, or in German: *echte Konkurrenz*, Art. 68 StGB und *unechte Konkurrenz*) already existing in the continental model of accusation and instead referred to the "alternative and cumulative charging" doctrine used in Anglo-Saxon systems—even if it has no justification in the judicial review model adopted before the International Criminal Court.[43] The only justification for this solution is the fact that it relies on the existing judicial practice of the *ad hoc* tribunals relating to this issue—having in mind though that it significantly narrowed the scope of application of the cumulative charging practice. It should be, however, noted that these tribunals operate on other assumptions, with the accusation model typical for common law states playing a dominant role.

4.2.3 *Consequences of a Defective Indictment*

In Anglo-Saxon systems, erroneous preparation of an indictment by a prosecutor has serious consequences: it may lead to acquittal of the accused or reversal of the judgement. A judgement issued on the basis of a wrongly formulated indictment will be reversed if the defence demonstrates that the entire trial should be considered as lacking integrity as a result of such a defect.[44] If the defect of an indictment, however, is not serious enough to lead to a miscarriage of justice, the conviction may be upheld by the court. Such is the case with so-called technical errors; as, e.g., it was decided in the *U.S. Federal Rules of Criminal Procedure*, unless the defendant was misled and thereby prejudiced, neither an error in a citation nor a citation's omission is a ground to dismiss the indictment or information or to reverse a conviction[45] or "trivial mistakes" (such as misspelling a name). Moreover, a procedure known as "a motion to quash the indictment" may be followed. However, this procedure signifies that after a successful motion to quash the

[43] Although there are many opposite opinions, as, e.g., in Friman et al. (2013), p. 488.

[44] See: Wiliński and Kuczyńska (2009), p. 196.

[45] In American federal law: *Federal Rules of Criminal Procedure*, Rule 7.1., version of 1 December 2012, http://www.law.cornell.edu/rules/frcrmp/rule_7. Accessed 1 Sept 2014.

indictment, the prosecution is entitled to commence fresh proceedings in respect of the same matters.[46]

In continental systems, the consequences of defective formulation of an indictment, whether formal or concerning the merits of the case, do not have to lead to acquittal. A defective indictment will be returned to the prosecutor as a result of a preliminary review of the indictment so that it can be cured. There are two ways to do this, the application of which is based on the stage of proceedings at which the indictment is found to be wrongly formulated: first, an indictment can be remedied under both the formal review and the review of its merits performed at the pre-trial hearing, as a result of which the case may be remanded to the state prosecutor in order to correct deficiencies of vital significance in the investigation (e.g., Article 339(3)(4) CCP[47]); second, when the case is already at the trial stage the court may refer the case back to the prosecutor in order to complete the investigation (Article 397 (1) CCP[48]). The first institution signifies that a deficient indictment can be remanded to the prosecutor so long until the prosecutor files a formally correct version thereof.

Whereas the former practice is used within the preliminary review of an indictment, the latter enables the deficiencies of investigation to be remedied at the stage of court proceedings. In the Polish criminal procedure, pursuant to Article 397 (1) CCP, if essential deficiencies of the investigation have become apparent at the trial, and their removal, were it to be done by the court, would prevent the court from issuing the correct judgement within a reasonable time, the court may discontinue or postpone the trial and refer the case back to the prosecutor, indicating a deadline to present evidence whose discovery would allow the remedy of the detected deficiencies.

This practice of returning a case to complete the investigation provides an opportunity to avoid an acquittal verdict by the court. The court may resolve doubts arising from the lack of adequate evidence for the benefit of the accused only as a result of the prosecutor's failure to present such evidence. The representatives of the Polish legal doctrine indicate that this practice should be applied only when there is no possibility of pursuing with the case any further.[49] Every time formal deficiencies are noticed, their nature and possibilities to remedy them by the court should be investigated thoroughly, as not every deficiency is significant enough to result in a return of the case for supplementary investigation to the prosecutor. "Major difficulties" do not necessarily entail the "impossibility" of eliminating the deficiencies by the court on its own. On the other hand, other authors believe that the prosecutor's duty to complete the investigation prevents the main trial from becoming a peculiar judicial investigation and, as such, counteracts situations in which the court takes over tasks inherent to investigation, simultaneously

[46] As in the English system—see: Ward and Wragg (2005), p. 586; Sprack (2012), pp. 253–254, an approach expressed also in: R v. Shields [2011] EWCA Crim 2343, the Appeal Court of 25 October 2011.

[47] As of the 1 July 2015 Article 339(4)(3) CCP is annulled (Dz.U. of 2013, pos. 1247).

[48] As of the 1 July 2015 Article 397 CCP is annulled (Dz.U. of 2013, pos. 1247).

[49] See: Razowski (2005), pp. 190–192; Olszewski (2004), p. 75; Stefański (1998), p. 28; Szyprowski (1999), p. 86.

guaranteeing that the responsibility to produce evidence rests with the prosecutor. It should be, however, noted that the above considerations will become unfounded when an amendment of the Code of Criminal Proceedings comes into force by way of the Act of 27 September 2013 (on the 1st of June 2015),[50] which enhances the adversarial nature of Polish criminal proceedings. It will repeal both of the aforementioned provisions, which will significantly affect the consequences of defective drafting of the indictment, as they will become similar to those existing in common law systems. One of the consequences of adopting the principle that the judicial authority is not responsible for collecting evidence, and is deprived of evidentiary initiative, is an assumption that it also cannot order the production of evidence in addition to that already presented during the trial by the parties. It does also mean that the prosecutor will not be able to remedy the deficiencies of the indictment. However, the amendments provide for another solution if the prosecutor deems production of new evidence necessary: the prosecutor may request a break in the hearing so as to enable him to gather additional evidence in support of the facts as presented in the indictment.

In proceedings before the *ad hoc* tribunals, the model typical for Anglo-Saxon systems has been adopted. It was assumed that the deficiencies of an indictment are impossible to remedy at the stage of court proceedings and as such should lead to acquittal of the accused. The correctness of the indictment is all the more significant since the legal characterisation of facts adopted by the Prosecutor is binding for the Trial Chamber. The adoption of an erroneous legal characterisation of facts or ambiguity and vagueness of charges may lead to overturning the entire conviction or the conviction as it relates to specific charges (as, e.g., in a case of wrongly adopted cumulative legal characterisation of facts).[51]

When an indictment is found to be defective—it fails to set forth the specific material facts against the accused or due to drafting errors it lacks the proper technical form—judges have two options. First, the Trial Chamber must decide whether the deficiencies may be remedied by way of amending the indictment by the Prosecutor, with the trial being postponed. Another solution is curing the deficiencies of the indictment during the court proceedings, by providing "timely, clear and consistent" information to the defendant on the factual basis of the charges and evidence to support them.[52] The judges will then assess whether the remedy of deficiencies of the indictment allows the accused to understand the nature of the alleged charges and to prepare properly for the defence.[53]

Second, it should be always considered whether a fair trial was ensured to the accused despite the errors in the indictment. Immaterial deficiencies may remain without any impact on the trial as long as the right to a fair trial of the accused is not

---

50 Act of 27 September 2013 amending the Act—Code of Criminal Proceedings, Dz.U. of 2013, pos. 1282.

51 See: *Prosecutor v. Kupreškić*, IT-95-16, judgment of the Trial Chamber of 14 January 2000, § 823.

52 See: Tochilovsky (2008), pp. 85–87, and the jurisprudence cited there and Locke (2012), p. 645.

53 *Prosecutor v. Naletilić*, IT-98-34, Trial Chamber, 31 March 2003, § 27.

affected. However, fundamental defects may result in the Trial Chamber disregarding the charge or the Appeals Chamber reversing a conviction that was decided on the basis of a deficient indictment.[54] For example, in one of its cases the ICTR ruled that an indictment could not be cured because the Prosecutor claimed that the accused controlled a different armed group that committed rape, not the one specified in the indictment. It was thus not possible to cure the indictment because to do so would amount to a "radical transformation" of the case.[55]

In proceedings before the ICC, the consequences of defective drafting of an indictment are not as critical. The confirmation hearing becomes a filter for improperly formulated indictments. If an indictment is imprecise or erroneously phrased out in formal terms, the Pre-Trial Chamber may postpone the hearing in order to enable the Prosecutor to carry on with the investigation or to amend the charges. It provides an opportunity for the Prosecutor to collect additional evidence or to correct the errors of this document. As far as the curing of the indictment is concerned after it has been approved by the Pre-Trial Chamber, pursuant to Article 61(9) of the Statute, "After the charges are confirmed and before the trial has begun, the Prosecutor may, with the permission of the Pre-Trial Chamber and after notice to the accused, amend the charges". If the Prosecutor seeks to amend charges already confirmed before the trial has begun, in accordance with Article 61, he may make a written request to the Pre-Trial Chamber (Rule 128). If the Prosecutor wants to present additional charges in the indictment or replace them with more serious ones, it is necessary to conduct proceedings to confirm the charges by the Pre-Trial Chamber pursuant to the basic procedure. However, once the trial has commenced, and specifically when the charges have been submitted to the Trial Chamber, the Prosecutor may only withdraw the charges upon the permission of the Trial Chamber; it is impossible, however, to supplement them or to replace them with more serious ones.

4.3 Judicial Control of Bringing an Accusation

4.3.1 Continental Model

The judicial review of both the merits and the formal contents of an indictment is a distinctive feature of the continental model of accusation.[56] The concept of the judicial review of an indictment in the Polish legal system covers the following aspects:

(1) the analysis of formal requirements of the indictment the filing of which to the court initiates court proceedings;

[54] *Prosecutor v. Krnojelac*, IT-97-25, Appeals Chamber, 17 September 2003, § 141–142.

[55] *Prosecutor v. Muvunyi*, ICTR-2000-55A, Trial Chamber, 29 August 2008, § 160–166. In general see: Cryer et al. (2010), p. 457; and Locke (2012), p. 645.

[56] See: Ambos (2000), p. 98.

(2) the analysis of legal and factual grounds for accusation;
(3) the analysis of correctness and completeness of the actions undertaken during the preparatory proceedings.[57]

First and foremost, however, the court analyses compliance with the formal requirements of the indictment. Pursuant to Article 337 § 1 CCP, if an indictment does not meet the formal criteria, the president of the court remands it to the state prosecutor in order that the deficiencies may be corrected within a 7-day period. The public prosecutor is obliged to file the corrected or supplemented indictment within the stipulated deadline. It is characteristic that the review may be performed both *ex officio* and as requested by a party to the judicial proceedings.[58]

The second group of the court's review competences pertains to the examination of the suitability of a petition (indictment) in terms of its merits. The review of the indictment's merits is performed during a hearing. During the hearing, first, the judicial authority controls if there are grounds to believe that the proceedings should be discontinued by reason of a manifest absence of any factual basis for charge (Article 339 § 3 CCP). A manifest absence of factual basis for an accusation is a situation in which it is evident and clear and there are no doubts that the collected evidence does not justify the accusation of a given person.[59]

Second, as a result of a completed review of an indictment's merits, the appointed judge may conclude that the case needs to be remanded to the state prosecutor in order to correct deficiencies of essential significance in the investigation (Article 339 § 4 p. 2 CCP). Pursuant to Article 345 § 1 CCP,[60] the court shall remand the case to the state prosecutor if the case's files indicate the essential deficiencies of the proceedings, especially the need to search for evidence, and where conducting necessary actions by the court would entail substantial hardship. Although the court is provided with powers to produce evidence *ex officio* (Article 167 CCP), it is not its responsibility to search for evidence or to secure it and to perform the necessary actions for its proper discovery.[61] When handing a case over to the prosecutor, the court indicates the specific deficiency in evidence. It may emphasise that there is a need for presenting specific evidence (e.g., an expert's opinion) or for conducting mandatory steps of the investigation (e.g., presenting charges to the suspect). The court may not, however, force the prosecutor to formulate charges in a given way, nor may it suggest the legal characterisation of facts that is, in its opinion, correct.[62] The prosecutor is bound by the court's decision to a limited extent. From the moment the indictment is returned, the prosecutor becomes the master of the proceedings again and may continue in any way: he may discontinue the proceedings, uphold the existing indictment, file a new

[57] After: Razowski (2005), p. 29.

[58] However, in 90 % of cases the control is realised ex officio. See: Stefański (1998), p. 28.

[59] See: Paprzycki (2010), pp. 1074–1081; Hofmański et al. (2011), pp. 352–354.

[60] Article 345 CCP is annulled as of 1 July 2015, Dz. U. of 2013, pos. 1247.

[61] See: Grzegorczyk (2008), p. 699; Razowski (2005), p. 181.

[62] See: Grzegorczyk (2008), p. 735.

one or suspend the proceedings. This will change with the coming into force of the amendment to the Code of Criminal Proceedings of 27 September 2013.[63] In the Explanatory Report to the draft, it was indicated that the judicial authority should have no right to review a filed indictment in terms of completeness of the accompanying evidence. In the planned model of proceedings the review of the sufficiency of evidence collected by the prosecutor will be the responsibility of the prosecutor himself and not of the court.

The evaluation of the indictment and of the presented evidence is performed by a judge, usually on the basis of the evidence presented in the case file, but such court hearings may become adversarial in nature. The parties, defence counsels and representatives may participate in the court hearing (Article 339 § 5 CCP). This offers the prosecutor the opportunity to take the floor during the hearing and present their reasons that may have an impact on the decision of the court.[64] He may present additional circumstances against discontinuation of the proceedings in addition to those included in the indictment (althought it rarely happens in practice).[65]

Also, in German criminal procedure strong judicial powers are manifested during the preliminary judicial review of the indictment. Upon completion of the investigation at the stage between instances, a judge is appointed, who examines in an *in camera* hearing whether the proceedings conducted by the prosecutor have provided sufficient grounds to suspect that a crime has been committed (*hinreichender Tatverdacht*, § 199(1) StPO). This decision is taken on the basis of the materials contained in the case file (*dossier*) without holding any adversarial hearing. When there is a well-founded suspicion that the act the accused is charged with has been committed, and the judge decides that the indictment is justified, the indictment can be admitted and the trial is opened. The judge may conclude, however, that the prosecutor has failed to demonstrate it and may order a further search for evidence during the same hearing or modify the charges by removing or amending certain allegations (then the prosecutor is obliged to read out the indictment in the version amended by the judge). He may then also refuse to open the trial (§202, §207(2), §204 StPO, respectively).

The powers of the judge during the pre-trial review of an indictment in German criminal procedure can be divided into two groups: the first type is a simple assessment of the investigation conducted by the prosecutor and the police; the second group of competencies relates to a specific type of a judicial investigation—conducting a judge's own enquiry. As a result of this preliminary judicial review of the case, which will be presented at the trial stage, the judge himself can eliminate existing prosecutorial deficiencies in the establishment of sufficient suspicion. The judge himself may use certain legal instruments to collect evidence and at this stage may, e.g., summon witnesses. It is a *proprio motu* power but can also be conducted on the initiative of the person charged. This power allows him "to raise additional

[63] Act of 27 September 2013 amending the Act—Code of Criminal Proceedings, Dz.U. of 2013, pos. 1282.

[64] Wąsek-Wiaderek (2003), p. 315.

[65] See: Syta (1999), p. 30; Razowski (2005), p. 185; Kardas (2012), p. 37.

evidence to support or weaken the necessary 'sufficient suspicion' that the accused committed the crime".[66] He may choose to take evidence himself during the trial or oblige the prosecutor to do so. The prosecutor may, but does not have to, collect the suggested evidence. In consequence, the preliminary judicial scrutiny shifts the responsibility for the matter of evidence to the judicial authority and clearly establishes a principle of a judge-led enquiry in trial.[67]

It may be noticed that in the German procedure the powerful role of the judge related to the screening of cases that "deserve" to be forwarded to the trial stage should be seen in conjunction with his powerful role during the trial, when he has broad competences related to conducting evidence *ex officio*. Owing to the powerful review functions performed during the preliminary hearing, he may more efficiently eliminate the cases that should not go to trial.[68] Thus, the judge is empowered to provide a "framework for the trial" in order to avoid unnecessary extension of the trial and clear up the case. The judicial authority is not bound by the indictment but obliged to independently search for the material truth and assess the legal value of the prosecutor's case. These powers of a judicial authority are referred to as an "inquisitorial principle" (*Untersuchungsgrundsatz,* § 155 (2) StPO). Moreover, it cannot be overlooked that in this model control of the proceedings lies with the judge, who deprives the prosecutor of the supervision over the indictment.

The continental systems are based on the assumption that the objective of the judicial review of prosecutor's actions is not to "undermine trust" in his actions but rather to "encourage him to be pro-active and diligent in the pursuit of the objective truth".[69] On the other hand some still believe that the impact of the judge on the contents of the indictment is in conflict with the judicial function of adjudicating and introduces an element of "inquisition" to the procedure.[70] They claim that if it is not the prosecutor who controls the contents and filing of an indictment, only the court, it is not the prosecutor, but the court, who is the real accusatory.[71] On the other hand, others appreciate a powerful interference of the judicial body in the prosecutor's activities.[72]

---

66 See in general: Ambos and Miller (2007), p. 355.

67 Cit. after: Hauck (2008), p. 48.

68 For more information, see: Hauck (2008), pp. 47–49; Hunt (2001), p. 139; Beulke (2005), pp. 205–209; Volk (2006), pp. 151–157. Although, as the last author concludes, only in 1 % of cases the proceedings is discontinued at this stage because of manifest absence of any factual basis for charge.

69 Kaftal (1974), p. 17. Similarily: Stachowiak S (1975) p. 109, Waltoś (1968) p. 23.

70 As "chasing after the criminal would undermine the authority of the court"—Mogilnicki (1929) Motywy ustawodawcze do Kodeksu postępowania karnego z 1928 r. cit. after: Kulesza (1988), p. 94.

71 As Glaser (1929) Zarys polskiego procesu karnego, Warszawa 1929, pp. 70–71, cit. after: Daszkiewicz (1960), p. 11.

72 As Kulesza (1988), pp. 93–104.

4.3.2 Common Law Model

In the common law model of accusation, judicial review of the prosecutor's activities during investigation is much more limited—judicial interference in this phase is seen as "an inconvenient element"[73] Judicial review of the filing of an indictment by the prosecutor at the inter-instance proceedings is performed during the preliminary hearing (preparatory hearing). The single objective of such a hearing is a review of merits—judges decide whether the evidence in possession of the prosecution provides a sufficient basis for acknowledging that a trial should be held (i.e., whether it justifies the presumption that a crime was committed by the accused), making sure that there is a *prima facie* case against the accused. The review of an indictment as regards technical requirements is not known here.[74]

In the United States, the preliminary hearing is the most significant aspect of the judicial review of the prosecutor's activities in investigation. Its aim is to prevent any "hasty, malicious, improvident and oppressive prosecutions" and to ensure that "there are substantial grounds upon which a prosecution may be based".[75] The prosecutor needs to prepare evidence to convince judges during this hearing that the case should be heard during the trial.[76] The standard of proof that rests with the prosecution is showing a "probable cause". The main objective of this stage is not yet to prove the defendant's guilt beyond any doubt but rather to present their responsibility as more probable. To require proof beyond a reasonable doubt, which is a higher evidentiary standard, would make holding a later criminal trial redundant.[77] Its only objective is to reject groundless cases.[78] The review takes place during an adversarial hearing, allowing the parties to undertake activities similar to those performed in the proceedings: they may, among others, interview witnesses (sometimes, however, only to a limited extent). At the preliminary hearing, the defendant may introduce evidence (present exculpatory testimony and cross-examine adverse witnesses).[79] However, a preliminary hearing certainly should not turn into a full-blown criminal trial. Usually, the parties themselves prevent the occurrence of such a situation, as they prefer to save their strategic moves for the trial itself. In the case of more serious crimes (e.g., those punishable by the death penalty), federal law and some states require that the review of an indictment in terms of its merits is performed by the grand jury. In such cases, it is usually an

---

[73] Hauck (2008), p. 50.

[74] For more, see: Stahn (2009), p. 253; Hunt (2001), p. 139.

[75] *Thies v. State* (178 Wis. 98 [1922]), Supreme Court of Wisconsin.

[76] *Federal Rules of Criminal Procedure*, Rule 5.1, version of 1 December 2012, http://www.law.cornell.edu/rules/frcrmp/rule_5.1. Accessed 1 Sept 2014.

[77] As decided in: *Coleman v. Alabama*, 399 U.P. 1 (1970), Supreme Court, 22 June 1970.

[78] See in general: Worrall (2007), p. 293; LaFave et al. (2009), pp. 744–746.

[79] However, the Supreme Court of the United States concluded that there is no constitutional right to cross-examine at the preliminary hearing. The courts have discretion over the extent of cross-examination. See: Worrall (2007), p. 293; LaFave et al. (2009), pp. 761–766.

internal procedure, in session *in camera*, without attendance of the prosecutor and the person charged. Sometimes only the prosecutor may present his arguments. However, in some states at this stage also the suspect may already present exculpatory testimony and even summon witnesses.[80]

If at the preliminary hearing judges find a probable cause to believe an offence has been committed and the defendant committed it, they must promptly require the defendant to appear for further proceedings.

The English legal system also knows preliminary hearings during which a judicial authority reviews the suitability of an indictment filed by a prosecutor. These include a preparatory hearing before the Crown Court (sections 28–38 CPIA).[81] During the preparatory hearing, the judge assesses whether there is a *prima facie* case. Only after such an assessment has been performed can a case be submitted to trial. However, it should be stressed that judges "do not investigate the case committed to trial but only control the evidence of the prosecution and thus 'filter out' the manifestly unfounded cases".[82] Moreover, the main aim of the hearing becomes an "active case management" in order "to reduce the number of ineffective and cracked trials and delays during the trial":[83] The hearing is usually committed to preparation of the case for trial in order to identify issues that are likely to be material to the verdict of the jury, to assist their comprehension of any such issues, to expedite the proceedings before the jury, to assist the judge's management of the trial or to consider questions as to the severance and joinder of charges. The hearing is summoned on the application of the prosecutor, on the application of the accused or on the judge's own motion. At the hearing, the judge may order the prosecutor to give the court and the accused a case statement that includes the principal facts of the case for the prosecution, including information about the witnesses who will speak to those facts, any exhibits relevant to those facts and the proposition of law on which the prosecutor proposes to rely. He may also be ordered to prepare the prosecution evidence and any explanatory material in such a form as appears to the judge to be likely to aid comprehension; this is a chance for the prosecutor to present any inferences that he is asking the jury to draw from the evidence. Once the prosecution has supplied such a case statement, the judge may order the defence to supply a statement setting out in general terms the nature of the defence and the principal matters on which they take issue with the prosecutor, including any objections that they have to the prosecution case statement. During this hearing, the accused is notified about the contents of the charges, and he has the opportunity to acquaint himself with the case statement. The hearing

---

[80] Federal Rules of Criminal Procedure, Rule 6, http://www.law.cornell.edu/rules/frcrmp/rule_6. Accessed 1 Sept 2014.

[81] *Criminal Procedure and Investigations Act 1996*: http://www.legislation.gov.uk/ukpga/1996/25/contents. Accessed 1 Sept 2014.

[82] Ambos and Miller (2007), p. 349.

[83] *Ibidem*.

is also adversarial in nature in that the accused may, when requested by the court, provide explanations and present the evidence of his innocence.[84]

In the past, also Magistrates' Courts decided whether there was a *prima facie* case to be sent to trial during a pre-trial judicial review called "committal proceedings". However, beginning in 1967, the procedure started to be reduced to a mere formality and reached the stage where the prosecutor could completely bypass the committal proceedings in certain cases by a process called "transfer for trial". Later, the possibility to interview witnesses was abolished, turning it into a written procedure. Finally, in 2003, the committal proceedings were abolished for all offences before these courts. In consequence, as on numerous other occasions, we can see that the English model of judicial review in this aspect is closer to the continental tradition than to its American counterpart.

4.3.3 Model Adopted by International Criminal Tribunals

Before international criminal tribunals as well, the review of justifiability of an indictment is performed at the inter-instance proceedings stage as "a linking interface between the investigation and trial".[85] These courts have adopted a *sui generis* solution for judicial review of an accusation in general and an indictment. The elements of the inter-instance stage are derived from various legal systems and, combined, create a solution that is unique and different from each of those systems. Confirmation of an indictment by a judicial authority became the element of the judicial authority review over the Prosecutor's activities in investigation that is common for all the tribunals. The procedure of confirmation of an indictment (before the *ad hoc* tribunals) or of charges (before the ICC) constitutes a preliminary review of the indictment by means of which the court assesses, first of all, its correctness in terms of merits.[86]

In proceedings before international military tribunals, there was no mechanism for preliminary judicial review of an indictment (or accusation in general) that would make it possible to assess at this stage whether the evidence collected by the Prosecutor was sufficient to commit the case to trial. There was no requirement to have the indictment approved by a judicial authority. Instead, the indictment was to be unanimously approved by four Chief Prosecutors: "The Chief Prosecutors shall act as a committee for the purpose to lodge the Indictment and the accompanying documents with the Tribunal" (Article 14 of the Charter of the International Military Tribunal in Nuremberg). The only example of judicial review over the work of the Prosecutors could be seen when the judges dismissed the motion to

[84] See in general: Sprack (2012), pp. 258–266 and 175–176.

[85] Cit. after: Ambos and Miller (2007), p. 335.

[86] See in general: Ambos (2007), p. 455; Schabas (2008), p. 732; Izydorczyk and Wiliński (2005), p. 70; Schabas (2010), p. 734; Hauck (2008), pp. 55–56.

amend the indictment by changing defendants.[87] The lack of judicial review of an indictment seemed to have a certain impact on further proceedings before the IMT in Tokyo: "it should nonetheless occasion no surprise that at the outset of its judgment the majority of the Tribunal dismissed forty five of the fifty five charges on grounds of redundancy, lack of jurisdiction, the merging of one count into another or because a charge was stated obscurely".[88]

The Statutes of the *ad hoc* tribunals for the first time introduced the possibility of reviewing the work of the Prosecutor as early as at the stage of issuing an indictment. In proceedings before these tribunals, while the decision to commence investigation is left to the discretion of the Prosecutor, the decision to lodge the indictment is subject to restrictions. Only after the review performed by a judicial authority—during the so-called review procedure—has shown that the Prosecutor provided evidence that, if accepted, would suffice to convict can the case be sent to trial.

The procedure for judicial confirmation of the indictment is provided by the Rules of Procedure and Evidence of the ICTY. The Prosecutor is to file an indictment when he is convinced that the "collected evidence is sufficient to become reasonably convinced that the accused committed the crime, which falls under the jurisdiction of the Tribunal". The appointed judge of the Trial Chamber confirms an indictment (he is then excluded from adjudication, Rule 47(A), Rule 15 (C) RPE). He is in charge of examining each of the presented charges and supporting evidence as presented by the Prosecutor in order to decide "whether there is a *prima facie* case against the accused" (Article 19(1) of the Statute). The judicial review aims to determine whether:

(a) the acts that the accused is charged with fall under the jurisdiction of the Tribunal or not; and
(b) the Prosecutor presented sufficient evidence to justify the charges formulated in the indictment.[89]

The term "*prima facie* case", as understood in common law systems, means a case in which the prosecutor produces evidence that provides a reasonable basis to believe that the guilt of the accused will be proven beyond any doubt in the trial. In the ICTY judicial practice, it has been assumed that the term designates a case that is "trustworthy and when approved and unchallenged, may provide a sufficient basis for the conviction of the accused", "a credible case, which would (if not contradicted by the Defence) be sufficient basis to convict the accused on the charge".[90] This phrase could be translated as "visible at first sight", "based on the

[87] See: deGuzman and Schabas (2013), p. 134.

[88] Cit after: Boister and Cryer (2000), p. 72.

[89] In general see: Hunt (2001), pp. 137 et seq.; Tochilovsky (2008), p. 51; Vasiliev (2012), pp. 740–742; Bassiouni and Manikas (1996), p. 900; Safferling (2001), p. 183.

[90] *Prosecutor v. Kupreškić*, IT-95-16, Decision on Review of the Indictment, 10 November 1995, § 14.

first impression", and the closest legal equivalent of the concept in Polish language would be "a reasonable suspicion that the crime was committed". It is, however, not clear what, if any, consequences arise from using two different phrases in the legislation of the *ad hoc* tribunals in relation to the same evidentiary threshold that should be met by the Prosecutor. The ICTY Statute provides that, first, the Prosecutor "shall assess the information received or obtained and decide whether there is sufficient basis to proceed", and then the court authority should analyse the presented evidence to verify whether the Prosecutor established a *prima facie* case. It seems that these notions are synonymous and that a *prima facie* case (whose existence is examined by the judge) occurs in a situation when the evidence collected by the Prosecutor leads to a conclusion that "there is sufficient basis to proceed" (which is to be proven by the Prosecutor while requesting the approval for the indictment).

When the appointed judge of the Trial Chamber is convinced that a *prima facie* case has been established by the Prosecutor, he shall confirm the indictment (Articles 18(4) ICTY and 17(4) ICTR). If not so satisfied, the indictment shall be dismissed. The judge may also request that the Prosecutor present additional evidence to support the charges, refuse to approve charges or postpone the hearing to give the Prosecutor the chance to amend the indictment. The refusal to confirm the indictment does not, however, exclude further proceedings in a given case: the Prosecutor may apply for a re-approval of the indictment if he presents additional evidence to support the charges.

4.3.4 *Judicial Control of Charges Before the ICC*

In proceedings before the ICC, the procedure for confirmation of charges also ends the stage of investigation (Article 61 of the ICC Statute). It is another stage of criminal proceedings during which the work of the Prosecutor is subject to a judicial authority's assessment: having granted authorisation for conducting the investigation and having issued an arrest warrant upon the Prosecutor's motion, it is the third occasion on which a judicial authority assesses whether the evidence and the information collected by the Prosecutor justify the transfer of the procedure to the next stage—this time, to court proceedings. The confirmation procedure has undergone a remarkable transformation compared to the *ad hoc* tribunals:

(1) A different form of document than that existing before the *ad hoc* tribunals has been used. The adopted nomenclature ("confirmation of charges" before the ICC and "confirmation of the indictment" before the *ad hoc* tribunals) reflects the negotiators' will to differentiate between these two practices; the Prosecutor presents charges rather than an indictment before the ICC;
(2) The confirmation procedure itself is different. Before the *ad hoc* tribunals, the review procedure is conducted by a single appointed judge and is an internal procedure. This is most similar to the grand jury review in the United States.

At this stage, the accused cannot challenge the outcomes of the investigation. Before the ICC, this practice has been significantly developed. The major differences are as follows:

(a) The confirmation is granted during a hearing of the Pre-Trial Chamber.
(b) This hearing is adversarial in nature. It is attended by the suspect and their defence counsel. In this way, the Prosecutor's claims may be immediately confronted with the response of the suspect, who has the right to participate in this hearing. It gives the suspect an opportunity to challenge the evidence presented by the Prosecutor and to present the evidence in his defence even prior to the formal commencement of court proceedings.
(c) The reference to the Anglo-Saxon procedural institution of "a *prima facie* case" was abandoned and replaced with the continental requirement to "have sufficient evidence to establish substantial grounds to believe that the person committed each of the crimes charged" (Article 61(7)).

4.3.5 Confirmation of Charges Before the ICC

When, according to the Prosecutor, the evidence collected during investigation substantiates the suspicion that the committed crimes fall within the jurisdiction of the Court, and the premise of Article 60(1) of the Statute has been met (the person has been surrendered to the Court or appeared before the Court voluntarily or pursuant to a summons), the Prosecutor files a motion with the Pre-Trial Chamber to approve the charges of the indictment.

Pursuant to the ICC Statute, the suspect (the Statute carefully avoids using the term "the accused" until the charges are confirmed) and the Prosecutor must participate in the confirmation hearing. At this stage, the suspect already has the right to be assisted by counsel. The Statute provides that if the suspect has waived his right to participate in the hearing or has fled (or otherwise cannot be found), this hearing may be held in his absence unless the Pre-Trial Chamber decides otherwise.

During this hearing, the Prosecutor presents charges, supporting them with evidence substantiating the belief that the suspect committed the alleged crime. The suspect has the chance to challenge the charges and produce evidence to support his statements. The parties may also raise their objections as to the Court's jurisdiction over a given case. If possible, they may also call witnesses. This depends on the adopted strategy and the decision as to whether using specific evidence will not be more useful if done during the course of the trial. It should be stressed that the parties are not obliged to present all evidence at the confirmation hearing but only the (supporting or refuting) "sufficient evidence" that is necessary "to establish substantial grounds to believe that the person committed each of the crimes charged" (or that he did not commit these crimes). During the confirmation hearing on the situation in Kenya, the Prosecutor decided against calling witnesses, but the defence called 43 witnesses. The Pre-Trial Chamber, however, indicating the objectives and the limited scope of the confirmation hearing, instructed the defence to limit the number of witnesses to 2 per suspect.[91] The defendant's strategy may also involve raising the grounds for excluding criminal responsibility pursuant to Article 31 of the Statute, or mistakes in procedural law or substantive law (in such case, it is, however, necessary to report such objections 3 days prior to the date of the hearing). The suspect may challenge not only the grounds for the charges but also the admissibility of evidence. It is characteristic that, since the Prosecutor's role is to establish the true facts of a case (the material truth), he may also raise such objections against the indictment during the hearing.

On the other hand, during the confirmation hearing, it is not necessary to examine the temporal and territorial jurisdiction of the Court. This examination is always performed by the Pre-Trial Chamber while analysing if there is sufficient basis to proceed with an investigation and authorising the commencement of the investigation by the Prosecutor. Therefore, it is not necessary to reassess the existence of *ratione loci* and *ratione materiae*. If the Court has already confirmed that it has the jurisdiction over a given case in the scope indicated by the Prosecutor, then, if the Prosecutor has conducted its investigation adhering to the scope authorised by the Pre-Trial Chamber, it is clear that it still has that jurisdiction.[92] This procedure is also designed to enable to evaluate evidence that may have been collected under different systems and in various countries before any decision as to whether the case may be sent to trial.[93]

The Pre-Trial Chamber shall, on the basis of the hearing, determine whether there is sufficient evidence to establish substantial grounds to believe that the person committed each of the crimes charged. Based on its determination, the Pre-Trial Chamber shall do as follows:

(1) Confirm those charges in relation to which it has determined that there is sufficient evidence and commit the person to a Trial Chamber for trial on the charges as confirmed. This decision cannot be appealed (*a contrario* Article 82 (d) of the Statute). Approval of the decision, which is a summary of the outcomes of the investigation, means that the judges claim there are grounds to commit the case to trial.
(2) If there is insufficient evidence to confirm the prosecution's charges, the Chamber declines to confirm them. Any and all previously issued warrants cease to have effect with respect to any charges that have not been confirmed by the Pre-Trial Chamber. The refusal to confirm the charges is not definitive. The Prosecutor may continue with the investigation. Article 61(8) of the Statute provides that "where the Pre-Trial Chamber declines to confirm a charge, the

[91] *The Prosecutor v. William Samoei Ruto*, ICC-01/09-01/11, Decision on the Confirmation of Charges Pursuant to Article 61(7)(a) and (b) of the Rome Statute, 23 January 2012, § 14.

[92] *The Prosecutor v. William Samoei Ruto*, ICC-01/09-01/11-1, Decision on the Prosecutor's Application for Summons to Appear for William Samoei Ruto, Hevol.y Kiprono Kosgey and Joshua Arap Sang, 8 March 2011, § 10–11.

[93] Such a conclusion presented in: Calvo-Goller (2006), p. 171.

Prosecutor shall not be precluded from subsequently requesting its confirmation if the request is supported by additional evidence". This leads to the conclusion that any subsequent request for confirmation can be filed only on the basis of additional evidence indicating the justifiability of the articulated charges.

(3) The Pre-Trial Chamber may also adjourn the hearing and request the Prosecutor to consider

(a) providing further evidence or conducting further investigation with respect to a particular charge; or
(b) amending a charge because the evidence submitted appears to establish a different crime within the jurisdiction of the Court.

Also, adjourning the hearing does not entail a definitive ruling on the justifiability of filing the indictment but only constitutes "a prima facie finding that the Pre-Trial Chamber has doubts as to the legal characterization of the facts as reflected in the document containing the charges".[94] The adopted regulation enables the Prosecutor to renew the search for evidence that could substantiate the presented charges. This procedure resembles the option of remanding the case to the Prosecutor at the preliminary hearing in order to correct deficiencies of essential significance in the investigation, known in the Polish legal system (Article 339 § 3 p. 4 CCP). Obliging the Prosecutor during the pre-trial hearing by the judge to complete the evidence is also known in German criminal procedure (§ 204 StPO).

The Pre-Trial Chamber can also confirm some of the charges and take one of the aforementioned decisions as regards the others (Rule 127).

The practice shows that the Pre-Trial Chamber also has a fourth option: rather than adjourning the hearing in order to enable the Prosecutor to present evidence to support the charges, it may modify the legal characterisation of facts allegedly committed by the defendant itself if submitted charges indicate that, in its opinion, another crime occurred within the Court's jurisdiction.[95] At this stage, the Pre-Trial Chamber may confirm that the presented evidence points to the commission of a crime different from the crime assumed by the Prosecutor.

The confirmation hearing proceeds pursuant to the agenda ordered by the presiding judge of the Pre-Trial Chamber. The presiding judge determines how the hearing is to be conducted and, in particular, may establish the order and the conditions under which he intends the evidence contained in the record of the proceedings to be presented (Rule 122(1)). During this hearing, the principles of the laws of evidence are applicable that were provided for the trial in Article 69 of the Rome Statute (pursuant to Rule 122(9) RPE). This means that the Pre-Trial Chamber may rule on the admissibility of charges as early as at this stage of the proceedings and may even request presentation of specific evidence by the parties

---

[94] *The Prosecutor v. Bemba*, ICC-01/05-01/08, Decision Adjourning the Hearing pursuant to Article 61(7)(c)(ii) of the Rome Statute, 3 March 2009, § 25.

[95] *The Prosecutor v. Lubanga*, Decision on the confirmation of charges, 29 January 2007, § 200–237.

and review such evidence on its own. As a result, the judicial authority may already become the organ that manages presentation of evidence during the inter-instance proceedings. This hearing also allows the judicial authority to perform a *quasi*-investigative function by indicating what type of evidence should be presented by the Prosecutor in order to make the charges more probable.[96] As early as this, the judicial authority has the competences to comply with the obligation to search for the material truth. For the representatives of the common law doctrine, this powers manifest an unwelcome phenomenon of "inviting the judiciary to take over the job of prosecuting which is incompatible with the Anglo-American adversarial model upon which the Court is principally based".[97] Interestingly, the proactive involvement of the judge in this hearing may depend, similar to the case of the trial phase, on the tradition from which the judge hails. Judges from the continental law tradition may demonstrate a natural tendency to be more involved. However, whereas a judge coming from the continental legal order may use his authority actively during a confirmation hearing, during the trial the Anglo-Saxon model of presenting evidence may prevail and the judge coming from that tradition may take on a passive role.[98]

4.3.6 Determination of Substantial Grounds for an Indictment Before the International Criminal Court

The Pre-Trial Chamber confirms the Prosecutor's charges if there is "sufficient evidence to establish substantial grounds to believe that the person committed each of the crimes charged". To establish "sufficient evidence", the Prosecutor needs to present specific and tangible proof in support of his belief that the crime was committed: "'substantial' can be understood as 'significant', 'solid', 'material', 'well built', 'real' rather than 'imaginary'".[99] For the Prosecutor to meet the evidentiary burden, he must offer concrete and tangible proof demonstrating a clear line of reasoning underpinning his specific allegations. The purpose of the confirmation hearing is to ensure that no case proceeds to trial without sufficient evidence to establish substantial grounds to believe that the person committed the crime or crimes with which he has been charged. This mechanism is designed to protect the rights of the defence against wrongful prosecution.[100] It also serves the

[96] In a manner typical for the continental model of prosecution—as it is claimed by: Hauck (2008), pp. 55–56.

[97] Cit. after: Jackson (2009), p. 35.

[98] See: Hauck (2008), pp. 56–57.

[99] *The Prosecutor v. Bemba*, ICC-01/05-01/08, Decision Pursuant to Article 61(7)(a) and (b) of the Rome Statute on the Charges of the Prosecutor Against Jean-Pierre Bemba Gombo, 15 June 2009, § 29.

[100] *The Prosecutor v. Lubanga*, 29 January 2007, § 63.

goals of judicial economy by allowing to distinguish between cases that should go to trial from those that should not.[101]

At this stage, the Prosecutor is still not required to present charges that would result in "being convinced of the guilt of the accused beyond reasonable doubt" as mentioned in Article 66 of the ICC Statute, which is the standard required for conviction—as the nature of evidentiary thresholds established in the Statute depends on the different stages of the proceedings and is also consistent with the foreseeable impact of the relevant decisions on the fundamental human rights of the person charged. The assembled evidence may still have less compelling power than that required for conviction, but the threshold is higher than for the purpose of initiating an investigation.[102] The Pre-Trial Chamber has only to assess whether there are grounds to proceed with the trial, refraining from adjudicating on the suspect's guilt. In the decision on confirmation of charges in *The Prosecutor v. Katanga*, the judges emphasised that the only objective of the confirmation hearing was to demonstrate that there were reasonable grounds to believe that the crime falling within the Court's jurisdiction had been committed. The Pre-Trial Chamber confirms charges if it is convinced that each of them has been sufficiently supported by evidence collected by the prosecution.

The fact that the adversarial hearing may be transformed into a "mini-trial", or "a trial before trial", may be considered a major disadvantage of this model for confirmation of charges.[103] When the Pre-Trial Chamber concludes that the indictment is justified and sends the case to the Trial Chamber, it establishes an inconvenient standard of "judicially confirmed guilt of the suspect", as is often emphasised in the legal doctrine.[104] Such a decision may be seen as a preliminary "guilty" ruling that adversely affects the impartiality of the proceedings, and the accused may find himself in a position where his guilt is prejudiced and he needs to prove his innocence.[105] Accordingly, it is necessary to ensure that evidence is not presented in its entirety during the hearing, but only in such part as substantiates a trial. The Pre-Trial Chamber itself emphasised that "the confirmation hearing has a limited extent and cannot be considered to be the goal in itself, but it should be considered as the means to distinguish between the cases that should go to trial and

---

[101] *The Prosecutor v. Bemba*, ICC-01/05-01/08, Public Document Decision Pursuant to Article 61 (7)(a) and (b) of the Rome Statute on the Charges of the Prosecutor Against Jean-Pierre Bemba Gombo, 15 June 2009, § 28.

[102] *The Prosecutor v. William Samoei Ruto*, ICC-01/09-01/11, Confirmation of Charges, 23 January 2012, § 40; *The Prosecutor v. Lubanga*, ICC-01/04-01/06-749, Prosecution's Document Addressing Matters that were Discussed at the Confirmation Hearing, document of 4 December 2006, § 9–14.

[103] *The Prosecutor v. Katanga*, ICC-01/04-01/07, Decision on the confirmation of the charges, 30 September 2008, § 63; *The Prosecutor v. Bahar Idriss Abu Garda*, ICC-02/05-02/09, Decision on the Confirmation of Charges, 8 February 2010, § 39.

[104] E.g., Calvo-Goller (2006), p. 171.

[105] Such possibility is noticed by: Ambos and Miller (2007), p. 348.

those that should not".[106] Such an opinion is expressed also in the continental legal doctrine, where it is claimed that "introduction of an adversarial debate to pre-trial proceedings, similar to that held during the trial, would challenge the purpose of the trial itself. Involvement of the parties in evidence proceedings renders such proceedings less provisional and enhances their reliability. Thus, it dispenses with the reasons for repeating them before the court".[107]

The broad scope of the pre-trial review of the Prosecutor's actions has become a distinctive feature of the ICC model of accusation.[108] The confirmation hearing is another, besides the requirement to authorise the decision to initiate an investigation, manifestation of the reinforced control of the Prosecutor's actions in pre-trial proceedings. This requirement was less prominent in the case of the *ad hoc* tribunals, as the competences of these courts were temporally and territorially limited. They faced significantly less pressure from the international community to review the actions of the Prosecutor empowered to make independent decisions on initiating proceedings in all cases. In the ICC, the early stage of judicial control over the Prosecutor's actions, manifesting itself not only in the requirement to obtain authorisation of initiation of an investigation and to confirm charges, but also in control over disclosure of evidence, in summoning of pre-trial hearings, brings to mind the institution of the examining magistrate (an investigative judge), who exercises judicial review over the entire course of pre-trial proceedings, or even of the hierarchically superior prosecutor.[109] As indicated in the legal doctrine, the powers of the Pre-Trial Chamber constitute "a unique combination of the competences that in Polish preparatory proceedings are held jointly by the hierarchically superior prosecutor and the court".[110]

However, it appears that concerns that the ICC Prosecutor will start proceedings in a case that is not sufficiently grave to be sent to trial are unfounded. The cases handled by international criminal courts' prosecutors are, by their very nature, sufficiently serious. The practice of international criminal courts shows that the prosecutor has never presented charges in a case that was intended only to intimidate the accused. Moreover, the gravity of cases is usually verified by the ICC Pre-Trial Chamber at the stage of authorisation of the Prosecutor's decision to start an investigation. Thus, it may be concluded that the basic objective of the confirmation proceedings, i.e. to reject insignificant cases, does not find justification.[111] It may even seem that the control over the Prosecutor's actions has become a goal in itself.

[106] *The Prosecutor v. Lubanga*, ICC-01/04-01/06, Decision on the confirmation decision, 29 January 2007, § 37.

[107] Cit. after: Waltoś (1968), p. 263.

[108] What is often highlighted: Shibahara and Schabas (2008), p. 1173; Wei (2007), p. 142.

[109] See: De Hert (2003), p. 98; Ambos (2007), p. 444.

[110] Cit. after: Izydorczyk and Wiliński (2004), pp. 85–86.

[111] See: Schabas (2010), pp. 734–735.

On the other hand, we may also find suggestions that the already powerful judicial review over the Prosecutor's actions should be further enhanced by establishing an "investigating chamber" based on the French model, which would ensure the involvement of judges in handling pre-trial proceedings, facilitating the latter, and ensure more effective enforcement of procedural guarantees.[112] This change—according to the opinions expressed on that topic—would lead to three important improvements in the functioning of the ICC: first, it would foster greater reliance on written evidence (the judge would interview witnesses "in the field", and consequently they would not have to appear at trial), as well as concluding of procedural agreements with the accused—as the judge would have the authority to ensure their enforceability at this stage of adjudication, which poses the most significant problem for the Prosecutor. Second, it would also strengthen the impartiality of the authority handling the pre-trial proceedings; the Prosecutor can never become fully impartial even though the law requires him to be so. Finally, through his involvement in the preparation of case files, the judge would be better acquainted with the particulars of cases and would be able to expedite their resolution. On the other hand, this proposal not only undermines the Prosecutor's independence but also shows a disbelief in the ability of the Prosecutor to be independent. Moreover, it cannot be stated for certain that "reliance on written evidence" and "concluding of procedural agreements" are positive phenomena before the ICC.

4.4 Political Control of Accusation

Supplementing judicial control with political review has become a distinctive feature of the review of bringing an accusation in cases conducted before the International Criminal Court. This model is certainly considered unacceptable in all the states' legal orders in question. Its most prominent characteristic is the requirement to abandon criminal proceedings as a result of a decision taken by a political rather than judicial authority.

The review performed by the States Parties to the ICC Statute and by the Security Council, after they have successfully "referred a situation" to the Court, can be viewed as the first manifestation of political control. These privileged entities become empowered to affect the course of pre-trial proceedings: having reported a crime falling within the Court's jurisdiction, they may initiate the Pre-Trial Chamber's review of the Prosecutor's decision to refuse to undertake investigation or to file an indictment (Article 53(2)(a)).

The second type of review, unrelated to referring a situation, is a *sui generis* political review conducted by the Security Council. Pursuant to Article 16 of the

[112] The idea of an "investigative chamber" appears quite often in the literature, e.g.: de Hemptinne (2007), p. 402; Harmon (2007), p. 377.

ICC Statue, "No investigation or prosecution may be commenced or proceeded with under this Statute for a period of 12 months after the Security Council, in a resolution adopted under Chapter VII of the Charter of the United Nations, has requested the Court to that effect; that request may be renewed by the Council under the same conditions". According to the Polish version of the Rome Statute, this power pertains both to the stage of the Prosecutor's decision to initiate proceedings as well as to the course of investigation initiated after the Pre-Trial Chamber's authorisation. In the English version of the Statute, however, this authority is shaped differently: the provision refers to stopping an investigation or prosecution. Here, the term "prosecution" means filing and supporting the charges before the Court. Thus, the English version of the Statute grants the Security Council a much broader scope of competences. In the English version, the Security Council is awarded with two additional types of authority. First, it may stop filing of the charges by the Prosecutor. The stage at which the investigation may be blocked starts with the official commencement of the investigation—both into a "situation" and a "case". This provision refers to "investigation" rather than to the "preliminary examination of a case". This means that the Security Council may not prevent the Prosecutor from examining a case as long as the latter does not officially commence an investigation. It may not block actions performed as part of the initial analysis of the case. This excludes the possibility of "preventive actions".[113] Therefore, it appears that the Prosecutor is not prevented from gathering information on the deferred case. As the preliminary examination or analysis of information phase precedes the investigation phase, the Prosecutor may undertake actions within the limits of the preliminary examination and thus continue to seek information from states, organs of the UN, inter-governmental or non-governmental organisations and other reliable sources and may receive written or oral testimony to this end.[114]

Second, according to some experts, it may be assumed that the Council may affect the course of a case already pending before the Trial Chamber because the term "prosecution" should be understood as the upholding of an indictment until adjudication.[115]

The relationship between the International Criminal Court and the Security Council was one of the main subjects of controversy among the states participating in the Rome Conference. The model adopted by the *ad hoc* tribunals suggested a close co-operation between the Council and the international court, with the Tribunal's actions subordinated to the Council.[116] Establishing broadly acceptable rules for the co-existence of the Security Council and the ICC, which would ensure

[113] As unanimously concluded by: Bergsmo and Pejić (2008), p. 601; also Stegmiller (2011), p. 157.

[114] Oosthuizen (1999), p. 334.

[115] See: Bergsmo and Pejić (2008), p. 602; Yañez-Barnuevo and Escobar Hernández (2003), p. 53; Milik (2012), pp. 132–133; Stegmiller (2011), p. 157.

[116] Schabas (2009), p. 325; Yañez-Barnuevo and Escobar Hernández (2003), p. 51; Płachta (2007), pp. 480–481; Krzan (2009), pp. 172–173; Stegmiller (2011), p. 154.

balance between political and judicial functions, has become one of the major challenges for the ICC founders. Some states (especially the United States) insisted that the Security Council should be given broad authority. They recommended adoption of a standard that would allow the Security Council to become a sort of a "filter" for proceedings before the Court. This solution was based on the assumption that cases should be investigated by the Prosecutor only when approved by the Council or when they had been reported by the Council. Had this approach prevailed, it would have significantly limited the authority of the Prosecutor and affected his role. A natural consequence would have been the impossibility of initiating proceedings against nationals of the Council members.

The current version of the ICC Statute provides for a narrower scope of powers for the Security Council than originally planned. Article 16 is the only basis for the Council's interference in the actions of the Court. However, even the competences to adjourn the commencement of investigation or proceeding with prosecution may notably restrict the Prosecutor's independence, especially since the request of deferral may be renewed. Because the Statute does not specify the number of times such a deferral may be requested, this may lead to the conclusion that the renewal may be repeated many times, resulting in an indefinite suspension of the investigation.[117] Potentially, the Security Council may see it fit to defer the proceedings "until the conflict in issue is resolved".[118] And although this provision does not foresee a permanent impossibility to conduct proceedings, repeating the resolution may have such consequences. Furthermore, the Statute does not envisage any mechanisms compensating for losses that may arise from the delay in hearing a case. In the meantime, the opportunity to find evidence that an international crime has been committed may be irretrievably wasted. Moreover, there are no guidelines as to how this "suspension" of the course of proceedings should work in practice. While arrest warrants do not become ineffective, they also may not be enforced and new warrants may not be issued. It is not entirely clear what happens with persons already deprived of liberty: should they await the end of the 12-month period (potentially extended) in a pre-trial detention? It may be assumed that in such a situation they could be released on parole (Article 60(2)).[119] This power is difficult to reconcile with the accused's right to "be tried without undue delay".

This institution enables a third-party authority to *veto* a case and to block international criminal proceedings and for reasons that have nothing to do with the administration of justice and criminal responsibility. This competence of the Security Council was a result of the compromise reached in Rome where the three permanent members of the Council in exchange agreed to vote in favour of the

[117] Against such danger warn: Arbour et al. (2000), p. 136; Bergsmo and Pejić (2008), p. 601; Safferling (2001), p. 83; Stegmiller (2011), pp. 153 and 167–168.

[118] Cit. after: Oosthuizen (1999), p. 334.

[119] See: Bergsmo and Pejić (2008), p. 602. Similarly: Stegmiller (2011), p. 159.

Statute.[120] It creates an opportunity to hinder and stop investigations that are considered political and irresponsible—or simply undesired.[121] The Security Council may use this power only when it has reasonable grounds to suspect that the Prosecutor's actions may pose a significant threat to peace and security, within the meaning of Article 39 of the UN Charter. It may, however, apply a broad discretionary margin when judging what situations are consistent with these conditions. On the other hand, if it may be assumed that investigating a case by the ICC Prosecutor may pose "a threat to the peace and security", such assumption questions the very grounds for the ICC's existence, accepting that justice could undermine international peace and security.[122] Moreover, in this way the Security Council questions its own operations under which on another occasion it "established international criminal jurisdictions (ICTY and ICTR) for the maintenance and restoration of peace".[123]

Despite the significance of this power, the Statute has not provided the Security Council with practical tools to review pending cases. This stems from the fact that there is no obligation to notify the Security Council of the initiation of an investigation.[124] Article 18(1) requires the Prosecutor only to notify States Parties and other States that "would normally exercise jurisdiction over the crimes concerned". The Regulations of the Office of the Prosecutor fill this gap to some extent, but only in relation to proceedings commenced under Article 13 of the Statute (Rule 30): the Prosecutor is obliged to notify the Council only if "a situation has been referred to the Prosecutor pursuant to Article 13(b)" and he decides that there is a reasonable basis to initiate an investigation. In all other situations, when the Prosecutor initiates proceedings *proprio motu*, he still does not have to notify the Security Council.

Until now, Article 16 of the Statute has been invoked only to protect members of peace forces who were citizens of states not a party to the ICC Statute from being prosecuted before the ICC. This goal was expressed in Resolution 1422 adopted at the request of the United States. The Security Council requested therein (already 11 days after the Statute became effective) that no investigation was commenced or proceeded with in relation to actions undertaken by citizens of a state not being a party to the Statute under the missions established or authorised by the UN since the ICC was established—unless the Security Council decides otherwise.[125]

[120] See: Yañez-Barnuevo and Escobar Hernández (2003), p. 54; La Haye (1999), p. 13; Cryer (2005), pp. 226–227 Coté (2012), p. 407; Wouters et al. (2008), p. 282; Krzan (2009), p. 163; Ohlin (2009), p. 193.

[121] As observed by Wouters et al. (2008), p. 282.

[122] Safferling (2001), p. 83. However, B. Krzan indicates how a proceedings started by the ICC might negatively influence, or even endanger, international peace, which may lead to a conflict between the Security Council and the Court—Krzan (2009), p. 171.

[123] Cit. after: Stegmiller (2011), p. 163.

[124] Probably as it was assumed that this provision had little chance of practical application—Stegmiller (2011), p. 152.

[125] Resolution UN Doc. S/RES/1422 of 2002: http://daccess-dds-ny.un.org/doc/UNDOC/GEN/N02/477/61/PDF/N0247761.pdf?OpenElement. Accessed 1 Sept 2014.

The Resolution also expressed the Council's intention to renew the request every 12 months "for as long as may be necessary". This Resolution met with a lot of criticism: first, there were claims that it was a contravention of Article 16 of the Statute, which provides a basis exclusively for the suspension (or prevention of initiation) of specific proceedings rather than of all cases in a group; it had never been meant to *a priori* immunise a whole category of persons. Since Article 16 granted an extraordinary authority to third parties, it should be interpreted in narrow terms rather than as the basis for any actions undertaken by such parties. Second, it was indicated that the Resolution was not a necessary measure to protect international security and peace, and, in consequence, the Security Council should not have issued it pursuant to the Charter of the United Nations.[126] In fact, the Resolution even failed to mention that the basis for the ICC to discontinue proceedings was to maintain international peace and security. There were opinions that, since the Security Council did not comply with legal conditions for issuing such a resolution, the ICC should not consider it as binding.[127] Despite this criticism, this Resolution was renewed in 2003. In 2004, after the reports of interrogation methods used by nationals of the United States in Iraq and its base in Guantanamo reached the public, the USA decided not to submit a motion to renew this Resolution for another year.

Resolution 1497, on the other hand, had a much broader impact. The Security Council decided that "current or former officials or personnel from a contributing State which is not a party to the Rome Statute of the International Criminal Court, shall be subject to the exclusive jurisdiction of the contributing State for all alleged acts or omissions arising out of or related to the Multinational Force or United Nations stabilisation force in Liberia, unless such exclusive jurisdiction has been expressly waived by that contributing State".[128] The impact of this Resolution is not limited in time, and the manner in which it was worded indicates that the Council delegated the jurisdiction over such acts solely to one state preventing the jurisdiction to be exercised by other states, e.g., based upon the passive personality principle or universal jurisdiction principle.

The request to apply Article 16 was also submitted to the Security Council by the African Union in 2008 after the ICC Prosecutor issued an arrest warrant for the President of Sudan, al-Bashir. The motion included a request to issue a resolution ordering adjournment of the indictment, but it was not endorsed by the Security Council.[129] This could serve as an indication that in the future, Article 16 of the Rome Statute should be used more carefully[130] or, simply, that the interests of the African Union were not deemed sufficiently important by the Council members. So far, neither of these Resolutions has impeded proceedings conducted by the

---

[126] Schabas (2010), p. 332.

[127] See: Stegmiller (2011), p. 173.

[128] Resolution UN Doc. S/RES/1497 of 2003.

[129] In general see: Schabas (2010), p. 331.

[130] See: Krzan (2009), p. 192.

International Criminal Court, and, consequently, the judicial authority has not found the opportunity to discuss their validity.

4.5 Judicial Control of Refusal to Prosecute

Both in common law and continental law systems, there is a judicial review of the grounds for bringing an accusation. The major difference between these systems as far as judicial powers are concerned pertains to judicial review of the prosecutor's decision not to initiate an investigation. This type of control is contemplated as a possibility to avoid arbitrary and non-transparent choices in the prosecutorial determinations concerning criminal action. Whereas in the common law model judicial review of the reasonableness of the prosecutor's decision not to hold the proceedings is (although existing) often considered to be an "interference with the powers of the prosecutor", in the continental model it is one of the assumptions of a fair criminal procedure.

Both the Polish and German Codes of Criminal Proceedings provide that the court reviews the decision both refusing to initiate an investigation or to discontinue it. The prosecutor's decision not to investigate, or not to investigate further because of insufficient evidence or because there was no violation of law, is not necessarily the end of a case. The court review may lead to compelling the prosecutor to prosecute by a judicial decision. J. H. Langbein proposes to describe this institution in Anglo-American terminology as a *mandamus action*.[131] Following reception of a party's complaint, the court may revoke the prosecutor's decision to discontinue investigation or to refuse to institute it. In such a case, the court must indicate the reasons for revoking and, if needed, also the circumstances that should be clarified or actions that should be conducted. These indications shall be binding on the state prosecutor. Revocation of a decision results in a "judicial order to investigate".[132] If the prosecutor, however, still does not find grounds to file an indictment, he again issues a decision on the discontinuance of proceedings or a refusal to institute it (this time the decision is final). In such a situation, the injured party may bring a private indictment (Article 330 § 1 and § 2 CCP). In German proceedings, this statutory procedure bears the name *Klageerzwingungsverfahren* (which could be translated into procedure for a forcible imposition of an accusation). If the court is persuaded that the prosecution is required, it orders it to be brought. The *mandamus procedure* permits judicial review of the prosecutor's evaluation under the rule of compulsory prosecution that he lacked "sufficient factual basis" for proceeding, that is, that there was no probable cause. Also, the German StPO provides that where the victim does succeed in *mandamusing* the prosecution, he is entitled to participate as an accessory accusing party (*Nebenkläger*) at the subsequent criminal trial. In both cases, however, the prosecutor cannot be forced to prosecute a case

[131] The terminology adopted, e.g., in: Langbein (1973–1974), p. 463, also Herrmannt (1973–1974), p. 476.

[132] As mentioned by: Turone (2002), p. 1165.

against his will.[133] According to German scholars, this judicial review is intended to be a "safeguard against prosecutorial abuse of power and is regarded as an important means for the citizen to enforce the rule of compulsory prosecution". Moreover, "because of the availability of these procedures, the prosecutor seems to be somewhat more reluctant to discontinue an investigation when there is a victim who can bring such a complaint".[134]

In Anglo-Saxon systems, the judicial control of accusation is unique in the sense that it is conducted "one-way only": the court verifies whether the filing of an indictment is justified and whether an indictment in an unimportant case would not be a waste of the court's time and efforts. Once the Prosecutor has decided not to file an indictment, the court cannot influence his decision.

This principle, which is a staple of the Anglo-Saxon model of accusation, is, however, being revisited, and a gradual departure from this restrictive view of the prosecutor's discretion may be observed. In England, the prosecutor's decision on whether to hold proceedings and file an indictment in the court, or whether to use other measures of criminal reaction (e.g., a caution), is more and more frequently subjected to judicial review.[135] In the first case dealing with judicial review of the prosecutor's discretion to prosecute, the House of Lords concluded that a decision not to prosecute should be open to judicial review only upon restricted basis, as the risk of "opening too wide the door of review of the discretion" should be avoided.[136] In its opinion, the review should be possible, but the actual interference of the court with the prosecutorial discretion should be a rare practice, employed only in extreme cases. Despite the discouraging tone of the ruling, a judicial review of the prosecutor's decision is now more frequently demanded.[137] Usually, however, the courts conclude that as long as the police and prosecutor act within the boundaries of the law, their decision on whether to finalise proceedings with a "caution" or to bring a case before the court should not be challenged as this would constitute an "inappropriate interference with the operational decisions of the police".[138] As a result, judges are quite reluctant to review the prosecutor's decision not to prosecute.

In the United States also, the judicial or instance review has been applied in practice. Some states have introduced the requirement that a decision not to prosecute must be approved by the court (the judicial approval of *Nolle Prosequi*—that is, of an entry on the record by the prosecutor declaring that he will not prosecute) or at least that a prosecutor must produce written reasons for his decision not to prosecute. The principal object of this requirement is to protect a

---

133 See these notions explained in: Langbein (1973–1974), p. 464.

134 Both citations after: Herrmannt (1973–1974), p. 477.

135 In the 1980s, the judicial control referred only to 2 % of cases where an indictment was filed. Kulesza (1987), p. 87.

136 *R v. Chief Constable of Kent County Constabulary, ex parte L, R v DPP, ex parte B*, [1993] 1 All ER 756, Watkins LJ. In: Padfield (2008), p. 181.

137 Padfield (2008), p. 164.

138 *R (F) v. CPS* [2003] EWHC 3266 (2004), 165 JP 93. In: Padfield (2008), p. 164.

defendant against prosecutorial harassment, e.g. charging, dismissing and recharging, when the prosecutor moves to dismiss an indictment over the defendant objection.[139] Although judicial review of the prosecutor's decisions is formally ensured, in practice courts rarely challenge the prosecutor's opinions. The Supreme Court of the United States has also expressed criticism of judicial review of prosecutorial discretion: "such factors as the strength of the case, the prosecution's general deterrence value, the Government's overall enforcement plan are not readily susceptible to the kind of analysis the courts are competent to make".[140] Depending on the jurisdiction, superior authorities (e.g., state prosecutor, attorney general) may also in some cases consider a prosecutor's decision to be inadequate. They may pursue a case then, but this happens rarely. It is equally rare for an indictment to be approved by the grand jury if the prosecutor opposes the prosecution.[141]

There is no remedy for a private citizen to force the prosecutor to file an indictment: as J. H. Langbein mentions, "what makes this problem of prosecutorial discretion so acute in American practice is that our prosecutor has a monopoly over the criminal process. (…) No other officer and no private citizen, not even the victim, may come forward to prosecute when the public prosecutor will not. No one else may make good the prosecutor's neglect".[142]

In the proceedings before the *ad hoc* tribunals, the judicial scrutiny of the grounds underpinning the refusal to prosecute is not known.[143] On the other hand, in the ICC proceedings that follow the continental model, the judicial review performed by the Pre-Trial Chamber covers the grounds for non-prosecution. This pertains to two groups of decisions: decisions not to proceed with an investigation and decisions not to file an indictment when the investigation has already been completed:

(1) The Prosecutor may refuse to investigate when he decides "that there is no reasonable basis to proceed" (Article 53(1) of the Rome Statute). He is entitled to do so even if a situation was referred by a state or the Security Council.
(2) The Prosecutor may refuse to prosecute when "upon investigation, [he] concludes that there is not a sufficient basis for a prosecution" (Article 53(2)).

However, the question remains whether the Prosecutor's decisions not to investigate made prior to the official initiation of the proceedings should be subject to the review of the Pre-Trial Chamber. The "preliminary examination" mentioned in Article 15 of the Statute held in order to examine whether there are grounds for investigation should be separated from the investigation held pursuant to Article 53 of the Statute. If, at this stage, the Prosecutor concludes that the initiation of

[139] As in *Rinaldi v. United States*, 434 U.S. 22 (1977).

[140] *Wayte v. United States*, 470 U.P. 598 [1985], Supreme Court, 19 March 1985.

[141] LaFave et al. (2009), p. 717; Worrall (2007), p. 313.

[142] Cit. after: Langbein (1973–1974), p. 440.

[143] Which was also noticed by: Reydams et al. (2012), p. 935.

proceedings is unjustified, his decision may also be reviewed by the Pre-Trial Chamber.[144]

The Pre-Trial Chamber may review the decisions not to proceed with an investigation or a prosecution in two different ways.

First, the review may be carried out upon request by the state presenting the situation or by the Security Council, if it has triggered the jurisdiction. The latter may submit to the Pre-Trial Chamber a motion to examine the grounds for the prosecutorial decision within 90 days from the Prosecutor's submission of the notification on refusal to investigate (to prosecute). If, on the other hand, a situation is referred to the Court by a state, pursuant to the interpretation adopted by the Prosecutor, only such reporting state is entitled to activate judicial review.[145] Having examined the Prosecutor's decision, the Pre-Trial Chamber requests the Prosecutor to review, in whole or in part, his decision not to initiate an investigation or not to prosecute, and "the Prosecutor shall reconsider that decision as soon as possible" (Rule 107 and 108). It may also request the Prosecutor to transmit the information or documents in his or her possession, or summaries thereof, that the Chamber considers necessary for the conduct of the review. The legal doctrine is not clear on whether his decision should be deemed final. Some experts indicate that the Statute does not specify whether the right of the Pre-Trial Chamber to refuse to approve the Prosecution's decision can be exercised only once or whether it can be used several times.[146] However, the wording of the provision in Rule 108(3) seems to be unambiguous in this regard: "Once the Prosecutor has taken a final decision, he or she shall notify the Pre-Trial Chamber in writing. This notification shall contain the conclusion of the Prosecutor and the reasons for the conclusion". It follows that this decision is final.[147] As a result, in the event that the Prosecutor refuses to pursue investigation following a "re-consideration" of the case, his decision becomes *res iudicata* for the Pre-Trial Chamber. This request is not, then, equivalent to a demand to pursue investigation, but rather it is only a motion to reconsider the decision. The Prosecutor may maintain his determination not to initiate an investigation. Thus, it is neither a "judicial order to investigate" (as known in continental systems) nor an "investigation on judicial command".[148] Only the Prosecutor has the right to alter it—Article 53(4) of the Statute provides that "the Prosecutor may, at any time, reconsider a decision on whether to initiate an investigation or prosecution based on new facts or information".

---

[144] See: Wei (2007), p. 82; Friman (2001), p. 497.

[145] *Situation in the Central African Republic*, ICC-01/05, Prosecution's Report Pursuant to Pre-Trial Chamber III's 30, November 2006 Decision Requesting Information on the Status of the Preliminary Examination of the Situation in the Central African Republic, 15 December 2006, § 10.

[146] See: Schabas (2010), p. 670; Bergsmo and Kruger (2008), p. 1075; and Turone (2002), p. 1165.

[147] But differently: Wouters et al. (2008), p. 302, who claim that a new review under the same conditions may follow.

[148] Turone et al. p. 1165.

Second, the Pre-Trial Chamber may undertake the review of the grounds for non-prosecution on its own initiative. When the Prosecutor refuses to investigate (Article 53(1)(c)) or to prosecute (Article 53(2)(c)) due to the fact that, despite taking the gravity of a crime and the interests of victims into account, there are reasons to believe that the investigation would not support the interest of the administration of justice, this decision will take effect only upon its confirmation by the Pre-Trial Chamber (Rule 109 (1)). The Chamber undertakes the review on its own initiative, and within 180 days from receipt of the Prosecutor's notification, it may establish a time limit within which the Prosecutor must provide his comments, additional information and supporting documents. If the Pre-Trial Chamber does not confirm the Prosecutor's decision, it orders him to pursue investigation (Rule 110). The Rules of Procedure and Evidence are clear about this: the Prosecutor is obliged to initiate the investigation. In consequence, if the Pre-Trial Chamber does not confirm the Prosecutor's decision, because it is of the opinion that it is in the interests of justice to start an investigation and due to the absence of other grounds not to initiate investigations, the Prosecutor has no possibility not to start investigations.[149]

This gives rise to a unique concept of a "judicial order to investigate", which is similar to that existing in the Polish procedure (Article 330 § 1 and §2 CCP). Similar to the case with its Polish counterpart, its consequences are somewhat vague: as the Pre-Trial Chamber does not have at its disposal any instruments for pursuing investigation, the Prosecutor is free to choose what kind of actions he will undertake. Certainly, the judges neither have tools to force the Prosecutor to do something that he manifestly has decided not to pursue, nor can they independently assign investigators.

However, it is clear that not in every case such a review will take place. There is no general obligation to confirm every decision based on Article 53(1)(c). It will happen only if the Pre-Trial Chamber wishes to review the decision of the Prosecutor.

As a result of adopting such a review model, the consequences of judicial review before the ICC will differ depending on the way in which the review was initiated and the basis for the Prosecutor's refusal to investigate or prosecute. If the Prosecutor does not cite "no interest for the administration of justice" as the reason why he refused to investigate or to prosecute, then his decision may be appealed only by an authorised state and the Security Council. Furthermore, when the Prosecutor relies on any other basis than "no interest for the administration of justice", his decision becomes final despite the Chamber's review, as the latter may oblige the Prosecutor only to "re-consider his decision" rather than to proceed with the case. In consequence, a model of "variable quantity" of independence of the Prosecutor has been adopted.[150] The Pre-Trial Chamber may order the prosecution to proceed with the case only if the question of no interest for the administration of justice has been

[149] As in: Wouters et al. (2008), p. 302.

[150] By: Turone (2002), p. 1146.

raised. In this way, the proper selection of a basis for refusal provides the Prosecutor with immunity against the judicial review that could challenge his decision.[151]

4.6 Authority of a Judicial Organ to Modify Legal Characterisation of Facts

4.6.1 Continental Model

One of the main differences in the accusation model between common law and continental law states is the court's binding with the legal characterisation of facts adopted in the indictment by the prosecutor. The right to amend such a characterisation may be considered to be an element of the judicial authority's control over the prosecutor's actions.

In accordance with the principle of *iura novit curia* (the court knows the law), continental law states do not deem the legal characterisation of facts offered by the prosecutor as binding for the court but rather see it as a suggestion (recommendation). It is the judge who decides on the applicable law, and it is upon him to issue a binding characterisation.

The basic assumption found in these systems is the preservation of identity of the act charged and the act for which the defendant has been convicted. The scope of the case tried is determined by acts the accused is charged with understood as facts and not as their legal characterisation. The judge is only bound as to the selection of situations by the prosecutor in the indictment and the corresponding factual allegations, but he is free to do his own legal evaluation of these facts. The factual allegations are set by a historical (factual) event described in an indictment, and such limits are considered to have been exceeded only when the factual basis of an event rather than the legal basis of criminal responsibility established by the prosecutor is overstepped. The adjudicating court is also not bound by the description of specific elements of the charged act, e.g., time of a specific conduct, the amount of the arising loss or its outcomes, if these modifications remain within the framework of the same factual event.[152] The court's modification of the legal characterisation of facts suggested by the prosecutor in an indictment is connected to the obligation to provide the accused with specific procedural guarantees. Pursuant to Article 399(1) CCP, if in the course of the trial it transpires that while remaining within the limits of the accusation an act may be classified under another legal provision, the court must advise the parties of this. The accused may request that the trial is suspended so as to enable him to prepare for defence. The legal characterisation of facts can even be modified at the appeal trial (Article 455 CCP).

[151] See: Schabas (2010), p. 669.

[152] Polish Supreme Court decision, 25 June 2008, IV KK 39/08, Biul.PK 2008, vol. 10, p. 17; Polish Supreme Court decision, 19 October 2010., III KK 97/10, OSNKW 2011, vol. 6, p. 50.

The German court is similarly not bound by the prosecutor's recommendation on the legal characterisation of facts. It may modify the substantive criminal law provision referred to in the charges admitted by the court, under two conditions: firstly, the defendant's attention should be specifically drawn to the change in the legal reference, and secondly he should be afforded an opportunity to defend himself (Article 265(1) and (2) StPO). The judge has to advise the accused about the possibility of investigating his legal responsibility under other provisions of substantive criminal law. However, the accused has the right not only to request the suspension of the trial in order to sufficiently prepare for defence (the court may also suspend the hearing *proprio motu*) but also to repeat evidentiary proceedings if the modification of legal characterisation of facts would enable the application of a more severe criminal law provision against the defendant than the one referred to in the charges admitted by the court.[153]

4.6.2 Common Law Model

As a rule, in common law states it is the prosecutor who decides on the legal characterisation of the act for which the accused may be convicted. The description of facts presented in an indictment is binding because it is assumed that the accused will prepare his defence with a view to a particular characterisation of facts. Consequently, the adoption of a different legal characterisation during trial would be an infringement of his right to information and defence. In Anglo-Saxon systems, defective formulation of legal characterisation of facts may lead to acquittal, as the jury has a simple choice between acquitting and convicting the accused. Sometimes, though, it is possible to find the accused guilty not as charged in the counts but of some other lesser offence (so-called lesser included offence). A distinctive legal concept is employed by which the accused is convicted for the commission of a different offence than the one alleged in the indictment if the former act by implication "amounts to or includes an allegation of another offence", e.g., in the case of a burglary that "includes allegation" of a theft.[154] This solution was introduced with the intention of facilitating the prosecutor's work—despite his not being able to prove an offence specified in the indictment, the accused is convicted; in accordance with the principle of *ne bis in idem,* no legal proceedings could be instituted twice for the same behaviour. In the Anglo-Saxon model, the consequence of binding force of a legal characterisation of facts presented by a prosecutor is the inclusion of a large number of alternative and cumulative charges in the indictment to avoid acquittal as a result of the judge's opinion that none of the presented legal characterisations of facts is supported by the evidence introduced in

[153] See: Schuon (2010), pp. 70–71; Beulke (2005), p. 163.

[154] Both citations after: Sprack (2012), pp. 357–363.

the prosecution case. If the jury acquits on the more serious (major) count, they can still convict on one of the less serious counts included in the indictment.

4.6.3 *Model Adopted by the* Ad Hoc *Tribunals*

International criminal courts had to choose between the different solutions for legal characterisation of facts adopted in the indictment, existing in two different legal traditions.[155]

In the proceedings before the ICTY, neither the Statute nor the Rules of Procedure deal with the problem of modification of legal characterisation of facts by the Trial Chamber. This issue was resolved *sui generis* in the case law. The judges concluded that the principle applied in common law states cannot be rejected. The advantages and disadvantages of the powers granted to the judicial authority were examined in the ruling issued in the case *Prosecutor v. Kupreškić*. The ICTY carried out a comprehensive, comparative assessment of various legal orders and the solutions adopted in them. Following that, the ICTY judges expressed a view that "for the time being it is questionable that the *iura novit curia* principle (whereby it is for a court of law to determine what relevant legal provisions are applicable and how facts should be legally classified) fully applies in international criminal proceedings".[156] However, they did not rule out the possibility of amending the legal classification of alleged acts at all. Thus, although the judges may not influence the classification of facts, the Trial Chamber connected the powers of the judicial authority to modify the legal characterisation included in the indictment, with the principles governing the alteration of charges by the Prosecutor.

The Trial Chamber distinguished between three different proceedings, depending on whether the amendment of characterisation pertains to

(1) a crime that is different from the charged one;
(2) *lex specialis*; or
(3) a more serious crime.

(1) When during court proceedings the Prosecutor concludes that he has failed to prove beyond reasonable doubt the commission of a crime but the presented evidence may prove that another crime has been committed or that it has been committed in another form, the Prosecutor should apply for the Trial Chamber's consent to amend the indictment. This will give the defence time to prepare to challenge the new charges. The Trial Chamber may also decline the legal characterisation of facts suggested by the Prosecutor. This pertains, in

[155] In general see: Stahn (2005), pp. 4–5; Ambos and Miller (2007), pp. 357–358; Safferling (2001), p. 341.

[156] *Prosecutor v. Kupreškić*, IT-95-16, Trial Chamber, 14 January 2000, § 723–748.

particular, to situations when elements of a crime have not been fulfilled and the judges decided that the acts of the accused could be characterised as a different international law crime falling under the jurisdiction of the Tribunal. In such a case, the judges may ask the Prosecutor to amend the indictment. If he is unwilling to do so, the Trial Chamber "will have no other choice, but to dismiss the petition".[157]

(2) If the Prosecutor finds that he is able to prove that a less serious crime has been committed, he does not have to turn to the Trial Chamber for permission to amend the legal characterisation of facts. It should be then assumed that if the accused was able to challenge charges of a *lex specialis* nature, he also could have challenged all *lex generalis* criteria (the doctrine of the lesser included offence). The Prosecutor, however, should always inform the defence that he intends to prove a less serious crime.[158] The same criteria that pertain to the amendment of the legal characterisation of facts by the Prosecutor should be applied in relation to the reclassification of facts by the Trial Chamber. If the Chamber concludes that commission of a more serious crime has not been proven, then it may consider the accused guilty of the less serious crime. It is sufficient that the judges mention this fact in their judgment, without asking the Prosecutor to amend the indictment. A similar principle applies in the case of adopting a less strict form of participation, e.g., aiding and abetting rather than complicity. It is worth mentioning that already in 1995 the ICTY judges refused to apply the doctrine of lesser included offence in *Prosecutor v. Tadić*, stating that they might only adjudicate on the basis of the legal characterisation of facts presented by the Prosecutor.[159]

(3) If the Trial Chamber concludes that the presented evidence proves that a more serious crime has been committed, then it should ask the Prosecutor to consider amendment of the indictment. Alternatively, it may find the accused guilty of committing a less serious crime than the one charged in the indictment.[160] It will always resort to the latter solution if the Prosecutor refuses to alter the indictment.

The Tribunal has not accepted the independence of judicial authority in modification of the legal characterisation of facts, based on two assumptions. First, it acknowledged that there was a gap in international criminal procedure, and, as a consequence, existence of such powers could not be confirmed beyond any doubt. Second, a potential adverse impact that the execution of this authority could have on the rights of the accused, in particular on their right to prepare effectively for defence, could not be ignored. This principle could violate the accused's rights

[157] *Prosecutor v. Kupreškić*, IT-95-16, Trial Chamber, 14 January 2000, § 748–748.

[158] This requirement is mentioned by: Stahn (2005), p. 16; Keegan and Mundis (2001), pp. 132–133.

[159] *Prosecutor v. Tadić*, IT-95-16, Appeals Chamber Decision on Jurisdiction, decision of 2 October 1995, § 87; *Prosecutor v. Kupreškić*, 14 January 2000, § 653.

[160] *Prosecutor v. Kupreškić*, 14 January 2000, § 747.

guaranteed in Article 21(4)(a) of the ICTY Statute, which provides that an accused shall be informed "promptly and in detail" of the "nature and cause of the charge against him". According to the judges' opinion, adoption of the continental approach would prevent the accused from preparing for defence, as he would not be familiar with the characterisation of facts.

On the other hand, they emphasised that the need for an efficient discharge of the Tribunal's functions in the interest of justice warrants the conclusion that any possible errors of the Prosecution "should not stultify criminal proceedings whenever a case nevertheless appears to have been made by the Prosecution and its possible flaws in the formulation of the charge are not such as to impair or curtail the rights of the Defence". Therefore, amendments to the indictment by the Prosecutor should be allowed in exceptional situations, when they do not deprive the accused of his rights or violate such rights.[161] Amendments are not, however, introduced by the judicial authority itself: the judges recommend alterations to the Prosecutor, linking their opinion on the necessity of amending the legal characterisation of facts to the principles governing the amendment of charges by the Prosecutor. As a result, the Prosecutor retains control over the legal assessment of the charged act, while the judicial authority always has some impact on the characterisation. This does not interfere with the powers of the Prosecutor, but does not leave it without any measures either.

4.6.4 Model Adopted by the ICC

Before the ICC Regulations of the Court were adopted, the judges in international criminal proceedings had no authority to modify the legal characterisation of facts adopted by the Prosecutor.

However, in the proceedings before the ICC, the applicability of the principle of *iura novit curia* was clearly favoured, and the judges had the right to modify the legal characterisation of facts formulated in the charges. Regulation 55 of the Regulations of the Court provides that "In its final decision the Trial Chamber may change the legal characterization of facts to accord with the crimes under articles 6, 7 or 8, or to accord with the form of participation of the accused under articles 25 and 28". Thus, the modification of characterisation pertains not only to acts but also to the forms of participation (e.g., aiding and abetting rather than complicity). The Trial Chamber may change the legal characterisation of facts only when "it does not exceed the facts and circumstances described in the charges and any amendments to the charges". If, at any time during the trial, it appears to the Chamber that the legal characterisation of facts may be subject to change, the Chamber shall give notice to the participants of such possibility and, having heard the evidence, shall, at an appropriate stage of the proceedings, give the participants

---

[161] *Ibidem*, § 743–748.

the opportunity to make oral or written submissions. The Chamber may suspend the hearing to ensure that the participants have adequate time and facilities for effective preparation, or, if necessary, it may order a hearing to consider all matters relevant to the proposed change.

Suspension of proceedings and repetition of evidentiary proceedings, as well as additional procedures, guarantee that the procedural rights of the accused, in particular the right to prepare adequately for defence, will be respected. The Trial Chamber may also hold a pre-trial hearing in order to prepare for the suggested modification of the legal characterisation of facts. As a result, the accused may bring new evidence into the proceedings, call witnesses and interview them again. The possibility to repeat evidentiary proceedings at a new hearing may be relevant in a situation where the Trial Chamber is already in deliberation deciding the questions of guilt. It should also be allowed for where the change in the legal characterisation requires a fundamental change of the strategy of defence.[162] The objective of these solutions is to address any concerns pertaining to the violation of the accused's rights expressed by the ICTY judges. This regulation's aim is supposed to cure the most serious—in the ICTY judges' opinion—disadvantage of the *iura novit curia* system.

In the case of modification of the legal characterisation of facts by the Trial Chamber judges, it is important that the limits of a historical event that determines the identity of the charged act and the alleged act are specified. In accordance with the Rome Statute, charges brought by the Prosecutor consist of two parts: a legal characterisation of facts and the "facts and circumstances contained in the Prosecution's charges". As in continental legal systems, the charges are composed of two elements: a factual element, the "statement of the facts, including the time and place of the alleged crimes", and a legal element, the "legal characterisation of facts". It is thus possible to change the legal characterisation of a crime without changing the charges. Changing the legal characterisation of facts, while still basing on the facts as set out in the charges, does not automatically lead to amendment of the charges.[163]

In *The Prosecutor v. Lubanga*, the Trial Chamber informed the parties that it intended to amend the legal characterisation of facts presented by the Prosecutor. Following the motion of the victims, it decided to expand the legal description in a manner that would allow the inclusion of a legal characterisation of facts that was not accounted for by the Prosecutor in the indictment but that was arising, in its opinion, from the evidence presented in the case. In the Chamber's opinion, the decision regarding the appropriate legal characterisation of facts can be taken only after the parties have presented evidence.[164]

---

[162] See: Stahn (2005), p. 23.

[163] Cit. after: Stahn (2005), p. 17.

[164] *The Prosecutor v. Lubanga*, ICC-01/04-01/06, Decision on the status before the Trial Chamber of the evidence heard by the Pre-Trial Chamber and the decision of the Pre-Trial Chamber in trial proceedings and the manner in which the evidence shall be submitted, 13 December 2007, § 42–48. A commentary to this decision by: Gallmetzer (2009), p. 518.

The Appeals Chamber declined this way of proceeding. It found that Regulation 55 did not authorise judges to expand *proprio motu* the scope of investigation to include facts and circumstances not charged by the Prosecutor. The judges emphasised that "facts described in the charges" should be distinguished from "subsidiary facts" included in the charges, which consists of the evidence put forward by the Prosecutor at the confirmation hearing to support a charge as well as from background or other information. In light of Article 74(2) of the Statute, which provides that "the decision shall not exceed the facts and circumstances described in the charges and any amendments to the charges", the charges should be understood as facts and circumstances that constitute "factual allegations which support each of the legal elements of the crime charged". Only the "facts described in the charges" determine the limits of examination for a case by the Trial Chamber. Subsidiary facts and additional information are treated as evidence proving that the main facts took place and may be subject to changes. Although they are included in the contents of charges, they do not affect the elements of the crime with which the accused is charged. This decision made it clear that it is the Prosecutor who determines the limits of the criminal procedure before the ICC, despite the judges' attempts to hijack these powers. This approach was further reflected in rulings by the Court. In its decision on the confirmation of charges in *The Prosecutor v. Samoei Ruto*, the Pre-Trial Chamber confirmed that only the evidence presented by the Prosecutor to support the charges, as well as subsidiary facts and additional information, may be subject to change and expansion, as opposed to the main facts that constitute the essence of charges and determine the limits for investigation of the case. Therefore, a distinction must be made between the facts underlying the charges—i.e., the "facts described in the charges", which, as such, are the only ones that cannot be exceeded by the Trial Chamber once confirmed by the Pre-Trial Chamber—and facts or evidence that is subsidiary to the facts described in the charges, serving the purpose of demonstrating or supporting their existence. Notably, subsidiary facts, although referred to in the document containing the charges or in the decision on the confirmation of charges, are of relevance only to the extent that facts described in the charges may be inferred from them.[165]

This brings to mind the principle adopted in Polish and German procedures pursuant to which it is not the description of the charged act or the legal characterisation of facts in the indictment that determines the scope of judicial proceedings but rather the historical event (before the ICC: "facts underlying the charges"), and the ruling court is not bound by the description of the specific elements of the charged act, e.g., the time of a specific conduct, the amount of the resulting loss or its outcomes, as long as the modifications remain within the framework of the same factual event. The court, however, may not exceed the scope of the historical event itself.

[165] *The Prosecutor v. William Samoei Ruto*, ICC-01/09-01/11, Confirmation of Charges, 23 January 2012, § 45, and later The Prosecutor v. Katanga, ICC-01/04-01/07, Decision on the implementation of regulation 55 of the Regulations of the Court and severing the charges against the accused persons, 21 November 2012, § 10.

The legal characterisation of facts may be amended "at any time during trial", so there is no temporal limitation. Therefore, the ICC assumed that the amendment may take place at both the stage of adjudication and the appeal proceedings. In *The Prosecutor v. Katanga*, the ICC concluded that, because the re-characterisation of facts pertained to the "facts described in the charges" included in the charges presented to the accused, it was within their framework, and there had been no violation of the right of information, despite the fact that the amendment of the legal characterisation of facts took place as late as at the stage of deliberations.[166] The basic requirement is, however, to ensure that the rights of the accused are duly respected. Therefore, each time the Court is making a decision as to whether in a given situation it is possible to re-characterise facts, it investigates whether the right of information and right of defence of the accused have not been violated.

Regulation 55 is the next step in the development of international criminal proceedings. It is a device designed to provide for the needs of the International Criminal Court and inspired by the legal heritage of specific states but adjusted to the character of procedures held before the ICC.[167] Its objective is to prevent the acquittal of the accused because of the lack of convincing evidence to support the given legal characterisation of facts even though such evidence indicates that another crime has been committed—which is a characteristic element of the Anglo-Saxon model of accusation. It is also beneficial from the viewpoint of judicial economy because it releases the Prosecutor (and the Chamber) from the burden to file (or recognise) large quantities of alternative or cumulative charges founded on the identical factual basis.[168] The adoption of such a solution proves that the procedural system of the ICC is exceptional when compared to any of the other models of criminal procedure that have served as a starting point for the development of the provision. These legal orders, as well as the jurisprudence of the ICTY, provided the foundations for the development of a unique model of judicial review that is not an exact copy of any of them.[169] Indeed, the jurisprudence of the ICTY "was very system-oriented and perhaps over-pessimistic in its general objection to the concept of the legal characterization of facts on the grounds of the protection of the accused".[170] Meanwhile, there can be no doubt that the continental model is better equipped to maintain the careful balance between the powers of the Trial Chamber and the Pre-Trial Chamber and the powers of the Prosecutor.[171] Regulation 55 is a clear example of giving preference to the continental model of

---

[166] *The Prosecutor v. Katanga*, ICC-01/04-01/07, Decision on the implementation of regulation 55 of the Regulations of the Court and severing the charges against the accused persons, 21 November 2012, § 15–20.

[167] See: Stahn (2005), p. 2.

[168] Ambos and Miller (2007), p. 360.

[169] Stahn (2005), p. 29.

[170] Cit. after: Stahn (2005), p. 29.

[171] Friman et al. (2013), p. 487 add "so long as an accused is protected against 'surprise' judicial re-characterisations and is not unduly burdened against any new legal re-characterisation".

relation between the charges and conviction: adopting the "modification of the characterisation of facts" doctrine rather than a common law methodology of "amendment of the charges". At the same time, it signals that the practice of the *ad hoc* tribunals "is an important, but by no means an exclusive parameter of legal and procedural design".[172]

4.6.5 Control of Legal Characterisation of Facts by the ICC Pre-Trial Chamber

A characteristic feature of the model of accusation before the ICC is not only the Trial Chamber's authority to modify the charges presented by the Prosecutor but also delegation of the same powers to the Pre-Trial Chamber, as the latter may modify the legal characterisation of facts during the confirmation hearing.

The ICTY Rules of Procedure and Evidence provide that only the Prosecutor may amend the legal characterisation of facts adopted in the indictment (Rule 50(A)(i)(C) ICTY RPE). If during the confirmation hearing the judges determine that, e.g., the legal characterisation of facts needs to be modified, they have to notify the Prosecutor of this fact or decline to confirm the indictment.[173]

Until 2007, Pre-Trial Chamber judges were bound by the legal characterisation of facts presented by the Prosecutor in the proceedings before the ICC. Regulation 55 of the ICC Regulations was designed to govern court proceedings and the powers of the Trial Chamber.[174] The legal doctrine, however, suggested that judges of the Pre-Trial Chamber should also have the right to confirm the charges with a modified legal characterisation of the facts, at the confirmation hearing stage, in line with the continental *iura novit curia* principle. It was proposed that Regulation 55 should be applied, by analogy to the pre-trial proceedings stage, or that such competences should be introduced pursuant to another, new provision.[175]

On February 2007, in *The Prosecutor v. Lubanga*, the Pre-Trial Chamber resolved this issue. The confirmation hearing was used by the judges as the occasion to modify the charges against the accused. The Prosecutor had motioned for an arrest warrant in relation to crimes committed "in international armed conflict" (Article 8(2)(b)(xxvi)), but when requesting confirmation of the charges, he referred to crimes committed "in armed conflicts not of an international character" (Article 8(2)(e)(vii) of the Rome Statute). The Pre-Trial Chamber was reluctant to confirm the "softened" legal characterisation of facts and instead opted for a stricter legal characterisation, indicating that the crimes with which the accused was charged had been committed in international military conflict. In this way, the

---

[172] Cit. after: Stahn (2005), p. 29.

[173] As in the case: *Prosecutor v. Kupreškić*, IT-95-16, Trial Chamber, 14 January 2000, § 728.

[174] Regulations of the Court ICC-BD/01-01-04, version of 29 June 2012.

[175] See: Ambos (2007), p. 464.

Chamber changed the contents of the indictment by amending the legal characterisation of the relevant facts.

The Pre-Trial Chamber referred to Regulation 55 of the ICC Regulations, which authorises the Trial Chamber to modify the legal characterisation of facts to accord with the relevant crimes under Articles 6, 7 and 8 of the Statute or with the appropriate form of participation of the accused. The Chamber applied a broad interpretation of the principle according to which judges are not bound by the legal characterisation of facts presented by the Prosecutor. This principle, used in court proceedings of the continental model, was expanded in the Court's jurisprudence to cover proceedings before the Pre-Trial Chamber. It bears a certain similarity to the German procedure, in which, at the stage of initial review of the indictment, the judge may conclude that the Prosecutor has failed to demonstrate the grounds for the presented charges and modify the contents of charges, e.g., by omitting some of them (§207(2) and (3) StPO).

The Prosecutor appealed against this decision, arguing that the Pre-Trial Chamber had no authority to modify the legal characterisation of facts at the confirmation hearing. First, the Prosecutor indicated that this decision was a violation of their independence that was guaranteed by the Statute. It interfered with the Statute-granted powers of the prosecution to amend charges if they are not confirmed by the Pre-Trial Chamber. Second, it imposed an onerous and undesired burden on the Prosecutor, who would have to collect evidence to support the charges articulated by the Chamber.[176] The Prosecutor indicated that the Chamber's decision materially interfered with the exercise of his independence from the judicial authority.

The prosecution's appeal was not accepted for formal reasons. The Appeals Chamber came to a conclusion that "according to the provisions of the Statute and to general principles of criminal law, an interlocutory decision can only be appealed in exceptional circumstances and to avoid irreparable prejudice to the appellant". Moreover, it found that "the drafters of the Statute [had] intentionally excluded decisions confirming charges against a suspect from the categories of decisions which may be appealed directly to the Appeals Chamber".[177] The Statute itself allows for granting leave to appeal only if two cumulative criteria are met, that is, first, it would significantly affect both the fair and expeditious conduct of the proceedings and the outcome of the trial, and second, its immediate resolution by the Appeals Chamber may materially advance the proceedings. Meanwhile, in the opinion of the Pre-Trial Chamber, an appeal of a decision confirming charges always delays commencement of court proceedings and significantly extends their duration. Such delays should be avoided especially when the accused is deprived of liberty. The Pre-Trial Chamber determined that appeals of the

---

[176] *The Prosecutor v. Lubanga*, ICC-01/04-01/06, Application for Leave to Appeal Pre-Trial Chamber "Decision sur la confirmation des charges", 7 February 2007.

[177] *The Prosecutor v. Lubanga*, ICC-01/04-01/06, Decision on the Prosecution and Defence applications for leave to appeal the Decision on the confirmation of charges, 24 May 2007, § 19–27.

confirmation decision would neither ensure a fair and expeditious conduct of the proceedings, nor would it advance them.[178]

Subsequently, the Prosecutor attempted to influence the Trial Chamber so that it refrained from adjudicating on the basis of the charges articulated by the Pre-Trial Chamber and to "strike down or declare null and void the charges as confirmed by the Pre-Trial Chamber"; he wanted the Chamber to separate such charges from those formulated by himself and rule only on the basis of the latter. The Trial Chamber, however, did not endorse the Prosecutor's motion and concluded that it did not have the authority to challenge the Pre-Trial Chamber's decisions. To support this conviction, the judges pointed out that the Pre-Trial Chamber had the exclusive competence to take decisions in relation to charges presented by the Prosecution during the confirmation hearing.[179] The Trial Chamber expressed a view according to which the Pre-Trial Chamber enjoys the sole authority (subject to revision by the Appeals Chamber) over any issue concerning amendments to the charges, certainly before the trial has begun. Although (as the Chamber observed) "it confirmed the charges in their current form by 'amending (the) charge' without specifically giving the prosecution an opportunity to make representations (. . .) the Pre-Trial Chamber observed in its Decision on the applications for leave to appeal that "i) the legal characterization of the conflict as of an international nature had already been mentioned in the Decision on the arrest warrant against Thomas Lubanga Dyilo and ii) the Defence itself raised the issue of the international character of the conflict at the confirmation hearing and all participants had the opportunity to present their observations on the matter". Even if the prosecution unsuccessfully sought leave to appeal the confirmation decision, that step does not nullify or remove the binding force of this decision. The power that the Trial Chamber has during this stage of proceedings does not involve altering the wording or the substance of the charges in any way. It is worth to mention that in case of exceeding the powers by the judges in some jurisdictions an institution of "invalidation" of decisions can be used.

In consequence, the authority of the judges to modify the legal characterisation of facts was used as the means to subject the Prosecutor's actions to judicial review. The judicial power to change the legal characterisation of facts at the confirmation hearing stage deprived the Prosecutor of the right to shape the contents of charges. In this way, during the confirmation hearing the judicial authority was not only able to control but also able to formulate the indictment, which, up to this point, had been a task reserved for the Prosecutor. This powerful position of the Pre-Trial Chamber arising from the above right is a response to the demand for strong control over the actions of the ICC Prosecutor—in a situation where he has almost unrestricted impact on the political situation by way of an indictment, and there

[178] See: Eckelmans (2009), pp. 539–541.

[179] *The Prosecutor v. Lubanga*, ICC-01/04-01/06, Decision on the status before the Trial Chamber of the evidence heard by the Pre-Trial Chamber and the decision of the Pre-Trial Chamber in trial proceedings, and the manner in which the evidence shall be submitted, 13 December 2007, § 39.

is no hierarchical or political review of his actions.[180] It may also be perceived as a manifestation of "a struggle between the Prosecutor and the Pre-Trial Chambers as to the adversarial or inquisitorial nature of the proceedings before the Court".[181]

Acquisition of this power by the Pre-Trial Chamber stirred up much controversy. As the Prosecutor argued, the Statute does not provide the grounds for the Pre-Trial Chamber to impose an obligation on the Prosecutor to charge with specific facts and to seek evidence to support charges he did not include in the charges. The prosecution cannot be expected to prove specific charges formulated by the Pre-Trial Chamber as the latter has no right to order the Prosecutor to conduct evidentiary proceedings in order to prove certain charges.[182]

It should be noted, however, that the legal characterisation of facts may be modified exclusively within the scope of facts described in the charges; using the continental law nomenclature: the Prosecutor is still the party determining the limits of a factual event examined by the Court. In another decision, the Appeals Chamber acknowledged that Regulation 55 does not authorise judges to extend *proprio motu* the scope of the criminal procedure by including subsidiary facts and circumstances not charged by the Prosecutor.[183] This decision eliminated doubts as to the fact that the limits of the criminal trial before the ICC are determined by the facts articulated by the Prosecutor. The factual basis of a conviction is still established by the Prosecutor, despite the judges' efforts to strengthen their influence on the contents of the charges.

4.7 Conclusion

The method and scope of the judicial control over bringing an accusation and specifically the form and contents of an indictment has a significant impact on the model of accusation, as it has on the role of the prosecutor before international criminal courts.

Compared to proceedings held before the *ad hoc* tribunals, there has been some extension of the scope of judicial control over the Prosecutor's actions in

[180] See: Ambos and Miller (2007), p. 349.

[181] Cit. after: Wouters et al. (2008), p. 314.

[182] See: Schabas (2010), p. 743; Shibahara and Schabas (2008), p. 1180; Schabas (2008), pp. 754–755; Cryer et al. (2010), p. 458.

[183] *The Prosecutor v. Lubanga*, ICC-01/04-01/06, Judgment on the Appeals of Mr Lubanga Dyilo and the Prosecutor against the Decision of Trial Chamber I of 14 July 2009 Entitled "Decision giving notice to the parties and participants that the legal characterization of facts may be subject to change in accordance with Regulation 55(2) of the Regulations of the Court", 8 December 2009; and similarly in decisions: *The Prosecutor v. William Samoei Ruto*, ICC-01/09-01/11, Confirmation of Charges, 23 January 2012, § 45; *The Prosecutor v. Katanga*, ICC-01/04-01/07, Decision on the implementation of regulation 55 of the Regulations of the Court and severing the charges against the accused persons, 21 November 2012, § 10. In general see: Boas et al. (2011), p. 43.

proceedings before the International Criminal Court. This broader extent has become a characteristic feature of ICC proceedings. The control goes far beyond the review of merits and the formal review of the charges. Its wide scope is a result of the compromise reached by the states that created the Rome Statute, which limited the Prosecutor's independence but granted him the power to initiate an investigation *proprio motu*. As a result, the Prosecutor was supposed to remain "accountable and with limited powers while [remaining] independent".[184] The ICC example shows how the role of the judicial authority matches the role of the Prosecutor in bringing an indictment before the Trial Chamber and these two cannot be considered separately. This "interplay" between the Prosecutor and the Pre-Trial Chamber may be also contemplated from the inter-systemic perspective and perceived as an example of "a subtle combination of elements derived from different legal traditions".[185] In comparison to the control applied in proceedings before the *ad hoc* tribunals, this model of judicial review has four additional elements.

First, judicial review before the ICC has been extended to cover the grounds for non-prosecution. Judges verify both the decision to refuse to investigate as well as the decision to refuse to prosecute after the investigation stage has been completed. The first type of review is performed at the request of the state referring a situation or of the Security Council. Following an evaluation, the Pre-Trial Chamber may only conclude that the Prosecutor should "reconsider the decision". If, in response to the Chamber's request, the prosecution issues another non-investigation or non-prosecution decision, such a decision is final. The second type of control involves evaluation of the grounds for non-prosecution, which is conducted by the Pre-Trial Chamber on its own initiative. This procedure, however, is applied only when the Prosecutor refuses to file an indictment due to the fact that, despite the gravity of the crime and interests of the victims, there are important reasons to believe that investigation would be in conflict with the interest of the administration of justice. As a result, the consequences of judicial review before the ICC differ depending on the way in which the review was initiated and the basis for the Prosecutor's refusal to investigate. When the Prosecutor cites grounds other than "no interest of the administration of justice" (in a case he initiated *proprio motu*), his decision becomes final. Analysis of this practice reveals that while review of the grounds for non-prosecution is limited, it still provides a method to restrict the Prosecutor's reliance on the principle of prosecutorial opportunism.

Second, the procedure of review of the charges filed by the Prosecutor has been also significantly developed in proceedings before the ICC: it is conducted at a hearing before the Pre-Trial Chamber and is adversarial in nature. This has resulted in the introduction of a *quasi*-trial already at the stage of confirmation of an indictment.

Third, the judicial authority may, during proceedings before the ICC, modify the legal characterisation of facts presented by the Prosecutor in the indictment. On the

---

[184] Cit. after: Wouters et al. (2008), p. 280.

[185] Cit. after: Kress (2003) p. 607.

one hand, this is a useful tool for the Prosecutor, as it helps to prevent the acquittal of the accused in the absence of convincing evidence to support the legal characterisation of facts adopted by him while such evidence points to the commission of a different crime. On the other hand, however, it deprives the Prosecutor of control over the adjudicated charges. Additionally, this competence of the judicial authority was extended to cover the stage of initial judicial review of the indictment, combined with the restricted application of alternative legal characterisation of facts, common in Anglo-Saxon systems. As a consequence, control was imposed over the adequacy of the Prosecutor's legal characterisation of facts, and the Prosecutor's influence over the contents of an indictment and charges was limited for the benefit of the judicial authority.

Fourth, there is the authority of the Pre-Trial Chamber to approve the decision to initiate investigation, analysed in the previous chapter. Its existence may lead to the conclusion that "the Prosecutor is far from independent: he needs to obtain permission before being allowed to go out in the field to initiate investigations".[186]

Analysis of the accusation model would not be complete without considering the political aspect of formulating the charges by the ICC Prosecutor. First, we should mention certain elements of control exercised by the Security Council over the investigation conducted by the Prosecutor. By issuing a resolution, the Council may postpone the commencement of or proceeding with investigation or prosecution for a period of 12 months pursuant to Chapter VII of the UN Charter. This power allows the Council to block prosecution for an indefinite period of time for strictly political reasons that have nothing to do with the interests of the administration of justice.

Moreover, reflections on this aspect of the Prosecutor's role should be related to a broader discussion of the objectives of international criminal law. The actions of the Prosecutor are the consequence of an ongoing discussion regarding the role of the ICC as the guarantor of international security—so-called *security court*, exercising almost diplomatic functions, designed to restore and improve regional peace and security—compared to its role as a criminal court and an organ fighting against impunity.[187]

Analysis of indictments prepared by the ICC Prosecutor and the circumstances of their filing reveals that the Prosecutor's role goes far beyond the prosecution and indictment of perpetrators of international law crimes. At issue is a fundamental debate over whether peace and justice can be pursued simultaneously—and whether justice should prevail. When deciding whether to indict, the Prosecutor must take into account the whole context of a situation and adjust actions to the existing political factors (as much as to the legal ones).[188] Most frequently, he is

[186] Cit. after: Wouters et al. (2008), p. 282.

[187] This notion in: Ohlin (2009), pp. 192 and 200. Similar conclusions: Goldstone and Fritz (2000), p. 13.

[188] Greenawalt (2007), pp. 619 and 658.

faced with the challenge of prosecuting offenders in the middle of a conflict. As a result, he may formulate the charges at various stages of negotiations undertaken by the parties to such conflicts.[189] Formulation of the charges—and their timing—undoubtedly exerts certain impact on the warring parties—however, not in a clear-cut and predictable way but more frequently in a way influenced by the complex and unique political realities on the ground. When deciding whether to indict a person, the Prosecutor must first consider whether his decision will not prompt such a person to undertake further war operations and to continue the conflict. If leaders of the warring parties expect to be prosecuted after the conflict ends, or after they abdicate, they are likely to hold tenaciously to the reins of power and continue fighting.[190] In Uganda, for example, prosecution of the rebellious forces (members of the *Lord's Resistance Army*) intensified attacks on the government's facilities and institutions. The rebels, however, were willing to enter into a peace agreement in exchange for the Prosecutor's withdrawing the indictment.[191] In this way, abandoning prosecution becomes a bargaining chip, a price for the entering into a peace agreement.[192] It should not be overlooked that when withdrawing an indictment in exchange for the restoration of peace, the Prosecutor contradicts the principle of legalism and the purpose for which the Court was appointed: to ensure that "the most serious crimes of concern to the international community as a whole must not go unpunished". However, while the Prosecutor does not bring the guilty before the Court, he achieves another, political goal and becomes an agent of peace, preventing further crimes.[193] This illustrates both the disadvantages and advantages of the Prosecutor's role, not known to national legal systems. Compared to national legal orders, the indictment has an additional role to play, which is a testament to the uniqueness of the ICC accusation model.

References

Ambos K (2000) Status, role, accountability of the Prosecutor of the International Criminal Court: a comparative overview on the basis of 33 national reports. Eur J Crime Crim Law Crim Justice 8:98

Ambos K (2007) The structure of international procedure: "adversarial", "inquisitorial" or mixed. In: Bohlander M (ed) International criminal justice: a critical analysis of institutions and procedures. Cameron May, London

189 See numerous authors on this topic, e.g.: Coté (2005), pp. 177 and seq.; Geis and Mundt (2009), pp. 7–8; Hall (2009), p. 227.

190 Damaška (2008), p. 332.

191 Schabas (2009), p. 238.

192 See: Geis and Mundt (2009), p. 15; Fish (2010), pp. 119 and 1703; Schabas (2010), pp. 664–665.

193 Unfortunately it is not possible to discuss this topic in more detail. Very detailed information can be found in: Hiéramente (2013), p. 28 et seq.

Ambos K, Miller D (2007) Structure and function of the confirmation procedure before the ICC from a comparative perspective. Int Crim Law Rev 7:355

Arbour L, Eser A, Ambos K, Sanders A (eds) (2000) The Prosecutor of a permanent International Criminal Court. International workshop in co-operation with the Office of the Prosecutor of the International Criminal Tribunals (ICTY and ICTR). Edition Iuscrim, Freiburg im Breisgau

Bassiouni MC, Manikas P (1996) The law of the International Criminal Tribunal for the former Yugoslavia. Transnational Publishers, New York

Bergsmo M, Kruger P (2008) In: Triffterer O (ed) Commentary on the Rome Statute of the International Criminal Court – observers' notes, article by article, 2nd edn. Hart/Nomos Verlagsgesellschaft/C.H. Beck, München/Oxford

Bergsmo M, Pejić J (2008) In: Triffterer O (ed) Commentary on the Rome Statute of the International Criminal Court – observers' notes, article by article, 2nd edn. Hart/Nomos Verlagsgesellschaft/C.H. Beck, München/Oxford

Beulke W (2005) Strafprozessrecht, 12th edn. C.F. Müller, Heidelberg

Boas G, Bischoff J, Reid N, Taylor BD III (2011) International criminal procedure. Cambridge University Press, Cambridge

Boister N, Cryer R (2000) The Tokyo Military Tribunal: a reappraisal. Oxford University Press, Oxford

Calvo-Goller K (2006) The trial proceedings of the International Criminal Court: ICTY and ICTR precedents. Martinus Nijhoff, Leiden/Boston

Coté L (2005) Reflections on the exercise of prosecutorial discretion in international criminal law. J Int Crim Justice 3:162

Coté L (2012) Independence and impartiality. In: Reydams L, Wouters J, Ryngaert C (eds) International prosecutors. Oxford University Press, Oxford

Cryer R (2005) Prosecuting international crimes: selectivity and the international criminal law regime. Cambridge University Press, Cambridge

Cryer R, Friman H, Robinson D, Wilmshurst E (2010) An introduction to international criminal law and procedure, 2nd edn. Cambridge University Press, Cambridge

Damaška M (2008) What is the point of international criminal justice? Chic Kent Law Rev 83:329

Daszkiewicz W (1960) Oskarżyciel w polskim procesie karnym. Państwowe Wydawnictwo Naukowe, Warszawa

de Hemptinne J (2007) The creation of investigating chambers at the International Criminal Court. An option worth pursuing? J Int Crim Justice 5:402

De Hert P (2003) Legal procedures at the International Criminal Court. A comparative law analysis of procedural basic rights. In: Haveman R, Kavran O, Nicholls J (eds) Supranational criminal law: a system *sui generis*. Intersentia, Antwerp/Oxford/New York

deGuzman MM, Schabas W (2013) Initiation of investigation and selection of cases. In: Sluiter G, Friman H, Linton S, Vasiliev S, Zappala S (eds) International criminal procedure. Principles and rules. Oxford University Press, Oxford

Eckelmans F (2009) The first jurisprudence of the Appeals Chamber of the ICC. In: Stahn C, Sluiter G (eds) The emerging practice of the International Criminal Court. Martinus Nijhoff, Leiden/Boston

Eser A (2008) The "adversarial" procedure: a model superior to other trial systems in international criminal justice? In: Kruessmann T (ed) ICTY: towards a fair trial? Neuer Wissenschaftlicher Verlag, Wien

Fish E (2010) Peace through complementarity: solving the ex post problem in International Criminal Court prosecutions. Yale Law J 119:1703

Friman H (2001) Investigation and prosecution. In: Lee RP (ed) The International Criminal Court. Elements of Crimes and Rules of Procedure and Evidence. Transnational Publishers, New York

Friman H, Brady H, Costi M, Guariglia F, Stuckenberg C-F (2013) Charges. In: Sluiter G, Friman H, Linton S, Vasiliev S, Zappala S (eds) International criminal procedure. Principles and rules. Oxford University Press, Oxford

Gallmetzer R (2009) The Trial-Chamber's discretionary power and its exercise in the trial of Thomas Lubanga Dyilo. In: Stahn C, Sluiter G (eds) The emerging practice of the International Criminal Court. Martinus Nijhoff, Leiden/Boston

Geis J, Mundt A (2009) When to indict? The impact of timing of international criminal indictments on peace processes and humanitarian action. The Brookings Institution-University of Bern Project on Internal Displacement, http://www.brookings.edu/~/media/research/files/papers/2009/4/peace%20and%20justice%20geis/04_peace_and_justice_geis.pdf. Accessed 13 Feb 2015

Glaser P (1929) Zarys polskiego procesu karnego. Księgarnia Powszechna, Warszawa

Goldstone R, Fritz N (2000) In the interest of justice and the independent referral: The ICC Prosecutor unprecedented power. Leiden J Int Law 13:655

Greenawalt A (2007) Justice without politics? Prosecutorial discretion and the International Criminal Court. NYU J Int Law Polit 39:583

Grzegorczyk T (2008) Kodeks postępowania karnego oraz Ustawa o świadku koronnym. Komentarz, 5th edn. Wolter Kluwer, Warszawa

Hall CK (2009) Developing and implementing an effective positive complementarity prosecution strategy. In: Stahn C, Sluiter G (eds) The emerging practice of the International Criminal Court. Martinus Nijhoff, Leiden/Boston

Harmon M (2007) The pre-trial process at the ICTY as a means of ensuring expeditious trial. A potential unrealized. J Int Crim Justice 5:377

Hauck P (2008) Judicial decisions in the pre-trial phase of criminal proceedings in France, Germany, and England. A comparative analysis responding to the law of the International Criminal Court. Nomos Verlagsgesellschaft, Baden-Baden

Herrmannt J (1973–1974) The rule of compulsory prosecution and the scope of prosecutorial discretion in Germany. Univ Chic Law Rev 41:468

Hiéramente M (2013) Internationale Haftbefehle in noch andauernden Konflikten. Rechtliche Rahmenbedingungen bei strafrechtlicher Intervention externer Akteure. Duncker & Humblot, Berlin

Hofmański P, Sadzik E, Zgryzek K (2011) Kodeks postępowania karnego. Komentarz. t. I, 4th edn. C.H. Beck, Warszawa

Hunt D (2001) The meaning of a "prima facie case" for the purpose of confirmation. In: May R, Tolbert D, Hocking J, Roberts K, Jia BB, Mundis D, Oosthuizen G (eds) Essays on ICTY procedure and evidence. In honour of Gabrielle Kirk McDonald. Brill Academic Publishers, The Hague/London/Boston

Izydorczyk J, Wiliński P (2004) Międzynarodowy Trybunał Karny. Zakamycze, Kraków

Izydorczyk J, Wiliński P (2005) Postępowanie przed Międzynarodowym Trybunałem Karnym. Państwo i Prawo 6:70

Jackson J (2009) Finding the best epistemic fit for international criminal tribunals. Beyond the adversarial-inquisitorial dichotomy. J Int Crim Justice 7:35

Kaftal A (1974) Kontrola sądowa postępowania przygotowawczego. Wiedza Powszechna, Warszawa

Kardas P (2012) Rola i miejsce prokuratury – w systemie organów demokratycznego państwa prawnego. Prokuratura i Prawo 9:37

Keegan MJ, Mundis DA (2001) Legal requirements for indictment. In: May R, Tolbert D, Hocking J, Roberts K, Jia BB, Mundis D, Oosthuizen G (eds) Essays on ICTY procedure and evidence. In honour of Gabrielle Kirk McDonald. Brill Academic Publishers, The Hague/London/Boston

Knoops G-J (2005) Theory and practice of international and internationalized criminal proceedings. Kluwer Law International, The Hague/London/Boston

Kress C (2003) The procedural law of the International Criminal Court in outline: anatomy of a unique compromise. J Int Crim Justice 1(3):603

Krzan B (2009) Kompetencje Rady Bezpieczeństwa ONZ w międzynarodowym sądownictwie karnym. TNOiK, Toruń

Kulesza C (1987) Rola sądu w postępowaniu przygotowawczym w systemach prawnych niektórych państw zachodnich. Państwo i Prawo 4:83

Kulesza C (1988) Sędzia śledczy w polskim modelu postępowania przygotowawczego (Uwagi de lege ferenda). Państwo i Prawo 12:94

La Haye E (1999) The jurisdiction of the International Criminal Court: controversies over the preconditions for exercising its jurisdiction. Netherlands Int Law Rev 46:1

LaFave W, Israel J, King N, Kerr O (2009) Criminal procedure, 5th edn. West Academic Publishing, St. Paul

Langbein JH (1973–1974) Controlling prosecutorial discretion in Germany. Univ Chic Law Rev 41:439

Locke J (2012) Indictments. In: Reydams L, Wouters J, Ryngaert C (eds) International prosecutors. Oxford University Press, Oxford

May R, Wierda M (2002) International criminal evidence. Transnational Publishers, Ardsley, NY

Milik P (2012) Komplementarność jurysdykcji Międzynarodowego Trybunału Karnego i trybunałów hybrydowych. Dom Wydawniczy Elipsa, Warszawa

Mogilnicki A, Rappaport ES (1929) Kodeks postępowania karnego. Motywy ustawodawcze. Cz. II, F. Hoesick, Warszawa

Ohlin JD (2009) Peace, security, and prosecutorial discretion. In: Stahn C, Sluiter G (eds) The emerging practice of the International Criminal Court. Martinus Nijhoff, Leiden/Boston

Olszewski R (2004) Usuwanie istotnych braków postępowania przygotowawczego w świetle znowelizowanego Article 397 kodeksu postępowania karnego. Prokuratura i Prawo 5:75

Oosthuizen G (1999) Some preliminary remarks on the relationship between the envisaged International Criminal Court and the UN Security Council. Netherlands International Law Review 46:313

Padfield N (2008) Text and materials on the criminal justice process, 4th edn. Oxford University Press, Oxford

Paprzycki LK (2010) In: Grajewski J, Paprzycki LK, Steinborn S (eds) Kodeks postępowania karnego. Komentarz, vol I. Wolters Kluwer, Warszawa

Płachta M (2007) Prokurator Międzynarodowego Trybunału Karnego: między legalizmem a oportunizmem ścigania. In: Menkes J (ed) Prawo międzynarodowego. Księga pamiątkowa Profesor Renaty Szafarz. WSHiP, Warszawa

Razowski T (2005) Formalna i merytoryczna kontrola oskarżenia w polskim procesie karnym. Zakamycze, Kraków

Reydams L, Wouters J, Ryngaert C (eds) (2012) International prosecutors. Oxford University Press, Oxford

Safferling C (2001) Towards an international criminal procedure, Oxford monographs in international law. Oxford University Press, Oxford

Schabas W (2008) Prosecutorial Discretion v. Judicial Activism at the International Criminal Court. J Int Crim Justice 6:731

Schabas W (2009) Prosecutorial discretion and gravity. In: Stahn C, Sluiter G (eds) The emerging practice of the International Criminal Court. Martinus Nijhoff, Leiden/Boston

Schabas W (2010) The International Criminal Court. A commentary on the Rome Statute. Oxford University Press, Oxford

Schuon C (2010) International criminal procedure. A clash of legal cultures. T. M. C. Asser Press, The Hague

Shibahara K, Schabas W (2008) In: Triffterer O (ed) Commentary on the Rome Statute of the International Criminal Court – observers' notes, article by article, 2nd edn. Hart/Nomos Verlagsgesellschaft/C.H. Beck, München/Oxford

Sprack J (2012) A practical approach to criminal procedure, 14th edn. Oxford University Press, Oxford

Stachowiak S (1975) Funkcje skargowości w polskim procesie karnym. Zakład Graficzny UAM, Poznań

Stahn C (2005) Modification of the legal characterization of facts in the ICC system. Crim Law Forum 16:1

Stahn C (2009) Judicial review of prosecutorial discretion: five years on. In: Stahn C, Sluiter G (eds) The emerging practice of the International Criminal Court. Martinus Nijhoff, Leiden/Boston

Stefański R (1998) Formalna kontrola aktu oskarżenia w nowym kodeksie postępowania karnego. Prokuratura i Prawo 9:28

Stegmiller I (2011) The pre-investigation stage of the ICC. Criteria for situation selection. Duncker & Humblot, Berlin

Syta M (1999) Udział prokuratora w posiedzeniach sądowych w świetle kodeksu postępowania karnego. Prokuratura i Prawo 10:30

Szyprowski B (1999) Kontrola warunków formalnych aktu oskarżenia w kodeksie postępowania karnego. Państwo i Prawo 12:86

Tochilovsky V (2004) International criminal justice: "Strangers in the Foreign System". Crim Law Forum 15:319

Tochilovsky V (2008) Jurisprudence of the International Criminal Courts and the European Court of Human Rights. Martinus Nijhoff, Leiden/Boston

Tochilovsky V (2009) Charging in the ICC and the relevant jurisprudence of the ad hoc tribunals. In: May R, Tolbert D, Hocking J, Roberts K, Jia BB, Mundis D, Oosthuizen G (eds) The legal regime of the International Criminal Court: essays in honour of Professor Igor Blishchenko. Martinus Nijhoff, Leiden/Boston

Townsend G (2012) Structure and management. In: Reydams L, Wouters J, Ryngaert C (eds) International prosecutors. Oxford University Press, Oxford

Turone G (2002) Powers and duties of the Prosecutor. In: Cassese A, Gaeta P, Jones WD (eds) The Rome Statute of the International Criminal Court: a commentary. Oxford University Press, Oxford

Vasiliev P (2012) Trial. In: Reydams L, Wouters J, Ryngaert C (eds) International prosecutors. Oxford University Press, Oxford

Volk K (2006) Grundkurs. StPO, 5th edn. C.H. Beck, München

Waltoś P (1963) Akt oskarżenia w polskim procesie karnym. Wydawnictwo Prawnicze, Warszawa

Waltoś S (1968) Model postępowania przygotowawczego na tle porównawczym. PWN, Warszawa

Ward R, Wragg A (2005) Walker and Walker's English legal system, 9th edn. Oxford University Press, Oxford

Wąsek-Wiaderek M (2003) Zasada równości stron w polskim procesie karnym w perspektywie prawnoporównawczej. Zakamycze, Kraków

Wei W (2007) Die Rolle des Anklägers eines Internationalen Strafgerichtshofs. Peter Lang, Frankfurt am Main

Wiliński P, Kuczyńska H (2009) Rzetelny proces karny w orzecznictwie międzynarodowych trybunałów karnych. In: Wiliński P (ed) Rzetelny proces karny w orzecznictwie sądów polskich i międzynarodowych. Wolter Kluwer, Warszawa

Worrall J (2007) Criminal procedure: from first contact to appeal, 2nd edn. Pearson Allyn & Bacon, Boston

Wouters J, Verhoeven S, Demeyere B (2008) The International Criminal Court's Office of the Prosecutor: navigating between independence and accountability? Int Crim Law Rev 8:273

Yañez-Barnuevo JA, Escobar Hernández C (2003) The ICC and the UN – a complex and vital relationship. In: Lattanzi F, Schabas W (eds) Essays on the Rome Statute of the International Criminal Court, vol 2. Il Sirente, Ripa di Fagnano Alto

Chapter 5
Obligations of the Prosecutor Related to the Accused's Right to Information

Abstract The realisation of the suspect's right to be informed imposes on the prosecutor an obligation to provide information in a manner and to the extent that guarantee observance of this right. Depending on the legal system, the prosecutor's obligation to inform the defence is performed using one of the following two procedures. In continental systems, the prosecutor may, and sometimes must, provide access to the case file. In common law states, an obligation to provide information on the evidence to the suspect and the accused is performed as part of the "disclosure of evidence". Before the ICC, the obligations of the Prosecutor to inform the accused about the evidence was solved utilising the model adopted in Anglo-Saxon states. The disclosure of evidence procedure was found to be strictly related to the assumption adopted by the ICC—that a trial was a dispute between two versions of a case prepared by the parties. In consequence, disclosure of evidence procedure constitutes a complicated procedure of gradual and multifaceted activities, including the application of the bilateral obligation to disclose and the specification of categories of evidence subject to disclosure, and complicated technical rules that are to be followed. However, is the disclosure of evidence procedure in the format existing in common law states compatible with the ICC's needs?

5.1 Model of Realisation of the Prosecutor's Obligations

5.1.1 Disclosure of Evidence as a Prerequisite of a Fair Trial

It is an element of the accused's right to information not only to get to know the contents of charges brought against him but also to familiarise himself with the evidence that the prosecution intends to use to support an indictment. In all legal systems, there is no doubt that knowledge of the evidence that is going to be used to prove guilt is one of the basic guarantees of a fair and adversarial trial. The European Court of Human Rights (ECtHR) considers it as a fundamental aspect of the right to a fair trial: "The right to an adversarial trial means, in a criminal case, that both prosecution and defence must be given the opportunity to have knowledge

© Springer International Publishing Switzerland 2015

H. Kuczyńska, *The Accusation Model Before the International Criminal Court*,
DOI 10.1007/978-3-319-17626-0_5

of and comment on the observations filed and the evidence adduced by the other party". In consequence, Article 6 § 1 (of the ECHR) requires that the prosecution authorities disclose to the defence all material evidence in their possession for or against the accused.[1] Also, the international criminal tribunals established that "the disclosure of exculpatory material is fundamental to the fairness of proceedings before the Tribunal".[2]

The issue of disclosure of evidence by the prosecutor to the accused (a suspect) is related to the broader matter of the overt nature of an investigation. Whereas the principle of transparency ("publicness") applies to judicial proceedings, the principle of confidentiality prevails at the investigation stage. The Polish Constitutional Tribunal emphasised that "the elements of openness in these proceedings, both internal and external, are very limited (for example, presentation of charges). It seems obvious that the possibility of achieving the objectives of the investigation is determined, inter alia, by keeping some information and evidence confidential. Therefore, the principle of open access to files in judicial proceedings gives way to 'discretionary' disclosure in the investigation. The legal situation and – most of all – the current facts of a case determine each time whether the suspect (or their defence attorney) may access files".[3] An investigation, however, may not be completely confidential either, by excluding any access to case files by the parties. The principle of confidentiality should be balanced with the accused's right of defence and with the principle of adversary trial. In each legal system, it is necessary to develop a reasonable compromise.[4] The interests of law enforcement should be reconciled with the rights of the suspect, including the right to defend his trial interests.

The realisation of the suspect's right to be informed imposes on the prosecutor an obligation to provide information in a manner and to the extent that guarantee observance of this right. Depending on the legal system, the prosecutor's obligation to inform the defence is performed using one of the following two procedures. In continental systems, the prosecutor may, and sometimes must, provide access to the case file (a *dossier* in the nomenclature of common law states). The case file is used to "ensure completeness and authenticity of documentation"[5] of the investigation conducted by the prosecutor and the police, and all the "traces of official activity must be preserved for future audits". Thus, the accused does not receive any information from the prosecutor, but from a case file.[6] In common law states, an obligation to provide information on the evidence to the suspect and the accused is performed as part of the "disclosure of evidence" procedure ("discovery" in the United States). This is an institution established in order to secure forced

[1] *Natunen v. Finland*, 31 March 2009, application No. 21022/04, § 39.

[2] *Prosecutor v. Kristić*, IT-98-33, Appeals Chamber 19 April 2004, § 180.

[3] Judgment of the Polish Constitutional Tribunal, 27 January 2004, SK 50/03.

[4] See: Ponikowski (2012), p. 138; Skorupka (2007), p. 73.

[5] Cit. after: Damaška (1986), p. 50.

[6] Heinze (2014), p. 319.

co-operation between litigants. These two institutions—despite the visible and diametric differences—fulfil the same procedural function, guaranteeing the realisation of the defendant's right to information.[7]

5.1.2 Access to a Case File in Continental Law Systems

In continental systems, the prosecutor fulfils his obligation to inform the defence through two institutions of investigation. The first of these is *access to case files of an investigation*, which includes both the right to request access of case files of a pending investigation and the institution of a *final inspection of materials of the case*. The second institution is the obligation to provide to the suspect specific documents drawn up in investigation: the decision on the presentation of charges and the indictment.

The first element of access to a case file is inspection of files during investigation. Article 156 § 5 CCP states that "unless provided otherwise by law, permission by the person conducting the investigation shall be required for the inspection of files of the investigation in progress, making copies and photocopies of the same by parties, defence counsels, legal representatives and statutory agents, and for the issuance of certified copies". This right of the defence is activated at the issuance of the decision on the presentation of charges and lasts till the end of investigation.[8]

The above is not, however, an absolute right. It can be exercised only if the authority carrying the investigation gives consent. In this system, then, an investigation's files are not disclosed automatically. Each time, the evaluation of suitability and feasibility of disclosure remain the responsibility of the authority managing the proceedings. The legislator, however, did not specify the criteria to be followed by the authority carrying out the proceedings when deciding to provide access to files to parties. The CCP does not even provide a general basis for refusal in the form of an "interest of the investigation".[9] As a result, the right of access to case files and the scope of this right are fully dependent on the discretion of the authority, and there is a risk that decisions are taken entirely arbitrarily. It has also been recognised in the legal science that the authority conducting investigation may express his consent to access the case files only in relation to some of the materials included in the case file or some fragments of files.[10] Naturally, "the trial authority should balance, with utmost care, on the one hand, the suspect's interests and rights protected by conventional standards, and on the other, the interest of effective prosecution in an investigation"; this does not, however, affect the fact that this decision is left to the authority's discretion.[11] Although it has been widely accepted

[7] See: Ambos (2003), p. 15; Orie (2002), p. 1484.

[8] See: Skorupka (2007), p. 65; Szczotka (2009), pp. 12–25; Kardas (2013), pp. 39–45.

[9] See: Skorupka (2007), p. 65; Wąsek-Wiaderek (2003a, b), pp. 65 and 247.

[10] See: Skorupka (2007), p. 73; Wiliński (2006), p. 79.

[11] Cit. after: Skorupka (2007), p. 73.

that the authority should indicate specific reasons for its refusal, this standard is rarely met in practice. The legal science proposes what kind of circumstances could be invoked in a decision justifying the refusal: e.g., the risk of premature disclosure of evidence, the distortion of evidence, the loss thereof, intimidation of witnesses or co-suspects, destruction of physical evidence, production of false evidence, as well as a reprehensible attitude towards the obligations of the accused, for example hiding or fleeing to another country.[12] In most cases, the practice shows that the authorities limit themselves to the reference to the contents of the legal provision underlying such a decision.

The access to case files always depends on the existence of a consent by the person conducting the investigation "unless provided otherwise by law". The law provides that two types of documents should always be disclosed. The party may not be refused permission to inspect documents as stipulated in Article 157 § 3 CCP, that is, a record of investigative steps in which it participated or had the right to participate, as well as a document obtained from such party or prepared with the participation of the same. Also, the suspect (later accused) and his defence counsel should be served with the decision on the admission of evidence based on an opinion issued by experts or a scientific institute and permitted to participate in the examination of such experts and to acquaint themselves with their opinions, if they have been prepared in writing (Article 318 CCP).

The institution of access to case files in the course of an investigation will be significantly remodelled effective as of 1st of June 2015 when the Act of 27 September 2013 amending the CCP[13] comes into effect. Pursuant to the new wording of Article 156 § 5 of the CCP, "(...) unless there is a need to safeguard the proper course of the proceedings or to protect a significant interest of the state, in the course of investigation the parties, defence counsels, legal representatives and statutory agents are provided access to files and allowed to make copies or photocopies and are issued certified copies or photocopies for a fee; the parties retain this right also upon completion of preparatory proceedings". This means that the parties will have access to files of an investigation that will not be conditional on an arbitrary decision of the prosecutor but made on the basis of statutory grounds (although drafted also as a general clause). Denial of access to the case files will be limited to statutory grounds: the significant interest of the state or the safeguarding of the proper course of the proceedings. It is important to compare these two provisions to see how the legislator amended the current shortcomings of the CCP by accepting and meeting the criticism of the legal doctrine.

The second important element of access to a case file is institution of final inspection of the case materials. Namely, if there are grounds to conclude the investigation, the authority conducting the investigation notifies the suspect and the defence counsel of the date of final inspection of the materials of the case, advising them of their right to examine files (Article 321 § 1 CCP). The suspect and

[12] See: Wiliński (2006), p. 81; Steinborn (2010), p. 558; Hofmański et al. (2011), p. 859.

[13] Dz. U. of 2013, pos. 1247.

his defence counsel can access the materials only upon request. This right does not depend on the consent of the authority carrying out the investigation. The suspect does not have to meet any additional conditions or demonstrate any basis for exercising his right—submission of the request automatically activates it. The scope of this right also covers the right of access to the materials that are not included in the files, that is, to the physical evidence kept in a deposit.[14]

Also in German criminal trial, a defence counsel has the right to inspect files that will be submitted to the court if charges are preferred even if investigations have not yet been designated as concluded on the file, as well as to inspect officially impounded pieces of evidence. It is, however, limited by two conditions: the counsel will be refused inspection of the files or of individual evidence if this may endanger the purpose of the investigation (also conducted in another case) and if overriding interests of third persons meriting protection do present an obstacle thereto (§ 147(6) and (7) StPO). The scope of inspection and the possibility to inspect files are decided by the prosecutor conducting investigation. Paragraph 147 (3) states: "At no stage of the proceedings may defence counsel be refused inspection of records concerning the examination of the accused or concerning such judicial acts of investigation to which defence counsel was or should have been admitted, nor may he be refused inspection of expert opinions". Access to files also includes the right to make copies and take notes. Similarly as in the Polish law, the suspect may submit such a request a number of times, and any previous denial of access does not prevent the case files from being made available when the reasons underlying the denial cease to exist.[15] Also, as in the Polish procedure, the case files are always made available to the defence prior to filing of an indictment and upon completion of an investigation. The defence counsel—but only him—always has the right to inspect the files of a case, in which investigation has been concluded. He also enjoys the right to take the files (with the exception of physical evidence), to his office or to his private premises for inspection, unless significant grounds present an obstacle thereto. We can see how the Polish new version of Article 156 § 5 CCP draws from the experience of the German StPO.

The second institution constituting realisation of obligation to inform the defendant about the evidence existing in his case is the obligation to disclose the contents of certain procedural decisions at specified stages of preparatory proceedings.

The first stage of realisation of this obligation takes place during the presentation of charges. A decision on the presentation of charges shall specify the identity of the suspect, detailed data on the act imputed to him and the legal characterisation thereof. The statement of reasons for such an order as demanded by Article 313 § 4 CCP should, in particular, indicate what facts and evidence were adopted as the grounds for the charges. The legal practice demonstrates, however, that the right to information is limited due to the prevailing practices of law enforcement services. The statement of reasons is usually very concise, "frequently omitting facts or

---

[14] Skorupka (2007), p. 67.

[15] See: Safferling (2001), pp. 196–197; Beulke (2005), p. 75.

evidence or indicating them only partially. Often, this statement only recounts the aspects of the alleged act, providing some limited elaboration, indicating the facts noted in a crime notification, and including a conclusion that the collected evidence provides a reasonable basis to suspect that the person named in the decision has committed the crime he is accused of, and therefore that the presentation of charges was necessary".[16] This tendency arises from the unwillingness to disclose information on evidence to the suspect. Most frequently the prosecutor assumes that the disclosure of all material facts and evidence could disrupt the course of proceedings already at their initial phase, opening the door to illicit destruction and obliteration of traces and evidence, as well as their distortion. As a result of such a practice, at this stage of the proceedings the suspect is rarely notified about the evidence to support the charges brought against him, despite the explicit statutory obligation.

The second stage of realisation of obligation to inform the defendant about evidence in his case is constituted by filing an indictment to the accused. In the indictment, the prosecutor indicates all the facts and evidence upon which the accusation is founded, and in an attachment he should include a list of the persons whom the prosecutor requests to be summoned and a list of such other evidence that the prosecutor will seek to obtain at the first instance hearing (Article 333 § 1 CCP, similarly § 200 StPO). Thus, an indictment is a comprehensive compendium for the accused and for the court on the evidence held by the prosecutor, on which the accusation will be based during the trial (this is the so-called informative function of an indictment, in German: *Informationsfunktion*). Only at this stage of criminal proceedings—upon completion of an investigation—is all evidence currently held by the prosecutor to support the charges brought against the accused disclosed in an obligatory and automatic manner, irrespective of the accused's request. An indictment should also include the information on the to-date line of defence adopted by the accused, which proves that this document is also informative for the court. The accused himself does not have the obligation of presenting any information or evidence pertaining to his line of defence, whether to the prosecutor or to the court.[17] At this stage, the prosecutor's obligation to inform ends, which is a characteristic of continental law systems. During the judicial proceedings, he does not have to disclose evidence prior to using it if he comes into possession of such evidence only at this stage of the proceedings (it may be percieved as a consequence of the fact - discussed in the previous chapters - that in general all the evidence presented by the prosecution at trial are gathered during the stage of investigation).

Again, the scope of the information as provided in the indictment changes beginning from the 1st of July 2015. First, there will be no obligation to present reasoned opinion of the indictment. Second, amendment is in favour of the accused: the prosecutor should not only present the list of all the evidence he requests to

[16] Cit. after: Ponikowski (2012), pp. 171–172.

[17] As highlighted by the representatives of both legal systems: Beulke (2005), pp. 163–164; Hofmański et al. (2011), p. 732; Waltoś (1963), pp. 15 and 109–110.

introduce during trial (grouped in three categories: witnesses, documents and physical evidence), but he is also obliged to explain what circumstances he is going to prove with a specific piece of evidence and indicate the method and scope of presentation of the evidence. Therefore, the prosecutor will be obliged to draft the evidentiary thesis relative to each piece of evidence, which should prompt him to analyse carefully the collected evidence. As we can see, also on this occasion the amendments require from the prosecutor more diligence in fulfilling his duties. The aforementioned solution will allow the other parties to prepare properly for interrogation of the individual witnesses. On the one hand, we can suppose that it will also force the parties to prepare properly, as the court may oversee whether the scope of the evidentiary motion is complied with, including by rejecting certain questions. On the other hand, it seems that in the new system of criminal procedure there are no obstacles to the evidentiary arguments set forth in an indictment being expanded in the course of the proceedings, upon request of the parties.

The last change is connected to the fact that together with the indictment, the prosecutor submits only some of the materials from the investigation to the court, rather than the complete investigation files, as has been the case so far. These are only the evidentiary materials that will be used by the prosecution in support of the charges formulated in the indictment.

On the basis of a theoretical analysis of the presented continental systems, we can draw a general conclusion on the access to case files. It may be concluded that there are various rules for disclosing evidence, depending on the stage of investigation. First, access to evidence contained in a case file during an ongoing investigation is possible only upon consent of the authority conducting the investigation; it is fully discretionary, and it is not always based on clear and objective criteria. It is advised to introduce criteria that are assessed by this authority, such as, most frequently, the "interest of the proceedings" or "interests of the state". Second, the access to materials of an investigation may not be denied upon its completion. In particular, the interest of the proceedings, which most frequently is the basis for denial of access to the case files of pending investigation, may not at this stage be referred to as a rational criterion. The full access to case files is, therefore, possible only upon completion of an investigation, during the stage of final inspection of the materials of the investigation. However, complete information on the evidence and the line of accusation is contained only in the indictment, which is the document from which the accused learns what evidence will be brought forth by the prosecutor in the trial to support his line of accusation. Finally, there are two groups of evidence that are always subject to disclosure, regardless of the opinion of the authority carrying out the proceedings: the opinions of experts and reports concerning procedures in which the party was or had the right to be involved (e.g., procedures performed at a party's request, unique investigative opportunities), as well as documents produced by him or prepared with his involvement.

It is characteristic of the continental law systems that if the accused wants to obtain information on evidence that may be favourable for him, he will not find such evidence in the indictment but must apply for access to case files, which should contain such evidence in line with the assumption that the prosecutor is obligated to collect it. Thus, he does not access the case file of the prosecution but an integrated case file, which organises the investigation into "a meaningful whole".[18] Another characteristic feature of this model is the fact that the obligation to disclose evidence is unilateral. Because all documents of a criminal case, both incriminating and exculpatory, are collected in a case file, known to the prosecutor and the court from the very beginning of the proceedings, it is assumed that the only party that should obtain the information on the content of this *dossier* is the accused and his defence counsel. Therefore, there is no balance between the obligations of the parties—as it was never the assumption in these legal systems.[19]

5.1.3 Disclosure of Evidence in Common Law Systems

The procedural institution referred to as the *disclosure of evidence* consists of establishing an obligation of a specific conduct of the parties upon completion or at the final stage of an investigation but prior to the initiation of the trial. It is defined as "the process by which each party to a case learns of the evidence that the opposition will present".[20] As the two parties prepare two sets of evidence separately, this institution enables communication between them and sharing (but only to the extent required by law) of information. The disclosure of evidence procedure plays a dual role. First, it constitutes an exercise of the accused's right to defence and to information. Second, it makes it possible to prepare the trial. It organises the work of the court, so that it is aware of what evidence will be presented by the parties, to support or to defend against specific charges. Third, it tempers some of the more unsatisfactory aspects of adversarialism.[21] It makes the course of the proceedings more efficient and also allows the parties to plan the presentation of evidence more effectively. The other party's familiarity with evidence enables the development of a certain strategy, which results in the trial becoming a carefully staged event. Disclosure of evidence in support of the indictment may even lead to the accused pleading guilty in the face of an obvious advantage of the prosecution.

In the Anglo-Saxon systems, the prosecutor's obligation resulting from the disclosure of evidence has two aspects. First, it consists in disclosing evidence to support an indictment pursuant to a general principle that presentation of evidence in trial that has not been previously disclosed to the opposite party is not possible. Second, the evidence that may be favourable for the accused is disclosed (exculpatory evidence).

---

[18] In the words of: Damaška (1986), p. 50.

[19] See: Heinze (2014), p. 319.

[20] Cit. after: Worrall (2007), p. 295.

[21] As it was observed by: Hannibal and Mountford (2002), p. 164.

The evidence disclosure process is usually much more complicated than the institution of access to case files in continental systems and constitutes a separate stage of the criminal procedure or, rather, two additional stages. The first stage of disclosing evidence is done prior to a confirmation of charges hearing, or a so-called preliminary hearing. The scope of disclosure of evidence is determined by the prosecutor's intention to rely upon it during this hearing. All the evidence that the prosecutor intends to present must be disclosed beforehand. The second stage is the disclosure of evidence prior to the trial, to the extent in which the prosecutor intends to use evidence at the trial to support an indictment. There are major differences between specific systems of the common law tradition as far as the scope of the disclosed evidence is concerned. This obligation may apply to all evidence of the prosecution, but it may also mean that the prosecutor presents to the defence only such evidence as is material for a given case. It may also refer to the disclosure of only the evidence in a specific category or only the information on (a list of) evidence intended to be relied upon.

The first basic difference between the common law and the continental tradition is the fact that each of the parties to the trial prepares separate sets of evidence that contain different versions of the case (*two cases approach*). The essence of a strictly adversarial trial is to convince the judge that one of these versions is true by way of a dispute between the parties to the trial. These versions are often entirely different, and using the lack of knowledge of the evidence of the opposite party seems to be a popular practice employed in trials. Such tactics, in turn, lead to the unpredictability of the course of the trial and the impossibility of planning its course. In continental systems, however, there is one case file and only the version prepared by the state law enforcement authorities and the public prosecutor is presented to the court.

Second, as it follows from the previous paragraph, in Anglo-Saxon systems there are no official case files controlled by a state authority that would contain all the evidence known to the prosecution and in its possession. The obligation of disclosure of evidence is inherently related to the position of the prosecutor. It is characteristic of states in which the prosecutor is an authority appointed solely to accuse. He looks only for incriminating evidence but does not have any obligation to perform an active search for evidence in the accused's favour. In the continental systems, on the other hand, the public prosecutor, in his official capacity, collects both incriminating and exculpatory evidence. As a result, all evidence and information on the evidence, both exculpatory and incriminating, is located in one place, accessible to both parties and to the court, namely in the *dossier* of the case. When the prosecutor submits the case to the court, the *dossier* is completed by the court, as the latter has the competence to call new evidence at trial and there is no preclusion for the parties to request including new evidence.

Third, in common law systems criminal proceedings are based on the basic principle that says that during the trial the parties may not rely on facts and evidence that have not been disclosed before. Therefore, as it is not possible to surprise the opposite party with new evidence, the strategy of presenting evidence and challenging evidence of the opposite party is of major importance. Disclosure obligation ends where strategy begins,[22] and the latter does not have to be shared with the opposite party.

The fourth basic difference in exercising the accused's right to information on evidence of the prosecution is the fact that in Anglo-Saxon systems of criminal proceedings it is not the "evidentiary mass" or "the bulk of evidence" (i.e., all that is contained in case files in the continental systems) that is subject to disclosure but rather individual categories of evidence, carefully specified in procedural laws. The court makes sure that the parties conscientiously meet the obligation to disclose evidence in the specific categories. In continental law jurisdictions, the defence simply has access to the whole of the prosecution's *dossier*.

Finally, the last difference is the right of inspection by the prosecution in Anglo-Saxon systems. Disclosure of evidence is of a reciprocal character. It is considered that provision of access to the outcome of the prosecutor's entire work only to the accused would result in inequality between the parties, unacceptable in this legal tradition.[23] Usually, disclosure of specific information by one party entails that the other party also has to disclose its evidence. For instance, the disclosure of the intention to use an *alibi* by the defence requires that the prosecutor disclose evidence that will be used to challenge this defence. On the other hand, in continental systems there is no doubt that only the prosecutor is obliged to enable inspection of the investigation files and there is no respective obligation on the part of the defence. The prosecution itself is also obliged to investigate exculpatory evidence, and—as he even enjoys greater practical and legal investigatory capacities—there is no need for the defence to disclose its evidence, as the prosecutor had both possibility and obligation to search for it.[24]

Moreover, the bilateral nature of disclosure of evidence also means that the evidence is transferred directly to the other party. The judge does not receive in advance any information pertaining to the evidence a party intends to present during the trial and therefore does not have any knowledge on the case. The court is only an authority managing and controlling the evidence disclosure procedure and also becomes an appeal authority if one of the parties raises objections as to the correctness of disclosure of evidence by the other party.

There are also certain similarities between both legal traditions. Common for them is the necessity to impose limitations on the access to evidence collected by the prosecution. These limitations are related to three basic areas: the need to protect witnesses, the need to protect classified information and the need to ensure effectiveness of prosecution by making specific evidence restricted for a defined period of time due to the interests of the investigation.

---

[22] This conclusion is unanimously repeated in the American doctrine: Worrall (2007), p. 295; LaFave et al. (2009), p. 957.

[23] As highlighted in: *The Prosecutor v. Lubanga,* ICC-01/04-01/06, Prosecution's Final Observations on Disclosure, 2 May 2006, § 8.

[24] In general see: Schuon (2010), p. 25; Orie (2002), p. 1450; Boas (2003), p. 22; Ambos (2007), pp. 472–473; Wiliński (2008), p. 640.

Both legal systems described above assume the confidentiality of an investigation, allowing, however, for certain exceptions to this rule. Two theoretical systems regulating access to investigation materials may be defined; the first one theoretically assumes "a general publicness of an investigation with specific secrecy concessions wherever same are necessary for the interest of the proceedings"; the second one assumes the confidentiality of an investigation with exceptions for disclosing specific materials to the defence.[25] In consequence, the mechanisms for applying exemptions to the confidentiality rule are different. There is no doubt that the continental model provides for much simpler means of access to information than the model of disclosure of evidence. The Anglo-Saxon model provides sets of highly complex technical rules determined by the case law and leading to a lack of clarity as to the extent of the obligation to disclose evidence, while the continental system simply offers access to all evidence. In common law states, there are major objections to the institution of disclosure. References are made to its misuse, as well as to its misapplication that leads to abuses of the trial. The basic objection applies to the lack of definition for specific categories of evidence—there is no certainty what evidence falls within the scope of the specific statutory categories. It has also been argued that the whole system is unnecessarily complicated.[26] Especially in England, it has been highlighted that the rules, only some of which were created by statute, while others were devised at common law, are not contained in one place. Therefore, while some of them have the force of law, some do not and are expressed in various guidelines.[27] Failure to comply with these rules by any of the parties may lead to further disputes and prolonging of a trial. In fact, a precise determination of evidence that should be disclosed pursuant to each of the rules is not possible in advance and depends on the circumstances of a specific case. Often, not all evidence may be found by the prosecutor at the investigation stage, which obliges him to an ongoing evaluation of the scope of evidence to be disclosed to the defence—also during trial. Moreover, there is one more disadvantage of this system that may be observed in the proceedings before international criminal courts that will be discussed later: the system of disclosure of evidence is not applied in a uniform manner. Attorneys from different jurisdictions seem to have different attitudes to the rules of disclosure and apparently brought this attitude with them to the international criminal court.[28]

It should be acknowledged that continental systems are much more favourable for the suspect and the accused in this respect. The prosecutor's scope of obligations is significantly broader in continental states, which makes it possible to disclose the entire case files, regardless of the fact of whether the evidence belongs to a specific category. The timing of disclosure makes preparation of the defence much easier. Moreover, files are disclosed at length, which gives an insight into the way the

[25] The citation and the theory can be found in: Wiliński (2006), p. 79.

[26] A remark often made, e.g., by: Everett (1964), p. 477; Schuon (2010), p. 27.

[27] Hannibal and Mountford (2002), p. 165; Tomaszewski (1996), p. 108.

[28] See: Tochilovsky (2004a), pp. 319–344.

investigation has developed. The system for handling case files is a straightforward one that does not require any complicated rules to govern the accused's (suspect's) access to the information on the charges brought against him and the evidence to support it.[29] In Anglo-Saxon states, access to such materials is highly formalised and divided into specific stages. Although at first glance it may seem that in the Anglo-Saxon system the suspect's situation is better, as the disclosure of evidence is not discretionary, the proper procedure of disclosing evidence takes place only upon completion of drafting an indictment—at which point it is the entire contents of case files that can be accessed by the accused in the continental procedure. In continental systems, case files can already be inspected during an investigation. It needs to be kept in mind at the same time that even in continental systems, this right depends solely on the consent of the authority handling the investigation, which does not always depend on transparent regulatory premises (although this major disadvantage of the system is soon going to be repaired in Poland). It should be also borne in mind that the suspect enjoys the right to submit requests to conduct certain investigative steps in investigation (Article 315 § 1 CCP). Thanks to this right, he has an impact on the contents of case files that arrive at the court.

5.2 Disclosure of Evidence by the Prosecutor

There was no doubt that it was necessary to introduce guarantees for the suspect's right to information in the proceedings before international criminal tribunals. This was done utilising the model adopted in Anglo-Saxon states. The disclosure of evidence procedure was found to be strictly related to the assumption adopted by all tribunals—both *ad hoc* tribunals and the ICC—that a trial was a dispute between two versions of a case prepared by the parties. In the proceedings before all international criminal tribunals, regulation of this obligation resembles the Anglo-Saxon solution, including the application of the bilateral obligation to disclose evidence, the specification of categories of evidence subject to disclosure and complicated technical rules of the disclosure procedure.

In proceedings before the International Military Tribunals, an obligation of disclosure of evidence was introduced in a rudimentary form. Article 16(a) of the Nuremberg Charter provided only for serving the defendants with a copy of the indictment and of all the documents lodged with the indictment, translated into a language that they understand, at a reasonable time before the trial. The Rules of Procedure supplemented this provision by stating that these documents should be received not less than 30 days before trial and that the defendants should also receive copies of the Charter and the Rules of Procedure "as may be adopted by the Tribunal from time to time". There was also an obligation to inform the Tribunal (but only the Tribunal) of "the nature of any evidence" before it is entered so that it

[29] See: Schuon (2010), p. 27; Tochilovsky (2002), p. 272.

may rule upon the relevance thereof (Article 20 of the Charter). This regulation, however, was intended solely to enable judges to assess whether evidence was acceptable as *per* the rules of acceptability of evidence adopted by this Tribunal. In practice, the defence complained about inadequate disclosure by the prosecution: receiving disorganised documents in English at a late date and only after repeated requests. The prosecution repeatedly used documents at trial that it had not listed in the list of evidence presented in the court and thus had not disclosed. This was done when the most drastic evidence was presented in order to achieve a better effect during cross-examination. When a defence counsel requested 25 copies of one of the documents for all the accused, the prosecution refused explaining that "the presses were already functioning to maximum capacity" and it was not possible to grant the request despite the fact that at the same time the prosecution delivered 250 copies of the same document to the press.[30]

The procedure of disclosure of evidence in the proceedings before the ICTY was adopted by incorporating the rules governing the discovery procedure in the United States. Not only does the procedure before the *ad hoc* tribunals rely upon procedural laws, sometimes adopting their contents literally, but also in their practice the tribunals refer directly to the decisions of American courts. Numerous authors have expressed an opinion that the adoption of such a form of disclosure of evidence first before the ICTY and ICTR and later before the ICC "is a clear expression of the adversarial model",[31] or at least that it "leans more towards an adversarial approach".[32] For continental lawyers, it was often the first time they were not given access to case files: "when a defence counsel from the former Yugoslavia made a request for a 'full' disclosure in one of the cases, he was directed by the Chamber to relevant United States and United Kingdom case-law".[33]

Similarly as in the case of other procedural institutions, before the ICC the institution of disclosure of evidence has been regulated in a different way than before the *ad hoc* tribunals. Drawing on the experience of the *ad hoc* tribunals, the ICC adopted a solution that, according to its creators, was best tailored to the specific role played by the International Criminal Court and its Prosecutor. At present, there are two basic differences between the *ad hoc* tribunals and the ICC when it comes to the disclosure of evidence. The first one is the specific "constitutionalisation" of the disclosure institution that was effected through the ICC Statute. In the Rome Statute, the right to be informed of the evidence on which the Prosecutor intends to rely is one of the fundamental rights of the accused (and

---

[30] Such information presented by: May and Wierda (2002), pp. 70–72; Bassiouni and Manikas (1996), p. 924.

[31] E.g., Ambos (2007), p. 472.

[32] E.g., Schuon (2010), p. 275; Brady (2001), p. 407.

[33] In the case: *Prosecutor v. Delalić*, IT-96-21, Decision on Motion by the accused Zejnil Delalić for the disclosure of evidence, 26 September 1996. The case and the reactions of the parties described in: Tochilovsky (2004a), pp. 319–344.

earlier of the suspect), constituting a guarantee of a fair trial (Article 61(3), Article 67(2)). Such institution is never mentioned in the Statutes of the ICTY and ICTR. The "statutory" rights of the accused include only the right to be informed promptly and in detail in a language that he understands of the nature and cause of the charge against him and the right to have adequate time and facilities for the preparation of his defence (Article 21(4)(a) and (b)). Thus, the issue of disclosing evidence was considered not only to constitute a separate right of the accused but also to be one of the rules of proceeding. The second significant difference is the fact that the ICC linked the procedure of disclosure of evidence with the new role of the Prosecutor as the authority seeking the material truth and obliged actively to collect evidence also in favour of the accused.

In the proceedings before all international criminal tribunals, there is a basic rule that the prosecutor discloses two groups of evidence to the accused. Firstly, it is the evidence he intends to use to support the charges brought against the accused, initially during the preliminary hearing and then during the trial (to the extent it has not been disclosed before). Secondly, he has an ongoing obligation of disclosing the entire evidence that may be favourable for the accused.

5.2.1 Disclosure of the Prosecution Evidence

Both in England and Wales and in the United States, the prosecution is always obliged to present the evidence to the accused by way of which it intends to prove his guilt in the trial. As there is an institution of a preliminary/preparatory hearing to confirm the charges, as early as at the stage of this hearing the prosecutor has to present the evidence showing that there is a reasonable basis to believe that the accused has committed a crime. In relation to the existence of such a separate adversarial hearing, two stages of disclosing evidence may be distinguished: the first one takes place prior to the preliminary hearing, and the second one is the actual disclosure that occurs after an indictment is brought before the court by the prosecutor and pertains solely to additional evidence not previously disclosed. At every stage of the disclosure of evidence, a general rule will be applied that the prosecutor may not use the evidence that has not been previously disclosed to the accused as the basis for prosecution.

In the English system, an obligation to disclose evidence (and its scope) depends on the procedure pursuant to which a given case is heard: basically, this applies to cases brought before the Crown Court (in the *trial on indictment* procedure). At the first stage of disclosure, the prosecution is required to serve on the defendant a committal bundle prior to the case being committed to the Crown Court. "The committal bundle" will comprise "used material", that is, the substance of the evidence the prosecution intends to rely on at trial. Based on this evidence, the examining judges may conclude that the prosecution has a case to answer and the defendant should be committed to stand jury trial in the Crown Court. In the Magistrates' Courts, the prosecution must disclose evidence to the defence only upon entering a not guilty plea.[34] Once the obligation is activated, its scope is set not only by Criminal Procedure and Investigations Act 1996[35] but also in the Guidelines on Disclosure drawn up by the Attorney General: "the prosecutor should, in addition to complying with the obligations under the Act, provide to the defence all evidence upon which the Crown proposes to rely in a summary trial. Such provision should allow the accused and their legal advisers sufficient time properly to consider the evidence before it is called" (section 57).[36] The second stage is disclosure of evidence within a certain period in the case of sending for trial.[37] As a rule, in the Crown Court the prosecutor discloses prosecution material to the defendant or serves on the defendant a written statement that there is no such material to disclose.[38] If some evidence is not disclosed, it is a customary practice of the court that the trial is postponed so that the prosecutor can disclose a given piece of evidence and the accused can prepare for the trial again, having the necessary knowledge. Separating the evidence to be used during the trial (or hearing) and the evidence in the prosecutor's possession that will not be used in line with the assumed strategy is of key importance for the scope of prosecutorial obligation. It is a continuous obligation. If the prosecution intends to broaden the scope of evidence as a result of disclosure of the defence's evidence, it is obliged to disclose supplementary evidence. For example, in the *R v. Lattimore* case, the police altered the scope of the expert's opinion when the *alibi* of the accused had been disclosed.[39] It did not notify the accused about it, as this information would provide an opportunity to prepare a new *alibi*. Such conduct was considered to be neglect of the obligation to disclose evidence and, in consequence, a violation of the right to a fair trial.

Also in the United States, the procedure of informing the accused about the evidence collected by the prosecution is a two-stage procedure. The information on incriminating evidence is received by the accused prior to the preliminary hearing, when the court confirms an indictment. At this stage, the prosecutor must disclose this evidence that he intends to present in the hearing and that is intended to convince the court that there is a reasonable basis to believe that the accused has committed the alleged offence. Depending on the state, the prosecutor may disclose evidence to support the entire line of prosecution, including the depositions of

[34] Magistrates' Courts; Act 1980, http://www.legislation.gov.uk/ukpga/1980/43/contents. Accessed 12 Feb 2015.

[35] Criminal Procedure and Investigations Act 1996, section 25: http://www.legislation.gov.uk/ukpga/1996/25/section/3. Accessed 6 Sept 2014.

[36] Attorney-General's Guidelines on disclosure, Pt 37(i-vi): http://www.cps.gov.uk/legal/a_to_c/attorney_generals_guidelines_on_disclosure/. Accessed 6 Sept 2014.

[37] In more detail described in: Hannibal and Mountford (2002), pp. 163–166; Ward and Wragg (2005), pp. 574–575; Ashworth and Redmayne (2005), pp. 93–99; Spencer (2004), p. 630.

[38] The Criminal Procedure Rules 2013, Part 22, at: http://www.legislation.gov.uk/uksi/2013/1554/part/22/made. Accessed 11 July 2013.

[39] *R v. Lattimore* (1976) 62 Cr App R 53; [1976] Crim Lr 45: cited after: Hannibal and Mountford (2002), pp. 163–166. Similar observations in: Kuczyńska H (2009), p. 60.

witnesses for the prosecution, or only to a limited extent, presenting only the selected material prior to this hearing.[40] The second stage takes place before the trial when the prosecutor discloses the remaining evidence to the extent that has not been disclosed before—in each of the categories specified below.

The United States Federal Rules of Criminal Procedure establish a detailed list of categories of evidence that should be disclosed by a prosecutor—before the preliminary hearing and later during the trial (Rule 16).[41] The first information subject to disclosure is *Defendant's Oral Statement* made by the defendant, before or after arrest, in response to interrogation by a person the defendant knew was a government agent if the government intends to use the statement at trial. Second, it is any relevant *Defendant's Written or Recorded Statement* that is within the government's possession, custody or control, and the attorney for the government knows—or through due diligence could know—that the statement exists (e.g., the defendant's recorded testimony before a grand jury relating to the charged offence). Third, the prosecutor must furnish the defendant with a copy of the defendant's prior criminal record that is within the government's possession, custody or control. Fourth, the government must permit the defendant to inspect and to copy or photograph books, papers, documents, data, photographs, tangible objects, buildings or places or copies or portions of any of these items, if the item is within the government's possession, custody or control and

(a) the item is material to preparing the defence;
(b) the government intends to use the item in its case-in-chief at trial; or
(c) the item was obtained from or belongs to the defendant.

Fifth, the government must permit a defendant to inspect and to copy or photograph the results or reports of any physical or mental examination and of any scientific test or experiment. Last, the government must give to the defendant a written summary of any testimony that the government intends to use during its case-in-chief at trial.

What is characteristic of this system is that the disclosure categories are not the same in every state. In most of them, however, legislation is adopted on the basis of federal law.[42] In many of the states, this obligation does not concern the contents of witnesses' testimonies but only their identity. In some other jurisdictions, the list of witnesses is disclosed to defence only when the court so requires.[43]

---

[40] LaFave et al. (2009), p. 746.

[41] Federal Rules of Evidence, Rule 16(a): http://www.law.cornell.edu/rules/frcrmp/rule_16. Accessed 7 Feb 2015.

[42] These general guidelines of the federal law may be narrowed or broadened in state law, e.g., by adding a list of witnesses, including their addresses of residence, who may have information on the case and who, hypothetically, could testify in the trial. See: Worrall (2007), p. 295; LaFave et al. (2009), p. 985.

[43] According to the followers of this solution, it is intended to prevent exercising any pressure on witnesses or the contents of their depositions, see: Schuon (2010), p. 20; Everett (1964), p. 481.

A second characteristic feature of this system is the fact that all the above-mentioned information is disclosed upon a defendant's request. It should all be made available for inspection, copying or photographing. Demand made by the private party triggers certain disclosure obligations for the state official in order to establish a certain procedural form of balance.[44] It is a double-edged weapon: a request to disclose a certain category of evidence leads to opening the possibility for the prosecutor to make a request to disclose the same category of evidence by the defence. On the other hand, as discovery is reciprocal, if a defendant requests disclosure of *Documents and Objects* and the government complies, then the defendant must permit the government, upon request, to inspect and to copy or photograph books, papers, documents, data, photographs, tangible objects, buildings or places or copies or portions of any of these items if

(a) the item is within the defendant's possession, custody or control; and
(b) the defendant intends to use the item in the defendant's case-in-chief at trial.

The same rule applies to *Reports of Examinations and Tests*, where the government is allowed to conduct the same activities in relation to the results or reports of any physical or mental examination and of any scientific test or experiment. In practice, though, not all the categories of evidence potentially subject to disclosure will be disclosed in every criminal process; however, the prosecution must be prepared to do it on request of the defence.

It is an obligation of the prosecutor in proceedings before international criminal tribunals to disclose evidence to support the charges formulated in an indictment. These tribunals adopted a broad understanding of the prosecutor's obligation to disclose evidence. As a rule, he is required to disclose any and all evidence and information that he intends to use in the trial (or in the preliminary hearing) regardless of the request of the accused or regardless of whether this evidence is material for the prosecution or not.

In the proceedings before the ICTY, the evidence to be disclosed by the Prosecutor to support the prosecution has been divided into three categories:

(1) The Prosecutor is under an obligation to disclose to the accused copies of the supporting material that accompanied the indictment when confirmation was sought within 30 days of the initial appearance of the accused (Rule 66(A)(i)). There was some controversy as to whether evidence should be disclosed solely to the parties of the proceedings or whether it should also be presented to the Trial Chamber. The case law of the *ad hoc* tribunals showed that it depended solely on the opinion of the Chamber, which could demand access to the disclosed material.[45]
(2) The Rules of Procedure and Evidence require the Prosecutor to disclose to the accused—within the same time limit—prior statements obtained by the

[44] See: Heinze (2014), p. 319.

[45] *Prosecutor v. Blagojević*, IT-02-60, Appeals Chamber, 8 April 2003, § 18.

Prosecutor from the accused (Rule 66(A)(i)). Their disclosure does not depend on whether they were oral or written, and neither does it need to be demonstrated (as is the case in the United States) that they are of material importance for the case or that they were obtained in the course of interrogation by the authorities of the Court. They may be statements delivered in any type of judicial proceedings, provided they are in the possession of the prosecutor.[46] This category of disclosure should be viewed in connection with the obligation of the prosecution to audio-record or video-record questioning of a suspect and to supply a copy of the recorded tape to the suspect (Rule 43).

(3) The Prosecutor must disclose copies of the statements of all witnesses whom he intends to call to testify at trial and copies of all transcripts and written statements within the time limit prescribed by the Trial Chamber (Rule 66A (ii)). This obligation is expressed in much broader terms than in the United States, where the prosecutor (usually) does not need to disclose the contents of depositions of such witnesses. This obligation has been additionally expanded relative to the original system adopted from the United States, as it also covers disclosing the contents of the opinions presented by court experts if the Prosecutor intends to summon them to the trial.[47] It is a continuous obligation: copies of the statements of additional prosecution witnesses shall be made available to the defence as soon as a decision is made to call those witnesses.

In proceedings before the ICC, the Prosecutor's obligation to disclose evidence to support the charges is also realised in stages. Its model follows the example of the ICTY.[48] The specific categories of evidence that is subject to disclosure are grouped in the following three sets:

(1) The first group consists of obligations of the Prosecutor before the confirmation of the charges hearing. According to Article 61(3) of the Rome Statute, within a reasonable time before the hearing, the suspect shall be provided with a copy of the document containing the charges on which the Prosecutor intends to bring the person to trial and be informed of the evidence on which the Prosecutor intends to rely at the hearing—also in order to argue with the defence's evidence. Rules of Procedure and Evidence specify that the Prosecutor is under an obligation to provide to the suspect (and the Pre-Trial Chamber), no later than 30 days before the date of the confirmation hearing, a detailed description of the charges together with a list of the evidence that he intends to present at the hearing (Rule 121(3)). This still does not constitute an obligation to disclose all incriminating evidence that is in the Prosecutor's possession.

---

[46] *Prosecutor v. Blaškić*, IT-95-14, Decision on the Defence Motion for Sanctions for the Prosecutor's Failure to Comply with Rule (66)(A) of the Rules and the Decision of 27 January 1997 Compelling the Production of All Statements of the Accused, 15 June 1998. See also: Pruitt (2001), pp. 308–309.

[47] See in general: Bitti (2008), p. 1210.

[48] There is a general agreement as to that fact, e.g. see: consequently Tochilovsky (2009), p. 844; Tochilovsky (2002), pp. 100 and 115.

It pertains solely to this evidence that he will present in order to prove that there is a reasonable basis to suspect that the accused has committed the alleged offence, which the Prosecutor is obliged to demonstrate during this hearing.[49]

(2) The second group of disclosure obligations is activated before the trial: upon assignment of a case for trial in accordance with this Statute, the Trial Chamber assigned to deal with the case shall provide for disclosure of documents or information not previously disclosed, sufficiently in advance of the commencement of the trial to enable adequate preparation for trial (Article 64(3)(c));

(3) The Rules of Procedure and Evidence complement both provisions, defining the scope of materials that are subject to disclosure. In this way, they establish two sets of rules pertaining to the evidence concerning:
- the prosecution witnesses and
- inspection of material in the possession or control of the Prosecutor.

When it comes to prosecution witnesses, the Prosecutor shall provide the defence with the names of witnesses whom the Prosecutor intends to call to testify and copies of any prior statements made by those witnesses. The statements of prosecution witnesses shall be made available in original and in a language that the accused fully understands and speaks. It should be done "sufficiently in advance to enable the adequate preparation of the defence" (Rule 76(1)). It is a continuous obligation. It extends also to additional prosecution witnesses, whom the prosecution decides to call subsequently, after the commencement of the trial. This decision needs to be communicated to the defence as soon as possible. The disclosure of evidence in respect of a witness is activated every time the Prosecutor makes a decision to summon this witness or even to present a part of his statement during the trial. Furthermore, it pertains to the stage of the confirmation of charges hearing: where the Prosecutor amended the charges, he should deliver a list of evidence he intends to bring in support of those charges at the hearing (Rule 121(4)).

Additionally, the suspect should be provided with a copy of his statements made during investigation before the Prosecutor—either a written copy or video- or audio-recorded one (Rule 112(1)(e))—but only materials being in possession or control of the Prosecutor and taken during the investigation.[50]

Regarding the inspection of material in possession or control of the Prosecutor, a distinction should be made between "providing the defence" (Rule 76) with evidence and the obligation to allow for "inspection" of evidence (Rule 77). Namely, the Prosecutor must permit the defence to inspect any books, documents, photographs and other tangible objects in his possession or control, which are intended for use by the Prosecutor as evidence for the purposes of the confirmation hearing or at trial, as the case may be, or were obtained from or belonged to the person. Inspection of a tangible document is not dependent on a prior request from the

[49] See in general: Shibahara and Schabas (2008), pp. 1176–1177; Schabas (2010), p. 739; Bitti (2008), p. 1208.

[50] And not notes taken by certain journalists and non-governmental organisations during interviews. See: Tochilovsky (2008), p. 174.

defence, although the use of the term "permit to inspect" might suggest, that the defence was interested in getting access to these documents—which interest is best expressed by the way of submitting a request. Additionally, the Pre-Trial Chamber may oblige the Prosecutor to "organise" a list of evidence, by matching each piece of evidence to the relevant fact and also by linking fragments of witnesses' statements with the elements of the crimes they pertain to.[51]

Interestingly, some similarities may be seen between the system adopted by international criminal tribunals and the continental systems with respect to evidence that is subject to mandatory disclosure. In the latter systems, also obligatorily, regardless of the prosecutor's consent, reports of procedures in which the party has participated or had the right to participate, documents coming from a party or that were prepared with its participation, as well as opinions of experts, research or a scientific institutions, need to be disclosed. In continental systems, however, this obligation is already activated during an investigation.

5.2.2 *Disclosure of the Evidence Material to the Preparation of the Defence*

It is the disclosure of evidence in favour of the accused by the prosecutor that is of major importance in common law systems. It is also the disclosure of exculpatory evidence that receives most attention in the Anglo-Saxon literature, and it is a key component of the disclosure of evidence procedure.

An element of this obligation includes recording certain categories of evidence set forth in the law and bringing favourable evidence to the prosecutor's attention, which rests with the police. An obligation of recording and then disclosing the evidence that may be favourable for the defence by the prosecution is intended to balance the disadvantaged position of the accused relative to the state authorities. What is meant here is not an active search for evidence but rather the recording and retaining of evidence that came into his possession.[52] If not for this obligation, the prosecutor would not be interested in recording such evidence, even if he came across it. The failure of the prosecution to preserve this evidence may lead to depriving the defendant of a fair trial. However, in order to demonstrate that the prosecutor violated this obligation, the defence needs to prove that the failure to retain specific evidence was intentional, namely that it arose from the ill will of the police (or the prosecutor). Failure to disclose evidence due to, for example, the

[51] See: Tochilovsky (2002), p. 173.

[52] Provisions of the Code of Practice, sections 3.1–3.7, on the basis of Criminal Procedure and Investigations Act 1996, section 23(1): http://www.xact.org.uk/information/downloads/CPIA/Disclosure_code_of_practice.pdf. Accessed 11 Sept 2014.

prosecutor's lack of knowledge about the fact that a piece of evidence may be used as exculpatory by the defence (when the favourable nature of the evidence was not obvious) will not constitute a violation of law.[53]

Another element of an obligation to disclose exculpatory evidence is the obligation to demonstrate the legitimacy of the origin of the evidence—the so-called *chain of evidence*. It means that the prosecutor is obliged to ensure that the evidence that is favourable for the accused is obtained and stored in a manner that would not be illicit and that would not infringe on its essence or make it unbelievable or inadmissible under the fruits of the poisonous tree doctrine.

In England and Wales, the prosecutor must disclose to the accused any prosecution material that "might reasonably be considered capable of undermining the case for the prosecution" against the accused or of assisting the case for the accused or give to the accused a written statement that there is no such material (so-called *unused material*—unlike the evidence that the prosecution intends to rely upon during the trial). Thus, an objective test for the notion "exculpatory material" has been adopted.[54] Disclosure of exculpatory information is regulated by Criminal Procedure and Investigation Act 1996, as recently amended by the Criminal Justice Act 2003. It states that "prosecution material" is not only

1) evidentiary material, which is in the prosecutor's possession, and came into his possession in connection with the case for the prosecution against the accused, but also
2) which he has inspected in connection with the case for the prosecution against the accused.[55]

Section 7(a) CPIA sets out the prosecution's obligation to constantly review the question of whether there is additional prosecution material that should be disclosed to the accused (constituting the so-called *continuous prosecutor's obligation*).

Very detailed guidelines according to which the English prosecutor must interpret these provisions have been drawn up by the Attorney General (recently, in 2005). In Guidelines on Disclosure, he gives examples of material that might reasonably be considered capable of undermining the prosecution case or of assisting the case for the accused, which is

(1) any material casting doubt upon the accuracy of any prosecution evidence;
(2) any material that may point to another person, whether charged or not (including a co-accused), having involvement in the commission of the offence;
(3) any material that may cast doubt upon the reliability of a confession;
(4) any material that might go to the credibility of a prosecution witness;

---

[53] As it was concluded in: *Arizona v. Youngblood*, 488 U.S. 51 (1988), U.S. Supreme Court, 29 November 1988. See in general also: in the US: LaFave et al. (2009), p. 1154. In England and Wales: Hannibal and Mountford (2002), p. 168.

[54] Heinze (2014), p. 338.

[55] Criminal Procedure and Investigations Act 1996 (section 25), http://www.legislation.gov.uk/ukpga/1996/25/section/3. Accessed 6 Sept 2014.

(5) any material that might support a defence that is either raised by the defence or apparent from the prosecution papers;
(6) any material that may have a bearing on the admissibility of any prosecution evidence.

It is underlined in the Guidelines that it should also be borne in mind that while items of material viewed in isolation may not be reasonably considered to be capable of undermining the prosecution case or assisting the accused, several items together can have that effect. Particular attention should be given to materials relating to the accused's mental or physical health, intellectual capacity or to any ill treatment that the accused may have suffered when in the investigator's custody.[56] The Guidelines on Disclosure also provide an interesting example, how the disclosure regime should be seen and interpreted by the practitioners: "It is vital that everybody in the criminal justice system operates these procedures properly and fairly to ensure we protect the integrity of the criminal justice system, whilst at the same time ensuring that a just and fair disclosure process is not abused so that it becomes unwieldy, bureaucratic and effectively unworkable". This is thus important in that the disclosure regime can only work "if there is trust and confidence in the system and everyone plays their role in it. If this is achieved, applications for a stay of proceedings on the grounds of non-disclosure will only be made exceedingly sparingly, and never on a speculative basis". Moreover, the "investigators must provide detailed and proper schedules. Prosecutors must not abrogate their duties under the CPIA by making a wholesale disclosure in order to avoid carrying out the disclosure exercise themselves. Likewise, defence practitioners should avoid fishing expeditions and where disclosure is not provided using this as an excuse for an abuse of process application".

A failure by the police to seize or retain evidence that may be of relevance to the accused's defence can give rise to an application to have the proceedings stayed for an abuse of process—especially if such evidence was earlier secured by the police.[57] In cases *R (Ebrahim) v. Feltham Magistrates Court* and *Mouat v. Director of Public Prosecutions*, the main objection of the defence related to the fact that the police failed to retain evidence that was of relevance to the defendant's guilt. As they failed to retain it, it was impossible to fulfil the disclosure of evidence obligation. In the first case, it was alleged that the police failed to secure possibly relevant video footage of a defendant captured on store security cameras. In the second case, the police had wiped clear a videotape (in order to reuse it) of the defendant speeding—having first viewed the tape in the presence of the defendant.[58]

[56] Attorney-General's Guidelines on disclosure, Pt 37(i-vi), at: http://www.cps.gov.uk/legal/a_to_c/attorney_generals_guidelines_on_disclosure/. Accessed 6 Sept 2014.

[57] For more detailed analysis, see: Padfield (2008), p. 271; Ward and Wragg (2005), pp. 574–575; Ashworth and Redmayne (2005), pp. 93–99; Sprack (2012), pp. 143–146; Hannibal and Mountford (2002), pp. 182–183.

[58] [2001] 2 Cr App R 427.

What is specific about the English system is the fact that the applicable disclosure obligations are influenced by the classification of offences. In summary trials, there is no prosecutor's obligation until the accused enters a plea of guilty. Disclosure provisions come into play only when the accused pleads not guilty. Disclosure should be undertaken by the prosecutor within 28 days of this plea.

Also in the United States, the prosecutor is obliged to disclose the evidence that is exculpatory for the accused. This obligation has been restricted by the Supreme Court of the United States in *Brady v. Maryland* to disclosing evidence that is "material" either to an accused's guilt or to punishment.[59] The Court concluded that suppression by the prosecution of evidence favourable to an accused who has requested it violates due process where the evidence is material either to guilt or to punishment, irrespective of the good faith or bad faith of the prosecution. This notion is defined as raising "a reasonable probability that its disclosure would have produced a different result at trial"—specifically—a different verdict by the jury.[60] In the next cases, the Supreme Court limited the scope of discovery; it concluded that "the Constitution does not demand such broad discovery; and the mere possibility that an item of undisclosed information (a criminal record) might have aided the defence, or might have affected the outcome of the trial, does not establish 'materiality' in the constitutional sense".[61] Moreover, in this case the fact that non-disclosure has not "harmed" the defence case was taken into consideration, especially that the defence did not request information about the victim's prior criminal record at trial, only on appeal. However, while the prosecution is not necessarily required to disclose every bit of information that might prove "helpful" to the defence, it must be "assigned the consequent responsibility to gauge the likely net effect of all such evidence and make disclosure when the point of 'reasonable probability' is reached".[62]

Similarly to the Anglo-Saxon systems, in proceedings before the ICTY the Prosecutor is under an obligation to disclose materials that are favourable to the accused. Also, there is no general obligation for him to disclose all evidence in his possession. According to Rule 68 RPE ICTY, the Prosecutor must disclose to the defence any material that in the actual knowledge of the Prosecutor

(1) may suggest the innocence or mitigate the guilt of the accused, or
(2) affect the credibility of Prosecution evidence.

Additionally, Rule 66(B) introduces an obligation to ensure the inspection of tangible evidence: the Prosecutor should, on request, permit the defence to inspect any books, documents, photographs and tangible objects in the Prosecutor's custody or control, which are "material to the preparation of the defence".

[59] *Brady v. Maryland*, 373 U.S. 83 (1963), Supreme Court, 13 May 1963, § 87.

[60] *Kyles v. Whitley*, 514 U.S. 419 (1995), Supreme Court, 19 April 1995.

[61] *United States v. Agurs*, 427 U.S. 97 (1976), Supreme Court, 24 June 1976.

[62] See: Worrall (2007), p. 302; LaFave et al. (2009), pp. 991–995; Heinze (2014), p. 327.

The condition that the physical evidence favourable for the defence was "material to the preparation of the defence" indicates that the prosecutor's obligation should not be interpreted as an obligation to provide the defence with all information that could be useful to it.[63] The criteria for establishing whether the evidence is actually "material to a case" have been set forth in *Prosecutor v. Delalić*.[64] In this case, the ICTY, citing the US Supreme Court's jurisprudence, expressed its opinion that "the requested evidence must be 'significantly helpful to an understanding of important incriminating or exculpatory evidence'"; it is material if there "is a strong indication that it will play an important role in uncovering admissible evidence, aiding witness preparation, corroborating testimony, or assisting impeachment or rebuttal".[65] On the other hand, it also invoked the English, wider understanding of the evidence material to the preparation of the defence, which might be also evidence that holds out a real (as opposed to fanciful) prospect of providing a lead on evidence that goes to exonerating evidence (as understood above).[66]

In 2001, the terminology used in Rule 68 RPE ICTY was changed, and exonerating "evidence" became exonerating "material". In this way, it has been highlighted that the scope of the disclosure of evidence material does not depend on the fact whether it would be admissible as evidence in a trial. Thus, the Prosecutor should disclose not only evidence in a strict meaning, but since the Rules refer to "material", the disclosure must not be restricted to material in a form that would be admissible as evidence but includes all information in any form.[67] As a result, any and all information that could be favourable for the accused is disclosed; for instance, it can be a combined fact of concluding favourable arrangements between the prosecution and a witness, and all information collected by the prosecution suggesting that any of its proposed witnesses may have committed or may have taken part in the commission of any criminal offence. Such a piece of information may indeed go to the credibility of prosecution's witness.[68] The prosecution's duty to disclose does not encompass material of a public nature—however, a distinction should be drawn between material of a public character in the public domain and material reasonably accessible to the defence. The ICTY emphasised that unless exculpatory material is reasonably accessible to the accused

63 *Prosecutor v. Blagojević*, IT-02-60, Joint Decision on Motions Related to Production of Evidence, 12 December 2002, § 26.

64 *Prosecutor v. Delalić*, IT-96-21-T, Decision on Motion by the Accused Z. Delalić for the Disclosure of Evidence, 26 September 1996.

65 *United States v. Jackson*, 850 F. Supp. 1481, 1503 (U.S. Dist. Ct. D. Kan. 1994); *United States v. Lloyd*, 992 F.2d 348, 351 (U.S. Ct. App. D.C. Cir. 1993).

66 As in case *R v. Keane*, 99 CRuleApp. R.1. Discussed in more detail: Tochilovsky (2004b), p. 8; Tochilovsky (2002), pp. 130–131; Schuon (2010), pp. 112–113; Pruitt (2001), pp. 309–311; and Harmon and Karagiannakis (2000), pp. 318–319.

67 *Prosecutor v. Kordić*, IT-95-14/2, Decision on Motions to Extend Time for Filling Appellant's Briefs, 11 May 2001, § 9; *Prosecutor v. Kristić*, IT-98-33, Appeals Chamber, 19 April 2004, § 178.

68 *Prosecutor v. Halilović*, IT-01-48, Decision on the Defence Motion for Identification of Suspects and other Categories Among the Proposed Witnesses, 14 November 2003, p. 3.

(with the exercise of due diligence), the prosecution has anyway a duty to disclose such material.[69]

This rule resembles the solution adopted in the United States. Moreover, the judges of the ICTY referred to the regulations of this country in the process of its interpretation.[70] They concluded that because, first, Rule 66(B) does not provide any guidelines on the type of physical evidence that is to be disclosed to the accused and, second, its wording is identical to that of Rule 16(a) of Federal Rules of Evidence,[71] the interpretation on the scope of application of this provision adopted by the US courts should serve as a guideline in the interpretation of the ICTY provisions. It is one of the numerous examples of the ICTY's reliance on national interpretations of provisions that have been transplanted into international criminal proceedings. However, the scope of disclosure is broader than in the case of the United States' system, as the obligation extends all the materials favourable for the defence and not only evidence that would have been admitted at trial. Moreover, the testimony of witnesses must be disclosed *in extenso*.[72]

Before the ICTY, the Prosecutor is an accuser who does not have an obligation to seek actively evidence in favour of the accused. Therefore, using the United States as an example, the ICTY also highlighted the need for introducing the requirement that evidence that is potentially favourable for the accused "should be in possession of the Prosecutor"—so as to avoid interpreting this obligation as one of performing an active search for evidence in favour of the accused.[73] This requirement has been stressed on several occasions. In *Prosecutor v. Blagojević*, the Trial Chamber stressed that the obligation to disclose exculpatory evidence is not intended to serve as a means through which the prosecution is forced to replace the defence in conducting investigations or gathering material that may assist the defence.[74]

If there is a doubt as to whether the Prosecutor is in possession of evidence that may be favourable for the defence, the latter may request that the Tribunal orders the Prosecutor to disclose it. In such a request, the defence must give its grounds for believing that an item of evidence may be favourable for it. In the ICTY jurisprudence, a high standard was adopted (on the basis of the US Supreme Court interpretation)—the defence may not rely on pure allegations or a general description of the information but must make a *prima facie* case showing of materiality and

[69] *Prosecutor v. Blaškić*, IT-95-14-A, Appeals Chamber, 29 July 2004, § 296; *Prosecutor v. Blagojević*, Joint Decision on Motions Related to Production of Evidence, 12 December 2002, § 26.

[70] As in e.g.: *Prosecutor v. Delalić*, IT-96-21-T, TC II, Decision on the Motion by the Accused Zejnil Delalić for the Disclosure of Evidence, 26 September 1996, § 7 and 9.

[71] *Federal Rules of Evidence*, Rule 16(a), at: http://www.law.cornell.edu/rules/frcrmp/rule_16. Accessed 7 Sept 2014.

[72] See: Schuon (2010), pp. 112–113; May and Wierda (2002), pp. 74–75.

[73] *Prosecutor v. Blaškić*, IT-95-14-PT, Decision on the Production of Discovery Materials, 27 January 1997, § 47, 50.

[74] *Prosecutor v. Blagojević*, IT-02-60-PT, Joint Decision on Motions Related to Production of Evidence, 12 December 2002, § 26.

that the requested evidence is in the custody or control of the prosecution.[75] Obviously, the fact that there is no way of learning what evidence is actually in the Prosecutor's possession does not make this task easier. Moreover, the defence may not submit a request for a general disclosure: it must always indicate what evidence it specifically demands to be disclosed. The institution of disclosure of evidence does not serve the purpose of facilitating the examination of all and any evidence in possession of the prosecutor by the defence.

The ICTY Prosecutor's obligation to disclose the exculpatory material acquired a very wide practical scope after obliging him to make available to the defence collections of relevant material held by the Prosecutor—in electronic form (Rule 68 (ii)). In 2003, the Electronic Disclosure System (EDS) was created. It is an electronic database where all material identified by the Prosecutor as being "relevant to the preparation of the defence" can be accessed by the defence. However, there is not only obligation to store (and make available) all the exculpatory material but also obligation to provide for "an appropriate computer software with which the defence can search such collections electronically". As the ICTY judges concluded, the Prosecutor should also enable its effective use. The Prosecutor's obligation, then, may not be considered to have been met if it simply offers access to all evidence collected in an electronic system.[76] It is not the task of the defence to comb through vast databases in order to find materials that meet the statutory premises of disclosure. It was concluded in the case law that the Prosecutor should single out the evidence that might be favourable for the accused, whether in the form of a separate database or in the form of a list of documents that the Prosecutor has qualified as potentially favourable for the defence in order to comply with the obligation of disclosure of evidence (ultimately, it was concluded that he should perform both of these actions).[77] The fact that even when providing access to materials potentially favourable to the defence it is necessary to provide a "guide" to these materials (so-called *meta-data*) in order to meet the fair trial standard, without which the navigation through the entire database is not possible, demonstrates the volume of evidence that is meant here. In one of the cases before the ICTY, following an analysis of 2.7 million documents, the Prosecutor identified 104,000 documents that were potentially significant to the defence.[78]

It is the Prosecutor who is in charge of qualifying evidence to this database. According to the ICTY's jurisprudence, a Chamber does not intervene in the exercise of this discretion by the prosecution, unless it is shown that the prosecution abused its discretion. Only if there is a dispute as to materiality of exculpatory

---

[75] *Prosecutor v. Delalić*, IT-96-21, Decision on the Motion by the Accused Zejnil Delalić for the Disclosure of Evidence, 26 September 1996, § 7, 9.

[76] We have to remember that "information loses heuristic value as its collective size begins to outgrow the capacity of humans to evaluate it"; cit. after: Ohlin (2009), p. 91.

[77] *Prosecutor v. Mladić*, IT-09-92, Decision on the defence motion for certification to appeal the decision on submissions relative to the proposed "EDS" method of disclosure, 13 August 2012.

[78] *Prosecutor v. Krajišnik*, IT-00-39, 23 May 2001, § 21–22. These cases and the consequences of the Prosecutor's actions analysed: Tochilovsky (2011), p. 605.

evidence that the Trial Chamber may become involved and act as a referee between the parties in order to determine the legal scope of disclosure.[79]

An obligation of disclosing evidence favourable for the defence also arises from the ICC Statute where it is one of the basic procedural rights of the accused. The Court has emphasised that the prosecutor's obligation to disclose to the defence the evidence that is favourable for the accused should be considered—in the light of the previous ICTY case law and, more importantly, the case law of the ECtHR—to be an element of a fair trial and of the right to defence.[80]

Article 67(2) obliges the ICC Prosecutor to disclose to the defence evidence in the Prosecutor's possession or control[81] that he or she believes

(1) shows or tends to show the innocence of the accused, or
(2) mitigates the guilt of the accused, or
(3) may affect the credibility of prosecution evidence.

The Rules of Procedure and Evidence additionally provide that, applying their exact wording, the Prosecutor should permit the defence to inspect any books, documents, photographs and other tangible objects in the possession or control of the Prosecutor, which are "material to the preparation of the defence" (Rule 77). This obligation extends only to materials that are "in the possession or control of the Prosecutor".[82] As it results from the ICC jurisprudence, a broad reading of this notion should be adopted. The ICC Appeals Chamber held that this term should be understood as referring to all objects that are relevant for the preparation of the defence.[83] The Chamber noted that the wording of Rule 77 is based on the wording of similar provision of RPE ICTY (Rule 66(B)) and concluded that the jurisprudence of the ICTY should be regarded as "relevant" as regards the meaning of this concept. Therefore, this concept should not be narrowed only to materials that would either undermine the case of the prosecution or support the line of argument of the defence (as it was done by the Trial Chamber in this case); it cannot be understood as material that is directly linked to exonerating or incriminating evidence. In further cases, the Trial Chamber concluded that "material" is also evidence that would "significantly assist the accused in understanding the incriminating and exculpatory evidence"

[79] A very detailed analysis in: Tochilovsky (2004b), p. 9; Tochilovsky (2002), pp. 148–150.

[80] *The Prosecutor v. Lubanga*, ICC-01/04-01/06, Decision on the consequences of non-disclosure of exculpatory materials covered by Article 54(3)(e) agreements and the application to stay the prosecution of the accused, together with certain other issues raised at the Status Conference on 10 June 2008, 13 June 2008, § 77–84, where the jurisprudence of the ECtHR was invoked as in the case of *Jaspers v. Belgium*, application No. 8403/78, § 58, and *Rowe and Davis v. United Kingdom*, application No. 28901/95, § 60.

[81] Which obligation is not limited to permitting the defence to inspect but extends also to providing the defence with an electronic copy of this material if requested. See: Ambos (2007), p. 471.

[82] See: Schabas (2008), p. 1270.

[83] *The Prosecutor v. Lubanga*, ICC-01/04-01/06, Judgment on the Appeal of Mr. Lubanga Dyilo against the oral decision of Trial Chamber I of 18 January 2008, Appeals Chamber, 11 July 2008, § 2.

and the issues of the case. The ICC went even further in stating (in *The Prosecutor v. Bemba*) that

> any prior information obtained from a prosecution witness will presumptively be material to the defence's preparation for that witness's testimony unless those items:
>
> 1) are truly repetitive in the sense that they are duplicates; or
> 2) bear no connection to the events relevant to the charges, such as items of a purely personal nature.[84]

Every document in every case should be carefully assessed by the Prosecutor in terms of whether it may be favourable for the defence: "the disclosure of truly relevant evidence presupposes an in-depth analysis by the Prosecutor of each piece of evidence prior to its disclosure, whether that evidence is incriminating or exculpatory".[85] Usually, the Prosecutor presents a plan of disclosing evidence to the defence under which he agrees to disclose all evidence potentially favourable to the accused that he has acquired in a given period, for example every 2 weeks.[86] The Prosecutor also needs to consider both the contents of a piece of evidence and its potential; evidence that may be potentially favourable for the accused, whether proving his innocence or leading to mitigation of guilt, should be subject to disclosure.[87] It has been established in the ICC's jurisprudence that this obligation relates also to the discovery of information regarding a possible criminal record and the suspect status (or the fact of being an accused) of any of the witnesses on whose statements or summaries the prosecution intends to rely at the confirmation hearing as these may affect the witness's credibility.[88]

Not only must the Prosecutor disclose this evidence, but he must also perform this duty in a certain way: in order to facilitate the defence in the analysis of the material disclosed, "the Prosecution shall provide a further elaboration of such material by including in the Disclosure Note, together with the list of the items disclosed and their reference numbers:

[84] *The Prosecutor v. Bemba*, Redacted Version of Decision on the "Defence Motion for Disclosure pursuant to Rule 77", 29 July 2011, § 23. See also analysis in: Tochilovsky (2013), p. 1091; and Heinze (2014), pp. 356–357.

[85] *The Prosecutor v. Bemba*, Decision on the Evidence Disclosure System and Setting a Timetable for Disclosure between the Parties, 31 July 2008, § 68.

[86] *The Prosecutor v. Lubanga,* ICC-01/04-01/06-102, Decision on the Final System of Disclosure and the Establishment of a Timetable, 15 May 2006, § 120.

[87] *The Prosecutor v. Lubanga*, ICC-01/04-01/06, Decision on the consequences of non-disclosure of exculpatory materials covered by Article 54(3)(e) agreements and the application to stay the prosecution of the accused, together with certain other issues raised at the Status Conference on 10 June 2008, 13 June 2008.

[88] *The Prosecutor v. Katanga*, ICC-01/04-01/07, Decision on the confirmation of charges, 30 September 2008, § 181.

1) a concise summary of the content of each item; and
2) an explanation of the relevance of such item as potentially exculpatory".[89]

Similarly, as regards the right to inspection of exculpatory material that the defence wishes to inspect physically, the Chamber was of a view that "the Prosecution shall include in the Pre-Inspection Report with respect to those items which are material to the preparation of the defence, together with the list of the items submitted and their reference numbers".

In *The Prosecutor v. Lubanga*, however, the Prosecutor noticed that it was not always possible to classify precisely a given item of evidence as being favourable for the accused, as some evidence may simultaneously be incriminating.[90] Even in the case of witness statements, it is obvious that they may be partially incriminating and at the same time in other parts exculpatory. Should such statements be disclosed only to the extent they are favourable to the accused? There is an even more complex, and more difficult to assess, situation when witness statements themselves can be interpreted both as being favourable and unfavourable for the accused. Such types of evidence are difficult to qualify definitely to a specific group of evidence.

In such a situation, the Prosecutor may demand that the Chamber resolves, as soon as possible, doubts concerning the nature of evidence favourable for the accused and, in consequence, determine whether it should be disclosed. For obvious reasons, the Chamber reviews the evidence *in camera*, as an open court hearing would render the process pointless, with the Prosecutor not being able to disclose all the desired details justifying his motion.

According to the ICC judges—just as it was the case before the ICTY—a final resolution on whether a given item of evidence "shows or tends to show the innocence of the accused" or "mitigates the guilt of the accused" is the task of judges.[91] In *The Prosecutor v. Lubanga* case, the judges expressed an opinion that this is a decision not for the prosecution but for the judges: once the prosecution believes that the evidence "shows or tends to show the innocence of the accused" (Article 67(2) of the Statute), it is to be disclosed to the defence, or in case of doubt put before the Court.[92] A thorough assessment will need to be made by the Pre-Trial Chamber of the potential relevance of the information to the defence on a case-by-case basis. If the information is relevant or potentially exculpatory, the balancing exercise performed by the Pre-Trial Chamber between the interests at stake will

[89] *The Prosecutor v. Abu Garda*, Second Decision on issues relating to Disclosure, 15 July 2009, § 15.

[90] *The Prosecutor v. Lubanga*, ICC-01/04-01/06, Prosecutor's observations on disclosure, 6 April 2006, § 14.

[91] *The Prosecutor v. Katanga*, ICC-01/04-01/-07, Decision on Article 54(3)(e) Documents Identified as Potentially Exculpatory or Otherwise Material to the Defence's Preparation of the Confirmation Hearing, 20 June 2008, § 2.

[92] *The Prosecutor v. Lubanga*, ICC-01/04-01/06, Decision on the consequences of non-disclosure of exculpatory materials covered by Article 54(3)(e) agreements and the application to stay the prosecution of the accused, together with certain other issues raised at the Status Conference on 10 June 2008, 13 June 2008, § 87.

require particular care. In the view of the Chamber, each individual document purporting to contain potentially exculpatory material must be individually examined by the Chamber in order to enable it to assess whether the trial will be "conducted with full respect for the rights of the accused" in accordance with Article 64(2) of the Statute. In the same case, the Trial Chamber decided even to send, *proprio motu*, "a suitably qualified and independent representative of the Registry to speak in person with each of them" in order to establish whether a witness who provides evidence that may be exculpatory in nature will co-operate with the Court. The judges decided that it would be wrong to leave it to the prosecution to decide whether such a witness is prepared to co-operate.[93] Therefore, although it is the Prosecutor who is responsible for identifying the relevant evidence, the Chambers "reserve for themselves the right to intervene whenever they see fit".[94]

While there is no doubt that the disclosure obligation works between two parties of the proceedings, it is still not clear to what extent this obligation extends to disclosing the evidence to the Pre-Trial Chamber. While in one case the Chamber requests communication of "all exculpatory evidence" as the Prosecutor's obligation is to investigate incriminating and exonerating circumstances equally,[95] in another case the Chamber takes a different view and states that only the exculpatory evidence on which the parties intend to rely at the confirmation hearing has to be communicated to the Chamber.[96] Interestingly, serious differences in the understanding of the scope of this obligation could have been observed in the judicial practice of the ICC. The Pre-Trial Chamber expressed two views: once it interpreted this obligation in a narrow way, while on other occasions it believed in a broad interpretation.[97] This case is a clear example of how the ICC provisions leave room for interpretation and the possibility to interpret the Statute and RPE on a case-by-case basis. In consequence, issues arising in different Chambers may be resolved in slightly different ways—which illustrates also how the composition of a certain Chamber can play an important role in the process of interpretation, as judges coming from different legal cultures tend to apply different methods of interpretation, depending on their legal background.[98] In consequence, as the Prosecutor cannot predict which method of interpretation will be adopted by a certain Chamber, he will have to adopt the broad understanding of the obligation to communicate the evidence to the Chambers. Similarly, not knowing what is the

---

[93] *The Prosecutor v. Lubanga*, ICC-01/04-01/06, Decision on Disclosure Issues, Responsibilities for Protective Measures and other Procedural Matters, 24 April 2008, § 100.

[94] Cit. after: Heinze (2014), p. 500.

[95] *The Prosecutor v. Bemba*, Decision on the Evidence Disclosure System and Setting a Timetable for Disclosure between the Parties, 31 July 2008, § 28.

[96] *The Prosecutor v. Lubanga*, Decision on the Final System of Disclosure and the Establishment of a Timetable, Annex, 15 May 2006, ICC-01/04-01/06, § 41. This case discussed by: Heinze (2014), p. 36.

[97] See: Heinze (2014), p. 39.

[98] As observed by A. Heinze, the narrow scope of interpretation was introduced by Judge Sylvia Steiner, who is a Brazilian judge.

precise scope of the "material to the case" clause he should adopt the broad understanding of this notion or risk claims of the other party that he violates his disclosure obligations.

In contrast to all the aforementioned solutions existing in Anglo-Saxon systems and in the proceedings before the *ad hoc* tribunals, in the case of the ICC the obligation to retain and to disclose evidence favourable for the defence may be derived from the role played by the Prosecutor, who is intended to be "an impartial organ of justice", "searching for the true facts of the case", and who "in order to establish the truth [is obliged to] extend the investigation to cover all facts and evidence relevant to an assessment of whether there is criminal responsibility under this Statute, and, in doing so, investigate incriminating and exonerating circumstances equally" (so Article 54(1)(a) of the Rome Statute).[99] At first glance, the provision pertaining to disclosure of evidence may seem a sort of "legislative surplus". As the ICC Prosecutor is anyway obliged to collect evidence favourable for the accused, it was not necessary to bind him with separate provisions. On the other hand, however, collection of favourable evidence under general legal provisions does not yet have to entail an obligation to disclose it to the accused. Without this obligation, the favourable evidence would stay in the files of the Prosecutor—which cannot be accessed by the accused in a manner similar to continental states. Moreover, the Prosecutor does not have an obligation to use it himself for the benefit of the accused. Due to the implementation of the disclosure of evidence institution, the Rome Statute imposes on the Prosecutor with a twofold obligation: an obligation not only to collect evidence favourable to the accused but also an obligation to provide the accused with such evidence collected by him.

5.3 Disclosure of Evidence by the Defence

It follows from the right to remain silent that the accused may not be forced to any proactive participation in criminal proceedings. Whereas in continental states this right is almost absolute, in Anglo-Saxon systems the accused is obliged to disclose some evidence that he intends to refer to in order to defend himself. Originally, there was no such an obligation in Anglo-Saxon states. Historically, the accused had no obligation corresponding to the prosecutorial obligation to disclose evidence. The right to remain silent also covered the right not to disclose the line of defence. Currently, however, the obligation to notify the prosecution about the intention to raise an *alibi*, or the circumstances excluding any criminal responsi-

[99] As the ICC highlighted in: *The Prosecutor v. Bemba*, ICC-01/05-01/08, Decision Regarding the Disclosure of Materials Pursuant to Article 67(2) of the Rome Statute and Rule 77 of the Rules of Procedure and Evidence, 13 November 2008, § 14.

bility, is typical for Anglo-Saxon systems, although there are still doubts as to the compatibility of this obligation with the right to avoid self-incrimination.[100]

In England, it was only in 1967 that an obligation of the defence to give notice of using the *alibi* defence was introduced. Presently, according to Criminal Procedure and Investigations Act 1996 (section 6A), the accused must produce a written statement setting out, first of all, the nature of his defence and including any particular defences on which he intends to rely. He should explain in this statement the problems at issue with the prosecution, as well as indicate any controversial point of law (such as admissibility of evidence). Second, the statement must disclose an *alibi*—if the accused wishes to bring it during trial. Then it should give particulars of it, such as the name, address and date of birth of any witness the accused believes is able to give evidence in support of the *alibi*, or as many of those details as are known to the accused when the statement is given. A similar obligation pertains to calling expert witnesses. This obligation is not only intended to prevent the so-called "trial by ambush", or the disclosure of the defence's evidence as late as at the end of the trial when the prosecutor has already presented all evidence in his possession, but also has positive outcomes for the accused. Having been informed about the line of defence, the prosecutor is able to analyse evidence in view of the information that may be useful for the defence and therefore requires disclosure.[101]

Also in the United States, there was a discussion whether the Fifth Amendment rights of the accused were violated on the ground that the *notice-of-alibi rule* required him to furnish the State with information useful in convicting him. The US Supreme Court concluded that the privilege against self-incrimination is not violated by a requirement that the defendant give notice of an *alibi* defence and disclose his *alibi* witnesses.[102] Not only disclosing the *alibi* cannot be considered to be "incriminating", but also the defendant cannot be considered to be "compelled" to incriminate himself, as he can make a choice between complete silence and presenting a defence.

In the United States, there is a distinction between *obligatory* and *reciprocal (conditional) discovery*.[103] In most states, it is obligatory to inform about an intent to present an *alibi* or defences, accompanied by a list of witnesses who are to testify on that topic. Conditional discovery refers to a broader range of evidence. Conditional disclosure by defence usually takes place only when previously the defence requested disclosure by the prosecution. This obligation is activated upon request of the prosecution. The first two categories of evidence that the defendant must permit the government to inspect and to copy or photograph—if they are within the

---

[100] E.g. in: Ashworth and Redmayne (2005), p. 136; Hannibal and Mountford (2002), p. 168; Sprack (2012), p. 147.

[101] See: Ward and Wragg (2005), pp. 574–575; Ashworth and Redmayne (2005), pp. 93–99.

[102] *Williams v. Florida*, 399 U.S. 78 (1970), Supreme Court, 22 June 1970, § 86.

[103] See: LaFave et al. (2009), p. 984.

defendant's possession, custody or control and the defendant intends to use the item in the defendant's case-in-chief at trial—are

(1) books, papers, documents, data, photographs, tangible objects, buildings or places or copies or portions of any of these items;
(2) the results or reports of any physical or mental examination and of any scientific test or experiment.

Moreover, the defendant should inform about an intent to present expert testimony on the defendant's mental condition to use as evidence at trial—if earlier he requested from the government disclosure of a written summary of any testimony that the government intends to use during its case-in-chief at trial.

Also, all the international criminal tribunals adopted the reciprocal model of disclosure of evidence.

In the IMT in Nuremberg, there was no express provision as to the obligation of the defence to disclose evidence. Nevertheless, the defence was instructed to submit to the Tribunal the evidence on which they intended to rely, including names of witnesses and matters to which they would testify: the Tribunal ordered the defence to disclose 3 weeks in advance the names of witnesses they intended to call and 2 weeks in advance the documents they intended to present to the Tribunal.[104]

Quite opposite than before the IMT in Nuremberg in proceedings before the *ad hoc* international criminal tribunals, there are extensive provisions on disclosure obligations for the defence. In the case of the ICTY, essentially, the defence is under an obligation to disclose three categories of materials:

(1) Permit the Prosecutor to inspect and copy any books, documents, photographs and tangible objects in the defence's custody or control, which are intended for use by the defence as evidence at trial—not less than 1 week prior to the commencement of the defence case (Rule 67(A)(i) RPE ICTY). Compared to the obligation of the Prosecutor, this obligation is limited, as it covers only physical evidence that the defence is going to use during the trial rather than all physical evidence in its possession (as is the case with the Prosecutor). It has been noticed that this late time limit makes efficient preparation of the prosecution case more difficult—taking into consideration the huge amount of case material that is usually involved before international tribunals.[105] It has even been raised that this provision should be amended and an obligation of prompt disclosure of all evidence should be imposed on the defence.[106] It would make the Prosecutor's task easier, first of all in the area of collecting incriminating material. He could collect the evidence rebutting the line of defence of the accused in a focused manner, not in a haphazard way, as is done now. Moreover, it would also be beneficiary for the accused himself, as the earlier

104 See: Klamberg (2013), p. 1100.
105 See: Schuon (2010), p. 120.
106 See: Harmon and Karagiannakis (2000), pp. 326–327.

knowledge of the line of defence would enable the Prosecutor to disclose evidence favourable for the accused that could be used to support his line of defence.

(2) The defence should provide to the Prosecutor copies of statements of all witnesses whom the defence intends to call to testify at trial or whose written statements the defence intends to present at trial (Rule 67(A)(ii)). Copies of the statements of additional witnesses who the defence decides to call at a later stage are to be made available to the Prosecutor "prior to a decision being made to call those witnesses". This rule was introduced in 2008, and prior to this date the defence's obligation was much narrower in scope: it pertained solely to disclosing statements of witnesses who had already testified in a trial, and the obligation itself was activated only upon request of the Prosecutor. At the beginning of using this procedure of disclosure, the Tribunal insisted on a strict interpretation of this obligation: "The Defence, in high contrast to the Prosecutor's obligations of disclosure, is not required to make any disclosure whatever, unless it intends to rely on an alibi defence or any special defence" and then "only to a quite limited extent, never involving disclosure of witness statements".[107] This opinion was changed, however, in a later case (*Prosecutor v. Delalić*), where the ICTY decided that the judges could order disclosure by the defence to the Prosecutor of its list of witnesses in order to give the prosecution time to prepare an effective cross-examination.[108]

(3) The defence should also notify the Prosecutor of its intent to use the defence of *alibi* or any special defence, including that of diminished or lack of mental responsibility. In such a case, the notification shall specify the place or places at which the accused claims to have been present at the time of the alleged crime. The Prosecutor should also be informed about the names and addresses of witnesses and any other evidence upon which the accused intends to rely to establish the alibi (Rule 67(B)(i)(a) and (b)). If the defence wishes to extend the scope of presentation of evidence, it needs to notify the Prosecutor about new evidence it intends to present.

Also the ICTR confirmed that "the requirement upon the Defence to disclose its intention to rely upon the defence of alibi reflects the well-established practice in the common law jurisdictions around the world. It is a requirement necessary in many jurisdictions, and in the jurisdiction of this Tribunal, in order to allow the Prosecution to adequately prepare its case. Once the accused has raised the defence of alibi, the burden to prove this defence may or may not rest upon him depending upon the jurisdiction concerned". However, although raising an *alibi* requires a reversed burden of proof, the material burden of proof rests upon the prosecution to

---

[107] *Prosecutor v. Tadić*, IT-94-1, Separate Opinion of Judge Stephen on prosecution motion for production of defence witness statement, 27 November 1996.

[108] *Prosecutor v. Delalić*, Decision on the Prosecution's Motion for an Order Requiring Advance Disclosure of Witnesses by the Defence, 4 February 1999, § 30–48.

prove its case beyond a reasonable doubt in all aspects notwithstanding that the defence raised *alibi*.[109]

In the proceedings before the ICC the disclosure obligation consists of two stages and first takes place before the confirmation of the charges hearing. If the defence intends to present evidence at the confirmation hearing, it must provide a list of evidence to the Pre-Trial Chamber no later than 15 days before the date of the hearing (Rule 121(6) RPE ICC). The Pre-Trial Chamber shall transmit the list to the Prosecutor without delay. The person shall provide a list of evidence that he or she intends to present in response to any amended charges or a new list of evidence provided by the Prosecutor. The Pre-Trial Chamber even demanded that the defence file the original statements of the witnesses on which they intended to rely at the confirmation hearing. Otherwise—it concluded—the Pre-Trial Chamber would be prevented from properly exercising its powers with regard to the relevance and admissibility of evidence.[110] At the same time, it stressed that this obligation of disclosure before the confirmation hearing does not apply to the witnesses the defence intends to call at trial.

Moreover, the second moment at which disclosure is due to happen takes place upon assignment of a case for trial.

At each of these two stages:

(1) The defence shall permit the Prosecutor to inspect any books, documents, photographs and other tangible objects in the possession or control of the defence, which are intended for use by the defence as evidence for the purposes of the confirmation hearing (if it intends to present any evidence at all) or at trial (Rule 78). This obligation, however, does not pertain to the contents of witness statements. It suffices to notify the Prosecutor about the identity of witnesses the defence is going to call in order "to enable the prosecution to conduct appropriate enquiries".[111]

(2) Moreover, similarly as before the *ad hoc* tribunals and in common law systems, the defence shall notify the Prosecutor of its intent to raise the existence of an *alibi* or a ground for excluding criminal responsibility—including any substantive factual or legal issues that it intends to raise. In such a case, the notification shall specify the place or places at which the accused claims to have been present at the time of the alleged crime and the names of witnesses and any other evidence upon which the accused intends to rely to establish the *alibi* or any other evidence upon which the accused intends to rely to establish the grounds for excluding criminal responsibility (Rule 79). This notification should be given sufficiently in advance to enable the Prosecutor to prepare adequately and to respond.

---

[109] *Prosecutor v. Kayishema and Ruzindana*, ICTR-95-1, Trial Chamber, 21 May 1999, § 233.

[110] *The Prosecutor v. Lubanga*, Decision on the Final System of Disclosure and the Establishment of a Timetable, 15 May 2006.

[111] *The Prosecutor v. Lubanga*, Decision on Disclosure by the Defence, 20 March 2008, § 41.

The scope of an obligation of the accused to provide the information is always narrower than in the case of the prosecutor. The obligation of the accused is restricted on the basis of his right to defence and the need to retain the guarantees arising from the right to avoid self-incrimination. However, it is also a consequence of the inequality of the parties to the proceedings—the prosecutor will always act from a privileged position.[112] This method of balancing rights of two parties to the trial is conducted by "reducing the rights of the party that is a state official, in order to react to the superiority of the party".[113] It is a method known and accepted in many national legal systems, not only in regard to disclosure obligations, according to which "state officials should be denied at least some procedural rights that are accorded to their private adversaries".[114] The particularly unfavourable position of the accused before international criminal tribunals that arises from the lack of, or at least an impeded, access to the evidence located in the territory of, frequently, very remote states should also be taken into account. It is only the prosecutor who has specific means to ensure the co-operation with the court or the tribunal on the part of the state. Ensuring the defence's access to this evidence is intended to be a remedy for the limited possibilities of acquiring evidence by the defence. Existing procedural solutions aim at providing some kind of procedural compensation for this unfavourable position in relation to the trial opponent and at guaranteeing at least statutory grounds for the implementation of the equality of arms. However, even full access to evidence collected by the prosecutor will not compensate for the lack of the actual possibility to collect evidence by the defence. Moreover, on the example of the disclosure obligations of the defence, we could observe how the equality-of-arms principle may be applied in favour of the prosecution. In *Prosecutor v. Aleksovski*, the ICTY ordered the defence to disclose to the prosecution its list of witnesses, stating that "the Prosecution acts on behalf of and in the interests of the community" and "it is difficult to see how a trial could ever be considered to be fair where the accused is favoured at the expense of the Prosecution beyond a strict compliance with those fundamental protections".[115]

The example of the defence's obligation to disclose evidence to the prosecution clearly shows the differences between legal systems. It should be the essence of the institution of disclosure of evidence to guarantee equal rights to parties in line with the model of strict adversarial principle. For the representatives of Anglo-Saxon legal orders, it is not acceptable that only one party to the trial is obliged to disclose the entire evidence, whereas the other party does not have such an obligation. It would not be consistent with the assumed equality of the parties and the equality of

[112] As to that fact the majority of authors seem to agree, e.g.: Schuon (2010), p. 119; Ambos (2007), p. 466; Hannibal and Mountford (2002), p. 164; Guariglia (2002), p. 1132.

[113] Cit. after: Heinze (2014), p. 317.

[114] Cit. after: Damaška (1986), p. 104.

[115] Cit. after: Klamberg (2013), p. 1105 and the case: *Prosecutor v. Delalić*, Decision on the Prosecution's Motion for an Order Requiring Advance Disclosure of Witnesses by the Defence, 4 February 1999, § 30–48.

arms in the trial. In continental systems, however, disclosure of evidence by the defence is not considered to be necessary and it is not considered to be inconsistent with the principle of equality of the parties. The lack of such an obligation is related to the manner in which the prosecutorial role has been shaped, the prosecutor being an authority that is also acting for the benefit of the defence and thus obliged to acquire evidence favourable for it. Therefore, it is assumed that he had both the opportunity and the obligation to obtain information on such evidence.

5.4 Infringement of the Duty to Disclose Evidence

Violation of the obligation to disclose evidence by the prosecutor has often provided grounds for complaints addressed to international criminal tribunals. The jurisprudence of the *ad hoc* tribunals shows that the prosecutor's failure to meet the obligations related to disclosure of evidence has a significant impact on the evaluation of the correctness of the trial. However, no regulations have been introduced to set forth sanctions for the violation of this obligation. The procedural response remains within the discretion of the judges. The pre-trial judge or the Trial Chamber may decide *proprio motu*, or at the request of either party, on sanctions to be imposed on a party that fails to perform its disclosure obligations pursuant to the Rules (Rule 69bis RPE ICTY). While deciding on an adequate sanction in a given situation, the judges must always take into account how seriously the rights to defence and fairness of the proceedings have suffered and how this violation can be remedied.

When it comes to evidence supporting the charges presented by the prosecution, as a rule, the failure to disclose evidence makes it impossible to refer to it during a trial (or a confirmation hearing). However, in practice this sanction is rarely applied. Most frequently, the failure to disclose evidence results in postponement of the trial (hearing) date in order to ensure effective service of the desired documents and provide enough time for the defence to examine its contents.[116] In the case of *Prosecutor v. Mladić*, 7,000 pages of incriminating materials sent to the defence under the disclosure procedure got lost.[117] In such a situation, the defence demanded that the hearing should be postponed by 6 months in order to make it possible for it to learn the contents of these materials. The same may result from failure to comply with the obligation to disclose exculpatory evidence. Here, in exceptional situations, the prosecutor's failure to comply with this obligation may even result in reopening of the case.[118] The ICTY case law shows that this happens only when the violation of this right by the ICTY Prosecutor led to a gross infringement of the fair trial rule through the infringement of the right to defence,

[116] See: May and Wierda (2002), pp. 84–85.
[117] "Ratko Mladic's war crimes trial postponed over evidence", BBC News, 17 May 2012.
[118] *Prosecutor v. Furundžija*, IT-95-17/1, Trial Chamber, 10 December 1998, § 22.

and damaged interests of the accused.[119] In *Prosecutor v. Furundžija*, the Prosecutor did not disclose information in relation to a psychiatric treatment that one of the witnesses allegedly received, which information might have had an impact on the witnesses' credibility. Despite the fact that the defence filed a motion either to strike the testimony of this witness due to what it considered to be misconduct on the part of the prosecution or, in the event of a conviction, for a new trial, the Trial Chamber did not decide to take such a step. Instead, it ordered that the proceedings were to be reopened only in connection with the medical, psychological or psychiatric treatment or counselling received by this certain witness, and the prosecution was ordered to disclose any other connected documents. Another possible solution is allowing the defence to re-examine any witnesses called by the prosecution during trial. Such a remedy is only possible in a situation where the defence could demonstrate that it would have put different questions to that witness on cross-examination if it had had access to the improperly withheld material.[120]

Also, before the ICC the procedural framework does not provide for any sanctions for improper disclosure by the prosecution. The drafters of the Rome Statute planned to determine such sanctions, but finally the delegates did not reach consensus on this issue as to what sanction would be most appropriate. Thus, the ICC was left a wide discretion to regulate this problem on a case-by-case basis and apply a measure that may be deemed necessary in a given case.[121] This method allows for a reaction that would be concordant with the scale of violation: e.g. to even stay the proceedings when the violation is considered by the Court to be "drastic".[122]

Moreover, sanctions may be imposed on the basis of provisions of a general character. First, some authors conclude[123] that failure to disclose materials may be ruled upon on the basis of Rule 121(8) RPE ICC: "the Pre-Trial Chamber shall not take into consideration charges and evidence presented after the time limit, or any extension thereof, has expired". Accordingly, the failure to oblige to the disclosure time limits by parties before the confirmation hearing would lead to the exclusion of evidence. Second, A. Heinze proposed that as for violation of disclosure rules during trial, sanctions may be imposed on the basis of Article 64(8)(b) of the Statute, which provides that "at the trial, the presiding judge may give directions for the conduct of proceedings, including to ensure that they are conducted in a fair and impartial manner. Subject to any directions of the presiding judge, the parties may submit evidence in accordance with the provisions of this Statute". This provision offers the Trial Chamber one of a wide range of instruments to manage and direct the proceedings.[124]

---

[119] *Prosecutor v. Blaškić*, IT-95-14, Appeals Chamber, 29 July 2004, § 303.

[120] *Prosecutor v. Stakić*, IT-97-24, Appeals Chamber, 22 March 2006, § 192.

[121] Gallmetzer (2009), p. 501.

[122] Heinze (2014), p. 452.

[123] As e.g. Brady (2001), pp. 403 and 412; Caianiello (2010), pp. 23 and 36; Heinze (2014), p. 425.

[124] Heinze (2014), p. 452.

According to H. Brady, it is possible to use disciplinary measures in the case of violation of this obligation by the Prosecutor. There are numerous legal basis for "disciplining" the Prosecutor. One option would be to impose it on the basis of Article 71 of the Statute if it is decided that the failure to disclose evidence was an intentional violation of the principles of proceeding before the Court. This provision allows the Court to sanction persons present before it who commit misconduct, including disruption of its proceedings or deliberate refusal to comply with its directions, by administrative measures other than imprisonment, such as temporary or permanent removal from the courtroom, a fine or other similar measures provided for in the Rules of Procedure and Evidence.[125] The second option is to use Article 47 of the Statute, which sets out the general terms of disciplinary measures: a judge, Prosecutor, Deputy Prosecutor, Registrar or Deputy Registrar who has committed misconduct of a less serious nature than that set out in Article 46 (1) (which is not amounting to the need to remove that person from the office) shall be subject to disciplinary measures, in accordance with the Rules of Procedure and Evidence. Both procedural possibilities are taken into consideration in the legal doctrine.[126] Disciplinary sanctions could also be imposed on the basis of the Staff Rules of the ICC[127] on those members of the OTP who did not act in accordance with "the official documents of the Court governing the rights and obligations of Staff members". Another possibility would arise from the Code of Conduct of the OTP, which obliges the members of the OTP to ensure compliance "with the applicable rules on disclosure of evidence and inspection of material in the possession or control of the Office in a manner that facilitates the fair and expeditious conduct of the proceedings and fully respects the rights of the person under investigation or the accused, with due regard for the protection of victims and witnesses" (section 52).[128] It is thought questionable if breaching these rules could lead to disciplinary sanctions as they are dealt with by another section of the Code. Moreover, it is not clear who would be held responsible for conduct constituting a breach of this provision—the Prosecutor himself or a member of the staff. Most importantly, however, the application of all the above mentioned disciplinary measures is still doubtful as, first, it is not always possible to define precisely the scope of evidence favourable for the accused and, second, it might be problematic to prove that the Prosecutor was aware of the favourable nature of the evidence for the defence and hid it intentionally.[129]

The issue of improper performance of this obligation by the ICC Prosecutor has been raised many times by the accused. Failure to comply with the disclosure obligations has resulted in a conflict between the judges and the Prosecutor.

[125] See the analysis of the relevant Rules: Brady (2001), p. 413.

[126] Heinze (2014), p. 465; Mégret (2009), pp. 416 and 479.

[127] Staff rules of the International Criminal Court, Annex to ICC/AI/2005/003, 25 August 2005, ICC-ASP/4/3.

[128] Code of Conduct for the Office of the Prosecutor: Date of entry into force: 5 September 2013.

[129] See: Brady (2001), p. 413.

Shortages in the disclosure of evidence in support of the charges presented in the confirmation hearing and particularly the failure to inform the defence about an intention to rely on the statements of additional witnesses by the Prosecutor in *The Prosecutor v. Bemba* became a reason for the postponement of the confirmation hearing "in order to ensure that the Defence may properly exercise its rights and, in particular, prepare adequately for the hearing". The Pre-Trial Chamber noted the existence of "significant problems that have emerged so far in the evidence disclosure system especially regarding the Prosecutor's obligation to disclose this material to the Defence correctly, fully and diligently".[130]

In *The Prosecutor v. Lubanga*, the proceedings have been stayed two times (on an "abuse of process" clause) in order to enable the Prosecutor to fulfil his disclosure obligations—when he refused to disclose the identity of certain "intermediaries" that the prosecution had used to find potential witnesses. The Prosecutor obtained a wide range of documents "under the cloak of confidentiality" in order to identify from those materials evidence to be used at trial—after obtaining the provider's subsequent consent. Although the ICC stated that there is no basis in the Statute for staying proceedings, nor is it "generally recognised as an indispensable power of a court of law", the Appeals Chamber concluded that "if no fair trial can be held, the object of the judicial process is frustrated and the process must be stopped".[131] Thus, not every violation of the disclosure obligations may lead to such serious results, but only gross violations, which make it impossible for the accused to "make his/her defence within the framework of his rights". In this case, the Prosecutor obtained more than 50 % of his evidence on the basis of confidentiality agreements. While according to the opinion of the ICC the Prosecutor is allowed to use evidence that was obtained on the basis of documents and information that had been received on a confidential basis solely for the purpose of generating new evidence—he may only do it as long as the amount of evidence obtained this way is relatively minor.[132] Even the Prosecutor himself admitted that the use of Article 54(3)(e) ICC Statute clause "may be seen as excessive". It was not acceptable that the majority of the evidence for the prosecution be based on information obtained from secret intermediaries whose identity could not be disclosed either during the trial or during the process of disclosing evidence. As a result of the assessment of the Prosecutor's actions, the judges had suspended the proceedings until the Prosecutor obtained permission to disclose the source of information, gave up such evidence or replaced it with other evidence. The Court

[130] *The Prosecutor v. Bemba*, ICC-01/05-01/08, Decision on the Postponement of the Confirmation Hearing, 17 October 2008, § 23–25.

[131] *The Prosecutor v. Lubanga*, Judgment on the Appeal of Mr. Lubanga Dyilo against the Decision of the Defence Challenge to the Jurisdiction of the Court pursuant to article 19(2)(a) of the Statute of 3 October 2006, 14 December 2006, § 37.

[132] *The Prosecutor v. Lubanga*, ICC-01/04-01/06, Decision on the consequences of non-disclosure of exculpatory materials covered by Article 54(3)(e) agreements and the application to stay the prosecution of the accused, together with certain other issues raised at the Status Conference on 10 June 2008, 13 June 2008, § 93.

pointed out that the Prosecutor had a duty to be "extremely cautious" when promising confidentiality to an informer, always bearing in mind his obligation of disclosing evidence to the accused. The trial crisis was averted, thanks to acquiring the information provider's permission to disclose the identity of the source.[133] After obtaining it, the stay was finally lifted. Thus, this sanction was only of a temporal character as the stay of proceedings was conditional.[134]

In his appeal, Mr. Lubanga alleged that late disclosure and the resulting stay of proceedings amounted to fair trial violations, such as violation of the right to be tried without undue delay.[135] He argued that these procedural errors should "lead the [Appeals] Chamber to recognise [Mr Lubanga]'s right to reparations in the form of a reduced sentence". The Appeals Chamber rejected such argumentation. It noted that—basing on the ICTR's jurisprudence—an effective remedy, such as reducing the length of sentence, should automatically be available only where there has been a serious violation of a person's fundamental rights—where a person was not being promptly informed of the nature of the charges against him for a significant period of time or a person was held in provisional detention for more than 3 years. In the present case, delay in disclosure did not amount to such a violation. Moreover, these allegations were dealt with as part of the trial proceedings.

The failure to comply with disclosure obligations on the part of the defence leads to entirely different consequences than in the case of the prosecution. In the United States, there is no differentiation, and a failure to comply with Rule 16 obligation leads to the same results for both parties, where the court may

(1) order that party to permit the discovery or inspection; specify its time, place and manner; and prescribe other just terms and conditions;
(2) grant a continuance;
(3) prohibit that party from introducing the undisclosed evidence; or
(4) enter any other order that is just under the circumstances.

However, in this respect the tribunals decided to reject this solution. According to the ICTY Rules, failure of the defence to provide notice under this Rule shall not limit the right of the accused to testify on the above defences (Rule 67 (C) RPE ICTY).

---

133 *The Prosecutor v. Lubanga*, ICC-01/04-01/06, Decision on the consequences of non-disclosure of exculpatory materials covered by Article 54(3)(e) agreements and the application to stay the prosecution of the accused, together with certain other issues raised at the Status Conference on 10 June 2008, 13 June 2008, § 92.

134 The history of this "crisis" described *in extenso* i.a. in: Re (2012), pp. 878–880; Vasiliev (2012), pp. 713–714; Scheffer (2009), pp. 596–597; Schuon (2010), p. 277; Ambos (2010), pp. 982–983; Schabas (2010), p. 819; Bitti (2008), pp. 1208–1209.

135 *The Prosecutor v. Lubanga*, ICC-01/04-01/06 A 4 A 6, Judgment on the appeals of the Prosecutor and Mr Thomas Lubanga Dyilo against the "Decision on Sentence pursuant to Article 76 of the Statute", 1 December 2014, § 109.

Also, although according to the ICC Rules disclosure by the defence should be done sufficiently in advance of the commencement of the trial to enable the Prosecutor to prepare adequately for trial, if the defence raises such circumstances only at trial, the Prosecutor may request to be granted an adjournment to address that ground (Rule 80(3) RPE ICC). Therefore, if the defence fails to disclose information about an intent to raise an *alibi* or rely on circumstances giving ground for excluding criminal responsibility, it cannot constitute an obstacle to present these defences during trial. It constitutes an example of a tendency to compensate the material advantages of the prosecution over the defence before international tribunals. This tendency, however, does not mean that there are no consequences for failure of the defence to disclose. The judges have the powers to decide *proprio motu*—similarly as in the case of failure on the part of the prosecution—on sanctions to be imposed on a party that fails to perform its disclosure obligations, in accordance with their conviction about the right procedural response. Usually, the most adequate sanction would be postponement of the trial (or the hearing). Alternatively, it may be assumed that if the defence fails to provide sufficiently precise witness statements that it intends to rely on to support the *alibi* defence, the Prosecutor will be allowed to interrogate the defence witnesses himself.[136]

5.5 Disclosure of Evidence and the Stage of Criminal Proceedings

The expansion of the inter-instance stage in proceedings before the ICC pertaining to the confirmation of the charges led to differentiation of the Prosecutor's disclosure obligation, both in terms of the time limit and the scope of disclosed evidence.

There is a major practical question related to the disclosure of evidence institution: to what extent should the evidence be disclosed prior to the confirmation hearing and to what extent just before the trial? The scope of evidence that should be disclosed at each of these stages is not entirely clear. Common law systems consider the confirmation hearing to be a simplified procedure intended solely as some sort of "filter" for cases that are obviously groundless. Because of this limited role, disclosure of evidence should take place mainly after this hearing and prior to the trial. Continental systems, on the other hand, recognise that the suspect should have an opportunity to acquaint himself with all evidence of the prosecution as early as upon completion of an investigation, prior to bringing an indictment before the court.

The provisions governing this institution before the ICC do not provide grounds for reliance on any of these systems. It seems that the limits of this obligation are determined by the function of each stage of the proceedings. This should entail that full and exhaustive information on the prosecution's evidence should be presented

[136] *Prosecutor v. Kupreškić*, IT-95-16, 11 January 1999.

just before the trial. Prior to the confirmation hearing, the evidence should be subject to disclosure only to the extent required to demonstrate the reasonable basis for the presented charges. A situation when the confirmation hearing turns into a "lengthy mini-trial" should be avoided. The hearing should rather summarise the situation that has taken place. This rule allows us to assume that the point is not to disclose all evidence but rather to enable keeping the majority of "the bulk of disclosure" for the stage of trial.[137] The prosecution should be obliged only to present "sufficient evidence", necessary to fulfil the standard provided for in Article 65(7) of the Statute. A different understanding of the regulations on the provision of access to the aforementioned data, which would assume an absolute obligation to provide the data immediately upon completion of an investigation, would lead to the conclusion that there is no need whatsoever to implement the regulations on the disclosure of evidence prior to the trial.[138]

Particular doubts have arisen in connection with the disclosure of evidence that is favourable for the accused. In *The Prosecutor v. Lubanga*, the Prosecutor proposed that the "bulk" of the disclosure of potentially exculpatory materials should take place after the confirmation hearing, in order to avoid excessive acceleration of the disclosure of evidence favourable for the defence. The Prosecutor intended to meet this obligation only after the confirmation hearing took place. He argued that since all evidence of the prosecution is disclosed before the trial, the same rule should apply to the evidence favourable for the defence. The Prosecutor also emphasised that only after acquainting himself with the line of defence would he be able to identify fully evidence that is potentially exculpatory. The judges, however, agreed with the defence and stated that the obligation of disclosing exculpatory evidence in possession of the Prosecutor does not in any way depend on the Prosecutor's disclosure of the evidence in support of the charges. The judges stressed that the Statute leaves no doubt as to the requirement for the prosecution to discharge this obligation "as soon as practicable", and thus the Prosecutor may not postpone this action to a moment he deems favourable, e.g., until the completion of the confirmation hearing.[139] According to the opinion of the judges, it is fully practicable to disclose most of the potentially exculpatory materials in the prosecution's possession or control before the confirmation hearing, regardless of whether the Prosecutor intends to use them in this hearing (the so-called *the bulk of the disclosure*). Only such an understanding of this obligation would allow the defence to be in a position to decide which of these materials it will present as evidence at the confirmation hearing. The judges stated that if the Prosecutor failed to disclose evidence that was favourable for the accused and

---

[137] Citations found in: Brady (2001), pp. 422–423; Tochilovsky (2009), p. 845; Jackson (2009), p. 36.

[138] *The Prosecutor v. Lubanga*, ICC-01/04-01/06-102, Decision on the Final System of Disclosure and the Establishment of a Timetable, 15 May 2006, § 124–133.

[139] *The Prosecutor v. Lubanga*, ICC-01/04-01/06-102, Decision on the Final System of Disclosure and the Establishment of a Timetable, 15 May 2006, § 120–131.

important for the assessment of the validity of presented charges, he would have to withdraw any such charges.[140] The rule according to which the prosecution might identify some materials as exculpatory only after such a hearing can only be an exception and not the general rule. The fact that the prosecution may not yet be obliged to disclose the evidence on which it intends to rely at the confirmation hearing—pursuant to the provisions regulating the prosecution's obligations in this respect—has no impact on the prosecution's obligation to disclose "as soon as practicable" any material that might fall within the ambit of exculpatory materials. In *The Prosecutor v. Bemba*, this obligation was stated even more clearly: the Chamber required the prosecution to "disclose evidence which is of true relevance to the case, whether that evidence be incriminating or exculpatory", that is, to disclose all evidence that is in possession of the prosecution before the confirmation hearing.

This case revealed a clear tendency of the judges to shift the balance of disclosure of evidence to earlier stages of criminal trial, that is, before the confirmation hearing. It would be highly unwelcome if this tendency were followed up by also shifting the weight of evidentiary proceedings to this stage.[141] On the other hand, on the basis of the detailed research presented by A. Heinze, we can conclude that there are serious variations in the interpretation of the Prosecutor's disclosure obligations.[142]

Despite the introduction of the two separate stages of disclosing evidence, it should not be forgotten that the disclosure obligation is of a continuous character. In proceedings before the ICTY, if either party discovers additional evidence or material that should have been disclosed earlier pursuant to the Rules, that party shall immediately disclose that evidence or material to the other party and the Trial Chamber (Rule 67(D) and Rule 68(v) RPE ICTY). The term "continuing obligation" is understood by the Tribunal as a responsibility of the prosecution to search for all "material known to the Prosecutor" on a continuous basis—including all its files, in whatever form, for the existence of material that in any way tends to suggest the innocence or mitigate the guilt of the accused or may affect the credibility of prosecution evidence—which on a given stage of proceedings and in the light of the present defence case would appear to be favourable for the defence.[143] In proceedings before the ICC, the Trial Chamber provides for the disclosure of documents or information not previously disclosed and for the production of additional evidence (Rule 84 RPE ICC). Additionally, the provision of Rule 76(2) establishes an obligation to advise the defence of the names of any additional prosecution

[140] *The Prosecutor v. Lubanga*, ICC-01/04-01/06, Decision on the consequences of non-disclosure of exculpatory materials covered by Article 54(3)(e) agreements and the application to stay the prosecution of the accused, together with certain other issues raised at the Status Conference on 10 June 2008, 13 June 2008, § 6.

[141] As observed by: Schuon (2010), p. 282; Ambos (2007), p. 472.

[142] Heinze (2014), p. 36.

[143] *Prosecutor v. Blagojević*, IT-02-60, Joint Decision on Motions Related to Production of Evidence, 12 December 2002, § 29.

witnesses and provide copies of their statements as soon as the decision is made to call those witnesses (Rule 76(2)). The prosecution's obligation to disclose exculpatory material also continues during proceedings before the Appeals Chamber if the Prosecutor intends to introduce new evidence.[144]

In common law states, disclosure of evidence may also be considered by dividing it into stages: disclosure of evidence by the prosecution, disclosure of evidence by the defence, secondary disclosure by the prosecution. Disclosure of evidence by the defence gives rise to the obligation of the prosecutor to disclose subsequent evidence under the so-called secondary disclosure. The secondary disclosure, first of all, covers the evidence the prosecutor is going to present in order to challenge the statements of the defence. Disclosure of an intention to refer to the *alibi* defence or the circumstances excluding criminal responsibility by the defence gives rise to the obligation to notify the defence of the names of the witnesses that the prosecutor intends to call in rebuttal of any defence plea (similarly Rule 67(B)(ii) RPE ICTY).

The ICC procedural regulations do not provide for a separate obligation in this form. It arises from the existence of an ongoing obligation of the Prosecutor to disclose the evidence and the obligation of each of the parties to the proceedings to disclose, appropriately in advance, the documents and information not previously disclosed in order to enable adequate preparation for trial (Article 64(3)(c) of the Statute). Second, upon disclosure of evidence by the accused, the Prosecutor is obliged to present evidence favourable for the accused that has not been previously disclosed and that could contribute to the preparation of the defence case, the plan of which was presented by the defence. Although the accused does not have a possibility of finding out whether the evidence helpful for him is in the Prosecutor's possession, if at any time of the trial the accused has any reason to suspect so, he can apply to the Trial Chamber to make any necessary orders for the disclosure of documents or information not previously disclosed and for the production of additional evidence (Rule 84 RPE ICC).

5.6 Limits to Disclosure of Evidence

The right of access to the case files is not absolute. In the course of an investigation, the most frequently cited reason for limiting access to case files includes an intention to ensure the efficiency of such proceedings. It is obvious that a premature disclosure of specific information could prevent the achievement of the objectives of an investigation. Moreover, competing interests, such as national safety, the need to protect witnesses against the risk of retaliation or the need to keep confidential

[144] However, there is no obligation if the evidence has already been disclosed at the trial stage—see: Harmon and Karagiannakis (2000), p. 328. See the case: *Prosecutor v. Blaškić*, IT-95-14, Appeals Chamber, 29 July 2004, § 267.

the methods of performing the investigation by the police need to be balanced against the rights of the accused. International criminal tribunals rely in this respect on the case law of the European Court of Human Rights and on the opinion that the right to a fair trial does not require disclosing the entire evidence to the accused. Consequently, in some cases, a denial of access to some part of the evidence to the defence may be necessary.[145]

In proceedings before international criminal tribunals, five groups of evidence are not subject to disclosure.

First, the prosecution does not have to disclose reports, memoranda or other internal documents prepared by a party in connection with the investigation or preparation of the case—by the Prosecutor himself, his assistants or representatives (so-called *work product privilege*).[146] It is one of the rules adopted from the system of the United States of America that has not been subject to any amendments in proceedings before international criminal tribunals.[147] In the case of disclosure of evidence by the defence, this rule covers also the liaison between the accused and the defence attorney (*legal professional privilege*).[148]

Second, if certain material or information has been obtained by the Prosecutor on the condition of confidentiality and solely for the purpose of generating new evidence, it cannot be disclosed. The Prosecutor may not disclose such material or information into evidence without the prior consent of the provider of the material or information.[149] Article 54(3)(e) of the Rome Statute gives to the Prosecutor the powers to agree not to disclose, at any stage of the proceedings, documents or information that the Prosecutor obtains on the condition of confidentiality and solely for the purpose of generating new evidence, unless the provider of the information consents. In turn, the evidence that required the collection of confidential materials or information can be disclosed only to the extent specified in the relevant disclosure consent. A witness who agrees to testify may not be interrogated for information pertaining to the circumstances not covered by his consent. However, as the lack of disclosure means that this evidence may not be used in the trial or the confirmation hearing,[150] it is in the Prosecutor's interest to make sure the consent for the disclosure of information has been obtained. As Rule 68 RPE ICTY explains: the Prosecutor shall take reasonable steps, if confidential information is provided to the Prosecutor by a person or entity, to obtain the consent

---

[145] The ECtHR cases: *Jasper v. United Kingdom*, 16 February 2000, application No. 27052/95, and *Rowe and Davis v. United Kingdom*, 16 February 2000, application No. 28901/95; *Natunen v. Finland*, 31 March 2009, application No. 21022/04; *Jałowiecki v. Poland*, 17 February 2009, application No. 34030/07.

[146] Rule 70(A) RPE ICTY and Rule 81(1) RPE ICC.

[147] See: Schuon (2010), p. 122.

[148] E.g., *Prosecutor v. Tadić*, IT-94-1-T, Separate Opinion of Judge Stephen on prosecution motion for production of defence witness statement, 27 November 1996.

[149] Rule 70(B)–(G) RPE ICTY; Rule 68(iii) RPE ICTY; Rule 81(4) and Rule 82(1) RPE ICC in conj. With Article 56(3)(e) of the Rome Statute.

[150] Rule 81(5) RPE ICC.

of the provider to the disclosure of that material, or the fact of its existence, to the accused.

As it was mentioned earlier, while collecting evidence pertaining to the situation in the Democratic Republic of Congo, the ICC Prosecutor accepted large quantities of material from the UN acting as an "intermediary". Pursuant to an agreement with the UN, the witnesses have been provided confidentiality and the Prosecutor had agreed not to disclose their identity without the UN's consent. In *The Prosecutor v. Lubanga*, the Prosecutor, based on the so-called lead evidence—evidence used in order to generate other evidence rather than production before the Court—obtained over 8,000 documents.[151] In consequence, he was unable to disclose it without the permission of the informers. When the Prosecutor, however, tried to use this evidence during the trial, the Trial Chamber decided that the right to a fair trial had been violated. In its opinion, this violation was so serious that it decided to stay the proceedings and at the same time issued an order to release the accused from detention (that was effectively contested by the Prosecutor). According to the judges, the Prosecutor should have either disclosed the entire evidence that had been obtained as classified material or resigned from using it in the trial altogether.

Third, the Prosecutor may apply to the Trial Chamber to be relieved from an obligation of disclosure of material if it might—at the given stage of the proceedings—lead to unfavourable consequences such as to prejudice further or ongoing investigations. This structure has also been known in continental systems where there is an option of restricting or denying access to case files of an ongoing investigation to the defence if the prosecutor finds that it might harm the proceedings. However, in proceedings before international criminal tribunals, disclosure of evidence may be denied for such reason only pursuant to the decision of a judicial authority. In the version adopted by the ICTY, when, according to the opinion of the ICTY Prosecutor, disclosure of specific information could prejudice ongoing investigations, and also in the situation when its disclosure would be against the public interest or could harm national security, he may apply to the Trial Chamber to release him from the obligation to disclose such information (Rule 68(iii)). The Chamber resolves the issue *in camera*. Also in the proceedings before the ICC, the obligation of the Prosecutor to disclose evidence to the accused at the stage of the confirmation hearing may be limited pursuant to the decision of the Pre-Trial Chamber. The Prosecutor may apply to the Chamber dealing with the matter for a ruling as to whether the material or information must be disclosed to the defence. The Chamber may give such a ruling if it concludes that disclosure at this given stage of proceedings may prejudice further or ongoing investigations (Rule 81(2) RPE ICC). However, if this is the case, the Prosecutor may not introduce such material or information into evidence during the confirmation hearing or the trial without adequate prior disclosure to the accused.

---

[151] *The Prosecutor v. Lubanga*, Judgment on the Appeal of Mr. Lubanga Dyilo against the Decision of the Defence Challenge to the Jurisdiction of the Court pursuant to article 19(2)(a) of the Statute of 3 October 2006, 14 December 2006, § 37.

Fourth, if there is a need to protect the safety of witnesses and victims and members of their families, the ICC Prosecutor may take necessary steps. He may apply to the Chamber to authorise the non-disclosure of their identity prior to the commencement of the trial. Based on the case law of the ECtHR, the ICC assumed that balance between the rights of the accused and the rights of witnesses should be sought in each case, and they should, if needed, be protected by the authorities of the Court.[152] Particularly, it should be taken into consideration whether the alleged danger involves an objectively justifiable risk to the safety of the person concerned. The risk must arise from disclosing the particular information to the defence (as opposed to disclosing the information to the public at large). The Chamber should consider, *inter alia*, whether the danger could be overcome by ruling that the information should be kept confidential between the parties.[153] This does not mean, however, that the statements of such witnesses may not be used. There is a special procedure provided for such an occasion in the Rules of Procedure and Evidence of the ICC. First, the Prosecutor may apply to the Pre-Trial Chamber to authorise the non-disclosure of their identity prior to the commencement of the trial. Second, in order to protect victims and witnesses or the accused, the Chambers of the Court may conduct part of the proceedings *in camera* or allow that their statements are presented by means of electronic transmission or other special means as an exception to the principle of conducting a trial in transparency of the ICC trial. Third, if disclosure of evidence or information may lead to a major risk to the witness's or his family's safety, the Prosecutor may, for the purpose of the proceedings and until the commencement of the trial, withhold such evidence or information and instead submit a summary thereof. Such measures shall be exercised in a manner that is not prejudicial to or inconsistent with the rights of the accused and a fair and impartial trial (Article 68(5) of the ICC Statute).

It follows from the case law of the ICC that in certain circumstances the Prosecutor may use a summary of material or information. It is generally agreed that the summary may not replace disclosure of evidence.[154] However, in some cases, it may be deemed sufficient to meet the disclosure of evidence standard even if it is presented in the form of a summary or a description rather than as direct

[152] *The Prosecutor v. Katanga*, ICC-01/04-01/07, Version publique expurgée de la: "Decision relative à la protection des témoins à charge 267 et 353" du 20 mai 2009, 28 May 2009, § 31, and the ECHR judgment cited there: *Dowsett v. United Kingdom*, 24 June 2003, § 43.

[153] *The Prosecutor v. Katanga*, ICC-01/04-01/07, Judgment on the Appeal of the Prosecutor against the decision of Pre-Trial Chamber I entitled "First Decision on the Prosecution Request for Authorisation to Redact Witness Statements", 13 May 2008, § 71.

[154] See: *The Prosecutor v. Lubanga*, ICC-01/04-01/06, Decision on the consequences of non-disclosure of exculpatory materials covered by Article 54(3)(e) agreements and the application to stay the prosecution of the accused, together with certain other issues raised at the Status Conference on 10 June 2008, 13 June 2008, § 86—and the ECtHR judgment cited there: *V. v. Finland*, 24 July 2007, application No. 40412/98, § 78.

evidence or interrogation reports.[155] If an objectively justifiable risk to the safety of the person in fact exists, the Chamber should assess whether certain redactions could overcome or reduce the risk (and also whether an alternative measure short of redaction is available and feasible in the circumstances of the case). Consequently, even some redaction of evidence does not always mean that the right to a fair trial will be violated. According to the ICC judges, the process of disclosure of evidence should always be assessed in the light of compliance with the fair trial standard, rather than strictly following the letter of law. For this reason, evidence that is material for the possibility of challenging the validity of charges brought by the Prosecutor may not be presented in a summarised form. However, if the Chamber concludes that the information concerned is not relevant to the defence, that is likely to be a significant factor in determining whether the interests of the person potentially placed at risk outweigh those of the defence. If, on the other hand, the information may be of assistance to the case of the suspect or may affect the credibility of the case of the Prosecutor, the Chamber will need to take particular care when balancing the interests at stake. If non-disclosure would result in a confirmation of the charges hearing or a trial, viewed as a whole, to be unfair to the suspect (accused), the requested redactions should not be authorised. It may not be forgotten either that the presentation of the summary of evidence is possible only upon authorisation by a judicial authority, as the application of all the aforementioned means of protection of witnesses depends on the judicial decision rather than on the decision of the Prosecutor.

Fifth, there is also a special procedure in the proceedings before international criminal tribunals that will be applied if disclosure of certain evidence may be contrary to the public interest or affect the security interests of any state. Both in the proceedings before the ICTY and the ICC, the issue of confidential information transferred in secret by the states has been regulated together with the issue of confidential materials, provided also by other entities.[156] It should not be forgotten that the Prosecutor's obligation to keep the evidence provided by the state confidential may be often applied.[157] After all, the ICC Prosecutor relies on the evidence submitted to him by the states, which often condition provision of such evidence on confidentiality. Introduction of this exception to the general disclosure of evidence

155 *The Prosecutor v. Katanga*, ICC-01/04-01/07, Judgment on the Appeal of the Prosecutor against the decision of Pre-Trial Chamber I entitled "First Decision on the Prosecution Request for Authorisation to Redact Witness Statements", 13 May 2008, § 71–73. In the same case: Version publique expurgée de la Decision relative à la protection des témoins à charge 267 et 353 du 20 mai 2009, 28 May 2009, § 52.

156 Rule 70(B) RPE ICTY; Rule 81(3) RPE ICC.

157 If a State learns that information or documents of the State are being, or are likely to be, disclosed at any stage of the proceedings, and it is of the opinion that disclosure would prejudice its national security interests, that State shall have the right to intervene in order to obtain resolution of the issue in accordance with this article (Article 72(4) of the Rome Statute).

requirement was intended as an encouragement for the states to co-operate more willingly.[158]

5.7 Conclusion

The rules governing disclosure of evidence show that international criminal tribunals have been drawing on the achievements of common law systems. This institution was shaped with the assumption that there are two parties to the proceedings, and each of them should present its "case" to the court (the *two cases approach*). It is characteristic that the institution adopted by the ICTY is wholly modelled on the US system, departing from it in only minor details, when it is expanded to allow for the disclosure of evidence that is favourable for the accused. The ICTY did not only regulate the disclosure of evidence institution using the common law states as an example but in its practice even referred to the jurisprudence of the US Supreme Court.

It is noteworthy, however, that as a result of the numerous amendments to the Rules of Procedure and Evidence, the structure of the disclosure of evidence institution before the *ad hoc* tribunals is no longer identical with the system from which it borrowed its procedural solutions. Also, the model of disclosure of evidence before the ICC has a lot of features of the "access to the case file", straying further and further from the Anglo-Saxon model of "disclosure of evidence".

First, access to the electronic database ensured to the accused by the ICTY—and now also by the ICC—Prosecutor resembles access to a case file known from continental systems. It is related to the Prosecutor's obligation of keeping a register of evidence. As a result, we should rather speak of "ensuring access" to a part of a *de facto* electronic case file rather than of evidence "disclosure". This solution resembles the "case file approach" used in continental proceedings, where there is no necessity of ensuring exchange of information on the evidence as, in line with the principle that there is one case and it covers solely the file prepared by the prosecutor, it is sufficient to offer the defence access to the case file handled by the public prosecutor.

Second, currently there is an obligation of exchange of evidence and information on evidence not only to the opposite party to the proceedings before the ICC but also to the judges of the Court, which in fact leads to the (successive) provision of the case file to the Trial Chamber. Thus, the scope of the principle, pursuant to which the judges could not have any previous access to case evidence, is no longer clear.

It may be noticed that before the ICC some convergence of two, seemingly entirely different, systems of implementation of the information obligation by the

[158] See in general: Tochilovsky (2004a), p. 859.

prosecutor has occurred in a manner that is intended to ensure that the right to defence is exercised to the highest possible extent without simultaneously jeopardising the interests of the proceedings.[159]

There are still major differences between the system of proceedings before international criminal tribunals and continental systems. The basic difference has been maintained—access to documents collected by the ICC Prosecutor covers only specific categories of evidence. As a result, the evidence of prosecution is still presented to the defence in a more limited scope than all materials collected by the prosecutor that are included in continental case files. The second difference pertains to the lack of access to the case file during the investigation before tribunals. Whereas such a right exists in the continental tradition, even if exercising it in practice is impeded, the procedure in common law states does not provide for such a right at all. In continental systems, finalisation of an investigation ends the stage of "confidentiality" and makes all information and physical evidence included in the case file (upon request) and in the indictment (always) be submitted to the attention of the defence. The third difference refers to the fact that the disclosure of evidence procedure is an obligation of the prosecutor, whereas access to the case file during an ongoing investigation or upon its conclusion is a right of the suspect that he may take advantage of only upon request. In the absence of such a request, the prosecutor is not obliged to enable the suspect to inspect the case file.[160] However, the full list of incriminating evidence is enclosed to the indictment.

The final outcome of the two institutions, disclosure of evidence and access to the case file, is identical: allowing the defence to acquaint itself with the evidence in possession of the prosecutor, either significant for the case of the prosecution or evidence that could be used by the defence. If the final outcome is the same, it may be suggested that the complicated system should be replaced with the simplified one. This proposal is even more justified in the situation when the proceedings before the ICC are lengthy, complicated and not always transparent. It has been noticed that the disclosure procedure in the format implemented by international tribunals has become even more complicated and unclear than it was in its original version existing in the common law systems.[161] The underlying reason was an exceptional volume of materials submitted by the parties to the proceedings due to the character of crimes to which the proceedings pertained. For example, while examining the case of the accused Thomas Lubanga Dyilo, the Prosecutor notified the ICC Trial Chamber that he was in possession of 27,500 documents with 92,500 pages, related to the charges brought against Mr. Dyilo. He also explained that he intended to submit 20,000 documents (74,000 pages)[162] to the Chamber prior to the trial. While the overwhelming amounts of the collected materials were a proof of

---

[159] See: Ambos (2007), pp. 472–473.

[160] Płachta (2004), p. 714.

[161] Heinsch (2009), p. 478; Tochilovsky (2004a), pp. 319–344.

[162] *The Prosecutor v. Lubanga*, ICC-01/04-01/06, Decision Regarding the Timing and Manner of Disclosure and the Date of Trial, 9 November 2007, § 2.

the Prosecutor's hard work, they also prevented rational assessment of these documents by the defence and their selection.

The information obligation arising from the disclosure of evidence institution is one of the major burdens related to the work of the prosecutors of international criminal tribunals. Development of the techniques for managing disclosure of evidence is a result of this obligation. As early as at the moment of obtaining evidence, the administration of the Office of the ICC Prosecutor analyses whether it should be disclosed to the defence and then prepares it for the disclosure of evidence procedure. A computerised system of managing the stages and the scope of disclosure of evidence has also been implemented. Replacing the disclosure of evidence institution in the proceedings before the ICC with the system of handling the case file by the Prosecutor and providing access to it to the defence at specific stages of the proceedings, naturally allowing for the limitations arising from the Rome Statute, would limit the disputes on the scope of disclosure of evidence and would shorten the entire procedure.[163] It would facilitate the work of the defence that is already in an unfavourable position relative to the Prosecutor when it comes to the possibility of collecting evidence in the territory of sovereign states. The element of "surprise" resulting from the tactical use of disclosure in trial would also disappear. An obligation of ensuring access to all case files would deprive the Prosecutor of the possibility of choosing which evidence may be disclosed at a later stage of the proceedings for strategic reasons. Moreover, such system would allow the judges to prepare for adjudication of the case as theories assuming that the judges should not have any prior knowledge of the case should be considered to be harmful for the operation of the international tribunals.[164]

On the other hand, the existence of the confirmation of the charges hearing in the proceedings before the tribunals impedes automatic transformation of the disclosure system into the system of access to files. The two-stage nature of proceedings on disclosure of evidence would have to be replaced by access to all materials of an investigation upon completion of the investigation (the so-called open-file disclosure model) and, therefore, before the confirmation hearing. It is worth to mention that this solution was suggested by the delegation of France during the negotiations in the course of proceedings before the ICC.[165] The other option could be dividing the access to the case file into two stages and subsequently creating a system of "separation of the case record for the Pre-Trial Phase and the Trial Phase".[166] At the first stage, the defendant's right to access to the case file would undergo restrictions; after transferring of the case file to the Trial Chamber (comprised of the records of the confirmation hearing in the part that includes evidence that has been admitted by

[163] The same conclusion in: Schuon (2010), pp. 284 and 134–135; Safferling (2001), p. 200; Schomburg (2009), p. 109; Bassiouni and Manikas (1996), p. 920.

[164] Similarly: Kremens (2010), p. 78.

[165] See: Tochilovsky (2004a), p. 844.

[166] The so-called double dossier model proposed by Heinze (2014), p. 522, on the basis of the example of Italy.

the Pre-Trial Chamber and of additional evidence that has been submitted at the trial stage), the defence would have unlimited access to it.

The suggested change would be in line with the amendment of the ICC Prosecutor's role—in proceedings before the ICC, he becomes more than a trial party. The essence of the role of the prosecutor in proceedings in Anglo-Saxon systems, and also in the initial period of functioning of the ICTY, is that he only acts as an accuser. The prosecutor is one of the two parties to the trial that hold a dispute. This role gives rise to mutual information obligations under the disclosure procedure. In the situation when, as is the case before the ICC, the Prosecutor is a searcher for the material truth, it is not necessary to maintain the illusion of the two cases approach and insist on keeping a complicated procedure of gradual and multifaceted disclosure of evidence. Handling the case file by the Prosecutor and providing access to its contents to the defence would only confirm the role played by the ICC Prosecutor. The disclosure of evidence procedure is reasonable only when two parties to the procedure prepare separate sets of evidence. Meanwhile, in practice, before the ICC, the accused himself has very limited opportunities to gather such evidence on his own. As a result, the court receives evidence derived mainly from the case file kept by the Prosecutor. In consequence, we can see that the disclosure of evidence procedure in the format existing in common law states has turned out to be incompatible with the ICC's needs. The Prosecutor's role has changed, and he is no longer only an accusing authority; also, the case file he develops contains more than just incriminating material. As a result, it should be assumed that the model of access to case files (or open-file disclosure) known from continental systems is better adjusted to the entire model of accusation currently existing before the ICC.

References

Ambos K (2003) International criminal procedure: "adversarial", "inquisitorial" or mixed? Int Crim Law Rev 3:1

Ambos K (2007) The structure of international procedure: "adversarial", "inquisitorial" or mixed. In: Bohlander M (ed) International criminal justice: a critical analysis of institutions and procedures. Cameron May, London

Ambos K (2010) The first confirmation decision of the International Criminal Court The Prosecutor v. Thomas Lubanga Dyilo. In: Kotsalis L, Courakis N, Mylonopoulos C (eds) Essays in honour of Argyrios Karras. Ant. N. Sakkoulas, Athens

Ashworth A, Redmayne M (2005) The criminal process, 4th edn. Oxford University Press, Oxford

Bassiouni MC, Manikas P (1996) The law of the International Criminal Tribunal for the former Yugoslavia. Transnational Publishers, New York

Beulke W (2005) Strafprozessrecht, 12th edn. C.F. Müller, Heidelberg

Bitti G (2008) In: Triffterer O (ed) Commentary on the Rome Statute of the International Criminal Court – observers' notes, article by article, 2nd edn. Hart/Nomos Verlagsgesellschaft/C.H. Beck, München/Oxford

Boas G (2003) A code of evidence and procedure for international criminal law? The rules of the ICTY. In: Boas G, Schabas W (eds) International criminal law developments in the case law of the ICTY. Martinus Nijhoff, Leiden

Brady H (2001) Disclosure of evidence. In: Lee RP (ed) The International Criminal Court. Elements of crime ad rules of procedure and evidence. Transnational Publishers, New York
Caianiello M (2010) Disclosure before the ICC: the emergence of a new form of policies implementation system in international criminal justice? Int Crim Law Rev 10:23
Damaška M (1986) The faces of justice and state authority. Yale University Press, New Haven/London
Everett R (1964) Discovery in criminal cases – in search of a standard. Duke Law J 3:477
Gallmetzer R (2009) The Trial-Chamber's discretionary power and its exercise in the trial of Thomas Lubanga Dyilo. In: Stahn C, Sluiter G (eds) The Emerging Practice of the International Criminal Court, Martinus Nijhoff Publishers, Leiden/Boston
Guariglia F (2002) The rules of procedure and evidence for the International Criminal Court: a new development in international adjudication of individual criminal responsibility. In: Cassese A, Gaeta P, Jones WD (eds) The Rome Statute of the International Criminal Court: a commentary. Oxford University Press, Oxford
Hannibal M, Mountford L (2002) The law of criminal and civil evidence. Principles and Practice, Longman, Harlow/New York
Harmon MB, Karagiannakis M (2000) The disclosure of exculpatory material by the prosecution to the defence under Rule 68 of the ICTY Rules. In: May R, Tolbert D, Hocking J, Roberts K, Jia BB, Mundis D, Oosthuizen G (eds) Essays on ICTY procedure and evidence. In honour of Gabrielle Kirk McDonald. Brill Academic Publishers, The Hague/London/Boston
Heinsch R (2009) How to achieve fair and expeditious trial proceedings before the ICC: Is it time for a more judge-dominated approach? In: Stahn C, Sluiter G (eds) The emerging practice of the International Criminal Court. Martinus Nijhoff, Leiden/Boston
Heinze A (2014) International criminal procedure and disclosure. An attempt to better understand and regulate disclosure and communication at the ICC on the basis of a comprehensive and comparative theory of criminal procedure. Duncker & Humblot, Berlin
Hofmański P, Sadzik E, Zgryzek K (2011) Kodeks postępowania karnego. Komentarz, t. I, 4th edn. C.H. Beck, Warszawa
Jackson J (2009) Finding the best epistemic fit for international criminal tribunals. Beyond the adversarial-inquisitorial dichotomy. J Int Crim Justice 7:17
Kardas P (2013) Jawność wewnętrzna i zewnętrzna postępowania przygotowawczego. In: Jasiński W, Nowicki K (eds) Jawność jako wymóg rzetelnego procesu karnego. Zagadnienia prawa polskiego i obcego, 1st edn. C.H. Beck, Warszawa
Klamberg M (2013) Prosecution access to the defence material. In: Sluiter G, Friman H, Linton S, Vasiliev S, Zappala S (eds) International criminal procedure. Principles and rules. Oxford University Press, Oxford
Kremens K (2010) Dowody osobowe w międzynarodowym postępowaniu karnym. TNOiK, Toruń
Kuczyńska H (2009) Rzetelny proces w orzecznictwie sądów angielskich. In: Wiliński P (ed) Rzetelny proces karny w orzecznictwie sądów polskich i międzynarodowych. Wolters Kluwer, Warszawa
LaFave W, Israel J, King N, Kerr O (2009) Criminal procedure, 5th edn. West Academic Publishing, St. Paul
May R, Wierda M (2002) International criminal evidence. Transnational Publishers, Ardsley, NY
Mégret F (2009) Beyond "fairness": understanding the determinants of international criminal procedure. UCLA J Int Law Foreign Aff 14:37
Ohlin J (2009) A meta-theory of international criminal procedure: vindicating the rule of law. UCLA J Int Law Foreign Aff 14:77
Orie A (2002) Accusatorial v. Inquisitorial approach in international criminal proceedings prior to the establishment of the ICC and in the proceedings before the ICC. In: Cassese A, Gaeta P, Jones WD (eds) The Rome Statute of the International Criminal Court: a commentary. Oxford University Press, Oxford
Padfield N (2008) Text and materials on the criminal justice process, 4th edn. Oxford University Press, Oxford

Płachta M (2004) Międzynarodowy Trybunał Karny. Zakamycze, Kraków

Ponikowski R (2012) Granice jawności wewnętrznej i zewnętrznej przygotowawczego stadium postępowania karnego. In: Skorupka J (ed) Jawność procesu karnego. Wolters Kluwer, Warszawa

Pruitt R (2001) Discovery: mutual disclosure, unilateral disclosure and non-disclosure under the Rules of Procedure and Evidence. In: May R, Tolbert D, Hocking J, Roberts K, Jia BB, Mundis D, Oosthuizen G (eds) Essays on ICTY procedure and evidence. In honour of Gabrielle Kirk McDonald. Brill Academic Publishers, The Hague/London/Boston

Re D (2012) Appeal. In: Reydams L, Wouters J, Ryngaert C (eds) International prosecutors. Oxford University Press, Oxford

Safferling C (2001) Towards an international criminal procedure, Oxford monographs in international law. Oxford University Press, Oxford

Schabas W (2008). In: Triffterer O (ed) Commentary on the Rome Statute of the International Criminal Court – observers' notes, article by article, 2nd edn. Hart/Nomos Verlagsgesellschaft/C.H. Beck, München/Oxford

Schabas W (2010) The International Criminal Court. A commentary on the Rome Statute. Oxford University Press, Oxford

Scheffer D (2009) A review of the experiences of the Pre-Trial and Appeals Chambers of the ICC regarding the disclosure of evidence. In: Stahn C, Sluiter G (eds) The emerging practice of the International Criminal Court. Martinus Nijhoff, Leiden/Boston

Schomburg W (2009) *Common Law* versus *Civil Law*: die Ad-hoc-Strafgerichtshöfe für das ehemalige Jugoslawien und Ruanda: ihre immanenten Grenzen auf der Suche nach der Wahrheit. Betrifft Justiz 99:108

Schuon C (2010) International criminal procedure. A clash of legal cultures. T.M.C. Asser Press, The Hague

Shibahara K, Schabas W (2008) In: Triffterer O (ed) Commentary on the Rome Statute of the International Criminal Court – observers' notes, article by article, 2nd edn. Hart/Nomos Verlagsgesellschaft/C.H. Beck, München/Oxford

Skorupka J (2007) Udostępnianie akt sprawy podejrzanemu. Prokuratura i Prawo 5:68

Spencer JR (2004) Evidence. In: Delmas-Marty M, Spencer JR (eds) European criminal procedures. Cambridge University Press, Cambridge

Sprack J (2012) A practical approach to criminal procedure, 14th edn. Oxford University Press, Oxford

Steinborn S (2010) In: Grajewski J, Paprzycki L K, Steinborn S (eds) Kodeks postępowania karnego. Komentarz, t. I. Wolters Kluwer, Warszawa

Szczotka A (2009) Dostęp do akt sprawy w postępowaniu przygotowawczym. Prokuratura i Prawo 2:12

Tochilovsky V (2002) Proceedings in the International Criminal Court: some lessons to learn from ICTY experience. Eur J Crime Crim Law Crim Justice 4:268

Tochilovsky V (2004a) International criminal justice: "Strangers In The Foreign System". Crim Law Forum 15:319

Tochilovsky V (2004(2)) Prosecution disclosure obligations in the ICTY and ICTR. Guest Lectures, 23 July, The Hague: http://www.icc-cpi.int/NR/rdonlyres/8243618E-59B1-4EFB-9A59-5DFB65F4F8C6/0/042307_Tochilovsky.pdf. Accessed 19 Dec 2012

Tochilovsky V (2008) Jurisprudence of the International Criminal Courts and the European Court of Human Rights. Martinus Nijhoff, Leiden

Tochilovsky V (2009) Prosecution disclosure obligation in the ICC and relevant jurisprudence of the ad hoc tribunals. In: Daria J, Gasser H-P, Bassiouni MC (eds) The legal regime of the International Criminal Court. Essays in honour of Professor Igor Blishchenko. Martinus Nijhoff, Leiden/Boston

Tochilovsky V (2011) Special commentary international criminal justice: some flaws and misperceptions. Crim Law Forum 22(4):593

Tochilovsky V (2013) Defence access to the prosecution material. In: Sluiter G, Friman H, Linton S, Vasiliev S, Zappala S (eds) International criminal procedure. Principles and rules. Oxford University Press, Oxford

Tomaszewski T (1996) Proces amerykański: Problematyka śledcza, Wyd. Comer, Toruń

Vasiliev S (2012) Trial. In: Reydams L, Wouters J, Ryngaert C (eds) International prosecutors. Oxford University Press, Oxford

Waltoś S (1963) Akt oskarżenia w polskim procesie karnym. Warszawa, WP

Ward R, Wragg A (2005) Walker and Walker's English legal system, 9th edn. Oxford University Press, Oxford

Wąsek-Wiaderek M (2003a) Zasada równości stron w polskim procesie karnym w perspektywie prawnoporównawczej. Zakamycze, Kraków

Wąsek-Wiaderek M (2003b) Dostęp do akt sprawy oskarżonego tymczasowo aresztowanego i jego obrońcy w postępowaniu przygotowawczym. Palestra 5–6:65

Wiliński P (2006) Odmowa dostępu do akt sprawy w postępowaniu przygotowawczym. Prokuratura i Prawo 11:79

Wiliński P (2008) Wpływ systemów *common law* i *civil law* na kształtowanie się międzynarodowego postępowania karnego. In: Jakubowska-Hara J, Skupiński J (eds) Reforma prawa karnego: propozycje i komentarze. Księga pamiątkowa Prof. Barbary Kunickiej-Michalskiej. Scholar, Warszawa

Worrall J (2007) Criminal procedure: from first contact to appeal, 2nd edn. Pearson Allyn & Bacon, Boston

Chapter 6
Influence of the Prosecutor on the Consensual Termination of Criminal Proceedings

Abstract The prosecutor's impact on the outcome of the proceedings is most visible when he has the power to enter into an agreement with the defendant, on the basis of which in exchange for a specific conduct of the defendant (usually pleading guilty), the outcome of the proceedings becomes more favourable for him compared to the one that could have been expected otherwise. The power to terminate proceedings in a consensual way can be regarded as the prosecutor's impact on the intensity of criminal prosecution and on the severity of the penal response. The key issue here is finding what significant concessions the prosecutor may offer to the defendant. Taking into consideration the functions of international criminal tribunals and the role they are intended to play, as well as the type of offences falling under their jurisdiction, we have to ask a question: is "bargaining over criminal responsibility" the right way to proceed? As we will see, the model of accusation before the ICC does not provide for an option for a consensual termination of proceedings pursuant to an agreement concluded between the ICC Prosecutor and the defendant, nor it envisages any basis for the guilty plea to have procedural effects such as elimination of a trial or reduction of a sentence.

6.1 Consensual Termination of Criminal Proceedings

6.1.1 Procedural Agreements

A consensual termination of criminal proceedings means (in general terms) the termination of criminal proceedings by reaching an agreement on the issue of the criminal responsibility of the defendant (in the broad sense of this notion, inclusive of the term "suspect"). The essence of such an agreement, which is concluded between a defendant and a public prosecutor (sometimes also with the participation of another authority or a victim), is that in exchange for a specific conduct of the defendant (usually pleading guilty) set forth in this agreement, the outcome of the proceedings becomes more favourable for him compared to the one that could have

© Springer International Publishing Switzerland 2015

H. Kuczyńska, *The Accusation Model Before the International Criminal Court*,
DOI 10.1007/978-3-319-17626-0_6

been expected otherwise.[1] Such a consensus is advantageous for both parties: not only is it beneficial for the defendant as he is served a more lenient punishment, or even in some cases held responsible for only some of the perpetrated acts, but also the state authorities conduct the proceedings more quickly and expeditiously, improving its statistical effectiveness. Such a consensus is then presented to the court as a suggested judgment finalising the proceedings. This competence may be described as the prosecutor's impact on the intensity of criminal prosecution and on the severity of the penal response of the court. It depends on the prosecutor whether there will be a confrontation of the parties at a trial or whether the criminal law conflict will be resolved in a non-confrontational manner. Also, other institutions such as discontinuation of prosecution, pursuant to the principle of opportunism, may be included in the category of powers affecting the intensity of criminal prosecution. However, only concluding a procedural agreement binding for the court provides an opportunity for the prosecutor to exert an impact on the contents of the decision on the merits. Depending on the system, the impact that the parties have on the contents of this judgment may be significant when the court is obliged to rule on the basis of this agreement or of smaller consequence when the court is only obliged to take this agreement as a suggestion into account. The essence of the institution of procedural agreements on the issue of criminal responsibility of a defendant is not only the possibility of negotiating with the prosecutor itself but first of all the significance of this consensus for the court and resolving the case in a merit-based manner.[2] If the court is obliged to issue the judgment in a form agreed on by the parties, then the prosecutor may have an impact not only on what the legal and penal response should be and the course of the proceedings but also on the contents of the ultimate resolution.

The actual significance of the prosecutor's authority to effect consensual disposition of criminal proceedings will always depend on what, within the limits of the law, may be offered to the defendant in exchange for pleading guilty. Therefore, the effectiveness and attractiveness of procedural agreements for the defendant are inherently related to other determinants of the model of accusation, including, foremost, the existence of the principle of procedural opportunism in a given legal order that enables the prosecutor to make a decision on whether, in his opinion, bringing charges (and what charges) is justifiable. This principle, combined with the rule that the court is bound not only by the scope of an indictment but also by the legal characterisation of an offence adopted by the prosecutor in the indictment, renders the prosecutor capable of offering to the defendant much more attractive concessions than in the systems that have the prosecutor act within the

[1] In the Polish criminal law literature, this concept has been widely discussed since the establishment of the statutory basis for concluding procedural agreements in 1997, e.g. by: Steinborn (2005), pp. 52 et seq.; Światłowski (1998a), p. 55; Waltoś (1992), p. 38.

[2] In a wide range of different types of procedural agreements this group is defined as "final agreements", as they relate to adjudicating on the issue of criminal responsibility of a defendant: e.g. Waltoś (2000), p. 24.

restricted principle of legalism and in which the legal characterisation of the offence charged to the defendant in an indictment is not binding for the court.

Despite following the assumptions of the accusation model typical for the common law tradition in numerous other cases, at the initial stage of their operations the international criminal tribunals have not adopted the procedural institution of the consensual termination of criminal proceedings—which in this model constitutes one of the most important powers of the prosecutor. Initially, no possibility of shortening the proceedings as a result of pleading guilty was provided for in the proceedings before the *ad hoc* tribunals. Neither was there a legal basis for concluding procedural agreements with the prosecutor. The impact of pleading guilty was restricted to it being taken into account, as a mitigating factor, at the sentencing stage. The original form of proceedings before the *ad hoc* tribunals in the area of pleading guilty was much more restrictive as far as the consequences of pleading guilty were concerned; as a matter of fact, they were even more restrictive than the criminal procedures of continental law states are at present. It was assumed that this component of proceedings would not be influenced by the common law model. However, characteristically for the *ad hoc* tribunals, the institution of pleading guilty gradually evolved, leading to the adoption of the institutions of guilty plea and plea bargaining in the form known in Anglo-Saxon states—quite opposite than other procedural institutions that evolved in the direction of the continental model.

First, nowadays, before both *ad hoc* tribunals if the defendant pleads guilty, there is no trial, and the case is heard in a sentencing hearing. Second, in the case the defendant pleads guilty to one or more charges, the prosecutor may conclude an agreement with the defence. This agreement may oblige the prosecutor to carry out three types of actions:

- bringing an indictment only on the charges related to the offences the defendant admitted to and promising to dismiss the proceedings related to the remaining charges;
- applying for a specific sentence;
- not opposing a request by the accused for a particular sentence or sentencing range that is less severe than the one usually imposed.

It is noteworthy that departure from the model adopted in the course of functioning of the *ad hoc* tribunals and a return to the original assumptions underlying the restrictive approach of international criminal tribunals to the institution of procedural agreements have become a characteristic feature of the proceedings held before the ICC. The defendant's pleading guilty before this Court only shortens the evidentiary proceedings and—at the sentencing stage—is treated as a mitigating factor, but it never leads to the elimination of a trial or presentation of evidence. The possibility to conclude a procedural agreement between the ICC Prosecutor and the defence to amend or not brings forward certain charges or to request a specific sentence has not been provided for either.

6.1.2 Procedural Agreements and Plea Bargaining

There are two institutions related to the notion of consensual termination of proceedings: a *guilty plea* and *plea bargaining* (understood as the procedure of negotiations prior to the consensual termination of criminal proceedings). These institutions are not always combined, and they may also occur in various procedural configurations, producing various effects. There are various concepts on the essence of all of the above-mentioned procedural institutions; however, what is certain, is that at the basis of any consensual termination of proceedings stands an agreement. In turn, the agreement is based on a confession of guilt or on not contesting the guilt.

In common law states, the process of concluding formal procedural agreements that terminate a case on merit-based terms has been known as plea bargaining. In the most general terms, plea bargaining is a process involving negotiations between the defendant and the prosecutor by way of which the defendant resigns of his chance for acquittal in exchange for a promise of a less severe punishment for his offences. Therefore, sometimes the process of negotiating between the parties concerning the outcome of a criminal case is referred to as "negotiated justice".[3] This usually involves the prosecutor agreeing to drop certain charges, not to bring them forward or to dismiss the proceedings to some extent, or to apply a more lenient legal characterisation of facts in exchange for the defendant pleading guilty to the charges in the form agreed with the prosecutor. These negotiations aim at a consensual termination of the criminal proceedings by executing a procedural agreement between the defendant and the prosecutor.[4]

The Anglo-Saxon procedure distinguishes various forms of negotiations regarding the form of the procedural agreement between the defence and the prosecutor (it is noteworthy that all the forms may occur in one criminal proceeding). Guilty pleas and negotiations can take place at all stages of criminal proceedings. *Charge bargaining* refers to the prosecutor's ability to negotiate with the defendant in terms of the charges that could be filed. This institution will be used at the stage of an investigation and takes place solely between the prosecutor and the defendant (or more frequently, his defence attorney). It may take one of the two forms: dropping of the original charges and presenting less serious charges or dismissing some charges in exchange for pleading guilty of others. *Fact bargaining* takes place

[3] Turner and Weigend (2013), p. 1376.

[4] Institution of plea bargaining was developed in the nineteenth century. It became a response to an increasing burden of some case loads. Up till this moment, criminal proceedings were short and not complicated and there was no need to speed up the proceedings. It was only when the defence counsels appeared in the courts, together with introducing more safeguards for the defendant, that the procedure became more complicated and more time consuming and the prosecutor began to search for methods of faster disposition of cases. As the system of adversary procedure and the law of evidence was developing, the trials with the use of a jury became more and more complicated and made it unworkable as a routine dispositive procedure. For more see: Langbein (1978–1979), p. 261; McConville and Mirsky (2005), pp. 2–4; Combs (2002), p. 13.

when the defendant agrees to stipulate to certain facts that will be more favourable for him. The prosecutor agrees to charge the defendant with a lesser crime (for example, manslaughter rather than murder) in exchange for pleading guilty to this act. In both cases, the consensus will be presented to the judge. Usually, the court is obliged to deliver the sentence suggested by the prosecutor, but it depends on a specific legal system. Even in systems in which this obligation does not occur, the judges usually grant the sentence requested by the prosecutor. Obviously, this power of the prosecutor may exist only in conjunction with the principle of prosecutorial opportunism. Applicability of the principle of legalism prevents making similar arrangements with the defendant.

The other type of negotiations is *sentence bargaining*. It takes place when the defendant agrees to plead guilty in exchange for a less serious sentence. In the case of the United States, it may be concluded between the prosecutor and the defendant, both at the stage of investigation and also at trial, when the defendant agrees to plead guilty to the charges in exchange for a more lenient sentence for which the prosecutor agrees to apply in the agreement.[5] While usually it must be subject to court approval, in most cases it is carried on between the defence and the prosecution with little judicial review. The second variant of this institution, found in England and Wales, requires that the judge is involved in the process of entering into an agreement with the defendant.[6] Also in Germany the judge may be involved in the negotiations from the beginning.

6.1.3 *Procedural Agreements and Pleading Guilty*

One should not identify the legal institution of procedural agreement with that of pleading guilty. Although these are often related, it is not a rule. Even in the legal systems in which both these institutions are known, pleading guilty does not always lead to the execution of a procedural agreement, and a legal agreement is not always based on pleading guilty (for example, in the case of the American *nolo contendere*—I do not plead guilty, but I do not contest this).[7] In the American procedure, *plea bargaining* institution (elimination of the trial stage as a result of execution of an agreement with the prosecutor on a specific sentence) is differentiated from *pleading guilty* (in such a case referred to in the Anglo-Saxon system as a *confession*).[8] Also in the English procedure, *a guilty plea* refers solely to the procedure of pleading guilty, whereas *plea bargaining* refers to the process of negotiations with justice authorities: both the prosecutor and the judge. Moreover,

---

[5] See: Worrall (2007), p. 345; LaFave et al. (2009), pp. 1000–1001.

[6] See in general: Baker (2004), p. 385; Padfield (2008), p. 322.

[7] Federal Rules of Criminal Procedure, version of 1.12.2012, Rule 11(a)(3): http://www.law.cornell.edu/rules/frcrmp. Accessed 1 Aug 2014.

[8] What is highlighted among others by: Bohlander (2001), pp. 151–159; Orie (2002), p. 1447.

confession is differentiated from a guilty plea: whereas a confession is "a statement of fact",[9] a plea of guilty is a procedural institution having certain consequences. We have to remember that in return for more lenient treatment on the part of state authorities, the defendant's concessions may vary. The defendant may promise "not to present certain evidence, to withdraw procedural motions, to cooperate with the prosecution in cases against other suspects, or not file an appeal".[10] Pleading guilty is just one in a wide range of possible concessions—the most straightforward one.

Depending on the legal system, there are two methods of shortening criminal proceedings as a result of the defendant's pleading guilty. The first group of systems, associated with continental law states, does not provide for waiving trial in case of pleading guilty but may rather reduce the proceedings to the presentation of evidence to confirm the defendant's explanations. A defendant's admission of guilt is not determinative of the issue of his criminal responsibility. In continental systems, it merely constitutes a part of the evidence that will be considered by the court in its ultimate determination of the case. Pleading guilty does not always need to lead to a conviction. It is possible that the defendant pleading guilty will be acquitted by the court if the court does not find the evidence confirming the admission of guilt convincing (pursuant to the principle of discretionary assessment of evidence, in the German procedure referred to as *Grundsatz der freien richterlichen Beweiswürdigung*). In the criminal proceedings of continental states, pleading guilty may constitute a sentence-mitigating factor, but whether this is true depends solely on the free assessment of all evidence presented during trial and is considered in light of the sentencing guidelines.

In the second group of systems (Anglo-Saxon), pleading guilty results in inability to conduct evidentiary proceedings and, in consequence, in the termination of the process of adjudicating guilt. A plea of guilty is considered to be more than a confession that admits that the accused did various acts. It becomes an equivalent of a conviction by the jury. By making this statement, the defendant consents that judgment of conviction may be entered without a trial—a waiver of his right to trial before a jury or a judge. No trial takes place. The court may proceed to the stage of giving a judgment and determining the punishment.[11] According to the logics of adversary trial, there is no need to conduct a trial if one of the parties consented to the claim of the other; their dispute cannot be continued. Since both adversaries are no longer willing to engage in disputation, any further proceeding would exceed the goal of conflict resolution.[12] It is an extreme consequence of the application of the strict adversality principle.[13]

---

[9] Turner and Weigend (2013), p. 1376.

[10] Turner and Weigend (2013), p. 1402.

[11] Such was the opinion expressed in: *Boykin v. Alabama*, 395 U.S. 238 (1969), Supreme Court, 2.6.1969.

[12] Damaška (1986), p. 110.

[13] As seen from the continental side.

In Anglo-Saxon systems, the possibility to conclude a procedural agreement stresses the character of criminal procedure as a contest between the equal parties that have the authority to terminate it at any time and in a manner agreed between them. It is also a consequence of perceiving criminal proceedings as a "contest between the parties" rather than as a process of seeking the material truth by a judge.[14] As there is no obligation of the court to establish the crime's true facts, lawyers with a common law background do not think the guilty pleas and plea bargaining have detrimental effect on the goals of a criminal trial; at least they certainly do not give so much attention to the existence of such a problem as the continental lawyers do.[15]

6.1.4 Common Law Model

The most representative example of a state where plea bargaining plays a decisive role in the functioning of justice is the United States of America. There, plea bargaining is taken to mean the negotiations between the defendant and the prosecution, held without any involvement of a judge, that result in, first, the defendant's deciding not to claim innocence and, second, the conclusion of a procedural agreement. Due to the powers to conclude procedural agreements, the prosecutor becomes the host (master) of the proceedings, leading to conviction of the guilty of the charged offences, and decides on the merits of the judgement. Termination of criminal proceedings by way of an agreement is a common way of resolving criminal law conflicts. According to general estimates, 95 % of the criminal cases that lead to conviction are disposed of by concluding an agreement between the parties and not as a result of a trial.

In the American system, the discretion related to the procedure of negotiating a guilty plea in return for a more lenient sentence is the main manifestation of applicability of the principle of prosecutorial opportunism.[16] No other state adhering to the principle of opportunism offers the prosecutor such a broad possibility for undertaking negotiations with the defendant.

The practice of plea bargaining was first introduced to the legal system by way of the case law of the US Supreme Court.[17] This preceded the formulation of written rules that determine the course of the procedure. Presently, according to the federal law (Rule 11(c) Federal Rules of Criminal Procedure),[18] an attorney for the

---

[14] Goodpaster (1987), p. 138.

[15] A phenomenon observed by: Schuon (2010), pp. 93–93 and 97; and Tulkens (2004), p. 662, and very clearly visible in the literature in question: Scott and Stuntz (1992), p. 1909.

[16] See in general: Worrall (2007), p. 346; Combs (2002), p. 23; Rogacka-Rzewnicka (2007), pp. 206 and 256; Petrig (2008), p. 4; Trüg (2003), pp. 146–148.

[17] *Brady v. U.S.* (379) U.S. (1970), Supreme Court, 4 May 1970.

[18] Federal Rules of Criminal Procedure, version of 1.12.2012: http://www.law.cornell.edu/rules/frcrmp/rule_11. Accessed 2 Sept 2014.

government and the defendant's attorney, or the defendant when proceeding *pro se*, may discuss and reach a plea agreement. The court must not participate in these discussions. If the defendant pleads guilty or makes a *nolo contendere* statement to either a charged offence or a lesser or related offence, the plea agreement may specify that an attorney for the government will

(1) not bring, or will move to dismiss, other charges;
(2) recommend, or agree not to oppose the defendant's request, that a particular sentence or sentencing range is appropriate or that a particular provision of the Sentencing Guidelines, or policy statement, or sentencing factor does or does not apply (such a recommendation or request does not bind the court); or
(3) agree that a specific sentence or sentencing range is the appropriate disposition of the case or that a particular provision of the Sentencing Guidelines, or policy statement, or sentencing factor does or does not apply (such a recommendation or request binds the court once the court accepts the plea agreement)

Pursuant to the federal law, the court is obliged to accept only agreements arising from *charge* or *fact bargaining*. It must adjudicate not only as to the facts covered by the indictment but also within the limits of the legal characterisation presented by the prosecutor. On the other hand, as far as *sentence bargaining* is concerned, the agreement concluded between the defendant and the prosecutor may pertain only to what sentence would be requested by the prosecutor. His sentence recommendation is not binding upon the judge. Moreover, any guilty plea negotiated between the prosecution and the defence is subject to judicial review and may be rejected.[19] However, in practice a judge nevertheless follows the prosecutor's recommendation in the majority of cases.

Although the prosecutor's discretion in presenting the offer to the defendant is broad, it is not unlimited. Detailed rules for executing such agreements are meant to provide a remedy for negative consequences for the accused. First of all, the proposed agreement must comply with law and constitutional guarantees. The second principle of a key importance is that the prosecutor should not threaten to take cases to trial where no reasonable jury could find the defendant guilty beyond a reasonable doubt. Third, the sentence that may be imposed according to the information given by the prosecutor may not be considered unfair, given the characteristics of the offence. Fourth, a conviction as an alternative to a guilty plea presented by the prosecutor must not be "vindictive". The prosecutor may not threaten a defendant with the consequence that more severe charges may be brought if he insists on going to trial and—if after plea negotiations fail—procure an indictment charging a more serious crime, as a strong inference is created that the only reason for the more serious charges is vindictiveness.[20] Moreover, the prosecutor should not charge defendants with offences that do not accurately characterise their conduct and are of a much more serious character or charge defendants for

[19] Damaška (1986), p. 111.

[20] *Bordenkircher v. Hayes*, 434 U.S. 357 (1978), Supreme Court, 18 January 1978. In more detail in: Ross PF (1978), p. 875.

relatively harmless behaviour; this applies especially to cases of overcharging, where prosecutors tend to charge the maximum provable offence and all the formally available offences.[21] Naturally, the guilty plea may not be obtained by means of force or deception (for example, by claiming untruthfully that the prosecutor is in possession of evidence proving the defendant's guilt). It should result from a voluntary and intelligent choice among the alternatives available to a defendant, choosing between the sentence in case he pleads guilty and that when he does not.[22]

One may frequently, however, encounter the opinion that the voluntary nature of the guilty plea often remains an illusion in the situation when, in the case of a trial by jury, the adjudicated sentences are disproportionally severe since "in practice, the defendant is under pressure of a more severe penalty if he/she insists on a public trial".[23] Such pressure may lead to entering into an agreement by innocent persons who prefer to accept a known penalty rather than risk a more severe sentence that may be adjudicated in a trial by jury. According to the Supreme Court, even the defendant's claim that he is innocent does not preclude conviction by the court pursuant to plea bargaining. In *North Carolina v. Alford*, several witnesses claimed that the defendant had committed a murder.[24] In face of such evidence, the defence attorney advised the defendant to settle with the prosecutor; he did so, agreeing to a sentence of 30 years of imprisonment. Although he informed the court that he made a guilty plea because its principal motivation was fear of the death penalty, and not because he had committed the murder, the Supreme Court accepted such a conduct as valid. It concluded that the courts must accept the validity of a guilty plea if it represents a voluntary and intelligent choice among the alternatives available to a defendant, especially one represented by a competent counsel, and there is evidence against him, which substantially negated his claim of innocence and he is not compelled—even if it was entered only to avoid the possibility of the death penalty.[25] According to the Supreme Court, criminal proceedings following such principles are compliant with the Constitution provided that the defendant pleaded guilty voluntarily.[26]

Execution of a procedural agreement imposes certain duties on the prosecutor. If the accused consents to the agreement, it is required that the prosecutor's plea bargaining promise must be kept. In *Santobello v. New York*, the Supreme Court found that "When a plea rests in any significant degree on a promise or agreement

---

[21] For more information on the conditions of plea bargaining see: Langer (2006), p. 225, and the literature cited there. Also: White (1979), p. 367.

[22] *Shelton v. U.S.*, 246 F.2d 571 (5th Cir. 1957), U. S. Court of Appeals Fifth Circuit, 25.6.1957.

[23] Por. Marek (1992), p. 61. Similarly: Gazal (2006), p. 103; Waltoś (2000), p. 22.

[24] 400 U.S. 25 (1970), Supreme Court, 23 November 1970.

[25] *North Carolina v. Alford*, 400 U.S. 25 (1970), Supreme Court, 23 November 1970. See also: Łamejko (2009), p. 211.

[26] Even in such a situation, the court believes that the guilty plea is an essential component of the administration of justice. Properly administered, it is to be encouraged. See also: Alschuler (1968), pp. 50 and 54; LaFave et al. (2009), pp. 1017–1025.

of the prosecutor, so that it can be said to be part of the inducement or consideration, such promise must be fulfilled".[27] Such was the conclusion in a case in which the prosecutor agreed with the defendant that in return for the guilty plea he would withdraw original charges and would raise only one of them. However, at trial another prosecutor had replaced the prosecutor who had negotiated the plea, and he had no knowledge of the agreement executed with the defendant and brought all original charges, which prompted the court to pronounce the maximum possible sentence. In this case, the Supreme Court decided that if the prosecutor's promise were not fulfilled, the defendant might withdraw his guilty plea. The staff of the prosecution is a unit, and each member must be presumed to know the commitments made by any other member. On the other hand, a couple of years later in *Mabry v. Johnson*, the same Supreme Court ruled that the prosecutor might amend the agreement and this would not amount to an "unfulfilled promise".[28] This case, however, was different from *Santobello* in that the defendant agreed to the new proposal made by the prosecutor. In *United States v. Benchimol* case, the Court "opened the door" for withdrawing from the bargain by the prosecutor. Namely, it concluded that the agreement entered by the defendant may not be challenged only in specific circumstances—the prosecutor must commit himself to make a certain recommendation to the sentencing court "enthusiastically" and explain to the court its reasons for making the recommendation; namely, he must "fully and in clear words support his/her offer", rather than in an implied manner, and demonstrate the basis for its existence; otherwise, the court is not obliged to respect such an agreement.[29]

The last manifestation of the development of the plea bargaining institution was addition of the following requirement: "before entering judgment on a guilty plea, the court must determine that there is a factual basis for the plea" (Rule 11(b)(3)) in the federal law. It means that regardless of the defendant's pleading guilty of committing a crime as *per* the prosecutor's version of events, it should be established whether the guilty plea is actually an informed (that is, whether the defendant knows exactly what crime he has admitted to have committed and knows its characteristics) and voluntary act. In case law, the "factual basis" is defined as "sufficient evidence at the time of the plea upon which a court may reasonably determine that the defendant likely committed the offense".[30]

The introduction of an obligation to examine the factual basis for pleading guilty may be a proof that the convergence of the systems in the area of procedural agreements works both ways. Not only have continental states adopted the plea bargaining institution, but also the Anglo-Saxon states have implemented the continental restriction of discretion of the court to approve procedural agreements. It is noticeable, however, that the US courts treat this obligation very superficially

[27] *Santobello v. New York*, 404 U.S. 257 (1971), Supreme Court, 20 December 1971.

[28] *Mabry v. Johnson*, 467 U.S. 504 (1984), Supreme Court, 11 June 1984.

[29] *United States v. Benchimol*, 471 U.S. 453 (1985), Supreme Court, 13 May 1985.

[30] *Schone v. Purkett*, 15 F.3d 785, 788 (1994), U.S. Court of Appeals, 7 February 1994.

and the examination of factual basis most often does not result in the dismissal of the defendant's plea or conduct of evidence discovery. This happens only in exceptional cases. It is claimed that therefore it does not constitute a reliable safeguard to ensure that the judgment will be based on real and true events.[31]

The system of justice in England and Wales differs from the American system in terms of both the form of agreements as well as the procedure of their execution.[32] The main difference between these two systems is that only *charge bargaining* is conducted with the involvement of the prosecutor. The Code for Crown Prosecutors highlights the prosecutor's competence to operate pursuant to the principle of prosecutorial opportunism, providing that it always depends on the discretionary decision of the prosecutor whether he brings a case to trial or suggests entering into a procedural agreement to the defendant. The Code sets down the conditions of legality of such a plea. Namely, the prosecutor should only accept the defendant's plea if he thinks the court is able to pass a sentence that matches the seriousness of the offending, particularly where there are aggravating features. Moreover, the Code provides that the prosecutor should ascertain whether a defendant pleads guilty to the charges on the basis of facts that are not different from the prosecution case. In consequence, it is clear that the English system demands from the prosecutor to establish the factual basis of the case and its true facts. Prosecutors must never accept a guilty plea "just because it is convenient".[33] It would seem that such an obligation excludes the possibility to conduct *fact bargaining*. Moreover, if there are any doubts as to the conformity of the guilty plea with the charges, the court is under an obligation to hear evidence to determine what happened and then sentence on that basis.

The Code also prohibits presenting the accused with more charges than are necessary just "to encourage" a defendant to plead guilty to a few. In the same way, prosecutors should never go ahead with a more serious charge just to encourage a defendant to plead guilty to a less serious one.

Charge bargaining in England usually takes place between the prosecutor and defence counsel outside court before the commencement of the trial. The prosecutor does not have any impact on the sentence pronounced by the judge, and for this reason he may not promise the defendant that a certain sentence will be pronounced. He may just request a specific sentence, and this may as well be the sentence agreed on with the defendant. On the one hand, the court may take into account the nature and intensity of co-operation as well as the prosecutor's suggestions regarding the sentence. On the other hand, the Court of Appeal observed that the judge is not a "rubber stamp" to sanction whatever counsel thought appropriate.[34] He must not ignore other elements of the sentence. Moreover, this Court concluded that even the prosecutor himself, in the situation in which the defendant

---

[31] Schuon (2010), p. 79.

[32] See in general: Sprack (2012), pp. 271–279.

[33] *Code for Crown Prosecutors*, sections 9.1–9.6.

[34] Cit. after: Sprack (2012), p. 277.

pleads guilty, is obligated to call the court's attention to the fact of existence of specific circumstances affecting the sentence, both those of a mitigating and an aggravating nature: "It is not satisfactory for a prosecuting advocate, having secured a conviction, to sit back and leave sentencing to the defence. Nor can an advocate, when appearing for the prosecution for the purpose of sentence on a plea of guilty, limit the assistance that he provides to the court to the outlining of the facts and details of the defendant's previous convictions. The advocate for the prosecution should always be ready to assist the court by drawing attention to any statutory provisions that govern the court's sentencing powers. It is the duty of the prosecuting advocate to ensure that the judge does not, through inadvertence, impose a sentence that is outside his powers. The advocate for the prosecution should also be in a position to offer to draw the judge's attention to any relevant sentencing guidelines or guideline decisions of this court".[35]

The process of negotiating a sentence before English courts (*sentence bargaining*) involving the defendant (defence counsel) and the judge usually takes place in a pre-trial hearing (the so-called *plea and case management hearing*).[36] The discussion between the judge, defence counsel and the defendant is of a confidential nature and may take place *in camera*, if necessary. The judge should not give an advance indication of sentence unless one has been sought by the defendant. However, the judge retains an unfettered discretion to refuse to give one. In *R v. Goodyear*, the England and Wales Court of Appeal concluded that "it may indeed be inappropriate for him to give any indication at all", as "it would be unwise for him to bind himself to any indication of the sentence after a trial in advance of it, in effect on a hypothetical basis". Both the advantages and disadvantages of this solution were analysed.[37] The Court of Appeal admitted that the judge's task is difficult: "he must find the right balance between the obligation of giving indications of a sentence" that a defendant should expect, but in such a manner as not to "become involved in discussions with him/her", "that could lead to the conclusion that he promises a specific sentence regardless of what the circumstances of the case turn out to be", as such a conduct was considered reprehensible. For some, the judge's involvement in negotiations of a sentence with the defendant challenges his independence. On the other hand, however, it is emphasised that the system reduces the risk of the prosecutor's failure to comply with the agreement. The judge is the person who provides "authorised", official information on the legal consequences in the form of a more lenient sentence.[38] Pursuant to the established practice of English courts, the defendant who pleaded guilty is served a less severe

---

[35] *R v. Cain* (Alan John) [2006] EWCA Crim 3233, [2007] 2 Cr. App. R. (S.) 25, England and Wales Court of Appeal (EWCA), Criminal Division, 5 December 2006 http://www.bailii.org. Accessed 13 Jan 2015.

[36] See in general: Padfield (2008), pp. 322–323; Combs (2002), p. 47.

[37] *R v Goodyear (Karl)* [2005] EWCA Crim 888, England and Wales Court of Appeal (EWCA), Criminal Division, 19 April 2005 (§ 54), http://www.bailii.org. Accessed 13 Jan 2015.

[38] As observed by: Darbyshire (2000), pp. 895–910; Tulkens (2004), pp. 667–668.

sentence than he would have been as a result of the trial—a defendant who admits committing an offence may count on a 20–30 % reduction in the sentence. Nowadays, this judicial practice has been given statutory basis.[39]

While plea bargaining and "negotiating justice" are considered to be an indispensable tool of administrating justice, they are not without reservations. Although seen as useful and efficient, these methods of conflict solving are also subject to criticism: "A rich body of literature has demonstrated that criminal laws are regularly stretched or disregarded by police and prosecutors as they choose among the crimes to be investigated and charged. Prosecutors accept pleas to lesser offenses because strict application of the law would produce too harsh a result. Charges are reduced, dismissed, or not brought at all in return for cooperation from a defendant or a potential defendant that will facilitate the conviction of another, more culpable offender. Particularly as the volume of crime increases and offense categories proliferate, even serious crimes are not fully prosecuted because it might be unduly time consuming to conduct a full investigation or to defend a search or confession against a claim of illegality".[40]

6.1.5 Continental Model

Until the 1980s, negotiated justice was considered a phenomenon of the common law tradition.[41] But in the course of the last 35 years, it has become accepted and introduced in most of the legal systems. Continental systems could not ignore the institution of procedural agreements as means to resolve criminal law conflicts and enhance the effectiveness of proceedings. There is no doubt that the concept of procedural agreements entered continental law states after they noticed its successful operation in the common law area.[42] S. Waltoś wrote that "its introduction in the Polish justice system results from a belief that the imperative model of resolving disputes (…) was not a sufficiently effective means to reduce the overload of the increasing number of pending criminal cases in courts and prosecution offices".[43] As a result of the adoption of the institution of consensual termination of criminal

[39] Powers of Criminal Courts (Sentencing) Act 2000, http://www.legislation.gov.uk/ukpga/2000/6/section/152. Accessed 13 Feb 2015. According to section 152, "In determining what sentence to pass on an offender who has pleaded guilty to an offence in proceedings before that or another court, a court shall take into account—(a) the stage in the proceedings for the offence at which the offender indicated his intention to plead guilty; and (b) the circumstances in which this indication was given". For more see: Baker (2004), p. 383; Padfield (2008), p. 322; Spencer (2004), p. 179.

[40] Goldstein and Marcus (1977–1978), p. 241.

[41] Turner and Weigend (2013), p. 1400.

[42] Waltoś (1992), p. 37. Moreover, consensual disposition of a criminal proceedings on the basis of procedural agreements was recommended by the Council of Europe as a method of making the administration of justice more effective: Recommendation R(87)18, 17 September 1987.

[43] Waltoś (1997), p. 25.

proceedings, also in continental systems adjudicating on the basis of an agreement concluded with the prosecutor differs from adjudication in the absence of such an agreement. The main effect of concluding of a procedural agreement is the limitation, or even elimination, of evidentiary proceedings. The only task of the court in such a case is to determine whether pleading guilty is consistent with the true course of events and also whether the agreement complies with the law. However, although institutions similar to plea bargaining were introduced to the criminal procedure of states of continental tradition, it may be noticed that despite the clear impact of the Anglo-Saxon model, they are very different from this original version. The concept of consensual disposition of criminal proceedings had to be adapted to fit the basic assumptions of the already-existing criminal proceeding systems.

First, in continental states it was obvious that offenders were prosecuted by law enforcement authorities, whereas in common law states until the end of the nineteenth century this competence belonged to individuals acting as private prosecutors (citizen prosecutors). Treating the prosecution function as a private function leads to a consequence that the method of its employment is within the discretionary powers of the prosecutor. As he was the *dominus litis* (the master of litigation), he enjoyed a full discretion to compromise his claim. In consequence, the conceptual forms of private discretion have been applied to the office of the public prosecutor.[44] The Anglo-Saxon tradition allows the parties to the proceedings to handle the subject of the trial at their discretion. In the conflict-solving type of procedure, the spirit of *laissez-faire* assumes that the "goals of justice can be attained when parties are left free to select the form of proceeding which best suits their interests".[45] In continental systems, on the other hand, it is just the opposite: from the very beginning, efforts were made to limit prosecutorial discretion. Interventionism, or aiming at the intervention of a state in order to have a criminal law conflict resolved, is what underlies this approach.

Second, as a rule, the systems of continental states give priority to the principle of legalism over the principle of procedural economics and the pragmatic approach. The prosecutor is not allowed to take any decisions as to the essence of the claim. In consequence, conducting negotiations on the legal characterisation of an offence or the contents of charges is unacceptable as the law dictates to prosecute every offence. It prevents the execution of procedural agreements in the form known in the United States, especially in the form of *charge bargaining*. The principle of legalism also means that the substantive criminal law is enforced accurately. Criminal prosecutions that are embedded in the style of private lawsuits seem to be indifferent to the need of accurate and effective enforcement of substantive criminal law.[46] Moreover, the compliance with these rules is controlled by the higher level in the prosecutorial hierarchy—hierarchically organised bureaucrats.

---

[44] Langbein (1978–1979), pp. 267–268.

[45] Damaška (1986), p. 100.

[46] Damaška (1986), p. 226.

Third, continental courts are obliged to seek the material truth. In continental systems, pleading guilty never means releasing the prosecutor from the obligation to collect evidence required to prove the guilt beyond any doubt. The basis for any kind of determination shall be the established "true fact situation" (Article 2 § 2 CCP). Therefore, the court's approval of the agreement in a form that is not consistent with the material truth is unacceptable. While representatives of the Anglo-Saxon legal science also admit that the elimination of the trial stage may lead to the permanent impossibility of disclosing all facts pertaining to the committed crime, or even other crimes, they do not go as far as the representatives of the continental system as to claim that "in such a situation, the trial may be distorted, and the decisions taken may even mean distortion of justice".[47]

Fourth, a hierarchical structure of the office of the prosecutor inhibits the development and use of plea bargaining. The prosecutor's subordination to his superiors does not allow him to handle the subject of the trial at his discretion or to take decisions freely. The less autonomy parties have to decide on their criminal case, the less possibilities there are to conclude agreements. As prosecutors are organised into "echelons", a decision to settle a case in a consensual way is always subject to control of the higher level of hierarchy. Interestingly, although (or maybe because) "the initial decision-makers are closer to the messy details of life, including human drama, and therefore can less readily be immunized from individual aspects of cases", the final decision belongs to "the top officials" who understand universal matters.[48]

And last, the prosecutor is not able to ensure that the court adjudicating in a case will follow the legal characterisation suggested in the indictment, as the court is unrestrained in its legal evaluation of the facts that are charged in the indictment and it is only the factual scope of the indictment that is binding.

The obligation of the court to accept the agreement and pronounce the sentence requested by the prosecutor—after certain terms and conditions have been met—is anyway the main indication of the prosecutor's impact on the consensual termination of a case.[49] As a result of the necessity to retain the basic assumptions of criminal proceedings, continental systems do not give the prosecutor many opportunities to offer major concessions to the defendant in return for a guilty plea. There is also another factor that is mentioned in the literature, which contributes to the fact that continental states do not need plea bargaining in such an extent as Anglo-Saxon courts. It is because the need for plea bargaining for non-trial disposition is not as urgent in the continental procedure. Continental trial procedure is more rapid and efficient than American procedure, and crime rates lower. Therefore, continental law can insist on a full trial for virtually every felony case.[50]

---

47 Cit. after: Marek (1992), p. 61. Similar conclusions in: Schuon (2010), pp. 76 and 206–207.

48 Damaška (1986), p. 20.

49 What was also observed by: Combs (2002), p. 50; Damaška (1975), pp. 480–481; Bohlander (2001), p. 151; Thaman (2008), p. 345; Trüg (2003), pp. 118–122 and 194–199; Waltoś (1997), p. 38.

50 Langbein (1978–1979), p. 467.

Procedural agreements are commonly found in Germany, but their form is different than that of the solutions known from the common law states. The first group of agreements is connected with the institution known as *resitutive discontinuation* of a case. An agreement may be executed at various stages of the proceedings: between the defendant and the prosecutor at the stage of an investigation and between the defendant and the judge at the trial stage. The first type of arrangements includes agreements on lesser offences (misdemeanours). On the basis of § 153a StPO, in a case involving a misdemeanour, the public prosecution office may, with the consent of the accused and of the court competent to order the opening of the main proceedings, dispense with preferment of public charges and concurrently impose conditions and instructions upon the accused (such as to pay a sum of money to a non-profit organisation, the victim or the Treasury). The public prosecution office sets then a time limit within which the accused is to comply with the conditions and instructions. If the accused complies with the conditions and instructions, the offence can no longer be prosecuted as a misdemeanour.[51]

Dispensing is only possible if the charges are of such a nature as to eliminate the public interest in criminal prosecution and if the degree of guilt does not present an obstacle. Moreover, the proceedings may be discontinued only when the prosecutor collects evidence sufficient to bring an indictment. The execution of such an agreement must always be approved by the court, which accepts the prosecutor's decision to discontinue the proceedings, provided the aforementioned preconditions are met and upon finding whether pleading guilty is consistent with the true course of events. If it is not, trial must take place.

Also, the court may conditionally discontinue the proceedings, if public charges have already been preferred, with the approval of the public prosecution office and of the indicted accused, up until the end of the main hearing and concurrently impose the conditions and instructions. However, during the hearing the findings of fact should be examined.

Moreover, it cannot be denied that there is also the practice of concluding *quasi*-formal agreements, not rooted in any legal regulations. As a result of such agreements both at the investigation stage and at trial, the defendant is able to negotiate some concessions with the prosecutor (or the court)—either a lower sentence or a suspended sentence—in return for pleading guilty. In the beginning, there were doubts as to, in the light of lack of statutory basis, whether such informal agreements are, first, admissible, and second, in any way binding for the court. The Federal Supreme Court (*der Bundesgerichtshof*) replied to both questions in the affirmative. It found that although such agreements are not provided for in the criminal procedure regulations, their execution does not violate the Constitution.[52] However, since they are not law based, the law does not guarantee their enforceability and automatic approval by the court. On the other hand, in another verdict

[51] See in general: Beulke (2005), pp. 193–201; Świątłowski (1998b), pp. 70–71; Girdwoyń (2004), pp. 9–11; Steinborn (2005), pp. 76–78; Trüg (2003), pp. 106–108; Płachta (2004a), p. 320.

[52] *Bundesgerichtshof* judgment, 7 June 1983 (BGHSt 210, 214).

the Federal Court emphasised that the court's failure to meet the conditions set out in such agreements is in conflict with the concept of a fair trial. This Court has also developed very detailed guidelines specifying the circumstances in which procedural agreements may be accepted by the court. Primarily, they provide that each time a procedural agreement is executed, the court first needs to make sure that the defendant's right to a fair trial has been complied with and that there has been no infringement of the principle of the material truth.[53]

On the one hand, the advantages of consensual termination of proceedings in this form cannot be overlooked. This mode of non-prosecution saves the prosecutor's and the court's time. The case does not go to trial. The offender saves the time and costs of trial. Much more important to him, he is spared the stigma of criminal conviction.[54] On the other hand, such conditional non-prosecution has been criticised in Germany because it does constitute a form of plea bargaining, and without any statutory basis. The offender or his lawyer haggles with the prosecutor, offering to waive judicial proceedings and accept a lesser "sanction" in exchange for lighter treatment (non-prosecution). The practice has also been criticised for allowing wealthy offenders, in particular white collar criminals, to buy their way out of criminal proceedings (as a *Freikaufverfahren*).[55]

During works on the introduction of the institution of procedural agreement to the Polish procedure, the concepts based on plea bargaining were decidedly rejected; instead, institutions following continental models (including the Italian model) were implemented, with the reservation that they could only be applied in relation to specific offences.[56]

There are two institutions in Poland that may be included in the category of procedural agreements terminating the case in a merit-based manner: *a motion for a conviction without conducting a trial* (Article 335 CCP, which may be applied after termination of the investigation) and *motion for a decision convicting an accused without evidentiary proceedings*, also known as *voluntary submission to penalty* (Article 387 CCP, applied during trial).

According to the first provision, a state prosecutor may attach to the indictment a motion to convict the accused for a misdemeanour (a lesser offence) that he is charged with without conducting a trial and to impose a specified penalty if circumstances surrounding the commission of the misdemeanour do not raise doubts, and the attitude of the accused indicates that the objectives of the proceedings will be achieved despite of lack of a trial. Only Article 335 § 2 CCP can be

---

[53] *Bundesgerichtshof* judgment, 28 August 1997 (BGHSt 43, 195–212). For more on this topic see: Trüg (2003), pp. 118–124; Bohlander (2001), pp. 159–161; Waltoś (2000), p. 17.

[54] Langbein (1978–1979), p. 460.

[55] Or even *Millionärsparagraph*. For more criticism see: Volk (2006), p. 114; Tulkens (2004), pp. 656–657; Herrmannt (1973–1974), p. 494. Such a sentence is not registered in the criminal record, so it is considered to constitute a method of "decriminalization" or "contraventionalization" of certain behaviours. This provision has always played the most important role in economic cases.

[56] Kardas (2004), p. 36; Steinborn (2005), p. 18; Świątłowski (1997), p. 115.

applied by a prosecutor. This provision additionally makes it possible to limit gathering of evidence not only at the stage of court proceedings but also at the stage of investigation. This is possible when the defendant's explanations do not raise any doubts, and conditions are met to file a motion for conviction without a trial. The only advantage the defendant derives from this agreement is that it will allow him to avoid a lengthy procedure and a public trial. In practice, however, this often works differently: the prosecutor proposes a specific sentence he will recommend to the court, provided the defendant pleads guilty.[57]

The second provision states that until the conclusion of the first examination at the first-instance hearing, the accused who is charged with a misdemeanour may submit a motion for a decision convicting him and sentencing him to a specified penalty or penal measure without evidentiary proceedings. The court may grant the motion of the accused to issue a decision convicting him only when the circumstances surrounding the offence and the guilt of the accused have not given rise to doubt and the state prosecutor and the injured party do not oppose. In this case, the prosecutor's role is limited to the possibility to oppose to the agreement. He has no influence on the merit-based decision.

Both of these provisions stipulate that in the case of concluding of a procedural agreement, the court itself does not carry out the evidentiary proceedings, but is obliged to examine, on the basis of the evidence collected in the course of investigation, whether there are reasonable grounds to find the defendant guilty beyond any doubt of the offence he has been charged with. The court may not accept such an agreement if there are doubts pertaining to the guilt of the defendant or the circumstances surrounding the commission of a crime. Beginning on the 1st of July 2015, the institution of voluntary submission to penalty is going to be applicable to all offences (both misdemeanours and crimes). As the Explanatory Report to the Act amending the CCP concludes: "there is no convincing reasons, why the institution of voluntary submission to penalty should not be applied to the most serious offences. We could even argue that the risk of incorrect decisions, resulting from an "instrumental" admission of guilt, is relatively lower in the case of crimes than it is in the case of lighter misdemeanours".

Both of these institutions provide for "a shortened form of handling a case". Their practical application is limited by the following two requirements: first, both of these institutions can be applied only "when the circumstances surrounding the offence and the guilt of the accused have not given rise to doubt". It is not required that the court has no doubts pertaining to a given case, because if such doubts are negligible from the point of view of the defendant's criminal responsibility, then sentencing is still possible. Second, an agreement between the prosecutor and the defendant must not pertain to the legal characterisation of facts; it should always arise from "the agreed factual circumstances and be a reliable reflection of the act

---

[57] See in general: Steinborn (2005), p. 53; Waltoś (1992), p. 39; Stefański (2003), p. 18; Sowiński (2009), p. 15.

that the defendant is validly charged with".[58] Only the prosecutor's commitment pertaining to the contents of the motion he will submit to the court in case the defendant expresses his consent may be the subject of an agreement, never the negotiations on the quantity and the type of charges (due to obvious limitations dictated by the principle of legalism). The relation between the guilty plea and the possibility of concluding of a procedural agreement is a characteristic feature of the Polish system. None of the aforementioned provisions of the Code of Criminal Proceedings instructs that the guilty plea is a precondition for concluding such an agreement. It can only be based on the remaining evidence (for example, catching the defendant in the act) that the court may assess whether the defendant is the perpetrator of an offence. However, whereas in reference to the contents of Article 335 CCP it is found in literature that it is not necessary to obtain the defendant's statement,[59] there is no such consent relative to Article 387 CCP. Some authors recognise that the defendant's consent for the prosecutor filing a motion with the court to have the defendant convicted without a trial establishes the presumption of pleading guilty.[60] As a result, it may be noticed that particularly the institution provided for in Article 335 of the CPP resembles the *nolo contendere* statement known from common law states.

The amendment of September 2013 has also empowered the prosecutor to use *compensatory (restitutive) discontinuation* in cases set forth in the new Article 59a of the Criminal Code (CC). This provision enables the discontinuation of the investigation as requested by the victim in relation to having the damage and/or harm caused by the offence remedied by the accused. This, however, needs to be the act of a person who has not been so far convicted for any act involving violence and an act that constitutes an offence carrying a risk of penalty of imprisonment of up to 3 years and—in the case of an offence against property—with a threat of imprisonment up to 5 years. This remedy for damage and/or compensation for harm needs to take place prior to the commencement of the evidentiary proceedings during the first main trial; it may, thus, take place in the course of investigation. The amendment assumes, therefore, that the discontinuation may take place already in the course of investigation, pursuant to the prosecutor's decision, and also when the case is heard before the court—in a case when the conditions for the discontinuation have been met after an indictment has been brought in. Article 59a § 1 CC focuses on the moment that the loss (harm) has been remedied by the accused rather than the moment of the victim's submission of the request for discontinuation of the proceedings. The *ratio legis* of this provision was the lack of purposefulness of further trial in a situation where the loss has been remedied by the perpetrator.

The provision is not yet in force, but yet it has awakened serious criticism. First, the incorporation of this provision into the Criminal Code, rather than into the CCP,

---

[58] Grzegorczyk (2008), pp. 736–739.

[59] Wysocki (2000), p. 93; Ważny (2003), p. 135; Grajewski (2010), p. 1052; Hofmański et al. (2011), pp. 314 and 530; Grzegorczyk (2008), p. 739.

[60] See: Waltoś (1997), p. 27; Grzegorczyk (2008), p. 819.

by the legislator is somewhat surprising. The basis for discontinuation specified in Article 59a CC is of a procedural, not of a substantive, nature.[61]

Another issue that is still not entirely clear is the question as to whether Article 59a CC is a manifestation of procedural opportunism.[62] This provision does not make any references to the social (public) interest, reasonable basis to proceed or any other criteria typical for opportunism that could be subject to assessment by a prosecutor or court. Neither does it contain any premises involving beyond-any-doubt guilt or negligible guilt that occur in the institution known from § 153 StPO. Moreover, the legislator used a definite phrase "it shall be discontinued" in Article 59a. This means that when the premises of paragraph 1 of this provision are met, the discontinuation of proceedings is mandatory. There is no room left for a discretionary prosecutor's decision. On the one hand, the lack of a broad margin for discretion by the procedural authorities supports equal treatment of citizens, but on the other, the facultative nature of discontinuation seems to be an essence of opportunism, differentiating *restitutive discontinuation* from simple *discontinuation* due to negative procedural premises. It is only in paragraph 3 of this provision where we find the information that the provision shall not be applied if there are exceptional circumstances that justify the decision not to discontinue proceedings in cases when this would compromise the objectives of the punishment. However, on the basis of the considerations presented in the previous chapters, pertaining to the interpretation of the evaluative premises, it can be distinctly seen that it is an example of the so-called "relative obligatority" rather than opportunism.

From the perspective of the consensual disposition of proceedings, it is important that the statute does not require pleading guilty. It is noteworthy, however, that this provision uses the term "perpetrator", which, in the context of pending proceedings, suggests that there are no doubts as to who committed the offence and what should be treated as attributing the guilt to this person. Moreover, the requirement of an earlier remedy of damage implies that the accused accepts his responsibility.

The example of this institution is particularly valuable from the point of view of the prosecutor's role in a consensual termination of the criminal proceedings—first, because the Polish procedure has adopted a structure of a *restitutive discontinuation of proceedings* known from the German trial. The prosecutor has gained a new instrument for influencing the merit-based judgment. More importantly, the prosecutor's power is not controlled by the court. He may discontinue the criminal proceedings on the merits with a binding adjudication. It also proves that the convergence of solutions occurs not only between various legal traditions but also within the same legal tradition and between specific national systems. The success of the procedural institution in one of the states (which has also borrowed it from another legal system) becomes a basis for its implementation in the legal system of another state. Second, from an objective perspective, it implements the components

[61] Lach (2015), p. 137.

[62] *Ibidem*, p. 138.

of the principle of opportunism even if this was not the authors' intention (and from what we hear, it was not).[63]

In the continental model of consensual termination of criminal proceedings, the prosecutor has never achieved such a high level of impact on the course of the trial as in the common law model, where the prosecutor's role goes far beyond negotiating the penalty for the charged offence.[64] The prosecutors in the latter systems have become some of the main *de facto* adjudicators of criminal trial. Both of these models, however, share the common goal of enhancing the effectiveness of administration of justice and preventing waste of financial and time resources. What differentiates them, however, is the type and scope of concessions they are willing to make for the sake of effectiveness of proceedings, at the cost of the principle of prosecutorial legalism and the material truth. Assuming that common law and continental law traditions present only "ideal models", as they do not exist in a pure form in any state, we may also assume that at one end of this continuum is the institution of plea bargaining unrestricted by any rules, and at the other end there is a system where it is not possible for the prosecutor to influence the course of a trial in any way or to offer procedural concessions to the defendant as a consequence of his pleading guilty. The scope of prosecutorial competence consensually to dispose of criminal proceedings as a result of execution of an agreement with the defendant in each legal system currently constitutes a hybrid between these two extremes.[65]

6.2 Model of Consensual Termination of Proceedings Before the Ad Hoc Tribunals

6.2.1 Consensualism on the Forum of International Criminal Justice

Administration of justice on the basis of an agreement concluded between the prosecution and the defendant has both advantages and disadvantages. On the one hand, this institution is praised for accelerating the course of the criminal trial, yet on the other, it is criticised for the "leniency of administration of justice" that results in imposing penalties that are disproportional to the social danger of an act in a manner that violates the judicial sentencing principles and involves the justice into "haggling" over the sentence.[66] Certainly, both these advantages and disadvantages of consensual termination of a case may be applied to the practice of international

[63] Compare the views presented by Andrzej Zoll, a Member of the Codification Commission of Criminal Law, expressed during a Conference: III Kraków Penalist Forum, 6th of February 2015, Kraków, Jagiellonian University.

[64] See: Marek (1992), p. 58; Trüg (2003), pp. 482–483.

[65] Langer (2006), pp. 226 and 252.

[66] As in: LaFave et al. (2009), p. 1005.

criminal tribunals. However, due to the function of these tribunals and the role they are intended to play, as well as the type of offences falling under their jurisdiction, certain aspects may be evaluated differently.

From the earliest days of international criminal tribunals, there were some doubts as to the possibility of application of the plea bargaining institution in the form known from Anglo-Saxon states.[67] There was a strong opposition against the possibility to allow for concluding of procedural agreements that would lead to the elimination of trial.[68] Avoiding a trial and moving directly to the determination of sentence—as characteristic of proceedings organised as a contest of two partisan cases—was undesirable in international criminal tribunals. Several arguments against such a possibility have been repeated most frequently.

First, consensual termination of the proceedings was considered to be in conflict with the tribunals' obligation to determine the material truth as it would lead to preventing the disclosure of historical truth pertaining to committed crimes. Attention was drawn to the fact that the conclusion of a binding agreement between the prosecutor and the defendant may not be in compliance with the actual course of events. That, in turn, would lead to administration of justice pursuant to the version of events negotiated by the parties and not based on the facts of the case. The tribunals were principally established to secure the right to truth and reveal factual circumstances of committed crimes. The historical role to be played by them was not compatible with expedited handling of cases and exculpation of defendants. The ICTY's judges have emphasised many times that the trial plays an irreplaceable role as the forum for disclosing historical truth and enables the victims to participate in the process of punishing the guilty ones.[69] They highlighted that the quality of the justice and the fulfilment of the mandate of this Tribunal, including the establishment of a complete and accurate record of the crimes committed in the former Yugoslavia, should not be compromised by avoiding the stage of trial and promoting guilty pleas. It has been observed that the "bipolar pressures", a "clash of conflicting positions" tends to "relativize, or weaken, both-including the courts' intended educational message" and the "didactic objective central to the mission of international criminal courts".[70]

The second factor giving rise to doubts relative to the implementation of the consensual institutions on the international criminal justice forum was the reluctance to give the prosecutor too much power to affect the contents of a merit-based judgment. When procedural agreements were first introduced, it has been indicated that this institution (especially in the form of *charge bargaining*) renders the judge

[67] These doubts described in more detail in: Terrier (2002), p. 1286; Calvo-Goller (2006), p. 239; Knoops (2005), pp. 260–261; Combs (2007), p. 76.

[68] As seen from the inside of the negotiations by: Morris and Scharf (1995), pp. 649–652; Scharf (2004), pp. 1070–1081. Also in: Harmon (2009), p. 166.

[69] This tendency has been on many occasions highlighted in the literature, e.g.: Combs (2007), p. 77; Combs (2002), p. 105; Schuon (2010), p. 253, Turner and Weigend (2013), p. 1406.

[70] A related reason was that the defence's freedom to mount its own case provides it with ample opportunity to spread ideas contrary to human rights values. See: Damaška (2008), p. 357.

incapable of deciding on the defendant's guilt and transfers this competence to the prosecutor.[71] Undoubtedly, having been granted the competence to dispose of criminal proceedings consensually, the prosecutor acquired the power to affect the contents of a verdict and sentence.[72] Having the power to decide on the contents of charges that will be brought, and being able to bring evidence to support them, the prosecutor in fact takes over some of the powers of an independent court. As a result of his decision, only some of the crimes charged to the perpetrator will come to light. The prosecutor becomes sort of a "barrier" that allows only certain cases to "pass" to the judge. He also determines the scope of the historical truth disclosed in the trial. The prosecutorial competence to decide, *de facto*, on the contents of the resolution on the criminal responsibility of the defendant brings the trial closer to the inquisitive model, vesting collection of evidence and decisions on the scope and form of criminal responsibility in the hands of a single person.[73] The prosecutor's powers before international tribunals are already significant: on his own initiative, he can initiate criminal proceedings and conduct them against persons selected by himself. If the competences to negotiate procedural agreements were also granted to him and the obligation to approve such agreements by the court was imposed, the prosecutor of the international criminal tribunal would become the most prominent person in the international administration of justice—a one-person inquisitive tribunal of justice, adjudicating in the most serious crimes of international law.

Third, the reluctance to allow a consensual termination of criminal proceedings is affected by the gravity of the crimes dealt with by the tribunals. It is hard to imagine that in a case of genocide, crimes against humanity or crimes of war, the prosecutor could ignore the violation of law in return for the defendant pleading guilty and having the proceedings expedited. Their very *raison d'être* is to have the persons most responsible for serious violations of international humanitarian law held accountable for their criminal conduct—not simply a portion thereof. A purposeful refusal to prosecute such crimes—to exclude criminally relevant facts

---

[71] However, we can also take into consideration a "modified real offence sentencing principle", which allows a court to determine a sentence also on the grounds of some elements of the offence that he was charged with in the beginning by a prosecutor, but finally these charged were dropped as a result of the bargain—and only on the grounds of the offence that the accused admitted to commit. See: Schuon (2010), pp. 82–83; Hessick and Saujani (2002), p. 189. Also in: Steinborn (2005), p. 68.

[72] When presenting to the defendant his suggestion as to the sentence in return for pleading guilty, the prosecutor *de facto* presents his theory on the trial that would have taken place, complete with his opinion on the possible sentence. This is the way to establish a sort of a "shadow-of-trial"—the trial that does not exist and, in the case of pleading guilty, will never take place. Litigants bargain toward settlement in the shadow of expected trial outcomes. In this model, rational parties forecast the expected trial outcome and strike bargains that leave both sides better off by splitting the saved costs of trial. The classic shadow-of-trial model predicts that the likelihood of conviction at trial and the likely post-trial sentence largely determine plea bargains. In consequence, the vision of the trial presented to the defendant differs depending on the prosecutor and the strength of the evidence collected by him. See: Bibas (2004), p. 2467.

[73] Gerard (1998), pp. 2120–2135; Langer (2006), p. 256.

from judicial scrutiny—would be inconsistent with the very reason the tribunals were established for—to bring gross human rights violations to justice.[74]

On the other hand, the most fundamental argument in favour of application of the plea bargaining method of convincing the court about the defendant's guilt has always been that "there are too many criminals and not enough prosecutors, court and prisons".[75] Plea bargaining minimises time the prosecutor spends on a case: less time spent on a case means more cases that can be handled with the available restricted budget. This argument is especially relevant in the case of trials pending in Anglo-Saxon states where a defendant's guilt is decided by the jury. This is not only very expensive but also time consuming, as there is much evidence to be presented. The pressure to end a case rapidly and convict a defendant grows in cases that are factually complex and therefore require a lot of time and funds. For certain, cases heard by international criminal tribunals are by nature much more time consuming than those heard before national courts.[76] This argument has been emphasised in the current line of adjudication of the *ad hoc* tribunals: voluntary admission of guilt that saves the International Tribunal the time and effort of a lengthy investigation and trial should be rewarded as it also saves resources of the Tribunal (which are limited, as has been noticed in numerous judgments issued under a guilty plea).

The efficiency argument is of a particular importance, the more complex are the rules of procedure. There is a correlation between eagerness of investigative organs to conclude a bargain and the level of complexity of criminal proceedings. For this reason, the guilty plea has become so significant in common law states where not only the rules of conducting a trial (combined with the rules for interrogating witnesses and the principles of admissibility of evidence), but also the rules governing the disclosure of evidence procedure, demand to deploy considerable resources in the conduct of trial. Thus, while the need for shortening criminal proceedings—not at any price, but at a significant one anyway—may be noticed in those states, it is not as conspicuous in the states where the criminal procedure is simpler and decisions are not made by the jury.[77] Indeed, the procedure before international criminal tribunals is complicated and time consuming. This has to do both with the level of complexity of procedural regulations and the scope of the examined factual situations, as well as with the need to offer adequate trial guarantees, both for the defendant and the victims. Considering the above, the search for methods to shorten such proceedings seems only like a natural response. The evolution of the consensual model of termination of criminal proceedings is

[74] See for more: Bohlander (2001), pp. 162–163; Combs (2002), pp. 7 et seq.; Schuon (2010), p. 253. Jean Kambanda, accused before the ICTR, was found guilty of *aiding* and abetting and participating in genocide of 800,000 persons in 100 days.

[75] Cit. after: Worrall (2007), p. 343. Similarly: Hessick and Saujani (2002), p. 192.

[76] Such data can be found in: Combs (2002), pp. 90 et seq.

[77] Such conclusion was expressed by an expert in this area: Combs (2002), pp. 46–49, and by many more authors, such as: Langbein and Wienreb (1978), p. 1562; Harmon (2009), p. 174; Schuon (2010), pp. 94–96 and 209; Langbein (1978–1979), pp. 267–268.

best exemplified in the practice of the ICTY. For the Tribunal's judges, preventing costly and lengthy trials turned out to be more important than complying with the initial assumptions that required the Tribunal to search for the material truth in a conscientious manner.[78] But this happened only after the Tribunal's effectiveness turned out to be the basic prerequisite of its further functioning and the ultimate deadline for completion of all the cases heard by the Tribunal had been set. As a result, there may be no doubt that the solution finally adopted is not a reflection of a planned and intentional development of the criminal trial but rather a manifestation of the pragmatic approach, a necessity arising from the threat that administration of justice will become paralysed, confronted with cases too numerous to be resolved by one tribunal established to deal with violations of international law.

It is noteworthy that the role of procedural agreements in the course of the criminal trial may not be limited solely to the acceleration of the proceedings or to financial savings. It has also been demonstrated that procedural agreements may play a special role in ensuring fulfilment of the social function of the administration of justice by alleviating conflicts occurring as a result of a crime and in the achievement of procedural justice. As such, they may constitute a fundamental step on the way to reconciliation.[79] This function of agreements could not be underestimated in the case of international tribunals. The international administration of justice system was established, in part, as a measure for the maintenance of international peace and security and fulfilling the aims of the so-called *post-conflict justice*. Especially in the areas of international conflicts, where people who used to fight on opposite sides are still living next to each other, the revealing of the historical truth and achievement of reconciliation must be the key objectives of all actions undertaken by these tribunals.[80] The goal of re-establishing peace and justice cannot be achieved unless the victims of international crimes are satisfied with the proceedings as well as with the outcome of the process.[81] Perhaps, stigmatisation of perpetrators and disclosure of truth about the conflicts and crimes should be more important than arriving at severe convicting sentences in a narrow range of cases. Providing the defendant with an opportunity to express regret in public, to explain the reasons for the commission of crimes and to provide information on other crime perpetrators lays the foundations for reconciliation between fighting parties. In their case law, the international tribunals started stressing the significance of guilty pleas as they provided to the prosecutor extensive information necessary for sketching the real picture of a conflict and for understanding why crimes have been committed. Guilty pleas became important for the purpose of

---

[78] See: Petrig (2008), p. 28.

[79] Steinborn (2005), pp. 60–61; Skorupka (2009), p. 17.

[80] As M. Damaška, puts it: The "desire to set the historical record straight, and to restore the integrity of human remembrance, is greatly strengthened by the belief that truth telling about the past is a necessary precondition for reconciliation and avoidance of future conflicts" (2008), p. 336. See for similar observations also in: Clark (2009), pp. 415–436; Harmon (2009), pp. 176–182; Combs (2002), pp. 150–151; Knoops (2005), pp. 264–266.

[81] Turner and Weigend (2013), p. 1406.

establishing the truth in relation to committed crimes. The judges pointed out that the will of co-operation of the defendant may become the only chance for the prosecutor to reveal information that he could not have obtained otherwise (in this or other cases).[82] The defendant's explanations often turn out to be of key importance for the case to be finalised with a conviction. Particularly valuable is information pertaining to the existence of a causal link between events and specific decision-makers. In this way, procedural agreements often became the method of arriving at the material truth.[83] The ICTY judges on many occasions stressed that "discovering the truth is a cornerstone of the rule of law and a fundamental step on the way to reconciliation: for it is the truth that cleanses the ethnic and religious hatreds and begins the healing process".[84] Moreover, one more argument cannot be neglected—offering major concessions to the perpetrators encourages them to conclude agreements with the prosecutor of the tribunal.

It is, therefore, very important to find the right balance between the advantages and disadvantages of a consensual termination of criminal proceedings. Pleading guilty may certainly provide valuable information about crimes and the circumstances surrounding their commission, but this information should not be "traded" for the victims' sense of justice. Similarly, effective and rapid conviction and saving of resources can never be treated as an overriding goal, with justice not being sought at all.[85]

6.2.2 *Pleading Guilty: Procedural Consequences*

During the trials before the International Military Tribunals in Nuremberg and in Tokyo, none of the defendants pleaded guilty. The charters of those tribunals provided that the Tribunal asked each accused whether he pleads "guilty" or "not guilty" after reading out the indictment in court (Article 24 Nuremberg IMT Charter and Article 15(b) IMTFE Charter). In the absence of the case law related to this issue, it is not known what consequences could have arisen from such a statement—whether it would have been possible to shorten or eliminate the discovery of evidence or to reduce a sentence.

The history of consensual termination of a case before the *ad hoc* tribunals is a history of a struggle between two legal traditions. Despite the fact that the procedure of these tribunals is based to a large extent on the principles borrowed from the legal systems of common law states, the model of consensual disposition of a case has not been adopted in the form known from these states. In the initial period of its

[82] Harmon (2009), pp. 170–171; Schuon (2010), pp. 208–209, s. 230, 252.

[83] Clark (2009), pp. 424–426; May and Wierda (2002), p. 46; Combs (2003), p. 936; Combs (2002), p. 149.

[84] *Prosecutor v. Erdemović*, IT-96-22, Trial Chamber, 5 March 1998, § 21.

[85] Tulkens (2004), pp. 641 and 669.

functioning, the policy of the ICTY assumed a total elimination of procedural agreements from the procedure before the Tribunal.[86] The possibility of eliminating or shortening the trial as a result of pleading guilty was not taken into account. But with the passage of time and appearance of new problems related to lengthy trials, and also in the face of ultimate deadlines for completion of the work by both the *ad hoc* tribunals, it turned out that they could not ignore the opportunities offered by procedural agreements. The judges' attitude evolved: while initially they did not approve of the plea bargaining institution, with time they presented a more pragmatic attitude. They decided to take advantage of the positive potential of this institution to accelerate and expedite the proceedings held in the international forum. Gradually, more and more elements of the model of consensual disposition of a case used in common law systems were introduced, to finally arrive at the legal status partially implementing the solutions of the US legal system.

At present, pleading guilty may trigger three types of legal consequences according to the Statutes of both the *ad hoc* tribunals. First, it may result in elimination of the trial stage and moving straight to the determination of sentence. Second, it is taken into account in the sentencing process where the judges assess whether it has constituted an element of co-operation with the prosecutor and as such can be considered a mitigating factor. Third, it constitutes an element enabling consensual termination of a case by way of concluding of a procedural agreement between the prosecutor and the defendant.

Before the ICTY, pleading guilty is possible at trial immediately after the indictment has been read out (Article 20(3) ICTY Statute). However, initially, there were no regulations dealing with this statement or its consequences. Characteristically for the common-law-based systems, various questions were first regulated in the case law, in specific cases, and only then that relevant regulations were reflected in procedural provisions. The guilty plea criteria were introduced in *Prosecutor v. Erdemović*. The latter was the first defendant who pleaded guilty. This case became a breakthrough not only due to the fact that these criteria were developed but first of all due to the impact of pleading guilty on a surprisingly lenient sentence (ultimately—5 years of imprisonment). The Tribunal concluded: "The common law institution of the guilty plea should, in our view, find a ready place in an international criminal forum such as the International Tribunal confronted by cases which, by their inherent nature, are very complex and necessarily require lengthy hearing if they are to go to trial under stringent financial constraints arising from allocations made by the United Nations itself dependent upon the contributions of States".[87] In this judgment, judges set up a framework for

[86] 1st Annual Report of the International Criminal Tribunal for the Prosecution of Persons Responsible for Serious Violations of International Humanitarian Law Committed in the Territory of the Former Yugoslavia Since 1991, U.N. Doc A/49/342, z 29.8.1994, § 74. A tendency described in detail in: Schuon (2010), pp. 196–197; D'Ascoli (2011), pp. 178–179; Tochilovsky (2008), p. 263.

[87] *Prosecutor v. Erdemović*, IT-96-22, Appeals Chamber, 7 October 1997, Joint Separate Opinion of Judge McDonald and Judge Vohrah, § 2.

the mitigating factors, expressing at the same time the key advantages of a guilty plea: "it might take into account that the accused surrendered voluntarily to the International Tribunal, confessed, pleaded guilty, showed sincere and genuine remorse or contrition and stated his willingness to supply evidence with probative value against other individuals for crimes falling within the jurisdiction of the International Tribunal, if this manner of proceeding is beneficial to the administration of justice, fosters the co-operation of future witnesses, and is consistent with the requirements of a fair trial".

In numerous subsequent proceedings before the *ad hoc* tribunals, the defendants took advantage of the opportunity to plead guilty, hoping that this would secure them a more lenient sentence.[88] At the same time, it turned out that lengthy proceedings before the *ad hoc* tribunals exceed their financial resources and forced them to find a remedy for this problem. Thus, there was a desire to regulate this issue on both sides.

The procedural consequences of pleading guilty were regulated in a manner known from Anglo-Saxon systems under the amendment of the Rules of Procedure and Evidence by adding Rule 62bis in 1997. It provides that during the Initial Appearance of the Accused, a judge should instruct the accused that he or she may either immediately enter a plea of guilty or not guilty on one or more counts or make such a statement within thirty days of the initial appearance. If the accused decides to enter such a plea and the Trial Chamber is satisfied that the conditions for its validity are fulfilled, it may "enter a finding of guilt and instruct the Registrar to set a date for the sentencing hearing". Currently, there is no doubt that pleading guilty may have trial consequences by shortening the proceedings. Where the defendant pleads guilty, a trial is not held and the case is immediately moved to the sentencing hearing. Theoretically, the information presented during this hearing should refer to the sentence rather than to the defendant's guilt. However, as the hearing creates an opportunity to present additional information, the ICTY has in many cases used it to clarify any discrepancies between the defendant's explanations and the remaining evidence in a case.[89]

If an accused pleads guilty, the Trial Chamber must be first satisfied that there is a sufficient factual basis for the crime and the accused's participation in it, either on the basis of independent indicia or on lack of any material disagreement between the parties about the facts of the case (Rule 62bis(iv) RPE ICTY). Thus, the guilty plea itself is not a sufficient proof of the defendant's guilt, and it is still necessary for the judges to find confirmation of the defendant's participation in a crime in the evidence collected in the case. In *Prosecutor v. Momir Nikolić*, the ICTY presented the criteria that have to be taken into consideration in order to ensure whether a sufficient factual basis for the crime exists. Namely, in questioning about the factual basis, a Trial Chamber should seek to ensure that the totality of the accused's criminal conduct is reflected and that an accurate historical record exists, as well as

[88] See in general: Combs (2003), p. 929; Bohlander (2001), pp. 153–156.

[89] As in the case of: *Prosecutor v. Deronjić*, IT-02-61, Appeals Chamber, 20 June 2005, § 47.

ensure that the accused is pleading guilty to no more than that for which he is, in fact, guilty.[90] It is worth mentioning that these criteria were set up in a Trial Chamber that was composed of two judges with a continental legal background and a third coming from a mixed system.[91] Due to the domination of the continental system judges, the procedural consequences of this judgment marked a departure of the guilty plea institution applied before the ICTY from the model used in the US trial. In consequence, in this respect "factual basis review at the ad hoc tribunals is more probing than factual basis review in common law systems, where judges rarely question the legal characterization of the facts by the parties".[92] For continental judges, the implementation of these criteria still guaranteed fulfilment of the Tribunal's mission, which consisted in determining of the historical truth. Despite the significant impact of the guilty plea on the course of proceedings before the Tribunal, the judges' obligation to determine the truth was given priority over arriving at conviction.

Therefore, before the *ad hoc* tribunals, when the defendant pleads guilty but his statement is not consistent with the version of events presented by the prosecutor in the indictment, the Chamber must not agree on issuing a verdict based on the indictment alone.[93] The obligation of the *ad hoc* tribunal judges to determine the material truth entails that when there is no consistency between the defendant's plea and the indictment, the former cannot be accepted. In such a situation, it is advisable to rely on supplementary evidence. The Trial Chamber may decide that it is necessary, for example, to summon and interrogate witnesses and may then summon them or have them summoned by the parties.[94] The ICTY has increasingly invited the parties (generally it was the Prosecutor) to submit additional documents and statements to support the facts as presented in the indictment by the Prosecutor.[95] It may also use the competence to ask witnesses and the defendant questions. For instance, in *Prosecutor v. Deronjić*, the Trial Chamber did not accept the guilty plea, claiming that it first needed to clarify the discrepancies found between the indictment and the contents of this plea.[96] Ultimately, it accepted the defendant's statement, and the proceedings were shortened by eliminating the trial stage. In *Prosecutor v. Babić*, the Chamber rejected the plea agreements, expressing doubts as to the "accuracy of the legal characterization" of aiding and abetting to a joint criminal enterprise, as it did not fulfil the actual basis requirement. In response, the

---

[90] E.g. in: *Prosecutor v. Nikolić*, IT-02-60/1, Trial Chamber, 2 December 2003, § 52.

[91] Schuon (2010), p. 199; Tochilovsky (2008), p. 267.

[92] Turner and Weigend (2013), p. 1382.

[93] In England and Wales, to address this problem a special procedure was developed of holding a "Newton hearing" (named after the first case in which the procedure was established) to resolve doubts. During this hearing, both sides present arguments with a view to the prosecution to prove its version of the facts "beyond reasonable doubt": "if it cannot, sentence is passed in line with the version claimed by the defence". Cit after: Baker (2004), p. 382.

[94] *Prosecutor v. Momir Nikolić*, IT-02-60/1, Trial Chamber, 2 December 2003, § 52 and 70.

[95] Turner and Weigend (2013), p. 1382.

[96] *Prosecutor v. Miroslav Deronjić*, IT-02-61, Appeals Chamber, 20 June 2005.

parties renegotiated their agreement and filed a new plea, one in which the defendant's participation was qualified as a co-perpetrator's.[97] However, in *Prosecutor v. Juvénal Rugambarara*, the ICTR took a more strict position. It observed that a guilty plea is considered to be valid as long as the accused confirmed that he was satisfied with the explanations provided in the indictment and that he did not challenge any of the facts alleged in the indictment after the plea. In such a situation, it is assumed that he pleaded to have committed the acts as described in the indictment and is informed and aware of the consequences of his plea.[98]

The adoption of this assumption has a major impact on the role to be played by the prosecutor. Rather than being satisfied with eliciting a guilty plea from the defendant, he must still proactively look for evidence to support his statement.

6.2.3 *Pleading Guilty: Influence on the Dimension of Penalty*

According to Rule 100(A) RPE ICTY, "If the Trial Chamber convicts the accused on a guilty plea, the Prosecutor and the defence may submit any relevant information that may assist the Trial Chamber in determining an appropriate sentence". Meanwhile, Rule 101(B) provides that in determining the sentence, the Trial Chamber shall take into account certain factors such as "any mitigating circumstances including the substantial cooperation with the Prosecutor by the convicted person before or after conviction". These two provisions have to be read and assessed separately. As a matter of fact, sentencing on the basis of a guilty plea and sentencing as a result of a full trial—while taking into consideration "substantial cooperation" with the Prosecutor—constitute two separate procedures. The Appeals Chamber indicated many times that using the guilty plea as an exculpatory factor, while refusing to consider the defendant's co-operation in the same way, was not a law infringement.[99]

Abundant case law of the ICTY addressed the issue of the guilty plea and its significance in reduction of a sentence. Right after the provision was first enforced, the Tribunal found that "a guilty plea should, in principle, give rise to a reduction in the sentence that the accused would otherwise have received".[100] Among the aspects that determined the weight in mitigation of the sentence, the most important was given to the timing of a guilty plea. Defendants pleaded guilty at various stages of proceedings: some did so when informed about the drafting of an indictment,

[97] *Prosecutor v. Babić*, IT-03-72, Trial Chamber, 29 June 2004. Described also in: Turner and Weigend (2013), p. 1383.

[98] *Prosecutor v. Juvénal Rugambarara*, ICTR-00-59, Trial Chamber, 16 November 2007, § 6. In this case, however, also other mitigating circumstances turned out to be decisive for the severity of the sentence: the accused's behavior after the committing of crimes. He was sentenced to 11 years of imprisonment and did not appeal.

[99] E.g. *Prosecutor v. Plavšić*, IT-00-39&40/1, Appeals Chamber, 27 February 2003, § 109.

[100] In the case: *Prosecutor v. Todorović*, IT-95-9/1, Trial Chamber, 31 July 2001, § 80.

during the initial appearance, others only during the trial when evidence then presented left no doubts as to their guilt. Pleading guilty at an early stage of the trial was considered to have a greater impact on the mitigation of a sentence. In *Prosecutor v. Babić*, the defendant pleaded guilty right after the indictment had been confirmed.[101] In this case, even the prosecution thought that the plea had a particular value, as it was entered at a very early stage of the trial. Also, B. Plavšić entered her guilty plea "months before" the commencement of the trial, which was considered to make a considerable contribution to the public advantage and the work of the International Tribunal. In *Prosecutor v. Zelenović*, the accused did not voluntarily surrender to the Tribunal, and he did not plead guilty at his initial appearance. His guilty plea therefore came late. However, it came before any trial proceedings in his case had commenced. The Trial Chamber therefore considered that the guilty plea could be given considerable weight in mitigation.[102] It seems that a guilty plea made on every stage of proceedings gave some credit to the accused. In *Prosecutor v. Sikirica*, the Trial Chamber stated that notwithstanding the timing of the guilty plea, a benefit accrues to the Trial Chamber because a guilty plea contributes directly to one of the fundamental objectives of the International Tribunal: namely, its truth-finding function; a guilty plea is always important for the purpose of establishing the truth in relation to a crime. Therefore, despite the lateness of his guilty plea, the accused should receive some credit.[103]

It was the sentence in *Prosecutor v. Biljana Plavšić*[104] that turned out to be a breakthrough as far as mitigation of the sentence as a result of pleading guilty is concerned. The defendant was the first high-ranking Bosnian Serb politician who voluntarily surrendered to the Tribunal and pleaded guilty. The indictment contained a statement that the prosecution did not make any promises in relation to the guilty plea of the defendant. The defence attorney also said that there was no agreement in place between the Office of the Prosecutor and the defence pertaining to the sentence, and the defendant confirmed that she did not expect any benefits in relation to the plea and was prepared for a life sentence. At the same time, she observed that since her life expectancy was 8 years, any sentence beyond that would amount to life imprisonment and would be inappropriate. In this case, the Prosecutor noted that the accused has expressed her remorse "fully and unconditionally", expressing her hope that her guilty plea will assist her people to reconcile with their neighbours. In consequence, he submitted that the appropriate sentence should be between 15 and 25 years of imprisonment. The prosecution stated moreover that this expression of remorse was noteworthy since it was offered from a person who had formerly held a leadership position and that it "merits judicial consideration".

---

[101] *Prosecutor v. Babić*, IT-03-72, Trial Chamber, 29 June 2004.

[102] *Prosecutor v. Zelenović*, IT-96-23/2, Appeal Chamber, 31 October 2007, § 46.

[103] The case of *Prosecutor v. Sikirica*, IT-95-8, Trial Chamber, 13 November 2001, § 150–151. More in: Combs (2002), p. 126.

[104] *Prosecutor v. Plavšić*, IT-00-39 & 40/1, Appeals Chamber, 27 February 2003, § 66–81. Also these judgments discussed in detail in: Combs (2007), p. 73; Combs (2003), p. 929.

However, the Trial Chamber considered that the prosecution in its submissions as to sentence has given insufficient weight to the age of the accused (the accused was 72 years old at the time) and the significant mitigating factors connected with her plea of guilty and post-conflict conduct. Finally, the Chamber imposed 11 years of imprisonment, well below the submissions of the Prosecutor. After this exceptionally lenient sentence was given, a growing number of guilty pleas were observed.[105]

However, the ICTY's approach to the factor of pleading guilty has constantly evolved. An analysis of the cases heard by the Tribunal proved that not only may it not be concluded that in return for pleading guilty the accused received specific benefits, but it also showed that the opposite might be true. In *Prosecutor v. Bralo*, while some counts were removed from the indictment by the Prosecutor, it is noteworthy that a new charge of persecution as a crime against humanity was added, which was possible thanks to information supplied by the accused in the frames of his co-operation with the Prosecutor.[106] The defendant himself, while testifying, disclosed his involvement in some other crimes (ethnic cleansing) than those to which the initially drafted indictment pertained. Moreover, this approach often has depended on the personal composition of a given Chamber.

6.2.4 Co-operation with the Prosecutor: Influence on the Sentence

Whereas pleading guilty is subject to a rational evaluation, the co-operation with the prosecutor may be assessed by judges only as a result of the prosecutor's presentation of an appropriate statement. Such an opportunity is provided by Rule 100(A) RPE ICTY, according to which if the Trial Chamber convicts the accused on a guilty plea, it must allow the Prosecutor to submit "any relevant information that may assist the Trial Chamber in determining an appropriate sentence". Rule 101(B)(ii), in turn, constitutes that, in determining the sentence, the Trial Chamber shall take into account (among other factors) "any mitigating circumstances, including the substantial cooperation with the Prosecutor by the convicted person before or after conviction". The co-operation with the Prosecutor may take on various forms: from providing comprehensive explanations on their case and pleading guilty through making testimonies in other cases and indicating other existing evidence of crimes and other perpetrators. It depends on the Prosecutor in what light the co-operation of the defendant will be presented. But the assessment on whether the co-operation with the Prosecutor was a "substantial cooperation" within the meaning of the provisions of Rule 101(B) is the responsibility of the judges.

---

[105] Combs (2003), pp. 929–933.

[106] *Prosecutor v. Bralo*, IT-95-17, Trial Chamber, 7 December 2005, § 73.

At the initial stage after introduction of this provision, it could not be concluded that when a defendant pleaded guilty and offered to co-operate with the Prosecutor, his co-operation would always be considered "substantial" and as such would be rewarded during sentencing. In *Prosecutor v. Jelisić*, the defendant pleaded guilty against the advice of his defence attorney, believing that his plea would be deemed to constitute a "substantial" co-operation with the Prosecutor.[107] Moreover, he did so despite the Prosecutor's statement that the prosecution could not offer anything in return, as they did not believe the co-operation to be substantial. In fact, the Prosecutor insisted on a life sentence.[108] And although the Trial Chamber did not grant the prosecution's request, it punished the defendant severely enough for him to feel deceived—with 40 years of imprisonment. It stated that although it must consider the accused's guilty plea out of principle, at the same time it could not ignore the photographs produced at trial that showed the accused committing crimes. Therefore "only relative weight" was given to his plea.

However, after the sentence in *Prosecutor v. Plavšić* and the Security Council Resolution setting the completion strategy, the Tribunal was willing to acknowledge the consistently increasing impact of co-operation with the Prosecutor on the mitigation of the sentence. As early as in 2003, in *Prosecutor v. Banović*,[109] the judges found that even the defendant's will to co-operate with the Prosecutor may, in certain circumstances, be a sign of co-operation, however modest. It was also found that pursuant to the Rules of Procedure and Evidence, even the promise of co-operation itself might be taken into account as a factor mitigating the sentence, provided it has been fulfilled. Also in *Prosecutor v. Vasiljević*,[110] the Trial Chamber indicated that the fact that the accused did make such a statement may in itself in some cases be a sign of co-operation, however modest. Although the Trial Chamber was not satisfied (neither was the Prosecutor) that the statement given by the accused represented "substantial" co-operation pursuant to Rule 101(B)(ii), at the same time it stressed that it did not interpret Rule 101(B)(ii) as excluding the possibility of taking into account such co-operation in mitigation unless such was "substantial". Next year, in *Prosecutor v. Bralo*, judges found that despite the fact that there is no evidence of "substantial" co-operation from the accused with the prosecution, there is still evidence of "some co-operation", in the form of provision of documents and a willingness to give information. Therefore, it is possible to consider even such moderate co-operation as a mitigating factor.[111] At the same time, they indicated that his willingness to give oral or written testimony in future

[107] *Prosecutor v. Jelisić*, IT-95-10, Trial Chamber, 14 December 1999, § 127.

[108] As it will be later explained, the prosecution did withdraw 8 of the 39 counts of war crimes and crimes against humanity, but it did so as a result of evidentiary deficiencies, not to grant *Jelisić* a concession—the history of this defendant presented in: Combs (2007), p. 62; and Combs (2002), pp. 115–117 and 142.

[109] *Prosecutor v. Banović*, IT-02-65/1, Trial Chamber, 28 October 2003, § 68.

[110] *Prosecutor v. Vasiljević*, IT-98-32, Appeal Chamber, 25 February 2004, § 299.

[111] *Prosecutor v. Bralo*, IT-95-17, Trial Chamber, 7 December 2005, § 81.

cases had a limited value, for it did not go beyond what was required of any individual who was called to give evidence to the Tribunal. However, in 2007 in *Prosecutor v. Zelenović* not only actual co-operation was rewarded but also the sole commitment to co-operate. In this case, the accused had not had the opportunity to demonstrate his co-operation in practice because of the short time period that had elapsed since the guilty plea, but nevertheless the defence asked the Trial Chamber to give full effect to the factor of "expressed intention" to co-operate. The Trial Chamber—surprisingly—concluded that even if due to the particular experiences of the convicted person his or her full and sincere assistance is judged to be of little or no value to ongoing investigations or trials, still some weight should be attached to this factor.[112] With the passage of time, each sign of the defendant's interest in co-operation with the Tribunal was more and more manifestly rewarded.

Similarly as before the ICTY, the judges of the ICTR Trial Chamber are obliged to take into consideration both the guilty plea and any mitigating circumstances, including "the substantial cooperation with the Prosecutor by the convicted person before or after conviction" (Rule 101(B)(ii)) RPE ICTR). The judges of the ICTR emphasised that the guilty plea and co-operation with the Prosecutor may not, in any way, affect the criminal responsibility of a defendant otherwise than as only one of the circumstances evaluated by the court when sentencing. However, even in the case law of this Tribunal it might be seen that the impact of the defendant's co-operation on the sentence tended to increase with time. In general, the ICTR was much less prone to make concessions to defendants than the ICTY.

The defendants who could potentially plead guilty were discouraged to do so by the consequences of the first guilty plea. The prime minister of Rwanda, Jean Kambanda, pleaded guilty and agreed to co-operate substantially with the Tribunal.[113] The Prosecutor requested the Trial Chamber to take into consideration the fact that Jean Kambanda has extended substantial co-operation and invaluable information to the Prosecutor (almost 90 h of testimony). The Prosecutor indicated that not only the co-operation in his own case before the trial should be regarded as a significant mitigating factor but also the future co-operation when the accused undertook to testify for the prosecution in the trials of other accused. At the same time, in the plea agreement submitted to the court the parties stated that "no agreements, understandings or promises have been made between the parties with respect to sentence". The Prosecutor was confronted with a difficult task: he had to reward the co-operation provided by the defendant if he wanted to encourage other defendants to co-operate and to plead guilty, but he could not ignore the nature of the crimes committed by the defendant. He demanded life imprisonment. Despite the substantial co-operation with the Prosecutor, the defendant was sentenced to this penalty. The Trial Chamber expressed the view that a finding of mitigating circumstances, such as a guilty plea, relates to assessment of sentence and in no way derogates from the gravity of the crime. It mitigates punishment, not the crime: "It

[112] *Prosecutor v. Zelenović*, IT-96-23/2, Appeals Chamber, 31 October 2007, § 68.

[113] *Prosecutor v. Jean Kambanda*, ICTR 97-23-S, Trial Chamber, 4 September 1998.

must be observed that mitigation of punishment does not in any sense of the word reduce the degree of the crime (. . .). The degree of magnitude of the crime is still an essential criterion for evaluation of sentence". In the submitted appeal, the defendant raised that before pleading guilty he should have been informed that he would be subject to a life imprisonment penalty for the crimes he had committed in each case and this could not have been changed by pleading guilty. The Appeals Chamber did not agree with this view. It stated that this sentence falls within the discretionary framework provided by the Statute and the Rules, and so it sees no reason to disturb the decision of the Trial Chamber, which was correct to assume that "the aggravating circumstances surrounding the crimes negate the mitigating circumstances".

One year later, a guilty plea made in *Prosecutor v. Serushago* had a diametrically different effect.[114] The co-operation in this case could be considered a model one. Even prior to his detention, the defendant provided the Prosecutor with access to information that made it possible to organise an operation to capture a number of persons suspected of committing war crimes during the civil war. He also committed himself to testify as the prosecution's witness in other trials pending before the Tribunal. He pleaded guilty to 4 out of 5 counts included in the indictment. Ultimately, he was sentenced to 15 years of imprisonment. The judges took into consideration the factors established by the *Prosecutor v. Erdemović* case and expressed their opinion "that exceptional circumstances in mitigation surrounding the crimes committed by Omar Serushago may afford him some clemency". They stressed that the accused voluntarily surrendered to the authorities of Côte d'Ivoire, although he had not yet been indicted by the Tribunal and was not included in the list of suspects wanted by Rwandan authorities, being fully aware of the fact that his surrender would lead to his indictment; his co-operation with the Prosecutor was substantial and ongoing; he has agreed to testify as a witness for the prosecution in other trials pending before the Tribunal, is a father of six children and expressed his remorse at length and openly. It is also noteworthy that the defendant was not satisfied with this sentence; in his appeal, he complained that despite his guilty plea he had been convicted for 15 years of imprisonment, whereas the sentence in *Prosecutor v. Erdemović* issued by the ICTY amounted to 5 years. The Appeals Court, however, upheld the judgment, emphasising the gravity of the committed crimes. The breakthrough in the ICTR case law came only with pronouncing the sentence in *Prosecutor v. Rutaganira*,[115] in which the Tribunal significantly mitigated the sentence as a consequence of the guilty plea. This change manifested itself also later, in *Prosecutor v. Bisengimana*, where the Prosecutor significantly

[114] *Prosecutor v. Serushago*, ICTR-98-39, Trial Chamber, 5 February 1999. In detail in: Bohlander (2001), p. 152.

[115] *Prosecutor v. Vincent Rutaganira*, ICTR-95-1C-T, Trial Chamber, 14 March 2005. Also in this case the accused did not appeal, what could have confirmed the authenticity of the expressed remorse.

altered the contents of charges in return for the co-operation offered by the defendant.

The proceedings before the ICTR clearly show that the Prosecutor himself supported the accused as the person who "may submit any relevant information that may assist the Trial Chamber in determining an appropriate sentence" (Rule 100(A)). He also raised the point that the information disclosed by the defendant constituted a "substantial" contribution to the case, as it resolved a lot of doubts and also disclosed crimes previously unknown to the prosecution. It happened, for example, in *Prosecutor v. Serugendo*,[116] in which the Prosecutor concluded the agreement with the defendant and in which he indicated that the defendant deserved a "credit of trust" for the early guilty plea and, in consequence, saving the Tribunal's modest funds. In *Prosecutor v. Bisengimana*, at the stage of judicial proceedings the Prosecutor indicated the necessity for a more lenient treatment of the defendant who pleaded guilty.[117] It was the Prosecutor who emphasised that pleading guilty was not only considered a factor mitigating the criminal responsibility in the majority of legal systems but also that, in the case at hand, it could contribute to the process of national reconciliation, as only disclosing the entire truth on the crimes would allow the nation to regain its unity. He also argued that it would provide an incentive for other defendants. The entire Trial Chamber agreed with these arguments emphasising, as usual, the defendant's sincere remorse and true intention to contribute to reconciliation. In this case, the defendant did not file an appeal, which might be the best indication of the sincerity of his remorse for having been involved in the crimes.

6.2.5 Procedural Agreements

The regulations underlying the functioning of the *ad hoc* tribunals did not provide for the possibility to conclude procedural agreements that could result in an alteration of the contents of charges or a reduction of the sentence. The impact of the ICTY Prosecutor on the merits of the judgment was, therefore, minor, apart from the possibility of informing the Tribunal that the defendant had co-operated with the prosecution in a "substantial" manner.

It turned out in practice, however, that—regardless of the absence of a statutory basis—the defence and prosecution did conclude agreements that resulted in the reduction of charges or in a request for a lower sentence as a result of the defendant's guilty plea. The growth in the number of such cases was affected by the factors pertaining to both parties to the agreement. On the one hand, defendants saw the growing significance of the guilty plea in the mitigation of the sentence as

[116] *Prosecutor v. Joseph Serugendo*, ICTR-2005-84-I, Trial Chamber, 12 June 2006, § 38. In more detail: Combs (2002), pp. 135–136.

[117] *Prosecutor v. Paul Bisengimana*, ICTR-00-60, Trial Chamber, 13 April 2006, § 128–131.

an encouragement. The prosecution, on the other hand, had to meet the busy schedule of the Tribunal and take into account its limited funds.[118] No wonder this practice had to be regulated and reflected in provisions. As a result, the subsequent amendment of the Rules of Procedure and Evidence led to the adoption of solutions already known in the common law states.

Rule 62ter adopted on 13 December 2001 provides that

> The Prosecutor and the defence may agree that, upon the accused entering a plea of guilty to the indictment or to one or more counts of the indictment, the Prosecutor shall do one or more of the following before the Trial Chamber:
>
> a) apply to amend the indictment accordingly;
> b) submit that a specific sentence or sentencing range is appropriate;
> c) not oppose a request by the accused for a particular sentence or sentencing range.

The judges should be informed about concluding such an agreement on the basis of Rule 100(A), similarly as about the scope of co-operation with the Prosecutor. The Prosecutor may at the same time request the mitigation of a sentence, referring to the defendant's co-operation and his guilty plea, as well as to the conclusion of an agreement. The significance of such an agreement should be evaluated in the light of Rule 62ter(B) RPE ICTY. According to this provision, even if such an agreement is concluded, the Trial Chamber shall not be bound by it.

This provision laid foundations for the adoption of a specific consensual model of termination of the case, offering a legal basis for negotiations between the Prosecutor and the defendant. It is of utmost importance for the ICTY Prosecutor's ability to act and the scope of his powers. It may not be assumed, however, that there is a consensus regarding the fact that all forms of plea bargaining known from the common law tradition may be applied by the ICTY Prosecutor.

Pursuant to the first approach, the *charge bargaining* institution, or dropping some of the charges in a situation where the defendant pleaded guilty to other charges,[119] turned out to be the basic mechanism whereby the Prosecutor may influence the substantive contents of a judgment before the ICTY. This approach acknowledges that at the stage of investigation, this practice is allowed without any limitations. This assumption finds confirmation in the practice. In 2001, in *Prosecutor v. Todorović*, the prosecution employed charge bargaining for the first time (despite the lack of a legal basis for conducting this type of negotiations).[120] The accused agreed to plead guilty to one count of a crime against humanity, promised to testify against his co-defendants and (what was considered to be his bargaining chip) to withdraw his motion challenging the legality of his arrest by the NATO troops. The prosecution, for its part, withdrew the remaining 26 counts of charges and agreed to recommend a sentence between 5 and 12 years to the Trial Chamber. The Trial Chamber sentenced the defendant to 10 years' imprisonment,

[118] See: Combs (2007), p. 62; Tochilovsky (2008), pp. 264–265.

[119] Harmon (2009), p. 169. Also in: Boas et al. (2011), p. 221.

[120] *Prosecutor v. Todorović*, IT-95-9/1, Trial Chamber, 31 July 2001, § 79. More details in: Combs (2002), pp. 120–121. Also in: Knoops (2005), p. 262.

emphasising the significance of his co-operation with the Prosecutor and of his guilty plea. In *Prosecutor v. Simić*,[121] upon presentation of the indictment by the Prosecutor, the defendant pleaded guilty to the more serious of the charged crimes. The Prosecutor amended the indictment, removing from it the offences to which the defendant had not pleaded guilty (he already had a legal basis at his disposal in the form of Rule 62ter). In this case, the defendant was sentenced to 5 years' imprisonment, which fell within the limits of the prosecution's motion (between 3 and 5 years). Also in *Prosecutor v. Obrenović*, the sentence was within the limits postulated by the Prosecutor.[122]

Another applicable variant of the plea bargaining institution is *fact bargaining*, involving replacement of one charge with another, as, for example, in *Prosecutor v. Plavšić*, where the accused voluntarily surrendered to the ICTY, and, even before the trial commenced, she pleaded guilty to one count of persecution as a crime against humanity. The prosecution dropped the remaining seven charges, including the genocide charges.[123] In *Prosecutor v. Deronjić*, in which the judgment was delivered in 2004, the charges pertaining to serious crimes committed under ethnic cleansing[124] were dismissed. Even the Prosecutor admitted that the limitation of charges was motivated by practical reasons—in this case, the necessity to expedite the proceedings. The Tribunal accepted the Prosecutor's tactics and limited the proceedings only to the acts charged in the indictment. In the convicting verdict, it indicated that holding the defendant responsible for other acts would require a lengthy trial and extensive funding. As the procedural agreement was executed prior to the commencement of the judicial proceedings, the trial did not take place. Later on, the correctness and the scope of the concluded agreement were questioned as it turned out during the initial hearing before the Tribunal that the contents of the indictment differed significantly from the scope of the defendant's plea, especially as regards the fact whether or not the defendant was present at the crime scene. Ultimately, however, the Tribunal decided that these differences had been satisfactorily explained by the defendant, and the judges moved immediately to sentencing (10 years).

However, there is also an opinion that neither *fact bargaining* nor *charge bargaining* may be applied before the ICTY and—as a matter of fact—that it has not been used by this Tribunal. Indeed, these notions have never been used by the Tribunal. According to its representatives, each time the ICTY Prosecutor decided to dismiss proceedings in relation to specific charges, he did so in the absence of sufficient evidence or because the charges to which a defendant pleaded guilty covered all of the incriminated acts and not because dropping charges took place.[125]

[121] *Prosecutor v. Simić*, IT-95-9/2, Trial Chamber, 17 October 2002. Noteworthy, on the 4th of November 2003 the convicted was conditionally released.

[122] *Prosecutor v. Obrenović*, IT-02-60/2, Trial Chamber, 10 December 2003.

[123] *Prosecutor v. Plavšić*, IT-00-39 & 40/1, Appeals Chamber, 27 February 2003, § 66–81.

[124] *Prosecutor v. Deronjić*, IT-02-61, Trial Chamber, 25 July 2005.

[125] See: Combs (2002), p. 140.

For instance, in *Prosecutor v. Simić*, it was emphasised that the disability of the defendant prevented carrying out a trial in normal conditions and allowed him only to be interrogated by means of a video connection established between the courtroom and the ICTY detention unit in The Hague. In its judgment, the Trial Chamber explained that the defendant would have received a much more severe punishment than the one requested by the Prosecutor in the agreement executed with the defendant[126] but for the aforementioned problems. In *Prosecutor v. Bralo*, the Prosecutor filed a plea agreement and the indictment was amended in the consequence of concluding the agreement. The agreement stated that the accused and the prosecution agree that the guilty plea "represents a full accounting of the accused's criminal behaviour for the events charged" and that "no promises or inducements have been made by the Prosecutor" to persuade him to enter into the agreement".[127] In *Prosecutor v. Todorović*, "although the withdrawal of 26 of 27 counts would seem a substantial prosecutorial concession, in fact, it had limited significance because the one count to which Todorović pleaded guilty encompassed the offences contained in the other 26 counts".[128]

It should be kept in mind that the Prosecutor's competence to reduce the number of charges or influence their contents needs to be taken together with the Trial Chamber's power to control the use of this competence. The Prosecutor is obliged to present to the judges, in addition to the agreement, the original indictment as it was presented to the defendant. If such an obligation did not exist, the Chamber would not be able to determine whether the Prosecutor dropped certain charges in exchange for the defendant pleading guilty or because he did not have sufficient evidence. The indictment drafted as a result of the conclusion of an agreement between parties may serve as a basis for sentencing only upon the consent of the Trial Chamber. If the judges reject the amendments made to an indictment as a result of the execution of an agreement, the procedural agreement ceases to be valid and binding upon the parties. Thus, it is ultimately up to the court to offer the defendant any concessions. First, the court has the right not to accept the presentation of a limited scope of charges by the Prosecutor and may insist on the presentation of supplementary charges reflecting the total criminal conduct of the defendant. Second, it is the court that imposes a penalty taking into account the fact of co-operation with the prosecutor if it deems it appropriate.

In the *Prosecutor v. Todorović* case, the judges stressed that "although the Plea Agreement does indicate a range within which the parties have agreed Todorović's sentence should fall, the Trial Chamber reiterates that it is in no way bound by this agreement. It is the Chamber's responsibility to determine an appropriate sentence in this case".[129] Also in *Prosecutor v. Nikolić*, the Trial Chamber rejected the Prosecutor's request for a more lenient sentence.[130] It stated that it cannot accept

[126] *Prosecutor v. Simić*, IT-95-9/2, Trial Chamber, 17 October 2002, § 84.

[127] *Prosecutor v. Bralo*, IT-95-17, Trial Chamber, 7 December 2005, § 6.

[128] Cit. after: Combs (2002), p. 120.

[129] *Prosecutor v. Todorović*, IT-95-9/1, Trial Chamber, 31 July 2001, § 79.

[130] *Prosecutor v. Momir Nikolić*, IT-02-60/1, Trial Chamber, 2 December 2003, § 156.

the sentence recommended by the prosecution (between 15 and 20 years) as it does not adequately reflect the totality of the criminal conduct for which the accused has been convicted and sentenced the accused to 27 years imprisonment. The Chamber emphasised the significant role of the defendant in the committed crimes. It also made an assessment of the credibility of Momir Nikolić, which ultimately impacts upon the value of such co-operation, and found that in numerous instances the testimony of Momir Nikolić was evasive, which should be treated as an indication that his willingness to co-operate does not translate into being fully forthcoming in relation to all the events, given his position and knowledge. In view of the other judgments issued in cases in which procedural agreements had been executed with the Prosecutor, it should be concluded that the verdict in *Prosecutor v. Nikolić* did not represent a permanent adjudicating line but was rather a signal that the judges took into account all circumstances of a case and that they did not accept automatically agreements concluded with the prosecutor (it is noteworthy that this judgment was delivered by a bench dominated by judges from continental legal orders). This sentence was, however, reduced by the Appeals Chamber—which found that the Trial Chamber committed several discernible errors when assessing the appellant's co-operation with the prosecution by failing to attach sufficient weight to the mitigating circumstance of his co-operation with the prosecution—to 20 years of imprisonment.[131]

Therefore, the Prosecutor's role in the ultimate outcome of a case may be significant, but only provided that the court is willing to accept the results of the defendant's co-operation. According to the judges of the Appeals Chamber, despite the fact that the prosecution is in a position to accurately assess the co-operation of an accused, the evaluation of the extent and nature of the accused's co-operation, and thus the weight, if any, to be given to this mitigating circumstance, is within the discretion of the Trial Chamber.[132] In most cases, the Trial Chamber agrees with the assessment made by the Prosecutor. However, there is always a risk for the accused, and he cannot be sure about the outcomes of the proceedings after the bargain.

6.2.6 *Evaluation of the Consensual Termination of a Case*

It may be noticed that the *ad hoc* tribunals were not entirely faithful to the principles adopted when they were first established. The early ICTY's policy explicitly rejected bargaining. However, after the initial period of strict adherence to the assumption that pleading guilty could not, in any way, affect the course of the proceedings and that there was no basis to conclude procedural agreements, this approach has undergone changes—first in the adjudicating line of the ICTY and

[131] *Prosecutor v. Momir Nikolić*, IT-02-60/1, Appeals Chamber, 8 March 2006, § 98–115. See for more details: Combs (2007), pp. 79 et seq.

[132] *Prosecutor v. Dragan Nikolić*, IT-94-2-A, Appeals Chamber, 4 February 2005, § 89.

subsequently in statutory provisions. These changes undoubtedly represented a triumph of pragmatism.[133] In the initial period of the Tribunal's operation, the defendants did not, indeed, plead guilty, knowing that this would not bring them any procedural benefits. It was not until the issue of the verdict in *Prosecutor v. Erdemović* and then the incorporation of Rule 62ter RPE ICTY to the Rules of Procedure and Evidence that each subsequent guilty plea leads to the concluding of an agreement with the Prosecutor. The judges, on the other hand, were quite willing to grant the Prosecutor's motions to impose a lower sentence following the defendant pleading guilty. While in the earliest cases the judges made only minor concessions due to the execution of an agreement, later on the impact of the agreement on a sentence became significant. As this influence continued to grow, the willingness of defendants to plead guilty and offer information that could become a factor of "substantial cooperation" with the Prosecutor influencing the imposed sentence increased.

When we consider the significant concessions the *ad hoc* tribunals make to defendants who plead guilty and their willingness to adjudicate on procedural agreements, it is worth mentioning that there were two non-legal factors that may have had the greatest impact on the introduction of the consensual termination of the case in the present shape.

First, we cannot omit the relationship between the publication of the Security Council resolution adopting a completion strategy for the closing down of the Tribunal[134] and the subsequent guilty pleas. The resolution calls "on the ICTY and the ICTR to take all possible measures to complete investigations by the end of 2004, to complete all trial activities at first instance by the end of 2008, and to complete all work in 2010". In effect, we have seen that in 2003 there were 5 guilty pleas, on January 2004–5, then by the end of 2008 a further 3, as compared to the number of pleas recorded in 1993–2001 (2) and in 2001 (4). It was observed that after 2003 the sentences of the Tribunal had become significantly more lenient compared to the earlier practice.[135] The Tribunal was delivering sentences that were two times lower for almost the same crimes. For instance, in *Prosecutor v. Jelisić*[136] of 2001, the sentence imposed was 40 years' imprisonment, and in *Prosecutor v. Dragan Nikolić*[137] in 2005, the imposed sentence for almost the same

[133] Jørgensen (2002), p. 407. And they were often seen as a symptom of the "Americanisation of the procedural system of the ICC through the introduction of plea bargaining mechanism"—see: Langer (2004).

[134] Resolution of the Security Council No. S/RES/1503 (2003), § 5–6, http://www.icty.org/x/file/Legal%20Library/Statute/statute_1503_2003_en.pdf. Accessed 12 Feb 2015; No. 1534 S/RES/1534 (2004), § 5, http://www.icty.org/x/file/Legal%20Library/Statute/statute_1534_2004_en.pdf. Accessed 12 Feb 2015 and then Resolution No. 1966, S/RES/1966(2010), § 3, which called on the tribunals to take all possible measures to expeditiously complete all their remaining work as provided by this resolution no later than 31 December 2014.

[135] Data found in: Combs (2002), pp. 29–30 and 76. The same conclusion can be found in: Raab (2005), p. 86 and Schuon (2010), pp. 202–203.

[136] *Prosecutor v. Jelisić*, IT-95-10, Trial Chamber, 5 July 2001.

[137] *Prosecutor v. Dragan Nikolić*, IT-94-24, Trial Chamber, 4 February 2005.

crime was 27 years' imprisonment. In addition to prosecuting only the highest ranking government officials and handing the prosecution of other perpetrators over to national courts, the consensual termination of a case became the third method of expediting trial and coping with the lengthy proceedings and the necessity to complete activities within a specific deadline.

The second group of factors that led to the broad application of the consensual disposition of a case were practical reasons and, more specifically, financial ones. Prior to 2003, which marked the introduction of procedural agreements, the ICTY spent US$650 million in 10 years of its operation, for hearing 18 cases. In turn, within the first 10 years of its operation, the ICTR spent over US$800 million for hearing 19 cases. On average, there were 100 witnesses involved in a case and the proceedings lasted 17 months, with their course being recorded on 10,000 pages.[138] As a result, financial issues became the main motivation behind the Tribunals' reaching for Anglo-Saxon solutions. Nearly all of the ICTY's sentencing judgments based on a guilty plea include an appreciative remark that the accused saved the Tribunal's considerable resources. The international criminal tribunals, as was similarly the case in the United States, had to face the problem of cost-effectiveness of the administration of justice. There was a question as to which was a better solution: to serve more lenient sentences to 10 persons, thus preventing their impunity, or to convict one person in a full-blown trial, sentencing him to 50 years of imprisonment, at the same cost. It was obvious that in the latter case, the remaining perpetrators would go unpunished. In the former case, on the other hand, the sense of justice could also be compromised, as the perpetrators of the most serious international law crimes would be released after having served only a few years in prison. It has been underlined that while savings of time and resources may be a result of guilty pleas, this consideration should not be the main reason for promoting guilty pleas through plea agreements.[139]

It may be noticed that the case law of the *ad hoc* tribunals lacked consistency in relation to treating a plea of guilty and co-operation with the Prosecutor as mitigating factors and to observing agreements concluded with the Prosecutor. On numerous occasions, the judges issued a sentence that went far beyond the expectations of both the defendant and even the sentence requested by the Prosecutor pursuant to an agreement. Despite what was said before, it is very difficult to determine what factors and to what extent they will affect the sentence in a specific case. The legal science suggested that uniform standards should be introduced in order to ensure higher predictability of adjudication. These standards could, for example, help to establish the mitigating effects of a guilty plea provided during an investigation versus a guilty plea provided at trial.[140] In the current situation, the

[138] Data found in: Combs (2007), pp. 28–40, and repeated in Combs (2003), p. 935. It is estimated that 17 years of the functioning of the ICTY consumed approx. US$1.5 million—so: Kranz (2009), p. 217.

[139] *Prosecutor v. Momir Nikolić*, IT-02-60/1, Trial Chamber, § 67.

[140] Beresford (2001), p. 65.

final sentence is always uncertain, and in consequence, the Prosecutor's task is extremely difficult. First, the judges are not obliged to take into account the agreement concluded with the defendant. Second, even if they do take it into account, there is no guarantee that they will deliver the sentence recommended by the Prosecutor. They do not have to consider the co-operation with the prosecution to be "significant" within the meaning of the Rules of the Procedure and Evidence and, as such, use it to issue a more lenient sentence. As a result, the Prosecutor may not guarantee the defendant that the sentence will reflect their arrangements. Neither can he promise that the Trial Chamber will agree to rule pursuant to an indictment limited to the charges to which the defendant pleaded guilty. And there's no doubt that enforceability of a concluded agreement provides the main basis for the Prosecutor's impact on the consensual disposition of criminal proceedings.

6.3 Model of Consensual Termination of Proceedings Before the ICC

6.3.1 Pleading Guilty: Procedural Consequences

The model of indictment before the ICC does not provide for an option for a consensual termination of proceedings pursuant to an agreement concluded between the ICC Prosecutor and the defendant. First, the Statute does not envisage any basis for the guilty plea to have procedural effects such as elimination of a trial or reduction of a sentence. Second, no legal basis has been provided for the concluding of a procedural agreement that would offer the possibility of any major concessions in return for pleading guilty.

The issue of procedural consequences of the defendant's guilty plea has become one of the basic points of dispute between representatives of the two legal traditions. The original draft of the Rome Statute suggested the introduction of a solution modelled after the institution existing in the United States, pursuant to which if the defendant pleads guilty, his case is not sent to trial but is moved straight to the sentencing stage. This solution was praised for its ability to prevent the lengthy and costly trials that had become a part of the *ad hoc* tribunals' experience. Proponents of this solution underlined obvious savings of time and funds, possible due to the elimination of evidentiary proceedings when the defendant pleaded guilty and also the possibility to obtain information on the circumstances of committed crimes and co-perpetrators due to encouraging the defendant to co-operation. It was also argued that the solution enabled reconciliation between the defendant regretting his acts and the victim. This solution was, however, widely criticised by the majority of national delegations, especially those coming from continental law systems. They demanded that any references to the possibility of concluding procedural agreements and shortening of proceedings as a result of a guilty plea should be eliminated from the Statute. They indicated that the plea bargaining institution was not consistent with the gravity of cases heard by an international tribunal. In their opinion, a judge needed to consider all evidence presented in a case, while a guilty plea was only a small part of it. An implementation of the basis for application of plea bargaining into the trial before the ICC would constitute a denial of the principle of the material truth, while the application of charge bargaining would allow perpetrators of the most serious crimes of international law to avoid responsibility. Moreover, there would always be a suspicion that the Prosecutor agreed to conclude an agreement for not having insufficient evidence to support the charges brought.[141]

In the end, when defining the consequences of pleading guilty, it was decided that the solution known from continental law systems should be applied. Of key importance here was the assumption that a guilty plea should never lead to elimination of the trial stage and moving to the sentencing stage, which is the practice employed before the ICTY. The defendant's pleading guilty may expedite the evidentiary proceedings and, later at the sentencing stage, be treated as a mitigating factor, but it never results in an elimination of trial and presentation of evidence. In this way, it was emphasised that the Tribunal could not accept the guilty plea as a means to release itself from the obligation to look for the material truth. At the same time, a new concept—the *admission of guilt*—was introduced to replace that of a *guilty plea*, which was a way to highlight the differences between this concept and the *plea bargaining* system known from the Anglo-Saxon tradition and to emphasise the non-binding nature of this statement for the court. It should also be noted that the authors were also reluctant to borrow from continental jargon and avoided using the notion of *confession*.[142] Another feature of this solution that should not escape our attention is that the final version of the Rome Statute was approved even before the implementation of Rule 62ter in the ICTY Rules of Procedure and Evidence, which established foundations to concluding procedural agreements before the ICTY.

According to Article 64(8)(a) of the Rome Statute, at the commencement of the trial, when the Trial Chamber has read to the accused the charges previously confirmed by the Pre-Trial Chamber, the accused is offered the opportunity to make an admission of guilt. It means that the only way to exert an impact on the course of a trial is by admitting guilt at the stage of proceedings specified in the Statute. Doing so at any other stage of proceedings does not have procedural consequences. Only the judges can decide whether the admission of guilt will result in shortening of proceedings. When the defendant decides to make such a statement, the Trial Chamber has three options:

[141] See for the complete picture of the course of negotiation on the shape of admission of guilt: Guariglia and Hochmayr (2008), p. 1220; Płachta (2004b), pp. 703–704; Safferling (2001), p. 275; Schabas (2010), pp. 775–776.

[142] As claimed alike by: Orie (2002), pp. 1480–1481; D'Ascoli (2011), p. 278; Bohlander (2001), pp. 156–158.

(1) when it is satisfied that the necessary conditions have been fulfilled, it may convict the accused;
(2) when it is not satisfied that the conditions have been fulfilled, it shall consider the admission of guilt as not having been made and it shall order that the trial be continued under the ordinary trial procedures;
(3) it may also require a more complete presentation of the facts of the case.

In the first case, the Trial Chamber must determine whether three conditions have been satisfied:

(a) the accused understands the nature and consequences of the admission of guilt;
(b) the admission is voluntarily made by the accused after sufficient consultation with defence counsel;
(c) the admission of guilt is supported by the facts of the case that are contained in

    (1) the charges brought by the Prosecutor and admitted by the accused;
    (2) any materials presented by the Prosecutor that supplement the charges and that the accused accepts;
    (3) any other evidence, such as the testimony of witnesses, presented by the Prosecutor or the accused.

The basic condition for shortening the presentation of evidence as a result of the admission of guilt is to examine whether the admission of guilt is supported by the facts of the case—both collected by the Prosecutor during an investigation and presented by the accused. It is only when the Trial Chamber is satisfied that the explanations of the accused find confirmation in the evidentiary material presented to the court by both parties that it may accept the admission of guilt and may convict the accused.

As far as this obligation is concerned, there are two major questions. First, there are some doubts as to the degree to which offences charged to the defendant have been proven or the question about the evidentiary standard that needs to be adopted. Some authors even indicate that the Trial Chamber must ascertain that there is sufficient evidentiary basis to "warrant a conviction if the defendant were to stand trial".[143] Thus, conviction on the basis of the admission of guilt would be possible only when the judges become certain that the guilt has been proven beyond any reasonable doubt in respect of all charges included in an indictment pursuant to Article 66 of the Rome Statute.

The second question is whether, if the Trial Chamber's task is seen this way, the Chamber should be obliged to conduct evidentiary proceedings or whether—to acknowledge that the admission of guilt is supported by evidentiary material—it is sufficient for the Chamber to rule on the basis of the evidence presented by the parties. The Statute does not provide for a mandatory elimination of evidentiary proceedings. Neither, however, does it provide for an obligation to conduct such proceedings, leaving the decision to the judges. The Trial Chamber, in order to

[143] So: Guariglia and Hochmayr (2008), p. 1229.

decide which of the three procedures to choose, may request the Prosecutor to present additional evidence, including the testimony of witnesses, and also invite the views of the Prosecutor and the defence (Rule 139 RPE ICC).[144] The opinions and supplementary evidence are to be decisive of a decision whether the admission of guilt is in compliance with the facts of the case and the truth and what decision should be taken on the admission of guilt. In case it is found that the prosecutor has not presented any additional evidence or that the evidence is still insufficient to determine whether the defendant is guilty or not, the Trial Chamber orders a further trial. In such a case, it shall consider the admission of guilt as "not having been made". The Rules of Procedure and Evidence do not specify whether the prosecutor's failure to respond to a request for presenting additional information will always lead to the Trial Chamber finding the admission of guilt as not having been made or whether it would be so only in a situation where the supplementary evidence is still not sufficient to convict the defendant. However, the wording of the provision seems clear, and the lack of prosecutorial response should always result in such a sanction.

When the Trial Chamber finds that the prosecution's charges are not consistent with the defendant's explanations or when the admission of guilt is not supported by the evidence of the case, it always considers the admission of guilt as not having been made. In such a case, it conducts evidentiary proceedings in such a way as if the defendant had pleaded innocent: "it shall order that the trial be continued under the ordinary trial procedures". Judges who took this decision have the right to refuse to adjudicate in such a case, for there may be doubts about their impartiality, as they had previously witnessed the admission of guilt by the defendant. The case may be remitted to another Trial Chamber.

The Trial Chamber finds that the admission of guilt is supported by the facts of the case only when it is clear to what extent and relative to which charges the defendant has pleaded guilty. If the accused admits guilt only for certain charges but not for others, it will be necessary to conduct evidentiary proceedings in relation to the remaining ones. The Trial Chamber could convict the accused of the crimes in relation to which he has made an admission of guilt and hold trial for the remaining charges.[145] If this would be the case, it would be possible to separate trials. There is also another option: concluding that it would not be appropriate to disaggregate the charges and it is necessary to have a full presentation of facts of the case in the interests of justice.[146] The Trial Chamber may refuse to accept the partial admission of guilt. It results *de facto* in considering the guilty plea to be invalid and proceedings as if it has not been made. It will be so when separate examination of charges presented in a case is impossible.[147] The third option

[144] Lewis (2001), p. 547.

[145] See: Terrier (2002), p. 1287.

[146] Examples of such a solution can be found in the case law of the ICTY, e.g. in: *Prosecutor v. Jelisić*, IT-95-10-T, Trial Chamber, 14 December 1999, § 127.

[147] See: Guariglia and Hochmayr (2008), p. 1230.

provides for withdrawal of the remaining charges by the Prosecutor. Such a decision would, however, require the Prosecutor to seek permission of the Trial Chamber to withdraw charges after the commencement of trial. The wording of Article 65(5) of the Rome Statue does not impose on the judges an obligation to consent to withdrawal of charges; it does not, however, prohibit them from doing so either. Therefore, it may be suspected that the provision concerning partial withdrawal of charges that are not covered by the admission of guilt may in the future lead to the Prosecutor (co-operating with Trial Chamber judges) using charge bargaining to consensually dispose of proceedings.[148] This has happened before in the adjudicating practice of the ICTY.

The third way the Trial Chamber may choose is to continue proceedings. Where it is of the opinion that a more complete presentation of the facts of the case is required in the interests of justice, in particular in the interests of the victims, it may decide to continue the trial under the ordinary trial procedures—despite the fact that the admission of guilt might be in compliance with the facts of the case. Also in this situation, the admission of guilt is considered as not having been made and the case may be remitted to another Trial Chamber. This provision enables the judges to conduct evidentiary proceedings and trial in order to determine the historical truth in the interests of justice. Although shortening of proceedings as a result of the admission of guilt does not distort history, it leads to presenting it "in a nutshell", whereas the role of the Court is to disclose the entire truth about the events that led to the commission of international law crimes. A full presentation of evidence may also be motivated by the care for the interests of victims who want to see the "administration of justice in action" and the perpetrator of the crime punished.[149] This solution enables the ICC to be more efficient in their efforts to determine the material truth than the ICTY, which, when the defendant pleads guilty, must only become convinced that independent sources provide sufficient evidence that crimes have been committed with the involvement of the defendant and that the defendant's explanations are consistent with the contents of the indictment.

Neither the Statute nor the RPE specially mentions that the admission of guilt may become a mitigating factor. However, on the basis of Rule 145(2)(a)(ii), which states that in the determination of the sentence the Court shall take into account as appropriate "the convicted person's conduct after the act, including any efforts by the person to compensate the victims and any cooperation with the Court", some authors conclude that it may take into consideration the admission of guilt as a mitigating factor or a sign of co-operation with the Tribunal. The practice of the ICTY and ICTR, which consequently considered guilty pleas as mitigating factors, would suggest that the ICC may adopt a similar practice.[150]

The discussion on the procedural consequences of a guilty plea in proceedings before the ICC has turned into a debate on the fundamental concept of the criminal

[148] See: Schabas (2010), p. 779.

[149] Terrier (2002), p. 1289; Orie (2002), p. 1489.

[150] Turner and Weigend (2013), p. 1391.

procedure and became an element of the polemics between the vision of the trial as a contest of equal parties (according to the concept of strictly adversarial trial) and a trial as a forum for arriving at the material truth (in compliance with foundations of tempered adversality of the continental trial). The parties to the discussion have also, however, stressed the diminishing differences between the assumptions of the different traditions of criminal proceedings, manifesting themselves in the growing significance of procedural agreements and consequences of the guilty plea in continental systems and in the demand for confirming the compliance of the guilty plea with the facts of a case in Anglo-Saxon states. These discussions have led this time not to reconciliation of the procedural solutions occurring in both legal traditions but to the development of a *sui generis* solution that would be best adapted to the needs of the Court.

6.3.2 Procedural Agreements

The execution of procedural agreements and the admission of guilt are treated as two separate issues in the proceedings before the ICC.

Article 65(5) of the Rome Statute provides that "any discussions between the Prosecutor and the defence regarding modification of the charges, the admission of guilt or the penalty to be imposed, shall not be binding on the Court". This provision was implemented at the final stage of the works on the Statute, and its aim was mainly to reassure the delegations from the continental systems that in no circumstances will the contents of the Rome Statute or the Rules of Procedure and Evidence "open the way to the introduction of plea-bargaining in the context of the Statute".[151]

This provision does not prohibit such plea bargains between the accused and the Prosecutor. Therefore, we can encounter opinions according to which despite the lack of procedural bases, charge bargaining is not explicitly prohibited and as such may be used by the Prosecutor. According to these opinions, it may even seem that, contrary to the intentions of its creators, the provision allows us to assume that negotiations may be conducted, with the reservation that the Court may set them aside: "ironically, the language in paragraph 5 presupposes exactly what it intends to avoid: the existence of discussions between the Prosecutor and the defence regarding modification of the charges, the admission of guilt or the penalty to be imposed".[152] Therefore, it is possible to undertake talks on the possible effects of a guilty plea as early as at the investigation stage.

[151] Guariglia and Hochmayr (2008), p. 1231.

[152] Cit. after: Guariglia and Hochmayr (2008), p. 1231. Similar conclusion in: Calvo-Goller (2006), p. 242. Friman (2003), pp. 373 and 393.

As in the case of general principles governing executing procedural agreements, finding what significant concessions the ICC Prosecutor may offer to the defendant is a basis for evaluation of the Prosecutor's impact on the consensual termination of criminal proceedings.

The ICC Prosecutor may, foremost, promise the defendant that he will file a request for a less severe sentence. This request is never binding for the judges. Therefore, it is claimed that, as the Prosecutor is in no position to guarantee a given outcome because his request is not binding on the court, this provision may be an insufficient encouragement for the defendant to plead guilty.[153] It is also worth indicating that in common law states and before the *ad hoc* tribunals, the contents of the agreement concluded between the prosecutor and the defendant, especially as regards the severity of a sentence, is not binding for the court either; however, the approval of this agreement by the court is usually a matter of judiciary custom and the practice adopted in a given legal system.

However, the basic competence of the Prosecutor is the appropriate drafting of charges, in which he may drop certain counts, while mitigating others. This competence arises from the adoption of the principle of opportunism in the proceedings before the ICC. The decision of who should be accused and what charges should be brought against him is solely the Prosecutor's responsibility. The Prosecutor also enjoys discretion in assessment of the premises in favour of and against the initiation of proceedings. As he always initiates the proceedings "in a case" on his own initiative, pursuant to information collected by himself or received from another source (including *notitia criminis* referred by the Security Council or a State Party to the Statute), he may, taking into account the gravity of the crime and the interests of justice, treat the potential defendants and the charges brought selectively. This power may lead the Prosecutor to acknowledge that it is possible to conclude agreements with the defendant.

The judicial authorities, however, always control whether charges are properly (correctly) drafted. First, the charges set the limits for hearing a case only when they are confirmed by the Pre-Trial Chamber. It was even adopted in recent case law that the Pre-Trial Chamber has the authority to change the legal characterisation of the facts charged by the Prosecutor in the indictment. Exercising such authority may obviously lead to the cancellation of the agreement concluded between the defendant and the Prosecutor if the Pre-Trial Chamber concludes that the charges, in the form presented by the Prosecutor to the defendant, need to be amended in terms of their legal characterisation. Second, it seems that it should be assumed that the Prosecutor is obliged to present to the Trial Chamber judges information that the charges have been amended, or drafted in a specific way as a result of the concluding of the agreement with the defendant, just as it is done before the ICTY. Without this requirement, they would not know if they are accepting results of "discussions between the Prosecutor and the defence". Hence, they would not be able to control the amendments made by the Prosecutor.

[153] See: Guariglia and Hochmayr (2008), p. 1232.

We may also consider an option to conclude an agreement between the Prosecutor and the defendant upon confirmation of the prosecution charges but prior to the commencement of the trial. This would be possible at this stage of proceedings due to the Prosecutor's authority to amend charges, yet it also requires the Pre-Trial Chamber's consent and notification to the defendant. Also, upon commencement of the trial, the Prosecutor may withdraw charges only upon the Trial Chamber's consent. Thus, a potential procedural agreement could be executed even when the arguments of both parties have been heard. The provisions of the Rome Statute do not exclude the possibility of amending charges, but this prosecutorial power is always subjected to judicial review. Therefore, the strong position of the court influences the frequency of plea bargaining, which, as a result, is "less likely to occur".[154]

Another question is whether—even if theoretically possible in the light of the wording of the Statute—charge or fact bargaining could be used by the ICC Prosecutor. In the light of the Tribunal's objectives, the representatives of the legal science are of the opinion that the use of fact bargaining and such presentation of facts that would lead to replacement of charges for more lenient ones and distortion of the actual course of events is out of the question. Despite the theoretical consideration of charge bargaining, the Prosecutor has not used this institution and has not conducted any negotiations with the defendants.

The prosecutorial use of negotiations before the *ad hoc* tribunals in order to conclude procedural agreements in the form of plea bargaining known from common law systems is an example of the often-encountered development of international criminal tribunal practices against the assumptions of the Statutes. The experiences of the ICTY have shown that despite the fact that the Tribunal in the first period was not bound by agreements between the Prosecutor and the defence, the judges still (usually) respected them. The first guilty plea was encountered in *Prosecutor v. Erdemović* and was a result of the execution of an informal agreement between the defendant and the Prosecutor.[155] The ICTY's practice also shows that despite the lack of the Trial Chamber's obligation to respect procedural agreements concluded between the defence and the prosecution, the Chamber has usually taken them into account. Despite the insistent wording of the Rome Statute, it cannot be excluded that the ICC judges will also take into account the information regarding procedural agreements. Some attention may be called to the fact that the Statute does not define the limits of a sentence. As a result, apart from the personal conviction of judges, there is nothing to prevent delivering a sentence as recommended by the Prosecutor. However, judges may also choose to accept the guilty plea to the extent presented by the defendant, although simultaneously they may not consider it possible to drop other charges to which the defendant failed to admit. In view of the lack of legal basis to approve the binding nature of the agreement concluded between the Prosecutor and the defence on the merit-based

---

[154] Turner and Weigend (2013), pp. 1390–1391.

[155] Guariglia and Hochmayr (2008), p. 1231; Schabas (2010), p. 777.

contents of judgement, it is solely up to the adjudicating judges whether they consider that such an agreement may provide a basis for issuing a merit-based judgement.

As a result of such a development of the rules of procedure—in confrontation with the already established adjudicating practice of the *ad hoc* tribunals—both the accuser and the defendant are in a state of uncertainty as to whether their case may be terminated consensually. Indeed, it is hard to predict at the moment what the practice and the scope of concessions will be that the defendant will be able to negotiate as a result of admitting guilt. Only after the first admission of guilt and potential concluding of a procedural agreement between the Prosecutor and the defence attorney will it be possible to determine the impact they exert on the course of the proceedings and the contents of the sentence and, as a result, the Prosecutor's impact on the intensity of criminal prosecution. The outcomes of the first proceedings will show the defendant whether pleading guilty is beneficial for him. Up till this moment,[156] *Bosco Ntaganda*, accused of war crimes and crimes against humanity allegedly committed in 2002–2003 in the Ituri Province, Democratic Republic of the Congo, voluntarily surrendered to the ICC's custody on 22 March 2013.[157] However, throughout the confirmation of charges hearing, he did not plead guilty. In the case of *The Prosecutor v. Bahar Idriss Abu Garda*, the accused, suspected of having committed war crimes in Darfur, Sudan, voluntarily arrived in the Netherlands by commercial aircraft. Despite this fact, the Pre-Trial Chamber declined to confirm charges against him.[158] Also, the accused in the case of *The Prosecutor v. Abdallah Banda Abakaer Nourain* appeared voluntarily when the summons to appear was issued. In this case, the charges presented by the Prosecutor have been confirmed.

6.4 Conclusion

In their early days, international criminal tribunals did not allow consensual termination of proceedings pursuant to an agreement concluded between the prosecutor and the defendant. All institutions ensuring effectiveness of this form of resolving criminal law disputes had been developed in such a manner as to minimise prosecutorial competence to influence the contents of a merit-based judgment. With time, however, appropriate legal solutions started to be introduced, as it turned out that procedural agreements based on a guilty plea and introducing prosecutorial concessions were nevertheless concluded, albeit without a legal basis. In this way, the use of specific practices led to amendment of regulations

[156] Till 1.2.2015.

[157] ICC-01/04-02/06.

[158] ICC-02/05-02/09.

and, in consequence, of the basic assumptions underlying the accusation model before the *ad hoc* tribunals.

In the proceedings before the ICC, however, the form of a consensual termination of a case has been regulated in an entirely innovative way. The form and consequences of pleading guilty resembled most the solutions adopted in continental systems. The acknowledgement of such—limited—consequences of a guilty plea by the defendant and the Prosecutor's inability to use consensual termination of criminal proceedings stemmed mainly from the fact that international justice had a supplementary role to fulfil relative to the national justice systems and that the meeting of defined objectives was crucial for the assessment of its efficiency.[159] The competence to dispose criminal proceedings consensually is an element of the accusation model, with the most evident differences observable in the proceedings before the ICC and the ICTY. These differences reflect the division into the two legal traditions: whereas the ICTY follows the assumptions of the Anglo-Saxon systems, the ICC adopted a model that is even more limiting for the Prosecutor's competence than the model encountered in continental systems.

The major difference between the proceedings before the *ad hoc* tribunals and the ICC is the fact that while the former provided a legal basis for the concluding of procedural agreements between the prosecutor and the defendant, the latter limited itself to stating that, if concluded, such an agreement does not have to be accepted by the judges. Since the agreements between the Prosecutor and the defence, pertaining to the contents of the charges, a guilty plea or the severity of sentence, are not binding on the ICC, the Prosecutor is not able to guarantee the defendant that conditions of the agreement will be fulfilled. As a result, the powers to offer concessions to the defendant rest with the judges. Thus, the Prosecutor does not have a well-defined competence to exert impact on the final merits of the judgment. This competence could not be totally eliminated either, as negotiations with the defendant have not been forbidden, but in its current form, it may be considered "soft". Therefore, the possibility to apply the consensual disposition of a case before the ICC may not be excluded. Even at this early stage of functioning, the ICC may face the same situation previously observed before the *ad hoc* tribunals. Namely, despite the lack of a legal basis, the judges may be willing to respect informal agreements concluded by the Prosecutor. The impact of the Prosecutor on the consensual disposition of the case may be significant, but only on the condition that the judges are willing to accept the outcome of co-operation between him and the defendant. If this practice turns into a custom, the Prosecutor will be able to ensure (at least to some degree) that the conditions of a concluded non-formal agreement will be met. This was the case with the *ad hoc* tribunals where, as a result of the development of *quasi*-formal agreements with the prosecutor, the basic factor that encouraged the formalisation of this practice was the fact that such agreements had been concluded anyway. It is obvious that in such a situation (at least in the international criminal tribunals' environment), it is necessary to either prohibit or

[159] Terrier (2002), p. 1288.

regulate the practice. However, one trait remains the same before all the tribunals: agreements between parties are not binding upon the court—even if before the *ad hoc* tribunals there are statutory basis to conclude such agreements.

In the legal science we can encounter also an opinion that the current form of the institution of the guilty plea before the ICC is a manifestation of the "excessive civil law reform of established common law institutions".[160] As a result, the current regulation is criticised for the limitations implemented by continental lawyers that had made the entire procedure "inoperable" and alien to the normal practice of common law and both for their systems and the parent system of this institution. One cannot agree with this criticism. First, theoretically, we cannot assume that the proceedings before the ICC should be seen, as a whole, as entirely Anglo-Saxon because the accusation model borrows only certain solutions from these systems. Second, from a practical point of view, we may conclude that in a situation where it turned out that Anglo-Saxon solutions do not meet the Tribunal's needs, they might be rejected and replaced with continental solutions, better adjusted to these needs.

Noteworthy is the fact that there is another disadvantage of the ICC model of consensualism that should be more concerning. It is the lack of clarity. As we have seen, although there is no legal basis for consensual termination of proceedings, there is no prohibition either. As a result, even now there is a quite common approach in the literature to negate on this basis the assumptions made by the makers of the Rome Statute and allow for concluding procedural agreements. In result, the defendant does not know what to expect of the Prosecutor and the Prosecutor does not know what he can procedurally afford.

It seems that the limits to development of the consensual disposition of the proceedings before the ICC are motivated ideologically. As has been shown above, all pragmatic reasons would rather encourage acceptance of this institution as a method to accelerate administration of justice and implementation of a statutory basis for concluding procedural agreements by the ICC Prosecutor. However, the question whether a consensual disposition of criminal proceedings, the so-called negotiated justice, is not a contradiction of the objectives set for international criminal tribunals[161] keeps coming back.

References

Alschuler A (1968) The prosecutor's role in plea bargaining. Chic Law Rev 36:50

Ambos K (2003) International criminal procedure: "adversarial", "inquisitorial" or mixed? Int Crim Law Rev 3:1

Ambos K (2007) The structure of international procedure: "adversarial", "inquisitorial" or mixed. In: Bohlander M (ed) International criminal justice: a critical analysis of institutions and procedures. Cameron May, London

---

[160] Cit. after: Ambos (2003), p. 18; Ambos (2007), pp. 474–475.

[161] Petrig (2008), pp. 1–31.

Baker E (2004) Guilty pleas and consensual dispositions: England and Wales. In: Eser A, Rabenstein C (eds) Strafjustiz im Spannungsfeld von Effizienz und Fairness. Konvergente und divergente Entwicklungen im Strafprozessrecht. Duncker & Humblot, Berlin

Beresford S (2001) Unshackling the paper tiger – the sentencing practises of the *ad hoc* International Criminal Tribunals for the former Yugoslavia and Rwanda. Int Crim Law Rev 1:33

Beulke W (2005) Strafprozessrecht, 12th edn. C.F. Müller, Heidelberg

Bibas S (2004) Plea bargaining outside the shadow of trial. Harv Law Rev 8:2463

Boas G, Bischoff J, Reid N, Taylor BD III (2011) International criminal procedure. Cambridge University Press, Cambridge

Bohlander M (2001) Plea-bargaining before the ICTY. In: May R, Tolbert D, Hocking J (eds) Essays on ICTY procedure and evidence. In honour of Gabrielle Kirk McDonald. Kluwer Law International, The Hague/London/Boston

Calvo-Goller K (2006) The trial proceedings of the International Criminal Court: ICTY and ICTR precedents. Martinus Nijhoff, Leiden/Boston

Clark J (2009) Plea bargaining at the ICTY: guilty pleas and reconciliation. Eur J Int Law 2:415

Combs N (2002) Copping a plea to genocide: the plea bargaining of international crimes. Univ Pa Law Rev 1:1

Combs N (2003) International decisions: *Prosecutor v. Plavšić*. Am J Int Law 97:929

Combs N (2007) Guilty pleas in international criminal law. Constructing a restorative justice approach. Stanford University Press, Stanford

D'Ascoli S (2011) Sentencing in international criminal law: the UN *ad hoc* tribunals and future perspectives for the ICC. Oxford University Press, Oxford

Damaška M (1975) Structures of authority and comparative criminal procedure. Yale Law J 84:480

Damaška M (1986) The faces of justice and state authority. Yale University Press, New Haven/London

Damaška M (2008) What is the point of international criminal justice? Chic Kent Law Rev 83:329

Darbyshire P (2000) The mischief of plea bargaining and sentencing rewards. Crim Law Rev 11:895

Friman H (2003) Inspiration from the international criminal tribunals when developing law on evidence for the International Criminal Court. Law Pract Int Courts Tribunals 3(2):373

Gazal O (2006) Partial ban on plea bargains. Cardozo Law Rev 27:2295

Gerard L (1998) Our administrative system of criminal justice. Fordham Law Rev 66:2117

Girdwoyń P (2004) Pozycja i zadania prokuratury w procesie karnym Republiki Federalnej Niemiec. Wojskowy Przegląd Prawniczy 3:9

Goldstein AS, Marcus MM (1977–1978) The myth of judicial supervision in three "inquisitorial" systems: France, Italy, and Germany. Yale Law J 87:240

Goodpaster G (1987) On the theory of the American adversary trial. J Crim Law Criminol 78:118

Grajewski J (2010) In: Grajewski J, Paprzycki L K, Steinborn S (eds) Kodeks postępowania karnego. Komentarz. t. I. Wolters Kluwer, Warszawa

Grzegorczyk T (2008) Kodeks postępowania karnego i ustawa o świadku koronnym. Komentarz, 5th edn. Wolter Kluwer, Warszawa

Guariglia F, Hochmayr G (2008) In: Triffterer O (ed) Commentary on the Rome Statute of the International Criminal Court – observers' notes, article by article, 2nd edn. Hart/Nomos Verlagsgesellschaft/C.H. Beck, München/Oxford

Harmon M (2009) Plea bargaining: the uninvited guest at the International Criminal Tribunal for the former Yugoslavia. In: Daria J, Gasser H-P, Bassiouni MC (eds) The legal regime of the International Criminal Court. Essays in honour of Professor Igor Blishchenko. Martinus Nijhoff, Leiden/Boston

Herrmannt J (1973–1974) The rule of compulsory prosecution and the scope of prosecutorial discretion in Germany. Univ Chic Law Rev 41:468

Hessick F, Saujani R (2002) Plea bargaining and convicting the innocent: the role of the prosecutor, the defence counsel, and the judge. B Y U J Public Law 16:189

Hofmański P, Sadzik E, Zgryzek K (2011) Kodeks postępowania karnego. Komentarz, t. I, 4th edn. C.H. Beck, Warszawa
Jørgensen N (2002) The genocide acquittal in the Sikrica case before the International Criminal Tribunal for the former Yugoslavia and the coming of age of the guilty pleas. Leiden Int Law Rev 15:407
Kardas P (2004) Konsensualne sposoby rozstrzygania w świetle nowelizacji kodeksu postępowania karnego z dnia 10.1.2003 r. Prokuratura i Prawo 1:36
Knoops G-J (2005) Theory and practice of international and internationalized criminal proceedings. Kluwer Law International, The Hague/London/Boston
Kranz B (2009) Międzynarodowe trybunały karne *ad hoc*. In: Kolasa J (ed) Współczesne sądownictwo międzynarodowe. Wydawnictwo Uniwersytetu Wrocławskiego, Wrocław
Lach A (2015) Umorzenie postępowania karnego na podstawie art. 59a k.k. Prokuratura i Prawo 1–2:137
LaFave W, Israel J, King N, Kerr O (2009) Criminal procedure, 5th edn. West Academic Publishing, St. Paul
Łamejko L (2009) Praktyczne aspekty *plea bargaining* w amerykańskim procesie karnym. In: Kulesza C (ed) Ocena funkcjonowania porozumień procesowych w praktyce wymiaru sprawiedliwości. Wolters Kluwer, Warszawa
Langbein J (1978–1979) Understanding the short history of plea bargaining. Law Soc Rev 13:261
Langbein JH, Wienreb LL (1978) Continental criminal procedure: myth and reality. Yale Law J 87:1562
Langer M (2004) From legal transplants to legal translations: the globalization of plea bargaining and the Americanization thesis in criminal procedure. Harv Int Law J 45:1
Langer M (2006) Rethinking plea bargaining: the practice and reform of prosecutorial adjudication in American criminal procedure. Am J Crim Law 3:223
Lewis P (2001) Trial procedure. In: Lee RP (ed) The International Criminal Court. Elements of Crime and Rules of Procedure and Evidence. Transnational Publishers, New York
Marek A (1992) "Porozumienia" w anglo-amerykańskim procesie karnym i w niektórych państwach Europy Zachodniej. Państwo i Prawo 8:61
May R, Wierda M (2002) International criminal evidence. Transnational Publishers, Ardsley, NY
McConville M, Mirsky CL (2005) Jury trials and plea bargaining: a true history. Oxford University Press, Oxford
Morris V, Scharf M (1995) An insider's guide to the International Criminal Tribunal for the former Yugoslavia. Documentary history and analysis. Martinus Nijhoff, Leiden/Boston
Orie A (2002) Accusatorial v. Inquisitorial approach in international criminal proceedings prior to the establishment of the ICC and in the proceedings before the ICC. In: Cassese A, Gaeta P, Jones WD (eds) The Rome Statute of the International Criminal Court: a commentary. Oxford University Press, Oxford
Padfield N (2008) Text and materials on the criminal justice process. Oxford University Press, Oxford
Petrig A (2008) Negotiated justice and the goals of international criminal tribunals. With a focus on the plea-bargaining practice of the ICTY and the legal framework of the ICC. Chic Kent J Int Comp Law 8:1
Płachta M (2004a) Kontrowersje wokół warunkowego umorzenia postępowania karnego w Niemczech. In: Marek A (ed) Współczesne problemy procesu karnego i jego efektywność. Księga pamiątkowa Profesora Andrzeja Bulsiewicza. TNOiK, Toruń
Płachta M (2004b) Międzynarodowy Trybunał Karny. Zakamycze, Kraków
Raab D (2005) Evaluating the ICTY and its completion strategy: efforts to achieve accountability for war crimes and their tribunals. J Int Crim Justice 3:82
Rogacka-Rzewnicka M (2007) Oportunizm i legalizm ścigania przestępstw w świetle współczesnych przeobrażeń procesu karnego. Zakamycze, Warszawa
Ross PF (1978) Bordenkircher v. Hayes: ignoring prosecutorial abuses in plea bargaining. Calif Law Rev 4:875
Safferling C (2001) Towards an international criminal procedure, Oxford monographs in international law. Oxford University Press, Oxford

Schabas W (2010) The International Criminal Court. A commentary on the Rome Statute. Oxford University Press, Oxford
Scharf M (2004) Trading justice for efficiency. J Int Justice 2:1070
Schuon C (2010) International criminal procedure. A clash of legal cultures. T.M.C. Asser Press, The Hague
Scott R, Stuntz W (1992) Plea bargaining as contract. Yale Law J 101:1909
Skorupka J (2009) Znaczenie porozumień procesowych dla modelu postępowania przygotowawczego. In: Kulesza C (ed) Ocena funkcjonowania porozumień procesowych w praktyce wymiaru sprawiedliwości. Wolters Kluwer, Warszawa
Sowiński P (2009) Przyznanie się oskarżonego a skrócone formy wyrokowania. In: Kulesza C (ed) Ocena funkcjonowania porozumień procesowych w praktyce wymiaru sprawiedliwości. Wolters Kluwer, Warszawa
Spencer JR (2004) The English system. In: Delmas-Marty M, Spencer JR (eds) European criminal procedure. Cambridge University Press, Cambridge
Sprack J (2012) A practical approach to criminal procedure. Oxford University Press, Oxford
Stefański R (2003) Skazanie bez rozprawy w znowelizowanym kodeksie postępowania karnego. Prokuratura i Prawo 6:18
Steinborn S (2005) Porozumienia w polskim procesie karnym. Zakamycze, Kraków
Światłowski A (1997) *Plea bargaining* (wytargowane przyznanie się do winy) w orzecznictwie amerykańskim. Palestra 9–10:115
Światłowski A (1998) Koncepcja porozumień karnoprocesowych. Państwo i Prawo 2:55
Światłowski A (1998b) Nieformalne i paraformalne porozumienia w praktyce niemieckiego procesu karnego. Prokuratura i Prawo 1:70
Terrier F (2002) The procedure before the Trial Chamber. In: Cassese A, Gaeta P, Jones WD (eds) The Rome Statute of the International Criminal Court: a commentary. Oxford University Press, Oxford
Thaman S (2008) The role of plea and confession bargaining in International Criminal Courts. In: Kruessmann T (ed) ICTY: towards a fair trial? Neuer Wissenschaftlicher Verlag, Wien/Graz
Tochilovsky V (2008) Jurisprudence of the International Criminal Courts and the European Court of Human Rights. Martinus Nijhoff, Leiden
Trüg G (2003) Lösungskonvergenzen trotz Systemdivergenzen im deutschen und US-amerikanischen Strafverfahren. Ein strukturanalytischer Vergleich am Beispiel der Wahrheitserforschung. Mohr Siebeck, Tübingen
Tulkens F (2004) Negotiated justice. In: Delmas-Marty M, Spencer JR (eds) European criminal procedure. Cambridge University Press, Cambridge
Turner JI, Weigend T (2013) Negotiated justice. In: Sluiter G, Friman H, Linton S, Vasiliev S, Zappala S (eds) International criminal procedure. Principles and rules. Oxford University Press, Oxford
Volk K (2006) Grundkurs. StPO, 5th edn. C.H. Beck, München
Waltoś S (1992) "Porozumienia" w polskim procesie karnym *de lege lata* i *de lege ferenda*. Państwo i Prawo 7:38
Waltoś S (1997) Nowe instytucje w kodeksie postępowania karnego z 1997 r. Państwo i Prawo 8:25
Waltoś S (2000) Porozumienia w europejskim procesie karnym: próba syntetycznego spojrzenia. Prokuratura i Prawo 1:24
Ważny A (2003) Czy przyznanie się oskarżonego do winy warunkuje stosowanie instytucji określonej w Artykule 387 k.p.k.? Prokuratura i Prawo 6:135
White T (1979) Alaska's ban on plea bargaining. Law Soc Rev 13:367
Worrall J (2007) Criminal procedure: from first contact to appeal, 2nd edn. Pearson Allyn & Bacon, Boston
Wysocki D (2000) Instytucja "porozumienia" w postępowaniu karnym. Państwo i Prawo 10:93

Chapter 7
Powers of the Prosecutor Before the Trial Chamber

Abstract The adopted model of adversarial (either strictly or tempered) trial determines the intensity of the prosecutor's activity during trial and in an investigation. A strictly adversarial trial (characteristic of common law states) assumes that both parties should actively engage in the search for evidence to support their claims. Meanwhile, in the continental tempered adversarial trial, a prosecutor's proactive role usually ends with the completion of an investigation and drafting of an indictment. As it is the court that is in charge of an active search of evidence during the trial, the accuser often settles for a passive role. The provisions regulating the course of judicial proceedings before the ICC demonstrate a departure from the strictly adversarial model of accusation (used before the *ad hoc* tribunals) and the introduction of numerous components of the continental trial. The role of the judge has changed from passive to active, and the Prosecutor's powers to control the scope and the manner of presentation of the prosecution case in the trial have been limited—both in terms of evidence and the content of charges brought against the accused. We have observed how the ICC judges have acquired managerial functions in regard to evidentiary material and how they have become active managers who try to expedite and simplify the Court's cases.

7.1 Model of a Contradictory Trial

7.1.1 *Two Models of a Contradictory Trial*

The major differences between the assumptions of the two models of accusation typical for the two legal traditions manifest themselves in the judicial proceedings quite clearly.[1]

The assumptions of the common law tradition oblige the prosecutor to take a proactive approach at the judicial proceedings stage, both in the process of

[1] These problems have been analysed in a number of positions, among others by the following authors: Ambos (2003), p. 18; Ambos (2007), p. 475; Safferling (2001), p. 371; Calvo-Goller (2006), pp. 142 et seq.; Schuon (2010), p. 56; Orie (2002), p. 1440; Langer (2005), p. 840.

© Springer International Publishing Switzerland 2015
H. Kuczyńska, *The Accusation Model Before the International Criminal Court*,
DOI 10.1007/978-3-319-17626-0_7

introducing evidence and in the presentation of this evidence before the court: witnesses appear in court when summoned by the prosecutor. The parties look for witnesses and then prepare them for the trial, practicing cross-examination. In common law adversarial criminal proceedings, the prosecutor is the master of his case; he determines the manner in which he will conduct his case, the number of witnesses and exhibits and the amount of testimony to be elicited. It is up to the parties to decide in what manner and sequence to present the evidentiary material. The parties manage evidentiary proceedings, interrogate witnesses and experts called by them and cross-examine the parties and experts summoned by the opposite party. The trial can end only when the parties decide to end it—as the length of the presentation of evidence depends on what the parties consider to be relevant to their case or on the number of available evidence. The judge is solely a passive observer of the dispute conducted by the parties to the proceedings. He may not influence the parties and demand that the time of the presentation of evidence is shortened. His role is limited to ensuring that trial participants properly apply the principles governing the trial. After the exchange of arguments and evidence is completed, the jury decides whether or not the prosecutor has proven the guilt of the accused beyond any doubt.[2]

Such a model of the contradictory trial could be referred to as a strictly adversarial approach (T. Grzegorczyk talks about the adversarial approach in a "pure" form).[3] The continental tradition uses the phrase "contradictory", where the common law tradition speaks of "adversarial". Both these phrases are best rendered in translation as "antagonistic" or "based on the evidence collected individually". This phrase is most commonly used to describe actual features of Anglo-Saxon criminal justice. However, as there is a need to apply one pattern to describing the accusation model, we will abandon "contradictory" nomenclature and settle for the principle of "adversarality". It can be understood in many ways: in a procedural way (where it means "procedural type designed by comparative law scholars to capture characteristic features of the common law process, particularly when contrasted with continental systems")[4], in a theoretical way (where it is used to describe the goal of the process: conflict resolution) or, as an ideal of procedure, in a purely normative meaning.[5] Here it will be used in the latter meaning.

Judicial proceedings in continental systems are also conducted contradictorily, but this principle is understood differently. Although it also means that the criminal trial is a dispute of two parties, in the case of such a dispute the court is neither passive, nor are the parties obliged to present the evidence during the trial. Here, the

---

[2] More information on this model of adversary trial, e.g. in: Eser (2008), pp. 216–217; Salas (2004), p. 505; Trüg (2003), pp. 25–27; De Smet (2009), pp. 409–412; Goodpaster (1987), pp. 118 et seq.; Safferling (2001), p. 217, and primarily in the works of Damaška (1986, 1972–1973).

[3] Grzegorczyk and Tylman (2007), p. 121; Cieślak (1984), p. 105. In similar words these two undestandings of a "contradicory trial" were described in: Kuczyńska H (2014b), p. 54–55.

[4] See: Damaška (2002), p. 27.

[5] See: Heinze (2014), pp. 119–121.

principle is deemed to be a directive "pursuant to which the parties have the right to fight for a resolution that is favourable for them".[6] There are a number of exceptions to this system that constitute a concession in favour of the inquisitorial approach, releasing the parties from the responsibility for the course of the trial and handing it over to the judge. First of those is the fact that it is the judge who controls the trial and presentation of evidence (it is so-called *judge-centered trial* or *judge-driven trial*).[7] Second, it is a special obligation of a judge to produce evidence *ex officio* in order to ensure that all circumstances of vital significance to the case shall be duly explained and elucidated (e.g. Article 366 § 1, Article 167 CCP).[8] The third limitation to the adversarial approach is the manner of introducing evidence to the trial by the court that has the right to evidentiary initiative, regardless of the parties' position on this matter. Moreover, it is the court that decides on the introduction of evidence requested by the party in an "evidentiary motion"—a motion to conduct a certain evidence. As a result, all evidence has the same status—that of evidence produced by the court. Moreover, the court not only introduces evidence to trial but also actively participates in the examination of the witnesses. In view of the situation, it is obvious that judges may always ask questions to the persons being interrogated without "waiting their turn" and at any moment of the trial. Fourth, there is only one "case"—that presented by the prosecutor, who submits the case file to court and is the only party obliged to be active in a trial. Such a trial structure may be referred to as a tempered adversarial approach. In Anglo-Saxon systems, this model is often termed "non-adversarial" or "inquisitorial".[9] Also, in the Polish legal science, there is a view that the Polish Code of Criminal Proceedings implements the principle of an adversarial approach "with an inquisitorial twist".[10] Although we have to remember, as of the 1st of July 2015, the Polish system ceases to be an example of a tempered adversarial (inquisitorial) model of trial.

The adoption of a specific model of the adversarial approach entails certain powers and obligations for the prosecutor.[11] An active role of a judge and a passive role of a prosecutor represent two sides of a coin. A judge in a more passive role results in the parties taking control over the course of the trial. In such a situation, it is solely the prosecutor who is in charge of the introduction of evidence to the trial. If the evidentiary material turns out to be ambiguous during the trial, he may not rely on the judge's support to elucidate on the matter—by requesting additional

---

[6] Cieślak (1984), p. 254; Waltoś (2005), p. 275.

[7] Although both models are determined more in a conventional, than normative, way. See: Damaška (1972–1973), pp. 510–511.

[8] See: Waltoś (2005), p. 276; Cieślak (1984), p. 257. Remembering that the new version of Article 366 § 1 and Article 167 CCP enters into force on the 1st of July 2015, Dz.U. of 2013 r. pos. 1247.

[9] Ambos (2003), p. 2; Trüg (2003), pp. 27–29; Bohlander (2012), p. 394; Eser (2008), p. 216; Langbein and Wienreb (1978), p. 1549.

[10] Grzegorczyk and Tylman (2007), p. 122.

[11] Cieślak speaks of the principle of contradictory trial that defines the structure of the criminal procedure: Cieślak (1984), p. 255.

evidence or by asking witnesses further questions—and to prevent adjudication that would be favourable for the accused. Evidentiary shortcomings are the responsibility of the prosecutor and result in acquittal. A proactive judge, on the other hand, takes over the evidentiary initiative and in this way outlines the scope of the evidentiary material. This problem can be perceived from the other perspective: when there is no activity on the part of the public prosecutor, the court is forced to look for evidence to enable conviction. If there are any elements of dispute that appear during the trial, they are usually related to the dispute between the defence and the court, which not only is ineffective but also does not help in promoting an image of the court as an independent and impartial authority entrusted with the task of guaranteeing respect for rights and freedom in a democratic state. Handling of the trial by the judge and introduction of evidentiary material solely pursuant to his discretionary decision deprive the prosecutor of his status as the master of the case. He enjoys specific powers only: he has the right to submit motions, especially evidentiary ones; to question the accused, witnesses and experts; to appeal judgements within the scope provided for in the law; to take the floor during the trial on the issues to be resolved; and to give an opinion on testimonies of the other party.

The adopted adversarial model determines the intensity of the prosecutor's activity during trial and in an investigation. A strictly adversarial trial assumes that both parties should actively engage in the search for evidence to support their claims. As early as at the investigation stage, they must collect extensive material in order to disclose it to the other party to the proceedings, thus meeting their trial obligations. However, for the prosecutor, this stage is only a preparation before his active performance in the trial. We could risk a thesis that the strictly adversarial system adopted in Anglo-Saxon states requires that the prosecutor prepare his case much more carefully and completely, not only in the legal aspect, as part of the investigation, but also in the practical aspect, pertaining to the preparation of evidentiary material to be presented: the clarity and transparency of the evidence presented to the jury, as well as the manner of presentation and the power of persuasion.[12]

Meanwhile, in the continental trial, a prosecutor's proactive role usually ends with the completion of an investigation and drafting of an indictment. As it is the court that is in charge of an active search of evidence during the trial, the accuser often settles for a passive role. It is assumed that he has already played his role as far as the search for evidence is concerned during an investigation, and all the evidence that needs to be submitted during the trial is included in the case file.[13] He is not

[12] As results from conclusions presented in: Damaška (1972–1973), p. 512; and Kremens (2010), p. 129.

[13] Beginning on the 1st of July 2015, evidence will be discovered by the parties before the court maintaining adversarial passivity rather than behind the investigators' desks during an investigation. If it is assumed that evidentiary proceedings will be fully conducted only before the court and that the evidence to be collected will serve as a basis for establishment of facts, then it also needs to be assumed that the prosecutor should conduct complete proceedings not prior to bringing an indictment but rather after that. The evidence will not be safeguarded—as has been the case until

considered to be obliged to participate actively in the trial dispute or in the conduct of evidentiary proceedings; although he is entitled to do so in line with the effective law, the lack of a proactive approach in the trial does not have any negative consequences, such as acquittal of the accused, as in Anglo-Saxon systems. This is related to the depreciation of the judicial stage of proceedings in the continental system, which—in extreme cases—is used solely for the presentation of findings made in an investigation.[14]

7.1.2 Model of a Contradictory Trial Before International Criminal Tribunals

Elements characteristic of both the aforementioned adversarial models have been used in proceedings before international criminal tribunals.

Proceedings before the International Military Tribunals had the features of both the strictly adversarial approach and the tempered adversarial approach but were predominantly shaped by the former. It was indicated for the first time that judicial proceedings could be regulated by using solutions borrowed from various legal systems. A compromise was needed to determine the course of the trial and the role of the judge: common law systems proved useful in lending the principle of bringing evidence by the parties and the cross-examination principle; simultaneously, a decision was made that the trial would be managed by the judge on the basis of the solutions taken from the continental trial model.[15]

At the very beginning of their operation, the *ad hoc* tribunals adopted a purely adversarial model of judicial proceedings. However, it turned out to be impossible to altogether exclude the judge's active involvement in such factually and legally complicated cases as adjudicated by the tribunals. This was mainly caused by the fact that the nature of and the principles governing the trial before the international criminal tribunal were different than in Anglo-Saxon systems, under which a judge is not obliged to determine the material truth. Conducting a trial pursuant to the assumptions of a strictly adversarial approach was in conflict with the main objective of the international tribunals, namely the determination of the so-called

now—for the court, but it will be safeguarded only for the public prosecutor, enabling him to perform the accusatory function before the court. Explanation of the circumstances of a case at the investigation stage should be limited to interviewing suspects and witnesses, without any formal interrogation of the latter, and the contents of depositions should be recorded only in the form of official memos; the district court or judge in charge of the investigation should be empowered to safeguard unrepeatable evidentiary activities, such as visual inspection or presentation and other evidence that is at risk of loss or distortion. See: Hofmański and Śliwa (2015), p. 77; and Grzegorczyk (2015), p. 35.

[14] See, e.g., conclusion presented by: Waltoś (1968), p. 98.

[15] Romano et al. (2004), p. 325; Ginsburg and Kudriavtsev (1990), p. 71.

historical truth, the truthful account of past events.[16] The makers of the Tribunal believed that if the judge had to choose between the versions of events presented by the parties, he would not be able independently to pursue the material truth. Also, the experience of the *ad hoc* tribunals has demonstrated that a model of trial closely following the strictly adversarial approach can bring international justice authorities to a standstill and reduce their effectiveness. During their operation, it had already become evident that this approach needed to be changed.

These changes had two main purposes: first, they were intended to expedite the course of the trial; second, they were intended to take into account the legal context of international criminal proceedings. It turned out that these objectives could be achieved by utilising solutions characteristic of the continental tradition. Following the example of continental judges, the ICTY judges were gradually broadening their powers to manage the course of a trial. They believed that it would enhance and improve the effectiveness of the trial. For example, they introduced solutions that would allow them to determine during the Pre-Trial Conference, prior to the commencement of the trial, the scope of evidentiary material presented by the Prosecutor at trial, the number of witnesses he may call and the time available to the Prosecutor for presenting evidence or even to limit the scope of the indictment itself, by directing the Prosecutor to select the counts in the indictment on which to proceed (Rule 73bis(C) and 73 bis(E)). The judges were also offered the power to produce evidence independently during the trial and while interrogating witnesses and experts. This authority was compatible with the simultaneous obligation to determine the material truth. Moreover, no jury was introduced, which simplified the rules of evidentiary proceedings and shifted the burden of deciding the accused's guilt to the judges. This burden turned the judges' attention to precise determination of the circumstances of the case. Ultimately, however, none of these changes affected the main assumptions of the trial that, as a rule, is conducted pursuant to the principles of the common law tradition: the Prosecutor does not prepare a case file, evidence is introduced by the parties, evidentiary proceedings are conducted in certain stages and according to a strict structure.

When drafting the ICC Statute, its authors did not want to follow the assumptions of a specific legal system but rather aimed at finding a balance between the rights of the parties and the effectiveness of the proceedings by incorporating elements of various legal systems. In its current form, this model cannot be definitely described as strictly adversarial because of the strong role given to the judges. It has been concluded that the continental tradition exerts a much greater influence on the proceedings before the ICC than on the proceedings held before the *ad hoc* tribunals.[17]

---

[16] May and Wierda (2002), p. 12; Turkivić (2008), p. 33.

[17] See e.g.: Bitti (2008), p. 1216; Orie (2002), p. 1442.

The characteristic features of this model include

- the powerful position of a judge as an authority managing the course of the evidentiary proceedings;
- the principle of introducing evidence by the parties;
- the judges' wide-ranging powers to introduce evidence *proprio motu*, to interrogate witnesses and to call the parties to submit additional evidence;
- limitation of the Prosecutor's role by granting judges the powers to affect the scope and organisation of the evidentiary material prepared by the prosecution for presentation at trial;
- flexible order of evidentiary proceedings, adjusted to the unique nature of each case;
- the judges' obligation to search for the material truth, combined with the obligation to draw up a reasoned opinion of a judgment;
- the existence of the register of case *dossiers*.

In the process of application of the ICC Statute, it can be observed that the individual elements characteristic of a specific adversarial model have gradually departed from their roots, becoming the components of a new criminal procedure. The *sui generis* development of the trial was adopted by using the legal institutions coming from both the common law and the continental law traditions, which have made the judicial proceedings stage the best example of a hybrid development of the accusation model before the ICC.

7.2 Obligations of the Prosecutor During Trial

7.2.1 Obligation to Act in Favour of the Accused

The decision whether the ICC Prosecutor should act as a "partisan actor" driven by the goal to prevail in a trial "combat" (as in the common law systems) or whether he should be an authority looking for the material truth (as a "guardian of the law", or "minister of justice", in German *Wächter des Gesetzes*[18]) turned out to be the basic factor affecting the scope of obligations and powers of the ICC Prosecutor. The question that had to be answered was whether the prosecutor of an international authority, whose role was diametrically different from that of a national prosecutor, should only seek conviction.

Whereas the assumptions of the accusation model before the ICTY were still unclear—the ICTY Prosecutor was, on the one hand, expected to act in the interests of justice, yet his powers were, on the other hand, limited to accusation—the powers of the ICC Prosecutor were clearly determined by his commitment arising from Article 54 of the Rome Statute, providing that "The Prosecutor shall, in order

[18] Mathias (2004), p. 479.

to establish the truth, extend the investigation to cover all facts and evidence relevant to an assessment of whether there is criminal responsibility under this Statute, and, in doing so, investigate incriminating and exonerating circumstances equally". There is no doubt he is expected to play the role of a "guardian of the law". The imposition of this obligation constituted a major difference relative to the proceedings before the *ad hoc* tribunals.

Two major problems arise in connection with the role to be played by the ICC Prosecutor.

First, it is not entirely clear whether the Prosecutor's obligation to act also in favour of the accused expires upon completion of the investigation. The Statute does not impose on the Prosecutor the obligation to undertake activities in favour of the accused during the trial. It seems that due to the lack of a direct prosecutorial obligation to actively engage in actions that would benefit the accused, the end of an investigation simultaneously terminates the Prosecutor's obligation to act as an authority seeking the material truth.[19] The only statutory manifestation of this obligation is the rule according to which the Prosecutor is under an obligation to disclose to the defence evidence in his possession or control that he believes shows or tends to show the innocence of the accused, or to mitigate the guilt of the accused, or that may affect the credibility of prosecution evidence (Article 67 (2) of the Rome Statute), in the frames of the disclosure of evidence procedure.

Second, it is not clear whether such a development of the Prosecutor's role also imposes on the Trial Chamber an obligation to ensure that the Prosecutor has properly fulfilled his task to collect evidence in favour of the accused.

We have seen that a question appeared whether the Pre-Trial Chamber has powers to examine the scope of fulfilment of the Prosecutor's obligation under Article 54 of the Statute during an investigation: whether the prosecution had sought enough to obtain exonerating information.[20] In the case law, it was concluded that the fulfilment of Article 54 duties is another one of the Prosecutor's powers that should fall into the scope of judicial control.[21]

Some representatives of the doctrine believe that the Trial Chamber also enjoys similar powers at the trial stage: to demand from the Prosecutor to establish certain facts or to bring additional evidence in order to supply also evidence in favour of the accused.[22] According to their opinion, it would be justified by limited human and technical resources of the defence, which leads to a lack of choice but to rely on evidence gathered by the Prosecutor; it is impossible for the accused to conduct an independent investigation on equal foot with the prosecution team. The Trial Chamber could—on request of the defence—oblige the Prosecutor to undertake

---

[19] See: Vasiliev (2012), p. 709.

[20] See on that topic comprehensively: Buisman (2014), p. 223.

[21] *The Prosecutor v. Uhuru Muigai Kenyatta*, ICC-01/09-02/11-728, Trial Chamber, Decision on Defense Application Pursuant to Article 64(4) and Related Requests, 26 April 2013, § 119.

[22] See e.g.: Kirsch (2008), p. 58; Heinsch (2009), p. 485. It is assumed that such an obligation can be imposed on the Prosecutor by the Pre-Trial Chamber, see: Tochilovsky (2002), p. 269.

such actions using its competence under Article 64(6)(d) of the Statute, to "order the production of evidence in addition to that already collected prior to the trial or presented during the trial by the parties". In practice, the exercise of these powers depends solely on the judges' visions of the trial and their personal views on the role of the ICC Prosecutor. This assumption could find confirmation in the phrase used by the Pre-Trial Chamber in *The Prosecutor v. Kenyatta*, where it found that the Prosecutor "is not responsible for establishing the truth only at the trial stage by presenting a complete evidentiary record, but is also expected to present a reliable version of events at the confirmation hearing". Such obligation could also be considered to be in compliance with the continental model of accusation, where the prosecutor is obliged to act according to the principle of objectivity. His obligation to establish the true account of events requires him to take into account circumstances that act both in favour of and against the accused also at the stage of judicial proceedings. He may not seek, at any cost, to demonstrate the guilt of the accused and should discontinue prosecution if the outcomes of judicial proceedings failed to confirm charges articulated in an indictment.

On the other hand, such an assumption could lead to a situation where the judges would determine the tasks of the Prosecutor in judicial proceedings and bindingly order him to produce certain evidence in favour of the accused. It seems that the existence of such a power would excessively complicate the fulfilment of prosecutorial tasks. Even at present, the ICC Prosecutor is not only expected to retain evidence to which he has had access and that could be used by the defence, but he also must actively seek such evidence during an investigation. If we also add the obligation to seek specific evidence upon request of the accused, the Prosecutor would be forced to play a dual role also in the judicial proceedings. Placing the burden on the Prosecutor to secure the "public interest" also in trial would contradict with his function as an accusatory and a partisan advocate. This burden would turn the Prosecutor into a "*quasi*-judicial authority" also during the court proceedings. It would also lead to an unequal treatment of the two parties to the proceedings—although the Prosecutor is entitled to be treated equitably by the Court. We should, however, notice that the wording of the Statute seems to be quite clear in demanding from the prosecution objectivity only within the scope of an investigation. The presentation of exonerating evidence at the trial stage should remain the realm of the defence—or eventually the Trial Chamber. It seems that it would be more reasonable to leave the collection of evidence requested by the accused to the Trial Chamber. During the judicial proceedings, the Prosecutor is to remain a solely accusing authority. It should be therefore assumed that the obligation to act and collect evidence in favour of the accused ends when an indictment is brought in. From this moment on, the Prosecutor's sole task is to accuse. This approach is consistent with the model of judiciary proceedings adopted before the ICC. Some authors claim that this approach is based on the strictly adversarial trial approach.[23] However, as the trial approach is a hybrid, it is better to conclude that it

[23] See: Vasiliev (2012), p. 709.

results from the adoption of the principle of general responsibility of the parties to submit evidence in support of their cases.

7.2.2 *Obligation of Active Argumentation*

International criminal tribunals introduce evidence in a manner borrowed from common law systems. Characteristically for these systems, witnesses are summoned by the parties. The Sixth Amendment to the United States Constitution, which forms a part of the US Bill of Rights, grants to the accused the right to be confronted with the witnesses against him and to have compulsory process for obtaining witnesses in his favour (on the basis of a court's order, so-called *subpoena*. In England, each participant of a criminal case not only can but must prepare and conduct the case in accordance with the overriding objective.[24] Pursuant to the concept of a strictly adversarial trial, each of the parties is expected to prove its arguments, taking a proactive approach. Since each party has its own witnesses, the witness for the prosecution cannot be (as a rule) used by the defence, and the prosecutor may not look for or call witnesses for the defence.

In continental states, the manner of introducing evidence to the trial is subject to more complex rules. There are three major assumptions that determine its unique nature.

First, it is the existence of a case file. During the investigation, the state law enforcement authorities collect a complete set of evidence provided to the court in the form of a case file that will be summarised in the indictment.

Second, there are three characteristic ways of introducing evidence into the trial. Evidence is produced

- which is included in the list of evidence formulated in the attachment to the indictment. According to Article 333 § 1 CCP and § 200(1) StPO, the indictment should contain a list of the persons whom the prosecutor requests to be summoned, a list of such other evidence that the prosecutor will seek to present at the first-instance hearing. This list is deemed as the prosecutor's motion pertaining to the evidence that should be produced;
- upon a motion of the parties. The parties have a right to request that certain evidence be produced. A judge has an obligation to produce such evidence at trial and can deny such motion only in exceptional circumstances as set out by the law.[25] An evidentiary motion shall be denied only in special and limited circumstances and only in a form of a judicial decision;
- *ex officio*, by the judges, regardless of the opinions of the parties.

[24] The Criminal Procedure Rules 2014, Rule 1.2: http://www.legislation.gov.uk/uksi/2014/1610/article/1.2/made. Accessed 9 Jan 2015.

[25] Article 170 § 1 CCP, § 244(3–5), and 245 StPO. In general see: Beulke (2005), pp. 258–259.

Finally, the third characteristic feature of this system is the fact that introduction of evidence to the trial is done solely upon the judge's decision (Article 167 CCP, § 244 StPO). Both in the Polish and the German systems, the evidence in the trial may not be introduced without the judge's authorisation.

In proceedings before the *ad hoc* tribunals, "each party is entitled to call witnesses and present evidence" (Rule 85(A)). Also, the Rome Statute provides in Article 69(3) that "The parties may submit evidence relevant to the case".

According to the opinion of the legal doctrine, formulation of this provision serves to emphasise the adversarial nature of the proceedings.[26] However, the application of the judicial proceedings model characteristic of common law states in proceedings before the ICC has negative consequences in the light of the functions of international justice. Namely, when certain persons are qualified as witnesses for a particular trial party right from the start of a case, it may put them in specific trial roles. As a result, both the parties and the witnesses act as the participants of a trial combat. Witnesses are expected not to present an objective course of events but rather to support the "case" presented in the trial by the party that has summoned them; a similar approach is expected from experts. Naturally, a party will not call a witness who could challenge the arguments it presents. This risk is further alleviated by the procedure of "witness proofing" during which both the defence attorney and the prosecutor prepare their witnesses for interrogation, practicing the correct replies to the questions that will be asked during the trial.[27] It has been observed that in the case of international tribunals, the trial combat reflects internal conflicts of an ethnic and religious nature underlying the committed crimes. It leads to unnecessary antagonisms throughout the trial. Taking into account the role played by international criminal tribunals, it has been suggested that the witnesses should appear before the tribunal upon the judge's summons rather than when called by the parties to the proceedings: "To make use of their investigative powers to intervene, the judges should in particular feel called upon when deadlocks between the parties which, for contrary reasons, restrict the presentation of evidence" should be "de-blocked".[28] In such a case, they would have witnesses called to determine the material truth rather than to win the trial combat.

We have experienced, however, a shift in understanding the role of a witness before the *ad hoc* tribunals, which have abandoned the doctrine of perceiving a witness as a partisan of solely one version of events. In *Prosecutor v. Tadić*, the Trial Chamber observed that after the witness has taken the solemn declaration, he becomes "a witness of truth" and is no longer a witness of the calling party: "a witness, either for the Prosecution or Defence, once he or she has taken the Solemn Declaration (. . .), is a witness of truth before the Tribunal and, inasmuch as he or she is required to contribute to the establishment of the truth, not strictly a witness for either party". In consequence of adopting a more neutral doctrine of

---

[26] Schabas (2010), p. 842; Terrier (2002a), p. 1295; May and Wierda (2002), pp. 144–145.

[27] Ambos (2009), pp. 599 et seq.; Jordash (2009), pp. 501–523; Kuczyńska H (2014a), p. 17.

[28] See: Eser (2008), p. 225.

presentation of evidence, the Chamber prohibited further communications between the party and a witness after he or she has commenced his or her testimony as it may lead both witness and party, albeit unwittingly, to discuss the content of the testimony already given so as to avoid the danger of "influencing the witness's further testimony in ways which are not consonant with the spirit of the Statute and Rules of the Tribunal".[29]

In proceedings before the ICC, it is clear that a witness should rather support the pursuit of the material truth rather than endorse a specific version of events. Due to this modification, a more neutral approach to the interrogation of witnesses, typically found in continental systems, is possible. Along with the increasingly proactive approach of the judge, this change is one of the significant exceptions in favour of the continental model of accusation. Based on the model of trial adopted in the continental procedure—and also before the ICC—the parties are expected not to conduct a trial combat but rather to participate in a dialogue to help the court to determine the material truth; this aim is highlighted by the fact that the Prosecutor is seen as an impartial authority who has investigated both the favourable and unfavourable circumstances for the accused in the course of the investigation.[30]

7.2.3 Obligation to Prove Guilt of the Accused

The aim of the actions undertaken in the trial by the prosecutor is to prove the guilt of the accused. However, this aim may be achieved in line with different rules.

First, the moment in which evidence is found sufficient to prove the guilt of the accused is defined differently in each legal system. In England and the United States, the theory is that the guilt of the accused must be established *beyond reasonable doubt*. In continental tradition, the court must not convict the accused except where it has *une intime conviction* that he is guilty.[31] It seems that in practice the degree of a judge's conviction sufficient to consider the accused guilty of the actions charged against him does not differ in these systems in any way except for the name and the manner in which it is defined in the law.[32]

[29] *Prosecutor v. Tadić*, IT-94-01, Decision on the Defence Motion to Prevent the Contamination of Testimony, 3 May 1996. Also: *Prosecutor v. Kupreskić*, Decision on Communications Between the Parties and their Witnesses, 21 September 1998.

[30] Eser (2008), p. 226; Damaška (2008), p. 342.

[31] Differences between these two thresholds are considered in: Spencer (2004), p. 601, coming to the same conclusion.

[32] Differently: Zappala (2002), pp. 1346–1348; Bassiouni (1993), p. 265, who binds these standards with a different understanding of a presumption of innocence concept in various legal systems. However, taking into consideration that the great bulk of offenders are processed through the negotiated guilty plea mechanism, "an opinion might even be hazarded that, on this broader plane, continental evidentiary standards for proving guilt are more demanding". Cit. after: Damaška (1972–1973), p. 552.

The *ad hoc* tribunals adopted the Anglo-Saxon standard requiring that a finding of guilt may be reached only when a majority of the Trial Chamber is satisfied that guilt has been proved beyond reasonable doubt (Rule 87(A) ICTY RPE). In *Prosecutor v. Tadić*, the ICTY Trial Chamber explained that the "beyond reasonable doubt" test signifies that "the proof must be such as to exclude not every hypothesis or possibility of innocence, but every fair or rational hypothesis which may be derived from the evidence, except that of guilt".[33] This formulation does not mean that the guilt should be proven "beyond a shadow of doubt" or with "an absolute certainty". "Reasonable doubt" means a doubt that is founded on a reason.[34] The Appeals Chamber in *Prosecutor v. Delalić* indicated "that only those matters which are proved beyond reasonable doubt against an accused may be the subject of an accused's sentence or taken into account in aggravation of that sentence".[35]

In proceedings before the ICC, according to the provision of Article 66(3) of the Rome Statute, "in order to convict the accused, the Court must be convinced of the guilt of the accused beyond reasonable doubt". So far, this concept has not been explained in the case law. It should be assumed that the ICC will adopt the common law understanding of this notion, following in the footsteps of the ICTY, which relies on the English and US doctrines in its rulings. The ICC in *The Prosecutor v. Lubanga* made it clear that the Court bases on a construction of "guilt proven beyond reasonable doubt". In this particular case, the Chamber concluded that when, based on the evidence, there is only one reasonable conclusion to be drawn from particular facts, this conclusion has been established beyond reasonable doubt.[36] Equally enigmatic was the Trial Chamber in the case of *The Prosecutor v. Ngudjolo Chui*, in which it gave an acquitting verdict assuming that there was a reasonable doubt as to the participation of the accused in the acts he was charged with (*une doute raisonnable*).[37]

Second, each model of proceedings needs to specify the party on which the burden of proof is placed. Article 66(2) of the Rome Statute provides that "the onus is on the Prosecutor to prove the guilt of the accused". Thus, it obliges the Prosecutor to get actively involved in the process of proving the guilt of the accused.[38] The Prosecutor's failure to engage in the process or the ineffectiveness of his evidence should be identified with a lack of incriminating evidence and therefore results in the accused's release from all or some of the charges brought

---

[33] In: *Prosecutor v. Tadić*, IT-94-1, Appeals Chamber, 15 July 1999, § 174.

[34] Schabas (2008), pp. 1241–1242; Schabas (2010), pp. 786–787; Boas et al. (2011), pp. 385–387.

[35] *Prosecutor v. Delalić*, IT-96-21, Appeals Chamber, 20 February 2001, § 763.

[36] *The Prosecutor v. Lubanga*, ICC-01/04-01/06, Trial Chamber, 14 March 2012, § 111, § 181.

[37] *The Prosecutor v. Mathieu Ngudjolo Chui*, ICC-01/04-02/12, Trial Chamber, 18 December 2012, § 490, 503.

[38] The active participation of the judges in the evidentiary proceedings cannot be perceived as a proof of the fact that *onus probandi* rests also on the judges. Compare interesting observations of Kremens (2010), p. 126, who argues that this conception is wrongly interpreted in the common law tradition.

against him. Moreover, it seems that the principle of presumption of innocence applicable before this Court is another indicator that the obligation of proving the guilt of the accused rests with the Prosecutor.

The acquittal of the accused is an obvious outcome of a prosecutor's failure to prove the guilt. There is, however, a major difference in how this problem has been addressed in the proceedings before various international criminal tribunals.

In proceedings before the *ad hoc* tribunals, a special mechanism derived from common law was adopted, which allows for entering a judgment of acquittal at the close of the prosecution's case and before the presentation of the defence's case. It may happen in a situation if at the close of the Prosecutor's case, the Trial Chamber is convinced that there is no evidence capable of supporting a conviction (so-called a *no case to answer* doctrine).[39] Thus, only when there is sufficient evidence to sustain a conviction on a particular charge is the defence called upon to produce exonerating evidence (Rule 98bis RPE ICTY).[40] A similar doctrine has not been so far adopted by the ICC. In *The Prosecutor v. Ngudjolo Chui*, the Trial Chamber acquitted the accused of charges made by the Prosecutor, but did so on the basis and under the influence of the evidence produced by the defence.[41]

The prosecutorial obligation to prove guilt proactively is balanced by the application of the so-called *reverse burden of proof*. It signifies an obligation imposed on the defence to prove its claims; for example, if the defence attorney challenges the credibility of a document presented by the prosecutor, he has to call an expert to establish the authenticity (or lack thereof) of the document. Before the ICTY, it has been assumed that the burden of proof is transferred in certain defined situations: when the defence demands exclusion of criminal responsibility due to the perpetrator's insanity, as well as in any other circumstances excluding or reducing the responsibility, for example, when a guilty plea is claimed to have not been entered voluntarily. Similar to common law systems, the ICTY does not require the defence to prove these circumstances "beyond any doubt" but requires it only to indicate some degree of its credibility.[42] In Anglo-Saxon systems, the accused has to meet a significantly lower evidentiary standard than the prosecutor. The standard of "balance of probabilities" borrowed from the civil law is sufficient.[43] For example, in *Prosecutor v. Delalić*, one of the accused claimed to be of

---

[39] See, e.g., the case of: *Prosecutor v. Jelisić*, IT-95-10, Trial Chamber, 14 December 1999, § 15–16; and Appeals Chamber, 5 July 2005, § 55–56. Also: *Prosecutor v. Milošević*, IT-02-54, Decision on the Motion for Judgment of Acquittal, 14 June 2004, § 11.

[40] See: Zappala (2002), p. 1345; Knoops (2005), p. 252; Boas et al. (2011), p. 279.

[41] *The Prosecutor v. Mathieu Ngudjolo Chui*, ICC-01/04-02/12, Trial Chamber, 18 December 2012.

[42] Kirsch (2008), p. 53; May and Wierda (2002), pp. 121–124; Bassiouni and Manikas (1996), p. 946; Wiliński and Kuczyńska (2009), pp. 208–209.

[43] In the United States, this standard was established in: *Davis v. United States*, 160 U.P. 469 (1895), Supreme Court, 16 December 1895; *Jackson v. Virginia*, 443 U.P. 307 (1979), Supreme Court, 28 July 1979. See in general: LaFave et al. (2009), pp. 566–567.

"diminished capacity" at the time of committing the acts he was charged with.[44] The Trial Chamber stated that there is a presumption of sanity (even despite an absence of prosecutorial evidence) and that "every person charged with an offence is presumed to be of sound mind and to have been of sound mind at any relevant time until the contrary is proven". In consequence, the Prosecutor did not have an obligation to produce evidence on the accused's sanity.

Contrary to the ICTY practice, the ICC Statute in Article 67(1)(i) introduces a quite original solution as to the *reverse burden of proof*, protecting the accused from placing on him a burden of proof in general. It provides that the accused is entitled "Not to have imposed on him or her any reversal of the burden of proof or any onus of rebuttal". This right was supposed to constitute an equivalent of a guarantee used in continental systems securing that the accused cannot be forced to be active in trial. However, according to some of the representatives of the Anglo-Saxon legal doctrine, these norms may create troublesome hurdles for the prosecution and provide the defence with a powerful tool. First, in the future jurisprudence, the ICC may adopt a conception that the accused is only required to raise a reasonable doubt as to his mental condition (demonstrating only the probability of this condition), and there will be no need to prove this fact beyond reasonable doubt (as it happened before the ICTY). The second conclusion is more extreme: the Court may apply this rule to impose the burden on the prosecution to establish sanity. Undoubtedly, adopting this theory would lead to consequences unintended by the drafters of the Statute and would place on the Prosecutor an impossible task. Such an interpretation of this provision seems to be contrary not only to the hitherto practice of the ICTY but also with the jurisprudence of the European Court of Human Rights. The latter Court has admitted that *reverse burden* provisions are known in all the domestic legal systems of criminal law, and therefore they are not contrary to the presumption of innocence principle.[45]

Third, in the case of evidentiary proceedings before international criminal tribunals, the basic problem associated with the unique nature of cases handled by these tribunals has to be taken into account for purposes of selection of the appropriate model of guilt proving. The nature of these cases forces the prosecutor to prepare them more extensively than in national proceedings and to prepare a comprehensive evidentiary material in support of each of his arguments. In the case of certain offences, such as crimes against humanity, the prosecutor has to present the circumstances that underlay the committed crimes falling within the tribunal's interest, for example, the evidence that "the act has been committed as part of a widespread or systematic attack directed against any civilian population, with knowledge of the attack" (Article 7 of the Rome Statute). This requirement signifies that he has to present evidence in support of the fact that not only "an attack" took place but that it was "widespread" and "systematic", conducted with a certain

[44] *Prosecutor v. Delalič*, IT-96-21, Trial Chamber, 16 November 1998, § 599, § 1157–1160. Also: *Prosecutor v. Simić*, IT-95-9/2, Trial Chamber, 17 October 2002, § 40.

[45] E.g.: Schabas (2008), p. 1239.

knowledge. It often requires evidence of a political and demographical character. Complex circumstances of the committed crimes and the type of crime elements that the prosecutor has to prove have led to acquittal in numerous cases, when one of the elements of a certain crime has not been proved adequately.[46]

7.3 Model of Presentation of Evidence

7.3.1 Order of Presentation of Evidence

The course of a trial before international criminal tribunals has taken on a form typical for common law systems. It is regulated by stiff rules (as it is aptly observed: "the adversarial debate is structured and painstakingly regulated").[47] First of all, the order of presentation of evidence by each party to the trial is strictly defined. Second, the manner of interrogating each of the witnesses and the sequence of asking questions by a given party to the trial are also subject to strict regulation.

It has been acknowledged in common law systems that since the evidence presented in the trial comes solely from the parties, and the judge has very limited options to interfere with the manner of the presentation, evidentiary material should be presented in a strictly defined order.[48] The trial begins with *opening statements*. In the United States, prior to the presentation of evidence, both parties may present their "opening statements", where they can state "what evidence will be represented, to make it easier for the jurors to understand what is to follow and to relate parts of the evidence and testimony to the whole" – it is an introduction to the evidentiary proceedings, "it is not an occasion for argument" yet.[49] It constitutes rather "an element of trial advocacy".[50] After the parties' opening statements, the prosecution is the first to present its *case-in-chief*. During the prosecution case, the defence may cross-examine prosecution witnesses but may not present any exculpatory material yet. The defence may only begin to present its case after the prosecution case is closed. The defence case may be then followed by *rebuttal* of the prosecutor, i.e. the response to the defence's arguments. *Rebuttal* evidence can only consist of evidence that refutes the defence case but not new evidence that merely supports the prosecution case. He may not continue to present charges and evidence to support them. Generally, once the prosecution case is completed, further evidence of the prosecution may not be presented. It is solely up to the

---

[46] E.g.: *The Prosecutor v. Mathieu Ngudjolo Chui*, ICC-01/04-02/12, Trial Chamber, 18 December 2012.

[47] Cit. after: Acquaviva et al. (2013), p. 638. Similarly: Schuon (2010), p. 58. Detailed rules of cross-examination in: LaFave et al. (2009), pp. 1159–1160, and 1169–1172.

[48] Orie (2002), p. 1445.

[49] LaFave et al. (2009), p. 1169.

[50] Acquaviva et al. (2013), p. 544.

judge's discretion whether he allows the prosecution to supplement its evidence. It requires the court's decision to reopen the prosecution's case. If the prosecution raises new issues in its rebuttal evidence, the defence can meet them by presenting evidence in *rejoinder*. In consequence, it also gives the defence the right to supplement its case with new evidence.

In England and Wales, the order of presentation of evidence in the trial is similar. In the beginning of the trial, the prosecution gives the members of the jury an overall view of the case (*the prosecution opening*). Then the prosecution calls witnesses to give oral statements and tender in evidence written statements that are read to the jury (*the prosecution case*). After the prosecution finishes hearing of witnesses, the defence may ask prosecution witnesses questions in cross-examination. After the prosecution evidence has been adduced, prosecuting counsel closes his case by saying "that is the case for the prosecution" or words to that effect. The prosecution may not in general call evidence after it has closed its case. There are, however, four exceptions to the general rule when a judge may allow the prosecution to call additional evidence: when in the course of the defence case, a matter arises "which no human ingenuity could have foreseen"; if a witness was not available to it before it closed its case (but only if the prosecutor shows that he had been sufficiently diligent in preparing his case); where the prosecution omits to present evidence of a purely formal nature (such as "a steamroller is made mainly of iron or steel")[51]; when evidence relates to matters going into the witness's credibility in order to rebut the answer the prosecution receives in cross-examination of the other party witness (such as proving the existence of previous convictions).

In continental states, the manner of presentation of evidence has taken on a more flexible form. Although it is also generally assumed that evidence should be presented in a specific order, the manner of presentation of evidence in the trial is subordinated to two major principles:

- the principle of seeking the material truth, and
- the principle of the judge's leading role.

Generally, the trial is structured as a uniform official enquiry by a trial judge, who plays a leading role in eliciting evidence from the witnesses. The hearing of evidence is managed by the judge in a way he deems best for the goal of ascertaining the truth. The parties' counsels can only "assist" the judge in the presentation of the evidence. According to Article 369 CCP, evidence in support of the charges should, if possible, be taken before evidence in support of the defence. There is nothing, however, that could prevent evidentiary proceedings from taking a different course—depending on the judge's decision. As a matter of fact, in practice he usually adopts his own vision of the course of proceedings. The

[51] Sprack (2012), pp. 343–344. Such information would be considered to constitute a so-called notorious fact in continental systems, encompassed by private knowledge of a judge, see: Damaška (1986), p. 138.

presiding judge should also permit the parties to express themselves on any matter that is to be resolved.

The judge also plays a leading role in the German trial: he both manages the presentation of evidence in the trial and interrogates the witnesses. He keeps bringing evidence to the trial until he is convinced that his vision of the case is consistent with the material truth. The sequence of presentation of evidence also depends on the judge's decision. The provisions of criminal procedure mention only one rule in relevance to the sequence of evidentiary proceedings: witnesses and experts named by the public prosecution office shall first be examined by the public prosecution office. Those named by the defendant shall first be examined by defence counsel (Article 367 § 1 CCP, § 238, 239 and 240 StPO). What is interesting is that in the continental systems, the prosecution presents its case only after the accused is called to give his statement at the very beginning of the trial. For the representatives of the common law tradition, this in fact means that the case of the prosecution is presented after the case of the defence.[52] There is little doubt that it is advantageous to the prosecution, "as the prosecutor may sit back and expect that leads or evidence damaging to the defendant will come out of his interrogation. Also, the prosecutor may hope that the concocted story of a guilty defendant will crumble in the light of testimony of subsequent witnesses".[53]

Before the International Military Tribunal in Nuremberg, there were only two rules related to the order of presentation of evidence. First, after the indictment was read in court and each defendant entered a plea, the prosecution was to make an opening statement (Article 24(c) of the IMT Charter). Second, the witnesses for the prosecution were to be examined first, and after that the witnesses for the defence. Thereafter, *rebutting* evidence could be called by either the prosecution or the defence, but only it was held by the Tribunal to be admissible.

In the proceedings before the ICTY, the evidence, as a rule, is presented in line with the order known from common law systems and the scheme according to which evidence is submitted is predominantly "strictly adversarial". The general principle is that evidence should be called at the proper time and in the order laid out in the Rules. Rule 85(A) provides that evidence at the trial is presented in the following sequence:

- evidence for the prosecution;
- evidence for the defence;
- prosecution evidence in rebuttal;
- defence evidence in rejoinder;
- evidence ordered by the Trial Chamber pursuant to Rule 98; and
- any relevant information that may assist the Trial Chamber in determining an appropriate sentence if the accused is found guilty on one or more of the charges in the indictment.

[52] See the conclusion presented by: D'Aoust (2009), p. 876.

[53] Damaška (1972–1973), p. 530.

The Trial Chamber characterised the nature of rebuttal evidence as "evidence to refute a particular piece of evidence which has been adduced by the defence", with the result that it is "limited to matters that arise directly and specifically out of defence evidence".[54] At the same time, rejoinder evidence is limited to those matters arising out of rebuttal that could not have been reasonably foreseen by the defence. The Prosecutor cannot hold back evidence as a matter of tactics, in order to use it later during the trial, e.g. during a cross-examination of a witness. If he fails to present all the evidence of a key importance to his case, there is no going back.

In *Prosecutor v. Kristić*, the Trial Chamber did not admit several pieces of evidence "that went into the heart of the prosecution case" as part of the rebuttal case.[55] The Chamber found that the Prosecutor appeared to have made a tactical decision to use a piece of evidence during cross-examination rather than during his case-in-chief in order to achieve a better "explosive effect", which, in his opinion, would not have been achieved if it had been presented earlier, together with other prosecution evidence.[56] For this reason, the judges concluded that this evidence did not meet the conditions that rendered it admissible at this stage of the proceedings. Producing new evidence is only possible when the Trial Chamber permits to reopen the case of the prosecution. Before the Chamber reopens the case, it must be satisfied that the evidence the prosecution seeks to introduce is "newly obtained", that is, obtained after the close of the case-in-chief, and moreover that it could not have been found and presented at the earlier stage of the proceedings, even though due diligence had been exercised. In *Prosecutor v. Delalić*, the prosecution was not permitted to call additional four witnesses as part of his rebuttal case, as their testimony related to issues that did not relate to the evidence called by the defence. However, when the Prosecutor sought leave of the Trial Chamber to reopen his case to call additional witnesses, this request was also rejected. It stated that "it is essential to the Prosecution that it should adduce all evidence critical to the guilt of the accused so as to establish his guilt at the close of its case".[57] It went further to state that the rebuttal case "must not be constructed as a *carte blanche* for the Prosecution to adduce evidence at a later stage in the proceedings which should properly have been presented as part of its original case".

Ten years later, this very restrictive rule was somewhat loosened: in *Prosecutor v. Popović*, the Trial Chamber concluded that the occurrence of new evidence made it possible to reopen the prosecution case, although it was not "newly obtained evidence". According to the Chamber, the term "new evidence" should also include

---

[54] *Prosecutor v. Delalić*, IT-96-21, Appeals Chamber, 20 February 2001, § 273.

[55] May and Wierda (2002), pp. 151 and 153.

[56] *Prosecutor v. Kristić*, IT-98-33, Decision on the Defence Motions to Exclude Exhibits in Rebuttal and Motion for Continuance, 4 May 2001, § 25, 26. In general see: Tochilovsky (2008), pp. 359–366; Tochilovsky (2005), p. 197; Vasiliev (2012), pp. 756–757.

[57] See: *Prosecutor v. Delalić*, IT-96-21, Decision on the Prosecution's Alternative Request to Re-Open the Prosecution's Case, 19 August 1998, § 18, 26–27 and 37.

evidence that existed before but has acquired new meaning only in the light of other "newly obtained evidence".[58] In this case, the Prosecutor could not have anticipated that specific documents would become significant until he discovered the meaning of other evidence. At the same time, we can find in the jurisprudence clear factors that were to be determinative of the discretion of the Trial Chamber to admit evidence: it was to be of "high probative value" and "significant", to the extent that "the injustice of rejecting it should be irresistible", and not merely circumstantial, corroborative or reinforcing the prosecution-case-in-chief.[59]

According to the common law doctrine, compliance with the rules pertaining to rebuttal is of key importance for the efficiency of the proceedings. Adoption of too flexible rules for challenging the opposite party's arguments could result in turning this stage into a repeated prosecution case. On the other hand, it has also been noted that an exceedingly restrictive approach to rebuttal prompts the prosecutor to present his evidence as exhaustively as possible so as to avoid the necessity of adding new evidence if the defence succeeds in challenging his arguments.[60] This attitude in turn leads to a protracted presentation of evidence. However, it can also be argued that it also obliges him to organise the evidentiary material in a comprehensive manner so as not to repeat the same arguments and call the same witnesses several times. It seems that the task of an international criminal tribunal judge is to strike the right balance between the following two obligations: on the one hand, he is expected not to handle the decision to admit new evidence too restrictively, in order to allow for submission of evidence presentation to be as comprehensive as possible. On the other hand, however, he is expected to deny the possibility to produce new evidence after closing the prosecution case that it failed to produce at an earlier stage when a party cannot show its diligence in finding it earlier. From the common law point of view, in such a situation, prosecution would expect that it can supply additional evidence at even the latest stage of the proceedings and would not be forced to apply due diligence during the case-in-chief presentation.[61]

However, there is also a possibility to react to certain extraordinary circumstances that may arise in a case. Namely, such an order of presentation of evidence is only obligatory if the Trial Chamber does not decide to vary it. It has discretion to do it "in the interests of justice". Such a variation may therefore be introduced when certain circumstances prevent the presentation of evidence in proper order, such as the necessity of interposing a witness due to illness.[62]

The ICC has adopted unique rules for presentation of evidence that do not follow the model of a strict adversarial approach.

---

[58] *Prosecutor v. Popović*, IT-05-88, Decision on Motion to Reopen the Prosecution Case, 9 May 2008, 28–29.

[59] *Prosecutor v. Delalić*, IT-96-21, decision of 19 August 1998, § 34–37.

[60] Eser (2008), p. 215.

[61] Schuon (2010), p. 58; LaFave et al. (2009), pp. 1169–1172.

[62] May and Wierda (2002), pp. 145 and 146; Knoops (2005), p. 251.

Its legal framework is silent on the issue in what sequence evidence is to be presented. The Statute merely provides that the presiding judge may give directions for the conduct of proceedings, including to ensure that they are conducted in a fair and impartial manner (Article 64(8)(b)). The Rules of Procedure and Evidence, on the other hand, provide for three ways in which the course of the evidentiary proceedings may be regulated.

In the beginning, there is no mention of *opening statements*—in contrast with *closing statements*, which are explicitly provided for in Rule 141(2). This solution seems rather characteristic of the conduct of trial in the continental tradition. This lacuna does not mean that there is no possibility to make such a statement: Regulation 54(a) of the Court Regulations stipulates that at a status conference the Trial Chamber may issue an order regarding "the length and content of (...) opening and closing statements". As a matter of fact, it has been concluded that such statements seem to be envisaged as "components of the ICC trial process".[63]

As to the order of presentation of evidence, firstly, the presiding judge shall determine how the hearing is to be conducted depending on the circumstances of the given case. In particular, he may establish the order and the conditions under which he intends the evidence to be presented (Rule 122 RPE). This power is only discretionary; the judge may also find that there is no need for him to get engaged in the course of the trial.

Secondly, when a judge does not give directions, the Rules offer to the parties a possibility to agree on the order and manner in which the evidence will be submitted. However, even the parties' agreement does not exclude the presiding judge's right to provide directions on the course of evidentiary proceedings. As priority should always be given to the provisions included in the Statute rather than those in the Rules, the latter are applied only when the provision of the Statute does not provide otherwise. In consequence, if, pursuant to the provisions of the Statute, the presiding judge considers it advisable and justified by the content of this provision that the course of evidentiary proceedings should be managed, the agreement of the parties may cover only those components of the evidentiary proceedings that have not been regulated by the judge's order.

Finally, if no agreement can be reached by the parties, the presiding judge shall issue directions (Rule 140(1) RPE).

Moreover, the Regulations of the Court provide that the presiding judge, in consultation with the other members of the Chamber, shall determine the mode and order of questioning witnesses and presenting evidence so as to make the questioning of witnesses and the presentation of evidence fair and effective for the determination of the truth and in order to avoid delays and ensure the effective use of time (Regulation 43). On the basis of the provision, it can be assumed that even if the time limit for the presentation of evidence by the Prosecutor is set, the Chamber may still review the length of questioning witnesses in order to prevent unnecessary delays and to maintain effective use of time.[64] Usually this is also what

[63] Acquaviva et al. (2013), p. 550.

[64] See: Solano Mc Causland and Carnera Rojo (2012), p. 429.

happens in judicial practice: judges indicate precisely how much time is given to the party to present its arguments. However, it is not clear if, in a situation when the parties agree on the sequence of questioning, the Chamber may still intervene in the mode and order of presenting evidence. We may assume that it is possible, as the Rules of Procedure and Evidence do not prevail in a situation of a conflict with Regulations of the Court; they are of the same legal force.

The manner of regulating the evidentiary proceedings may then follow the way known from the *ad hoc* tribunals, as well as any other way that the parties or the judge considers appropriate for a given case. It is thus left to the discretion of a judge to decide whether the style of trial is to be judge-steered or adversarial, that is, whether the trial should be conducted by a judge with wide powers as in continental law systems or whether the parties as the main actors should present evidence as in common law systems; as it can be put: the Statute remains open for both forms.[65]

In the first ICC's case, the parties concluded an agreement in which they opted for an adversarial model at trial, where the order of presentation of evidence was strictly followed.[66] "This is not surprising given the fact that the bench's presiding judge, Sir Adrian Fulford from the United Kingdom, has a common law background".[67] It should be stressed that the agreement was concluded basing on the prosecution's proposal. According to the prosecution, it was more favourable to them to present all of its incriminating evidence at the beginning of the trial. The Prosecutor concluded that only having a complete picture of such evidence would enable the accused to decide how to exercise his procedural rights—whether to use the right to silence.[68] In his opinion, this model will also allow to present the prosecution case in a well and effectively organised manner. However, on the request of the defence and with the co-operation of the Chamber such a trial order was incorporated: after presentation of the prosecution case, the Chamber's evidence and evidence submitted by the participating victims in person were submitted and the defence presented its evidence in the final stage after which the prosecution's response in the form of rebuttal was authorised. Also, although the defence objected to the prosecution's proposal to present a response to evidence *via* rebuttal, such right was authorised by the Trial Chamber, which concluded that the Statute and the Rules are "sufficiently broadly framed to allow this kind of evidence to be introduced".[69] However, in the second trial, in *The Prosecutor v Katanga*, the Trial Chamber chose to issue the consolidated directions on the conduct of the proceedings from the outset. According to these directions, trial was to be organised in distinct phases, including the right of the Chamber to intervene at all times and to

---

[65] Tochilovsky (1999), p. 344.

[66] *The Prosecutor v. Lubanga*, ICC-01/04-01/06, Decision on the Status before the Trial Chamber of the Evidence Heard by the Pre-Trial Chamber and the Decisions of the Pre-Trial Chamber in Trial Proceedings, 13 December 2007, § 2–3. In general see: Gallmetzer (2009), pp. 512–514 and 519–520.

[67] Schuon (2010), p. 292.

[68] Vasiliev (2012), p. 761.

[69] Acquaviva et al. (2013), p. 602.

order the production of evidence necessary to assist the Chamber in establishing the truth. These directions did not envisage rebuttal stage, as the Chamber concluded that this stage may be permitted in exceptional circumstances only. In *The Prosecutor v. Bemba*, the ICC followed the previous example and issued consolidated directions on the conduct of the trial pursuant to Rule 140.[70] However, in this case the Trial Chamber approach was less "managerial", as it granted the parties greater autonomy in developing their cases: "it is for the parties to determine the manner in which they will present their cases"—it concluded.[71] Nonetheless, it continued to state that this discretion is not unlimited but subject to the Chamber's statutory duties to ensure a fair and expeditious trial and to guarantee full respect to the rights of the accused. Finally, quite oppositely, in *The Prosecutor v. Banda and Jerbo*, the sequence of presenting evidence is governed by the parties' joint submissions filed upon the Trial Chamber's invitation.[72] Flexibility of solutions was particularly important in this case, as the parties agreed on the facts of the case. It seemed most appropriate to leave them full discretion as to the organisation of the presentation of evidence in such a case. Usually, the order of presentation of evidence follows the scheme of adversarial debate with two parties presenting their arguments then submitting replies to the other party's arguments with the judge giving the floor to the parties in sequence.

If we think about the consequences of the model of evidentiary proceedings before the ICC for the Prosecutor, the most important difference in relation to the regulations applied before the *ad hoc* tribunals is that there is no reference to "prosecution case" and "defence case".[73] Therefore, there is no obligation to present first all the evidence in support of the accusation and only then proceed to the evidence prepared by the defence (by all the stages of cross-examination). This attitude resulted in both the *ad hoc* tribunals in unacceptable delays in presenting evidence. The restrictive approach to rebuttal prompts the parties to present their evidence as excessively as possible in order to avoid the necessity of bringing additional evidence in case the other party successfully challenges the presented reasoning. Regardless of the merit-based preparation of evidentiary material, the ICTY Prosecutor's failure to follow the rules of evidentiary proceedings resulted in the rejection of his arguments by the court and the acquittal of the accused. The separation of a trial into a prosecution case and a defence case, which both relate to a plurality and variety of counts, each of which may furthermore cover numerous events, and then the presentation of evidence with regard to the same count and event by the prosecution on the one side and the defence on the other side leads to a

[70] *The Prosecutor v. Bemba*, ICC-01/05-01/08-1023, Decision on Directions for the Conduct of the Proceedings, 19 November 2010.

[71] Cases described in: Acquaviva et al. (2013), p. 606.

[72] *The Prosecutor v. Banda and Jerbo*, ICC-02/05-03/09-155, Order requesting submissions on procedures to facilitate the fair and expeditious conduct of the proceedings following the Joint Submission of 16 May 2011, 30 May 2011, § 7.

[73] Bitti (2008), p. 1217.

consequence that it takes months, if not years, to present the case. In such a case, it was all the more difficult to keep the presentation of evidence with regard to its relevance under control (both for the parties and for the judges).[74]

At present, due to the application of a more flexible procedure before the ICC, the Prosecutor does not need to submit the entire evidentiary material during the presentation of his case for fear that he will not be able to return to this phase at a later stage. Thanks to this procedural flexibility, the parties do not overwhelm the Court with a vast amount of evidence from the very beginning of the trial "just in case". The flexible order of evidence presentation makes it possible to assume that the evidence will be presented by topic, in a sequence, relative to specific charges or to specific elements of the crime, instead of being presented all at once. This model of evidence presentation is often referred to as a "thematic organisation model".[75] In this model, neither prosecution nor defence has a distinguishable case of their own of which they are "masters". Instead, the order in which the hearing of evidence at trial progresses is organised *per* substantive topics and specific charges rather than by formal adversarial requirements. The model follows substantive rather than procedural logic. Before the prosecution and the defence can continue to the next fact that requires proving, they need to present all evidence, pertaining to a specific charge or its element or even topic. Each stage of presentation of evidence—evidence for the prosecution, evidence for the defence, rebuttal and rejoinder—may address subsequent charges one by one. However, as both the Rome Statute and the Rules are not conclusive as to whether the parties should present their evidence in a coherent block or organised by topics, the presentation may also take up a model adopted by the parties for the needs of a given case. Therefore, trials may follow either the approach of organising the trial enquiry *per* party or the approach under which the presentation of evidence is structured *per* topic, basing on the continental model of trial ("a variable model").[76] However, it seems that in practice the ICC has been consistent in considering the evidence for the prosecution and evidence for the defence as the two phases of the trial *par excellence*.[77] The same practice shows that it cannot be stated that the prosecution's right to rebut evidence submitted by the defence can be taken for granted. In spite of full flexibility of rules of conduct of the evidentiary proceedings, it seems that the ICC judges most often follow a certain pattern—the one used before the *ad hoc* tribunals.

7.3.2 Method of Presentation of Evidence

The rules of evidentiary proceedings relate also to the manner of interrogating witnesses. In the common law tradition, the central meaning is given to cross-

[74] Eser (2008), p. 214.

[75] See: Vasiliev (2012), p. 757. Similar commentary in: Kuczyńska H (2014b), p. 61.

[76] Eser (2008), p. 224; Vasiliev (2012), p. 760.

[77] Acquaviva et al. (2013), p. 607.

examination. The common law lawyers put emphasis on cross-examination as the central safeguard and truth-seeking mechanism of the criminal trial, seen as a contest between two parties and their versions of events. It is perceived as a major instrument of the prosecution and the guarantee of the rights of the accused; it is the most secure method of verifying the authenticity and completeness of a witness's claims and of his credibility.[78] At the same time, it is an institution in which major differences between the two legal traditions in question manifest themselves.

In the United States, this right is guaranteed by The Sixth Amendment to the US Constitution. The order of the subsequent stages of witness interrogation is strictly defined. The first examination of a witness is called *direct examination*, which is conducted by the party calling the witness. The next step is *cross-examination* by a party other than the one who called the witness. The scope of questioning is restricted here. It may relate only to matters covered on direct examination and enquiries into the credibility of the witness. Afterwards, the party calling the witness conducts *redirect examination*, which is limited to the issues raised during the cross-examination. New issues cannot be raised. This stage is used to clarify any ambiguities that had occurred in cross-examination, as well as to strengthen the credibility of the evidence challenged by the defence. The introduction of new evidence is not possible. At each of these stages, there are different rules for asking questions. For instance, leading questions should not be used on direct examination (except as necessary to develop the witness's testimony). However, ordinarily, the court should allow leading questions on cross-examination.[79] Each deviation from the strictly defined rules may lead to the opposite party's objection and to the judge's overruling of the question.

In England and Wales, following the *examination-in-chief*, a witness will be cross-examined by the advocate for the party not calling the witness. The purpose of *cross-examination* is to challenge each component of the witness's deposition that is at odds with the version presented by the party, to obtain information that could support cross-examiner's version and to undermine the witness's credibility. This stage is used to "weaken the testimony of the witness, either by casting doubt about his testimony, or by eliciting facts favourable to the cross-examiner, or by discrediting the credit of the witness in the eyes of the jury".[80] During the cross-examination, a party may only ask questions that are relevant. A question is relevant if it concerns "an issue in the case, i.e. it relates directly to whether the accused committed the offence, or relates to the fact which increases or decreases the likelihood of his having done so".[81] However, it differs from the United States in

---

78 See: *Mechanical and General Inventions Co and Lehwess v. Austin and Austin Motor* Co [1935] AC 346. Case cited after: Hannibal and Mountford (2002), p. 306. See also in general: May and Wierda (2002), p. 146; Safferling (2001), p. 283.

79 Federal Rules of Evidence, Rule 611(c), http://www.law.cornell.edu/rules/fre/rule_611. Accessed 9 Feb 2015.

80 Ward and Wragg (2005), p. 608.

81 Cit. after: Sprack (2012), p. 328.

that the cross-examination may go beyond the issues raised during the main hearing and the witness's credibility—it may tackle any issue relevant for the case. As far as the witness's credibility is concerned, the questions asked are usually aimed at demonstrating that his current testimony is in conflict with the depositions made earlier in the proceedings. The cross-examiner may also want to demonstrate that the witness has been bribed by the other party, that there exists a special personal relationship between the witness and the other party, that he has previously been penalised or that his personal or health-related conditions and characteristics render his testimony unbelievable. If any of these circumstances has been proven during the cross-examination, the judge is obliged to instruct the jury that the testimony of such a witness may have only a limited evidentiary effect.[82] In England, however, the witness has a chance to explain any testimony contradictions that arose during the cross-examination. The cross-examination ends with the witness providing a final answer to a question (the so-called *finality rule*). Cross-examination is followed, sometimes, by *re-examination* by the advocate for the party calling the witness. The purpose of re-examination is limited to clarifying matters that have arisen out of testimony that has been shaken under cross-examination. Its objective is to remedy any damage to the witness's credibility arising from the cross-examination and to explain the contradictions that have occurred in his statement.[83]

In the continental system, the rules pertaining to the sequence of questioning are optional. Usually, trials follow the unitary mode of questioning, which is applied indiscriminately to all witnesses whether they are called to testify in favour or against the accused. This is a consequence of the fact that all witnesses are considered to be "witnesses of the court" rather than "partisan witnesses". The Polish criminal procedure provides that after a person examined has expressed himself freely, other persons may ask questions in the following order as called by the presiding judge: the state prosecutor, subsidiary prosecutor, attorney of the subsidiary prosecutor, private prosecutor, attorney of the private prosecutor, civil plaintiff, attorney of the civil plaintiff, expert, defence counsel, the accused and members of the panel of judges (Article 370 CCP). The optional character of the questioning sequence leaves plenty of liberty to the judge in shaping the course of an interrogation. As a rule, however, the party upon whose request the witness has been admitted asks questions before the other parties. This is also the case in the German procedure, where both the prosecutor and the defence counsel are the first to interrogate witnesses they have called. Usually, however, it is the judge who is in charge of asking questions of key importance for the case. He conducts the bulk of examination. In German criminal trial, the presiding judge shall conduct the hearing, examine the defendant and take the evidence. In the Polish model of trial, the members of the panel of judges may, when necessary, ask additional questions at any time. In German trial, however, the presiding judge may ask the witnesses and experts such questions as he deems

[82] Criminal Procedure Act 1864, Section 6(1), http://www.legislation.gov.uk/ukpga/Vict/28-29/18/contents. Accessed 9 Feb 2015.

[83] Hannibal and Mountford (2002), p. 315.

necessary for further clarification in the case, but only after the examination conducted by the parties (§ 239 StPO).[84] It is worth mentioning that also this rule changes in the Polish system of criminal procedure. The new Article 370 § 1 CCP states that the members of the bench are allowed to pose questions to an interrogated person only when all the other parties finished their interrogation. In those systems, the cross-examination, although possible, does not play as significant a role as in the Anglo-Saxon systems. In the majority of cases, it is not held at all during the trial due to the insignificant activity of the parties.

The Charter of the IMT in Nuremberg regulated the principles of the interrogation to only a limited extent. It provided that "the Prosecution and the Defense shall interrogate and may cross-examine any witnesses and any Defendant who gives testimony". It was concluded that this right, however, does not adduce to the questioning of a witness by a represented defendant. Additionally, the Tribunal could ask any question to any witness and to any defendant at any time (Article 24 (g) and (f) of the Charter).

In proceedings before the ICTY, the right to examine, or have examined, the witnesses against him and to obtain the attendance and examination of witnesses on his behalf under the same conditions as witnesses against him became one of the rights guaranteed to the accused by the Statute (Article 21(4)). The provisions regulating this stage of proceedings replicate a classical common law model of conduct of examination: cross-examination is subject to restrictive rules. Evidentiary proceedings follow a prescribed pattern: the *examination-in-chief*, *cross-examination* and *re-examination*. As a rule, the party calling the witness manages the examination.[85] As in the Anglo-Saxon model of trial, cross-examination is limited to the subject matter of the evidence-in-chief and matters affecting the credibility of the witness and, where the witness is able to give evidence relevant to the case for the cross-examining party, to the subject matter of that case (Rule 90(H) RPE ICTY). Cross-examination is a testimonial case following the examination-in-chief of the other party's witnesses. Its objective is to elicit information that has emerged from examination-in-chief that would serve to undermine the case of the other party: e.g., aim to show that the witness is testifying falsely, incompletely or inconsistently with his previous statements or refuses to answer a question.[86]

The Trial Chamber may, in the exercise of its discretion, permit enquiry into additional matters. If it considers it necessary, it may admit further questions, including those that do not pertain to the main subject of the examination. The scope of interrogation may also be expanded when it turns out that the witness's statements contradict the case of the party that called him. The party may explain to

---

[84] Volk (2006), p. 201.

[85] *Prosecutor v. Kordić*, IT-95-14/2, Decision on Prosecutor's Motion on Trial Procedure, 19 March 1999. See in general: May and Wierda (2002), pp. 147–148; Vasiliev (2012), pp. 769–770.

[86] See: *Prosecutor v. Halilović*, IT-01-48-T, Decision on Admission into Evidence of Prior Statements of a Witness, 5 July 2005.

the witness the nature of the problem—in order to provide the witness with an opportunity to comment on the contradictory versions of the events, to deal with any matters in his evidence that are disputed and not to limit him only to responding to questions.[87] During the re-examination, on the other hand, the party calling the witness may ask him questions to clarify any ambiguities or new issues that have resulted from the cross-examination. Thus, the party that summoned the witness is given the "final word". However, if during the re-examination other issues are brought up than those revealed during the examination-in-chief, the opposite party may subject the witness to the cross-examination procedure, but only in relation to these new issues. A judge may at any stage put any question to the witness (Rule 85 (B)). Also, upon his intervention, the party may continue with an examination to clarify any new issues that have arisen.[88] As a result, the scope of cross-examination held before the ICTY is broader than the scope of examination conducted before US courts. It is more similar to the English system in that it leaves the judge more liberty to go beyond the basic examination principles.

The process of witness examination in proceedings before the ICC has become much more flexible than in the case of the *ad hoc* tribunals.

The Rules of Procedure and Evidence provide only for general rules that should be applied during an examination. According to Rule 140(2), a party that submits evidence by way of a witness has the right to question that witness. In the second phase, the prosecution and the defence have the right to question that witness about relevant matters related to the witness's testimony and its reliability, the credibility of the witness and other relevant matters. The defence shall always have the right to be the last to examine a witness. This model resembles the common law structure of examination. However, the Rules do not use the term *cross-examination*. It is assumed that this "culturally neutral" phrasing of this provision was deliberate in order not to predetermine the use of this procedural element in a spirit of one legal system but to establish a *sui generis* solution.[89] Moreover, the Rules are silent as to the problem of re-examination—whether a party has the right to repeatedly question the same witness after the cross-examination by the other party. From the judicial practice, it would seem that there is such a possibility. However, even if the party considers that is has no right to re-examine the witness, questions posed by a judge may clarify certain issues. The Trial Chamber has the right to question a witness before or after a witness is questioned by a party (but never within the questioning). Therefore, the judges should abstain from interrupting the party during an examination. The same solution was adopted in the German criminal trial—notwithstanding the wide powers of a judge. It is claimed that this solution

[87] May and Wierda (2002), p. 150; Vasiliev (2012), p. 770; Tochilovsky (2008), pp. 329 and 340.

[88] Existence of such a possibility is indicated by: Tochilovsky (1999), p. 195.

[89] As noticed by most of the authors, *inter alia*: Ambos (2003), p. 20; Orie (2002), p. 1488; Schuon (2010), p. 294; Lewis (2001), pp. 548–549.

before the ICC allows avoiding a situation when a judge interferes with a party's line of questioning and thus frustrates the adopted tactics. However, as it is observed, the ICC judges in practice "have interpreted the quite unambiguous provision of Rule 140(2)(c) as authorizing their intervention not only before, or after, the questioning by the parties, but virtually any time".[90]

No limits have been determined in proceedings before the ICC within which the cross-examination of the opposite party's witnesses is permissible. No decision was made to implement the principle present in the RPE ICTY to limit cross-examination to the claims raised in the examination-in-chief or to questions pertaining to the witness's credibility. At the ICC, according to Rule 140(2)(b), both parties may question the witness of the other party not only about relevant matters related to the witness's testimony and its reliability, the credibility of the witness, but also about all the "other relevant matters". The concept of "other relevant matters", as it was explained in the case law, should be understood to include "*inter alia*, trial issues (e.g. matters which impact on the guilt or innocence of the accused such as the credibility or reliability of the evidence), sentencing issues (mitigating or aggravating factors), and reparation issues (properties, assets and harm suffered)".[91] In *The Prosecutor v. Lubanga*, the ICC Trial Chamber pointed out that a party may question a witness it has not called about matters that go beyond the scope of the witness's initial evidence. Quite oppositely than in the common law model, the parties were encouraged to put such part of their case as is relevant to the testimony of a witness, *inter alia*, to avoid recalling witnesses unnecessarily.

Moreover, the Regulations of the Court grant to the judges the power to control (and intervene in) the examination of witnesses. Regulation 43 provides that the presiding judge shall, in consultation with the other members of the Chamber, determine the mode and order of questioning witnesses and presenting evidence so as to

(a) make the questioning of witnesses and the presentation of evidence fair and effective for the determination of the truth, and
(b) avoid delays and ensure the effective use of time.

However, this power has not been used frequently. It has served more to adjudicate current problems of protection of witnesses rather than to influence the line and sequence of questioning by a party.[92]

The lack of a definitive verb and the use of the phrase "may be questioned" cause that the order in which the evidence would be presented is left open.[93] Moreover,

---

[90] Acquaviva et al. (2013), p. 621. The judges argued that the model of examination should not be interpreted in such a strict way as in the case of the Anglo-Saxon model; see: Kremens (2010), pp. 135 and 141.

[91] Cit after: *The Prosecutor v. Lubanga*, ICC-01/04-01/06, Decision on Various Issues Related to Witnesses Testimony During Trial, 29 January 2008, § 32. See also: Calvo-Goller (2006), p. 273.

[92] Acquaviva et al. (2013), p. 727.

[93] May and Wierda (2002), pp. 145–146. Differently: Płachta (2004), p. 735.

there is no direct indication that any cross-examination could take place. Due to the application of the flexible rules of evidentiary proceedings, it is possible to go beyond the fixed structure of interrogation adopted in common law states. On the other hand, it is also possible to stick to it. Despite the effort of the drafters of the Statute to avoid the term "cross-examination", the participants of the trials before the ICC appear to ignore the difference between this term and the term used in the Statute: "questioning by the party other than calling a witness".[94] In practice, the examination of witnesses is conducted in compliance with the principles of cross-examination and "resorting to the adversarial language for the sake of convenience".[95] However, although in cases against Mr. Bemba and Mr. Lubanga Trial Chambers preferred using neutral terms, in *The Prosecutor v. Katanga and Ngudjolo*, the ICC did formally adopt the traditional common law terminology.[96]

There is a tendency to "clear" the course of a trial before the ICC of stiff rules of evidentiary proceedings that are applied in common law systems. As there is no jury, there is also no need to protect the jurors from improperly presented evidence. The provisions provide only a framework for the procedures to be adopted. The details are left to the presiding judge to decide. The absence of rigid rules of examination makes it likely that the debate during trial at the ICC will be much more free and open than it is in the case of ICTY or in adversarial trial in general.[97] As an example, we can imagine such an order of a trial: first, the judges may put questions at the beginning of the testimony or ask the witnesses to "testify freely" (as it is the case in the Polish criminal trial or even in some cases adjudicated before the ICTY[98]), only then to proceed to the questioning by the parties stage. The "free witness narration" allows the judge to make his own determinations. Moreover, he does not have to rely on the list of questions that both parties prepared for the given witness. It may help the judges to figure out the course of events and not limit themselves to listening to the witness's testimony as guided by the parties. There is no doubt this model means a stronger judicial control over the course of a trial.

The lack of rigid rules leads to a situation in which managing the course of evidentiary proceedings in each case is left to the presiding judge. It is noted that the uncertainty as to how trials are to be conducted and leaving the matter in the hands of the judges may give rise to numerous doubts and necessitate the development of defined rules for witness examination during initial proceedings before the Court.[99]

---

[94] See the remarks of: Vasiliev (2012), pp. 765 and 771.

[95] Acquaviva et al. (2013), p. 610.

[96] *Ibidem.*

[97] Bitti (2008), p. 1216.

[98] As in *Prosecutor v. Blaskić*, IT-95-14-T, Decision of Trial Chamber I on Protective Measures for General Philippe Morillon, Witness of the Trial Chamber, 12 May 1999.

[99] The price for flexibility becomes the lack of certainty as to how the proceedings will be conducted, which is brought up by: Guariglia (2002), p. 1133. Similarly: Bitti (2008), p. 1217.

7.4 Interrelation of the Powers of a Judge and the Model of Accusation

More and more often—also in common law systems—it is considered that the judges' role consists not only in deciding on the criminal responsibility of the accused but that judges have an increasingly important case management role, also as regards controlling trial proceedings.[100] The judge is responsible for the implementation of the trial "concentration of evidence" principle (this phrase could be treated as the Polish equivalent of the "management" of the course of the trial).[101] The principle of concentration of evidence is a directive pursuant to which the trial resources should be focused on the subject of the trial exclusively for trial purposes; this objective is realised through the sequence of actions (and their concentration in time), as well as their content: "the trial should be a contained, consistent sequence of actions and events without any breaks or impediments",[102] performed "without unnecessary delay, focusing evidence around the subject of the trial".[103]

International criminal tribunals deal with cases involving vast and complex factual material, which from the very beginning forced the judges to take care of the effective handling of proceedings. Lengthy proceedings before the *ad hoc* tribunals led to the adoption of certain solutions aimed at the acceleration and facilitation of the course of a trial. In order to expedite the proceedings, ICTY judges began to manage procedure using a complicated set of managerial powers, which includes not only making judges more active at a trial and increasing their procedural controlling powers relative to the presentation of the evidence by the prosecution and defence but also calling pre-trial hearings organising the conduct of trial, plea bargaining, meetings *inter partes* to discuss issues related to the preparation of the case and trying to reach agreements on as many factual and legal issues as possible. The managing of a trial may also include broader disclosure duties toward the other party (and the court), as well as an obligation of a pre-trial judge to submit to the Trial Chamber a complete file consisting of all the filings of the parties, transcripts of status conferences and minutes of meetings held, which are functionally equivalent to a written *dossier* and give the Trial Chamber considerable information about the case.[104] These managerial powers have even become a characteristic feature of the *ad hoc* tribunals, and, as they proved effective, they were adopted for proceedings before the ICC.

---

[100] In the case of the English system, a whole chapter is devoted to this issue in: Padfield (2008), p. 322.

[101] This principle is discussed by: Cieślak (1984), pp. 343–344.

[102] See: Cieślak (1984), p. 343.

[103] See: Kwiatkowski (1992), pp. 53–55.

[104] Langer (2005), pp. 837, 874, 898, although it is also demonstrated that the judges could be making a better use of managerial judging techniques. Also: Langer and Doherty (2011), p. 279.

The first of the mechanisms chosen as one of the characteristic features of the model of conducting trial is the control exercised by the judge over the evidence prepared for presentation in trial by the parties during a pre-trial hearing. The second one is an ongoing control of the duration and the manner of presentation of evidence in trial. The third one includes the instruments offered to the judge that enable him to exert impact on the evidence in the case and to be more active during evidentiary proceedings. Last, there is a general duty to ensure the integrity of the proceedings in order to prevent different types of disruption of the proceedings. Due to it, the judge becomes not only a passive observer of the dispute of two parties but also a proactive participant of evidentiary proceedings.

7.4.1 Role of the Pre-trial Conference

Pre-trial hearings are the main instrument in the common law tradition that enables the judges to exert control over the course of the trial. In English criminal procedure, so-called *plea and case management hearing* and *preparatory hearings* before the Crown Court[105] are known, which are supposed to "enable the judge to start the business of managing the trial before it begins".[106] The purpose of this hearing is to ensure that any steps necessary for trial have been taken and that the court is provided with sufficient information to fix a trial date. The judge can then obtain information from the parties as to the issues and the way in which they intend to conduct their case. In consequence, the judge "can act upon such information by making any orders which seem necessary in order to assist the efficient conduct of the trial".[107] Also in the magistrates' courts there are pre-trial hearings. At such a hearing the accused may, e.g., plead guilty. If he pleads not guilty, the magistrates are empowered to make during such a hearing all the binding rulings that are in the interests of justice: on questions of law and admissibility of evidence, application for special measures in relation to witnesses, disclosure, expert evidence, granting the accused legal representation at public expense. It seems that the hearing is a response to the judge's lack of control over the evidence that the parties present in the trial; it allows the judge to obtain information at least on the scope and type of such material—even if they cannot control its contents.

In the continental trial, however, the judge's power to outline the limits of the evidence presented in the trial is obvious. It is the judge who decides whether given evidence is to be introduced.[108] Due to his proactive role in the trial as the authority managing evidentiary proceedings, there was no necessity for introducing an institution of pre-trial hearing in a form known from Anglo-Saxon states (although

[105] Sections 28–38 CPIA.

[106] Both citations after: Sprack (2012), p. 237.

[107] *Ibidem.*

[108] Article 171 § 1 CCP, § 244 (3)–(6) StPO.

this assumption is currently re-evaluated as the possible positive impact of such a hearing on the organisation of a trial cannot be ignored—see new Article 349 CCP).

Prior to the commencement of the trial before the ICTY, a *Pre-Trial Conference* may be held pursuant to Rule 73bis RPE. Before the Conference, the Prosecutor is under an obligation to present to the Chamber the final version of the Prosecutor's pre-trial brief, including, for each count, a summary of the evidence that the Prosecutor intends to bring regarding the commission of the alleged crime and the form of responsibility incurred by the accused. Before this Conference also any admissions by the parties and a statement of matters that are not in dispute, as well as a statement of contested matters of fact and law and a list of witnesses the defence intends to call with the name or pseudonym of each witness, a summary of the facts on which each witness will testify, the points in the indictment as to which each witness will testify should be presented. During this Conference, judges can seriously influence not only the scope of evidentiary material presented by the Prosecutor but even the contents of the indictment.

One of the major shortcomings of international justice has always been the length of the proceedings. Before the ICTY upon completion of one of the most factually complicated cases (*Prosecutor v. Tadić*)[109] in 1998, the judges decided to implement Rule 73bis RPE. This rule obliges the Prosecutor to inform the Chamber of the total number of witnesses and the number of witnesses who will testify for each accused and on each count and the estimated length of time required for each witness and the total time estimated for presentation of the prosecution's case. The Trial Chamber may refuse to hear a witness whose name does not appear on the list of witnesses presented by the Prosecutor before the Conference (Rule 90(G)). In addition, it gives the power to the Trial Chamber to call upon the Prosecutor to shorten the estimated length of the examination-in-chief for some witnesses.

Later, in 2001, there was a further strengthening of the control of judges over evidentiary material that the parties intend to present in trial. Rule 73bis(C) was introduced, giving the pre-trial judge the authority not only to "suggest" but also to "determine" the number of witnesses the Prosecutor may call and the time available to the Prosecutor for presenting evidence.

This solution was suggested by a group of experts who had been assessing the effectiveness of the ICTY and ICTR.[110] They decided that without some amendments to the procedure, it would not be possible to expedite the handling of cases before these tribunals. They found that the most advisable solution would be for the judges to assert greater control over the proceedings; the experts concluded that this

[109] *Prosecutor v. Tadić*, IT-94-0, Trial Chamber, 17 May 1997.

[110] Report of the Expert Group to Conduct a Review of the Effective Operation and Functioning of the International Criminal Tribunal for the former Yugoslavia and the International Criminal Tribunal for Rwanda, UN Doc. A/54/634, 22 November 1999, § 76, Recommendation 7, 8 and 10. See also: Comprehensive report on the results of the implementation of the recommendations of the Expert Group to Conduct a Review of the Effective Operation and Functioning of the International Tribunal for the Former Yugoslavia and the International Criminal Tribunal for Rwanda, 4 March 2002, UN Doc. A/56/853, http://www.un.org/documents/ga/docs/56/a56853.pdf. Accessed 11 Feb 2015.

would allow to expedite trials while ensuring the legal rights of the accused and the rights and security of witnesses.[111]

The implementation of such solutions, however, turned out still to be insufficient, and there was an increasing number of lengthy proceedings. Moreover, the Security Council has called on the Tribunal to "take all possible measures" to complete all trial work by 2008 and all appeal work by 2010. In response to this appeal, the Tribunal was to "plan and act accordingly".[112] With this consideration in mind, the judges amended Rule 73bis again on July 2003 in order to secure a greater control over the scope and method of presentation of the case. Newly included Rule 73bis(D) allows the Trial Chamber just before the beginning of trial—"in the interest of a fair and expeditious trial" and "after having heard the Prosecutor"—to "invite the Prosecutor to reduce the number of counts charged in the indictment" and to "fix a number of crime sites or incidents comprised in one or more of the charges in respect of which evidence may be presented by the Prosecutor which, having regard to all the relevant circumstances, including the crimes charged in the indictment, their classification and nature, the places where they are alleged to have been committed, their scale and the victims of the crimes, are reasonably representative of the crimes charged". The idea behind this provision is to invite or oblige the prosecution to focus its case on the more important charges against the accused and to eliminate or simply not proceed to trial on the less important charges (which are not reasonably representative of the crimes charged).[113]

This wording was considered to be "remarkably ambiguous", leaving uncertain the question as to whether "a chamber's powers to 'direct' or the prosecution's authority to 'select' should prevail".[114] In view of the Prosecutor, such directions by the Chambers could only be interpreted as advisory in nature.[115] He claimed that any other interpretation would encroach upon his independence should the Chamber use this rule in other than merely advisory way. In response to this statement, the judges of the Tribunal observed that these powers should not be seen as to serve to affect the Prosecutor's independence in drafting an indictment, but rather to enhance the Prosecutor's responsibility to submit the indictment properly drafted: "This amendment to Rule 73bis of the Rules of Procedure and Evidence is intended to further enhance the accused's right to a fair and expeditious trial while at the same time respecting the Prosecution's independence".[116]

---

[111] Kwon (2007), p. 361. The same conclusions in: Tochilovsky (2008), p. 271.

[112] U.N. Doc. Security Council Resolution S/Res/1503 (2003), 28 August 2003, http://www.un.org/en/ga/search/view_doc.asp?symbol=S/RES/1503(2003). Accessed 11 Feb 2015.

[113] Kwon (2007), p. 374.

[114] Schuon (2010), p. 175.

[115] Tribunal's Prosecutor Addresses Security Council on Completion Strategy Progress, 7 June 2006 r., The International Criminal Tribunal for the former Yugoslavia, News Archive, Press Releases, www.icty.org/sid/8739. Accessed 11 Feb 2015.

[116] President Pocar Updates Security Council on Tribunal's Mission and Completion Strategy, 7 June 2006, The International Criminal Tribunal for the former Yugoslavia, News Archive, Press Releases, www.icty.org/sid/8740. Accessed 11 Feb 2015.

In view of those doubts, the Rules of Procedure and Evidence were amended one more time and Rule 73bis(E) was adopted in 2006. This amendment of the Rules went one step further and allowed the judges not only to "invite" but also to "order" the prosecution to select the counts in the indictment on which it will proceed at trial. This time, there was no doubt that the judges could "order" the Prosecutor in a binding manner to give up specific charges. Nonetheless, despite the fact that it had already been made possible, the judges never decided to apply the procedure of ordering the reduction of counts. The first decision that incorporated a Chamber's order to reduce the counts in *Prosecutor v. Šešelj* was based not on the controversial Rule 73bis(E) but rather on Rule 73bis(D).[117] It "invited" the Prosecutor to propose means of reducing the scope of the indictment by at least one-third by reducing the number of counts charged in the indictment and/or crime sites or incidents comprised in one or more of the charges in the indictment.[118] The Prosecutor declined the Chamber's invitation on the basis that reduction in the indictment is unnecessary and would result in submitting an indictment that is "not reasonably representative of the crimes charged" and would thus impede the prosecution's ability to prove its case. However, the Prosecutor submitted a proposal for reducing the indictment in other way, which was accepted by the Chamber. This intervention of judges was a hint that the prosecution should concentrate its cases on a handful of representative (which best describe the criminal conduct of the suspect) crime bases.

The decision of Trial Chamber judges to exclude specific evidence from the evidentiary material of the parties has not always been acknowledged by the ICTY Appeals Chamber as the right decision. In *Prosecutor v. Orić*, the Appeals Chamber stated that the Trial Chamber failed to find the appropriate balance in reducing the time available to the prosecution for the presentation of its case. It found that some evidence must not be considered redundant in the process of presentation of arguments. It should be borne in mind that the duty to ensure the fairness and expeditiousness of proceedings will often entail a delicate balancing of interests, particularly in a trial of this scope and complexity. The Trial Chamber is required to ensure that the allotted time is reasonably sufficient in light of the complexity and number of issues to be litigated.[119] It concluded that the considerations of economy should never violate the right of the parties to a fair trial. Also in another case, *Prosecutor v. Prlić*, the Appeals Chamber indicated that the Trial Chamber had unreasonably limited the prosecution's ability to fairly and effectively present its

---

[117] *Prosecutor v. Milutinović*, IT-05-87, Trial Chamber, Decision on Application of Rule 73bis, 11 July 2006, § 13. See also: Kwon (2007), pp. 375–376.

[118] *Prosecutor v. Šešelj*, IT-03-67, Decision on the Application of Rule 73bis, § 13, 8 November 2006, § 3–7. Also: Request to the Prosecutor to Make Proposals to Reduce the Scope of the Indictment, 31 August 2006, p. 2.

[119] *Prosecutor v. Orić*, IT-03-68, Interlocutory Decision on Length of Defence Case, 20 July 2005, § 6–8. See also in general: Ackerman and O'Sullivan (2000), p. 122; D'Aoust (2009), pp. 875–876; Coté (2012), p. 332; Boas et al. (2011), p. 245.

case by limiting the initially granted 400 h for presentation of the case-in-chief to 293 h.[120] It stressed that judges should indeed asses on every occasion whether the reduction of time would allow the prosecution a fair opportunity to present its case in light of the complexity and number of issues of the case. However, according to the Appeals Chamber's view, the Trial Chamber judges appeared to have rendered their calculations based on the amount of time they wished the trial to take rather than on the amount of time the prosecution fairly needed. The Appeals Chamber also indicated that it was necessary to keep the time offered to the prosecution and the defence proportionate (ultimately, the prosecution was granted 316 h for the presentation of the case whereas the defence was granted 336 h). Moreover, taking decisions solely with the aim of expeditiousness of trial without taking into consideration the real interest of the parties may lead to suspect that they are not being in the interests of justice but are in fact dictated by the Security Council completion strategy.

The Rome Statute obliges the Trial Chamber to "confer with the parties and adopt such procedures as are necessary to facilitate the fair and expeditious conduct of the proceedings" (Article 64(3)(a)). This obligation may be fulfilled by holding *status conferences* in order to facilitate the fair and expeditious conduct of the proceedings, promptly after the Trial Chamber is constituted to deal with the case. The Regulations of the Court specify what issues may be discussed at a status conference (Regulation 54).[121] At a status conference, the Trial Chamber may, in accordance with the Statute and the Rules, issue any order in the interests of justice for the purposes of the proceedings on, *inter alia*, the following issues:

(1) the length and content of legal arguments and the opening and closing statements;
(2) a summary of the evidence the participants intend to rely on;
(3) the length of the evidence to be relied on;
(4) the length of questioning of the witnesses;
(5) the number and identity (including any pseudonym) of the witnesses to be called;
(6) the production and disclosure of the statements of the witnesses on which the participants propose to rely;
(7) the number of documents or exhibits to be introduced, together with their length and size;
(8) the issues the participants propose to raise during the trial;
(9) the extent to which a participant can rely on recorded evidence, including the transcripts and the audio- and video-record of evidence previously given;
(10) the presentation of evidence in summary form;
(11) the extent to which evidence is to be given by an audio- or video-link;

---

[120] *Prosecutor v. Prlić*, IT-04-74, Decision on Prosecution Appeal Concerning the Trial Chamber's Ruling Reducing Time for the Prosecution Case, 6 February 2007, § 23.

[121] Regulations of the Court, ICC-BD/01-03-11, Adopted by the judges of the Court on 26 May 2004, http://www.icc-cpi.int/NR/rdonlyres/50A6CD53-3E8A-4034-B5A9-8903CD9CDC79/0/RegulationsOfTheCourtEng.pdf. Accessed 11 Feb 2015.

(12) the disclosure of evidence;
(13) the joint or separate instruction by the participants of expert witnesses;
(14) evidence as regards agreed facts;
(15) the conditions under which victims shall participate in the proceedings;
(16) the defences, if any, to be advanced by the accused.

The list of these actions is only exemplary. The phrase "may issue any order" provides grounds to believe that this provision offers powers to the Trial Chamber to influence the reduction of evidence prepared by the Prosecutor for the trial. This order may refer to each of the above-mentioned circumstances: shortening of the time of witness examination, reduction of the number of witnesses, reduction of the list of issues the parties are going to raise during the trial and guaranteeing that the manner of their presentation will not lead to lengthy proceedings. It may also set deadlines for completing certain tasks necessary to proceed with the case, such as preparing translation of produced documents to the other party or drafting of their final arguments. This provision builds a foundation for exercising wide managerial powers at the pre-trial stage. The maximum rationalisation of the proceedings is to be ensured by allowing to hold a status conference by way of audio- or video-link technology or by way of written submissions. As a matter of fact, sometimes it seems that these managerial activities that were supposed to be dealt with at a status conference moved smoothly to the trial stage as well, where the judges address similar issues with their orders.

It is symptomatic that the ICTY significantly expanded the powers of the judges in the pre-trial hearing compared to the ICC. This was related to the fact that the ICTY judges were intended to complete their work within a specific, foreseeable deadline. The judge's power to influence the content of charges presented by the Prosecutor was only to be exceptional means to be used in exceptional situations. Already before the ICC the judges may not reduce the content of charges but only limit the evidence presented in the trial. The ICC judges enjoy unlimited time for the investigation of cases.

As the provisions presented above indicate, the judge's power to influence the role played by the prosecutor during the judicial proceedings should be analysed in two aspects.

The first aspect is the possibility of managing and organising the evidence prepared to support the prosecution case. Indeed, as "excessively charged indictments" are the "basic evil" leading to an extensive length of proceedings, the most easily available measure to secure expediency by shortening the length of trials is to limit the scope of indictments.[122] It encourages the prosecutor to review and select evidence and to present only such items of evidence that are directly related to the prosecution charges. The need to use such a procedural instrument in proceedings before the ICC clearly resulted from the experience of the *ad hoc* tribunals. Presentation of an evidence list to the court before the commencement of the trial

---

[122] Compare conclusions presented in: Eser (2008), p. 212; Tochilovsky (2002), pp. 377–379; Tochilovsky (1999), p. 186.

and the planning of the trial's course turned out to be indispensable in light of the requirement to limit the duration of trials before international criminal tribunals.

This solution serves as a remedy to the prosecutorial "pathology" seen before international criminal tribunals, which involves the presentation of excessive charges supported by excessively vast evidence. Such "pathology" arises from the adherence to a common law principle that the prosecutor's failure to prove that the crime charged to the accused meets the elements of the offence acknowledged in the legal characterisation drafted in the indictment leads to an acquittal. It encourages prosecutors to collect vast evidence "just in case" the evidence pertaining to the main facts turned out to be insufficient, in the hope that it at least proves that the elements of another crime have been fulfilled; for example, if the prosecutor is not able to demonstrate that an armed conflict was of an international character (Article 8(2b) of the Rome Statute), he may at least try to prove that the crimes were committed as part of a conflict that did not have an international character (Article 8(2c)). "The more the prosecution is afraid that should a count fail or evidence expected to be successful turn out to be insufficient modifying an indictment and/or bringing additional evidence is precluded, the more the prosecution will be inclined, if not forced, to frame the indictment as broadly and comprehensively as possible and to present as many witnesses and exhibits as are available".[123] As the adversarial system establishes a very clear distinction between the roles of accusing—the responsibility of the prosecutor—and adjudicating—the responsibility of the court, it is solely dependent on the prosecutor how much evidence will be enough to persuade the decision-maker. He has to make a speculative assessment well in advance. "This uncertainty may lead a prosecutor to obtain and present more evidence than what the prosecutor, or even the judges, might consider necessary to support a conviction – especially in long investigations and trials where an acquittal might be especially painful". It will lead him to "undertake especially lengthy investigations, produce an excess of evidence at trial, and spend a great deal of time in the interrogation of witnesses and experts".[124] Moreover, the prosecution has to take into account the fact that if it fails to present certain evidence during the prosecution case, it will be precluded from adducing any further evidence; as a result of this belief, it tends to present more evidence in its case-in-chief in order to avoid the risk of foreclosure of evidence at the rebuttal stage of the proceedings. The introduction of the judges' power to limit the scope of evidence is intended to ensure that the parties do not keep overwhelming the court with evidence that could have negligible or secondary relevance to the issue of criminal responsibility of the accused. Managing the course of a trial by judges involves mainly filtering out of irrelevant evidence on the pre-trial stage rather than leaving it until the final judgement. Thus, the judges can take control of what evidence to admit as relevant—while the parties usually

[123] Eser (2008), p. 213.

[124] Langer (2005), p. 872.

define the relevance of evidence as broadly as possible to avoid running the risk of not having presented evidence that might have been considered as relevant.

On the other hand, one should agree with the opinion expressed by the representatives of the common law systems that every intervention of a judge in the evidence may be regarded as a manifestation of a lack of impartiality. In a strictly adversarial trial, only the parties may decide what evidence will be presented. The judge should not be able to reduce the evidence presented by the parties. If the aim is to expedite the proceedings, the judge's role should be limited to restricting the time available to the parties for the presentation of the evidence rather than limiting the number of witnesses.[125] Naturally, the prosecutor knows best what evidence is necessary to prove the presented charges and how to conduct his case. The court's intervention may distort the coherent entirety of the prosecution case.

The second aspect of influencing the prosecutor's powers in judicial proceedings involves the court's ability to restrict effectively the charges proposed by the prosecutor. This has a significant impact on the model of prosecution, as these powers go beyond controlling the pace and length of a trial and managing the proceedings.

This institution was implemented to prevent the prosecutorial practice of presenting excessive charges of little weight that "jammed" the tribunal and impeded its efficiency. Similar to the case of evidence collection, when drafting charges, the ICTY Prosecutor was inclined to outline broadly the limits of an act charged to the perpetrator and to bring numerous cumulative or alternative charges. The excessively broad and comprehensive framing of an indictment resulted from the Prosecutor's concern that the legal characterisation suggested by him would turn out to be inadequate and that the court would decide that the collected evidence supported the commission of a different crime than the one included in the indictment.[126] The more the prosecution is afraid that should a count fail or evidence expected to be successful turn out to be insufficient and at the same time modifying an indictment and/or bringing additional evidence is precluded, the more the prosecution will be inclined, if not forced, to frame the indictment as broadly and comprehensively as possible and to present as many witnesses and exhibits as are available.[127] Conversely, by charging the accused with more crimes or through more modes of responsibility, the Prosecutor believes that he stands a greater chance of convicting the accused on at least one of the presented charges—what is commonly referred to as a "hunting expedition".[128]

However, there are some justified doubts as to the suitability of this solution. First, the reduction of the number of charges leads to a partial impunity of the accused. One may ask what should prevail: the efficiency of the proceedings or holding the perpetrators of the most serious crimes under international law

125 May and Wierda (2002), p. 342.

126 See: Eser (2008), p. 213.

127 *Ibidem.*

128 Kwon (2007), p. 375.

responsible. It seems, however, that the nature of jurisdiction of international criminal tribunals leads, as a matter of necessity, to the impunity of some of the perpetrators responsible for the crimes falling within their jurisdiction, and the powers of judges to reduce the content of charges brought against such perpetrators should be interpreted together with the principle of prosecutorial opportunism and the prosecutor's power to select perpetrators and charges brought against them.

The second doubt seems to be more concerning: it pertains to whether the impact of judges on the content of an indictment is reconcilable with a correctly understood principle of accusation and a division into the accusatory authority and the court.[129] Undoubtedly, it infringes the independence of the Office of the Prosecutor and constitutes a judicial limitation of the accusation. It sets aside part of a legally confirmed indictment for the sole reason of expediency, similar to a refusal to adjudicate. A judicial authority gets involved in a domain that seems clearly to infringe the independence of the accusation.[130] It may be, however, noticed that this is a "soft power" of the judges. Confronted with the possibility of it being used, the ICTY Prosecutor has two options: first, he may draft charges in such a manner as to render the application of this provision by the Trial Chamber unnecessary. Second, it has been indicated that as long as the Prosecutor agrees to co-operate with the judges, his independence is not jeopardised. As a result of arrangements, it is left to the Prosecutor to decide on the reduction of charges or the number of witnesses called.

The efficiency of trials held before tribunals has become one of the greatest challenges for international justice. It is indicated in the doctrine that the prosecutor is expected to join in the efforts to facilitate the course of proceedings even at the price of refraining from prosecuting certain acts or certain defendants. It means that the prosecutor should restrict his freedom of action and drafting an indictment in order to contribute to the achievement of efficiency of proceedings. It is suggested that—in order to avoid judicial intervention—he should follow specific indictment drafting principles: the document should focus not only on the persons who are the most responsible for the committed crimes but also on the most serious acts charged to them; he should always take into consideration that the size of the cases should be manageable so that the prosecution's case-in-chief does not last longer than 1 year.[131] Faced with the risk that the outcomes of his work will be disregarded or even ignored, the prosecutor should be careful not to formulate excessive charges and should present them concisely from the very beginning of the proceedings.

The implementation of the judge's control over the evidence and the content of the indictment, both in terms of its scope and specific pieces of evidence, resulted in a departure from the assumptions of the model of accusation typical for the strictly adversarial procedure. The introduction of the judge's power to limit the evidence presented by the prosecutor—despite the fact that the leading role of the parties in

[129] Compare: Eser (2008), p. 212; Tochilovsky (2002), pp. 383–384.

[130] Coté (2012), p. 332.

[131] As proposed by: Kwon (2007), pp. 375–376.

evidence presentation has been maintained—is one of the examples for the convergence of the legal systems. Currently, it is not possible to state that trial before the tribunals is strictly adversarial within the meaning of common law states. The outcome constitutes a hybrid of the strictly adversarial approach in which proceedings are conducted by the parties and the tempered adversarial approach with its active role of the judge in trial management, including the control of evidence presented by the parties.[132]

7.4.2 *Role of a Judge in the Common Law Model*

The different scope of the judges' powers in the continental and the common law traditions is related to the different roles of judges in these systems. The judge's activity during the trial is determined by the essence of the trial. In systems, where the very essence of criminal trial lies in establishing the objective truth, there is a natural need for the judge to get involved in evidentiary proceedings and to be able to introduce evidence to the trial. This is the case for the continental trial, where the proactive approach of the judge is subjected to the principle of the material truth and discovery of the objective truth is considered to be a mandatory prerequisite to a just decision.[133]

In the common law tradition, the judge is not expected to seek the material truth. This system leaves the outcome of the proceedings to the ability and discretion of the parties, as the role of a judge is limited to a mere formal control of the trial: chairing the trial and to function as a mediator between the parties.[134] He even does not take a decision as to the guilt of the accused, as it is the jury that decides which of the versions presented by the parties is more convincing. In systems that involve a contest between two parties, the judge does not have to participate in this process. The Anglo-American adversarial system focuses more on the "just settlement of dispute", and therefore the truth must be subordinated to other competing interests.[135]

Indeed, the goals of a judge in common law are not clearly defined.[136] Whereas the trial in continental states serves as an official pursuit of the material truth, in common law it is simply a contest between the parties led according to strict rules of evidence. If the trial is not aimed at establishing a true version of events, its main

---

132 *Ibidem*. Also: Boas et al. (2011), p. 301.

133 Trüg (2003), pp. 59–66, 203–209, 477; Safferling (2001), p. 217; Fairlie (2004), p. 248.

134 Eser (2008), p. 218; Safferling (2001), pp. 218 and 269; LaFave et al. (2009), p. 1176.

135 Although it is often argued to the contrary, as in: Grande (2008), p. 145; Goodpaster (1987), p. 121.

136 Schuon (2010), p. 63; Trüg (2003), pp. 66–67, who writes about aiming at determination of the "formal truth". See also comprehensive discussion in: Damaška (1972–1973), pp. 580–589; Goodpaster (1987), pp. 122 et seq.

objective is the victory of one of the parties. Hence, the course of the trial is subjected to the "contest" between the parties. It is not the material truth that wins but rather the party that is better prepared for the trial and its vision of the case. It leads to an uncertainty as to which ends an active involvement in trial would serve, if not only the judge does not have to establish the true facts of the case but even is not obliged to deliver a reasoned judgment. This uncertainty of a role he is to play results in a passive behaviour.

The judge's influence on the contents of the evidentiary material is not, however, excluded in Anglo-Saxon states.

First, both in the United States[137] and in England and Wales,[138] the judge has the right to call witnesses out of his own initiative. The case law of the Anglo-Saxon courts shows that there are certain categories of cases when calling a witness by a court is considered to be justified. It would be the case of a witness who had not been called by either party where his testimony is "clearly required by the interests of justice",[139] as well as in the case of a witness who is "untrustworthy" (e.g., due to a prior record). The parties prefer to avoid calling such a witness, fearing that his "untrustworthiness" will be revealed during cross-examination (and being associated by the court with such a "delinquent" witness). If, however, the witness has information of relevance for the case, his testimony is in the interests of justice.[140] The second category of evidence a court may produce *proprio motu* is calling expert witnesses. It allows an expert to deliver an objective opinion. Usually, the parties call only such experts who are willing to confirm their case. Intervention of a judge aims at avoiding a "battle of experts" called by the parties and acting on their commission.[141]

Second, the judge has the right to ask questions to witnesses, both called by himself and by a party.[142] However—considering the precise regulation of both the manner and the order of presentation of evidence—the judge very rarely takes advantage of this power. The adopted convention and practice of Anglo-Saxon courts lead to the conclusion that the judge uses this power only exceptionally, leaving the parties freedom as to the presentation of evidence as long as they follow the statutory scheme. The precise regulation of the course of the trial lets the judge remain passive and interfere only in situations where the parties fail to comply with these rules. It is argued that during an interrogation, the judge would have to reveal his attitude to a case, which would undermine his impartiality.

Even if the judge formally enjoys the same powers in both adversarial models, he uses them in an entirely different manner. An Anglo-Saxon judge rarely

---

[137] Federal Evidence Rules, Rule 611(a), Rule 614(a).

[138] Padfield (2008), p. 323; Sprack (2012), pp. 344–345.

[139] See cases: *R v. Roberts* (1985) 80 Cr App R 89, *R v. Haringey Justices ex parte DPP* [1996] QB 351.

[140] See: Sprack (2012), p. 323; Schuon (2010), p. 60.

[141] Acting as mere "hired guns", Schuon (2010), p. 61.

[142] Federal Evidence Rules, Rule 614(b).

exercises these powers. Numerous reservations related to the proactive role of a judge in a trial discourage him from taking practical advantage of them. In common law states, the proactive approach of a judge may not exceed specific boundaries beyond which he would become an active participant in a dispute. Despite the fact that there is a formal basis to act, this action is considered to be in conflict with the assumption of impartiality of the judge. Calling a witness by a judge is viewed with great scepticism by common law lawyers: they tend to believe that the calling of a witness by a court is "generally an unwarranted intrusion into the adversary system and should be undertaken only when clearly required by the interests of justice".[143] According to the opinion of the Anglo-Saxon courts, expressed in a case where a questioning by the judge has passed (according to their opinion) outside judicial discretion to an inquisitorial undertaking, "it is far better for the trial judge to err on the side of abstention from intervention in the case rather than on the side of active participation in it".[144]

The English judges are considered to be generally more eager to participate actively in the evidentiary proceedings than their US counterparts. In the Report of the Royal Commission on Criminal Justice, it was recommended that judges be prepared in suitable cases, where they become aware of a witness who may have something to contribute, to ask the counsel in the absence of the jury why the witness has not been called and, if they think it appropriate, urge them to rectify the situation. In the last resort, however, "judges must be prepared to exercise their power to call the witness themselves". It seems that not without a reason, the Report speaks only of calling the witness of the defence. In *R v. Grafton*, the prosecutor made a decision not to call any more witnesses. The judge disagreed with this decision and called the last witness for the prosecution. This decision was questioned by the Court of Appeal. It emphasised that the judge's power to call witnesses should be taken advantage of "carefully". Its point is to ensure a fair trial. Continuation of the case for the prosecution could never be considered to be the judge's power.[145]

It seems that the representatives of the common law model of accusation tend to equate every intervention of a judge in the course of a trial with a lack of impartiality. It is, however, harmful for the efficiency of the trial to equate a judge's passivity with his impartiality.[146] It is noteworthy that this aspect of the Anglo-Saxon model has been widely criticised. On the one hand, the representatives of these systems guard the absolute principle of impartiality of a judge, but on the other, they agree that the system leads to certain problems and gives rise to undesired consequences. However, seen from the continental perspective, his

---

143 Schuon (2010), p. 60; Trüg (2003), pp. 382–383 and 474.

144 *U.S. v. Liddy*, 509 F.2d 428, Court of Appeals, 8 November 1974.

145 [1992] QB 101. Report of the Royal Commission on Criminal Justice, section 18, p. 123, https://www.gov.uk/government/uploads/system/uploads/attachment_data/file/271971/2263.pdf. Accessed 11 Jan 2015.

146 As, e.g., Damaška (1997), p. 851, and after him: Fairlie (2004), p. 273.

activity, the scope and timing of involvement are completely unpredictable; "His detachment at trial is essentially an exercise in self-restraint, buttressed by ideology of non-involvement. However, like a dormant volcano, he may under certain circumstances erupt into vigorous activity".[147]

First of all, some attention should be paid to the interrelation between the length of a trial and the proactive approach of the judge. The Anglo-Saxon trial style encourages the parties to prolong the case. The necessity of presenting convincing arguments at the very beginning of the trial forces the prosecutor to expand his evidence in order to create as convincing and powerful a case as possible. He knows that he will not be allowed to adduce any evidence at a later stage. This, combined with the lack of judicial intervention to shorten or organise the presentation of evidence, inevitably leads to a prolonged trial. In the United States, it is considered that the judge's lack of intervention at trial is one of the most crucial factors why criminal trials tend to be so protracted.[148] Also, the ICTY judges have noticed that the judge's intervention facilitates the course of the trial and shortens it significantly: "the prolonged nature of Tribunal proceedings was attributed to a significant degree to not enough control having been exercised over the proceedings by the judges, and also to the manner in which the prosecution and defence presented their cases. (. . .) From the beginning, the judges have been scrupulous in their respect for the distribution of responsibilities implicit in the common law adversarial systems and have tended to refrain from intervening in the manner of presentation elected by the parties. This surely contributes to the length of the proceedings and is recognized as having done so by the judges".[149]

Second, the fact that turning a criminal trial into a contest between two parties appearing on equal footing may exclude the possibility of establishing the true course of events has become the main shortcoming of the strictly adversarial model of judicial proceedings.

Third, the passive role of a judge is connected with his lack of knowledge of a case. This lack of knowledge, in turn, is caused by two factors. First, in common law systems there is no *dossier* of a case in the meaning of continental law, which consists of a collection of documents containing the results of pre-trial investigation collected by a prosecutor. The common law judges do not have an access to the files of an investigation and learn about the facts of the case only when the parties present them during trial. Each party collects its evidence and presents it only at trial. The judge (jury) can only take a decision on the basis of the facts presented by the parties during the trial proceedings—in the process of presenting the evidence, challenging the evidence of the other party, examining and cross-examining.

---

[147] Damaška (1986), p. 216.

[148] Schuon (2010), p. 75; Eser (2008), p. 217; Orie (2002), p. 1442; Tochilovsky (2008), pp. 270–271.

[149] Report of the Expert Group to Conduct a Review of the Effective Operation and Functioning of the International Criminal Tribunal for the former Yugoslavia and the International Criminal Tribunal for Rwanda, UN Doc. A/54/634, 22 November 1999, § 77, http://www.un.org/en/ga/search/view_doc.asp?symbol=A/54/634. Accessed 11 Feb 2015.

Second, the judge *has to* be completely ignorant about the evidence he will be asked to evaluate, to be *tabula rasa* (a virgin mind) adjudicator at the start of the trial.[150] He can be tutored only "through the bilateral process of evidentiary presentation and argument".[151] This belief results from a conviction that knowledge by a judge of a case before the trial starts would render him biased. Indeed, it should be borne in mind that if the prosecutor submitted his materials to the judge, this would only reveal a biased version of the case, as the prosecutor collects only incriminating evidence. In result, lacking prior knowledge of the case makes it difficult for a judge to intervene reasonably during the presentation of evidence, even if he intended to make it more efficient: "the passive stance of the coordinate adjudicator is located on pragmatic grounds: unfamiliar with the dispute he is ill prepared to take charge of the procedural actions himself".[152] For instance, it is difficult for him to ask a witness meaningful questions if he has no knowledge what evidence will be presented by the party and what the party's tactics are. "If the judge does not participate in the pre-trial investigation or have access to the case through a written dossier that contains this investigation – as the judges did not in the initial years of the tribunal – she cannot be very active in the interrogation of witnesses even if she wants to, because she does not have enough information to ask meaningful questions".[153] As the judge has no prior knowledge of the facts of the case and sees the evidence for the first time at trial, the trial "can be packed with excitement and drama: the vivacity of first impressions is not adversely affected by a documentary curtain over the trial"; therefore "coordinate officials are accustomed to deciding on the basis of might be called 'astonished reflection'".[154]

7.4.3 Role of a Judge in the Continental Law Model

The judge's activity in the continental trial is an entirely different matter. The judge has a legal duty to establish the true facts of the case. Both in the Polish trial and in the German trial, the main role in the evidentiary proceedings is entrusted to the court. If the parties have failed to provide the complete evidence to the court and the court can see certain gaps in the evidence, it is obliged to supplement it.[155] The court's obligation to establish the material truth renders the continental limited

150 This notion is used in: Damaška (1986), p. 137, and repeated, inter alia, by: De Smet (2009), pp. 409–410.

151 Damaška (1986), p. 138.

152 Cit after: Damaška (1986), p. 216. Similar observations are made by the majority of authors, e.g.: Schuon (2010), p. 64; Schomburg (2009), p. 110; Tochilovsky (2004), pp. 319–344; Heinsch (2009), p. 488; Fairlie (2004), p. 278.

153 Langer (2005), p. 860.

154 Damaška (1986), p. 62.

155 Skorupka (2011), p. 125. There is also a theory of imposing on the court a "formal burden of proof". See e.g.: Śliwiński (1959), p. 300.

adversarial approach better equipped with much more efficient instruments to achieve this objective than the strictly adversarial system.

The Polish criminal procedure obliges the presiding judge not only to direct the trial and ensure that it follows the correct course but also to take a special care in order to ensure that all circumstances of vital significance to the case shall be duly explained and elucidated (Article 366 § 1 CCP). Also in the German procedure, the judge is obliged to look for the material truth: § 244 StPO provides that "in order to establish the truth, the court shall, proprio motu, extend the taking of evidence to all facts and means of proof relevant to the decision".[156] The judge has both an obligation and a right to lead an official enquiry into the crime's true events. As part of this obligation, he needs to handle the evidentiary proceedings on his own and actively search for evidence to establish the true course of events, even against the will of the accused or the prosecutor. It is considered in the above-mentioned systems that optimal investigative strategies require a viewpoint independent of "narrow partisan perspectives".[157] The parties may request introducing of additional evidence, but it is the judge who makes the ultimate decision on whether or not a given piece of evidence will be presented in trial. The court introduces evidence during the evidentiary proceedings (e.g., summons witnesses) and controls the manner of their presentation (e.g., interrogation, § 238(1) and 214 (1) StPO). Search for the material truth becomes the basic means to achieve the objective of serving justice.[158]

Representatives of the common law tradition consider this as a confusion of the adjudicating and investigative functions. Indeed, in a trial the judge plays the role usually played by the prosecutor in the investigation. It may be seen as an infringement of "the duty of an objective and impartial adjudication".[159] This belief is shared by an increasing number of representatives of the Polish legal doctrine. They indicate that such a model leads to a distortion of the triangle, the base of which should be constituted by the accuser and the accused and whose vertex should be a neutral court.[160] Moreover, it is badly perceived by society, as people believe that there are two prosecutors in the courtroom (one with a chain, the other with a red jabot). The judge is thought to be turning into a prosecutor, acting against the accused and losing his impartiality. This often gives rise to reluctance or even hostility towards the court and stirs aversion towards the prosecutor, who is believed to be sitting in trial, doing nothing and taking money for it. It has often been indicated that if the court introduces *ex officio* evidence that should have been introduced at the prosecutor's motion (for example, if significant shortcomings are found in the investigation that the judge decides to eliminate, Article 397 § 1 CCP *a contrario*), "the accused has reasons to lose trust in the court finding it not to be

[156] So-called: *materielle Wahrheit*, also: *Untersuchungsgrundsatz*. See: § 155(2), § 160(2), § 244 (2) StPO. See in general: Volk (2006), pp. 170–171 and 269; Beulke (2005), p. 233.

[157] Cit. after: Damaška (1986), p. 161.

[158] See: Trüg (2003), pp. 60–62 and 203–209; Salas (2004), p. 509; Kremens (2010), p. 117.

[159] Skorupka (2011), p. 137.

[160] Waltoś (2015), pp. 193–194. Similarily: Kremens (2010), p. 118.

objective, as it is looking for evidence for his guilt that will make it possible to convict him".[161] It should also be assumed that in the continental systems, despite the fact that the judge may look for the material truth, the burden of evidence should be placed on it very carefully. It is believed that there should be emphasis on the obligation to assess evidence rather than to introduce it. The court's evidentiary initiative means doing all the work for a public prosecutor and should be used only in exceptional cases. Therefore, the obligation to explain and elucidate all circumstances of vital significance to the case will be erased when the law reforming the model of the criminal trial to make it more adversarial becomes effective.[162]

Beginning from 1st of June 2015, the obligation of the presiding judge will be limited to "directing the trial and ensuring that it follows the correct course". Interestingly, what is one of the most discussed issues at the moment, erasing of this obligation does not change the general goal of criminal proceedings: there is still an obligation to establish the "true fact situation". It results from Article 2 CCP, which demands that "The basis for any kind of determination shall be the established true fact situation". This could lead to a conclusion that changing Article 366 § 1 CCP is a "cosmetic" change and does not have any impact on the obligation of a judge.

In continental systems, the judge has a complete overview of all the evidence from the start of the trial that he derives from the *dossier*, passed by the prosecutor, together with an indictment, which constitutes a complete investigation file. The *dossier* contains the outcomes of an investigation carried out by the prosecutor. Having this knowledge, which is equal to that of the prosecutor, the judge may actively participate in the trial, ask questions to witnesses and introduce new evidence. This knowledge is a factor encouraging intervening in the course of evidentiary proceedings. He can use the *dossier* as the basis for organising the trial and especially for introducing the evidence. Continental lawyers are not concerned that it leads to a lack of impartiality in the judge, as the version of events that he receives in the case file is a "materially true" version, since the prosecutor is also obliged to look for the material truth and collect exculpatory evidence. Evidence is therefore considered to be neutral.[163] As a matter of fact, the judges prefer to decide on the basis of written records—the *dossier* contains sources of information on which both original and reviewing decisions are based.[164] On the other hand, often concerns are expressed that in the case file "a clear hypothesis is established as to somebody's guilt and the investigating magistrate's job is to verify it". After reading the case file, therefore, "the investigating magistrate cannot start from the premise that the defendant is innocent".[165] He must adopt an initial

[161] *Ibidem*; also: Stefański (2010), p. 67.

[162] Act of 27 September 2013 amending the Act—Code of Criminal Proceedings, Dz.U. of 2013 r. pos. 1282.

[163] Schuon (2010), p. 71; Orie (2002), p. 1444; De Smet (2009), p. 409; Fairlie (2004), p. 253.

[164] Damaška (1986), p. 50.

[165] Cited after: Heinze (2014), p. 519.

hypothesis or assumption that necessarily favours one disputant over the other. Therefore, as it is seen by the Anglo-Saxon authors, under such circumstances, the trial becomes little more than a ritual confirmation of the police report or the prosecutor's file.[166]

The considerations regarding the adversarial model and the proactive approach of the judge in judicial proceedings are the more significant in the light of the current discussion on the re-modelling of judicial proceedings in Poland to enhance their adversarial character. The representatives of the Polish legal science came to a conclusion that strict adversality creates the best conditions for finding the material truth and best respects the rights of the parties to the proceedings. Accordingly, the amendment to the Code of Criminal Proceedings shifts the burden of evidentiary proceedings onto the parties, and the court is expected to limit (significantly) its role to issuing its decisions upon producing of evidence by the parties.[167] Evidence will be discovered before the court rather than by the court. The rules of the evidentiary proceedings are divided into two stages: rules of introducing of the evidence and rules of conducting of the evidentiary proceedings (interrogation of witnesses and experts, reading out a document). The evidence is to be introduced to the trial upon request of the parties on the basis of an "evidentiary motion". Only in exceptional cases justified by "extraordinary circumstances" may the court use its evidentiary initiative and act *ex officio*. However, even if introduced by the parties, the evidence may be presented only upon an authorisation by a court. The parties will also be responsible for the presentation of the evidence once it is confirmed by the court. The court will be able to conduct the evidentiary proceedings (only within the limits of an evidentiary thesis) only in situations defined by law: in case of failure to appear by a party, upon whose request the evidence has been confirmed, and also in exceptional cases justified by "extraordinary circumstances".

The amendment's authors assume that the lack of a proactive approach and of involvement in a dispute between the parties should allow the court to remain more objective and should eliminate suspicions that the court is biased, as well as reduce the risk of basing appeal charges on the claim that "the court has failed to take advantage of the evidentiary initiative"—which is raised in the majority of appeals when a party is not satisfied with the outcome of the case.

Undoubtedly, the implementation of such requirements would have the greatest impact on the work of the prosecutor's office. It would necessitate an enhancement of the proactive approach of the prosecutor and his active involvement in handling the evidentiary proceedings. In a model of criminal proceedings that has been designed in this way, there is no room for passivity from the parties, who are

---

[166] Goldstein and Marcus (1977–1978), p. 280. However, it can also be claimed that the judge can also engage on the side of the accused. Nonetheless, the result is similar: one of the parties loses faith in the fact-finder's neutrality: Damaška (1986), p. 120.

[167] Act of 27 September 2013 amending the Act—Code of Criminal Proceedings, Dz.U. of 2013, pos. 1282. See also the Explanatory Report: p. 5 and the extensive literature on this topic, e.g. Jodłowski (2012); Nita and Światłowski (2012); Lach (2012), p. 137, and the whole review entitled: Prokuratura i Prawo 2015 no. 1–2.

burdened with handling the dispute and who face the consequences of failing to prove their arguments. Until now, the prosecutor could remain passive before the court, which was determined by both normative and non-normative (organisational) factors. Currently, he needs to take over the responsibility for the presentation of evidence to support the indictment and become a fully fledged party to a dispute. Therefore, it is necessary for him to prepare better to act before the court; at present, this practice is (most frequently) limited to reading out the indictment—a natural consequence of an active judge's participation. It seems, at the same time, that the presence of "any" prosecutor at trial will not resolve the problem of a lack of a proactive approach by a public prosecutor and therefore will not strengthen the adversarial nature of the proceedings. The main reason for the passivity of prosecutors is the fact that the prosecutor in charge of the investigation does not participate in the trial. As far as the main hearing is concerned, 81.2 % of cases involved prosecutors who were not handling the investigation, and the information on the proceedings was taken only from the reference files containing only copies of the main trial decisions. Concerns about procedural obstruction arise also from inadequate organisation of work and the too-large number of prosecutor bureaucrats standing higher in the hierarchy [Pol. *prokuratorzy funkcyjni*] relative to the overall number of prosecutors. No wonder that the changes have caused a stir, if not concern, especially among prosecutors. Prosecutors have voiced their concerns, arguing that they will not be able to apply the amended provisions of the CCP and that their implementation will trigger an avalanche of acquittals of perpetrators, even for serious offences.

As this amendment enhances the adversarial nature of the trial, one of its effects will be the increased length of the judicial proceedings. In the manner typical for adversarial systems, the parties will make an attempt to present the evidentiary material to the fullest extent possible, knowing that if it is found deficient, the court would not have the authority to call additional evidence to clarify additional issues that arose in the course of evidentiary proceedings or to perform "additional questioning" of a witness. Therefore, the implementation of an enhanced adversality had to be followed by the introduction of other components of criminal procedure that would make it compatible—indeed, in the case of newly introduced systemic components of the criminal procedure, it is necessary to ensure their compatibility with other components of the system to create a coherent and logical whole. In this case, it was necessary to, first, implement components that would cause fewer cases to reach the trial stage and, second, support efficient planning of the trial so that it could be conducted without obstacles or unnecessary delays. Therefore, this amendment implements numerous, interesting solutions known from foreign systems of criminal proceedings that are aimed at expediting the trial. The first of these components is the greater scope of cases that may be resolved in a consensual mode (as we have seen in the previous chapters, presenting the institution from Article 59a of the Criminal Code). Second, it also leads to increasing the role of judicial proceedings relative to an investigation. Another new mechanism in the Polish criminal procedure model is intended to be the pre-trial conference, which should meet the same objectives as in the proceedings before international criminal tribunals. Such an organisational hearing provided for in the newly drafted Article 349 CCP makes it possible to plan the course of the trial. Such a solution provides an option for both the judge and the participants in the proceedings to plan properly their participation in the trial and to reduce the risk of schedule conflict. During this hearing (which is mandatory in more complex cases—more complex meaning expected to last for more than 5 trial days), any and all issues that may contribute to expediting the trial may be heard. The catalogue of issues that may be subject to arrangements and decisions in the pre-trial hearing is not closed but only determined by their relevance to the efficient handling of further proceedings.

The re-codification of the CCP has drawn so much attention because it is the result of an operation that is similar to establishing a certain model of criminal procedure before the ICC. It is a consequence of the vigorous discussion now taking place in Poland on comparative law. This discussion is also fuelled by the example of the ICC itself. It shows how a new model of criminal procedure has been established and new procedural solutions have been introduced in order to find the best way to achieve the goals of criminal litigation. This re-codification raises also the question as to how much the culture of criminal adjudication that exists presently in Poland will influence the new procedural situation: whether those active in criminal justice will acknowledge the existence of the new adversary trial model and adapt their behaviours accordingly, or will they just behave in the same way as under the previous model.

7.4.4 *Re-evaluation of the Role of a Judge Before the* Ad Hoc *Tribunals*

In the trial before the IMT in Nuremberg, evidentiary material was not handed over to the court prior to trial, but the prosecutors submitted it only during the hearings. This practical solution was used due to the fact that delegations of the interested states (surprisingly also continental delegations) expressed a concern that if the judges have access to a case file at the stage of pre-trial proceedings, it might be regarded as "contaminating the Court".[168] Although the IMT's judges had the power to "summon witnesses to the Trial and to require their attendance and testimony and to put questions to them", as well as the power to "require production of documents and other evidentiary material", they did not actually call any witnesses to appear.[169]

Despite initially conducting their trials following the common law model, international tribunals had to change their assumptions as was necessary in the light of the unique nature of their operation. Indeed, the essence of the proceedings

[168] Cassese (2003), p. 378.

[169] Acquaviva et al. (2013), p. 691.

before the tribunals has changed relative to the common law model. Before the tribunals, establishing the material truth and historical truth is of major importance. Although there is no such obligation in the statutory provisions, it is interpreted from the general role played by them.[170] Their task is to explain the course of events leading to the commission of international law crimes, their background and triggers. The change in the trial essence was followed by a change in the trial style. The adjudicated issues were too complex, and the "partisan polarisation" of two "self-interested individuals" became impediments to truth discovery.[171] An obligation of arriving at the material truth has been related to the principle of the proactive participation of the judge in evidentiary proceedings. The power to make a decision on the guilt of the accused also forces the judge to demonstrate a proactive approach to pursuing the material truth. Moreover, he has a duty to produce a reasoned opinion of a judgment in writing (Article 23(2) ICTY Statute).

The activation of the judicial role was, in principle, at odds with the assumptions of the strictly adversarial trial. It turned out, however, to be necessary in the case of international tribunals. Confronted with factually complex and time-consuming cases, the judges had to take more and more initiative in order to ensure a more effective operation.[172] As a result, international criminal tribunals turned to the continental law. Both the ICTY and the ICC judges are expected to take a proactive approach in establishing the material truth. They may fulfil this task, first of all, thanks to the relevant powers granted to them. Second, the trial lasts, and the parties present their evidence until the judges decide that all the factual circumstances have been clarified and it is possible to issue the ruling on the basis of true factual findings. When this happens, it is left to the judges to decide. Also, in the situation when they find the material presented by the parties insufficient to present a reasoned opinion of a judgement, they need to continue with the evidentiary proceedings in order to clarify all the issues.

In the proceedings before the ICTY, first, the Trial Chamber may order either party to produce additional evidence (Rule 98 RPE ICTY). The practice shows that the judge may order evidence when, upon presentation of the evidence by the parties, there are still some circumstances that need explaining in order to arrive at the material truth.[173]

Second, it may *proprio motu* summon witnesses and order their attendance (Rule 85(A)(v)).[174] Witnesses called by the judges usually appear after the closing of the parties' cases. In the system of lack of *dossier* of a case, it is only towards the end of

---

[170] Kremens (2010), pp. 72 and 125.

[171] Damaška (2008), p. 337.

[172] Terrier (2002a), p. 1295; D'Aoust (2009), pp. 877–878; Tochilovsky (2008), p. 270; Jackson and M'Boge (2013), p. 950.

[173] E.g. *Prosecutor v. Kupreškić*, Trial transcript, IT-95-16, Trial Chamber II, 27 August 1998, pp. 1213–1214.

[174] Piragoff (2008), p. 1304; Schuon (2010), p. 181.

a trial that they can assess which evidentiary material they lack to deliver the judgment. These additional witnesses are called to clarify the doubts that have occurred during the presentation of the case by the parties and complete the picture of events rather than to present new circumstances. Moreover, the judge will not call the witness for the defence upon its direct request. He will do it only as a result of his own decision. The Trial Chamber acknowledged in one of the cases that calling witnesses upon request of the defence is not its task.[175] This would lead to distortion of the judge's position as an impartial arbiter. During the earliest proceedings before the ICTY, such a restrictive approach continuously surprised Yugoslavian lawyers who requested the Prosecutor, and then the judges, to call such witnesses in line with the continental approach.

Third, a judge may at any stage put any question to the witness (Rule 85(B)). They have the right to ask witnesses questions both during and after the examination.

There are various opinions as to their proactive involvement in evidentiary proceedings.

Most often it is concluded that the right to actively pose questions to witnesses arises from the adoption of the continental model of trial. Many authors indicate that the actions undertaken by the ICTY judges have shown that they eagerly take advantage of their powers and do so in the manner adopted by the judges of the continental system.[176] The ICTY judges (or at least some of them) have frequently used their powers in order to clarify or complete the testimony of the witnesses called by the parties or to clarify inconsistencies or discrepancies in the testimony of a witness.[177]

However, the representatives of the Anglo-Saxon tradition perceive the proactive approach of the ICTY judge as a threat to the adversarial nature of the trial. They warn that this activity should not reach so far as to allow the judge to become an active participant in the dispute between the parties and to get involved in the exchange of arguments.[178] The passive approach of judges, however, often leads to restraint—deemed excessive by representatives of continental states—in asking questions to witnesses or calling their own witnesses, while even a small intervention could clarify doubts or establish circumstances relevant to the case. Such a situation appeared in *Prosecutor v. Tadić*, where the prosecution failed to elicit clear and definitive evidence from witnesses about the condition of the four prisoners after they had been assaulted. The witness was not asked whether or not the victim was dead, and no further details regarding his condition were produced

---

[175] *Prosecutor v. Kupreškić*, Trial transcript, IT-95-16, Trial Chamber II, 27 August 1998, pp. 1220–1221. Cases described in: Tochilovsky (2004), pp. 319–344.

[176] See: Acquaviva et al. (2013), p. 579; Schuon (2010), p. 181; May and Wierda (2002), p. 158; Tochilovsky (2008), p. 271; Kremens (2010), p. 79.

[177] Orie (2002), p. 1464; Tochilovsky (2008), pp. 271 and 387.

[178] Damaška (2008), p. 342; Ntanda Nsereko (1994), p. 538; Wald (2001), pp. 87 and 90; Tochilovsky (2004), pp. 319–344.

by the Prosecutor. For these reasons, the Trial Chamber, instead of examining the witness *proprio motu*, in order to extract this crucial information, found that the prosecution has failed to establish that any of these four victims died as a result of actions undertaken by the accused and there is no causal link between his actions and the death of the victims. The judges stated that it was not their task to "ask additional questions" to the witness. They could not take the place of the prosecution and prove the guilt of the accused.[179]

It seems that the above three powers do not render the rights of the ICTY judges identical to those enjoyed by continental judges. The burden of examining and calling witnesses is still placed on the parties to the proceedings rather than on the judges. The judges play only a supplementary role.[180] It should be rather stressed that the ICTY judges continue to look for the balance between the obligation to seek the material truth and the necessity of remaining impartial. They always have to make a decision in what situation they should take advantage of their powers to participate actively in evidentiary proceedings and when they need to acknowledge that the evidence presented by the Prosecutor is insufficient and must lead to the acquittal of the accused.

7.4.5 *Role of a Judge Before the ICC*

The power of the judges to participate actively in a trial and to exert an impact on the evidence has become an indicator regarding the role that delegations wanted to give to the judges in trial proceedings before the ICC. It is often remarked that this power became a "battlefield" for the delegations, each of which considered its trial model as the best one. The position of judge in a trial has led to a "clash between legal cultures": the culture of a passive judge and the culture of an active judge.[181] Representatives of the continental law systems insisted that the court's role should not be limited to the analysis of evidence presented by the parties. It was suggested that the judges should be granted powers similar to those enjoyed by judges in continental systems so that they could call witnesses and order the presentation of evidence.[182] During the works of the Preparatory Committee, the German delegation even proposed to grant the judges not only the authority but also the duty to call evidence that they consider necessary for the determination of the truth.[183] This obligation would ensure that the Court was not restricted to adjudicating solely on

[179] *Prosecutor v. Tadić*, IT-94-1, Trial Chamber, 7 May 1997, § 238–241. See in general: Tochilovsky (2004), p. 333.

[180] E.g.: Schomburg (2009), p. 109.

[181] This "clash" comprehensively described in: Ambos (2003), p. 20; Bitti (2008), p. 1216; Orie (2002), pp. 1475 and 1492.

[182] See: the Report of 22 November 1999. The Report analysed also in: Kirsch (2008), pp. 48–49.

[183] Piragoff (2008), p. 1304.

the basis of the evidence presented by the parties, which is often incomplete and insufficient to establish the true version of events. The lawyers hailing from the common law states claimed, in turn, that an arbiter who may participate in a dispute ceases to be an arbiter.[184]

The main point of contention was not so much the judicial power to influence the scope of evidence—which was ultimately considered necessary—but rather the manner in which the judge should be able to exert this influence: whether he should be authorised to introduce the evidence on his own or whether his powers should be limited to obliging a party to supplement the evidentiary material with a specific piece of evidence. In the end, the judge was granted three powers to influence the content of the evidentiary material.

First, the judge does not need to be satisfied with the evidentiary material presented by the parties but may demand that they present supplementary evidence that he considers necessary to establish the material truth. He "may order the production of evidence in addition to that already collected prior to the trial or presented during the trial by the parties" (Article 64(6)(d)). Moreover, on the basis of Article 69(3) of the Rome Statute, although the responsibility to submit evidence relevant to the case rests primarily on the parties, at the same time "the Court shall have the authority to request the submission of all evidence that it considers necessary for the determination of the truth". Naturally, similarly to the parties, the judges may require the presentation of only the evidence that is "relevant to the case". The judges seem to be able to take advantage of this power only after the parties have already presented their evidence. It is implied by the use of the phrase: "evidence in addition to that already presented during the trial by the parties".

Second, the Trial Chamber may "require the attendance and testimony of witnesses and production of documents and other evidence by obtaining, if necessary, the assistance of States as provided in this Statute" (Article 64(6)(b)). The current case law shows that this phrase is taken to mean that judges may introduce evidence to the trial on their own initiative. In *The Prosecutor v. Lubanga*, the Trial Chamber considered that the right to introduce evidence during trials before the Court is not limited to the parties. If the Court may oblige a party to submit specific evidence, regardless of its consent, it may do so on its own as well.[185] In consequence of adopting this interpretation, the judges are not dependent on the co-operation or the consent of the parties to request the presentation of all evidence necessary for the determination of the truth. The judges decided to consult an expert witness, who was a UN Special Repporteur. Although the parties had made clear their intention to call witnesses who were to deal with the background and context of the conflict, the Chamber stated that "it is crucial that we have a thorough understanding of the general circumstances, historical and otherwise, in which

---

[184] Kirsch (2008), p. 50.

[185] See: *The Prosecutor v. Lubanga*, ICC-01/04-01/06, Decision on victims' participation, 18 January 2008, § 108.

these general events occurred".[186] The defence complained against this decision, indicating that the content of this provision should be understood only as the power to require presentation of evidence by the parties, but the Appeals Chamber agreed with the interpretation adopted in the first instance. It acknowledged that although the right to introduce evidence rests mainly with the parties, this provision does not exclude the possibility of calling witnesses by the Court. So far, this power has not been abused.

Third, the Trial Chamber has the right to question a witness before or after a witness is questioned by a party that submitted this evidence (Rule 140(2)(c)). This power is used quite frequently. The ICC judges virtually ask questions not only clarifying minor issues but also relating to all types of issues—even to other criminal acts of the defendant—as such information may be relevant to a possible sentencing stage as pertaining to mitigating or aggravating factors. The Trial Chamber in *The Prosecutor v. Lubanga* dismissed the defence's arguments that judges must avoid questions going beyond the "facts and issues that have been ignored, or inadequately dealt with, by counsel" or facts described by the charges, as well as leading questions.[187] In consequence, as the judges seem to be reluctant to set any limits on themselves as to the questions' topics, they enjoy in practice almost unfettered discretion in this regard. Nonetheless, there are certain boundaries that the judges should be careful not to overstep. Namely, the judge must not aim to support either of the parties to the trial or to develop this party's version. His proactive approach may be only focused on explaining the real circumstances of the case.

All these three powers enable the ICC judges to go beyond the traditional role of the Anglo-Saxon arbiter.[188] They are not limited to ruling on the basis of the evidence presented by the parties, which was the greatest fear of the representatives of the continental tradition. Granting these powers to the judge does not, however, mean that he is obliged to seek evidence. The principle that the parties are in charge of introducing the evidence to the trial, and that they are responsible for the scope and quality of the evidence, remains a basic rule.

The example of a proactive participation of the judge in the evidentiary proceedings shows how procedural style and tradition influence the practice and behaviour of judges. Despite the existence of the same statutory formulations both in the Anglo-Saxon system and before the ICC, which grant judges the same powers to call and question witnesses, the manner of use of these powers is entirely different. An Anglo-Saxon judge rarely takes advantage of his authority to call witnesses or to question them. Judicial powers of evidentiary initiative and interrogation "are used as means of last resort when party-propelled presentation of facts fails; even then, these powers are used gingerly and within narrow limits".[189]

[186] Schabas (2010), p. 843.

[187] This case analysed by: Acquaviva et al. (2013), pp. 622 and 702.

[188] This fact admitted, *inter alia*, by: Terrier (2002a) and (2002b), respectively p. 1292 and p. 1296; Calvo-Goller (2006), p. 254; Safferling (2001), p. 288.

[189] Damaška (1986), p. 124.

Whereas in the Anglo-Saxon system "it has not been established" that a judge conducts an examination, some of the ICC judges proactively take advantage of their powers. It is not uncommon that the Presiding Judge directs a question to the bench: "I would just ask my colleagues whether they do have any questions?" Moreover, there are numerous issues that require from a judge active management of a case, such as arranging an effective translation (as the parties or their counsels present arguments in different languages and the proceedings cannot be paralysed or even delayed by excessively long delays in translation) or proposing solutions for the problems that have appeared in the previous sessions and require intervention. At the same time, there are still judges who do not take active part in the evidentiary proceedings. They have a tendency to regard these powers as a "kind of fall back right which will be invoked only exceptionally".[190] This seems to be a consequence of a different legal culture and style of trial handling.[191] The judicial activity during the proceedings before the ICC is an example of how the legal culture affects the perception of the scope of judicial powers and the manner in which they are used and how the perception of criminal proceedings affects the behaviours of trial participants. These factors are known as "internal dispositions of legal actors".[192] While judges with a common law background remain uncomfortable with the active participation in trial approach, the continental judges have used the same powers much more broadly.[193] In practice, it seems that the proactive approach of a judge in a trial depends on a specific style of trial handling rather than the content of a provision that regulates his powers. This style stems from a combination of the procedural culture, the trial handling tradition and the legal habits, and is combined with the general assumptions of the criminal trial model—whether strictly adversarial or tempered adversarial.

On the other hand, we may also encounter opinions that not only "naturally" judges from common law jurisdictions because of their internal dispositions generally tended toward the judge's role as an umpire, but "besides these ingrained tendencies of common law judges, even the majority of the civil law judges basically behaved as umpires or passive decision-makers during the initial years of the Tribunal".[194] There is also a third group of judges: the quickly adapting ones. It seems that some of the ICC judges have internalised a specific legal tradition of the international criminal trial and have come to consider the role prescribed for a judge in the system of the *ad hoc* tribunals as the proper role of a judge. They have adapted to a new environment, in which, as they assume, they should act according

[190] Heinze (2014), p. 502.

[191] And the authority and respect the judge enjoys in these systems could lead to a situation where the method of interrogation of a witness by a judge, showing his attitude towards the witness, could undermine the trustworthiness of the witness in the eyes of the jury. See: Kremens (2010), p. 131.

[192] This notion used by: Langer (2004), p. 12; and Heinze (2014), p. 127.

[193] Tochilovsky (2004), p. 398; Schuon (2010), p. 182, similar observations made in: Kuczyńska H (2014b), p. 65–66.

[194] Cit after: Langer (2005), p. 871.

to new rules. They will usually act accordingly, e.g. censoring a judge who participates too actively in the interrogation of witnesses.

Hence, even if we attempt to present a general conclusion as to the scope of and intensity of judicial activism, the behaviour of the ICC judges seems to be quite unpredictable. Such diversity among the Trial Chamber of a single tribunal and in the broader dimension of international justice may appear "undesirable and counterproductive" as the fragmentation of practice reflects negatively on the legal certainty and foreseeability of court practice and the way of interpretation of the procedural provisions for the parties to the trial.[195] A coherent system of law should not allow for such discrepancies.[196] There is no doubt that balancing the right amount of activism is not an easy task. On the one hand, if judicial interference can be expected in the normal run of events, the parties lose their willingness to present their cases on their own. Moreover, as soon as an official takes over the responsibility for adducing proof, it is no longer appropriate to justify factual findings in terms of burdens unsustained or requirements unfulfilled by the parties: "if any protagonist has failed to sustain a burden, it must be the official fact-finder himself".[197] On the other hand, a complete passivity of a judge may exclude the possibility of establishing the true course of events and accomplishing his fact-finding mission. Therefore, the ICC judge should adopt a "coordinate officialdom" attitude, characteristic of the continental tradition: in view of the objectives that the ICC is straining to achieve, the balanced approach should signify that even if the judge appears to superficially play umpire of a contest, he remains duty bound to seek the correct result, the right result meaning establishing the true course of events.

7.5 Conclusion

The provisions regulating the course of judicial proceedings before the ICC demonstrate a departure from the purely adversarial model of accusation and the introduction of numerous components of the continental model. The role of the judge has changed from passive to active, modelled on the continental systems. At the same time, the prosecutor's powers to control the scope and the manner of presentation of the prosecution case in the trial have been limited—both in terms of evidence and the content of charges brought against the accused.

The ICTY founders decided to use the adversarial model adopted in the common law tradition. At the initial stage of the ICTY operations, the judges diligently complied with the trial order derived from the US system. They avoided any intervention in the evidence presented by the parties. With time, it turned out, however, that in the practice of international justice these assumptions could not be

195 Criticism presented in: Acquaviva et al. (2013), p. 648.

196 Kremens (2010), p. 142.

197 Damaška (1986), p. 121. Although Kremens (2010), p. 128, argues the contrary.

followed strictly. The practice of the *ad hoc* tribunals showed that it was the limited adversarial model adopted in the continental systems that made it possible to finalise proceedings in a more efficient and expeditious manner than in the case of strictly adversarial systems.[198] An analysis conducted by a group of experts has shown that the phenomenon of notoriously prolonged proceedings before the ICTY was caused by the lack of control of the judge over the course of the trial.[199] "These problems arose from the difficulties that the adversarial system had in dealing with complex criminal cases within the international context".[200] The Tribunal itself concluded that the very own characteristics of international criminal cases cause that there is a demand to have a more proactive judge controlling the conduct of the parties and not allowing them to prolong the trial *ad infinitum.*[201] In order to expedite the proceedings, judges resorted to a managerial judging system, which combined different elements from both legal traditions. On the one hand, they were the continental system solutions, where it was the judge rather than the parties that had the sole power to make decisions on the scope of evidence presented in the trial.[202] On the other hand, we have observed how the managerial functions of the ICTY judge in regard to evidentiary material have been moved mainly to the pre-trial stage, instead of being applied during the trial (as in continental examples). The goal of its activism was not to be an active judge modelling his activities on the example of a continental judge but to be an active manager who tries to expedite and simplify the court's cases.

Only when the ICC judge has been burdened with an obligation to seek the material truth the perception of the trial model had to change. At present, the model of accusation in judiciary proceedings before the ICC differs considerably from both the common law and the continental system models. After almost two decades of experience of international criminal adjudication, which was largely based on adversarial model, the makers of the ICC concluded that the strictly adversarial mode of presenting evidence at trial should not normally be the first choice for an international forum.[203] At the same time, the adopted solution does not favour any of the models. Judicial proceedings before the ICC, despite the fact that they are partially based on the adversarial model in its pure form, also have distinct features of the continental law system (the tempered adversarial model). The ICC makers concluded that the course of the trial would ensure reliability, and simultaneously

[198] See: Heinsch (2009), p. 487; Tochilovsky (2002), p. 269; Terrier (2002a), p. 1295; Jackson (2009), p. 22.

[199] See the two reports: Report of the Expert Group to Conduct a Review of the Effective Operation and Functioning of the International Criminal Tribunal for the former Yugoslavia and the International Criminal Tribunal for Rwanda, UN Doc. A/54/634, 22 November 1999, § 76 and Report of the International Commission of Inquiry on Darfur to the Secretary-General Pursuant to Security Council resolution 1564(2004), 18 September 2004, UN Doc. S/2005/60, § 572–574.

[200] Cit. after: Langer (2005), p. 871.

[201] E.g. in: *Prosecutor v. Jelisić*, IT-95-10, Appeals Chamber, 5 July 2001, § 15–16.

[202] Tochilovsky (2002), pp. 269–270; Sluiter et al. (2013), p. 45.

[203] Acquaviva et al. (2013), p. 645.

the efficiency of the proceedings, in a manner adjusted to the specific conditions of an international criminal tribunal, only if they combine components of the continental and common law trial. They have not chosen between these two legal traditions but combined them to produce their own, unique, adversarial model that may be referred to as “a tempered adversality of proceedings model”.[204] It is a new system for arriving at the material truth. In this way, an international criminal procedure is developing, responding to specific needs of this type of administration of justice. Some may claim that the need to expedite the administration of justice and avoid delays accounted for the slow shift away from a largely accusatorial procedure, toward one that is “increasingly interspersed with inquisitorial correctives”.[205] However, a more accurate conclusion could be that the main aim of introduced procedural solutions was to adopt an effective managerial judging system that led to adopting of a hybrid model between the adversarial and inquisitorial systems.[206]

Before the ICC clear distinctions can be seen between specific components borrowed from each of the models. The technical rules of evidentiary proceedings follow the adversarial system in its pure form. First, evidence is introduced to the trial by parties. Second, the course of the trial itself may take on a form characteristic of those systems: both the order of presentation of evidence and the manner of interrogating witnesses and expert witnesses in the form of cross-examination. However, the basic assumptions of the criminal trial are identical to the assumptions of the continental systems: the aim of the criminal trial is to determine the material truth, the prosecutor performs the functions of an impartial authority of justice and the judges are expected to carry out a proactive search for the material truth. In order to ensure the expeditiousness of the proceedings, which may only be relative, taking into account the complexity of cases heard by the Tribunal, efficient management of the course of the trial by judges has turned out to be of key importance.

The ICC Prosecutor and the defence continue to present their dispute to an impartial arbiter, but their dispute has been subordinated to time-framework requirements and the necessity of organising vast evidentiary material and of complying with a reasonable case resolution deadline. Moreover, the judge has ceased to be an impartial arbiter and turned into an entity with a lot of options to influence the course of the trial, often at the cost of the Prosecutor’s self-sufficiency and independence—for the sake of the effectiveness of the proceedings. The Prosecutor’s role has also changed; he could not be solely the opposite party in the trial before the ICC, being at the same time an authority appointed to seek the material truth, not solely an accuser but also an active player in a historical and cultural process of seeking international justice.[207] Simultaneously, this model of

---

[204] Keen (2004), pp. 792–794, cited also in Wiliński and Kuczyńska (2009), p. 223. Similar conclusions in: Mégret (2009), p. 44.

[205] Mégret (2009), p. 62.

[206] Langer (2005), pp. 885 and 890.

[207] Eser (2008), p. 209.

accusation has not shared the most serious shortcomings of the continental model. The judges' obligation to conduct active search for evidence cannot result in a passive attitude by the ICC Prosecutor during a trial. More importantly, it is not the Trial Chamber that decides what evidence will be presented in a trial. The model has also managed to avoid the second serious shortcoming of the continental model, namely a situation where the court becomes acquainted with only one version of events—that presented by the prosecutor in a case file. In the case of the ICC, however, such a solution would not infringe the principle of the equality of the parties and would not lead to the superiority of the incriminating evidence, as the Prosecutor is also obliged to collect evidence in favour of the accused. This leads to an additional aspect that should also be mentioned, that is, the compatibility of procedural institutions: how introducing of one element of criminal procedure must be necessarily combined with adapting other determinants of criminal trial. For example, there is only a need for rigorous rules of cross-examination and producing evidence when a judge is trained in being a neutral arbiter, not taking part in the presentation of the parties' cases. Another example of this theory would be that the passing of a *dossier* of an investigation to a judge is in compliance with the principle of a fair trial only if this *dossier* has been assembled by an impartial prosecutor.

References

Ackerman J, O'Sullivan E (2000) Practice and procedure of the international criminal tribunal for the former Yugoslavia. With selected materials. Kluwer Law International, The Hague/London/Boston

Acquaviva G, Combs N, Heikkila M, Linton S, McDermott Y, Vasiliev S (2013) Trial process. In: Sluiter G, Friman H, Linton S, Vasiliev S, Zappala S (2013) International criminal procedure. Principles and rules. Oxford University Press, Oxford

Ambos K (2003) International criminal procedure: "adversarial", "inquisitorial" or mixed? Int Crim Law Rev 3:1

Ambos K (2007) The structure of international procedure: "adversarial", "inquisitorial" or mixed. In: Bohlander M (ed) International criminal justice: a critical analysis of institutions and procedures. Cameron May, London

Ambos K (2009) 'Witness Proofing' before the ICC: neither legally admissible nor necessary. In: Stahn C, Sluiter G (eds) The emerging practice of the International Criminal Court. Martinus Nijhoff, Leiden/Boston

Bassiouni MC (1993) Human rights in the context of criminal justice: identifying international procedural protections and equivalent protections in national constitutions. Duke J Comp Int Law 3:235

Bassiouni MC, Manikas P (1996) The law of the International Criminal Tribunal for the former Yugoslavia. Transnational Publishers, New York

Beulke W (2005) Strafprozessrecht, 12th edn. C.F. Müller, Heidelberg

Bitti G (2008) In: Triffterer O (ed) Commentary on the Rome Statute of the International Criminal Court – observers' notes, article by article, 2nd edn. Hart/Nomos Verlagsgesellschaft/C.H. Beck, München/Oxford

Boas G, Bischoff J, Reid N, Taylor BD III (2011) International criminal procedure. Cambridge University Press, Cambridge

Bohlander M (2012) Principles of German criminal procedure. Hart, Oxford and Portland/Oregon
Buisman C (2014) The prosecutor's obligation to investigate incriminating and exonerating circumstances equally: illusion or reality? Leiden J Int Law 27:205
Calvo-Goller K (2006) The trial proceedings of the International Criminal Court: ICTY and ICTR precedents. Martinus Nijhoff, Leiden/Boston
Cassese A (2003) International criminal law. Oxford University Press, Oxford
Cieślak M (1984) Polska procedura karna. PWN, Warszawa
Coté L (2012) Independence and impartiality. In: Reydams L, Wouters J, Ryngaert C (eds) International prosecutors. Oxford University Press, Oxford
D'Aoust J (2009) The conduct of trials. In: Daria J, Gasser H-P, Bassiouni MC (eds) The legal regime of the International Criminal Court. Essays in honour of Professor Igor Blishchenko. Martinus Nijhoff, Leiden/Boston
Damaška M (1972–1973) Evidentiary barriers to conviction and two models of criminal procedure: a comparative study. Univ Pa Law Rev 121:508
Damaška M (1986) The faces of justice and state authority. Yale University Press, New Haven/London
Damaška M (1997) The uncertain fate of evidentiary transplants: Anglo-American and continental experiments. Am J Comp Law 45:839
Damaška M (2002) Adversary system. In: Encyclopedia of crime and justice, 2nd edn. MacMillan, New York
Damaška M (2008) What is the point of international criminal justice? Chic Kent Law Rev 83:342
De Smet P (2009) A structural analysis of the role of the Pre-Trial Chamber in the fact-finding process of the ICC. In: Stahn C, Sluiter G (eds) The emerging practice of the International Criminal Court. Martinus Nijhoff, Leiden/Boston
Eser A (2008) The "adversarial" procedure: a model superior to other trial systems in international criminal justice? In: Kruessmann T (ed) ICTY: towards a fair trial? Neuer Wissenschaftlicher Verlag, Wien/Graz
Fairlie M (2004) The marriage of common and continental law at the ICTY and its progeny, due process deficit. Int Crim Law Rev 4:315
Gallmetzer R (2009) The Trial-Chamber's discretionary power and its exercise in the trial of Thomas Lubanga Dyilo. In: Stahn C, Sluiter G (eds) The emerging practice of the International Criminal Court. Martinus Nijhoff, Leiden/Boston
Ginsburg G, Kudriavtsev VN (eds) (1990) The Nuremberg trial and international law. Martinus Nijhoff, Leiden/Boston
Goldstein AS, Marcus MM (1977–1978) The myth of judicial supervision in three "Inquisitorial" systems: France, Italy, and Germany. Yale Law J 87:240
Goodpaster G (1987) On the theory of the American adversary trial. J Crim Law Criminol 78:118
Grande E (2008) Dances of criminal justice: thoughts on systemic differences and the search for truth. In: Jackson I, Langer M, Tillers P (eds) Crime, procedure and evidence in a comparative and international context. Essays in honour of Professor Mirjan Damaška. Hart, Oxford
Grzegorczyk T (2015) Postępowanie przygotowawcze w świetle nowelizacji z dnia 27 września 2013 r. i rola w nim prokuratora w aspekcie sądowego stadium procesu. Prokuratura i Prawo 1–2:35
Grzegorczyk T, Tylman J (2007) Polskie postępowanie karne. LexisNexis, Warszawa
Guariglia F (2002) The Rules of Procedure and Evidence for the International Criminal Court: a new development in international adjudication of individual criminal responsibility. In: Cassese A, Gaeta P, Jones WD (eds) The Rome Statute of the International Criminal Court: a commentary. Oxford University Press, Oxford
Hannibal M, Mountford L (2002) The law of criminal and civil evidence. Principles and practice. Longman, Harlow/New York
Heinsch R (2009) How to achieve fair and expeditious trial proceedings before the ICC: is it time for a more judge-dominated approach? In: Stahn C, Sluiter G (eds) The emerging practice of the International Criminal Court. Martinus Nijhoff, Leiden/Boston

Heinze A (2014) International criminal procedure and disclosure. An attempt to better understand and regulate disclosure and communication at the ICC on the basis of a comprehensive and comparative theory of criminal procedure. Duncker & Humblot, Berlin
Hofmański P, Śliwa J (2015) Dwugłos w sprawie nowego kształtu postępowania przygotowawczego. Prokuratura i Prawo 1–2:77
Jackson J (2009) Finding the best epistemic fit for international criminal tribunals. Beyond the adversarial-inquisitorial dichotomy. J Int Crim Justice 7:17
Jackson J, M'Boge Y (2013) The effect of legal culture on the development of international evidentiary practice: from the 'Robing Room' to the 'Melting Pot'. Leiden J Int Law 26:947
Jodłowski J (2012) Wpływ ograniczenia inicjatywy sądu na realizację zasady prawdy materialnej w postępowaniu karnym, e-Czasopismo Prawa Karnego i Nauk Penalnych 2012:6
Jordash W (2009) The practice of 'Witness Proofing' in international criminal tribunals: why the international criminal court should prohibit the practice. Leiden J Int Law 22:501
Keen PC (2004) Tempered adversality: the judicial role and trial theory in the international criminal tribunals. Leiden J Int Law 17:725
Kirsch S (2008) Finding the truth at international criminal tribunals. In: Kruessmann T (ed) ICTY: towards a fair trial? Neuer Wissenschaftlicher Verlag, Wien/Graz
Knoops G-J (2005) Theory and practice of international and internationalized criminal proceedings. Kluwer Law International, The Hague/London/Boston
Kremens K (2010) Dowody osobowe w międzynarodowym postępowaniu karnym. TNOiK, Toruń
Kuczyńska H (2014a) Instytucja "*proofing of witnesses*" przed międzynarodowymi trybunałami karnymi. Palestra 7–8:17
Kuczyńska H (2014b) Model kontradyktoryjności przed Międzynarodowym Trybunałem Karnym. Państwo i Prawo 10:54
Kwiatkowski Z (1992) Koncentracja materiału dowodowego w fazie przygotowania do rozprawy głównej w procesie karnym. Problemy Prawa Karnego 18:53
Kwon O (2007) The challenge of an international criminal trial as seen from the bench. J Int Crim Justice 2:360
Lach A (2012) Zasada kontradyktoryjności w postępowaniu sądowym w procesie karnym *de lege lata* i *de lege ferenda*. Palestra 5–6:137
LaFave W, Israel J, King N, Kerr O (2009) Criminal procedure, 5th edn. West Academic Publishing, St. Paul
Langbein JH, Wienreb LL (1978) Continental criminal procedure: myth and reality. Yale Law J 87:1549
Langer M (2004) From legal transplants to legal translations: the globalization of plea bargaining and the Americanization thesis in criminal procedure. Harv Int Law J 45:1
Langer M (2005) The rise of managerial judging in international criminal law. Am J Comp Law 53:835
Langer M, Doherty JW (2011) Managerial judging goes international, but its promise remains unfulfilled: an empirical assessment of the ICTY reforms. Yale J Int Law 36:241
Lewis P (2001) Trial procedure. In: Lee RP (ed) The International Criminal Court. Elements of Crime and Rules of Procedure and Evidence. Transnational Publishers, New York
Mathias E (2004) The police and public prosecutor. In: Delmas-Marty M, Spencer J (eds) European criminal procedures. Cambridge University Press, Cambridge
May R, Wierda M (2002) International criminal evidence. Transnational Publishers, Ardsley, NY
Mégret F (2009) Beyond "Fairness": understanding the determinants of international criminal procedure. UCLA J Int Law Foreign Aff 14:37
Nita B, Światłowski A (2012) Kontradyktoryjny proces karny (między prawdą materialną a szybkością postępowania). Państwo i Prawo 1
Ntanda Nsereko DD (1994) Rules of Procedure and Evidence of the International Tribunal for the former Yugoslavia. Crim Law Forum 5:507
Orie A (2002) Accusatorial v. Inquisitorial approach in international criminal proceedings prior to the establishment of the ICC and in the proceedings before the ICC. In: Cassese A, Gaeta P,

Jones WD (eds) The Rome Statute of the International Criminal Court: a commentary. Oxford University Press, Oxford
Padfield N (2008) Text and materials on the criminal justice process, 4th edn. Oxford University Press, Oxford
Piragoff D (2008) In: Triffterer O (ed) Commentary on the Rome Statute of the International Criminal Court – observers' notes, article by article, 2nd edn. Hart/Nomos Verlagsgesellschaft/ C.H. Beck, München/Oxford
Płachta M (2004) Międzynarodowy Trybunał Karny. Zakamycze, Kraków
Romano C, Nollkaemper A, Kleffner J (2004) Internationalized criminal courts. Oxford University Press, Oxford
Safferling C (2001) Towards an international criminal procedure, Oxford monographs in international law. Oxford University Press, Oxford
Salas D (2004) The role of the judge. In: Delmas-Marty M, Spencer J (eds) European criminal procedures. Cambridge University Press, Cambridge
Schabas W (2008) In: Triffterer O (ed) Commentary on the Rome Statute of the International Criminal Court – observers' notes, article by article, 2nd edn. Hart/Nomos Verlagsgesellschaft/ C.H. Beck, München/Oxford
Schabas W (2010) The International Criminal Court. A commentary on the Rome Statute. Oxford University Press, Oxford
Schomburg W (2009) Common Law versus Civil Law: die Ad-hoc-Strafgerichtshöfe für das ehemalige Jugoslawien und Ruanda: ihre immanenten Grenzen auf der Suche nach der Wahrheit. Betrifft Justiz 99:108
Schuon C (2010) International criminal procedure. A clash of legal cultures. T.M.C. Asser Press, The Hague
Skorupka J (2011) Ciężar dowodu i ciężar dowodzenia w procesie karnym. In: Grzegorczyk T (ed) Funkcje procesu karnego. Księga jubileuszowa Profesora Janusza Tylmana. Wolters Kluwer, Warszawa
Śliwiński S (1959) Polski proces karny przed sądem powszechnym. PWN, Warszawa
Sluiter G, Friman H, Linton S, Vasiliev S, Zappala S (2013) International criminal procedure. Principles and rules. Oxford University Press, Oxford
Solano Mc Causland J, Carnera Rojo E (2012) Developments at the International Criminal Court. Law Pract Int Courts Tribunals 10:429
Spencer JR (2004) Evidence. In: Delmas-Marty M, Spencer J (eds) European criminal procedures. Cambridge University Press, Cambridge
Sprack J (2012) A practical approach to criminal procedure. Oxford University Press, Oxford
Stefański R (2010) Rzetelne postępowanie przed sądem pierwszej instancji. In: Skorupka J, Jasiński W (eds) Rzetelny proces karny. Materiały z konferencji naukowej. Wolters Kluwer, Warszawa
Terrier F (2002a) Powers of the Trial Chamber. In: Cassese A, Gaeta P, Jones WD (eds) The Rome Statute of the International Criminal Court: a commentary. Oxford University Press, Oxford
Terrier F (2002b) Proceedings before the Trial Chamber. In: Cassese A, Gaeta P, Jones WD (eds) The Rome Statute of the International Criminal Court: a commentary. Oxford University Press, Oxford
Tochilovsky V (1999) Rules of Procedure for the International Criminal Court: problems to address in light of the experience of the ad hoc tribunals. Netherlands Int Law Rev 46:343
Tochilovsky V (2002) Proceedings in the International Criminal Court: some lessons to learn from ICTY experience. Eur J Crime Crim Law Crim Justice 4:268
Tochilovsky V (2004) International criminal justice: "Strangers in the Foreign System". Crim Law Forum 15:319
Tochilovsky V (2005) Charges, evidence, and legal assistance in international jurisdictions: the jurisprudence of the ICTY, ICTR and SCSL. Wolf Legal Publishers, Nijmegen
Tochilovsky V (2008) Jurisprudence of the International Criminal Courts and the European Court of Human Rights. Martinus Nijhoff, Leiden

Trüg G (2003) Lösungskonvergenzen trotz Systemdivergenzen im deutschen und US–amerikanischen Strafverfahren. Ein strukturanalytischer Vergleich am Beispiel der Wahrheitserforschung. Mohr Siebeck, Tübingen

Turkivić K (2008) The value of the ICTY as a historiographical tool. In: Kruessmann T (ed) ICTY: towards a fair trial? Neuer Wissenschaftlicher Verlag, Wien/Graz

Vasiliev S (2012) Trial. In: Reydams L, Wouters J, Ryngaert C (eds) International prosecutors. Oxford University Press, Oxford

Volk K (2006) Grundkurs. StPO, 5th edn. C.H. Beck, München

Wald PM (2001) The International Criminal Tribunal for the former Yugoslavia comes of age: some observations on day-to-day dilemmas of an international court. J Law Policy 5:87

Waltoś S (1968) Model postępowania przygotowawczego na tle prawnoporównawczym. PWN, Warszawa

Waltoś (2005) Proces karny. Zarys systemu, 8th edn. LexisNexis, Warszawa

Waltoś S (2015) Panel I. Kontradyktoryjna rozprawa główna – sytuacja procesowa stron. Prokuratura i Prawo 1–2:193

Ward R, Wragg A (2005) Walker and Walker's English legal system, 9th edn. Oxford University Press, Oxford

Wiliński P, Kuczyńska H (2009) Rzetelny proces karny w orzecznictwie międzynarodowych trybunałów karnych. In: Wiliński P (ed) Rzetelny proces karny w orzecznictwie sądów polskich i międzynarodowych. Wolters Kluwer, Warszawa

Zappala P (2002) The rights of the accused. In: Cassese A, Gaeta P, Jones WD (eds) The Rome Statute of the International Criminal Court: a commentary. Oxford University Press, Oxford

Chapter 8
Powers of the Prosecutor in the Appeal Proceedings

Abstract The right to appeal in international criminal proceedings has developed steadily. Although in the beginning the judgments issued by international military tribunals were final, the ICTY and ICTR provided for the right to appeal. The fundamental feature for the model of accusation adopted by these tribunals became the prosecutor's right to appeal on equal terms with the accused. But even the acceptance of the existence of the prosecutor's right to appeal does not end the discussion on the scope of his powers in the appeal proceedings. There is the crucial question of whether the prosecutor should act as a guardian of law and lodge an appeal in favour of the accused. Equally important is the establishment of whether the prosecutor should be granted the right to appeal acquittals. For the model of accusation, it is also decisive to outline the grounds for prosecutorial appeal, as well as to define the extent to which the prosecutor is allowed to use evidence in proceedings before the appellate court. All these issues could be resolved in one of the two ways: either as adopted in common law states or in a manner known from continental states.

8.1 The Right to Appeal Before International Criminal Tribunals

At the initial stage of the functioning of the international administration of justice, the mere possibility of performing an instance review over the judgments issued by international criminal tribunals gave rise to serious doubts. Judgments of the IMTs in Nuremberg and Tokyo were final. Article 27 of the IMT in Nuremberg Charter provided that "the Tribunal shall have the right to impose upon a Defendant, on conviction, death or such other punishment as shall be determined by it to be just". The only opportunity to influence the character and dimension of the sanction was provided in Article 29 of the Charter, which stated that "in case of guilt, sentences shall be carried out in accordance with the orders of the Control Council for Germany, which may at any time reduce or otherwise alter the sentences, but may not increase the severity thereof".

© Springer International Publishing Switzerland 2015

H. Kuczyńska, *The Accusation Model Before the International Criminal Court*,
DOI 10.1007/978-3-319-17626-0_8

Currently, there is no doubt that the proceedings before international criminal tribunals have to be two-instance proceedings.[1] In the time that passed between the establishment of the IMT Charters and the Statutes of the *ad hoc* tribunals, numerous legal acts protecting human rights were enacted, which recognise the right to an appeal as a fundamental component of due process in criminal proceedings. Both Article 14(5) of the International Covenant on Civil and Political Rights and Article 2(1) of the Protocol No. 7 to the Convention for the Protection of Human Rights and Fundamental Freedoms provide that "Everyone convicted of a criminal offence by a tribunal shall have the right to have his conviction or sentence reviewed by a higher tribunal". The ICTY was the first international criminal tribunal that provided for the right to appeal. It was also the first time when a two-instance appeal structure was introduced with the establishment of the Appeals Chamber. Thanks to this solution, it was possible to sustain the principle of devolution of the appellate measures. When analysing the necessity to secure the right to appeal against a judgement of the Tribunals, the ICTY indicated that a right to appeal is imposed not only by the Statute but also by customary law: "The right to a fair trial requires and ensures the correction of errors made at trial".[2]

During the development of the proceedings before the ICC, it was not initially obvious that the proceedings were intended to be two instance. The opposition against the introduction of the right of appeal resulted not only from the conviction that this Court should follow the assumptions of the Anglo-Saxon tradition but also from the view that "judgments rendered by the highest criminal Court should not be subject to appeal".[3] Ultimately, however, it was decided that judgments issued by the ICC's Trial Chamber may be subjected to instance review. Article 81 of the Rome Statute provides that the parties are entitled to "an appeal against decision of acquittal or conviction or against sentence". It seems to have been a good decision that in the Polish version of the Statute this measure is not referred to as *apelacja* (an "appeal") but rather as *odwołanie* ("referral"), which differentiates it from the classically understood continental concept of the "appeal".

8.2 Power of the Prosecutor to Appeal

The introduction of the two-instance system does not mean, however, that the prosecutor is also entitled to appeal. The international human rights acts clearly give the right to appeal only to the defendant. None of them orders the states to allow the state authority to appeal against a court's judgment. Indeed, it is not a

---

[1] See: Staker (2008), p. 1022; Schabas (2010), p. 930; Boas et al. (2013), p. 954.

[2] See: *Prosecutor v. Aleksovski*, IT-95-14/1, Appeals Chamber judgment, 24 March 2000, § 106.

[3] Cit. after: Schabas (2010), p. 931.

right in the narrow sense but rather a prerogative of a state authority that must be rooted in adequately drafted law.

The prosecutor's power to appeal against the judgments adjudicating guilt and sentences depends on the development of the internal national proceedings, as well as on the assumptions as to the tasks of the public prosecutor's office. The states following the continental law tradition usually opt for equal rights to appeal for the parties of the proceedings (e.g., Article 444 CCP, § 312 StPO). The prosecutor, as a guardian of the law, is obliged to challenge the judgments of first instance courts if there is a basis for appeal. The continental tradition sees the process continuing until the time appeal is recognised or the time limit for lodging an appeal has expired. In turn, the Anglo-Saxon systems provide solely for limited powers of the prosecutor to appeal. First, there is still a conviction in the legal science of these states that the *ne bis in idem* principle should apply from the moment a court of first instance issues its judgment. Second, there is the frequently asked question of whether the powers to challenge a state authority's judgment by another state authority do not violate human rights. And third, in a situation when there is a jury that decides on the guilt, it is rather difficult to subject their decision to instance review. This power is also limited by the prosecutor's inability to lodge an appeal—or to undertake any other action—in favour of the accused. Such a limitation leads, in consequence, to a situation in which the prosecutor may only appeal against acquittals—in relation to the adjudication of guilt—or sentences that are too lenient.[4]

Faced with the major differences between the legal systems, international criminal tribunals had to choose a specific solution. Proceedings before the *ad hoc* tribunals had mainly features of the *common law* system. But already during the functioning of these tribunals, similar to the case of other legal institutions, it turned out that it was necessary to make use of certain solutions from the continental appeal proceedings, which, according to the judges of the *ad hoc* tribunals, was to ensure efficiency and reliability of the proceedings; for example, it was necessary to accept the possibility of bringing new evidence to the appeal proceedings or amending a judgment by the appellate court (rather than only accept the powers to reverse a judgment back to the first instance). But the fundamental feature of this model of accusation, implemented from the early days of the *ad hoc* tribunals, is the prosecutor's right to appeal on equal terms with the accused.

Article 25 of the ICTY Statute empowers both the accused and the Prosecutor to appeal against the decision of the Trial Chamber: "The Appeals Chamber shall hear appeals from persons convicted by the Trial Chambers or from the Prosecutor". The grounds for an appeal are the same for both parties. The model of appeal adopted by the ICTY allows the Prosecutor to act in order to correct errors of justice by way of

[4] Similar discussion in: Safferling (2001), p. 331; Worrall (2007), p. 451; Nieto-Navia and Roche (2001), p. 478; LaFave et al. (2009), p. 1303; Sprack (2012), p. 512; Ward and Wragg (2005), p. 688.

an appeal acknowledging in this way that such errors may take place not only to the detriment of the accused.[5]

During the works on the Rome Statute, negotiations were initiated on the scope of powers of the Prosecutor in the appeal proceedings. There was a clash of two opposite views: whereas a group of lawyers coming from continental states were forcing the idea of equal rights for both parties to the trial, the lawyers hailing from common law states were defending the argument that the Prosecutor should have a power to appeal against the judgment of the Trial Chamber solely on grounds of errors of law.[6] In the end, the system argument turned out to be decisive: the *ad hoc* tribunals had already established a precedent of ensuring equal powers to both parties in the proceedings.[7] Currently, both the accused and the Prosecutor have equal rights to appeal in proceedings before the ICC. On the ground of Article 81 (1), the Prosecutor may appeal against a decision of acquittal or conviction, and on the ground of Article 81(2)(a), against a sentence.

But even the acceptance of the existence of the ICC Prosecutor's right to appeal does not end the discussion on the scope of his powers in the appeal proceedings. There is also the crucial question of whether the Prosecutor should act as a guardian of law and lodge an appeal in favour of the accused. Equally important from the practical point of view is the establishment of whether the Prosecutor should be granted the right to appeal acquittals. For the model of accusation, it is also decisive to outline the grounds for prosecutorial appeal against a first instance court's decision, as well as to define the extent to which the prosecutor is allowed to use evidence to achieve this goal in proceedings before the appeal court. The actual scope of examination of a case depends not only on the manner in which the prosecutor has drafted charges but also on the extent the appeal court may go beyond the scope of appeal. All these issues could be resolved in one of the two ways: either as adopted in common law states or in a manner known from continental states. Ultimately, the appeal proceedings before the ICC came to be the second stage of proceedings (next to the Prosecutor's power, or rather lack thereof, of consensual termination of the proceedings) in which the continental model of accusation prevailed.

8.2.1 Appeal in Favour of the Accused

In the discussion on the development of the model of accusation before international criminal tribunals, the basic issue at dispute pertaining to the powers of

[5] See: Safferling (2001), p. 333. Differently: Bassiouni and Manikas (1996), p. 979; Nieto-Navia and Roche (2001), pp. 473–494; Izydorczyk and Wiliński (2004), pp. 105–108.

[6] However, even in the ILC Draft Statute the Prosecutor was equipped with the power to appeal on the same rights as the defence and on the same grounds: 1994 ILC Draft Statute, Article 25(1), http://legal.un.org/ilc/texts/instruments/english/draft%20articles/7_4_1994.pdf. Accessed 13 Feb 2015.

[7] Staker (2008), p. 1451; Behrens (1998), p. 440.

the prosecutor was whether he should be allowed to act in favour of the accused, or in other words, used in the continental nomenclature, what "the direction of the appeal" should be (in favour of the accused or to the detriment of the accused).

As a rule, a party may appeal against a decision only to the extent that the latter violates its rights or harms its interests. A court will accept the appeal if it finds that there is a *gravemen*, i.e., that a party has legal interest in appealing against a verdict. Continental systems adhere to the rule that the public prosecutor is the only party that may appeal the decision in any direction, as he is also entitled to file appellate measures in favour of the accused (Article 425 § 4 CCP, § 296 II StPO).[8] The prosecutor may use this power in a situation where he considers it necessary to bring an appeal to "defend law", which appeal is, as a rule, considered to benefit the accused, or when the interests of the accused have not been properly represented, e.g., the lack of proper representation did not guarantee the accused a fair trial. This solution is characteristic of the systems in which the prosecutor is considered to be the guardian of the law. But it is quite obvious that in common law states the principle of strict adversality of trial seen as a contest of two opposite parties prevents the application of this type of solution.

There is no precedent in international criminal law concerning the prosecutor appealing on behalf of the accused. In the case of proceedings before the ICTY, there was no legal basis to adopt the powers of the ICTY Prosecutor to act in favour of the accused in the appeal proceedings. Although formally the regulations do not forbid the Prosecutor to lodge an appeal on behalf of the accused, he has not been unequivocally designated as an authority searching for material truth, neither in the regulations nor in the case law. Even the legal science does not offer views supporting the existence of the Prosecutor's competence to act in favour of the accused by lodging an appeal against the Trial Chamber's judgments. Neither the Prosecutor has yet used his (supposed) power to lodge an appeal in favour of the accused.

It was only in proceedings before the ICC that it was confirmed that the ICC Prosecutor should be granted such a right. This right stems directly from the content of the provision in Article 81(1)(b) of the Statute, which states that the Prosecutor is also entitled to appeal on behalf of the convicted person: "The convicted person, or the Prosecutor on that person's behalf, may make an appeal on any of the following grounds (...)". As a result, if the convicted person fails to appeal on his own behalf, the Prosecutor may, based on the same grounds, request the amendment of the judgment in favour of the convicted person. Thus, the Prosecutor may appeal not only against judgments that are too lenient but also against those that are too severe. The Rules of Procedure and Evidence provide also that if the Prosecutor has filed an appeal on behalf of a convicted person before filing any notice of discontinuance, he may discontinue the appeal only if the convicted person agrees. Thus, he should

[8] See: Waltoś (2008), p. 533; Beulke (2005), p. 316; Grajewski (2010), p. 35; Hofmański et al. (2011), p. 721.

give him the opportunity to step into the position of the appealing party and to continue the appeal proceedings (Rule 152(2)).

This power arose from the general provisions pertaining to the tasks of the ICC Prosecutor. The fact that he had been entrusted with the task of searching for material truth turned out to be of major importance for the Prosecutor's role in the appeal proceedings. This assumption meant that consistently at all stages of the proceedings, the Prosecutor should be able not only to act as an accusatory authority but also to undertake actions that benefit the accused. At the stage of the appeal proceedings, this could only be achieved through granting the Prosecutor the power to file an appeal on behalf of the accused. Such regulation of the direction of filing an appeal neutralises the Prosecutor's role as an accusatory authority and, again, emphasises his task as a seeker and defender of the material truth.[9] It is one of the provisions of the Rome Statute that order the Prosecutor to act in the broadly understood "interests of justice". The ICC Prosecutor's power to lodge an appeal in favour of the accused represents one of the instances in which the authors of the Rome Statute departed from the Anglo-Saxon trial model that affected many other provisions of the Statute pertaining to the role of the Prosecutor and adopted a solution based on the continental model of accusation.

8.2.2 *Appeal from an Acquittal*

Another crucial element of the model of accusation in the appeal proceedings is the Prosecutor's right to appeal against an acquittal. It was a problem most debated when the international criminal tribunals were established.[10]

Common law states reject this possibility as contrary to the principle of *res iudicata* and violating international human rights standards.[11] It is worth remembering, however, that the differentiation between acquittals and convictions is a direct consequence of the existence of the two decisions finalising proceedings: foremost, the court (jury) delivers a convicting verdict, and only when the accused has been found guilty may the court adjudicate on the sentence; this model of adjudication arises from the assumption that the sentence may not be determined before the accused is found guilty of the acts charged against him. In the first model, submission and evidence on sentencing may be considered at one (or more) distinct (from hearings on guilt) hearing, to be held only after a verdict of guilt is pronounced (*bifurcated trial*). The other approach, characteristic of continental tradition, allows for hearing evidence and submissions together, without issuing two separate decisions on the guilt and on the sentence (*single trial*).[12]

[9] Roth and Henzelin (2002), p. 1543.

[10] Ibidem, p. 1542.

[11] Cryer et al. (2010), p. 471; Bassiouni (1993), p. 288.

[12] Notions used by: Acquaviva et al. (2013), p. 534.

In the United States, the concept of granting a sort of "automatic" right to challenge acquittals is, for a majority of lawyers, an "uncivilized" and "disturbing"[13] concept. The prosecutor's filing of an appeal against an acquittal verdict has been considered to be an infringement of the double jeopardy clause of The Fifth Amendment to the US Constitution. It aims to prevent the state from repeatedly subjecting a person to prosecution for offences arising out of the same behaviour. In most states, the first instance rulings can sometimes be appealed by the prosecution—but only those besides those deciding the issue of guilt: "in a criminal case an appeal by the United States shall lie to a court of appeals from a decision, judgment, or order of a district court dismissing an indictment or information or granting a new trial after verdict or judgment, as to any one or more counts, or any part thereof, except that no appeal shall lie where the double jeopardy clause of the United States Constitution prohibits further prosecution. An appeal by the United States shall lie to a court of appeals from a decision or order of a district court suppressing or excluding evidence (. . .). An appeal by the United States shall lie to a court of appeals from a decision or order, entered by a district court of the United States, granting the release of a person charged with or convicted of an offense, or denying a motion for revocation of, or modification of the conditions of, a decision or order granting release".[14]

The Supreme Court of the United States made an explicit statement on this subject: "appeals by the Government in criminal cases are something unusual, exceptional, not favoured. The history shows resistance of the Court to the opening of an appellate route for the Government until it was plainly provided by the Congress, and after that a close restriction of its uses to those authorized by the statute".[15] Much more significant are interlocutory appeals, which, when filed at the right moment of the trial, may have similar effects as the appeal. This power may be exemplified by the prosecutor's right to lodge an interlocutory appeal of a district court's decision to suppress or exclude evidence from trial (which is usually a result of the defence challenging the legality of its acquisition), but this always takes place during the first instance proceedings. The prosecutor must restrict himself to this type of response and use it reasonably because if the evidence he presented to support the accusation is considered unacceptable, he may not appeal from the acquittal verdict.

Also in England, the prosecutor, as a rule, has no right to file an appeal against an acquittal (the doctrine known as *autrefois acquit* which prevents the defendant from being re-tried for the same offence). The English system provides, however, for

---

13 See for more: Ambos (2007), p. 494; Worrall (2007), p. 451; Nieto-Navia and Roche (2001), p. 478; LaFave et al. (2009), p. 1303.

14 E.g., Criminal Appeals Act (18 U.P.C.A., § 3731): http://www.law.cornell.edu/uscode/text/18/3731. Accessed 28 Jan 2015.

15 See e.g.: Carroll v. United States, 354 U.P. 394 (1957), Supreme Court, 24 June 1957, and similarly in: *United States v. DiFrancesco*, 449 U.P. 117 (1980), Supreme Court, 9 December 1980.

some exceptions to this rule, the most prominent of which has been implemented quite recently.

First, pursuant to the Criminal Justice Act 2003, the prosecution is to have the rights of appeal in relation to a trial on indictment to the Court of Appeal; however, such an appeal may be brought only with the leave of the judge or the Court of Appeal.[16] This Act allows the prosecutor to file an appeal against acquittals in the most serious cases, which are defined as cases punishable with imprisonment for life and whose consequences for the victims and the society as a whole are particularly serious. This right can be exercised in a situation when new evidence has appeared that makes it "highly likely" that the accused committed an offence. It also follows from the Act that the complaint is considered the most prominent appellate measure in the English system. Under the Criminal Justice Act 2003, the prosecution may also appeal in respect of a "qualifying evidentiary ruling", that is, an evidentiary ruling of a judge that is made before the opening of the case for the defence. The relevant condition is that the ruling significantly weakens the prosecution's case. This may be regarded as a way for the prosecutor to affect the judgment of the court before it has been issued.[17]

The second unique structure is the appeal against the judgment issued in the summary trial procedure when the case is heard by lay magistrates before a magistrates' court, where the prosecutor may question the proceedings before the High Court on the ground that it is wrong in law or is in excess of jurisdiction. According to Magistrates' Courts Act 1980, the prosecutor can apply for the opinion of the High Court on the question of law or jurisdiction involved, also in the case of acquittal (the Act mentions the right of "any person who was a party to any proceeding before a magistrates' court or is aggrieved by the conviction, order, determination or other proceeding of the court").[18] This procedure has not, however, been considered an "appeal", but rather a review of the expertise of persons who are not specialists, using certain specific grounds. This procedure is normally used where the magistrates made an error of substantive law or acted in excess of jurisdiction. The prosecution is then responsible for pointing to a wrong ruling on a point of law "before it spreads dangerously around the lower courts".[19]

There are also two procedural institutions that aim at challenging the decision of the first instance court, which allow the prosecutor to exert his impact where a person tried on indictment has been acquitted. These powers, however, do not

[16] Criminal Justice Act 2003, Part 9 (Prosecution Appeals): http://www.legislation.gov.uk/ukpga/2003/44/part/9. Accessed 1 Sept 2014.

[17] Criminal Justice Act 2003, Part 9 (Prosecution Appeals), section 62.

[18] Magistrates' Courts Act 1980, p. 111: http://www.legislation.gov.uk/ukpga/1980/43/section/111. Accessed 1 Sept 2014.

[19] Padfield (2008), p. 409.

constitute "an appeal" in the strict sense. The first of these is the power granted in 1972 to the Attorney General who, if he desires the opinion of the Court of Appeal on a point of law that has arisen in the case before the Crown Court, may refer that point to the court.[20] Regardless of the opinion expressed by the Court of Appeal, even if it decides that the first instance court was wrong to find the accused not guilty, the acquittal may not be challenged. Following the judgment of the Court of Appeal, which can "consider the point and give their opinion on it", confirming that the law has been infringed, the Attorney General may only obtain the Court's opinion to which he may refer in other cases.[21] Second, in 1988 the prosecution was granted the power to file an appeal against the sentencing ruling issued by the Crown Court. This power is also extraordinary because only the Attorney General may refer the case for them to review the sentencing if he considers "that the sentencing of a person in a proceeding in the Crown Court has been unduly lenient".[22] He may use this competence only with the leave of the Court of Appeal. On such a reference, the Court of Appeal may quash any sentence passed on him in the proceeding and in place of it pass such sentence as they think appropriate for the case and as the court below had power to pass when dealing with him. Implementation of this power was related to the assumption that the court may infringe the rules regulating the severity of sentence not only to the convict's detriment. However, the Court of Appeal stressed that it will not intervene unless there was some error of principle in the Crown Court sentence, so that public confidence would be damaged if the sentence were not altered. Moreover, even where the sentence is increased, in most cases it will be mitigated because of the fact that the "offender has had to face the prospect of being sentenced twice over".[23]

In continental systems, the prosecutor's appealing powers are not limited. The judgment at trial is not considered to constitute the end of criminal proceedings, and the appeal only leads to another stage of criminal proceedings. According to "hierarchical system of judicial organisation, associated with the continental tradition, a regular and comprehensive system of appeals is regarded as an essential guarantee of fair and orderly administration of justice".[24] At the same time within the "coordinated", Anglo-Saxon, model of judicial organisation, the adjudicator at first instance is primarily responsible for decision-making, and appellate review is in the nature of an extraordinary and independent proceeding.

Although the international criminal tribunals seem to incline towards the second approach (as the ICTY Appeals Chamber stressed on several occasions that it does not lightly disturb findings of fact made by a Trial Chamber, as "the task of hearing,

[20] Criminal Justice Act 1972, section 36(1): http://www.legislation.gov.uk/ukpga/1972/71/section/36. Accessed 1 Sept 2014.

[21] Padfield (2008), p. 411.

[22] Criminal Justice Act 1988, section 36: http://www.legislation.gov.uk/ukpga/1988/33/section/36. Accessed 1 Sept 2014.

[23] Sprack (2012), p. 496.

[24] Damaška (1986), pp. 49–50.

assessing and weighting the evidence is left primarily to the Trial Chamber"), it was obvious that the prosecutor may file appeals against both convictions and acquittals.[25]

The wording of Article 25 of the ICTY Statute provides clear grounds for assuming that both parties to the proceedings are given equal rights to appeal: the accused may appeal against the conviction, whereas the Prosecutor may do so both against the acquittal and the conviction.[26] Both parties may also appeal the sentence. The granting of equal appeal rights to the parties to proceedings gives rise to the assumption that if the accused may appeal against a sentence that is unfavourable for him, it should be accepted that the Prosecutor may proceed similarly. His powers to appeal are not dependent on the content of a ruling. As in the continental tradition, it has been understood that the accused is not the only party that may be harmed by a court's mistake. The Rules of Procedure and Evidence also provide a basis for this power. They mention that it is possible to deliver the judgment resulting from the appeal from the prosecution where the accused is not present because of having been acquitted on all charges. In such a situation, the Appeals Chamber may deliver its judgment in the absence of the accused and shall, unless it pronounces an acquittal, order the arrest or surrender of the accused to the Tribunal (Rule 118(B)).

In proceedings before the ICC, appeals against convictions and acquittals are filed pursuant to identical rules. The Rome Statute provides that, first, "a decision under article 74 may be appealed" (Article 81(1)) and, second "a sentence may be appealed" (Article 81(2)(a)). Decisions under Article 74 are treated as one group: it may be both *decision of acquittal* or *conviction*. Therefore, the rules pertaining to appealing judgments by both the accused and the Prosecutor apply to both of them. This principle is also confirmed by the Rules of Procedure and Evidence, providing that an appeal can be filed against a decision of conviction or acquittal under article 74 (Rule 150(1)). The Rome Statute also directly mentions the possibility of filing an appeal against an acquittal by the Prosecutor in Article 81(3)(c)(i), which provides that "in case of an acquittal, the accused shall be released immediately"; however, "under exceptional circumstances, and having regard, inter alia, to the concrete risk of flight, the seriousness of the offence charged and the probability of success on appeal, the Trial Chamber, at the request of the Prosecutor, may maintain the detention of the person pending appeal". This provision clearly indicates that not only does the Prosecutor enjoy such a power but also that this power may be applied to maintain temporary detention of the accused. As a matter

[25] See also: Waltoś (2008), p. 533; Beulke (2005), p. 316; Grzegorczyk (2008), p. 961.

[26] See for more: Re (2012), pp. 806–810; Nieto-Navia and Roche (2001), p. 473. However, in 1996 Bassiouni and Manikas concluded that permitting the Prosecutor to appeal convictions could raise the issues of "double jeopardy" in any case where the Prosecutor's appeal is successful and the Appeals Chamber reverses an acquittal by the Trial Chamber. Therefore, they expressed an opinion that "it appears that the Statute was not intended to reverse an acquittal" (1996), p. 979.

of fact, on 20 December 2012, the Prosecutor filed the Notice of Appeal against the Acquittal Decision in the case of *The Prosecutor v. Ngudjolo Chui.*[27] In this case, the ICC Appeals Chamber established a method of dealing with appeals against acquittals. It adopted the standard articulated by the Appeals Chamber of the *ad hoc* tribunals with respect to alleged factual errors in an acquittal decision and assumed that "considering that it is the Prosecution that bears the burden at trial of proving the guilt of the accused beyond reasonable doubt, the significance of an error of fact occasioning a miscarriage of justice is somewhat different for a Prosecution appeal against acquittal than for a defence appeal against conviction. A convicted person must show that the Trial Chamber's factual errors create a reasonable doubt as to his guilt. The Prosecution must show that, when account is taken of the errors of fact committed by the Trial Chamber, all reasonable doubt of the accused's guilt has been eliminated. Furthermore, the Appeals Chamber notes that the ICTY Appeals Chamber held in relation to an acquittal decision that "[it] will reverse only if it finds that no reasonable trier of fact could have failed to make the particular finding of fact beyond reasonable doubt and the acquittal relied on the absence of this finding".[28]

As we have seen, in relation to the prosecutor's power to appeal an acquittal, the solution typical for the continental model of accusation has been adopted in proceedings before the international criminal tribunals. Both the *ad hoc* tribunals and the ICC grant the prosecutor the power to appeal against acquittals. Although the Anglo-Saxon division into two rulings ending proceedings has been maintained—there is the decision on guilt and the decision on the sentence[29]—which further leads to the distinction between convictions and acquittals, both of these groups of sentences can be appealed according to the same rules. The view that the prosecutor of the international criminal tribunal is the representative of the international community, which should have the right to challenge an acquittal, provided the basis for adopting this approach. It has also been assumed that constant control over the prosecutor (the *ad hoc* tribunals' prosecutors are controlled by the Security Council and the UN finance, and the ICC Prosecutor by the judicial authority) will prevent any abuse of this right, bullying of the accused and repeated prosecution for the same act.[30] Indeed, in several cases the ICTY Prosecutor's appeal led to the challenging of acquittal (in relation to some charges) by the Appeals Chamber.[31]

---

[27] *The Prosecutor v. Ngudjolo Chui*, ICC-01/04-02/12 A, Judgment on the Prosecutor's appeal against the decision of Trial Chamber II entitled "Judgment pursuant to article 74 of the Statute", 27 February 2015.

[28] *The Prosecutor v. Ngudjolo Chui*, ICC-01/04-02/12 A, Appeals Chamber, 27 February 2015, § 25 referring among other to the case of *Prosecutor v. Brđanin*, IT-99-36 Appeals Chamber, 3 April 2007, § 12–14 and *Prosecutor v. Blagojević and Jokić*, IT-02-60, Appeals Chamber, 9 May 2007, § 9.

[29] Boas et al. (2011), p. 390.

[30] Nieto-Navia and Roche (2001), pp. 481–482.

[31] Np. *Prosecutor v. Tadić*, IT-94-1-T, Appeals Chamber, 15 July 1999.

8.3 Grounds of Appeal

Grounds of appeal in proceedings before international criminal tribunals are limited, which might suggest that this institution is akin to the Anglo-Saxon appeal while remaining the characteristic feature of the continental review (cassation). The appeal is intended to be an extraordinary measure. According to the ICTY jurisprudence, "the appeal process of the International Tribunal is not designed for the purpose of allowing parties to remedy their own failings or oversights during trial or sentencing".[32] Thus, in the opinion of the Tribunal's judges, the Prosecutor should appeal a judgment issued by the Trial Chamber not to have a case re-examined but rather to identify and eliminate law infringement.[33]

Grounds of appeal in proceedings before the international criminal tribunals were grouped pursuant to the common law model into two categories: those pertaining to a decision on guilt and those pertaining to the sentence. Depending on the grounds of the scope of appeal, the powers of the prosecutor are also different.

In the case of proceedings before the *ad hoc* tribunals, similar to the common law systems, a decision was made to divide the grounds of appeal related to the decision on the guilt into two groups. The grounds to appeal, pursuant to Article 25 of the ICTY Statute, include *an error on a question of law invalidating the decision* and *an error of fact which has occasioned a miscarriage of justice*.

Not every "error on a question of law" is an error "invalidating the decision". According to the ICTY jurisprudence, an appellant must demonstrate that the Trial Chamber committed a factual error and the error resulted in a miscarriage of justice. Moreover, the appellant must establish that the error of fact was "critical to the verdict reached by the Trial Chamber", thereby resulting in a "grossly unfair outcome in judicial proceedings", as when a defendant is convicted despite a lack of evidence on an essential element of the crime.[34] Not every error can lead to a reversal or revision of the Trial Chamber's decision; the appellate party must demonstrate that "the error renders the decision invalid" and that it has occasioned "a miscarriage of justice".[35] The Appeals Chamber has also emphasised that it would not handle charges that were presented in an unclear, unjustified manner without a precise reference to specific fragments of the ruling of the Trial Chamber.

"An error of fact which has occasioned a miscarriage of justice" is, in turn, an error in factual findings. It has always been the most controversial ground of appeal. Error in factual findings cannot be, as a rule, used in appeals in Anglo-Saxon systems. It would mean challenging the decision of the jury. It was decided,

---

[32] As, e.g., in the case: *Prosecutor v. Erdemović*, IT-96-22, Appeals Chamber, 7 October 1997, § 15; *Prosecutor v. Kupreškić*, IT-95-16, Trial Chamber, 23 October 2001, § 408.

[33] E.g., *Prosecutor v. Tadić*, IT-94-1, Decision on Appellant's Motion for the Extension of the Time-Limit and Admission of Additional Evidence, 15 October 1998, § 72.

[34] *Prosecutor v. Kupreškić*, IT-95-16, Appeals Chamber, 23 October 2001, § 29.

[35] *Prosecutor v. Furundžija*, IT-95-17/1, Appeals Chamber, 21 July 2000, § 36.

however, in the proceedings before the ICTY that errors of fact may provide a ground for appeal. These errors may pertain to the manner of evaluation of evidence or to reliance on insufficient evidence.

The Appeals Chamber stressed that they will not lightly disturb findings of fact by a Trial Chamber: "The Trial Chamber has the advantage of observing witnesses in person and so is better positioned than the Appeals Chamber to assess the reliability and credibility of the evidence. Accordingly, it is primarily for the Trial Chamber to determine whether a witness is credible and to decide which witness' testimony to prefer".[36] It is also the responsibility of the Trial Chamber to resolve any inconsistencies that may arise within and/or among witnesses' testimonies. Such a view did not prevent the Appeals Chamber from acknowledging in the *Prosecutor v. Kupreškić* case that the Trial Chamber had wrongly assessed the witness's statements as reliable. Relying solely on the trial record, the Appeals Chamber concluded, although it had not seen the witness and had not heard her statement, that there was an error of fact. It concluded that "there are several strong indications on the trial record that her absolute conviction in her identification evidence was very much a reflection of her personality and not necessarily an indicator of her reliability".[37]

The Appeals Chamber's restraint in adjudication on facts is related to its practice of reversing judgments of the Trial Chamber: the Appeals Chamber refers cases for revision rather than amends judgements on its own on the basis of new facts. The Appeals Chamber believes that it is not competent to perform an assessment of facts. It may only establish whether or not the first instance court made an error and infringed law in a given trial.[38] The ICTY Appeals Chamber held that it may substitute its own finding for that of the Trial Chamber only if evidence relied on by the Trial Chamber "could not have been accepted by any reasonable tribunal" or where the evaluation of the evidence is "wholly erroneous", especially, as "it must be borne in mind that two judges, both acting reasonably, can come to different conclusions on the basis of the same evidence".[39] This, however, has been changing recently. We can even speak of a new standard in the Appeals Chamber's adjudication practice: it has started amending the judgments of the Trial Chamber instead of reversing them, e.g., in *Prosecutor v. Blaškić* it concluded that based on both trial record and additional evidence (when admitted) it can examine whether the accused's guilt has been proved beyond reasonable doubt.[40] More and more frequently, the Appeals Chamber accepts the admissibility of new facts and evidence in the appeal proceedings, thus acquiring competencies for adjudicating "in

36 *Prosecutor v. Kupreškić*, IT-95-16, Appeals Chamber, 23 October 2001, § 31.

37 *Ibidem*, § 154.

38 As in the case: *Prosecutor v. Tadić*, IT-94-1, Appeals Chamber, 15 July 1999, § 64.

39 *Prosecutor v. Tadić*, IT-94-1, Appeals Chamber, 15 July 1999, § 64. See in general: Ackerman and O'Sullivan (2002), pp. 146–147; Boas et al (2011), p. 445.

40 *Prosecutor v. Blaškić*, IT-95-14, Appeals Chamber, 29 July 2004, § 24. See also: Knoops (2005), p. 299; Cryer et al. (2010), p. 472.

place" of the Trial Chamber. The Appeals Chamber, however, will amend the judgment of the Trial Chamber only when the former makes "a discernible error" in the exercise of discretion with regard to its analysis that is serious enough for the Appeals Chamber to issue a decision reversing the Appeals Chamber's decision.[41] This tendency stemmed from the need to prevent remitting the case back for re-investigation in the first instance; it was intended to prevent making the lengthy proceedings before the Tribunal even longer. But in the opinion of common law commentators, such practice is unacceptable, as it does not allow the parties to challenge the new factual findings made by the second instance court.

The ICTY Statute does not provide for a legal basis for appealing against decisions on the sentence. But such an option has been admitted in the case law of this Tribunal, where it was assumed that it is a particular type of error in substantive law. Concerning the general overall standard of review in appeals against sentence, it was established that the Appeals Chamber will only intervene if it finds that the Trial Chamber's error in exercising its discretion in sentencing was "discernible". The Appeals Chamber indicated that the Trial Chamber's decision may be disturbed on appeal if it is demonstrated that "the Trial Chamber imposed sentences outside the discretionary framework provided by the Statute and the Rules"[42] or by abusing its discretion "either by taking into account what it ought not to have or by failing to take into account what it ought to have taken into account in the weighing process involved in the exercise of its discretion".[43] This interpretation, however, is narrower than the "disproportion between the crime and the sentence" grounds used in the Rome Statute.

Also, appeals before the ICC must be filed exceptionally. Not every infringement of law in a trial must necessarily lead to reversal or amendment of a judgment: it must have a significant effect on the contents of judgment. During the work on the Rome Statute, the International Law Commission explained that it would be "desirable, having regard to the existence of only a single appeal from decisions at trial".[44] It is the appeal model applied in Anglo-Saxon states (where the right to appeal depends on whether the court of higher instance issued a leave for its filing, independently and making a decision at the very beginning whether the infringement of law indicated in the appeal "might have been significant for the contents of judgement"). This model is also characteristic of continental cassation (or German *Revision*, that is an appeal on the point of law only), where it needs to be demonstrated that the indicated infringement of law (not only being "a flagrant breach of law") might have had a significant effect on the contents of judgement (e.g., Article 523 § 1 CCP) or where "the judgment was based upon a violation of the law" (§ 337 StPO). What is typical for such a limited form of appeal is referring

[41] *Prosecutor v. Tadić*, Appeals Chamber, 26 January 2000, § 22.

[42] See: *Prosecutor v. Kupreškić*, IT-95-16, Appeals Chamber, 23 October 2001, § 406–407; *Prosecutor v. Blaškić*, IT-95-14, Appeals Chamber, 29 July 2004, § 680.

[43] *Prosecutor v. Deronjić*, IT-02-61, Appeals Chamber, 20 July 2005, § 8.

[44] Cit. after: Schabas (2010), p. 934.

to the accused as "the convicted person" in the regulations on the appeal proceedings.

In the case of proceedings before the ICC, the grounds of appeal are defined differently compared to the *ad hoc* tribunals. They also cover a much broader spectrum of cases. Indeed, the manner in which they are drafted mostly resembles the model adopted in continental systems (as they expressly allow for the appeal on grounds of both fact and law, e.g. Article 438 CCP, § 312 StPO). The ICC Prosecutor may appeal against a decision of guilt on the following grounds:

(1) procedural error;
(2) error of law;
(3) error of fact;
(4) disproportion between the crime and the sentence.

Making an appeal on the ground of a procedural error may include non-compliance with mandatory procedural requirements of the Statute and the Rules by the Trial Chamber. But it may also relate to a failure to comply with mandatory requirements by the Prosecutor (as in the case of disclosure of evidence) or the Registry.[45] This ground of appeal may also be presented in a case when a Trial Chamber exercised discretion (as to admit or exclude certain evidence), but the appealing party considers it to be exercised erroneously. Regarding procedural errors in *The Prosecutor v. Lubanga*, the Appeals Chamber stated that "an allegation of a procedural error may be based on events which occurred during the pre-trial and trial proceedings. However, as with errors of law, the Appeals Chamber will only reverse a decision of acquittal if it is materially affected by the procedural error. In that respect, the appellant needs to demonstrate that, in the absence of the procedural error, the decision would have substantially differed from the one rendered".[46] As procedural errors can relate to alleged errors in a Trial Chamber's exercise of its discretion, the Appeals Chamber has stressed that it will not interfere with the Pre-Trial Chamber's exercise of discretion "merely because the Appeals Chamber, if it had the power, might have made a different ruling. To do so would be to usurp powers not conferred on it and to render nugatory powers specifically vested in the Pre-Trial Chamber".

In relation to an error of law, the Trial Chamber's erroneous application of the substantive or procedural law of the Court or any issue of international law generally that arises in the case may become the ground for appeal, as a result of incorrect interpretation of a regulation. Thus, in a way unknown to continental systems, the error in law may pertain to application of both the substantive and

[45] Staker (2008), p. 1458.

[46] *The Prosecutor v. Lubanga*, ICC-01/04-01/06 A 4 A 6, Judgment on the appeals of the Prosecutor and Mr Thomas Lubanga Dyilo against the "Decision on Sentence pursuant to Article 76 of the Statute", 1 December 2014, § 20.

procedural laws. It has been claimed that in such cases, the Appeals Chamber is the final arbiter in the interpretation of a regulation.[47] However, in *The Prosecutor v. Lubanga*, the Appeals Chamber expressed a more balanced opinion. Namely, it concluded that with respect to legal errors, the Appeals Chamber "will not defer to the Trial Chamber's interpretation of the law. Rather, it will arrive at its own conclusions as to the appropriate law and determine whether or not the Trial Chamber misinterpreted the law. If the Trial Chamber committed such an error, the Appeals Chamber will only intervene if the error materially affected the Impugned Decision".[48] Furthermore, a decision is "'materially affected by an error of law" if the Trial Chamber "would have rendered a decision that is substantially different from the decision that was affected by the error, if it had not made the error".

Error of fact in most cases concerns allegation that the Trial Chamber erred in reaching the conclusion of fact that it did on the basis of the evidence that was before it, but it can also relate to a situation where reaching that conclusion was justified, however, there is additional evidence presented by a party that casts doubt on those findings. This ground of appeal may also be invoked when the Trial Chamber made erroneous findings with respect to the national law of a certain state.[49] Also regarding errors of fact, the Appeals Chamber noted in another case that:

"it will not interfere with factual findings of the first-instance Chamber unless it is shown that the Chamber committed a clear error, namely, misappreciated the facts, took into account irrelevant facts, or failed to take into account relevant facts. As to the 'misappreciation of facts', the Appeals Chamber has also stated that it 'will not disturb a Pre-Trial or Trial Chamber's evaluation of the facts just because the Appeals Chamber might have come to a different conclusion. It will interfere only in the case where it cannot discern how the Chamber's conclusion could have reasonably been reached from the evidence before it'"[50]

The grounds of appeal have been expanded by an additional premise in the case of filing an appeal in favour of the accused, either by the accused or by the Prosecutor. According to Article 81(1)(b), the convicted person or the Prosecutor on that person's behalf may make an appeal on one or more of the appellate grounds: on "any other ground that affects the fairness or reliability of the proceedings or decision". The Prosecutor may not rely on these grounds when lodging an appeal to the detriment of the accused. It is the broadest ground, covering all other reasons for dissatisfaction with the judgment of the Court that could not be

[47] Ibidem, p. 1465.

[48] *The Prosecutor v. Lubanga*, Appeals Chamber, 1 December 2014, § 18.

[49] See: ibidem, p. 1459; Safferling (2001), pp. 334–335.

[50] *The Prosecutor v. Ngudjolo Chui*, ICC-01/04-02/12 A, Appeals Chamber, 27 February 2015, § 23.

invoked on the basis of the remaining grounds of appeal, the so-called *catch all provision*.[51] It seems, however, that its implementation not only contradicts the objectives of the limitation of appellate grounds but that it is also unnecessary, as the previously existing grounds of appeal would be sufficient to refer to any type of infringement of law that could have taken place. In the legal science, several examples have been demonstrated of what grounds for appeal were not covered under the other items; they may include, e.g., ineffective assistance of a counsel[52] or the fact that evidence significant for the defence could not be presented in the trial as it was located in the territory of a state that does not co-operate with the Court. These grounds relete to circumstances that put the accused in an unfavourable position, although not by reason of the Court's erroneous application of law or its proceeding.

Both parties: the Prosecutor or the convicted person may appeal the sentence. The ground of appeal is a disproportion between the crime and the sentence. It may be applied when the Trial Chamber, according to the Appeals Chamber, has acted outside the discretionary margin when adjudicating a sentence. Article 81(2) of the Statute is silent about the Prosecutor's right to invoke this ground for appeal to the benefit of the accused. But it follows from the content of the previous paragraph that, due to his role as a guardian of law, he may also appeal against a sentence when he considers it too severe. In the first appeal judgment in the case *The Prosecutor v. Lubanga*, the Appeals Chamber presented its opinion on the nature of this ground of appeal: namely, "the Appeals Chamber's role is not to determine, on its own, which sentence is appropriate, unless it has found that the sentence imposed by the Trial Chamber is 'disproportionate' to the crime. Only then can the Appeals Chamber 'amend' the sentence and enter a new, appropriate sentence".[53] It further explained that the imposed sentence is "disproportionate to the crime" when "as a result of the Trial Chamber's weighing and balancing of the relevant factors" it "is so unreasonable as to constitute an abuse of discretion". The Chamber assumed that it may interfere with a discretionary decision only under limited conditions. They identifed the conditions justifying appellate interference in the dimension of a sentence to be:

(1) where the exercise of discretion is based on an erroneous interpretation of the law;
(2) where it is exercised on patently incorrect conclusion of fact; or
(3) where the decision is so unfair and unreasonable as to constitute an abuse of discretion.[54]

---

[51] In the words of: Staker (2008), p. 1466.

[52] Ibidem.

[53] *The Prosecutor v. Lubanga*, Appeals Chamber, 1 December 2014, § 2 and 39.

[54] *The Prosecutor v. Lubanga*, Appeals Chamber, 1 December 2014, § 41–42.

It is, however, impossible to challenge the sentence on procedural grounds or due to an error in substantive law. There are opinions that this should be considered an oversight.[55] But this shortage is, to some extent, remedied by the powers of the Appeals Chamber that may act in one of the two ways: first, if while examining an appeal against sentence the Chamber considers that there are grounds on which the conviction might be set aside, wholly or in part, it may invite the Prosecutor and the convicted person to submit relevant new grounds of appeal and may render a decision on conviction in accordance with the new scope of appeal. The Appeals Chamber proceeds in the same way if, while handling the appeal only against the conviction, it establishes the grounds for decreasing the sentence. Second, it may also find that the proceedings appealed from were unfair in a way that affected the reliability of the decision or sentence or that the decision or sentence appealed from was materially affected by error of fact or law or procedural error (Article 83(2)), which prompts it to evaluate the disproportion of the sentence in view of the infringement of procedural or substantive law. It then proceeds to revert or amend the decision or sentence or refers the case for revision to another Trial Chamber. In order to do that, the Appeals Chamber may turn to the previously adjudicating Trial Chamber to establish and submit necessary findings of fact, or it may conduct evidentiary proceedings on its own. In *The Prosecutor v. Lubanga*, the Appeals Chamber dispelled any doubts as to the possibility to undermine the sentence on grounds of error in law or error in procedure: it concluded that it is possible to intervene in a Trial Chamber's exercise of its discretion in determining the sentence both if:

(1) the Trial Chamber's exercise of discretion is based on an erroneous interpretation of the law, and
(2) the discretion was exercised based on an incorrect conclusion of fact.[56]

In the case of proceedings before the ICC, the appellate grounds are considerably broader than in the case of the *ad hoc* tribunals. Indeed, they are very comprehensive. Especially broad are the grounds to appeal a judgment in favour of the accused because of "affecting the fairness or reliability of the proceedings or decision". They have been drafted similarly to the continental systems and cover, as a result, all infringements of law that could have taken place in the first instance proceedings. The content of Article 83(2) of the Statute, establishing the scope of powers of the Appeals Chamber, is the only element that has an impact on the limitation of the appellate grounds. Namely, it may reverse or amend the decision or sentence or order a new trial before a different Trial Chamber only in a situation when it concludes "that the proceedings appealed from were unfair in a way that affected the reliability of the decision or sentence or that the decision or sentence appealed from was materially affected by error of fact or law or procedural error". It follows

[55] Staker (2008), p. 1454.

[56] *The Prosecutor v. Lubanga*, Appeals Chamber, 1 December 2014, § 2.

from the content of this provision that only a "serious" error or infringement of law should provide the ground for appeal.

8.4 Scope of Appeal Proceedings

The actual scope of the Appeals Chamber examination of a case depends not only on the manner in which the appeal has been drafted by the Prosecutor but also on whether the Chamber has the power to go beyond the scope of appeal. In German legal science, this theory is bound with the notion of the "extent of review" (§ 352 StPO) and it signifies that the "scope of appeal" as specified by the grounds formulated in an appellate measure sets the limits for the "extent of review" by an appellate court. Going beyond the scope of appeal is a concept typical for the continental model of appeal proceedings, in which the court is not only allowed to but also obliged to act in this way. No decision was made to implement before the international tribunals the solution known from continental law systems, where the law provides for specific situations in which there is an option of going beyond the scope of appeal: first, there is a whole statutory list of absolute grounds of appeal that an appellate court is obliged to examine *proprio motu*, irrespective of the scope of the appellate measure and the limits established for the appellate measure and even of the effect of the violation on the contents of the decision (Article 439 § 1 CCP; in the German trial, these are *absolute Revisionsgründe*—§ 338 StPO). The second exception concerns a situation when upholding of the decision would be manifestly unjust. Thirdly, if the appellate court considers it necessary to correct an incorrect legal characterisation of facts, it may do it irrespective of the scope of the appeal and grounds raised therein.

Pursuant to the strictly adversarial model of accusation, the Appeals Chamber of the ICTY adopted a very restrictive understanding of the scope and nature of the appeal proceedings. But whereas the ICTY Statute does not provide formally for the possibility of going beyond the limits of appeal against a decision on guilt or the sentence, in some instances the Tribunal's Appeals Chamber did so at its own will, as if *proprio motu*. For example, in *Prosecutor v. Erdemović*, it examined *proprio motu* the question of the validity of the plea of guilty entered by the accused that—as it judged—was inadequately assessed by the Trial Chamber in view of the mental condition of the accused—although none of the parties entered such a motion. The Appeals Chamber found that there was "nothing in the Statute or the Rules, nor in practices of international institutions or national judicial systems, which would confine its consideration of the appeal to the issues raised formally by the parties".[57] In consequence, it has been assumed that the ICTY Appeals Chamber is not confined by the scope of an appeal and may, at its own discretion, consider circumstances that may result in the reversion of a verdict or reduction of a

[57] *Prosecutor v. Erdemović*, IT-96-22, Appeals Chamber, 7 October 1997, § 16.

sentence. The legal doctrine assumes, however, that this rule should only work in favour of the accused: the prohibition against *reformationis in peius* (worsening of an earlier verdict) safeguards the convicted from changing the sentence to his detriment if only he appeals.[58]

The restrictive interpretation of the scope of appeal, which is so characteristic of Anglo-Saxon systems, manifested itself in the refusal to address procedural deficiencies occurring in the first instance proceedings that had not been raised earlier by the party.[59] Pursuant to this principle, any infringement of law occurring in the judicial proceedings should be reported to the Trial Chamber itself. The party cannot remain silent on the matter only to return on appeal to seek a trial *de novo*. The party should not be permitted to refrain from making an objection to a matter that was apparent during the course of the trial and to raise it only in the event of adverse findings against that party. In general, the accused should raise all possible reservations, especially those concerning the issues of key importance for the criminal responsibility, during the trial, and therefore cannot raise a defence for the first time on appeal.[60] This limitation stems from the principles of procedural pragmatism: if the Trial Chamber has all the data pertaining to a potential infringement of law, then it will be able to satisfactorily address the issue of the criminal responsibility of the accused, and there will be no need to appeal against its ruling—which could lead to lengthy proceedings. It is also important that the prosecution should be allowed the opportunity to cross-examine witnesses testifying in support of any defence put forward and to call rebuttal witnesses, if necessary. This solution is typical for Anglo-Saxon systems, in which the interlocutory appeal is the main appellate measure applied by the prosecutor. Despite such strict limitations, the adjudicating practice of these two *ad hoc* tribunals shows that they are far from ignoring the charges that could have been raised before the first instance and rejecting the appeal for formal reasons.[61] It may be indicated that in the ruling in the *Prosecutor v. Kambanda*, the Appeals Chamber of the ICTR referred to a general rule according to which if the appellant made no objection before the Trial Chamber, it means that he has waived his right to adduce the issue as a valid ground of appeal. In this case, "the Appellant had several opportunities to raise any issues of fact on the basis of which he now alleges that his guilty plea was invalid, but failed to do so until after receiving a life sentence for the guilty plea. In the absence of a satisfactory explanation of his failure to raise the validity of the guilty plea in a timely manner before the Trial Chamber, the Appeals Chamber could find that the Appellant has waived his right to later assert that his guilty plea was invalid". However, the ICTR decided to consider the question of the validity of the guilty plea even if they were raised only during the appellate proceedings, as "this is the Chamber of last resort for the Appellant facing life imprisonment on the

[58] Cryer et al. (2010), p. 471.

[59] See: *Prosecutor v. Tadić*, IT-94-1, Appeals Chamber, 15 July 1999, § 55, *Prosecutor v. Kambanda*, ICTR-97-23, Appeals Chamber, 19 October 2000, § 25–28, 55.

[60] *Prosecutor v. Aleksovski*, IT-95-14/1, Appeals Chamber, 24 March 2000, § 51.

[61] See: Staker (2008), p. 1457, and the jurisprudence analysed there.

basis of his guilty plea", and "the issues raised in this case are of general importance to the work of the Tribunal".

Based on the experience of the *ad hoc* tribunals, the ICC Statue has—since the very beginning—provided for a much more flexible approach to the impact of the scope of the appeal on the extent of case review. Article 81(2)(b) provides that in specific cases, the Appeals Chamber may go beyond the limits of appeal. If examining an appeal against sentence it considers that there are grounds on which the conviction might be set aside, wholly or in part, it may invite the Prosecutor and the convicted person to submit grounds of appeal as provided by the Statute. Then it may examine the grounds of appeal thus extended and render a decision on conviction. This entails a judicial indication of grounds that should be raised in an appeal. The Court acts in the same way if, during review of an appeal only against a conviction decision, it finds that there are grounds for a reduction of the sentence due to its disproportion. From the theoretical perspective, the institution of "indication of grounds" by a judicial authority leads to a situation in which, after a party extends grounds for appeal according to the "judicial indication", the appellate authority adjudicates within the scope of appeal. However, from the practical perspective, it is an institution of going beyond the limits of the original appellate measure. There are two main questions here: first, how precise might the judges' indication of "grounds for appeal pertaining to the decision on guilt" be? Does it mean that there should be a general invitation to supplement the grounds for appeal or that the judges will indicate a specific deficiency of the Trial Chamber (or the Prosecutor) that in their opinion should lead to an amendment or to a reversal of its ruling? And second, the Statute does not mention whether such an "invitation to submit" is binding on the Prosecutor. If we assume that it is binding, it would significantly limit the prosecutorial discretion in drafting appeal grounds and would lead to a situation where the grounds would be drafted by the authority that is meant to examine them.

It is also interesting to see how the ICC addressed the problem of procedural deficiencies occurring in the first instance proceedings. Namely, in the case *The Prosecutor v. Ngudjolo Chui*, the ICC Appeals Chamber concluded that "it must be possible to raise procedural errors on appeal pursuant to article 81 (1) (a) (i) of the Statute in relation to decisions rendered during trial, and such errors may lead to the reversal of a decision under article 74 of the Statute, provided that it is materially affected by such errors. The Appeals Chamber considers that to decide otherwise would deprive the parties of the ability to raise procedural errors on appeal".[62]

The above consideration provided another occasion to see how the initial restrictive approach to the limits of appeal, characteristic of Anglo-Saxon systems, was gradually abandoned by the *ad hoc* tribunals. Despite being lauded for its pragmatism and guaranteeing the effectiveness and expediency of proceedings, the approach that obliged the tribunals to pass decisions solely within the scope of the grounds of appeal formulated by the parties turned out to be inadequate for the cases

[62] *The Prosecutor v. Ngudjolo Chui*, ICC-01/04-02/12 A, Appeals Chamber, 27 February 2015, § 3.

examined by the international criminal tribunals. Another interesting question is the casuistic approach to cases in which the *ad hoc* tribunals accepted going beyond the scope of appeal. However, there was not a general rule in place that would provide a basis to specify when it could happen. Such rules were introduced only in the proceedings before the ICC, and they remained very general, as there were no references to lists of situations, commonly found in continental systems, where the appellate court would be obliged to go beyond the scope of appeal. Moreover, no obligation was introduced for the judges to extend a review beyond the grounds of an appeal, leaving them discretion as to whether this is necessary in a particular case.

In the proceedings before the international criminal tribunals, there appeared another principle known from continental systems—the prohibition of *reformationis in peius*. In its basic sense, the principle provides that the appellate court may adjudicate to the detriment of the accused only when an appellate measure has been brought against him, and only within the limits of the appeal, unless the law provides otherwise. This prohibition is out of the question if the appellate measure has been brought in to the detriment of the accused. It can be used solely for the benefit of the accused. An appeal filed to the detriment of the accused may always result in a more favourable ruling. Additionally, in Polish criminal procedure there are restrictions on discretion in adjudicating when a case is submitted for re-examination to the first instance court. The prohibition of *reformationis in peius* signifies also that in the event that the case is remanded for re-examination, the court of the first instance in such further proceedings may sentence the accused to a penalty more severe than that decided in the judgement reversed, only if the appeal thereof was an appeal prejudicial to the accused (Article 434 and 443 CCP).[63] Also in German criminal procedure, a judgment may not be amended to the defendant's detriment where only the defendant or his statutory representative filed the appeal on fact and law or the public prosecution office appealed on fact and law in his favour (§ 331 and § 358 StPO).[64] In these states, the broad application of appeal by prosecutors, combined with the binding prohibition of *reformationis in peius*, often leads to abuse of the right to appeal when the prosecutor appeals against a sentence only to guarantee that a second instance court will have the possibility of ruling against the accused.

The *ad hoc* tribunals do not know the prohibition of *reformationis in peius*, although it has been mentioned that the Appeals Chamber should analyse, at the sentencing stage, whether a successful prosecution appeal should put the person in a worse position than that at the end of trial (the so-called *reformatio in peius* principle).[65] Interestingly, the legal science understands this principle as all the negative effects a challenge to an acquittal can have on the accused. Therefore, the

[63] See in general: Waltoś (2008), p. 534; Grzegorczyk (2008), pp. 978–979 and 959.

[64] See in more detail: Beulke (2005), p. 318.

[65] *Prosecutor v. Tadić*, IT-94-1, Appeals Chamber, 15 July 1999, Declaration of Judge Nieto-Navia, § 11.

reformatio in peius principle also pertains to the fact that the accused had to appear before the tribunal for a second time, and in addition to this, he was detained a second time after a period of release and deprived of liberty on the basis of the same charges as before.[66]

As far as proceedings before the ICC are concerned, the *reformationis in peius* principle has been implemented, but in its most general, basic form. Namely, the ICC, when examining the appeal filed in favour of the accused—whether by the person convicted or the Prosecutor on that person's behalf—cannot amend the judgment to the detriment of the accused (Article 83(2) *in fine*). These limits can be, however, overstepped where the opposite is true—when the Prosecutor brought in the appellate measure to the detriment of the accused, the Chamber may amend the judgment in favour of the accused.[67]

8.5 New Evidence in Appeal Proceedings

The restriction in the presentation of evidence before an appellate court can be found in all systems of criminal proceedings. This rule pertains both to new evidence and to the re-presentation of the evidence already known to the first instance court. The rules of evidentiary proceedings held before a second instance court reveal an interesting phenomenon—the convergence of objectives in both traditions. Both the continental and the common law systems intend the admission of evidence in the appeal proceedings to be exceptional. However, this objective is achieved through different means. The rules for the introduction of new evidence to criminal proceedings at this stage of the proceedings are related to the essence of the appeal proceedings that may be perceived as a trial *de novo* (as in continental systems) or as a procedure that is used only to control proceedings before first instance courts (as in common law systems—in the continental tradition, a similar role is played by cassation or a revision).[68] The principles of admissibility of evidence in continental systems are the same as in the first instance proceedings (see Article 170 CCP), and admissibility of evidence may be denied only pursuant to enumerative criteria. At the same time, in common law states the evidence may be accepted in appeal proceedings only exceptionally, having met specific conditions. Another basic difference can be found in the timing of evaluation of evidence: while in the continental tradition evaluation of the materiality and credibility of evidence is left to be dealt with at the final adjudication stage, in common law states the law itself establishes a "barrier" to evidence and places it before the appellate hearing; the evidence is not even admitted to the hearing. The same rule is besides true as regards the first instance hearing.

---

[66] Nieto-Navia and Roche (2001), p. 485.

[67] Cryer et al. (2010), p. 471.

[68] On this agree: Featherstone (2001), p. 497; Knoops (2005), p. 290; Cryer et al. (2010), p. 472.

In the Polish criminal procedure, according to the general rule, an appellate court should not be allowed to conduct evidentiary proceedings pertaining to the intrinsic nature of the case (Article 452 § 1 CCP). However, paragraph 2 of this article in its current wording provides for a rather broad exception to this general rule: in exceptional cases, the appellate court, if it finds the completion of a judicial examination necessary, may nevertheless take evidence directly at the appellate trial, if this will expedite the judicial proceedings, and there is no necessity to conduct the whole of it, or a major part thereof, anew. Despite the existence of this apparently restrictive principle, the appellate court, similar to the first instance court, may refuse to discover the evidence only on the basis of a list of the criteria included in Article 170 CCP.[69] Additionally, if the pieces of evidence indicated in the appeal are numerous and pertain to the intrinsic nature of the case, then, as a rule, it is necessary to reverse the first instance court judgement. However, pursuant to the Act of 27th of September 2013, the new wording of Article 452[70] was implemented. The Codification Commission of Criminal Law established that it is necessary to enable the appellate court to complete a case by issuing a reformatory ruling without the need to reverse cases and remit them for re-examination. Therefore, the phrases "in exceptional cases" and "may nevertheless take evidence directly" were deleted (the latter was replaced with "takes evidence directly"), together with the phrase "a major part thereof". From the date of enforcement of the amendment to the CCP, the appellate court will be obliged in every case when it finds the completion of a judicial examination necessary, to take evidence directly at the appellate trial, if this will expedite the judicial proceedings. As a result of the amendment, the appellate court may not issue a reformatory ruling only in the case when it was necessary to conduct the whole judicial proceedings anew (but not in a major part—this additional barrier was introduced through the provision of Article 452(2) prior to the amendment). It is still not important whether the evidence is new and has not been presented in the main trial, which is a matter crucial to Anglo-Saxon systems. The continental appellate court cannot exclude evidence from the appeal proceedings only because a party could have adduced it at an earlier stage of the proceedings.

In Germany, it is also possible to admit evidence pursuant to general principles—evidentiary proceedings are conducted in line with rules that are similar to those applied before the first instance court. There is not only the possibility of taking evidence and calling witnesses, but there are also no limitations as to admitting new and additional evidence (§ 323, 324, 325 StPO).[71] It is also possible to summon the witnesses and experts examined at first instance. However, if their repeated examination does not seem to be necessary for clearing up the case, it can be dispensed

[69] Grajewski (2010), pp. 132–133; Hofmański et al. (2011), pp. 932–937; Grzegorczyk (2008), pp. 974–976.

[70] Act of 27 September 2013 amending the Act—Code of Criminal Proceedings, Dz.U. of 2013, pos. 1282.

[71] Beulke (2005), p. 324.

with. In so far as it appears necessary, the appeal court may also order the transposition of a tape recording of an examination into a written transcript. The person who produced the transposition shall affix his or her signature with additional wording confirming the accuracy of the transposition. Also, the written transcripts may be read out during the hearing.

In the case of common law states, the reluctance to open the possibility of submission of evidence at the appeal trial is an obvious consequence of the existence of a jury acting as an authority competent to evaluate the evidence before the first instance court. There are three characteristic features related to the admission of evidence in appellate proceedings in these systems:

(1) There are precise guidelines instructing the court when it may admit evidence.
(2) Evidence must be new (which means that either the party did not dispose of it during the trial or it was available but not called at trial—but usually after fulfilling certain conditions, such as the interest of justice or offering a reasonable explanation for the failure to adduce it at trial).
(3) A party needs to demonstrate that it exercised due care to obtain the evidence in the proceedings before the first instance court—the focus is thus on a conscientious handling of a case by the parties.

Section 23 of the Criminal Appeals Act 1968[72] allows the Appeal Court to take a discretionary decision as to order the production of evidence. If it thinks it is necessary for the determination of the case or expedient in the interests of justice, it may order the production of any document, exhibit or other things connected with the proceedings, as well as order any witness to attend for examination and be examined before the Court, whether or not he was called in those proceedings, and also receive any evidence that was not adduced in the proceedings from which the appeal lies. The court is obliged, in considering whether to receive any evidence, to have regard in particular to

- whether the evidence appears to the Court to be capable of belief;
- whether it appears to the Court that the evidence may afford any ground for allowing the appeal;
- whether the evidence would have been admissible in the proceedings from which the appeal lies on an issue that is the subject of the appeal; and
- whether there is a reasonable explanation for the failure to adduce the evidence in those proceedings.

The necessity to demonstrate that it was not possible to use evidence at an earlier stage of the proceedings is intended to prevent a situation in which the accused will be "saving up" evidence awaiting the appeal. When assessing the admissibility of evidence in the appeal proceedings, the court should first of all consider whether it

---

[72] Criminal Appeals Act 1968, section 23: http://www.legislation.gov.uk/ukpga/1968/19/section/23. Accessed 1 Sept 2014.

may lead to the amendment of the ruling, that is, whether new evidence hints to the possibility that the accused is not guilty.

More and more frequently, there are arguments that the English Court of Appeal should be more ready to "overturn the verdict of a jury" and consider arguments that the jury has made a mistake and to admit evidence that might favour the defendant even if it was, or could have been, available at trial.[73] It is also the view of the Royal Commission on Criminal Justice.[74] Currently, it is being considered whether evidence should be admitted on the same basis at the appeal proceedings stage also. It has been indicated that "an appellate court genuinely concerned to avoid miscarriages of justice should admit all evidence which could be believed by a reasonable jury, which could have affected the outcome of the case (and) that has not been deliberately saved up for appeal, should the accused be convicted".[75] It may be noticed that continental system states came to this conclusion a long time ago, and rightfully so. This conclusion may, however, lead to a change in the manner of perceiving the essence of the appeal proceedings: if, as a rule, "all evidence which could have affected the outcome of the case" may be admitted, the appeal proceedings turn into a trial *de novo*.

In the United States, most of the jurisdictions differentiate between appeals lodged to demonstrate the error of law that occurred before a first instance court and appeals based on the error of fact, which are aimed at achieving a trial *de novo*.[76] In the latter case, the appeal court is required to conduct a new, independent trial at the appellate level. This procedure, however, is very rarely used, and it is usually limited to cases related to misdemeanours. The appellate court's task is to pass an opinion on the law rather than on the facts. Representatives of the American doctrine believe that where the appellate court is entitled to issue opinion on facts, this might lead to a situation in which the accused would be penalised again for the same act (double jeopardy). Establishing the facts by the appellate court is, however, accepted in the so-called *habeas corpus* procedure pertaining to the infringement of the constitutional rights of the accused by the first instance court. This procedure may be applied only when ordinary appellate measures (i.e., the appeal) have been exhausted, and for this reason it bears greater resemblance to continental cassation. The Supreme Court of the United States found that the appellate court adjudicating in this procedure may take evidence anew and establish facts if:

- the procedure employed by the State Court appeared to be seriously inadequate for the ascertainment of the truth;

[73] Ward and Wragg (2005), p. 682; Sprack (2012), pp. 491–492.

[74] [1992] QB 101. Report of the Royal Commission on Criminal Justice, p. 162, https://www.gov.uk/government/uploads/system/uploads/attachment_data/file/271971/2263.pdf. Accessed 11 Jan 2015.

[75] Padfield (2008), p. 407, and the case *R v. McIlkenny* (1992) 93 Cr App R 287, Lloyd LJ, p. 310, cit. at p. 418.

[76] Worrall (2007), pp. 443–444.

- it is alleged that there is newly discovered evidence that could not reasonably have been presented to the State Court (unless the allegation of newly discovered evidence is irrelevant, frivolous or incredible);
- evidence crucial to the adequate consideration of his constitutional claim was not developed at the state hearing (for any reason not attributable to the inexcusable neglect of the applicant);
- the State Court has not reliably found the relevant facts.[77]

The characteristic features of the common law model of appeal proceedings manifest themselves in the proceedings before the *ad hoc* tribunals.[78] Both the ICTY and the ICTR showed some restraint in admitting new evidence.[79] First of all, they adopted the nomenclature used in these systems. Therefore, the necessity to prove that the requested evidence is new and that it could not be presented by a party in the proceedings before the first instance court, despite demonstrating due diligence, is of key importance for the admittance of evidence. According to Rule 115 RPE ICTY and ICTR, the motion to present additional evidence before the Appeals Chamber must be either in the appeal or served on the other party and filed with the Registrar not later than 30 days from the date for filing of the brief in reply to appeal. The party must first file a motion to the Chamber in which it clearly identifies with precision the specific finding of fact made by the Trial Chamber to which the additional evidence is directed, as well as describe the potential impact of the additional evidence. Additionally, this evidence should be served upon the opposite party under the disclosure of evidence procedure. The Appeals Chamber will consider the additional evidence only if it finds that certain conditions have been fulfilled:

- the additional evidence was not available at trial;
- it is relevant and credible;
- it would have been a decisive factor in reaching the decision at trial.

The party that requests the admission of new evidence must demonstrate the existence of all of the above circumstances. Only after such an initial assessment of admissibility of evidence does the Appeals Chamber undertake the evaluation of merits of such evidence. Only then may the evidence presented at the appeal proceedings become the material on which it will arrive at a final judgment.[80]

Despite the formal possibility of using new evidence, such requests are rarely granted by the Appeals Chamber. In *Prosecutor v. Tadić*, the ICTY Appeals Chamber expressed its view that additional evidence should not be admitted lightly at the appellate stage. The right to a full appeal process must be carefully balanced against the equally important requirement that the appeal be dealt with

[77] *Townsend v. Sain*, 372 U.P. 293 (1963), Supreme Court, 18 March 1963.

[78] Boas et al. (2013), p. 1003.

[79] Roth and Henzelin (2002), p. 1556; Tochilovsky (2008), pp. 569–582.

[80] Featherstone (2001), pp. 495–508; May and Wierda (2002), pp. 305–309.

expeditiously. Moreover, the Chamber formulated four conditions applying to the admissibility of evidence:

- it can be admitted only if the interests of justice required admission of additional evidence;
- the evidence was relevant to a material issue;
- the evidence was credible; and
- the evidence was such that it would probably show that the conviction was unsafe.

The ICTY refused to admit evidence requested by the accused, finding that it could not prove the erroneousness of the conviction, as it had not been demonstrated to be related to the subject of the case.[81] In the same case, the Appeals Chamber determined that additional evidence should not be admissible in the absence of a reasonable explanation as to why the evidence was not available at trial as such unavailability may result from the lack of due diligence on the part of counsel. There will be no possibility of presenting it before the Appeals Chamber if the counsel has chosen not to present the evidence at trial because of his litigation strategy.[82] However, if there is a reasonable explanation for the failure to produce the evidence at trial, it may still be admitted. As a result of this interpretation, the Chamber did not give its permission for admission of new evidence as, in its opinion, the defence could have obtained it earlier had it acted with due diligence. The party is obliged to present its case in the best possible way and may not retain evidence "as a stand-by", hoping to win the appeal. In both these rulings, the Appeals Chamber emphasised that the appeal proceedings may not turn into a trial *de novo*. The Appeals Chamber may not function as another Trial Chamber. Its role is limited to remedying the errors that render decisions invalid as well as the errors of facts resulting in a judicial mistake. Also, the ICTR has shown a tendency to a strict approach: in the case of *Prosecutor v. Barayagwiza*, the defence counsel motioned for the admission of new documentary evidence that had been recently disclosed by the state and had not been available before. Although the Appeals Chamber considered that the evidence was new according to the interpretation given to this notion in the jurisprudence of the *ad hoc* tribunals and there was no lack of due diligence of the party, it finally stated that it could not be admitted as it could not have prompted the Trial Chamber to make a different decision.[83]

On the other hand, in another case the ICTY Appeals Chamber has held that it possesses an "inherent power" to admit additional evidence to ensure that no miscarriage of justice would result, even if such evidence was available at the

[81] *Prosecutor v. Tadić*, IT-94-1, Appeals Chamber, 15 July 1999, § 16.

[82] *Prosecutor v. Tadić*, IT-94-1, Decision on Appellant's Motion for the Extension of the Time-Limit and Admission of Evidence, 15 October 1998, § 49.

[83] *Prosecutor v. Barayagwiza*, ICTR-99-52, Decision on Appellant J. B. Barayagwiza's Motion for Leave to Present Additional Evidence Pursuant to Rule 115 of the Rules of Procedure and Evidence, 8 December 2006, § 40–44.

trial and could have been produced earlier.[84] Also, in respect of admission of evidence, the attitude of the Appeals Chamber seems not to be coherent and easy to foresee.

The scope of evidence to be presented during appeal proceedings depends in most parts on the essence of the appeal proceedings: if it is intended to be a hearing *de novo* or if it is more in the nature of a review procedure. The ICC Statute is not entirely clear on the nature of the hearing on appeal.[85]

The presentation of evidence, both new and previously produced before the first instance, which is adduced again to support the appeal, is possible in appeal proceedings before the ICC. This power of the Appeal Chamber to admit evidence in such an extensive manner can be concluded from the general rule that for the purposes of appellate proceedings, the Appeals Chamber shall have all the powers of the Trial Chamber. Article 83(2)(b) states that the Appeals Chamber in order to determine the issues that arise in consequence of the appeal may itself call evidence. Moreover, the Rules of Procedure and Evidence explain that the rules governing proceedings and the submission of evidence in the Pre-Trial and Trial Chambers shall apply *mutatis mutandis* to proceedings in the Appeals Chamber (Rule 149). Therefore, no separate rules for the presentation of new evidence are foreseen in the appeal proceedings. Ultimately, the admissibility of such evidence is decided by the judges of the Appeals Chamber. Thus, it has not been clearly resolved which of the systems of evidentiary proceedings will be adopted by the ICC before the appellate court. On the one hand, it could be argued that the lack of limitations on the scope of evidentiary proceedings opens the possibility of conducting the trial *de novo*. On the other, it might also be assumed that the Court will rely on the experience of the *ad hoc* tribunals. If the ICC judges adopt the approach functioning before the *ad hoc* tribunals, they will be able to draw on their experiences[86] and, following the rules adopted by the ICTY, will conclude that the party may present in the appeal proceedings only new evidence, and only such evidence as was not available during the judicial proceedings, and moreover that the party needs to demonstrate that the lack of availability did not arise from the lack of due diligence.

Due to the possibility of conducting evidentiary proceedings, the Appeals Chamber may acquire a factual basis to revise the sentence of the Trial Chamber rather than remit the question of sentencing back to the Trial Chamber. It will have a legally guaranteed possibility to establish facts of the case on its own. However, whether or not it should use this competence is an entirely different matter.[87] It seems that in a specific case, it should always make a decision on whether it is

---

[84] *Prosecutor v. Jelisić*, Appeals Chamber, 15 November 2000, § 40–41.

[85] Kress (2003), p. 614.

[86] Such proposition presents: *ibidem*.

[87] According to C. Staker, "for the Appeals Chamber itself to make findings of fact at first instance would deprive the defendant of any possibility of appeal against those findings": Staker (2008), p. 1484.

possible and consistent with the rights of the accused to establish its own factual circumstances or whether it is necessary to remit the case back for re-examination to the Trial Chamber. Establishing facts may turn out to be problematic, especially in the case of reversing a verdict of acquittal and imposing a sentence. It is considered—not only by common law scholars—to be not compatible with fundamental human rights principles (see, e.g., the *reformations in peius* and *ne peius* rules known in the continental tradition).[88]

From the recent case law, it results that the ICC Appeals Chamber has taken a strict view on the admissibility of admitting evidence, known from the *ad hoc* tribunals. When Mr. Lubanga in his appeal requested producing additional evidence during the appeal proceedings in response, the Appeals Chamber made several observations on the general issues connected to the admissibility of evidence during a second instance hearing. First, it stressed that Trial Chamber is better positioned than the Appeals Chamber to assess a piece of evidence in light of all the other evidence presented at trial. Accordingly, evidence should, with only limited exceptions, be presented at trial. Second, it set out criterion specifying when additional evidence on appeal is admissible:

(a) the Appeals Chamber is convinced of the reasons why such evidence was not presented at trial, including whether it could have been presented with the exercise of due diligence;
(b) it is demonstrated that the additional evidence, had it been presented before the Trial Chamber, could have led the Trial Chamber to enter a different verdict, in whole or in part;
(c) it is necessary for purposes of demonstrating that the proceedings appealed from were unfair and thereby rendered the decision pursuant to Article 74 of the Statute unreliable.

In applying these criterion to the case of Mr. Lubanga, the Appeals Chamber found that "all of the proposed additional evidence is inadmissible because it was either available at trial, would have been available with the exercise of due diligence, or is inadmissible because the Appeals Chamber does not find that the additional evidence, had it been presented during the trial, could have led the Trial Chamber to enter a different verdict, in whole or in part".[89]

8.6 Conclusion

In the case of appeal proceedings before the ICC, it may also be seen that the model was developed by combining components of the common law and continental law systems.

[88] What is highlighted by: Schabas (2010), p. 955.

[89] *The Prosecutor v. Lubanga*, Appeals Chamber, trial transcript, 1 December 2014, pp. 4–5.

Anglo-Saxon law had a greater impact on the proceedings before the *ad hoc* tribunals. The tribunals used this tradition as the "basis", establishing a "structure" or a "backbone" for their appeal proceedings. More specifically, the revisionary nature of the appeal and the dichotomy between error of law grounds and the error of fact grounds were drawn from the common law systems. Also, the principles of introducing evidence in the appeal proceedings come from this tradition. At the same time, the *ad hoc* tribunals followed the example of continental courts in that they granted the prosecutor the power to appeal against acquittals on the same basis and on the same grounds as convicted persons could appeal against convictions. Also, in the case law there have been examples of the adjudicating practice aiming at expanding the competences of the Appeals Chamber judges to adjudicate beyond the scope of appeal.

The limited nature of appeal in the appeal proceedings before the ICC was taken over from common law systems (although it may be claimed that it came from the cassation model adopted in the continental law states). On the other hand, the ICC Prosecutor was entrusted with the role of a guardian of law, which is a characteristic feature of continental systems that is of key significance for the accusation model. The prosecutor is able to fulfil this role at the appeal proceedings stage mainly due to the possibility of filing an appeal in favour of the accused. The competence to challenge acquittals as the key power of the Prosecutor in the appeal proceedings is also derived from the continental system. Another solution adopted from the continental tradition is the formulation and the broad scope of the grounds for appeal that in fact cover all infringements of law that could have taken place in the proceedings before the first instance. The principles of introducing new evidence that is admitted pursuant to the same rules as before the Trial Chamber account for another component of the continental model of accusation. The ICC Statue also provides for the statutory premises for adjudicating beyond the scope of appeal.

It could be seen that specific components of the appeal proceedings were gradually transformed as the system of proceedings before the ICC developed. There were no doubts as to the direction of the changes: while at the beginning the *ad hoc* tribunals copied components of the common law procedure, later the focus was put on the continental model of accusation; in proceedings before the ICC, the continental solutions prevailed. During the operation of the *ad hoc* tribunals, the continental model of appeal proceedings again turned out to be more compatible with the goals of effective and efficient completion of proceedings before international criminal tribunals. As the appellate instance has been granted the competence to take evidence, it may independently assess whether the facts of the case established by a first instance court are in compliance with the true course of events. Combined with the power to amend judgements of the first instance court, it facilitates the completion of proceedings without the necessity of sending cases back to the Trial Chamber for re-examination. The expansion of the Prosecutor's competences to appeal against judgements may, in turn, be considered to be derived from the need to have the contents of international court judgements controlled by the international community.

References

Ackerman JE, O'Sullivan E (2002) Practice and procedure of the International Criminal Tribunal for the former Yugoslavia. Kluwer Law International, The Hague/London/Boston

Acquaviva G, Combs N, Heikkila M, Linton S, McDermott Y, Vasiliev S (2013) Trial process. In: Sluiter G, Friman H, Linton S, Vasiliev S, Zappala S (2013) International criminal procedure. Principles and rules. Oxford University Press, Oxford

Ambos K (2007) The structure of international procedure: "adversarial", "inquisitorial" or mixed. In: Bohlander M (ed) International criminal justice: a critical analysis of institutions and procedures. Cameron May, London

Bassiouni MC (1993) Human rights in the context of criminal justice: identifying international procedural protections and equivalent protections in national constitutions. Duke J Comp Int Law 3:235

Bassiouni MC, Manikas P (1996) The law of the International Criminal Tribunal for the former Yugoslavia. Transnational Publishers, New York

Behrens HJ (1998) Investigation, trial and appeal in the International Criminal Court Statute. Eur J Crime Crim Law Crim Justice 6:429

Beulke W (2005) Strafprozessrecht, 12th edn. C.F. Müller, Heidelberg

Boas G, Bischoff J, Reid N, Taylor BD III (2011) International criminal procedure. Cambridge University Press, Cambridge

Boas G, Jackson J, Roche B, Taylor D (2013) Appeals, reviews and reconsideration. In: Sluiter G, Friman H, Linton S, Vasiliev S, Zappala S (eds) International criminal procedure. Principles and rules. Oxford University Press, Oxford

Cryer R, Friman H, Robinson D, Wilmshurst E (2010) An introduction to international criminal law and procedure, 2 edn. Cambridge University Press, Cambridge

Damaška M (1986) The faces of justice and state authority. Yale University Press, New Haven/London

Featherstone Y (2001) Additional evidence in the appeals proceedings and review of final judgment. In: May R, Tolbert D, Hocking J, Roberts K, Jia BB, Mundis D, Oosthuizen G (eds) Essays on ICTY procedure and evidence. In honour of Gabrielle Kirk McDonald. Brill Academic Publishers, The Hague/London/Boston

Grajewski J (2010) In: Grajewski J, Paprzycki LK, Steinborn S (eds) Kodeks postępowania karnego. Komentarz, vol I. Wolters Kluwer, Warszawa

Grzegorczyk T (2008) Kodeks postępowania karnego oraz Ustawa o świadku koronnym. Komentarz, 5th edn. Wolter Kluwer, Warszawa

Hofmański P, Sadzik E, Zgryzek K (2011) Kodeks postępowania karnego. Komentarz. t. I, 4th edn. C.H. Beck, Warszawa

Izydorczyk J, Wiliński P (2004) Międzynarodowy Trybunał Karny. Zakamycze, Kraków

Knoops G-J (2005) Theory and practice of international and internationalized criminal proceedings. Kluwer Law International, The Hague/London/Boston

Kress C (2003) The procedural law of the International Criminal Court in outline: anatomy of a unique compromise. J Int Crim Justice 1:603

LaFave W, Israel J, King N, Kerr O (2009) Criminal procedure, 5th edn. West Academic Publishing, St. Paul

May R, Wierda M (2002) International criminal evidence. Transnational Publishers, Ardsley, NY

Nieto-Navia R, Roche B (2001) The ambit of the powers under Article 25 of the ICTY Statute: three issues of recent interest. In: May R, Tolbert D, Hocking J, Roberts K, Jia BB, Mundis D, Oosthuizen G (eds) Essays on ICTY procedure and evidence. In honour of Gabrielle Kirk McDonald. Brill Academic Publishers, The Hague/London/Boston

Padfield N (2008) Text and materials on the criminal justice process, 4th edn. Oxford University Press, Oxford

Re D (2012) Appeal. In: Reydams L, Wouters J, Ryngaert C (eds) International prosecutors. Oxford University Press, Oxford

Roth R, Henzelin M (2002) In: Cassese A, Gaeta P, Jones WD (eds) The Rome Statute of the International Criminal Court: a commentary. Oxford University Press, Oxford

Safferling C (2001) Towards an international criminal procedure, Oxford monographs in international law. Oxford University Press, Oxford

Schabas W (2010) The International Criminal Court. A commentary on the Rome Statute. Oxford University Press, Oxford

Sprack J (2012) A practical approach to criminal procedure, 14th edn. Oxford University Press, Oxford

Staker C (2008) In: Triffterer O (ed) Commentary on the Rome Statute of the International Criminal Court – observers' notes, article by article, 2nd edn. Hart/Nomos Verlagsgesellschaft/C.H. Beck, München/Oxford

Tochilovsky V (2008) Jurisprudence of the International Criminal Courts and the European Court of human rights. Martinus Nijhoff, Leiden

Waltoś S (2008) Proces karny. Zarys systemu, 9th edn. LexisNexis, Warszawa

Ward R, Wragg A (2005) Walker and Walker's English legal system, 9th edn. Oxford University Press, Oxford

Worrall J (2007) Criminal procedure: from first contact to appeal, 2nd edn. Pearson Allyn & Bacon, Boston

Chapter 9
Conclusion

9.1 The Model of Accusation Before the ICC

During the functioning of the international criminal tribunals, certain features and solutions have been developed that presently determine the specific nature of the model of accusation before the International Criminal Court. From the first international military tribunals in Tokyo and Nuremberg, through the experience of the *ad hoc* tribunals to the universal ICC, the institutions defining the position and the powers of the prosecutor on international law crimes were transformed from scattered and very simple into advanced catalogues of powers and detailed regulations governing all of his activities in international criminal proceedings. The proceedings before the international tribunals were also subjected to a different type of transformation: they have come a long way from a procedure based on common law to the mixed procedure, exemplifying the convergence of the continental and Anglo-Saxon legal systems. Whereas initially the *ad hoc* tribunals used mainly common law solutions to conduct their proceedings, with time, as they started seeing the need to balance the expediency and effectiveness of prosecution with the fairness of trial, they began to resort to procedural solutions known from continental states. The functioning of the *ad hoc* tribunals has proven that a strictly adversarial trial is not compatible with the tasks of international tribunals and the specific conditions of their work. In the situation where international justice strives to establish the historical truth and to participate in restoring international peace and safety, the criminal trial may not be subjected to a contest between parties. This was particularly noticeable in the accusation model: the prosecutor could not play a strictly accusatory role and, at the same time, seek the material truth and act "in the interest of justice". It turned out to be necessary to utilise the potential of certain institutions of the continental model of accusation. On the other hand, it would be a mistake to claim that the continental system better serves the objectives of international administration of justice. Taking into account the experience of the *ad hoc* tribunals, the creators of the ICC model of accusation reached freely to both of these

© Springer International Publishing Switzerland 2015

H. Kuczyńska, *The Accusation Model Before the International Criminal Court*,
DOI 10.1007/978-3-319-17626-0_9

legal systems to find procedural institutions that, in their opinion, could be best suited to the tasks imposed on the Court and tried to balance them. This inevitably led to the selection of the most pragmatic solutions. As a result, the ICC Prosecutor turned into "a *sui generis* organ of international justice" that operates in an entirely different legal and factual environment.[1] Being an authority of a new institution of justice, he must define his competences from scratch, try them out in confrontation with judicial authorities and with external factors.

9.2 The Model of Accusation Before the ICC and the Two Legal Traditions

The crucial elements of the ICC model of accusation were analysed in the light of their development in the continental law systems of Poland and Germany and in the common law systems represented by the United States and England. Based on the findings of the analysis, it was possible to establish which of the two legal systems lent specific procedural institutions or solutions to the model of accusation found before the ICC.

In the ICC's case, the components of the model of accusation transplanted from these legal orders had to be adapted to suit the needs of the Court and to become compatible with the remaining procedural solutions that often came from another legal tradition. As a result, the analysis had to focus on the manner in which specific procedural institutions taken from the two legal systems are used in the new context, acquiring a new meaning and new content. The monograph presents the modifications implemented to the ICC proceedings in relation to models adopted in specific states, as well as the reason for their introduction; it reveals the specific needs of the international administration of justice that triggered these modifications. The analysis concerned also how the model solution had to be transformed when transferred from the source legal system to the legal system of the ICC and whether the transformation led to a "faithful but autonomous restatement" between the original and the ICC procedure, or whether the translation constituted a substantial variation of the original system, when the main goal of translation was to create a provision that is effective and appealing in the final system.[2] It was also demonstrated what aim an institution was intended to achieve in its final form before the ICC and whether it has actually achieved it. The analysis also tackled how the ICC judges took practical advantage of the achievements of the legal science and case law pertaining to specific components of the model of accusation coming from different legal systems, which resulted in the mixing of legal traditions from common law and continental law systems, not only within one model of accusation but even within one procedural institution.

[1] See: Coté (2012), p. 322.

[2] In: Langer (2004), p. 33.

Due to the fact that the specific components of the procedural model are derived from various legal orders, the applied solutions are not always compatible with each other. Indeed, it is not always possible to "pluck" specific procedural institutions from various legal systems and treat them as ready-to-use products. Each system is internally coherent[3]—it is not only a complete whole, but it also follows a specific "vision" of justice. Taking a procedural institution out of an entire system of criminal proceedings or a legal culture may lead to its wrong interpretation and, in consequence, erroneous evaluation. The effectiveness and benefits of a procedural institution may not be assessed in isolation from its legal, procedural or even cultural context. Legal constructs and techniques of legal interpretation upheld in national law should not be automatically applied at the international level.[4] Therefore, "it is more appropriate in the interpretation of the provisions of a rule to rely essentially on the words of the rule as promulgated, rather than to assume an a priori position as to the origin of the rule. A rule may have a common law or civilian origin but the final product may be an amalgam of both common law and civilian elements, so as to render it sui generis".[5] For every procedural solution, there are many other determinants that need to be considered. The use of a specific institution of criminal proceedings in an international context always requires a detailed analysis of the characteristics and conditions of an international criminal tribunal. The institution has to be adjusted both to the tribunals' tasks and to the remaining components of the procedure.

The role played by the ICC Prosecutor in the model of accusation before the ICC should be considered to be the most significant feature taken over from the continental procedure. Before the international military tribunals, as well as at the initial stage of functioning of the *ad hoc* tribunals, the prosecutor used to play the role of an accusatory authority in a form known from the strictly adversarial system of common law states—his only task was to accuse. As the *ad hoc* tribunals continued to operate, however, it turned out that such a model was not compatible with the tasks addressed by the international administration of justice. It became necessary to balance the chances of the parties to the proceedings, which resulted in an obligation of the Prosecutor to look also for evidence in favour of the accused. From the earliest days of the international administration of justice, it was obvious that the collection of evidence at the location of the crime made it significantly more difficult for the accused to prepare properly for the defence. Taking these difficulties into consideration, the ICC finally adopted a solution offering support to the accused in the preparation of exculpatory evidentiary material based on the assumption that the Prosecutor should act in the broadly understood interests of justice. As a result, in proceedings before the ICC the Prosecutor plays not only the role of an

[3] Wąsek (1999), p. 160. Similarly: Luderssen (2004), p. 20; and Ambos (2007), p. 501.

[4] *Prosecutor v. Erdemović*, Separate and Dissenting Opinion of Judge Cassesse, 7 October 1997, § 2.

[5] *The Prosecutor v. Delalić*, IT-96-21, Decision on the Motion on Presentation of Evidence by the Accused, Esad Landzo, 1 May 1997, § 15.

accuser but also that of a guardian of the law. He is expected to strive to establish the material truth rather than only to have the accused convicted.

The development of the investigation stage based on the Anglo-Saxon tradition accounts for another characteristic feature of the accusation model before the ICC. This model is based on the principle of procedural opportunism. In view of its almost unlimited range of jurisdiction and limited personal and financial resources, it turned out that the ICC Prosecutor could not avoid the selection of defendants. Therefore, the broad prosecutorial discretion in the selection of cases he is going to handle has become a basic component of the model of investigation. The ICC Prosecutor's right to select the suspects is limited only by the factual (and financial) capacity of the Court. Another significant feature is that the investigation, similar to the Anglo-Saxon model of accusation, is aimed at establishing whether "there is sufficient evidence justifying the suspicion that the suspect committed the crime he/she is charged with" and therefore whether filing an indictment is reasonable. Contrary to the practice as in the continental tradition, the Prosecutor is not obliged to clarify a case comprehensively or to handle the proceedings every time there is a justified suspicion that a crime has been committed that falls within the jurisdiction of the Court. At the same time, components characteristic of the continental model of accusation were introduced to the investigation, including: subjecting the decision on the commencement of an investigation to judicial review; judicial review of a decision on the refusal of initiation and conducting of proceedings; implementing the preliminary examination of a case due to the Prosecutor's need to collect evidence to convince the judicial authority that there is a sufficient basis for authorisation of initiation of an investigation.

Another characteristic component of the accusation model before the ICC is the broad scope of judicial review over the Prosecutor's actions in the investigation. This review goes beyond a strict review of merits and formal review of an indictment. The Prosecutor's autonomy has been subjected to an extensive judicial control, unknown in the majority of legal systems. The Pre-Trial Chamber does not only exercise the powers traditionally secured for investigative judges in a manner taken from the continental law tradition but also performs the functions reserved for the hierarchically superior prosecutors in the absence of a hierarchical structure in the ICC Office of the Prosecutor. First, the scope of review has been expanded: not only the decision to initiate an investigation has been authorised, but the judicial review before the ICC also covers the justifiability of the Prosecutor's decision not to file the charges. Thus, scrutiny is given both to the refusal to conduct an investigation and to the refusal to file an indictment after an investigation has been completed. Second, the manner of performing the review has been expanded: a *quasi*-trial was implemented to confirm the charges drafted by the Prosecutor. It is an adversarial procedure, held on the forum of the Pre-Trial Chamber. Third, the scope of evidence the Prosecutor intends to present at trial was subjected to judicial review during a status conference. Another component of judicial control over prosecutorial actions is the Trial Chamber's competence to modify the legal characterisation of facts formulated by the Prosecutor in the charges. Moreover, this has also become possible at the stage when the indictment is presented for confirmation by the Pre-Trial Chamber. As a result, the Prosecutor's independence in drafting the charges has been limited in favour of the judicial authority. In this way, the system of "checks and balances"[6] was intended to be achieved within the scope of the investigation, where the role of the court would be aligned with the role of the Prosecutor in filing the indictment before the Trial Chamber. In consequence, however, the numerous components of judicial review—frequently introduced in the case law—further complicate the Prosecutor's work.

The institution of disclosure of evidence was, in turn, transferred, almost in its entirety, from the legal system of common law states. This institution is a consequence of the adoption of a strictly adversarial model of trial and the assumption that there are two parties to the proceedings, each of them presenting its case to the court. Characteristically, the ICTY modelled this institution almost completely on the United States system, introducing only small modifications to expand the scope of the Prosecutor's disclosure obligation. The ICC has adopted the model applied and tested by the ICTY without any major changes. Simultaneously, two fundamental components of the continental procedure were adopted, which rendered the established solution incoherent. First, the ICC Prosecutor has the obligation not only to disclose all evidence in favour of the accused but also to search for it proactively. Taking into account that the accused should have ensured access to the electronic database containing also exculpatory evidence, which the Prosecutor is obliged to keep, it can be concluded that the ICC model of prosecutorial disclosure obligation has taken on many features of "access to the case file", departing further away from the Anglo-Saxon "disclosure of evidence" model. Second, it was assumed in the proceedings before the ICC that the materials disclosed to the other party should be also submitted to the Pre-Trial Chamber and the Trial Chamber. This gave rise to an obligation that resulted in the establishment of a *quasi-dossier* (the register) of the case.

As far as consensual termination of proceedings is concerned, at the initial stage of functioning of the *ad hoc* tribunals, the model known from common law states was eliminated. Later on, however, the tribunals reached for solutions provided for in this model: before the ICTY, it was decided that the trial would be terminated if the accused pleaded guilty and broad grounds for the execution of agreements between the Prosecutor and the accused were established—pursuant to such agreements, the Prosecutor could file an indictment only on the charges relating to offences that the accused admitted to have committed while promising to discontinue the proceedings in relation to other charges; moreover, the Prosecutor could request adjudication of a specific sentence. Thus, a solution similar to the American plea bargaining institution was adopted. And there, the largest differences between the proceedings before the ICTY and the ICC manifested themselves. The creators of the ICC decided that plea bargaining between the Prosecutor and the accused could not provide a basis for adjudicating on the criminal responsibility of the accused and for issuing a merit-based ruling. Currently, the ICC rules for

[6] See: Turone (2002), p. 1138.

consensual termination of criminal proceedings are even more restrictive than in the majority of continental law states. The Trial Chamber is not allowed to adjudicate exclusively on the basis of guilty plea. It has to establish whether the plea is based on the facts of the case arising from the collected evidence. This solution is negatively evaluated in the legal science: it has been suggested that despite the imperative character of the Rome Statute, it cannot be excluded that the ICC judges will behave as Anglo-Saxon judges do, taking into account informal agreements concluded between the parties without any legal basis, as there are clear practical and procedural advantages to this solution. This practice will then need to be formally regulated.[7]

The development of an accusation at trial before the ICC is the best example of the convergence of the legal systems. In general, the "basic structure" for evidentiary proceedings has been adopted from common law systems. At the same time, numerous components from the continental tradition were implemented. The rule that the parties are responsible for the presentation of evidence in the case comes from the common law tradition. At the initial stage of functioning of the *ad hoc* tribunals, the judge's role was also taken from this tradition. However, even during the earliest proceedings, it turned out that the needs of the international administration of justice are not compatible with the judge's passivity. Learning from the *ad hoc* tribunals' experience, the ICC adopted a solution that departed from the Anglo-Saxon model and where the judge became obliged to manage the course of the trial and the presentation of evidence, similar to continental systems. The adoption of the objectives and the essence of the trial known in continental systems should be considered as the fundamental change. Namely, the trial before the ICC nowadays aims at establishing the objective historical truth. This objective has numerous implications. First, the judge must have knowledge of the case and be able to access case records held by the Registry. Second, the judge must be "activated" by being able to use broad competences in introducing evidence to the trial and interrogating witnesses. Third, every judgment must be accompanied by a reasoned statement of findings. Last, the judge's role manifests itself in a lack of binding rules for evidentiary proceedings, as a result of which a judge may manage the course of evidentiary proceedings. The growing judicial competence has led to limitation of the Prosecutor's role. Greater judicial impact on the scope and organisation of evidence prepared by the prosecution means that it is not the Prosecutor but rather the judge who can have an exclusive right to decide on the scope of evidence presented in a trial. The judge ceased to be an impartial arbiter and became an authority with plenty of options to affect the course of the trial, often at the cost of the Prosecutor's autonomy and independence—in the name of the effectiveness of the proceedings. We should not, however, overlook the fact that the Prosecutor's role has also changed—he cannot confine himself to being the opposite party in a trial when at the same time he is an authority appointed to look for the material

[7] See e.g.: Stegmiller (2008), p. 330; Friman (2003b), pp. 373 and 393; Calvo-Goller (2006), p. 242.

truth. All these implications arising from the obligation to determine the material truth constitute the components of a trial model known from continental systems.[8]

As far as appeal proceedings are concerned, it seems that the model of accusation before the appeal instance of the ICC is a reflection of the features found in continental systems. It is demonstrated, principally, by two components of the procedure: the Prosecutor's competence to file an appeal in favour of the accused and his power to appeal against acquittals. Numerous other components of the continental appeal model have been implemented: the drafting of the appeal grounds and their broad scope covering all infringements of law that could have taken place before the first instance, the rules for submitting new evidence that is admitted in the same way as before the Trial Chamber and statutory premises for adjudicating beyond the scope of appeal. However, the essence of the appeal, its uniqueness manifesting itself in the possibility of being filed only in case of "significant infringements of law", was developed following the example of the Anglo-Saxon model, although it also bears much resemblance to the continental institution of revision (cassation).

The question of whether the procedure before the ICC is in principle strictly adversarial or whether it has become predominantly continental cannot be unequivocally answered. The most popular opinion is that it has been modelled on the Anglo-Saxon example but that it also incorporates numerous components borrowed from the continental tradition.[9] Almost as popular is a conviction that criminal procedure before the ICC does not represent pure forms of *either* the adversarial or the inquisitorial models: "the ICC Statute indeed represents an admirable attempt to achieve the right mixture – the golden mean – between the inquisitorial and accusatorial systems".[10] It seems that it is no longer possible to define the ICC model of accusation as having been developed based on a single system. Although a majority of the institutions and solutions of the model may be identified as having been sourced from a specific legal system, they have become a *sui generis* solution due to their use and functioning before the international criminal tribunal. Some stages of the proceedings are conducted pursuant to the Anglo-Saxon model. Others, however, have been transferred in their entirety from the continental system, which has also had a crucial impact on the development of the procedure. Therefore, in the case of the ICC, the following basic question should be asked: have these two legal traditions been successfully reconciled?[11] Taking into account the short, 12-year period of this Court's functioning, which has seen only three cases completed and has seen two appeal proceedings finalised, only a tentative

[8] And these features can be also seen as "hallmarks of a hierarchical model of authority". See: Langer (2005), p. 867; and Heinze (2014), pp. 543–544.

[9] See also: Roberts (2001), p. 561; Knoops (2005), p. 8.

[10] Delmas-Marty (2003), p. 20; Kress (2003), p. 605; Sluiter et al. (2013), p. 50.

[11] Usually the answer is affirmative. See e.g.: Ambos (2007), pp. 429 and 500; Ambos (2003), p. 35; Fernandez de Gurmeni (2001), pp. 250–253; Schuon (2010), p. 273; Friman (2003a), p. 202. Though there are also negative answers, e.g.: Kremens (2010), p. 247. According to the last author, this system is moreover neither complete nor coherent.

answer may be given. The model of accusation seems to be functioning properly, but undoubtedly it is enormously complicated.

9.3 The Model of Accusation Before the ICC and the Legal Culture

International criminal proceedings exemplify how it is possible to separate a criminal proceedings system from a specific legal, cultural and moral system, associated usually with a specific state. As it is not anchored in any given national tradition, the analysed model of criminal proceedings is sometimes referred to as "artificial".[12] The assessment of the impact of different legal systems on the development of the ICC criminal procedure occasions the question on how the legal culture affects the competences of the accuser in criminal trial.

The accusation model in a given system of criminal procedure is difficult to consider without taking into account the cultural and social context of a particular state: "to consider forms of justice in monadic isolation from their social and economic context is – for many purposes – like playing Hamlet without the Prince".[13] The criminal procedure is, to a large extent, a social process, rooted in a specific legal environment.[14] The entire system of justice authorities and the course of the trial are a reflection of the needs and visions of a society on justice, political objectives and economic factors. Also, the decision-making process of justice authorities has a social basis: decisions depend on the place and context in which they are issued. Seen in this way, the criminal procedure becomes a sociological phenomenon. Sociology provides, among others, the framework for all cases where an authority may use discretion of operation. The prosecutor's decisions on whether to initiate proceedings in a given factual situation, how to handle them and what factors to take into account are all sociologically conditioned. Moreover, the structure and role of the government cannot be ignored: *M. Damaška* builds the whole structure of "the faces of justice" basing on the assumption that "where government is conceived as a manager, the administration of justice appears to be devoted to fulfilment of state programs and implementation of state policies. In contrast, where government mainly maintains the social equilibrium, the administration of justice tends to be associated with conflict resolution".[15] Economical factors cannot either be ignored: "While Continental rulers continuously expanded the agenda of government – from the army to the

[12] Hauck (2008), p. 14.

[13] Damaška (1986), p. 7.

[14] See: Findlay and Henham (2005), p. 5; Gerecka-Żołyńska (2009), pp. 19–21; Rogacka-Rzewnicka (2007), pp. 47–49; Waltoś (2002), p. 18; Kardas (2012), p. 20. Detailed analysis of this phenomenon in: Andrzejewska (2013), pp. 141 et seq.

[15] Damaška (1986), p. 11.

maintenance of internal order, education, even to public health and social security – England and America seemed until recently to rely to a far greater measure on private or 'voluntaristic' action for the fulfilment of social needs. Outsiders marvelled about the feasibility of such 'minimal statism' and proposed a variety of theories to explain the mystery. One theory that has gained wide currency attributes the comparatively minor importance of government in Anglo-American lands to the allegedly greater success there of capitalist markets. The more pervasive and effective the mechanisms of the market, it is said, the lesser the need for direct governmental involvement; power can be exercised mainly in the economic and social spheres, and the state apparatus can often be bypassed".[16]

The assumption that the legal procedure has social and cultural foundations leads us to conclude that the development of specific models of accusation not only is a task of criminal procedure but also is conditioned by politics, social engineering and psychological factors. In consequence, the specific development of the prosecutor's office structure, tasks and powers affects its role and is also adjusted to the expectations of a given society as to its operation and effectiveness. The objectives and tasks of the prosecution are not, and may not be, identical in each state. Regardless of their title (the public prosecutor, public prosecution director, office of prosecution), and their place in the structure of the judicial or executive power, both the detailed competences and the practical functioning of public prosecutors in each legal order depend not only on the existing legal system and the criminal law system but also on the history and historical development of the law, the cultural and juridical influences of other states, the existing moral system and the culture that goes beyond the legal culture.

In the case of the ICC at the same time, the model of accusation was shaped not in the frames of historical development but as a result of a diplomatic compromise.[17] Borrowing components of the accusation model from two different legal traditions led to the convergence of not only legal systems but also the systems of legal ideology and culture. On the one hand, the "freedom of choice" of the creators of the ICC procedural institutions made possible the departure from troublesome legal traditions and repeatable models, and for the first time in history it triggered a search for pure effectiveness in the criminal procedure.[18] One may even risk the statement that this separation from national traditions allowed the creation of a separate legal culture—that of international criminal tribunals.[19]

On the other hand, the mixture and coexistence of cultural circumstances related to specific legal solutions have had many negative consequences.

---

[16] Damaška (1986), p. 91. See also detailed analysis on the phenomenon of Soviet system of "central control", which had to result in swallowing conflict solving by the administrative officialdom and focus on legalism of prosecution, on pp. 197–204.

[17] De Smet (2009), p. 418; Tochilovsky (2002), pp. 274–275.

[18] Schuon (2010), p. 308.

[19] Very detailed analysis of this concept is presented in: Campbell (2013), p. 159 and next.

The lack of consistency in interpretation of legal norms turned out to be the first negative consequence. The judges cannot avoid making references to concepts they know from their own legal systems (including arguments and terminology, methods of application of law).[20] It is said that practitioners before the international criminal tribunals "have a natural tendency to bring their domestic culture with them".[21] Judges associated with particular traditions, consciously (or unconsciously), promote certain interpretation of criminal procedure from their own legal system, with which they are familiar. They are often found to reach for the justification of a given institution that comes from a specific (their own) country. As a consequence, the application of the same regulations (even the same provision) may lead to different outcomes, depending on the background of the persons who use them—as the two analysed legal traditions offer not only "two different techniques to handle criminal cases" but also "two different procedural cultures – including structures of interpretation and meaning".[22] Moreover, where one judicial authority comprises judges and prosecutors hailing from various legal orders, it is often time consuming for them to reach a common stance and there appear obstacles to its effective operation. In consequence, we can observe a lack of systemic coherence in the activities of the judges seen as a group. Indeed: "while in domestic legal systems the method of thinking is rather fixed (because it is influenced by a legal tradition that has evolved over centuries and shaped the minds of individuals), at the ICC level, the method of legal thinking must be determined first".[23]

The activity of judges during a trial before the ICC is an example of how cultural background affects the perception of regulations governing the operation of the ICC. Whereas the judges with a common law background were hesitant to use their competence to participate actively in the presentation of evidence—producing evidence, questioning witnesses and experts—the judges coming from continental systems were much more inclined to exercise these powers.[24] In a survey based on two trials at the ICTY, it was found that the trial presided over by a judge with a continental background adopted the style of the continental (inquisitorial) tradition, whereas in another trial presided over by an Anglo-American judge, this judge adopted a role characteristic of an adversarial proceeding approach, acting as a referee between the two belligerent parties. Also, the activity of the judge in a confirmation of charges hearing before the ICC, during which the same principles of conducting evidentiary proceedings apply as during the trial, depends, similarly as in the trial, on the judge's tradition. It may also be noticed that even if judges with a continental background demonstrated a natural tendency to be more active during

[20] See for more details: Bohlander (2014), p. 505; and Mégret (2009), p. 44.

[21] Cit. after: Langer (2005), p. 852.

[22] Cit. after: Heinze (2014), p. 200.

[23] Cit. after: Jackson and M'Boge (2013), p. 952.

[24] Tochilovsky (2004), p. 398; Schuon (2010), p. 182.

this hearing, this approach was not necessarily maintained during the trial. Indeed, the trial may have been dominated by the Anglo-Saxon model of evidentiary proceedings, with the judge assuming a more passive role.[25] Also, the flexibility of the ICC's rules of evidence reveals how the legal culture influences the development of evidentiary proceedings in practice. During the first case heard by the ICC's Trial Chamber, the parties agreed on the sequence of the presentation of evidence that was based on the strictly adversarial model adopted by the *ad hoc* tribunals. It was emphasised that both the presiding judge and the Prosecutor came from the common law tradition.[26]

Another occasion where noticeable difference could be seen was the manner in which indictments were formulated before the international criminal tribunals. In the absence of a coherent standard and certainty as to what legal system should be followed, the prosecutor was expected to decide what form the indictment should take. As a result, the prosecutor's legal background came to determine the contents and form of an indictment (especially its level of detail).[27] The model adopted before the *ad hoc* tribunals is, in turn, continued before the ICC.

It also turned out that the materials provided to the judge under the disclosure procedure before the ICTY depended on the trial culture of the ICTY Prosecutor's country of origin. The Prosecutor with a continental background adopted the practice of sending a significantly larger amount of material than he was obliged to. Thus, as a result of his unilateral decision, judges gained access to an investigation file—for which there was no basis in the legal provisions. According to his opinion, in order to be able to reasonably and effectively control the trial (and parties), a judge's knowledge of the case prior to trial was essential.[28] In consequence, we could quite often observe how deviations from the adversarial system were not so much a result of adopting a special provision, as came from its interpretation by an organ of the Tribunal.[29] Also, the developments in the plea bargaining practice before the ICTY demonstrate "that the internal dispositions of legal actors include not only a disposition to act and react in certain ways to procedural issues, but also to understand them in certain ways".[30]

Another adverse consequence of the ICC procedure's lack of rooting in a specific legal system is the unfamiliarity of this procedure to its participants. Negative results of this phenomenon could be seen in the proceedings before the *ad hoc* tribunals. They were created as strictly adversarial in nature, following the adoption of the draft Rules of Procedure and Evidence as presented by the American

---

[25] Hauck (2008), pp. 56–57.

[26] *The Prosecutor v. Lubanga*, ICC-01/04-01/06-1084, Decision on the Status before the Trial Chamber of the Evidence Heard by the Pre-Trial Chamber and the Decisions of the Pre-Trial Chamber in Trial Proceedings, 13 December 2007, § 2–3. In general see: Gallmetzer (2009), pp. 512–514 and 519–520; Schuon (2010), p. 292; Vasiliev (2012), p. 761.

[27] In more detail see: Keegan and Mundis (2001), pp. 124–125.

[28] Schuon (2010), p. 183. These circumstances described also in: Fairlie (2004), p. 316.

[29] As observed by Kavran (2003), p. 139.

[30] Cit. after: Langer (2005), p. 865.

delegation. In many cases, specific procedural solutions and institutions were borrowed directly from the American procedure (for example, the entire institution of disclosure of evidence). At the same time, the *ad hoc* tribunals function in states that adhere to the continental legal tradition. Thus, international trials not only created too great a distance between the place where the crime was committed and the place where it is judged, "uprooting the crimes", but also led to the creation of a "legal distance" between the perpetrator and the environment in which the crimes will be judged that have little connection with local legal reality.[31] As a result, they administered justice according to rules that were entirely different from the national rules and in different languages. This was the reason why the population of the former Yugoslavia and Rwanda did not easily see their advantages.[32] As a result of the adoption of the common law model, the continental lawyers were never on an equal footing with the lawyers coming from common law systems. Moreover, this system adopted English language as the main *lingua franca*, which causes that international criminal justice sees itself through the eyes of that language of law, and it all leads to an excessive use of the cultural luggage that comes with it.[33] Even the most comprehensive training in the rules of procedure before the ICTY (or the language used before the Tribunal) could not compete with the years of experience and immersion in a specific model of accusation.[34] Each institution had accumulated vast case law and practice. Theoretical training could not substitute the years of practical experience gained in using an institution. This could be seen, for example, especially in the "witness proofing" institution of which the continental lawyers were often not even aware and which has a great impact on the preparation of evidence by the parties. In view of the above, it is certainly a challenge for the practitioners to operate under the new model of criminal proceedings that was established before the ICC. Development of an entirely new system of criminal procedure resulted in a situation where representatives of no country are sufficiently familiar with it. Both the accused and the witnesses, and often their defence counsels, have to deal with an unfamiliar legal order. Often, the accused use the different institutions (e.g., the guilty plea), without knowing their implications and consequences. The "mixed" procedure undoubtedly requires much more effort and knowledge of different legal systems from its actors: judges, prosecutor's office, defence attorneys; they are certainly expected to have broad legal expertise and knowledge of both the continental and the common law orders.[35]

---

[31] Notions used by: Mégret (2009), p. 730.

[32] What is noticed by: Clark (2009), p. 422, and also: Boas et al. (2011), p. 467.

[33] Not even mentioning the topic of the level of knowledge of the official languages of the Court. See: "Languages spoken by the former and current judges of the ICC (May 2013)" in Bohlander (2014), pp. 499 and 513, who indicates that the language barrier of originally English-speaking judges who do not speak any other language leads to the limitation in the use of legal sources—and therefore concepts—stemming from other than English-speaking states.

[34] And there are such trainings, e.g., "trial advocacy courses" for the defence counsels. See: Kremens (2010), p. 144.

[35] However, the research analysed in Jackson and M'Boge (2013), p. 954, proves that the practitioners adopted very quickly to the new legal environment of work.

The provisions of criminal procedure before international criminal tribunals have become an indicator of the amendments that will concern the provisions of the national criminal proceedings. The convergence of legal systems has become a characteristic feature of the procedure. With increasing frequency, the various institutions of criminal procedure are being "liberated" from the context of a particular legal system and are penetrating from one legal system to another. The rules of procedure are no longer associated with the culture and territory of a given state. In their search for effectiveness, states are reaching for procedural institutions and solutions adopted in other legal systems. The problem of creating a model of accusation before international criminal tribunals is very important as it has the potential of becoming a starting point for discussions on the most effective model of accusation—and not only in relation to international law crimes.

References

Ambos K (2003) International criminal procedure: "adversarial", "inquisitorial" or mixed? Int Crim Law Rev 3:18

Ambos K (2007) The structure of international procedure: "adversarial", "inquisitorial" or mixed. In: Bohlander M (ed) International criminal justice: a critical analysis of institutions and procedures. Cameron May, London

Andrzejewska M (2013) Adaptacja koncepcji Thomasa Kuhna dla postępowania karnego. Prokuratura i Prawo 3:136

Boas G, Bischoff J, Reid N, Taylor BD III (2011) International criminal procedure. Cambridge University Press, Cambridge

Bohlander M (2014) Language, culture, legal traditions, and international criminal justice. J Int Crim Justice 12:499

Calvo-Goller K (2006) The trial proceedings of the International Criminal Court: ICTY and ICTR precedents. Martinus Nijhoff, Leiden/Boston

Campbell K (2013) The making of global legal culture and international criminal law. Leiden J Int Law 26:155

Clark J (2009) Plea bargaining at the ICTY: guilty pleas and reconciliation. Eur J Int Law 2:415

Coté L (2012) Independence and impartiality. In: Reydams L, Wouters J, Ryngaert C (eds) International prosecutors. Oxford University Press, Oxford

Damaška M (1986) The faces of justice and state authority. Yale University Press, New Haven/London

De Smet P (2009) A structural analysis of the role of the Pre-Trial Chamber in the fact-finding process of the ICC. In: Stahn C, Sluiter G (eds) The emerging practice of the International Criminal Court. Martinus Nijhoff, Leiden/Boston

Delmas-Marty M (2003) Comparative law to a pluralist conception of international criminal law. J Int Crim Justice 1:13

Fairlie M (2004) The marriage of common and continental law at the ICTY and its progeny, due process deficit. Int Crim Law Rev 4:315

Fernandez de Gurmeni S (2001) Elaboration of Rules of Procedure and Evidence. In: Lee RP (ed) The International Criminal Court. Elements of Crimes and Rules of Procedure and Evidence. Transnational Publishers, New York

Findlay M, Henham R (2005) Transforming international criminal justice: retributive and restorative justice in the trial process. Willian Publishing, Portland

Friman H (2003a) Procedural law of the criminal court – an introduction. In: Lattanzi F, Schabas W (eds) Essays on the Rome Statute of the International Criminal Court, vol 2. Il Sirente, Ripa di Fagnano Alto

Friman H (2003b) Inspiration from the international criminal tribunals when developing law on evidence for the International Criminal Court. Law Pract Int Courts Tribunals 3:373

Gallmetzer R (2009) The Trial-Chamber's discretionary power and its exercise in the trial of Thomas Lubanga Dyilo. In: Stahn C, Sluiter G (eds) The emerging practice of the International Criminal Court. Martinus Nijhoff, Leiden/Boston

Gerecka-Żołyńska A (2009) Internacjonalizacja współczesnego procesu karnego w Polsce. Warszawa

Hauck P (2008) Judicial decisions in the pre-trial phase of criminal proceedings in France, Germany, and England: a comparative analysis responding to the law of the International Criminal Court. Nomos Verlagsgesellschaft, Baden-Baden

Heinze A (2014) International criminal procedure and disclosure. An attempt to better understand and regulate disclosure and communication at the ICC on the basis of a comprehensive and comparative theory of criminal procedure. Duncker & Humblot, Berlin

Jackson J, M'Boge Y (2013) The effect of legal culture on the development of international evidentiary practice: from the 'Robing Room' to the 'Melting Pot'. Leiden J Int Law 26:947

Kardas P (2012) Rola i miejsce prokuratury – w systemie organów demokratycznego państwa prawnego. Prokuratura i Prawo 9:37

Kavran O (2003) The *sui generis* Rules of Procedure and Evidence. In: Haveman R, Nicholls J (eds) Supranational criminal law: a system *sui generis*. Intersentia, Antwerp/Oxford/New York

Keegan MJ, Mundis DA (2001) Legal requirements for indictment. In: May R, Tolbert D, Hocking J, Roberts K, Jia BB, Mundis D, Oosthuizen G (eds) Essays on ICTY procedure and evidence. In honour of Gabrielle Kirk McDonald. Brill Academic Publishers, The Hague/London/Boston

Knoops G-J (2005) Theory and practice of international and internationalized criminal proceedings. Kluwer Law International, The Hague/London/Boston

Kremens K (2010) Dowody osobowe w międzynarodowym postępowaniu karnym. TNOiK, Toruń

Kress C (2003) The procedural law of the International Criminal Court in outline: anatomy of a unique compromise. J Int Crim Justice 1:603

Langer M (2004) From legal transplants to legal translations: the globalization of plea bargaining and the Americanization thesis in criminal procedure. Harv Int Law J 45:1

Langer M (2005) The rise of managerial judging in international criminal law. Am J Comp Law 53:835

Luderssen K (2004) Overview of different types of procedure from a German point of view. In: Eser A, Rabenstein C (eds) Strafjustiz im Spannungsfeld von Effizienz und Fairness. Konvergente und divergente Entwicklungen im Strafprozessrecht. Duncker & Humblot, Berlin

Mégret F (2009) Beyond "Fairness": understanding the determinants of international criminal procedure. UCLA J Int Law Foreign Aff 14:37

Roberts K (2001) Aspects of the ICTY contribution to the criminal procedure of the ICC. In: May R, Tolbert D, Hocking J (eds) Essays on ICTY procedure and evidence. In honour of Gabrielle Kirk McDonald. Brill Academic Publishers, The Hague/London/Boston

Rogacka-Rzewnicka M (2007) Oportunizm i legalizm ścigania przestępstw w świetle współczesnych przeobrażeń procesu karnego. Zakamycze, Warszawa

Schuon C (2010) International criminal procedure. A clash of legal cultures. T.M.C. Asser Press, The Hague

Sluiter G, Friman H, Linton S, Vasiliev S, Zappala S (eds) (2013) International criminal procedure. Principles and rules. Oxford University Press, Oxford

Stegmiller I (2008) The pre-investigation stage of the ICTY and ICC compared. In: Kruessmann T (ed) ICTY: towards a fair trial? Neuer Wissenschaftlicher Verlag, Wien

Tochilovsky V (2002) Proceedings in the International Criminal Court: some lessons to learn from ICTY experience. Eur J Crime Crim Law Crim Justice 4:268

Tochilovsky V (2004) International criminal justice: "Strangers In The Foreign System". Crim Law Forum 15:319

Turone G (2002) Powers and duties of the Prosecutor. In: Cassese A, Gaeta P, Jones WD (eds) The Rome Statute of the International Criminal Court: a commentary. Oxford University Press, Oxford

Vasiliev S (2012) Trial. In: Reydams L, Wouters J, Ryngaert C (eds) International prosecutors. Oxford University Press, Oxford

Waltoś S (2002) Prokuratura – jej miejsce wśród organów władzy, struktura i funkcje. Państwo i Prawo 4:6

Wąsek A (1999) Europejski modelowy kodeks karny. In: Nowak T (ed) Nowe prawo karne procesowe. Zagadnienia wybrane. Księga ku czci Wiesława Daszkiewicza, vol III. Prace Wydziału Prawa i Administracji UAM w Poznaniu, Poznań

MIX
Papier aus verantwortungsvollen Quellen
Paper from responsible sources
FSC® C105338

If you have any concerns about our products,
you can contact us on
ProductSafety@springernature.com

In case Publisher is established outside the EU,
the EU authorized representative is:
Springer Nature Customer Service Center GmbH
Europaplatz 3, 69115 Heidelberg, Germany

Printed by Libri Plureos GmbH
in Hamburg, Germany